Interpreting Daniel for Preaching and Teaching

# Interpreting Daniel for Preaching and Teaching

A Model for Moving from Exegesis to Exposition to Teaching

THOMAS J. FINLEY
*and* BRANDON R. CASH

*Foreword by Don Sunukjian*

WIPF & STOCK · Eugene, Oregon

INTERPRETING DANIEL FOR PREACHING AND TEACHING
A Model for Moving from Exegesis to Exposition to Teaching

Copyright © 2024 Thomas J. Finley and Brandon R. Cash. All rights reserved. Except for brief quotations in critical publications or reviews, no part of this book may be reproduced in any manner without prior written permission from the publisher. Write: Permissions, Wipf and Stock Publishers, 199 W. 8th Ave., Suite 3, Eugene, OR 97401.

Wipf & Stock
An Imprint of Wipf and Stock Publishers
199 W. 8th Ave., Suite 3
Eugene, OR 97401

www.wipfandstock.com

PAPERBACK ISBN: 978-1-6667-6497-0
HARDCOVER ISBN: 978-1-6667-6498-7
EBOOK ISBN: 978-1-6667-6499-4

VERSION NUMBER 01/22/24

Scripture quotations marked (CSB) have been taken from the Christian Standard Bible, copyright © 2017 by Holman Bible Publishers. Used by Permission. Christian Standard Bible© and CSB© are federally registered trademarks of Holman Bible Publishers.

Scripture quotations marked (ESV) are from The Holy Bible, English Standard Version, copyright © 2001 by Crossway, a publishing ministry of Good News Publishing. Used by permission. All rights reserved.

Scripture quotations taken from the (NASB©) are from the New American Standard Bible©, Copyright © 2020 by The Lockman Foundation. Used by permission. All rights reserved lockman.org.

Scripture quotations marked (NLT) are taken from the *Holy Bible,* New Living Translation, copyright © 1996, 2004, 2007 by Tyndale House Foundation. Used by permission of Tyndale House Publishers, Inc., Carol Stream, Illinois 60188.

Scripture quotations marked (NRSV) are from the *New Revised Standard Bible,* copyright © 1989 National Council of the Churches of Christ in the United States of America. Used by permission. All rights reserved worldwide.

Scripture quotations marked (NRSVue) are from the *New Revised Standard Version Updated Edition,* copyright © 2021 National Council of the Churches of Christ in the United States of America. Used by permission. All rights reserved worldwide.

Scripture translations not from any of the preceding versions are translated by the authors of this book.

Dedication (Thomas): In memory of my parents, Ken and Jenny Finley, who provided a stable family life and modelled a vibrant faith.

Dedication (Brandon): To my parents, Ron and Jeanie Cash. Their faithfulness to God, love for his word, and pursuit of his wisdom have been an example for our family and countless others (Daniel 12:3).

"May God's name be blessed forever and ever" (Daniel 2:20).

# Contents

*List of Figures* | ix
*List of Tables* | x
*Abbreviations* | xi
*Forword by Don Sunukjian* | xvii
*Preface and Acknowledgements* | xix

Introduction | 1
Who's in Control? (Daniel 1:1–21) | 39
Dreams of Greatness (Daniel 2:1–49) | 63
Three Men Who Refused to Obey the King of Babylon (Daniel 3:1–30) | 100
A Proud King is Humbled (Daniel 4:1–37 [3:31—4:34]) | 125
Belshazzar Is Overthrown (Daniel 5:1–31 [6:1]) | 163
Daniel in the Lion's Den (Daniel 6:1–28 [6:2–29]) | 196
Vision of Beasts and Kingdoms (Daniel 7:1–28) | 222
The Ram and the Male Goat (Daniel 8:1–27) | 263
Prophecy of Seventy Weeks (Daniel 9:1–27) | 298
Prelude to the Final Revelation (Daniel 10:1—11:1) | 349
Prophetic History (Daniel 11:2—12:2) | 370
Waiting Patiently for God to Act (Daniel 12:3–13) | 419

*Bibliography* | 435

# List of Figures

Figure 0.1: Moving from Background and Textual Work to Teaching | 3
Figure 0.2: The Chiastic Structure of Daniel 2 to 7 | 27

# List of Tables

Tabe 0.1: **Aspects of God's Sovereignty According to the Book of Daniel** | 5

Table 0.2: **The Neo-Babylonian Kings** | 7

Table 0.3: **Chronology of Babylonian Attacks on Judah** | 8

Table 2.1: **Terms for Babylonian Wise Men: Aramaic, Hebrew, and English** | 74

Table 2.2: **Daniel 2:20–23 as a Theme Verse** | 81

Table 5.1: **The Traditional Interpretation of the Writing on the Wall** | 183

Table 9.1: **Suggested Starting Points for Daniel's Prophecy of Seventy Weeks** | 324

Table 9.2: **Renderings of Daniel 9:27b** | 334

Table 11.1: **The Kings of the North and the Kings of the South** | 413

# Abbreviations

1Qap$^{Gen}$ ar = *Genesis Apocryphon* from Cave 1 at Qumran

1QDan$^a$ = first manuscript of Daniel from Cave 1 at Qumran

1QDan$^b$ = second manuscript of Daniel from Cave 1 at Qumran

1QIsa$^a$ = first manuscript of Isaiah from Cave 1 at Qumran

1QM = a manuscript from Cave 1 at Qumran called *Milchamah*

1QS = a manuscript from Cave 1 at Qumran called *Serekh*

4Q174 [Florilegium] = a manuscript called *Florilegium* numbered 174 from Cave 4 at Qumran

4Q213 [Levi$^a$ ar] = a manuscript called *Testament of Levi* numbered 213 from Cave 4 at Qumran

4Q550$^c$ [4QPrEsther$^d$ ar] = a manuscript called *Prayer of Esther* numbered 550 from Cave 4 at Qumran

4QDan$^a$ = first manuscript of Daniel from Cave 4 at Qumran

4QDan$^c$ = third manuscript of Daniel from Cave 4 at Qumran

4QDan$^d$ = a fourth manuscript of Daniel from Cave 4 at Qumran

4QDan$^e$ = a fifth manuscript of Daniel from Cave 4 at Qumran

4QFlor (see 4Q174)

4QPrNab ar = Aramaic manuscript of the *Prayer of Nabonidus* from Cave 4 at Qumran

11QMelch = a manuscript mentioning Melchizedek from Cave 11 at Qumran (also 11Q 13)

AB = Anchor Bible

*ABC* = *Assyrian and Babylonian Chronicles*

## ABBREVIATIONS

*ABD* = *Anchor Bible Dictionary.* Edited by David Noel Freedman. 6 vols. New York: Doubleday, 1992

ACCSOT = Ancient Christian Commentary on Scripture, Old Testament

AD = *Anno Domini,* "in the year of the Lord"

*A.J.* = *Antiquities of the Jews* by Josephus

*ANEP* = *The Ancient Near East in Pictures Relating to the Old Testament.* 2nd ed. Edited by James B. Pritchard. Princeton: Princeton University Press, 1994

*ANET* = *Ancient Near Eastern Texts Relating to the Old Testament.* Edited by James B. Pritchard. 3rd ed. Princeton: Princeton University Press, 1969

AOAT = Alter Orient und Altes Testament

AOTC = Abingdon Old Testament Commentaries

ApOTC = Apollos Old Testament Commentary

Ar = Aramaic

*AUSS* = *Andrews University Seminary Studies*

BC = Before Christ

BDB = Brown, Francis, S. R. Driver, and Charles A. Briggs. *A Hebrew and English Lexicon of the Old Testament*

BETL = Bibliotheca Ephemeridum Theologicarum Lovaniensium

BHS = *Biblia Hebraica Stuttgartensia.* Edited by Karl Elliger and Wilhelm Rudolph. Stuttgart: Deutsche Bibelgesellschaft, 1983

*BibSac* = *Bibliotheca Sacra*

*BR* = *Biblical Research*

ca. = circa, "approximately"

*CAH* = *Cambridge Ancient History*

*CANE* = *Civilizations of the Ancient Near East*

*CBQ* = *Catholic Biblical Quarterly*

CBQMS = Catholic Biblical Quarterly Monograph Series

Chap. = chapter; chaps. = chapters

DJD = Discoveries in the Judaean Desert

*EBC* = *Expositor's Bible Commentary*

GKC = *Gesenius' Hebrew Grammar,* Edited by E. Kautzsch. Translated by A. E. Cowley. 2nd ed. Oxford: Clarendon, 1910.

## ABBREVIATIONS

EBTC = Evangelical Biblical Theology Commentary

GELS = *A Greek-English Lexicon of the Septuagint*. Takamitsu Muraoka. Leuvain: Peeters, 2009

HALOT = *Hebrew and Aramaic Lexicon of the Old Testament*. Ludwig Koehler, Walter Baumgartner, and Johann J. Stamm. Translated and edited under the supervision of Mervyn E. J. Richardson. 5 vols. Leiden: Brill, 1994-2000.

*Hist.* = *Histories* by Herodotus

*HTR* = *Harvard Theological Review*

*HUCA* = *Hebrew Union College Annual*

*IDB* = *The Interpreter's Dictionary of the Bible*. Edited by George A. Buttrick. 4 vols. New York: Abingdon, 1962

*JAOS* = *Journal of the American Oriental Society*

*JBL* = *Journal of Biblical Literature*

*JBQ* = *Jewish Biblical Quarterly*

*JETS* = *Journal of the Evangelical Theological Society*

*JHebS* = *Journal of Hebrew Scriptures (online)*

*JHNES* = *The Johns Hopkins Near Eastern Studies*

*JNES* = *Journal of Near Eastern Studies*

*JSJ* = *Journal for the Study of Judaism in the Persian, Hellenistic, and Roman Periods*

JSNTSup = Journal for the Study of the New Testament Supplement Series

*JSOT* = *Journal for the Study of the Old Testament*

JSOTSup = Journal for the Study of the Old Testament Supplement Series

JSPSup = Journal for the Study of the Pseudepigrapha Supplement Series

LA = Late Aramaic

LCL = Loeb Classical Library

LNTS = The Library of New Testament Studies

LXX = Septuagint

MA = Middle Aramaic

MT = Masoretic Text

NAC = New American Commentary

NICOT = New International Commentary on the Old Testament

ABBREVIATIONS

NIDOTTE = *New Interational Dictionary of Old Testament Theology & Exegesis*. Edited by Willem A. VanGemeren. 5 vols. Grand Rapids: Zondervan, 1997

NIGTC = New International Greek Testament Commentary

NT = New Testament

NTS = *New Testament Studies*

OA = Old Aramaic

OG = Old Greek of Daniel

OLA = Orientalia Lovaniensia Analecta

OT = Old Testament

OTL = Old Testament Library

OTP = *The Old Testament Pseudepigrapha*. Edited by James H. Charlesworth. 2 vols. New York: Doubleday, 1983, 1985

P967 = papyrus manuscript of the Old Greek of Daniel

PN = *The Prayer of Nabonidus*

RevQ—*Revue de Qumran*

SB = Stuttgarter Bibelstudien

SLA = Standard Literary Aramaic

TBC = Torch Bible Commentaries

TCS = Texts from Cuneiform Sources

TDOT = *Theological Dictionary of the Old Testament*. Edited by G. Johannes Botterweck and Helmer Ringgren. Translated by John T. Willis et al. 16 vols. Grand Rapids: Eerdmans, 1974--2018

Th = Theodotion of Daniel (Greek)

TJ = *Trinity Journal*

TOTC = Tyndale Old Testament Commentaries

v. = verse; vv. = verses

Vg = Vulgate

VT = *Vetus Testamentum*

VTSup = Supplements to Vetus Testamentum

WAW = Writings from the Ancient World

WBC = Word Biblical Commentary

ABBREVIATIONS

WGRW = Writings from the Greco-Roman World

*WTJ* = *Westminster Theological Journal*

YOSR = Yale Oriental Series, Researches

*ZAW* = *Zeitschrift für die alttestamentliche Wissenschaft*

*ZNW* = *Zeitschrift für die neutestamentliche Wissenschaft und die Kunde der älteren Kirche*

Note: Comments that lead the reader to the theological thrust of each chapter are emboldened.

# Foreword

It's hard to think of two men more qualified to write a commentary which combines Hebrew scholarship with preaching excellence. Tom Finley was professor of Old Testament and Semitics at Talbot School of Theology for forty years, while Brandon Cash currently chairs and teaches the preaching and ministry courses at the school. For many years, Brandon has also been the preaching pastor of Oceanside Christian Fellowship. The cumulative experience and expertise of these two men have produced this first-rate commentary.

The authors' goal is to model the flow from the historical meaning of the text, to the underlying theology of the text, to the application of that theology to the experiences of contemporary listeners. Eternal truths are underneath the stories known from childhood and the appearances of fantastic beasts. These are not simply things which *did* happen or *will* happen; they are things which *always* happen. And the job of preachers is to prepare their listeners for when they might happen to them.

Tom and Brandon are to be commended for helping preachers do their job well.

Don Sunukjian

# Preface and Acknowledgements

WE BELIEVE THAT THE New Testament account of Jesus is true, and therefore we are reading Daniel with a presupposition that much of it was fulfilled in Christ. However, as students of the Hebrew Bible, who believe that the Hebrew Scriptures are as much God's Word as the New Testament, we read Daniel in its context and not primarily through the lens of the New Testament.

As concerned leaders in the church we desire that God's Word will be faithfully proclaimed in such a way that good exegesis and hermeneutics are modeled for the people in the pews. Trends in Christianity and churches come and go, popular teachings come and go, but God's Word abides forever. We hope to correct misconceptions, both liberal and conservative, by following the text rather than theology. In the process we hope to demonstrate our exegetical method that leads to our theological conclusions.

Much has been written about the book of Daniel, and we hope to break some new ground and to explore new methods of interpreting the Bible. We work from the Hebrew and Aramaic as the basis for our exegesis, always seeking to understand what God is saying through the book of Daniel. We are also cognizant of the context of the ancient Near East in which not only the book of Daniel, but also the entire Old Testament came into existence. Modern interpreters must beware of importing modern ways of interpreting Scripture that would have been foreign to the original authors. Some attention to the history of the interpretation of the book of Daniel also helps to moderate the influence of methods of interpretation that may seem reasonable but that are not helpful in discerning clearly what the book of Daniel teaches. Our ultimate hope is that God will be glorified through our meditations on the book of Daniel.

To quote a common cliché, we are "standing on the shoulders of giants." Both of us have had teachers, pastors, and professors who have shaped our outlook on exegesis and theology. Both of us are thankful for the fine

PREFACE AND ACKNOWLEDGEMENTS

education we received at Biola University, Talbot School of Theology, Fuller Seminary, and University of California at Los Angeles. We would give special thanks to Jim Weaver, who started us on the journey to melding exegesis with hermeneutics, homiletics, and theology. Special thanks to the JLH Foundation, which provided some funds to complete the project, and to Esther Cash, who has given valuable assistance in making sure the manuscript meets professional standards. And we would be remiss if we did not give thanks to our students over many years of teaching. Their inquisitiveness, insights, and pursuit of truth have inspired much of what we have written.

Finally, I (Brandon) would like to thank Tom for the journey this project has been. Our relationship began as teacher/student in 1996 and grew into a mentor/mentee relationship as I traveled down the road of marriage and doctoral studies. While I continue to count Tom as a mentor, the time we've spent together discussing Daniel, among other things, has forged a friendship, and for that I am most grateful.

# Introduction

FEW OLD TESTAMENT BOOKS influenced the teachings of Jesus and the writers of the New Testament as did Daniel. Jesus and the Gospel writers needed to explain to God's people, in a way they could understand, that the kingdom of God had arrived and King Jesus would soon take his throne. But the arrival of the kingdom and the enthronement of the King would defy expectations. To help the people understand that this was, in fact, what was taking place, Jesus often alludes to the book of Daniel. It's as if he was saying, without explicitly stating it, "Remember what Daniel said? All of this is happening according to God's sovereign plans which were revealed to Daniel."

Not only are there significant and specific prophecies concerning the future, but the book of Daniel also serves as a scenic set design for the performance of Jesus. When Jesus mentions "the abomination that causes desolation" (Matt 24:15–16 // Mark 13:14–15; cf. Dan 9:27), the book of Daniel is the scenic setting that adds force to Jesus's words. When Jesus repeatedly identifies himself as the "son of man" (esp. Matt 24:30; 26:64; Mark 13:26; 14:62; Luke 21:27; 22:69), the book of Daniel is the stage set containing thrones in the background that remind the audience that Jesus will soon be seated by the "Ancient of Days" (Dan 7:13). When the angel Gabriel announces the births of John the Baptist (Luke 1:19) and Jesus (Luke 1:26), it is only the book of Daniel that sets the scene for the significance of who Gabriel is and what these births portend (Dan 8:16; 9:21).

Much more could be said, and will be said throughout this book, but two closing illustrations will serve to show that Daniel's influence continues to shape God's people for all time. Daniel's influence on NT eschatology is second to none. If one is not acquainted with Daniel 7–12, the imagery in the book of Revelation cannot be understood according to John's intention.[1]

---

1. For example, the "beast coming up out of the sea, having ten horns and seven heads" (Rev 13:1) draws heavily on the imagery of Dan 7:3, 7–8.

And the hope of resurrection, the central hope of the Christian faith, is most clearly articulated among OT books, in Daniel. Daniel's final vision reveals that one day everyone will be raised, some to "everlasting life" and some to "everlasting contempt" (12:2).

The book of Daniel is so much more than an ancient book or a mystery to be solved. It is a portrait of our sovereign God, the scenic stage set for the leading performance of Jesus, and an invitation to all of God's people to be wise so they will "shine like the brightness of the sky, and those who lead many to righteousness, like the stars forever and ever" (12:3).

## OUR APPROACH TO THE BOOK OF DANIEL

The relationship between exegesis, hermeneutics and homiletics garners much discussion and debate. Generally speaking, exegesis focuses on establishing the text and what the text says; hermeneutics focuses on what the text means; and homiletics focuses on the application(s) of the text. While such a division clarifies helpful distinctions, it can lead to the impression that these are individual components of biblical studies rather than complementary aspects of the ministry of God's Word to his people. An unfortunate byproduct of such delineations are two unintended consequences. First, when a hard separation is made, exegesis and hermeneutics become academic endeavors, something for scholars to debate and write about, but with little perceived relevance for the church and the life of God's people. The second consequence, which flows from the first, is that preachers are tempted to skip the hard work of exegesis and hermeneutics and settle for sermons that focus on *an aspect of the text* rather than a sermon that captures the flow and point of *an entire text*. No doubt, exegesis and hermeneutics require hard work, and they are time-intensive. It is difficult to carve out the necessary time amid all of the other pressing pastoral responsibilities. However, the hard work pays great dividends, and we believe that the transition to faithful, life-changing application flows naturally and more easily from good hermeneutics. In other words, the crafting of sermons becomes easier when good hermeneutics are employed.

In the following commentary we have attempted to model the hard work of exegesis and hermeneutics and to show how sermons flow naturally from such labors. Our goal for this book is threefold. First, we want to help the preacher to understand the meaning of the book of Daniel. It is a book containing two distinct genres, narrative and apocalyptic, and the interpretation of the book must consider these distinct genres. Second, we want to show preachers how to move from the interpretation of a text to the preaching of a text. Though exegesis is imperative, sermons are not exegesis. Understanding history is necessary, and for most preachers, quite interesting; but sermons are not history lessons. Commentaries are crucial; after all, we're writing one! However, sermons are not running commentaries. Sermons are the application of God's word for the life of God's people—no matter when or where God's people are located. And that flows into the third goal; we want this book to serve as a model for the interpretation and preaching of other biblical books. We include here a visual illustration of what we believe to be the process of exegesis and hermeneutics and the move to homiletics. We have applied the model to the book of Daniel and its two genres, but we believe the model is appropriate for all genres of Scripture.

**Figure 0.1**

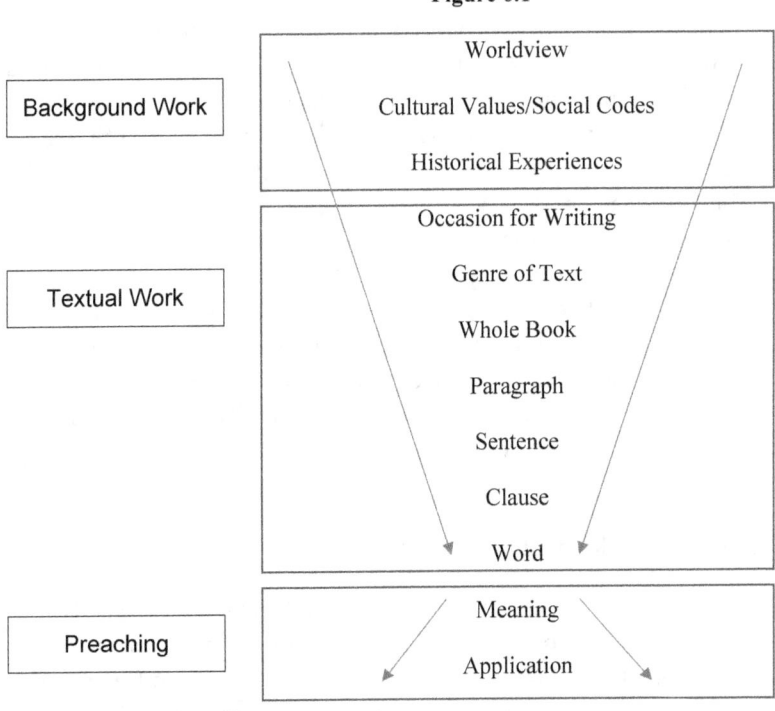

Figure 0.1 highlights three phases of the process: *background work*, *textual work* and *preaching*. The *background work* and *textual work* are exegesis, which flows naturally into the hermeneutical and homiletical portion of the chart, *preaching*. Though on the chart the *preaching* section appears

disproportionately small, it is the section that will have the greatest impact on the people you serve.[2]

The remainder of the Introduction will follow the format of Figure 0.1; that is, the Introduction moves from the top of the funnel (background issues) to the bottom of the funnel (textual issues). The rest of the commentary works through the chapters of Daniel, addressing additional *background* and *textual* issues as they arise. The meaning of the text (the theological thrust, which is the most significant aspect in the move to homiletics) is highlighted throughout the exegetical work, so that readers can see how the move to sermon preparation is made.

## PREACHING THE BOOK OF DANIEL

Sermon preparation begins with exegesis, moves to hermeneutics, and ends with application. Preachers must concern themselves with what *happened*, but they must be equally concerned with what *happens*. As the apostle Paul reminds us, preachers study Scripture to "convince, rebuke, and encourage, with the utmost patience in teaching" the people of God (2 Tim 4:2, NRSVue). It is not enough to explain the text; preachers need to move beyond the exegetical and hermeneutical in order to appropriate God's Word for people today. Northrop Frye's description of the poet is apropos for preachers: "The poet's job is not to tell you . . . what did take place, but the kind of thing that always does take place. He gives you the typical, recurring, or what Aristotle calls the universal event."[3] One way for preachers to do this is to think theologically, that is, to keep God at the center of the move from hermeneutics to homiletics.

### Thinking Theologically for Preaching

As one works through Daniel, it becomes clear that God's sovereignty is the preeminent message of the entire book. However, if each sermon speaks only generally to the sovereignty of God, a sermon series on Daniel will be repetitious, and the encouragement and particular aspects of God's sovereignty will be lost.

The stories contained in Daniel are literary masterpieces, and the apocalyptic revelations are awe-inducing accounts of world history. Woven through the stories and revelations is the thread of God's sovereignty. Each chapter contributes a unique vantage point from which to see a particular

---

2. More on the *preaching* section follows Figure 0.1.
3. Frye, *Educated Imagination*, 63–64.

## INTRODUCTION

aspect of this sovereignty. Therefore, one aspect of our approach to preaching Daniel will focus on the unique revelation of God's sovereignty contained in each chapter. By focusing on these unique revelations, Daniel's God becomes our God; the same God who did things in Daniel's lifetime is the same God who does things in our lifetime. What *happened* becomes what *happens* when we focus on God. The way that we see God's sovereignty played out in each chapter of Daniel is shown in Table 0.1.

| Table 0.1: Aspects of God's Sovereignty According to the Book of Daniel | |
|---|---|
| Chapter in Daniel | Aspects of God's Sovereignty |
| Daniel 1:1–21 | God demonstrates his sovereignty through the faithfulness of his people. |
| Daniel 2:1–49 | God reveals his plans to display his superior wisdom and sovereign kingdom. |
| Daniel 3:1–30 | God demonstrates his sovereign ability to rescue his faithful people. |
| Daniel 4:1–37 (3:31—4:34) | God demonstrates his sovereignty by humbling the proud and exalting the humble. |
| Daniel 5:1–31 | God, the Creator and Sustainer of life, will judge those who do not honor him. |
| Daniel 6:1–28 (2–29) | God exalts over their enemies those who are faithful to him. |
| Daniel 7:1–28 | God as sovereign over time determines the end time of all earthly kingdoms and the beginning time of his everlasting kingdom. |
| Daniel 8:1–27 | God is sovereign over those who persecute his people and the extent of the persecution. |
| Daniel 9:1–27 | God is faithful to his promises in Scripture, forgiving his people and fulfilling his decrees. |
| Daniel 10:1—12:3 | God is sovereign over the rise and fall of earthly kingdoms, and he will bring all of them to a close when he establishes his everlasting kingdom. |
| Daniel 12:4–13 | God will sanctify the wise and raise them to eternal life. |

## Thinking Instructionally for Preaching

In addition to the unchanging character of God, Daniel speaks to what *happens* through instruction. As the Apostle Paul notes to the churches in Rome, "Whatever was written in former days was written for our *instruction*, that through endurance and through the encouragement of the Scriptures we might have hope" (Rom 15:4, ESV). The book of Daniel doesn't just teach us about God, it teaches us *how to live* in light of who God is. There is a didactic element to Daniel that instructs God's people on how to navigate the complexities of life in a way that pleases and honors our sovereign King. Therefore, as expositors work through the stories and the apocalyptic revelations, they need to pay attention to how the story is told; for in the telling of the story there is implicit instruction for how to live.

God and the biblical authors chose not to teach God's people through a bullet-point list of propositional statements, but rather through carefully crafted narratives subtly embedded with instruction for God's people. The stories are told with intention. By paying careful attention to the way in which the stories are told, preachers can discern how God intends his people to respond to the teaching of the text. Through careful exegesis and theological hermeneutics, the preacher can discern the divine instruction, and that instruction becomes the application of the sermon. We have attempted to model careful exegesis, theological hermeneutics, and faithful transitions to sermons that focus on the character of God and instruction for God's people. To do this we conclude each chapter with three potential approaches to preaching/teaching the text: *The Big Idea, Following the Exegetical Flow, Following a Theme*.

## HISTORICAL CONTEXT

Understanding the historical context of Daniel highlights the sovereignty of God as the focus of the book. Two of the most significant events in the history of the ancient Near East were the rise and fall of the Babylonian and Medo-Persian empires. Daniel shows that even these two events were a part of God's sovereign plans in the unfolding of salvation history. Therefore, it is crucial to understand the history of these two empires and Israel's place in them, in order to properly interpret the book of Daniel.

### The Neo-Babylonian Empire

The Neo-Babylonian Empire was founded by Nebuchadnezzar's father, Nabopolassar, after he conquered and destroyed Nineveh, the capital of Assyria. The Medes and other peoples also participated in this destruction in 612 BC. The Assyrians set up a new government at Haran, the town in northwest Mesopotamia where Abraham had stayed until his father died (Gen 11:31–32). The end finally came for Assyria at Carchemish (northern

Syria on the Euphrates River) in 605 BC, where Nebuchadnezzar defeated the remnants of the Assyrian army. Neco, the king of Egypt, was on his way to Carchemish to aid the Assyrians when Josiah king of Judah tried to stop him and was killed in the effort (2 Chr 35:20–24). Shortly after the battle of Carchemish, Nabopolassar died, and Nebuchadnezzar hurried to Babylon to be crowned the new king. It was during this period, either before Nebuchadnezzar was officially the king or shortly after, that he laid siege to Jerusalem and the Lord delivered Jehoiakim into his power (Dan 1:2).[4]

Contemporary sources show that Nebuchadnezzar's son Evil-Merodach reigned for two years after his father's death in 562 BC. Two more kings came to the throne of Babylon and reigned until Nabonidus, the father of Belshazzar, became king as a usurper. In the third or fourth year of his reign, Nabonidus left for a stay of ten years in Arabia, entrusting the kingdom to Belshazzar. Upon his return to Babylon, Nabonidus resumed the duties of king and reigned another few years until 539 BC, when Cyrus of Persia conquered Babylon.[5]

| Table 0.2: The Neo-Babylonian Kings[6] ||
| --- | --- |
| Nabopolassar (626–25 BC) | Not mentioned in the Bible, but see Jer 46:2. |
| Nebuchadnezzar II (605–562 BC) | Mentioned ninety-one times in the OT. |
| Evil-Merodach (562–560 BC) | Son of Nebuchadnezzar; mentioned in 2 Kgs 25:27 and Jer 52:31. |
| Neriglissar (560–556 BC) | Brother-in-law of Evil-Merodach, possibly mentioned in Jer 39:3, 13. |
| Labashi-Marduk (556 BC) | Son of Neriglissar, not mentioned in the Bible. |
| Nabonidus (556–539 BC) | Possibly married a daughter of Nebuchadnezzar, not mentioned in the Bible. Spent ten years in Arabia and left control of Babylon to his son Belshazzar. |
| Belshazzar (553/552–539 BC) | Possibly a grandson of Nebuchadnezzar; in charge of Babylon when it fell to the Medes and the Persians in 539 BC; mentioned in Dan 5; 7:1; 8:1. |

4. See Hallo and Simpson, *Ancient Near East*, 141–47.

5. Beaulieu, *Reign of Nabonidus*, 95–160; Beaulieu's evidence is based on detailed analysis of documents contemporary with Nabonidus. For a list of Babylonian kings from Nabopolassar to Belshazzar, see Table 0.2.

6. Sources for Table 0.2 are Wiseman, "Historical Problems"; Parker and Dubberstein, *Babylonian Chronology*; Beaulieu, *Reign of Nabonidus*; Bracke, "Nergal-Sharezer"; and Bright, *History of Israel*.

Nebuchadnezzar made at least five incursions into Judah. At first, he was demanding allegiance to Babylon and receiving tribute. After about fifteen years of enduring rebellions against his authority, he ordered his forces to sack and destroy Jerusalem and the temple. Table 0.3 shows the historical sequence of these attacks.

| Table 0.3 Chronology of Babylonian Attacks on Judah[7] ||
|---|---|
| 605 BC | Nebuchadnezzar lays siege to Jerusalem; Jehoiakim surrenders; temple articles taken to Babylon (Dan 1:1–2) |
| 604 BC | Jehoiakim surrenders to Nebuchadnezzar in a formal ceremony that included all the kings of Syria-Palestine (2 Kgs 24:1) |
| 597 BC | Jehoiachin surrenders to Nebuchadnezzar and is taken to Babylon along with other captives; Zedekiah is appointed king of Judah by Nebuchadnezzar (2 Kgs 24:12–18) |
| 589/588 BC | Nebuchadnezzar's forces lay siege to Jerusalem in Zedekiah's ninth year, because he had rebelled against Babylonian rule (2 Kgs 25:1) |
| 587/586 BC | Nebuchadnezzar's forces take Jerusalem and burn the temple; Zedekiah's sons are executed in his sight before he is blinded and taken to Babylon; many captives are taken to Babylon (2 Kgs 25:2–11) |

## The Medo-Persian Empire

Very little information exists about the ancient Medes. Some historical evidence points to a small Median kingdom from the end of the seventh century BC to about 550 BC in central West Iran, centered around ancient Ecbatana. The fifth century Greek historian Herodotus describes the rise of the Medes.[8] A certain Deioces founded a Median kingdom and reigned for fifty-three years. He was followed by his son Phraortes who was in turn followed by his son Cyaxares, who defeated the Assyrians but was then attacked and defeated by the Scythians. Eventually the Medes defeated the Scythians and aided in the destruction of Nineveh. Cyaxares was succeeded by his son Astyages, who had a daughter who married Cambyses, a Persian. Cyrus the Great was born from their union,[9] and he eventually led a successful revolt against Median rule. The account of Herodotus has been

---

7. Edwards, "Year of Jerusalem's Destruction"; Wiseman, *1 and 2 Kings*; Rodger Young, "When Did Jerusalem Fall?"

8. Herodotus, *Hist.* 1:97–130 (Godley, LCL).

9. Xenophon (*Cyropaedia* 1:2:1, Walter Miller, LCL) supports Herodotus in describing these familial connections.

questioned, especially his narrative about Deioces and Phraortes, for which no independent evidence exists. Scholars dispute the full extent of the Median kingdom, or even if it should be considered a kingdom.[10]

The Medo-Persian empire, also known as the Achaemenid empire, was founded by Cyrus the Great, who conquered Babylon in 539 BC and died in 530 BC. In one respect Cyrus, being the son of a Median mother and a Persian father, simply continued and expanded Median rule when he defeated Astyages, his grandfather, in 550 BC. The Bible describes the conquest of Babylon as accomplished by the Medes (Isa 13:1-17; Jer 51:11, 28; Dan 5:31 [6:1]), but it describes as Persian the benevolent rule that the Jews experienced under the new regime (2 Chr 36:20-23; often in Ezra; and Neh 12:22). The continued unity of the Medes and the Persians is emphasized with reference to certain laws (Esth 1:19; Dan 6:8 [9], 12 [13]) and other organizational terminology (Esth 1:3, 14; 10:2; Dan 8:20). Occasionally there are also references in ancient Greek literature to the "Persians and Medes" or even to the "Medes" alone with reference to the Persian empire.[11]

## Israel in Exile

According to the OT, those who went into exile from Judah and Jerusalem were mostly from the educated and prosperous upper classes. The contingent of captives who came with Daniel, for example, were young men from the royal family and the nobility who could be educated in the Babylonian language and its literature. The next wave of captives included king Jehoiachin and his mother, along with their servants, government and military officials, and "all the nobles of Judah and Jerusalem" (2 Kgs 24:14). Then when Jerusalem and the temple were destroyed (586 BC), the Babylonians exiled King Zedekiah, some deserters who had defected to the Babylonian forces, and various craftsmen (2 Kgs 25:1-12; 2 Chron. 36:17-18; Jer. 52:15-16, 29).[12] 2 Kings 25:12 states that "some of the poor people of the land were left to be vinedressers and farmers." A few years later more Judeans were deported to Babylon (Jer 52:30). All told, some 4,600 Judeans were taken captive to Babylon (Jer 52:30).

10. See Muscarella, "Median Matters," 60-62; Sancisi-Weerdenburg, "Orality of Herodotus' *Medikos Logos*," 39-55.

11. See Hallo and Simpson, *Ancient Near East*, 147-49; cf. Briant, *From Cyrus to Alexander*, 25; Allen, *Persian Empire*.

12. 2 Kgs 25:11 refers to "the rest of the multitude" (יֶתֶר הֶהָמוֹן), but the parallel passage in Jer 52:15 has "the rest of the craftsmen" (יֶתֶר הָאָמוֹן). Since 2 Kgs 25:11 already mentioned "the rest of the people," it is likely that Jer 52:15 has the better reading. The *HALOT* accepts that reading for the Kings passage.

## Jews in Babylonia

Some Babylonian documents list Jehoiachin and his five sons among various captives who received food rations during the reign of Nebuchadnezzar.[13] After Nebuchadnezzar died and Evil-Merodach became king, Jehoiachin was released from prison and even dined with the new king of Babylon "all the days of his life," being supplied with a regular food allowance (2 Kgs 25:27–30; Jer 52:31–34).

While Daniel and his friends were held and educated at the court of Nebuchadnezzar in Babylon, it appears from extra-biblical data that most of the deported Judeans were placed in settlements in the area of Nippur, a Babylonian city located in the plain between the Tigris and the Euphrates rivers, southeast of Babylon and northeast of Ur. Ezekiel was at Tel Abib (exact location unknown) on the Chebar Canal (Ezek 3:15), which flows by Nippur.[14]

Three settlements in the general area of Nippur came to light recently from Babylonian documents: Judahtown (*Al-Yaḫudu* in Babylonian); Nashar; and Bit-Abi-ram.[15] The cuneiform clay tablets are part of a private collection published in 2014. The texts from Judahtown date from 572 BC to about 485 BC. A sizeable number of names in these economic documents (loans, receipts, or legal settlements) have a form of "Yahweh" in them. Judeans clearly made up "the predominant part" of the population.[16] Names with Yahweh are less common in the texts from Nashar and Bit-Abiram, but they illustrate similar economic activities in which Judeans were involved.[17]

Another group of Babylonian documents from Nippur detail the business of the Murashu family. They date to the last half of the fifth century BC and are contemporary with Ezra and Nehemiah. They attest to the presence of some Jews still present in the Nippur area, but the named individuals who were Jews "figure as smallholders, as petty officials, or as witnesses."[18] The Murashu family members were not themselves Jewish.[19]

The exiles from Judah, then, were either high ranking members of the royal families, or nobility who were kept in Babylon, or other persons of the upper class who were settled in certain towns in the area of Nippur. There

---

13. *ANET*, 308.
14. See *Macmillan Bible Atlas*, map 163.
15. Pearce and Wunsch, *Judean Exiles*, 7–9.
16. Pearce and Wunsch, *Judean Exiles*, 6.
17. Pearce and Wunsch, *Judean Exiles*, 9.
18. Stolper, "Governor of Babylon," 927–28.
19. D. W. Thomas, *Documents*, 96.

the Judeans followed the instructions of Jeremiah's letter to the exiles: "Build houses and settle. Plant gardens and eat their fruit. Get married and have sons and daughters. Marry off your sons and daughters that they may have sons and daughters. Increase in number and do not decrease" (Jer 29:5-6).

Given the prominence of these exiles, it is plausible that many were literate, or at least that someone could have read aloud for a larger group. And whether oral or written, the stories of Daniel and his friends must have circulated widely in both Babylon and in the Nippur area. For these exiles who prospered and increased in number, Daniel's visions recorded in chapters 7 to 12 served as an inspiration for them to remember their Israelite roots and to continue to worship the God of their ancestors. The Babylonian documents are not the type to include such information, but something along these lines can be deduced from them.

From Daniel's book there are hints of some prejudice against the Jews.[20] While at least some were able to prosper and become important entrepreneurs, their concentration around the area of Nippur likely represented a Babylonian attempt to confine them to a specific area. Judahtown was a Jewish enclave that is likely representative of other such concentrations of Jews. In such settlements they could carry on their affairs in peace, somewhat removed from the taunts of their captors (cf. Ps 137). Evil-merodach, successor to Nebuchadnezzar, may have elevated Jehoiachin to a place of honor in the royal court because of the reputation of Daniel. By the time of Belshazzar, however, Daniel had been pushed out of his prominent position. He would not be restored to a position of high leadership until the Medes and the Persians captured Babylon (Dan 6).

## Jews in Egypt

Even prior to when Nebuchadnezzar took Daniel and his friends to Babylon, some Judeans had settled on an island in the Nile known as Elephantine. Many papyri that were found enabled scholars to reconstruct details about this Jewish settlement. The men mostly served in Pharaoh's army and worshiped Yahweh, but at the same time they worshiped some Egyptian deities as well. They built a temple for Yahweh (spelled $Y^eho$) that was eventually destroyed by an army that was commanded by the Persian governor.[21]

---

20. See the commentary on 3:8-12, 29; 5:13; 6:4 (5)-18 (19).

21. There are different theories about why the Jews built a temple in Egypt. Porten and Yardeni (*Aramaic Documents from Egypt*, 456-61) concluded that it may have been built by priests who fled to Egypt to escape from Manasseh's persecution (2 Kgs 21:2-16), finding authorization for building a temple from Isa 19:19.

Later, they sent a letter to the governor of Judah, asking for help to rebuild their temple.[22] Several Judean officials and army commanders fled to Egypt in order to escape from captivity in Babylon (Jer 43:1–7). Jeremiah also went there but against his will. Some of this contingent may have joined the colony at Elephantine.

While Daniel himself ministered to the kings of Babylonia and Media-Persia, chapter 11 has prophecies that concern various rulers of Egypt, always called "the king of the South." Those prophecies that involved "the king of the South" and "the king of the North," then, would have been relevant both for the Jews who had returned to Judah and Jerusalem and also for the large number of Jews who were in Egypt. Josephus records that Alexander the Great was shown the book of Daniel at the temple in Jerusalem (A.J. 11.337), from which Alexander deduced that he was the fulfillment of a prophecy in Daniel. Most scholars reject the historicity of Josephus's account, but that is largely because they don't believe that the book of Daniel was in existence as early as 332 BC.

After Alexander the Great established Alexandria in Egypt in 331 BC, many Jews settled in the city (J.W. 2.487). Though the origins of the Greek translation of the Pentateuch or Torah are much debated, there is general consensus that it was completed sometime in the third century BC in Alexandria. Then by about 100 BC the remainder of the OT was complete.

Another Jewish temple was also built in Egypt, founded either by the high priest Onias III in the time of Antiochus III or by Onias's son, Onias IV. The sources from First and Second Maccabees and two works of Josephus (A.J. 13.62–73; J.W. 1.31–33) give conflicting accounts, but in either case the building of a temple in Leontopolis in the delta area of Egypt is noted.

*Jews in Persia*

The post-exilic books of Ezra, Nehemiah, Esther, Haggai, Zechariah, and Malachi have valuable information about the Jews in Persia and Judea during the sixth and fifth centuries BC under the Persian kings. Ezra and Nehemiah record two occasions when Jews returned from Babylonia to Judah and Jerusalem. Their numbers were not large; most of the Jewish exiles remained in Babylonia and Egypt. Those who did return succeeded in rebuilding the temple in Jerusalem, building a wall around Jerusalem, and establishing the observance of the Mosaic law. All this was done, however, under the authority of the Persian government. The post-exilic prophets, Haggai and

---

22. Lindenberger, *Aramaic and Hebrew Letters*, AP 30, 31, 63–68.

INTRODUCTION

Zechariah, encouraged the people to rebuild the temple and called them to account for their continued straying from God's requirements.

Information from the area of Persia itself is sparse, but the book of Esther illustrates an intense anti-Semitic attitude, also felt by Daniel and his companions in Babylon. Esther, like Daniel, shows the possibility for a Jew to attain a high government post in the Persian administration. Mordecai was "second only to King Ahasuerus" (Esth 10:3). Esther was made queen to Ahasuerus (i.e., Xerxes) but only before she revealed her identity as a Jew (Esth 2:10).

## *Summary of Israel in Exile*

Schiffman summarizes the situation of the Jews in the Persian period as follows: "While at times the Judeans had trouble with the government, Jews throughout the empire were able to rise in the civil service and even formed military units that were deployed on the frontiers of the Persian Empire. Under Persian rule Jerusalem was rebuilt and its sacrificial ritual reconstituted. In addition . . . temporal (and not just religious) authority was granted to the high priesthood."[23]

Schiffman's comments are applicable even during the Babylonian period. For the most part the Jews who were deported were able to prosper in Babylonia and Egypt. Some became quite wealthy and even, like Daniel and his three companions, found favor with the king. There was no denying, however, that they were no longer part of an independent nation. Yes, the Persians allowed the Jews who returned to Jerusalem to reestablish the worship of the Lord, and yes, they had governors and religious leaders who favored them. Yet even so they were subject to the whims of different rulers and sometimes felt the sting of anti-Semitism. They were in a precarious position, in danger of losing their identity as the people of the Lord. In some cases they compromised with local religions, mixing the worship of the Lord with the worship of other deities. They would have had feelings of abandonment, feelings stated with strong emotion in Ps 137. Hearing the stories of Daniel, Shadrach, Meshach, and Abednego would have encouraged them greatly. And Daniel's own visions, while portending hard times ahead, taught them that the Lord was still sovereign over the nations and had plans for a kingdom that his people would someday inherit.

---

23. Schiffman, *Text to Tradition*, 34.

## HISTORICAL ISSUES

### Date and Authorship

Traditionally, Daniel's book is thought to have been composed by an historical figure named Daniel who lived in the sixth century BC. Early testimony to the authorship of Daniel may be found in one of the Dead Sea Scrolls, where the writer quotes Dan 12:10 from "the book of Daniel the prophet" (4Q174 2:3–4).[24] What Jesus Christ taught about the book is of key importance for his followers. In his discourse on the Mount of Olives he referred to the "abomination of desolation that was spoken of by Daniel the prophet" (Matt 24:15; see Dan 9:27; 11:31; 12:11), giving Daniel the authority of a prophet. If, as some scholars think, a writer in the second century BC was using the name *Daniel* as a pseudonym and framing as prophecy what was only history to him, then it is hard to understand how Jesus could have called Daniel a prophet. Jesus also adopted the title "Son of Man" from Dan 7:13,[25] showing that he identified himself with that key figure in Daniel's vision. Jesus' use of Daniel's book makes the theory of a legendary Daniel theologically problematic.

While scholars who posit a Maccabean date for the writing of Daniel previously thought of a unified book,[26] the recent consensus among historical critics is that the book is a combination of two parts originally composed at different times. John Collins, for example, holds that though the court stories of Daniel 1 to 6 would have been relevant for the persecution the Jews suffered under Antiochus Epiphanes, "close consideration of the stories does not support the view that they were composed with that situation in mind."[27] The positive view of Nebuchadnezzar and "the hazards of the Jewish minority who sought to succeed in the gentile world" don't fit well with a situation of general religious persecution under Antiochus.[28] Moreover, "there is no passage in Daniel 1—6 that is necessarily understood as an allusion to the time of Antiochus Epiphanes or is now generally accepted as such."[29] But for chapters 7 to 12, according to Collins, "there is no mistaking the allusions to the Maccabean era."[30]

---

24. This document is also known as 4Q Florigium.
25. Matt 19:28; 24:27–44; 25:31; 26:64; Mark 13:26; 14:62; Luke 12:40; 17:24, 30; 18:8; 21:27; 22:69; John 5:27; 13:31–32; Acts 7:56; Rev 14:14.
26. See Rowley, "Unity of the Book of Daniel."
27. John Collins, *Daniel*, 33.
28. John Collins, *Daniel*, 33.
29. John Collins, *Daniel*, 33.
30. John Collins, *Daniel*, 33.

There are significant reasons, however, to think of the book of Daniel as a unified work. Daniel 7 makes a link between the court stories and chapters 8 to 12. Chapter 7, Daniel's own vision, is written in Aramaic rather than the Hebrew of chapters 1 and 8 to 12. It also presents a scheme of four world kingdoms that parallels Nebuchadnezzar's dream in chapter 2. The introduction to the book in Hebrew makes an additional linguistic connection with Daniel 8 to 12, while its story of how Daniel and his friends arrived at the Babylonian court both introduces and parallels Daniel 2 to 6. And Daniel 12, with its emphasis on wise people, parallels chapter 1 with its emphasis on the wisdom of Daniel and his friends.[31]

Since the two parts of the Hebrew-Aramaic book are joined together, the argument that the first part has nothing to do with Antiochus Epiphanes can cut both ways. The neo-Babylonian and early Persian setting of the first half of the book should determine the time of the entire book. Saying that reference to Antiochus Epiphanes in the second half must date it to his time denies the possibility of predictive prophecy. The sovereignty of God over history is a major theme throughout Daniel (esp. 2:20-22). God "gave" Jehoiakim of Judah into the power of Nebuchadnezzar (1:2). He "gave" Nebuchadnezzar kingdom authority on earth (2:37). The same thought is found in the second part of the book when God limits the time for defiant rulers (8:25; 9:27; 11:45). If God was unable to predict the times of Antiochus, then how could he have the kind of authority over history that Daniel continually reinforced?

The dominant view in critical scholarship holds that an unknown author or authors living in the second century BC either wrote or compiled the book about 164 BC, based on a legendary figure known as Daniel. The stories of chapters 1 to 6 are then merely entertaining and inspiring "tales," while the visions that comprise chapters 7 to 12 were written by the author to appear that they are prophetic when they record past history.

Some evidence from the Dead Sea Scrolls helps to support an earlier date for Daniel. The earliest scrolls (4QDan^c and 4QDan^e)[32] were copied around the late second or early first century BC. One scroll (4QDan^a) copied in the first century BC contains portions of Daniel 1 to 5, 7, 8, 10, and 11. All the remaining scrolls were copied in the first century BC or the first

---

31. The young men that Nebuchadnezzar chose for his court were to be *wise* (מַשְׂכִּילִם, *maskilim*, 1:4), and the *wise* (*maskilim*), according to 12:3, are destined to "shine like the brightness of the sky." The *Hiphil* of the root שׂכל also occurs in Dan 1:17; 9:13, 22, 25; 11:33, 35; and 12:10.

32. 4Q means the fourth cave at Qumran, and the superscripted letter identifies which one of the Daniel manuscripts is meant.

century AD.[33] The number of scrolls found as well as the reference in one of the sectarian documents to "Daniel the prophet" (4QFlor [4Q174], late first century BC) indicate that the community of Qumran considered the entire Hebrew/Aramaic book authoritative. Another document from the first century BC (11 QMelch 2:15–19 [11Q13]) interprets Isa 52:7 based on Daniel's prophecy at 9:25.

Considering the scenario painted by those who date Daniel to about 164 BC, it is remarkable that the book was copied and given prophetic authority within about fifty to sixty-five years of its alleged composition. Martin Hengel, who accepts the late date for the book of Daniel, makes this telling comment: "The fact that the book of Daniel . . . was received so quickly and without hesitation seems to be almost a miracle given its late origins . . . ."[34] Surely many would have known about the true author or authors of the book. Unlike Daniel's book, other works from the third to first century BC whose authorship was in question, such as the "Testaments of the Twelve Patriarchs" and "Enoch," did not gain acceptance as canonical.[35] More evidence for an early date of Daniel comes from the Greek translations, which reflect an early first or late second century BC translation.[36]

While certain scholars have raised historical and linguistic objections to a date for the book of Daniel in the sixth century BC, reasonable responses can be given in favor of that date. That is, after all, the way the book portrays itself. More decisive, though, is the near impossibility for a date as late as about 164 BC. The evidence of language, of the unity of the book, of the early date of the Greek translations, and of the Qumran scrolls, the earliest of which dates to within about fifty years of 164 BC—all these factors make a late date for the writing of the book nearly impossible. Most decisive of all, however, is the authority of Jesus Christ and the NT authors. For them Daniel was a real person and a true prophet of God.

## Chronological Issues in Daniel 1:1–2

The "third year" of Dan 1:1 appears at first glance to conflict with Jer 25:1 and 46:2. The latter passages equate the first year of Nebuchadnezzar and Pharaoh Neco's defeat at Carchemish with the fourth year of Jehoiakim.

33. See Ulrich, "Text of Daniel," for details and analysis.

34. Hengel, *Septuagint as Christian Scripture*, 95.

35. Early translations of Daniel into Greek, also evidence for the antiquity of the book, will discussed later under "The Greek Translation of Daniel."

36. For more detail about the Greek translations, see below under "The Greek Translations of Daniel."

INTRODUCTION

Many have consequently attributed an error to the author of Daniel,[37] but it seems odd that the author would contradict Jeremiah when he took such a strong interest in that prophet's book (Dan 9:2). Since there is a difference of only one year between Jeremiah's "fourth year" and Daniel's "third year," the apparent contradiction can be solved by assuming different methods of calculation and different starting points for a new year.[38]

Another issue concerns what happened in Jehoiakim's third year. The text says that Nebuchadnezzar "besieged" (וַיָּצַר) Jerusalem, made Jehoiakim submit to him, and took vessels from the temple to Babylon. The historical issue here is that there is no independent account of these events, either in the rest of the OT or in the Babylonian records. Some have said that the events as described are historically implausible in light of the Babylonian records that we do have.[39]

According to 2 Kgs 24:1-2, Jehoiakim was a vassal of Nebuchadnezzar for three years and then rebelled. Gowan thinks that the three years "must have come at the end of [Jehoiakim's] eleven-year reign,"[40] but the text nowhere indicates this. It could well be that Jehoiakim's period of servitude began late in 605 BC. or that it was measured from early 604 BC, the start of Nebuchadnezzar's official first year.[41] Daniel indicates only that Nebuchadnezzar laid siege to Jerusalem in the third year of Jehoiakim; the actual capture could have taken some time and occurred only after Nebuchadnezzar was forced to return to Babylon because of the death of his father.[42]

A more important issue concerns Jer 36:9. If Jehoiakim was still loyal to Egypt in his fifth year and worried about an impending Babylonian invasion (Jer 37:5-10), then it would contradict the import of Dan 1:1. The text of Jeremiah mentions a fast but does not specify why there was fasting. Keil thought it was to commemorate the first taking of Jerusalem by Nebuchadnezzar as described in Dan 1:2.[43] Nebuchadnezzar suffered a major defeat at the hands of the Egyptians in his fourth year (601 BC) and was forced to

---

37. John Collins, *Daniel*, 131.
38. See Millard, "Daniel in Babylon," 263-66.
39. See Gowan, *Daniel*, 43.
40. Gowan, *Daniel*, 43.
41. See Finegan, *Handbook of Biblical Chronology*, 28.
42. *Babylonian Chronicle* 5:12-13 states: "In (his) accession year Nebuchadnezzar (II) returned to Hattu. Until the month Shebat [January/February of 604 BC] he marched about victoriously in Hattu" (Grayson, *ABC*, 100). If Nebuchadnezzar took Jerusalem in December of 605 BC, then he would already be king, though it would not be his "first" regnal year yet according to the Babylonian reckoning.
43. Keil, *Ezekiel, Daniel*, 66; *Jeremiah, Lamentations*, 94-95.

return to Babylon.[44] This defeat can be correlated with Jehoiakim's submission to Nebuchadnezzar in late 605 BC, if the three years of submission to Nebuchadnezzar ( 2 Kgs 24:1) were calculated from the start of Nebuchadnezzar's official first year. According to the *Babylonian Chronicle*, near the end of that year (November or December of 604 BC), "all the kings of Hattu [Syria-Palestine] came into his presence and he received their vast tribute."[45] Jehoiakim would have become officially a vassal of Nebuchadnezzar at that time, and then rebelled three years later, being emboldened by the Egyptian victory in 601 BC.[46]

## The Identity of Darius the Mede

According to Dan 5:31 [6:1], a certain Darius the Mede "received the kingdom when he was sixty-two years old." This statement is surprising, because according to the rest of the OT, Cyrus should have been the one to receive the kingdom after the death of Belshazzar. Isa 45:1 states that Cyrus is Yahweh's "anointed one . . ., whom he holds by his right hand to subdue nations before him." The Chronicler notes that the exiled remnant of the Jews became servants of Babylonian kings "until the rule of the kingdom of Persia" (2 Chr 36:20). The land had its "sabbath rests" in fulfillment of Jeremiah's prophecy of seventy years, and it was "in the first year of Cyrus king of Persia" that he issued his proclamation granting the permission to rebuild the temple in Jerusalem "to fulfill seventy years" (2 Chr 36:21–23; cf. Jer 25:11–12; 29:10–14). Even so, Daniel's search of the prophecy of Jeremiah regarding the seventy years is dated "the first year of Darius son of Ahasuerus of the seed of the Medes" (9:1).

The book of Daniel mentions Cyrus only three times (1:21; 6:28 [29]; 10:1), while in the rest of the OT he is mentioned twenty times. Darius the Mede is mentioned eleven times in Daniel 6 and twice elsewhere in Daniel (9:1; 11:1). Outside of the book of Daniel, no individual who is called Darius the Mede is mentioned in Scripture or anywhere else. The only Darius the rest of Scripture knows is Darius (Hystaspes), the king of Persia by whose reign the books of Haggai and Zechariah are dated, and his reign did not begin until about 520 BC.

The king who conquered Babylon is known as Cyrus in extra biblical sources,[47] and Darius the Mede is not mentioned anywhere else in the Bible

---

44. Grayson, *ABC*, 101.
45. Grayson, *ABC*, 100.
46. Wiseman, *1 and 2 Kings*, 328.
47. Herodotus; Xenophon; Babylonian Chronicle 7:15–17 (Nabonidus Chronicle);

or in ancient sources outside of the Bible.[48] Many argue that the author of Daniel made a blunder when he said that Darius the Mede "received the kingdom" of Babylon rather than Cyrus. Jeremiah 51:11 states that the Lord would use the Medes to conquer Babylon, so perhaps, according to the argument, the author of Daniel got the name from the biblical references to the later Persian king known as Darius (e.g., Ezra 4:5).[49] It should be noted, though, that the book of Ezra, which was written much earlier than the second century BC, places Cyrus earlier than Darius Hystaspes (4:5 and 6:14), whereas in Daniel, Darius the Mede is situated either prior to or simultaneous with Cyrus (Dan 6:28 [29]).

Whitcomb equated Darius the Mede with a certain Gubaru, who was appointed governor of Babylon by Cyrus.[50] His view has two major problems. First, there is general agreement that the names Gubaru and Ugbaru in the Nabonidus Chronicle refer to one individual, not two different persons as Whitcomb thought. The two forms of the name are simply phonetic variants, and it is clear that the general who conquered Babylon for Cyrus died some eight days after Babylon fell.[51] Secondly and more importantly, according to cuneiform sources Cambyses, the son of Cyrus, was appointed king of Babylon in the first year of Cyrus, and it was another individual named Gubaru who was appointed governor of Babylon only several years later.[52] It could also be objected that it is unlikely that a mere governor would be treated like a king as chapter 6 of Daniel portrays Darius.

Recently, Steven Anderson has revised an older view that Darius the Mede is to be identified with a certain Cyaxares, said by the ancient Greek writer Xenophon to be the uncle of Cyrus the Great.[53] Herodotus and the Babylonian sources do not mention Cyaxares, but Josephus and Jerome agree that a certain Darius, the king of the Medes, was the maternal uncle of Cyrus. Jerome cites Xenophon for his information, and it is quite likely that Josephus relied on Xenophon as well.[54] If Cyaxares is indeed a throne name for Darius the Mede, then Xenophon has Cyrus become ruler of Babylon

---

the Cyrus Cylinder; and Berossus (Greek).

48. Some sources, such as Josephus (*A.J.* 10), are exceptions that had knowledge of the book of Daniel.

49. See Rowley, *Darius the Mede and the Four World Empires* rev, 59.

50. Whitcomb, *Darius the Mede*.

51. Beaulieu, *Reign of Nabonidus*, 227.

52. Grabbe, "*Gestalt* of Darius the Mede," 201–3; Shea, "Darius the Mede," 97; Nicolò, *Prosopographie neubabylonischer Beamten*, 63.

53. Steven Anderson, *Darius the Mede*; Xenophon, *Cyropaedia* 1:4:9.

54. Josephus, *A.J.* 10:248; Jerome, *Commentary on Daniel*, 55; Steven Anderson, *Darius the Mede*, 4.

immediately after conquering it but, according to Anderson, as a subordinate king to Cyaxares/Darius. For Anderson's view to work, Cyaxares/Darius would be taking an active role at first, doing all the things described of Darius the Mede in chapter six of Daniel. Then when Cyaxares/Darius dies, Cyrus becomes king (Dan 6:28 [29]). Anderson, however, says that Cyrus was actively involved in organizing "Medo-Persian rule over Babylon," with Cyaxares ruling officially from his palace in Media.[55] Daniel, however, clearly assigns the organization of Babylon to Darius the Mede, something he could hardly do if not present in Babylon.

Most historians view Cyaxares the uncle of Cyrus as "wholly unhistorical."[56] Herodotus and the ancient Babylonian texts have Cyrus defeating Astyages and thereby becoming king of the Medes, but Xenophon introduced Cyaxares as the successor of Astyages and helpful uncle of Cyrus. Anderson prefers Xenophon's account over Herodotus and the Babylonian texts, arguing that those accounts became contaminated with bias for which Cyrus himself was responsible. Cyrus, according to Xenophon, was the ideal ruler and became the ruler of the Persian empire through force of his leadership qualities more than through physical force. Cyrus, then, was portrayed by Xenophon as an ideal ruler.

A more likely solution to the identity of Darius the Mede was proposed by Wiseman, namely that Darius the Mede is an alternate name for Cyrus the Persian.[57] This would entail reading Dan 6:28 (29) as "in the reign of Darius, that is, in the reign of Cyrus the Persian." Such a reading is linguistically justifiable and assumes that *Darius*, a name borne by three later Persian kings, was an alternate name for *Cyrus*.[58] Precedent for dual names for a king is known from the Bible and from other ancient sources. For example, Tiglath-pileser was also known as Pul, as attested both in the Bible and in cuneiform inscriptions.[59] In 1 Chr 5:26 the two names occur together: "the spirit of Pul, king of Assyria, *even* [Hebrew 1] the spirit of Tilgath-pilneser, king of Assyria." More to the point, Daniel and his companions had dual names; dual languages were used in the book; and "the Medes and the Persians" is best taken as referring to a single kingdom with two parts.[60] Cyrus the Great, according to Herodotus and the *Babylonian*

---

55. Steven Anderson, *Darius the Mede*, 124.
56. Rowley, *Darius the Mede and the Four World Empires*, 42.
57. Wiseman, "Historical Problems," 9–16.
58. Both ancient Greek versions (OG and Th) have *Cyrus* instead of *Darius* at Dan 11:1.
59. Grayson, "Tiglath-pileser," 552.
60. Colless, "Cyrus the Persian and Darius the Mede," 113–26.

*Chronicles*, conquered Media in 550 BC, so when he conquered Babylon in 539 BC, his kingdom could already be called *Medo-Persian*.[61] Prophets previous to Daniel also predicted the overthrow of the Babylonians by both the Medes (Isa 13:17; 21:2; Jer 51:11, 28) and the Persians (*Elam* in Isa 21:2).

According to Herodotus and Xenophon, Cyrus's father Cambyses, who was Persian, married the daughter of Astyages, the king of the Medes.[62] This would make Cyrus part Persian and part Median. At Dan 9:1 the father of Cyrus is said to be Ahasuerus, but this may refer to his grandfather Astyages or to "an ancient Achaemenid royal title" given to one of Cyrus's ancestors.[63] Darius is never called king of the Medes. Only his Median ancestry is mentioned, following the Jewish custom of tracing the ancestry of a person of mixed parents through the mother (cf. Deut 7:3). Cyrus, on the other hand, is called "the king of Persia" at Dan 10:1, and at 11:1 both ancient Greek versions substitute Cyrus for Darius the Mede. Bulman offers the following explanation for the prominence of the name Darius the Mede over Cyrus: "The author of Daniel pondered the problem of the restoration from reading Jeremiah (Dan 9:2). Unlike the authors of Chronicles and Ezra, however, he does not represent Cyrus as the agent of fulfillment of prophecy. But since Jeremiah, who mentioned no name, emphasized the Medes as conquerors of Babylon, Daniel was led . . . to use the name which was associated with them."[64] While it is difficult to prove that Cyrus was also known as Darius without extra-biblical verification, until further data become known, this appears to be the best solution to the identity of Darius the Mede.[65]

## LITERARY GENRE

On a general level there are two types of literature in the book of Daniel—narratives about Daniel and his friends in the royal court and apocalyptic visions narrated by Daniel himself.

---

61. The Greeks often called Persians "Medes" (Tuplin, "Persians as Medes," 235).
62. Herodotus, *Hist.* 1:107–23; Xenophon, *Cyro.* 1:2:1.
63. Wiseman, "Historical Problems," 15.
64. Bulman, "Darius the Mede," 267.
65. See also Steinmann, *Daniel*, 290–96; cf. Sprinkle, *Daniel*, 30–33. Colless treats the book of Daniel "as a veritable mystery story, full of puzzles to be solved by the reader." He considers the names Darius and Cyrus as alternate names for the same person, thus contributing to the "mystery" ("Cyrus the Persian and Darius the Mede," 113).

## Court Narrative

As for the stories, they have a certain exaggerated quality about them, as though they were caricatures of the events. Daniel and his young companions, for example, were *ten times* wiser than *all* the wise men in Nebuchadnezzar's *whole realm* (1:20). Chapter 3 has constant repetition of lists of government officials, musical instruments, and terms for the general population. Even the names "Shadrach, Meshach, and Abednego" occur over and over. The story about Belshazzar (chapter 5) uses a repeated pun to highlight his dismal failure as a king. He was in such terror at seeing the writing on the wall that the "knots" of his loins were "untied." Eventually, Daniel was summoned because he was able "to untie knots" (i.e., "solve difficult problems," 5:12, 16). The king's embarrassment showcased Daniel's special ability to solve mysteries. In short, literary techniques like hyperbole, repetition, and word play heighten the emotional impact, increase the sense of wonder, and add to the entertainment value of the stories.

None of the literary techniques by which the stories are told need mean that they were only folk legends.[66] Historical characters can also be caricatured and made to look larger than life. One could think of the separate accounts of David in Samuel and Kings versus that found in Chronicles. Both give accurate historical information, but the reader is left with a different impression of David in each. And even if one thinks of a narrator/editor who attached stories about Daniel and his friends to Daniel's own recorded visions, that also does not have to mean that the stories are fictitious. The miraculous elements are unusual but surely not beyond the God of Scripture, who often injects himself into human affairs in unusual ways. Our assumption is that as part of inspired Scripture it makes good sense to treat the narratives of Daniel as true stories that are told in an entertaining and impressive manner.

Daniel is portrayed in the narratives as a wise man who excels beyond Babylonian and Persian wise men, and his wisdom is different from theirs. They must rely on various techniques of divination to interpret mysteries, but Daniel had no need of such methods. Through his faith in the Lord and prayer he received the wisdom he needed to interpret Nebuchadnezzar's dreams or Belshazzar's handwriting on the wall. It was his direct, personal connection to God that made all the difference, even as the book of Proverbs and many other OT Scriptures present the possibility of wisdom for all who seek it. And when it came to knowing practical ways of wisdom, Daniel surpassed the leaders of Persia and received the top administrative position in the kingdom.

---

66. *Contra* John Collins, *Daniel*, 44–45.

## Apocalyptic

Chapters 7 to 12 of Daniel have been broadly described as "apocalyptic." Older studies tended to make lists of characteristics that would identify literature as apocalyptic,[67] but more recently the thought has been to view "a body of texts sharing a family resemblance."[68] These features "interconnect family members, but they are not necessary, fixed features or any ultimate essence."[69] John Collins famously defined the genre: *"'Apocalypse' is a genre of revelatory literature within a narrative framework, in which a revelation is mediated by an otherworldly being to a human recipient disclosing a transcendent reality which is both temporal, insofar as it envisages eschatological salvation, and spatial insofar as it involves another, supernatural world."*[70]

Daniel's visions are given "within a narrative framework" and involve interpreting angels who bring him special revelation from God. Also, they climax in "eschatological salvation" when God's eternal kingdom supplants all the kingdoms of this world. Daniel's "eschatological salvation" also includes "some form of personal afterlife," making reference to a future resurrection (Dan 12:2).[71] According to Collins's definition, then, the visions in Daniel fit well the genre of an apocalypse.

John Collins also classifies Daniel with a group of Jewish apocalypses that according to him were composed between about 250 BC and AD 150.[72] He further considers Daniel 7 to 12 a type of apocalypse that gives a survey of history that is presented as though it were revealed in advance by heavenly intermediaries. In reality, though, all the so-called predictions were past history for the author (*ex eventu* prophecy). Also, the "visionary is always pseudonymous."[73] That is, the person who receives the vision is falsely claimed to be a great figure of the past, as for example Enoch in the books that bear his name (cf. Gen 5:18–24). For reasons to be discussed shortly, however, we see that the book of Daniel differs from other Jewish apocalyptic visions in that a historical Daniel had real visions through which he received genuine revelations about the future.

Other biblical books also have apocalyptic features, such as angelic mediation and a theology of eschatological salvation. Examples would be

---

67. E.g., Russell, *Jewish Apocalyptic*, 9.
68. Cook, *Apocalyptic Literature*, 22.
69. Cook, *Apocalyptic Literature*, 22.
70. John Collins, "Morphology of a Genre," 9. (Emphasis his.)
71. John Collins, "Morphology of a Genre," 9.
72. John Collins, "Morphology of a Genre," 22–23.
73. John Collins, "Morphology of a Genre," 24.

portions of Ezekiel and Zechariah. While apocalyptic features are more pronounced in Daniel (at least for chapters 7 to 12) than in other biblical books, that is due to Daniel's unique situation in Babylon and Persia. Being among the wise men in the royal court, imagery that was latent with symbolic meaning conveyed through dreams would have been natural for him.[74] The apocalyptic features of Daniel, then, can be related to features found in other books of the OT but enhanced through the cultural milieu of the Babylonian court. God revealed himself through Scripture in ways that were reflective of the writer's own cultural situation, and that was true of Daniel's visions as well.

## Wisdom and Prophecy

The German scholar Gerhard von Rad thought that Jewish apocalyptic literature arose from wisdom circles rather than from earlier prophetic works.[75] His view has not gone unchallenged. According to John Collins, "There is no doubt that Daniel also stands in continuity with the prophetic tradition, especially as it developed in the post-exilic period."[76] While we would argue that Daniel's connections should rather be with pre-exilic (e.g., Isa) or exilic prophets (e.g., Ezek), the debate illustrates well the variant positions of the book of Daniel within Jewish and Christian traditions. In Christian Bibles Daniel is placed as the last of the Major Prophets, while in Jewish Bibles the book is found in the section known as the "Writings" (*Ketubim*).[77] Daniel is thus included with biblical wisdom literature (Job, some Pss [e.g. Ps 1], Prov, Eccl, and Song) in Jewish traditions.[78]

Prophetic analogs to Daniel's apocalyptic material would include Isa (24–25, 56–66), Ezek (37–39), Joel, and Zech. Wisdom material within Daniel is pervasive in the court narratives, with Daniel and his friends said to be wiser than all the other wise men at the Babylonian court (cf. Dan 1:17-20; 2:47-48; 4:7-9 [4-6]). Daniel appears at court as a wise interpreter of dreams, and in the apocalyptic material he receives his own dreams and

---

74. For discussion about dream interpretation in ancient Mesopotamia see Oppenheim, *Interpretation of Dreams*.

75. Von Rad, *Wisdom in Israel*, 263–83.

76. John Collins, *Daniel*, 59.

77. The Hebrew Bible has three sections: *Torah*; *Prophets*; and *Writings*. The *Torah* consists of the five books of Moses, and the *Prophets* division consists of Joshua, Judges, I and II Samuel, I and II Kings, Isaiah, Jeremiah, Ezekiel, and *The Twelve* (Minor Prophets). All the rest of the books are in the *Writings*, including the book of Daniel.

78. For the view that it was only in the post-NT age that Daniel was classified among the Writings rather than as a prophet, see Finley ("Daniel in the Canon").

# INTRODUCTION

visions with an angelic interpreter. The reader first encounters Daniel and his companions among the מַשְׂכִּילִים ("wise ones") that Nebuchadnezzar placed in his Babylonian school (1:4), and the rest of the book demonstrates how perfectly Daniel fits that description. At the end of the book there is reference to the מַשְׂכִּילִים (*wise ones*) who will give insight to others, and the reader has no doubt that Daniel is among them as well (11:33, 35; 12:3, 10). The theme verse of the book, 2:20–22, states that all *wisdom* comes from God and that he is responsible for removing and establishing kings. Daniel's own visions show how dependent he is on divine interpretation, and they show how God controls the movement of history through the ages as well. So while Daniel follows in the train of the prophets, he also blossoms as one of God's greatest wise men (cf. Ezek. 28:3). Both characteristics, wisdom and prophecy, show up in the book that he has bequeathed to Scripture.

The significance of the book's dual pedigree—prophecy and wisdom—lies in its abiding message. If we focus only on the wisdom elements, then we could miss how the book centers our hope on God, who works not only in the future but who also controls the future. And if we dwell only on the prophetic elements found in apocalyptic, we miss how the book can shape us in our faithfulness to God. Moreover, there is a tension within the book between these two streams of revelation. In the narratives about the royal court the issue of human faithfulness comes to the fore, whereas in the apocalyptic visions God's sovereignty over all of history reigns supreme. And chapter 9 heightens the tension when Daniel first prays for forgiveness, but then hears about an historical framework that includes even greater hardship for his Jewish people in the future. This tension represents the human condition for the believer. On the one hand, God's followers are responsible to remain faithful and to repent when they depart from his ways; and their faithfulness can in some mysterious way influence the outworking of history. On the other hand, they need to trust that God is always and everywhere in complete control of events, and that he will judge all wickedness in due time.

## THE STRUCTURE OF THE BOOK OF DANIEL

### The Bipartite Structure of the Book of Daniel

The book of Daniel divides into two parts. The first part consists of episodes in the lives of Daniel and his three friends at the court of the king, recorded from the perspective of a narrator (Dan 1–6). The events of chapters 1–4 take place at the court of Nebuchadnezzar, the king of Babylon; chapter

5 concerns the last Babylonian king, Belshazzar; and chapter 6 ushers in the era of the Medes and Persians under "Darius the Mede" (5:31) and concludes with "Cyrus the Persian" (6:28). The second part of the book, chapters 7—12, contains Daniel's own visions recorded in first person style, although the voice of a narrator is not entirely absent (7:1; 10:1).

When the book of Daniel is examined in its standard form as embraced by Jews and Protestants (as opposed to an expanded form in the Septuagint), the surprising fact emerges that it was written in two languages, namely Hebrew and Aramaic. The following general outline will be based on both language and genre.

## General Outline of the Book of Daniel

I. 1:1–21 Introduction to the Book

II. 2:1—6:28 [29] Court Stories

III. 7:1–28 Daniel's First Vision

IV. 8:1–27 Daniel's Second Vision

V. 9:1–19 Daniel's Prayer for His People

VI. 9:20–27 Gabriel's Message of the Seventy Weeks Given to Daniel

VII. 10:1—11:1a Introduction to Daniel's Third Vision

VIII. 11:1—12:2 Daniel's Third Vision

IX. 12:3–13 Epilogue to Daniel's Visions

The way the book divides by language highlights three distinct sections. The introduction in Hebrew provides the historical setting of the book and brings Daniel and his three companions onto the scene, at the same time explaining how these four Judean exiles received important positions in the Babylonian court. The Aramaic section details the activities of these men in the court but also includes the first of Daniel's personal visions. Like Nebuchadnezzar's dream found in chapter two of the Aramaic section, Daniel's vision of chapter seven uses the same scheme of four successive kingdoms or empires to outline the remaining history of the world; and it brings the Aramaic portion to an end. The visions recorded in Hebrew for the remainder of the book then give more detailed prophecies concerning the third or Greek kingdom as well as concerning the fourth and final kingdom.

INTRODUCTION

The contents of the six Aramaic chapters are arranged in a *chiastic* or inverted literary pattern.[79] Figure 0.2 illustrates the chiastic pattern. The first and last parts (A and A') have the theme of four kingdoms. They show how God reveals mysteries and as the Ancient of Days is Lord over all history. The next set of chapters (B and B') display how God can deliver those who are faithful to him. The center chapters (C and C') focus on human response to who God is. That response is either humility or pride. If we refuse to humble ourselves, then God will humble us, according to chapter 4. Chapter 5 shows the disastrous results when people attempt to exalt themselves over God. That is a central theme of the book—God will humble the proud and exalt the humble (cf. Prov 3:34 [LXX]; Jas 4:6; 1 Pet 5:5).[80]

**Figure 0.2. Chiastic Structure of Daniel 2–7**

A Chapter 2: Nebuchadnezzar's dream of four kingdoms

    B Chapter 3: The three men rescued from the fiery furnace

        C Chapter 4: Nebuchadnezzar's downfall through pride

        C' Chapter 5: Belshazzar's downfall through pride

    B' Chapter 6: Daniel rescued from the lions' den

A' Chapter 7: Daniel's vision of four kingdoms

## THE TWO LANGUAGES OF THE BOOK OF DANIEL

Despite S. R. Driver's confident assertion that the Aramaic of Daniel "permits" and its Hebrew "demands" a date in the second century BC,[81] there are good reasons to situate the Aramaic and Hebrew of the book no later than the third century BC.

### Aramaic

Daniel 2:4b–7:28 is in the Aramaic language. Using language as a basis for assigning an approximate date to a written document requires works of known date as points of reference. The history of Aramaic is commonly

---

79. Lenglet, "Daniel 2–7," 170–89.

80. See also Davis (*Message of Daniel*, 22–24) for further ideas about the intricate structure of chapters 2–7.

81. Driver, *Book of Daniel*, lxiii.

divided into Old Aramaic (OA, inscriptions from the tenth to the seventh century BC), Standard Literary Aramaic (SLA, various documents, especially papyri, from the sixth to the third century BC), Middle Aramaic (MA, texts from the second century BC to the second century AD, especially the Aramaic of the Dead Sea Scrolls), and Late Aramaic (LA, writings from the third to the ninth century). After my own detailed study of the Aramaic of Daniel, I concluded that Daniel falls into the period of SLA and not MA. Some salient points are as follows:

1. The Aramaic of Daniel is like that of Ezra (fifth century BC with correspondence from the sixth century BC).

2. The Qumran scrolls of Daniel show that some scribal updating took place in the Masoretic Text that can help to account for spelling differences and some minor morphological differences from SLA texts of the sixth and fifth centuries BC.

3. Some features, such as the overwhelming presence of *Haphel* patterns of the verb as opposed to *Aphel* patterns, point to a period earlier than the second century BC.

4. Daniel's Aramaic contains numerous loanwords from Akkadian and Old Persian.[82] Since Daniel was schooled in "the literature and language of the Chaldeans" (Dan 1:4), the presence of Akkadian loanwords would hardly be surprising if the book was authored as early as the sixth century BC. Many of the Akkadian loans are attested elsewhere in SLA.

5. As a book that was transmitted by scribes, it makes sense that scribes from the MA or later periods would have made spellings that were variable in SLA consistent.[83]

From Kitchen's discussion of the Aramaic of Daniel the following important points about the Persian loanwords should be noted:[84]

1. They were taken from Old Persian (prior to about 300 BC), not Middle Persian.

---

82. A convenient listing of all loanwords in biblical Aramaic may be found in Rosenthal (*Grammar of Biblical Aramaic*, 57–59).

83. E.g., wherever a Qumran scroll of Daniel has preserved a word for which a choice could be made between a spelling with either *zayin* (ז) or *dalet* (ד), the spelling with *dalet* was chosen, whereas in SLA the spellings were more variable.

84. Kitchen, "Aramaic of Daniel," 37–44.

2. The translators of the Old Greek, working about 100 BC,[85] had difficulty understanding certain Persian loanwords.

3. Daniel presumably wrote during the reign of Cyrus when he had a high administrative post, accounting for the many Persian terms.

There is nothing about the Aramaic of Daniel, then, to indicate that the book could not have been composed earlier than the second century BC, and there is some evidence to indicate composition of the book even earlier.

## Hebrew

S. R. Driver compiled a list of twenty-five words and idioms in Daniel that he thought substantiated his observation that *"in all distinctive features [the Hebrew of Daniel] resembles, not the Hebrew of Ezekiel, or even of Haggai or Zechariah, but that of the age subsequent to Nehemiah."*[86] To this list he added the evidence of various Persian words, Aramaisms, and a style that is "often laboured and inelegant."[87] John Collins thinks that the Hebrew of the book of Daniel has more in common with Second Temple Hebrew than with exilic Hebrew. As part of his evidence, he cites with approval Driver's list and adds several arguments of his own.[88]

Others have defended an earlier dating of the Hebrew of Daniel. Robert Wilson challenged seven "assumptions" that he ascribed to Driver, all relating to the root עמד (e.g. that עמד in the *Qal* with the sense *stand up* is a feature of Hebrew after the age of Nehemiah). Wilson concluded that the various uses of the root עמד in Daniel show evidence of Babylonian influence rather than Aramaic.[89] Martin also responded to Driver, finding

---

85. John Collins (*Daniel*, 8–9) thinks a date for the OG of Daniel in the late second century BC is "most probable." Kitchen gave a range from 100 BC to AD 100 for "the first important Greek translation of Daniel" ("Aramaic of Daniel," 14), but anything after the first century BC is probably too late.

86. S. R. Driver, *Introduction*, 506–8.

87. S. R. Driver, *Introduction*, 506–8. Polak ("Written and Oral Narrative," 33–103) presented some ways to discern the difference between oral and written styles based on sociolinguistics. He referred to a "complex-nominal style" that "reflects the language skills of the professional and experienced scribe" (80). Many examples of the characteristics that Polak adduced for the "complex-nominal style" can be found in the Hebrew portions of Daniel (e.g., 1:3–4, which includes complex subordination and long noun groups), and this could account at least partly for Driver's characterization of the style of Daniel's Hebrew as "laboured," given that Daniel wrote as an "experienced scribe."

88. John Collins, *Daniel*, 20–21.

89. Robert Wilson, "Hebrew of Daniel," 177–99.

that some of his allegedly late terms can be found in earlier books as well.[90] As an example, the term מַלְכוּת for *kingdom* or *reign* is found in Numbers, 1 Samuel, Jeremiah, Ezra, and Nehemiah. "It is not only well attested but it is a pattern of noun widely used in all periods of Hebrew, and is found in Akkadian as early as Hammurabi."[91]

Archer compared the Hebrew of Daniel with that of two Qumran sectarian documents, *The Rule of the Congregation* (1QS) and *The War of the Sons of Light against the Sons of Darkness* (1QM).[92] He successfully indicated a few late traits in these documents that do not appear in the Hebrew of Daniel or in the OT generally (e.g., אנו for *we* versus אֲנַחְנוּ and a preference for *lamed* with the infinitive in place of an imperfect).[93] Especially telling is the term קץ, which occurs in the Qumran sectarian documents in the sense of *time* (e.g., 1QS 10:1) but with the standard biblical sense of *end* in Daniel (8:17 and often).

For the Hebrew of Daniel many of the allegedly late features are related to the influence of Aramaic. Taken captive to Babylon as a youth, perhaps around the age of fifteen, Daniel was immediately immersed into the "language and literature of the Chaldeans" (Dan 1:4). He continued to live in Babylon throughout the Neo-Babylonian and early Achaemenid (Persian) periods. In the court of Nebuchadnezzar he would have studied Akkadian and Aramaic, perhaps even Sumerian. By the time he recorded his visions he was likely more fluent in writing Aramaic than in writing Hebrew. And he used both languages for the visions, with chapter 7 in Aramaic but chapters 8 to 12 in Hebrew. For Daniel, then, to use a vocabulary laced with Aramaisms would have been natural even in the late sixth century BC. That some of those Aramaisms survived into post-biblical Aramaic and/or Hebrew could have been due to scribes such as Ezra.

There is no question that Daniel's Hebrew is "late" in the sense of having been written towards the end of the exile. Keeping in mind that the text of Daniel was transmitted over a long period of time by scribes and that the circumstances of the prophet Daniel must be related to the two languages in the book, there is reason to believe that the book could have been composed in both languages in the sixth century BC.

---

90. Martin, "Hebrew of Daniel," 28–30.
91. Martin, "Hebrew of Daniel," 28.
92. Archer, "Hebrew of Daniel," 470–81.
93. In Jer 42:6 אנו occurs as the *kethiv*, with אֲנַחְנוּ as the *qere*.

INTRODUCTION

## THE TEXTS OF DANIEL

Individual comments on the text of Daniel will be in translation footnotes or exposition. Here we will make some general comments about the textual history of the book of Daniel.

### The Qumran Scrolls and Daniel

Eight different fragmentary scrolls of Daniel came from the caves near the site of Qumran on the northwestern shore of the Dead Sea. A full list of the scrolls, their content, and their approximate date may be found in Ulrich, "The Text of Daniel in the Qumran Scrolls."[94] The earliest scroll (4QDan$^c$) was copied in the late second or early first century BC.[95] Notably, it contains portions of chapters 10 and 11, the very chapters that mainstream scholarship dates to about 165 BC. Several other Daniel scrolls date to the first century BC (4QDan$^a$, 4QDan$^d$, and 4QDan$^e$). The rest were copied sometime during the first century AD but prior to AD 70.[96]

### The Greek Translations of Daniel

Two ancient Greek translations of Daniel are known. One, the Old Greek (OG), was done about 100 BC.[97] The other, *Theodotion* (Th), is a translation that replaced the Old Greek in the main manuscripts of the Septuagint.[98] Since the Old Greek was quoted in 1 Maccabees, it must have been translated at least as early as 100 BC and possibly even earlier.[99] Since the apocryphal additions to Daniel, found in both Greek versions, appear to be

---

94. Ulrich, "Text of Daniel," 574; see also Steinmann, *Daniel*, 62, fig. 5.

95. Ulrich, "Text of Daniel," 574.

96. For discussion about determination of the date of the book of Daniel based on the scrolls from Qumran, see "Date and Authorship" above.

97. The OG of Daniel is attested in three sources: Papyrus 967 (second or third century AD); the Syro-Hexapla (seventh century); and the Chisian manuscript 88 (ninth to eleventh century). P967 preserves a pre-hexaplaric form of the text, but it was not discovered until 1931 and only fully published by 1976. It is fully utilized in the revised Göttingen edition of the Septuagint of Daniel, edited by Ziegler and Munnich (*Susanna-Daniel-Bel et Draco*).

98. Jerome attributed the later Greek translation of Daniel to Theodotion, who did his work in the second century. The translation must have been much older, however, because there are readings from Theodotion's translation of Daniel in the Greek NT (Hartman and Di Lella, *Book of Daniel*, 81).

99. John Collins, *Daniel*, 8–9.

secondary to the Hebrew/Aramaic text, it is clear that the Hebrew/Aramaic text had to be in existence some time prior to 100 BC. Thus, the Old Greek of Daniel in combination with the Qumran Daniel scrolls at least complicates the frequent assumption that the book was not composed until the Maccabean era.

## DANIEL IN THE LARGER BIBLICAL CONTEXT

The prophet Daniel is also known from the book of Ezekiel, and Daniel supplies much of the background to the imagery in the book of Revelation.

## "Daniel" in the Book of Ezekiel

Three passages in the book of Ezekiel mention a figure named Daniel: Ezek 14:14, 20; and 28:3. Is it possible that Ezekiel knew of the Daniel of the book when both were in Babylonia at the same time? The traditional answer is that Ezekiel refers to the Daniel who was part of the court of Nebuchadnezzar. If so, then it becomes strong evidence for an historical Daniel of the sixth century BC.

In Ezek 14:14, 20 *Daniel* occurs between Noah and Job, both of whom are ancient figures and non-Israelite. Some have looked for a figure more ancient than the prophet Daniel, then, who was also non-Israelite.[100] Critical scholars suggest that *Daniel* in Ezekiel refers to a legendary figure named *Dan'el* known from the Ugaritic story of *Aqhat* (ca. 1200 BC). The theory is that the name *Daniel* for the figure at Nebuchadnezzar's court was derived from this early legendary figure.[101]

The "Dan'el" of the story of *Aqhat* worshiped idols, and there is no obvious indication that he was known for wisdom. He was a king who "judged the cases of widows, [and] presided over orphans' hearings" but that was the expectation of rulers in the ancient world and did not necessarily indicate either wisdom or righteousness.[102] The Daniel who was among the wise men in Babylon, though, was clearly righteous (Dan 1:8) and wise (Dan 1:20). Moreover, his wisdom was imparted by the God of Israel (Dan 2:21), and he was not devoted to any pagan deity.

Ezek 28:3 shows that Daniel was well known in Phoenicia as a wise man. Using sarcasm, the Lord said to "the ruler of Tyre": "Behold, you are

---

100. Eichrodt, *Ezekiel*, 188–99.
101. John Collins, *Daniel*, 1.
102. Dressler, "Identification of the Ugaritic Dnil," 154.

wiser than Daniel; no secret amazes you." Ezekiel's oracle can be dated to about 587 BC.[103] Since Daniel went into captivity in 605 BC, that means he would have been in Babylon for about eighteen years already. During this time, he had at a minimum interpreted Nebuchadnezzar's first dream. And Daniel's close relationship with Nebuchadnezzar as seen in Daniel 4 shows many more years must have passed. If Daniel's interpretation of Nebuchadnezzar's second dream was a few years prior to the fall of Jerusalem, then the letter about Daniel's wise counsel that the king sent "to all the peoples, nations, and languages that live in all the earth" would have gone to Tyre as well. The ruler of Tyre and Nebuchadnezzar were enemies at that time (Ezek 26:7–14), and Ezekiel's reference to Daniel's wisdom would have given the king of Tyre pause. The contest would be between Daniel, whose wisdom stemmed from God, and the ruler of Tyre, whose wisdom stemmed from his own pride. The prophet Daniel fits better with Ezekiel's *Daniel* than the figure Dan'el in the story of Aqhat. The wisdom of the three figures in Ezekiel 14 was more important than their ancient status or their Israelite or non-Israelite background.

## Allusions to Daniel in the New Testament

What Jesus taught about the book of Daniel is of key importance for his followers. In his discourse on the Mount of Olives he referred to the phrase "abomination of desolation," which he said was "spoken of by Daniel the prophet" (Matt 24:15; see Dan 9:27; 11:31; 12:11). The most natural way to understand his statement is that Jesus gives Daniel the authority of a prophet. Additionally, when Jesus adopted the title *Son of Man* from Daniel 7:13, he identified himself with that figure and saw himself as the fulfillment of the vision at some future point.[104]

Some allusions to Daniel's vision of the four beasts from the great sea are in Revelation 17, especially verses eight and twelve. John saw a "beast" with seven heads and ten horns (v. 3), calling to mind both the fourth beast that Daniel saw that had ten horns (7:7) and the third beast that had four heads (7:6). John's beast "was and is not and is about to ascend from the abyss" (17:8). The *abyss* (ἄβυσσος) alludes to the "great sea" from which Daniel's beasts arose (Dan 7:2). The Greek term is used in the Septuagint to translate תְּהוֹם ([the] *deep*), which often implies the deep waters of the sea (Gen 1:2; 7:11; 8:2; Pss 33:7; 77:16 [17]; 104:6; 107:26; 135:6; Job 38:16;

---

103. Block, *Ezekiel 25–48*, 31.

104. France, *Jesus and the Old Testament*, 144–50; Bock, "Daniel 7 in Jesus' Trial," 78–100; cf. Adela Collins, "Christian Interpretation," 90–105.

Jonah 2:5 [6]; Isa 51:10; Ezek 26:19). Even as for Daniel the different beasts represented the demonic forces behind the nations in their opposition to God, so the abyss stood for the abode of demons (Luke 8:31; Rev 9:11; 11:7; 20:1–3). Also, both Daniel and John saw a horn or horns from a beast that will wage war against the faithful in a future world kingdom. Then God will win the victory, and the saints will inherit an everlasting kingdom. For Daniel it was the king symbolized by the "little horn" that was defeated in battle (Dan 7:24–26), while for John it was the last of the kings represented by the seven heads and seven mountains in addition to the ten kings represented by the ten horns (Rev 17:9–14).

It is interesting how elements of Daniel's vision were blended into the elements of John's vision. The imagery of Revelation is more complex and varied than Daniel's visions. The beast that John saw had seven heads that were seven "mountains" (ὄρη) that also represented seven "kings" or "kingdoms," and these in turn correspond to the four beasts that Daniel saw. Even as interpreters have struggled to identify Daniel's beasts, so they have wrestled with the interpretation of the seven "mountains" and other symbols in the book of Revelation.

Daniel's fourth beast would have its counterpart in John's vision in both the king (kingdom) who "is" and the one who "has not yet come." That is, Rome was ruling in John's time, and in the future the Antichrist will arise as leader of the seventh kingdom, making an "eighth" (Rev 17:11).

An important point for the discussion about Daniel 7 concerns how the beast of Revelation 17 is said to be "of the seven" (ἐκ τῶν ἑπτά). It shares its identity with all the kingdoms of this world. In a similar fashion, as we will discuss in the exposition of Daniel 7, the fourth beast of Daniel 7 need not be limited to Rome. It represents more simply the ultimate human kingdom that stands against God. As sovereign rule in the human sense passed from one people to another, there were not necessarily sharp boundary lines between them. That is how the smiting stone in Nebuchadnezzar's dream crushed the various parts of the image "all at once" (Dan 2:35) and why the four beasts in Daniel's vision all participated together in the judgment. There is some pertinence to deciding which historical kingdoms are represented, but in the final analysis the theological message pronounces the ultimate sovereignty of the Ancient of Days, of the Lord of lords and King of kings (Rev 17:14).

In addition to the influence of Daniel's apocalyptic theology on Jesus and John, one also finds certain allusions in the rest of the NT that probably came from the book of Daniel. Not only is the angel Gabriel (8:16; 9:21) mentioned in the NT, the angel Michael (Dan 10:13, 21; 12:1) also makes an appearance (Jude 1:9 and Rev 12:7). An echo of Dan 2:44 may be found in 1

Cor 15:24. Both passages refer to the time of the end when all kingdoms will be done away and replaced by God's kingdom. Paul, like Daniel, was "rescued from the lion's mouth" (2 Tim 4:17), though in Paul's case it was not a literal lion. The great heroes of the faith mentioned in Heb 11:33–34 include also "those who shut the mouths of lions" and those who, like Shadrach, Meshach, and Abednego, "quenched the power of fire."

Clearly the book of Daniel is critical for correctly interpreting the NT, especially for understanding the apocalyptic theology of Jesus and John.

## EXCURSUS: THE GREEK ADDITIONS TO DANIEL

Both Greek versions of Daniel contain additions to what is found in the Hebrew/Aramaic text. These additions are known as "The Prayer of Azariah and the Song of the Three Young Men," "Susanna," and "Bel and the Dragon." The additions are accepted officially as part of the canon (*deutero-canonical*) by the Roman Catholic Church. The Greek Orthodox Church also uses the expanded Greek version of the book of Daniel. These additions, along with the rest of the books known as the Apocrypha, were rejected by Jerome (fifth century) and by Protestants. Translations of all of the Apocrypha, including the additions to Daniel, are available in Catholic Bibles and in the NRSV. They were also included as a group placed between the Old and New Testaments in earlier editions of the KJV. The KJV translation of the Apocrypha is now available online.

### The Prayer of Azariah and the Song of the Three Young Men

At Dan 3:23 the Old Greek and Theodotion have an insertion of sixty-eight verses that consists of three parts: the *Prayer of Azariah*; an account of how the angel of the Lord delivered Azariah and his companions; and the *Song of the Three Young Men*. There is strong agreement among scholars that this section was inserted into the narrative and was not originally part of it, especially since for the most part it is not suited to its context.[105] Two manuscripts of Daniel from Qumran clearly do not contain the addition, 1QDan[b] and 4QDan[d], and none of the other Qumran texts of the book contain any portion of the additions. "The rationale for the additions is obvious enough: they are pious embellishments of the story, like the prayers in Greek

---

105. For example, the Prayer of Azariah contains a national confession of sin, whereas the three men were thrown into the fire because of their righteous behavior. For details see John Collins, *Daniel*, 195–207.

Esther."[106] The *Prayer of Azariah* resembles "national laments as those in the Psalter (e.g., Pss 44, 74, 79 and 80) and in prose confessions elsewhere, notably, Dan 9:4–19; Ezra 9:6–15; Neh 9:6–37; and 1 Bar 1:15—3:8."[107] The Old Greek introduces the name *Azarias* (i.e., Abednego) at 3:20, whereas Theodotian still refers to Shadrach, Meshach, and Abednego in that verse. Both versions then have Azarias taking the lead and start his prayer. Following Azarias's prayer and the song the three of them sang, translation of the canonical text resumes at verse twenty-five.

## Susanna

The story of Susanna, a married woman falsely accused by two Jewish elders of adultery but vindicated by a young Daniel, is placed as chapter 1 of Daniel in *Theodotion* but after the canonical book in the Old Greek (P967). The order in *Theodotion* serves to introduce the reader to the young Daniel, although it is strange that the story places Daniel in Babylon in circumstances that are markedly different from those of the biblical account. The two Greek versions also differ from each other significantly in other ways, especially in a series of additions in *Theodotion*. Moore concludes that there must have been two different Semitic texts from which the translators drew.[108] Daniel shows his wisdom by cleverly proving that the two elders have falsely accused Susanna.

## Bel and the Dragon

The story of *Bel and the Dragon* at the end of the canonical book (either after Susanna in Th or before it in the OG) contains three originally separate stories that have been put together to "constitute a coherent and artistic whole."[109] In the first of these stories Daniel arranges a test with Nebuchadnezzar to discover if the god Bel is real, and he is able to prove satisfactorily to the king that Bel is only a false idol. In the second story Daniel kills a serpent that the people were worshiping, stirring them to anger. The king then gave Daniel to them and they threw him into a lions' den. The third story, then, is a second story of Daniel in a lions' den. This time the angel of

---

106. John Collins, *Daniel*, 198.
107. Moore, *Additions*, 41.
108. Moore, *Additions*, 22.
109. John Collins, *Daniel*, 409.

the Lord carries the prophet Habakkuk to Daniel with a specially prepared meal for him. Afterward the king came and found Daniel still alive.

*Bel and the Dragon* has a preface in the Old Greek that introduces the story and Daniel: "From the prophecy of Habakkuk, son of Yesu, of the tribe of Levi. There was a man who was a priest, whose name was Daniel, son of Abal, a companion of the king of Babylon." In *Theodotion* this reads: "And the king, Astyages, was gathered to his fathers, and Cyrus the Persian received his kingdom. And Daniel was a companion of the king and was highly esteemed above all his friends." It is clear from these verses, which presume the need to reintroduce Daniel, that the story was never an integral part of the book of Daniel. Moore sees the underlying narratives as originating in the Persian period "as haggadic elaborations of Jer 51:34–35, 44," with its addition to the Semitic text of Daniel "several decades after 163 BC, that year being the approximate date of canonical Daniel."[110] The biblical book of Daniel does not imply that he was a priest. The variant form of the preface in Theodotion then seems like an attempt to connect the Daniel of Bel and the Dragon with the Daniel of the biblical book.[111]

Possibly *Susanna* and *Bel and the Dragon* may serve to refocus the court conflicts in Daniel 1 to 6 to conflicts among the Jews in the land in the Maccabean or Hasmonean periods. Both stories portray Daniel as someone who reveals the truth about false people (elders or priests of Bel) by a clever ploy. In the context of *Bel and the Dragon*, Daniel as priest came into direct conflict with the priests of Bel, even as Daniel as court official had conflict with the other court officials of Darius the Mede (Dan 6). The elders in *Susanna* may represent a conflict of the second or first century BC which was occurring in Palestine among rival factions of Jews.

The Old Greek of Daniel, with the additions, can be interpreted as in some sense dependent on the original biblical book. It tends to move away from the court contests of the Hebrew/Aramaic book. Chapter four of the Old Greek nearly eliminates the element of the court contest, and chapter five makes Belshazzar's banquet more of a private affair than an official banquet.[112] The Greek story focuses more on the prophet himself than the Hebrew/Aramaic account, and there is a more overt exaltation of Daniel's God.[113]

---

110. Moore, *Additions*, 128.
111. Moore, *Additions*, 133.
112. See Meadowcroft, *Aramaic Daniel and Greek Daniel*, 32–33, 66–67.
113. For an argument that the variations in Daniel 4—6 are a product of the Greek translator rather than the original Aramaic, see A. G. Daniel, "Translator's Tell," 723–49.

Some see the variants in Daniel 4 to 6 as evidence for a literary theory by which independent stories were edited together.[114] We propose a different model based on Jewish literature that was prevalent in the first and second centuries BC. The Aramaic *Genesis Apocryphon* discovered among the scrolls from Qumran (1QGenAp ar), while clearly based on biblical Genesis, includes other stories as well as interpretive additions to the text, some of them major. Here is a helpful description of this fragmentary text: "The narrative has a Biblical text as its basis, which is followed verse after verse so that one gets the impression now and then that it is a Targum."[115]

The Dead Sea Scrolls bear witness to a flourishing literature in the third to first centuries BC that expanded, interpreted, or in some sense rewrote various parts of the OT.[116] The book of Daniel, assuming a composition in the late sixth or early fifth century BC, likewise generated additional Daniel stories, interpretations, and embellishments. Possibly a Semitic text that lies behind the Greek versions (*Vorlage*) included all or some of the additions and could be viewed as a "Daniel Apocryphon." In other words, rather than saying that the Hebrew/Aramaic form of the book came about through the selection of various independent stories, in this model a core book authored by Daniel that is fairly close to the current Masoretic Text spawned variations and interpretations, some of which were added directly to a Semitic text that eventuated in the *Vorlage* of the Old Greek.[117] The source of the variations in this view need not be merely the book of Daniel itself. Materials originally extraneous to Daniel could also have been inserted into the "Daniel Apocryphon" where it seemed appropriate. And of course, some variations of stories about Daniel still could have circulated independently.[118]

---

114. Hartman and Di Lella, *Book of Daniel*, 13; John Collins, *Daniel*, 38.

115. Jongeling, Labuschagne, and van der Woude, *Aramaic Texts from Qumran*; a *Targum* is a translation of the biblical text into Aramaic, often with additions that are traditional or homiletical.

116. For recent work on this type of literature see Zahn, *Genres of Rewriting*.

117. *Vorlage* is a German term that refers to the hypothetical manuscript that a translator was translating from. In the case of Daniel, it would be a Hebrew/Aramaic text that is only indirectly accessible through the Greek translation.

118. At Qumran additional fragmentary texts in Aramaic seem enough like the biblical book of Daniel to call them "pseudo-Daniel" texts. See Flint ("Daniel Tradition at Qumran") for a detailed study of the full scope of Daniel material at Qumran.

# Who's in Control?
## (Daniel 1:1–21)

**Chapter 1 Summary:** After handing the king of Judah over to the king of Babylon, God works on behalf of, and through, the faithfulness of Daniel, Hananiah, Mishael, and Azariah to demonstrate that he is sovereign over the Babylonian kingdom and superior to the Babylonian king.

**Chapter 2 Preview:** Chapter 2 introduces for the first time the theme of four kingdoms that follow one another until God sets up an eternal kingdom that will not pass away. This theme is presented through Nebuchadnezzar's dream and Daniel's interpretation of it based on what God had revealed to him.

## THEOLOGICAL FOCUS OF CHAPTER 1

IN HIS SOVEREIGNTY GOD may allow what is seemingly evil to flourish. When God's people remain faithful in such circumstances, their faithfulness may be tested. But when it is tested, God works on behalf of, and through, their faithfulness in order to display his sovereignty and to enable his people to endure through the trial.

  I. *In his sovereignty God may allow what is seemingly evil to flourish.* (1:1–2)

  II. *When God's people remain faithful in difficult circumstances, their faithfulness may be tested.* (1:3–17)

  III. *When their faithfulness is tested, God works on behalf of, and through, their faithfulness in order to demonstrate his sovereignty and to enable his people to endure through the trial.* (1:18–21)

## BIG PICTURE (1:1–21)[1]

Chapter 1 tells how Nebuchadnezzar king of Babylon conquered Judah and took select youths captive to Babylon in order to train them to serve in the royal court. Nebuchadnezzar ordered them to be fed food and wine from the king's table and gave them Babylonian names (Daniel, Hananiah, Mishael, and Azariah). Knowing that their allegiance was to their God and not to the king of Babylon, Daniel persuaded the steward who oversaw their rations to give them vegetables and water for ten days. After that the four young men **appeared healthier and better nourished than the others who dined on the king's fare**, and so the steward continued their diet throughout the training. When their preparation ended, they appeared before the king and amazed him with their superior intelligence and social ability. **They could answer all his questions, and he found them "ten times beyond" even all of his own wise men.**

While this is a testament to Daniel and his friends' faithfulness, the narrator makes it clear that the successes were God's doing. The emphasis on the sovereignty of God is made abundantly clear in the telling of the story; *God gave* Jehoiakim to Nebuchadnezzar; *God gave* Daniel favor with the chief official; and *God gave* Daniel and his friends understanding ten times greater than the rest of those in the Babylonian court. And because God gave them these successes, they became favored officials in the king's court.

## TRANSLATION (DANIEL 1:1–21)

1    In the third regnal year of Jehoiakim king of Judah, Nebuchadnezzar[2] king of Babylon came to Jerusalem and besieged it.

2    And **the Lord**[3] **delivered Jehoiakim** king of Judah into his power along with some of the articles of the house of God. And he brought them to the land of Shinar to the house of his god, and the vessels he brought to the treasury of his god.[4]

---

1 Comments that lead the reader to the theological thrust of each chapter are emboldened throughout the book.

2. Nebuchadnezzar is spelled three different ways in Daniel: נְבֻכַדְנֶאצַּר; נְבוּכַדְנֶאצַּר; and נְבוּכַדְנֶצַּר. A spelling with *resh* occurs only in Jeremiah and Ezekiel (נְבוּכַדְרֶאצַּר). According to Wiseman (*Nebuchadrezzar and Babylon*, 2–4) the form with *nun* instead of *resh* represents a phonetic variant with dissimilation.

3. אֲדֹנָי (the Lord) in BHS, but some Masoretic manuscripts have יהוה (YHWH).

4. Most likely the "treasury" or "storehouse" refers to a more specific area within the temple complex.

## WHO'S IN CONTROL?

3  The king commanded Ashpenaz, his chief official,[5] to bring youths[6] from the Israelites of the royal line and of the nobility,

4  who have no blemish, are good looking, are skilled in all (kinds of) wisdom and endowed with knowledge and insightful understanding, and who are capable to serve in the king's palace. (And he commanded him) to teach them the literature and language of the Chaldeans.[7]

5  And the king assigned them a daily portion from the king's provisions and from the wine that he drank. And (he commanded him) to educate them for three years, after which they were to stand before the king.

6  Now there happened to be among them from the descendants of Judah—Daniel, Hananiah, Mishael, and Azariah.

7  And the chief official gave them names. To Daniel he gave the name *Belteshazzar*, to Hananiah *Shadrach*, to Mishael *Meshach*, and to Azariah *Abednego*.[8]

8  Then Daniel resolved that he would not defile himself with the king's provisions or with the wine that he drank. So he requested from the chief official that he would not have to defile himself.

9  Now **God put Daniel into a position of favor and compassion** in the presence of the chief official.

10  And the chief official said to Daniel:

"I fear my master the king who assigned your food and your drink.

For why should he see your faces (looking) worse than the young men who are your age? Then you would put my head in jeopardy to the king."

11  So Daniel said to the overseer[9] whom the chief official had appointed over Daniel, Hananiah, Mishael, and Azariah:

---

5. Or "chief eunuch"; see the Exposition.

6. *Youths* (יְלָדִים) has been transposed from v. 4 for the sake of good English.

7. The correspondence of כַּשְׂדִּים (*kaśdîm*) with "Chaldeans" is due to a change in Assyrian of the consonant cluster /šd/ to /ld/, a change preserved through the Greek versions (see Koch, *Daniel 1—4*, 4).

8. For the meaning of the Babylonian names see the exposition.

9. Various terms have been chosen as equivalents for הַמֶּלְצַר—*overseer* (NASB), *guard* (NRSVue), *steward* (ESV), and *attendant* (NLT). The KJV followed the Vulgate, taking it as the proper name *Melzar*. A name is unlikely, since the term is used with

| 12 | "Please test your servants for ten days by giving us vegetables[10] to eat and water to drink. |
|---|---|
| 13 | Then inspect our appearance and the appearance of the young men who eat the king's provisions. And in accordance with what you see deal with your servants." |
| 14 | So he agreed with this proposal and tested them for ten days. |
| 15 | At the end of ten days their appearance looked better and fatter in flesh than the young men who ate the king's provisions. |
| 16 | So the overseer continued to take away their provisions and the wine that they were to drink and kept giving them vegetables. |
| 17 | Now as for these four young men, **God gave them understanding and comprehension** in every (kind of) scribal skill and wisdom, and Daniel could understand all (sorts of) visions and dreams. |
| 18 | At the end of the days after that the king had commanded to present them, the chief official brought them before Nebuchadnezzar. |
| 19 | The king spoke with them, and among all of them none were found like Daniel, Hananiah, Mishael, and Azariah. So they served before the king. |
| 20 | Whatever matter of wisdom and understanding that the king sought from them, he found them ten times beyond all the soothsayer-priests and conjurers that were in his whole realm.[11] |
| 21 | And Daniel continued (in the service of Babylon)[12] until the first year of Cyrus the king. |

## TEXTUAL OUTLINE (1:1–21)

I. God Transfers the Kingdom to Nebuchadnezzar. (1:1–2)

*[In his sovereignty God may allow what is seemingly evil to flourish.]*

---

the definite article. Hebrew probably borrowed a Babylonian term that means *guard* (*HALOT*), but the person's duties indicate that he was something like an *overseer* or *attendant*.

10. The term for *vegetables* here is זֵרֹעִים, but it is זֵרְעֹנִים in 1:16; 1QDan[a] has זרעים in both verses; cf. *BHS*.

11. See Table 2.1 for the various terms used for the Babylonian wise men.

12. The context stresses Daniel's Babylonian service, not his entire career (see also the Exposition).

II. Daniel and His Companions Remain Faithful to Their God. (1:3–17)

*[When God's people remain faithful in difficult circumstances, their faithfulness will be tested.]*

    A. The king commands to raise and educate the young men. (1:3–5)

    B. Daniel and his three companions undergo a test. (1:6–17)

III. Daniel and His Companions Excel at the King's Inspection. (1:18–21)

*[When their faithfulness is tested, God works on behalf of, and through, their faithfulness, to demonstrate his sovereignty and to enable his people to endure through the trial.]*

## EXPOSITION (1:1–21)

## God Transfers the Kingdom to Nebuchadnezzar. (1:1–2)

Theological Point: In his sovereignty God may allow what is seemingly evil to flourish.

**1:1–2.** As an introduction to the book, the first two verses indicate that **the Lord transferred the arena of his main activity on earth from Judah to Babylon.** The key thought here is that the Lord (אֲדֹנָי) is sovereign over world history and gives authority to govern to whomever he chooses (cf. 2:21). The remainder of the book emphasizes a scheme of four successive world empires followed by God's own eternal kingdom. One kingdom gives way to the next until finally God breaks into history and establishes the realm that "will not pass away" (Dan 7:14). The succession of world empires began when the Lord removed Judah from the scene and raised up Babylon through Nebuchadnezzar.

Three verbs express the main actions in these opening verses. First, Nebuchadnezzar "laid siege" (וַיָּצַר) to Jerusalem. Then **the Lord "gave"** (וַיִּתֵּן) **Jehoiakim and some items from the temple in Jerusalem into Nebuchadnezzar's power** (בְּיָדוֹ, "into his hand"). Then Nebuchadnezzar "brought them" (וַיְבִיאֵם) to the temple of his god in Shinar. The first verse gives the background for these actions. They took place in Jehoiakim's third year, at which time Nebuchadnezzar arrived at Jerusalem.[13]

**The most significant statement in verse two is that "the Lord," that is,** *Adonai* **(אֲדֹנָי) delivered or "gave" (וַיִּתֵּן) king Jehoiakim to**

---

13. For a discussion of the historical issues associated with 1:1–6 see the Introduction.

Nebuchadnezzar, along with some articles from the temple in Jerusalem. The divine name Adonai occurs only here and in chapter nine of the book of Daniel. The name Yahweh appears some eight times in the book but only in chapter nine, so Daniel's use of the names appears deliberate. **Adonai means "Lord" or "Master" and stresses God's sovereign authority to deliver earthly kingdoms to whomever he pleases** (Dan 2:21). **Since Yahweh is God's name that strongly relates to his covenant relationship with Israel, the choice of "Lord" rather than Yahweh points to his new relationship in the realm of the nations.**

It was not uncommon for a victorious king to take images of the defeated country as a symbol of his victory over their god(s). **The text makes it clear—the Lord "gave" not only Jehoiakim but also these temple items to Nebuchadnezzar.** The king of Babylon did not somehow gain a victory over Judah's God. **The God of Daniel and his companions was still in control, and the proof for that would be their phenomenal success in the Babylonian court.** God infused them with wisdom that confounded the wisest of the Babylonians and even brought Nebuchadnezzar himself to his knees. Later, when Belshazzar dared to use some of Jerusalem's temple vessels for common purposes, it cost him his kingdom.

It is not entirely clear what happened to Jehoiakim at this point. Certainly, he surrendered to Nebuchadnezzar, but whether the Babylonian king brought him to Babylon along with the temple vessels is unclear. The issue is complicated by 2 Chr 36:6: "Nebuchadnezzar king of Babylon came up against [Jehoiakim] and imprisoned him in chains in order to bring him to Babylon." If he was taken to Babylon, he must not have stayed there very long. According to 2 Kgs 24:1–6, Jehoiakim was a "servant" of Nebuchadnezzar for three years, after which he rebelled (see Introduction).[14]

Babylonia is called "the land of Shinar" in verse two. Used only eight times in the Bible, *Shinar* refers to the area of southern Mesopotamia that includes Babylon (Gen 10:10; 11:2; 14:1, 9; Josh 7:21; Isa 11:11; Dan 1:2; Zech 5:5–11).[15] **All of these instances of "Shinar" fit well with Dan 1:2 in that they deal with some kind of rebellion against God. It was only with God's permission that Nebuchadnezzar was able to take Jerusalem, but taking the temple articles to Shinar foreshadowed the king's pride that**

---

14. Myers (*II Chronicles*, 219) posits that Jehoiakim was only "threatened with deportation," and McConville (*I & II Chronicles*, 266–67) thinks the binding could have been "a symbolic demonstration of his status" without requiring deportation to Babylon.

15. The OG of Daniel gives Βαβυλῶνα (*Babylonia*) as its equivalent for *Shinar*. Possibly the term *Shinar* is related to *Sumer*, although that is uncertain (Toorn and Horst, "Nimrod," 3–4; *HALOT*).

would be magnified according to chapter 2 and brought into submission according to chapter 4.[16]

## Daniel and His Companions Remain Faithful to Their God. (1:3–19)

Theological Point: When God's people remain faithful in difficult circumstances, their faithfulness may be tested.

Nebuchadnezzar planned to develop faithful servants from his captives, but **the Lord intervened on behalf of Daniel and his friends with a better educational plan.** The first thing that Nebuchadnezzar did was to issue a command regarding his captives. He appeared to be in control of the situation. But was he? He set up a training program for the elite among his captives, hoping to develop young men who could serve in administrative posts. God, however, had his own plans. **The king wanted to take the very best of Israel's young men to become, in all respects, elite Babylonians whom he could consult regarding matters of the kingdom, but God planned to develop four of these young men as his own agents within the Babylonian government.** Nebuchadnezzar issued orders, but his orders were subverted by the Lord in ways that actually proved beneficial, in the long run, even to Nebuchadnezzar. His three-year educational program was to be followed by a test to see if the pupils would be ready for public service, but God's program was to infuse these young Israelites with a special divine wisdom that would overpower anything that Babylon had to offer. And while these young men would learn Babylonian ways, even excel in them, they would do it without compromising their fidelity to their God. They might receive Babylonian names and instruction in Babylonian literature and language, but they would not compromise when it came to matters of covenantal commitment to Yahweh. They would continue to do things God's way and to worship him alone. In the process they would become much more valuable to Nebuchadnezzar than even any of the other wise men who served him.

**God arranged for Daniel to impress favorably the chief official so that he would not interfere with a test that would challenge Nebuchadnezzar's wisdom. The miraculous looks of the Hebrews after only ten days of their special diet proved that Daniel's God was acting behind the scenes.** When the time for the crucial test before Nebuchadnezzar came, it was not the Babylonian science and learning that created the wisest of

16. See excursus, "The Land of Shinar."

captives; **it was God himself who "gave" them their skill, even as he had "given" Nebuchadnezzar control of Jehoiakim and the temple vessels.**

*The king commands to raise and educate the young men. (1:3–5)*

Daniel 1:1–2 does not mention that Nebuchadnezzar brought the captives to Babylon.[17] **The abruptness of the text highlights that it was the Lord who delivered Jehoiakim into Nebuchadnezzar's power.** As soon as the kingdom shifted from Jerusalem to Babylon we find Judeans who are under the Babylonian king's sway. They are now simply pawns to help the king carry out his designs. Moreover, they are young men (יְלָדִים) of great potential; Judah and Jerusalem no longer have such men to guide them in the ways of wisdom. Instead the king planned to educate them in Babylonian ways so that they would be capable to serve at the royal court of Babylon.

**1:3a.** According to some translations, Ashpenaz was the chief eunuch, not the chief official. Hebrew סָרִיס can mean either "eunuch" or "official." Here the text wants to make readers think of Ashpenaz's official capacity, not that he was a eunuch.[18]

**1:3b–4a.** Most often the plural of יֶלֶד denotes the offspring of parents, whether young (Gen 33:14) or grown (Ruth 1:5). In another usage it means something like "minors" (Ezra 10:1; Neh 12:43) or "boys" (Zech 8:5). The closest parallel to Daniel's use occurs in the account of Jeroboam I seeking the counsel of "the young men" (הַיְלָדִים) he grew up with rather than the "elders" (1 Kgs 12:8, 10, 14; 2 Chr 10:8, 10, 14). Since it would take about three years to educate these יְלָדִים, they were probably teenagers, and the best translation for Daniel's passage is "youths" or "young men."

These young men were taken מִבְּנֵי יִשְׂרָאֵל ("from the sons of Israel") since the Lord had just delivered the city into Nebuchadnezzar's power. It is interesting that the text says they were from "Israel" rather than from

---

17. Should the reader assume that Nebuchadnezzar had brought them there along with the temple articles? Did Ashpenaz have to go to Judah to fetch them? One might be tempted to think that there was a time gap between verses two and three, so that verse three would refer to 597 BC when Nebuchadnezzar took Jehoiachin and various officials captive to Babylon (2 Kgs 24:14–15). Dan 2:1 militates against that understanding. It was in Nebuchadnezzar's second year that Daniel was called in before him to interpret the king's dream. That could not have been later than 602 BC. So, the time when Nebuchadnezzar brought the temple articles to Babylon must have coincided with his order to Ashpenaz (see. Keil, *Ezekiel, Daniel*, 72; Miller, *Daniel*, 59; and Koch, *Daniel 1—4*, 42).

18. Péter-Contesse and Ellington, *Handbook on the Book of Daniel*, 13. The term סָרִיס derives from Babylonian *ša rēš (šarri)*, "official of the king," attested on documents from the time of Nebuchadnezzar.

Judah, as in verse six. "Israel" occurs only here and in chapter 9; elsewhere in Daniel the reference is always to "Judah." "Israel" can refer either to the northern kingdom as opposed to Judah (Hos 1:1) or to the entire nation that God called out of Egypt, his special elect people (Jer 25:15; Amos 3:1). When Daniel later prayed to the Lord on behalf of his people, he called them "Israel" (9:7, 11, 20). **Here the use of "Israel" may further emphasize that God's dealings with his people will no longer be through the kingdom of Judah but through the Gentile powers.** Later (v. 4), when the narrative focuses on Daniel and his companions, they are called מִבְּנֵי יְהוּדָה ("from the sons of Judah") to underscore their tribal heritage.

These Israelite youths were also of royal lineage (מִזֶּרַע הַמְּלוּכָה, "from the offspring of the kingdom") and from aristocratic families (מִן־הַפַּרְתְּמִים, "from the nobles"). In other words, some of these youths were members of the royal family and/or from the elite class of society.

**1:4b.** In addition to concern about the birth heritage of the young men, Nebuchadnezzar also wanted youths who were physically perfect (אֵין־בָּהֶם כָּל־מאוּם, "without any blemish") and good looking (טוֹבֵי מַרְאֶה, "good with respect to appearance"). They were also to be highly intelligent and insightful. These qualities of mind and body needed to be of the sort that would enable them to serve in the royal court. An ancient Egyptian text (late thirteenth century BC) describes the ideal scribe as "choice of heart, persevering of counsel. . . . a youth distinguished of appearance and pleasing of charm, who can explain the difficulties of the annals like him who composed them."[19]

"Wisdom" (חָכְמָה) often refers to various kinds of skills (Exod 28:3; 31:3) as well as to different areas of knowledge (1 Kgs 4:30-33 [5:10-13]). Presumably, these young men had already received enough instruction at the Jerusalem court that Ashpenaz could discern in them capacity to learn diverse subjects. It is not entirely clear what יֹדְעֵי דַעַת ("knowers of knowledge") references. An identical expression occurs in Prov 17:27, where it indicates "one who . . . has knowledge" (NASB) or "a knowledgeable person." The final expression that refers to the intelligence of these youths uses, like "knowers of knowledge," a form of the root ידע. HALOT glosses the term מַדָּע with "understanding," and מְבִינֵי means "those who understand." Thus, מְבִינֵי מַדָּע would have a literal sense of "those who understand understanding."

**One could legitimately ask how much stress should be placed on exact definitions for these terms. To some extent synonymous, the list of terms simply emphasizes that, regarding intelligence, Nebuchadnezzar**

---

19. Pritchard, *ANET*, 475.

wanted the top of the class. Unbeknownst to him, he also got the top of the class regarding faithfulness, and because of that faithfulness the wisdom of these young men was multiplied many times over.

1:4c. Their education was to include scribal arts and "the language of the Chaldeans" or Babylonian.[20] The term for "language," לָשׁוֹן, helps to clarify that "Chaldeans" refers to the Babylonians and not to the special class of Chaldean wise men as found elsewhere in Daniel (2:2, 4, 5, 10; 4:7; 5:7, 11). Most modern English versions take סֵפֶר, which normally means "written document," as "literature" and modify it by "Chaldean" or "Babylonian." This skill would involve learning Babylonian literature and script, but it would also include the ability to write and communicate in Aramaic, important skills for a palace administrator in the neo-Babylonian empire.

1:5a. Quality food and drink would be essential for these young men, and the king made sure that they received the very best. The term פַּת־בַּג is derived from an Old Persian word and means "food" or "provisions."[21] It occurs only here and in Dan 11:26. It probably implies some special food appropriate for a king. Also, the wine was from the king's own special stock. Nebuchadnezzar obviously had a strong interest in seeing these young men develop healthy minds and bodies.

1:5b. Ashpenaz was to raise these youths for a period of three years, at the end of which they would enter the king's service. The wording of the Hebrew could also imply that an audience with the king would occur after three years. An audience did occur for the four Hebrew youths "at the end of the days that the king had commanded to present them" (1:18), and the term מִקְצָת ("at the end of") occurs in both places. So, it seems likely that the primary referent for יַעֲמְדוּ (*they were to stand*) in this case refers to that time when they would "stand" before the king. This was the king's way to assure himself that each candidate was worthy of an important position in the administration of the palace.

## *Daniel and his three companions undergo a test. (1:6–18)*

Among the young men that Ashpenaz assembled were four from the tribe of Judah. They were also to have royal blood and be from noble families. As Joseph had been sent ahead into Egypt to preserve Jacob's family in

---

20. Keil (*Ezekiel, Daniel*, 74–78) showed that the "language of the Chaldeans" was Babylonian, not Aramaic. For the latter the Hebrew term was אֲרָמִית (see 2 Kgs 18:26; Ezra 4:7; Isa 36:11; Dan 2:4). The term "Chaldean" is still sometimes used incorrectly for Aramaic. Perhaps the confusion stems from Dan 2:4, but as Collins (*Daniel*, 156) points out: "Aramaic was the lingua franca of the Near East from the eighth century [BC]."

21. *HALOT* 3:984.

advance of their becoming a great nation, so Daniel and his friends would obtain high positions in the Babylonian government and ensure the survival of their people. **Nebuchadnezzar had a plan to nourish and instruct the captives, but God also had his own plans for these four from Judah. And his plans were superior.** These young men were able to thrive in a foreign land, because they were faithful to God, who in turn showed his faithfulness by endowing them with outstanding qualities that led to their success (cf. Gen 39:2–9; 41:38–45). The stories of both Joseph and Daniel illustrate themes of God's sovereignty on the one hand and of the believer's faithfulness on the other hand. What would have happened if Joseph had surrendered to Potiphar's wife or exacted revenge on his brothers by having them executed? Or what if Daniel had consumed the king's food and drink, quietly studied his lessons, and adopted the comfortable lifestyle afforded the king's men? The issue of divine sovereignty versus human responsibility remains a mystery, but Joseph and Daniel illustrate how both elements work hand in hand.

1:6–7. Three key cultural identity markers occur in the text—language, name, and food. Daniel and his friends were to receive an education in the Babylonian language and literature. For that they were captive pupils. They also had to accept the new names that their captors gave them. **But because of Daniel's faithfulness to God and God's faithfulness to Daniel, they were able to change their diet and thereby maintain their identity as servants of God.**

The king determined that his charges must become good Babylonian citizens. Consequently, they were given Babylonian names. As recorded in the Hebrew of the MT of Daniel, these names require some reconstruction to determine their original form and meaning. While some of the names are not entirely clear, it is evident that they reflect worship of Babylonian gods.

Three possible derivations have been suggested for Daniel's new name of בֵּלְטְשַׁאצַּר (Belteshazzar): (1) Balaṭ-su-uṣur, "(The god) protect his life"; (2) Balaṭ-šar-uṣur, "(The god) protect the king's life"; and (3) Bēlet-šar-uṣur, "Lady [the god's wife] protect the king." The first option is most likely in that it refers more directly to Nebuchadnezzar's god (Dan 4:8) and to Daniel himself rather than to the king.[22]

---

22. Shea ("Bel(te)shazzar," 67–81) thinks that Daniel's Babylonian name was actually the same as Belshazzar's name, the king of Babylon. A *ṭet* was added by a scribe in order to avoid the mention of the god Bel, even as Abednego was changed from an original Abednebo. Shea's further point that Daniel may be identified with another Belshazzar mentioned in Babylonian texts during the reign of Evil-merodach is interesting but speculative.

Shadrach's name (שַׁדְרַךְ) is difficult to explain. One suggestion is "I have been made to feel very much afraid" (*HALOT*), probably meaning fear of a god. "Command of Aku" has also been posited (BDB), although a divine name *Aku* is uncertain.[23] Meshach (מֵישַׁךְ) might mean "Who is like Aku?" or "Who belongs to Aku?"[24] If either explanation is correct, then Mishael's Hebrew name (מִישָׁאֵל), which signifies either "Who is like God?" or "Who belongs to God?," is the only name whose Babylonian meaning corresponds roughly to its Hebrew meaning. Abednego (עֲבֵד נְגוֹ) appears to mean "Servant of Nego," but there is no Babylonian god known as *Nego*. The common opinion is that the name of the god "Nebo" has been altered by the scribes by changing the *beth* to *gimel*, the letter in the alphabet that immediately follows it (*HALOT*).

1:8. Daniel purposed "not to defile himself" (לֹא־יִתְגָּאַל) with the king's food or wine. The exact nature of the king's food is not clear, and it is described with a rare word, פַּתְבַּג, evidently a Persian loanword (*HALOT*). Many commentators have assumed that the king's food must have included meat that came from unclean animals (cf. Lev 11) or animals that had not had their blood drained when they were killed (cf. Lev 17:10–14), or animals that had been offered to idols. Likewise, the wine could have been that which was poured out as a libation to the gods.[25]

While it is true that Daniel was concerned about the issue of obeying the Law of Moses, is that what the text emphasizes? The text is explicit that it was the king's provisions and his personal stock of wine that Daniel refused. Later when Daniel asked for vegetables and water, there is no reference to their source (1:12); they also could have been involved in idolatrous rites. Regarding wine, at a much later time Daniel fasted from food and wine (10:3), inferring that he did not abstain normally. It does not seem, therefore, that "keeping kosher" or abstaining from food and drink offered to idols were the primary issue for Daniel.

Daniel feared that he would "defile himself" by eating and drinking what came from the king's table. "Having to live in a foreign country is an inherently defiling experience."[26] In refusing the Babylonian food and drink Daniel thereby refused to identify completely with Babylonian culture.[27] Although Daniel's name had been changed and he had been enrolled in a compulsory educational regimen, he purposed not

---

23. Koch, *Daniel 1—4*, 6.
24. BDB; *HALOT* considers the name unexplained.
25. Wood, *Daniel*, 37; Miller, *Daniel*, 66–67.
26. Goldingay, *Daniel*, 18.
27. Baldwin, *Daniel*, 83.

to pledge allegiance to the king rather than to God. The parallel use of the same verb (וַיָּשֶׂם) for both "appointing" names to the men and for Daniel's "purposing" not to defile himself stresses the antithetical nature of the actions.[28] The names were meant to make the men Babylonians, while Daniel's resolve was meant to avoid assimilation to Babylonian religion and total loyalty to the king. Daniel chose to show his devotion to the Lord rather than to the king through the one thing he could control—his diet.

In many respects followers of Jesus Christ also live in an alien culture. Certain assimilations are perhaps unavoidable, but it is also important for the believer to purpose in his or her heart to be different in a way that matters. Daniel's diet mattered in that his food and drink had the potential to direct his total loyalty to the king. The lesson of Daniel is clear—God will honor those who choose to follow him completely.

**1:9.** According to a familiar Hebrew idiom, someone either finds favor in the eyes of another (Gen 39:4),[29] or God gives or puts someone's favor in the eyes of someone else (Gen 39:21).[30] The idiom in Daniel resembles the example from Genesis 39:21 but also differs from it in several respects: "And God put Daniel to graciousness [חֶסֶד] and to compassion [רַחֲמִים] before the chief official." **The thought is that God arranged for Daniel to experience not only graciousness but also compassion from the official.** Nehemiah expressed a similar thought: "Place him [your servant] to compassion before this man" (Neh 1:11). **When Daniel needed to ask a favor from such an important man as Ashpenaz, he also needed God to instill compassion and a gracious attitude in Ashpenaz's heart. When God's servants need help from an outsider to do God's will, they can count on him even to work in the heart of that outsider.**

**1:10–16.** Despite the grace and compassion that the chief official felt for Daniel, it was not enough to overcome his fear of displeasing Nebuchadnezzar. Not letting that stop him, Daniel proceeded to arrange for a test to be supervised by Ashpenaz's subordinate. Ashpenaz had to agree to this test as well.[31] **The reference to three tiers of leadership over the cap-**

---

28. Koch, *Daniel 1—4*, 58.
29. וַיִּמְצָא יוֹסֵף חֵן בְּעֵינָיו, "And Joseph found favor in his eyes."
30. וַיִּתֵּן חִנּוֹ בְּעֵינֵי שַׂר בֵּית־הַסֹּהַר, "And [God] put his favor [Joseph's] into the eyes of the chief jailer."
31. In the OG it is still the "chief eunuch" (ἀρχιευνοῦχος) that Daniel deals with (v. 11). Instead of an equivalent for הַמֶּלְצַר (*the chief steward*), the OG has "Abiesdri," the name assigned by the OG to the "chief eunuch" known as Ashpenaz in the Hebrew. This eliminates the difficulty of the second official that Daniel and his companions encountered, but the MT supports the historicity of the passage. It seems unlikely that

tives—Nebuchadnezzar, Ashpenaz, and the overseer—emphasizes God's sovereignty over the whole of the Babylonian empire. It extends from the least to the greatest of her authority figures.

The test was simple enough. For ten days Daniel and his companions would eat a vegetarian diet and drink only water. Then the overseer could inspect them to see how they looked in comparison to the others who hadn't followed such a diet. If they looked better than the others, then it would be to Ashpenaz's advantage to continue to authorize that diet for these young men. Rather than putting his life in jeopardy he would instead be commended for having done such a fine job of raising the youths. **The message of the text is that these men prospered because of their God, not because of their diet per se as moderns might think. The diet showed their loyalty to God over against loyalty to Babylon.**

**All four youths received an education that surpassed that which the Babylonians were giving them. God himself granted them the necessary ability to understand scribal skills (סֵפֶר) and wisdom (חָכְמָה).** It would be interesting to know exactly how this wisdom that God gave them went beyond that of their Babylonian instructors. It would include at least a divine viewpoint on their subjects. They would have understood that true wisdom and understanding must begin with "the fear of the Lord" (Prov 1:7). The grounding point in education is crucial; the Babylonians had a polytheistic outlook that could accommodate other gods if their worshipers would subordinate themselves to the Babylonian gods. Daniel and his friends, as worshipers of the one and only God, could discern the true nature of what they were learning. Such insight permitted them to advance beyond their young contemporaries who did not know Daniel's God.

Even among the four, Daniel stood out for his special ability to understand visions and dreams. The Babylonians also claimed to communicate with the gods through visions and dreams, but they practiced things like divination or magic to obtain their knowledge, practices that were forbidden to the Jews (Deut 18:10–12).

The reference to Daniel's skills anticipates how he would later interpret Nebuchadnezzar's two dreams (chapters 2 and 4), solve Belshazzar's puzzling writing (chapter 5), and experience the visions described in chapters 7 to 12. **In each instance Daniel was careful to ascribe his abilities to God rather than to his own skills.** He told Nebuchadnezzar that "there is a God in heaven who reveals secrets" (Dan 2:28). **While the Babylonians also specialized in interpreting dreams, Daniel came to his interpretations**

---

a fictional story would be so complicated as to have a threefold chain of command from Nebuchadnezzar through Ashpenaz and finally through the chief steward.

through divine insight.[32] The text emphasizes that God's ways are superior to the Babylonian ways. Daniel is specially enabled by God to discern truth through dreams and visions, but the Babylonians themselves, as the book will show later, are powerless to come to any real knowledge through their efforts. Their so-called gods are ineffective in the kinds of situations that Daniel's God will use to reveal his will.

## Daniel and His Companions Excel at the King's Inspection. (1:19–21)

Theological Point: When their faithfulness is tested, God works on behalf of, and through, their faithfulness in order to demonstrate his sovereignty and enable his people to endure, and even thrive, through the trial.

Nebuchadnezzar finds Daniel and his friends far superior to all his wise men. In his audience with the youths the king noticed that the four Judean men stood out from all the others. As a result, they entered the king's service. The situation has some irony to it. Nebuchadnezzar, who had ordered the finest Babylonian food and drink along with the best education for these young men, sees the top of the class. And who are they? They are the men who refused the king's choice foods and fine wine and who excelled because their wisdom came from God rather than from men.[33]

1:19. The section about the training of Daniel and his companions comes to its conclusion with the statement, "So they served before the king." The text could be translated "they stood" rather than "they served," but the context here indicates that they entered the king's service.

1:20. The last two verses of the chapter maintain continuity with the previous segment by maintaining the theme of the superiority of Daniel and his companions. Previously they were superior among their fellow students; now as the king continues to question them, he finds that they are superior to all the Babylonian wise men. They are wiser and more skilled than even all the king's entourage of professionals scattered throughout his entire realm.

1:20. Most English translations have "magicians" for חַרְטֻמִּים, but English speakers would normally think of performers who use sleight of hand when they hear that term. Interpreters have various ideas about what

---

32. See Walvoord, *Daniel*, 41–42.

33. That true wisdom comes from God rather than from men is a common biblical theme (Gen 41:38; 1 Kgs 4:29 [5:9]; Job 28:20–28; Prov 1:7; 3:5–8; 9:10; 1 Cor 1:18—2:13; 3:18–19; Eph 1:17; Col 1:9; 2 Tim 3:15; Jas 1:5; 3:13–17).

the Hebrew means. *HALOT* recommends "soothsayer-priests." Soothsayer is not a common term, but it probably gets closer to the sense of the Hebrew than magician in that it refers to people who claim to be able to tell the future. *Soothsayer-priests* also has the advantage of associating religion with the people involved, a connection that was normal in the ancient Near Eastern world. *Magicians* is an appropriate term if the reader realizes that in the ancient world "magic" was a way of determining the future and of somehow manipulating the gods to do what one wanted. The term חַרְטֻמִּים (soothsayer-priests) also occurs in the story of Joseph (Gen 41:8, 24) and in the encounter between Moses and the wise men of Egypt (Exod 7:11, 22; 9:11).

**Given that the soothsayer-priests and conjurers used magic to determine the meaning of a dream or to deflect any harmful effects of it, how is it that these four Jewish men who worshiped the Lord were "ten times better"? The answer must be not that they were better at the magical arts but that they got better results.** The second chapter of Daniel illustrates this well. The Babylonian diviners insisted that Nebuchadnezzar tell them the dream so they could then practice their magical arts to determine its meaning. Daniel and his friends prayed that God would reveal the matter to them, which he then did. **These men didn't have to somehow manipulate the "gods" to get answers to Nebuchadnezzar's questions. They either knew the answers intrinsically because of their God-given wisdom, or they could get the answer through their relationship with the one true God to whom they prayed.**[34]

**1:21.** Some perceive a chronological problem with "the first year of Cyrus," since Daniel must have lived until at least the third year of Cyrus (Dan 10:1). Goldingay connects the statement with the end of the exile as described in 2 Chr 36:22–23 and Ezra 1,[35] but more likely it marks the end of the Babylonian era, the first of the four kingdoms mentioned in Daniel 2

---

34. Prayer is a key issue regarding wisdom in Daniel. He gained insight into Nebuchadnezzar's dream through prayer (2:17–23). As a customary practice he prayed three times a day (6:10 [11]), and he prayed earnestly to the Lord when he sought forgiveness for the national sins of Israel (9:2–23). This concept of praying for wisdom continued into NT times. James directed his readers to ask God for wisdom if they lacked it, being careful to trust him for the answer (Jas 1:5–6). Any believer who seeks wisdom concerning a difficult or puzzling issue may bring it before the Lord to discover an answer. While God may not offer direct revelation to believers in the same way he did to Daniel, believers do have the Holy Spirit, and he gives guidance and understanding to those who seek it through prayer. Scholars also find it important to pray concerning their study. Specific items of exposition need to be a matter of study and research, but the significance of what has been learned, how it is applied to the human heart, always relates to their own spiritual communion with the Lord.

35. Goldingay, *Daniel*, 27–28.

and 7. For Daniel the fact that the end of the Babylonian exile did not usher in a new era of independence for the Jews was problematic, and his passionate prayer concerning the issue resulted in the famous prophecy of seventy "weeks" in chapter 9.

Daniel was able to serve at the Babylonian court through the remaining tenure of the Babylonian empire, more than sixty years. His lengthy period of service to Babylon forms a fitting conclusion to the first chapter. Nebuchadnezzar's attempt to raise up new leaders in Babylonia succeeded beyond all his expectations, but that success was not because of him but because of the God of Daniel, Hananiah, Mishael, and Azariah.

The concluding remark about Daniel's service until the first year of Cyrus aptly refers to the opening statement of the chapter. The kingdom passed from Jehoiakim to the Babylonians under Nebuchadnezzar, and throughout that long period of Babylonian rule Daniel, a man infused with the wisdom of God, continued to serve as a high government official. **God not only gave the authority to rule the world to Nebuchadnezzar, but he also put in place someone who could offer sound advice to all the Babylonian kings until the authority shifted once again to Persia under Cyrus.**

## SHARPENING THE THEOLOGICAL FOCUS

The book of Daniel teaches the complete sovereignty of God over the nations and indeed, over history itself. The biblical doctrine of his sovereign reign comes not so much from explicit teaching as from stories, from narratives regarding God's dealings with his people through time.

From the time God called Abraham out of Ur of the Chaldees to the point where he permitted Nebuchadnezzar to exile the nation that descended from Abraham, the Lord was working out his plan, a plan that included growing Abraham's offspring into a great nation, entering a covenant relationship with that nation, and blessing all the peoples of the earth through that nation (Gen 12:1–3; 22:16–18). Unfortunately, the nation, whether led by "judges" or kings, did not live up to its calling to bless the peoples of the earth. Eventually the nation split in two, and God used the Assyrians to judge the northern kingdom, and, as Daniel portrays, the Babylonians to judge the southern kingdom of Judah.

Prior to Nebuchadnezzar the Lord had worked his will on earth mainly through Israel and Judah, using their kings, priests, and prophets to instruct and direct the people. When Nebuchadnezzar came to power in Babylonia, God shifted to Babylon the central focus of his work in the world. Rather than working through the king of Judah he now would grant wisdom and insight to his faithful servants held captive in Babylon and accomplish his purposes through them as well as through Gentile nations. In this way he would graciously maintain solidarity with his covenant people even though they no longer possessed the Promised Land but lived as exiles in foreign countries.

**As exiles it was hard for God's people to accept the fact that God was sovereign over the nations, that he was still in control. That is why the key word in chapter 1 is *gave*. The Lord *gave* Jehoiakim and the temple vessels to Nebuchadnezzar (1:2). He *gave* Daniel and his companions favor in the sight of the king's chief official (1:9). And he *gave* these men their superior knowledge and wisdom (1:17).** This theological concept of the Lord's control over who receives the kingdom and how his own followers will fare helps to prepare the way for the apocalyptic chapters (7 to 12) that map out the future for the Jewish people. When they find themselves oppressed under tyrannical rulers, they can be confident that the Lord is still in control. Even the worst tyrant cannot rule apart from the Lord's permission. The Lord's ways may be mysterious, but those who trust him can still prosper through his small acts of favor and through the wisdom that he grants them. And even if they do not prosper but struggle under the yoke of slavery, they can still trust in God, whose plans are always and ultimately for their good (Rom 8:28).

The Lord uniquely positioned Daniel to assume the role of a wise man for all the kings of Babylon—from Nebuchadnezzar to Belshazzar and on into the Medo-Persian empire. Because Daniel and his companions were faithful, loyal to God first, God was able to use them to influence the Babylonian and Persian governments.

**The relationship between God's sovereignty and human faithfulness is a recurring theme throughout not only Daniel, but also through the whole of Scripture. Clearly, God is sovereign, but Scripture also affirms that humans make choices and that these choices have consequences. As the book unfolds, each chapter of Daniel seems to highlight a different aspect of God's sovereignty and its interaction with human faithfulness. While the book of Daniel does not resolve the tension, it does offer insights into how God's people may live in the tension.**

In the first chapter of Daniel God shows himself sovereign on the one hand, on the other hand the faithful obedience of Daniel and his companions is manifest. In light of God's sovereignty did it really matter whether Daniel and his friends chose to serve him or not? They were willing vessels in God's hands, but even Nebuchadnezzar was used of the Lord, as an unwilling vessel. The Lord can and does use anyone, even unbelievers, to carry out his plans, but those who are faithful get the blessing of knowing that God is using them to accomplish his plans. Whether or not Daniel experienced success in the Babylonian kingdom, he was willing to submit to God's will.

Nebuchadnezzar thought that he had defeated Judah's God and was bringing the temple articles to Babylon in triumph, but the Lord had a better and more effective plan. When his plan succeeded by producing wise men vastly superior to Babylonian wise men, it became evident who the real victor was.

These theological themes emerge from a text that was written long ago. Though ancient, the text contains eternal truths that must be communicated and applied to contemporary life. The transitions from exegesis to theology to preaching should be rooted in the contours of a particular text.

Walking through Daniel 1, it becomes clear that the sovereignty of God is the central theme. In fact, God's sovereignty is the preeminent message of the entire book. Each chapter in Daniel contributes to this overall message by offering a unique vantage point from which to see a particular aspect of God's sovereignty. Here in chapter 1, the vantage point is from the chaos of exile and the struggle to remain faithful in a foreign and pagan culture. It was a culture in which Daniel and his friends, with their privileged status as court officials, could easily have found a comfortable life through conformity. However, chapter 1 communicates that because God's sovereignty extends even to these situations, he can, and will, work through the trusting faithfulness of his people.

## THE FOCUS OF DANIEL 1 FOR PREACHING AND TEACHING

In chapter 1 the faithfulness of Daniel and his friends introduces us to a major theme that runs throughout the book—the relationship between God's sovereignty and our free will. It's not so much that Daniel reconciles or explains how they can both be true, it simply affirms, repeatedly, that God is sovereign and that our faithfulness, or lack thereof, makes a difference. Here in chapter 1 this is affirmed both through the actions of an unbelieving king (Nebuchadnezzar) and believing youths (Daniel and his three friends). Additionally, Daniel highlights the difference between the participation of believers and unbelievers in the sovereign plans of God; believers know that their faithfulness will be rewarded. Here the rewards are immediate (success in the Babylonian royal court). But this is not always the case. The Bible, church history, and life experience teach us that often the rewards are not realized in this life. But, as the apostle Paul makes clear, the sovereign God of whom Daniel speaks will reward our faithfulness (1 Cor 4:5; 15:58).

In addition to future rewards, there is, in the present, a rest available to believers who realize that results are in God's hands and not theirs. Daniel and his friends were not on the hook for the fate of the remnant of Israel—God was. All they had to worry about was being faithful in the circumstances in which they found themselves. While the book of Daniel will not fully and finally reconcile the relationship between God's sovereignty and the choices people make, it will repeatedly reveal that choices do matter and that no one, not even the most powerful man on earth, can do something that will thwart God's will.

As people hear this story, at least three questions are naturally going to arise. First, they are going to wonder whether or not God truly is sovereign. In light of all the chaos and evil in the world today, can they really trust that God is in control? The second question that people are going to wonder about is whether or not God still works on their behalf just as he did with Daniel and his friends. When God's people take a stand for God, can they expect that he will bless and protect them as he did for these four young men? The third question is about God working through the faithfulness of his people. Does God still work through faithfulness in order to demonstrate his sovereignty? To all three questions the answer is a categorical "yes!" However, an intellectual, philosophical, or purely historical defense will not do much to convince people that this is true. Rather, they need to hear personal and contemporary examples of God's sovereign interventions on behalf of his people. To preach with power and relevance, "argue" your case (the Bible's case!) with concrete examples. Personal examples (preacher and congregation) are best, but examples from the Bible and church history are also effective. Stories of missionaries who ministered in pagan cultures can convince people that the God of Daniel is the same yesterday, today, and forever. Whenever biblical preachers proclaim the sovereignty of God, they should assume that some of the listeners are skeptical. The problem of evil is ubiquitous, and listeners tend to judge the veracity of the Scriptures by their own experience of pain. It often appears that God is *not* in control, and this text provides an opportunity for preachers to acknowledge that with empathy. Surely Daniel and the friends were tempted to doubt, despair, and compromise. But in the dark, they trusted what they had learned about God in the light, he is faithful and sovereign. They staked everything on that hope and thus experienced the grace of God.

## FROM TEXTUAL WORK TO TEACHING

## The Big Idea

- *Exegetical Idea:* After handing the king of Judah over to the king of Babylon, God works on behalf of, and through, the faithfulness of Daniel, Hananiah, Mishael, and Azariah to demonstrate that he is sovereign over the Babylonian kingdom and superior to the Babylonian king.
- *Theological Idea:* God works on behalf of, and through, the faithfulness of his people in order to demonstrate his sovereignty and supremacy.
- *Preaching Idea:* Because God is sovereign, trust him to work for you and through you in difficult times.

## Outline One: Following the Exegetical Flow

I. In his sovereignty God may allow what is seemingly evil to flourish. (1:1–2)

  A. The fall of Jerusalem, Jehoiakim and the temple was among the darkest days in Israel's history.

  B. God was in control; *he gave* them to Nebuchadnezzar.

  C. Application—move to relevance: When the darkest of days hit God's people, individually and collectively, God is still in control.

  1. Examples of dark days for the church.

  2. Examples of dark days for individual Christians.

II. When God's people remain faithful in difficult circumstances, their faithfulness may be tested. (1:3–17)

  A. Daniel and his friends had no choice when it came to their Babylonian education and name changes.

  B. Daniel and his friends did have a choice with regard to the food and drink they would consume and they chose faithfulness.

  C. Because Daniel and his friends chose faithfulness they were tested.

  D. Application—move to relevance: God's people will face temptations and if they choose faithfulness they can expect to be tested.

III. When their faithfulness is tested, God works on behalf of, and through, their faithfulness in order to demonstrate his sovereignty and enable his people to endure and thrive through the trial. (1:18–21)

  A. God worked on behalf of, and through, the youths' faithfulness in order to demonstrate his sovereignty and enable them to endure and thrive through the trial.

    1. God gave them favor with the king's officials.

    2. God gave them wisdom superior to any Babylonian wise men.

  B. God works on behalf of, and through, the faithfulness of his people in the same way today.

    1. Examples of God's faithfulness in response to his peoples' faithfulness.

    2. Examples of people enduring and thriving through trials.

## Outline Two: Following a Theme

I. Daniel chapter 1 is filled with chaos.

  A. The fall of Jerusalem, Jehoiakim and the temple.

  B. Youths are taken from their home court and planted in the royal court of a foreign king.

  C. A new way of life is imposed on them.

II. Because Daniel and his friends were more concerned with who they belonged to than they were with success, comfort and even survival, they had the confidence they needed to stay faithful in the chaos.

  A. They knew they belonged to Yahweh and this brought confidence.

  B. The comforts and temptations of the king's court held no power over them.

III. When God's people understand that who they belong to is more important than success, comfort and survival, they will have the confidence they need to remain faithful.

A. Because we belong to God, our identity is not in our success.

B. Because we belong to God, comfort takes a back seat to faithfulness.

C. Because we belong to God, survival is an eternal issue.

## EXCURSUS: *THE BABYLONIAN CHRONICLES*

*The Babylonian Chronicles* consist of a list of Babylonian kings in chronological order with significant events recorded for their reigns year by year. Scribes composed these chronicles in Babylonian cuneiform, probably extracting their information from running accounts of a king's reign. The specific set of chronicles known as Babylonian covered a period from the eighth century BC to the Seleucid era in the fourth to second centuries BC. They are a valuable source of historical information. Wiseman first published part of the Babylonian Chronicles; later Grayson also published them, including new material that had surfaced since Wiseman's edition and some Assyrian chronicles as well.[36] Grayson's publication of the Babylonian Chronicles is divided into two parts—chronicles from the Neo-Babylonian period (1–7) and chronicles from the Persian period (starting in 539 BC) to the Seleucid period. Wiseman's publication included only Grayson's numbers one through six. Grayson's Chronicle 7 is also known as the "Nabonidus Chronicle"; it is significant for its information about Nabonidus, the literal father of Belshazzar.

## EXCURSUS: THE LAND OF SHINAR

The world's first kingdom began with Nimrod at Babylon in the land of Shinar (Gen 10:10). There the people rebelled against the Lord's command to scatter over the earth, and the Lord had to confuse their languages (Gen 11:2). The first conflict between the man that God chose to be the progenitor of his elect people, Abram/Abraham, happened with a group of kings that included the king of Shinar (Gen 14:1, 9). At a crucial point when the people were starting to possess the land that the Lord had given them, they were almost stopped by Achan, who coveted a "cloak from Shinar" (Josh 7:21). The prophet Isaiah foresaw a time when God's people would be delivered from various locales, including Shinar (Isa 11:11). Finally, Zechariah had a vision of "wickedness" carried away from the land (of Judah) to "the land of Shinar" (Zech 5:5–11).

---

36. Wiseman, *Chronicles of Chaldean Kings*; Grayson, *ABC*.

While the NT does not use the term "Shinar," it does use "Babylon" to describe the leader of the nations that the Lord will judge in the time before he sets up his kingdom on earth (Rev 14:8; 16:19; 17:5; 18:2, 10, 21). When it came time for the Lord to send his people into exile because of their wickedness, he delivered them into the power of Nebuchadnezzar, who ruled over the land of "Shinar" (Dan 1:2).

# Dreams of Greatness
(Daniel 2:1–49)

**Chapter 1 Review**: Daniel 1 tells of the fall of Judah at the hands of Nebuchadnezzar. However, the author skillfully makes it clear that Nebuchadnezzar could do no more than besiege Jerusalem. It was God who gave Jehoiakim over to the king of Babylon. Just as it was God who gave Daniel favor in the eyes of the chief official, so it was God who gave Daniel and his friends superior wisdom. God is sovereign over all, and he sovereignly works on behalf of, and through, the faithfulness of his people.

**Chapter 2 Summary:** Much like chapter 1, chapter 2 highlights God's sovereignty. However, in this chapter the focus is on God's omniscient and sovereign control of history. He is the only all-knowing one, and there are mysteries only he can reveal. Through Nebuchadnezzar's dream and Daniel's God-given interpretation, God reveals his supreme wisdom and the ultimate superiority of his heavenly kingdom over all earthly kingdoms.

**Chapter 3 Preview:** Chapter 2 concludes with Daniel's appointment as "ruler over the whole province of Babylon and chief administrator over all the wise men." At Daniel's request, Shadrach, Meshach and Abednego are appointed to positions of leadership over the administration of the province of Babylon. From this new perch of prominence, the faithfulness of these Jews is tested as the *image* in Nebuchadnezzar's dream gives way to the reality of an *image* that he erects for his subjects to worship.

## THEOLOGICAL FOCUS OF CHAPTER 2

THERE ARE MYSTERIES THAT intelligence, ingenuity, and investigation will never figure out apart from the gracious revelation of God; therefore, God's people are to humbly seek the mercy and wisdom of God, trusting that he will graciously guide them and reveal what they need to know in order to be prepared for what will come to pass.

   I. *There are mysteries that intelligence, ingenuity, and investigation will never be able to figure out apart from the gracious revelation of God. (2:1–13)*

  II. *God's people are to humbly seek the mercy and wisdom of God. (2:14–18)*

 III. *God's people are to trust that God will graciously reveal to them what they need to know in order to be prepared for what will come to pass. (2:19–49)*

## BIG PICTURE (2:1–49)

Chapter 2 tells of Nebuchadnezzar's first dream and Daniel's interpretation of it. Narratively speaking, this story connects with the previous story through the words of Daniel's weighty prayer of praise. According to 2:21a, Daniel acknowledges that God "changes times and epochs; he removes kings and sets up kings." Chapter 1 noted the removal of Jehoiakim and the "setting up" of Nebuchadnezzar's reign over God's people. In 2:21b Daniel confesses that God "gives wisdom to wise men and knowledge to those who have understanding." This connects back to chapter 1:17–20 and points forward to what will happen here in chapter 2.

While the details about Nebuchadnezzar and the wise men can seem like a caricature or have a cartoon-like quality, they are historical. However, classifying Daniel 2 as a true story does not mean that it should be considered like a video that captured every detail of what happened. Even a video can capture only some details, not all of them. The narrator was selective in what was included, and he also chose to caricature the events and the people in it. Perhaps there were additional verbal exchanges between Nebuchadnezzar and the wise men before he declared their doom if they couldn't tell him the dream and its interpretation (2:5), but his declaration was recorded immediately following their seemingly innocent question in order to highlight Nebuchadnezzar's autocratic authority. And why condemn Daniel and his friends in the decree when they weren't there? Reasonable explanations could have been given, but again, Nebuchadnezzar's arbitrary rule is placed in stark relief by omitting them. Did Nebuchadnezzar respond to anything that Daniel said during his telling of the dream and its interpretation (2:26–45)? Perhaps, but Daniel's complete control of the situation would not be so obvious if additional conversations were recorded.

That the narrator told the story in such a foreshortened and dramatic fashion made it both entertaining and penetratingly theological at the same time. Here the most powerful man in the world comes face to face with dreams that threaten his world, but not even the wisest men in his kingdom can help him. Instead, a young Judean captive steps forward and gives the king his answer in a convincing and forceful way, at the same time ascribing the power and wisdom to do such a thing to "a God in heaven" (2:27–30, 45). The whole chapter turns out to be a powerful statement of God's sovereign control of history, highlighted in a direct way through Daniel's prayer (2:20–23). These would have been comforting words indeed to the Jewish people in exile, scattered throughout the world, and they still bring comfort to believers in the face of incredibly difficult events that happen around the world.

## TRANSLATION (DANIEL 2:1–49)

1   And in the second year of Nebuchadnezzar's reign Nebuchadnezzar had dreams.[1] And his spirit was troubled[2] so that he couldn't sleep any longer.

2   So the king commanded to summon the soothsayer-priests, the conjurers, the sorcerers, and the Chaldeans so they could tell the king his dreams. So they came and stood before the king.

3   Then the king said to them, "I have had a dream and my spirit is troubled to understand the dream."

4   Then the Chaldeans[3] spoke to the king in Aramaic[4]:

---

1. Since Daniel interprets only one dream, the plural indicates that the king had more than one dream that referred to the same elements (Montgomery, *Book of Daniel*, 141). Cf. the Pharaoh's dream that had different elements but the same interpretation (Gen 41).

2. The *Hithpael* of פעם occurs here for the king's agitation, and the *Niphal* of the same root occurs in Gen 41:8 of the Pharaoh's agitation after his troubling dream. The king also uses the *Niphal* to describe his agitated state (Dan 2:3a).

3. The NLT has "astrologers" instead of "Chaldeans," but that is too narrow. "Chaldeans" is a cover term for all the categories of wise men.

4. Possibly a gloss to inform the reader that the narrative switches the language

| | "O king, live forever! Tell your servants the dream and we will explain the interpretation." |
|---|---|
| 5 | The king responded by saying to the Chaldeans: |
| | "My word is firm.[5] If you don't tell me both the dream and its interpretation, you will be dismembered, and your houses will be made into a dump. |
| 6 | But if you explain the dream and its interpretation, you will receive gifts and a present and great honor from me. Therefore, make known the dream to me and its interpretation." |
| 7 | They responded a second time, saying: |
| | "Let the king tell the dream to his servants. Then we will explain the interpretation." |
| 8 | The king responded, saying: |
| | "I know for sure that you are buying time. For you have seen that the matter from me is firm—that if you don't tell me the dream, there is only one sentence for you. |
| 9 | So you have agreed together[6] to tell me a lying and corrupt word until the time might be changed. Therefore, tell me the dream; then I will know that you can explain its interpretation to me." |
| 10 | The Chaldeans responded before the king, saying: |
| | "There isn't a man on the earth who would be able to explain the king's matter. For no great and powerful king[7] has ever asked a matter like this of any soothsayer-priest, conjurer, or Chaldean. |
| 11 | The thing that the king is asking is difficult, and there is no one else who could declare it before the king except gods, whose dwelling is not with mortal beings." |

---

to Aramaic.

5. אַזְדָּא could mean *publicly known* (cf. NRSV), but more likely it has the sense *firm* or *irrefutable* (*HALOT*). "Has gone from me" in the KJV is in error, even though it is supported by Th (ἀπ' ἐμοῦ ἀπέστη) and the Vulgate (*recessit a me*).

6. The *kethiv* (הזמנתון) is a *Hithpeel* with complete assimilation of the *taw*. The *qere* (הִזְדְּמִנְתּוּן) shows partial assimilation of the *taw* to *daleth*. It is in the main text in some Masoretic manuscripts (*BHS*).

7. Or, "great king or ruler." The Chaldeans were seeking to convince Nebuchadnezzar that even one such as himself would never ask something so difficult.

## DREAMS OF GREATNESS

12. Because of this the king became angry and very furious and commanded that all the wise men of Babylon should be destroyed.

13. So the ruling was issued, and the wise men were about to be put to death. And Daniel and his companions were sought so they might be put to death.

14. Then Daniel wisely and discretely went to Arioch,[8] the captain of the king's bodyguards, who had gone out to put to death the wise men of Babylon.

15. He responded to Arioch, the king's commander, saying:

    "Why is the ruling from the king so harsh?"

    Then Arioch informed Daniel about the matter.

16. So Daniel went in and requested of the king that he would give him time to explain the interpretation to the king.

17. Then Daniel went to his house and informed Hananiah, Mishael, and Azariah, his companions, about the matter.

18. This was so that they could request mercy from the God of heaven about this mystery, so that Daniel and his companions would not be executed with the rest of the wise men of Babylon.

19. Then the mystery was revealed to Daniel in a vision of the night, and Daniel praised the God of heaven.

20. Daniel responded by saying:

    "May God's name be blessed forever and ever,

    for wisdom and power belong to him.

21. And he changes times and epochs;

    he removes kings and sets up kings.

    He gives wisdom to wise men

    and knowledge to those who have understanding.

22. He reveals the deep and hidden things;

    he knows what is in the darkness,

    for the light abides with him.

23. To you, O God of my fathers, I offer thanksgiving and praise, for you have given me wisdom and might.[9] Even now you have

---

8. Literally, "He gave Arioch counsel and advice."
9. For MT's וּגְבוּרְתָא (and might) 4QDan[a] has ונהי[רא] or ונהי[רתא] (and light),

| | |
|---|---|
| | made know to me what we requested of you. For you have made known to us the king's matter." |
| 24 | In light of this Daniel went to Arioch, whom the king had appointed to execute the wise men of Babylon. He went and said to him as follows: |
| | "Do not execute the wise men of Babylon! Bring me before the king, and I will explain the interpretation to the king." |
| 25 | Then Arioch quickly brought Daniel before the king and said to him as follows: |
| | "I have found a man of the exiles of Judah who will make known the interpretation to the king." |
| 26 | The king responded by saying to Daniel, whose name was Belteshazzar: |
| | "Are you able to make known to me the dream I had and its interpretation?" |
| 27 | Daniel responded to the king by saying: |
| | "The mystery that the king is asking about, wise men, conjurers, soothsayer-priests, or diviners cannot disclose to the king.[10] |
| 28 | But there is a God in heaven who reveals mysteries, and he has made known to King Nebuchadnezzar what will take place in future days. As for the visions in your head (that you saw in) your dream, here they are. |
| 29 | As for you, O king, while on your bed your concerns[11] about what will be in the future came up, and the revealer of mysteries has made known to you what will happen. |
| 30 | As for me, it is not by any wisdom that I have more than any other living being that this mystery was revealed to me, but it was so that the interpretation might be made known to the king, and you might know about the concerns in your mind. |
| 31 | O king, as you were looking there appeared a great statue. That statue was large; and its brilliance was dazzling as it stood before you; and its appearance was frightening. |

---

probably influenced by the same term in the previous verse.

    10. For the different types of Babylonian wise men see Table 2.1.

    11. See Gzella, "רעי," *TDOT*, 16.

| 32 | As for that statue, its head was of fine gold. Its chest and arms were of silver. Its belly and thighs were of bronze. |
|---|---|
| 33 | Its legs were of iron. Its feet were partly of iron and partly of baked clay. |
| 34 | You kept looking until a stone was cut out without hands, and it struck the statue on its feet of iron and clay and crushed them. |
| 35 | At that time they were crushed all at once—the iron, the clay, the bronze, the silver, and the gold. And they became like chaff from a threshing floor in summer. The wind took them away, and no trace of them was found. And the stone that struck the statue became a great mountain and filled the whole earth. |
| 36 | This was the dream, and we[12] will tell its interpretation before the king. |
| 37 | You, O king, are the king of kings[13] to whom the God of heaven has given the kingdom, the might, the power, and the glory. |
| 38 | Wherever people, wild animals, and birds of the sky live, he has given them into your control and given you authority over all of them.[14] It is you who are the head of gold. |
| 39 | And after you another kingdom will arise that is inferior to you, and another third kingdom of bronze that will rule over the whole world. |
| 40 | And a fourth kingdom will be strong like iron in that iron smashes and crushes everything. So like iron that breaks in pieces all these metals, it will smash and shatter all the earth.[15] |
| 41 | And in that you saw the feet and the toes[16] partly of potter's clay and partly of iron, it will be a divided kingdom, but some of the |

---

12. It is unlikely that Daniel meant to include his companions in the statement (Lacocque, *Book of Daniel*, 47) or to state that he and God were giving the interpretation (Miller, *Daniel*, 92). Probably it is a "plural of modesty, a way of showing the humility of the speaker" (Péter-Contesse and Ellington, *Handbook on the Book of Daniel*, 59).

13. Cf. Ezek 26:7.

14. See Jer 27:6; 28:14.

15. Following 4QDan[a] (first century BC) and the OG. The reading is adopted by Koch, *Daniel 1—4*, 102, but cf. Goldingay, *Daniel*, 35. The MT has "all these it will smash and shatter."

16. The OG omits "toes"; Th supports the MT; 4QDan[a] has a gap at this point, but there may not be enough room for the word אֶצְבְּעָתָא (*and the toes*) in the gap (Collins, *Daniel*, 151).

| | |
|---|---|
| | strength of iron will be in it since you saw the iron mixed with common clay. |
| 42 | As the toes of the feet were partly of iron and partly of clay, part of the kingdom will be strong and part of it will be brittle. |
| 43 | And[17] in that you saw the iron mixed with common clay, people will intermingle with the offspring of men but will not stick with one another, even as[18] iron does not mix with clay. |
| 44 | And in the days of those kings the God of heaven will raise up a kingdom that will never be destroyed, and the kingdom will not be left for another people. It will smash and bring to an end all these kingdoms, and it will endure forever. |
| 45 | In that you saw a stone cut out from a mountain without hands and it smashed the iron, the clay, the silver, and the gold, a great God[19] has made known to the king what will happen after this time. The dream is certain, and its interpretation is trustworthy." |
| 46 | Then king Nebuchadnezzar fell on his face and paid homage to Daniel, ordering sacrifice and incense to be offered to him. |
| 47 | The king responded to Daniel by saying: |
| | "Truly your God is a God of gods and a Lord of kings and a revealer of mysteries, for you have been able to reveal this mystery. |
| 48 | Then the king promoted Daniel and gave him many great gifts. And he made him ruler over the whole province of Babylon and chief administrator over all the wise men of Babylon. |
| 49 | Then Daniel petitioned the king to appoint over the administration of the province of Babylon Shadrach, Meshach, and Abednego, but Daniel served at the king's court.[20] |

---

17. The *qere* inserts the conjunction *waw* (*and*); 4QDan[a] supports the *qere*.

18. The MT has הָאּ־כְדִי, translated "even/just as" in many versions. *HALOT* proposes reading הָאּ דִּי with the same translation. 4QDan[a] has הכא די, probably to be read *aheka di*.

19. The Aramaic does not have the definite article.

20. The term תְּרַע (*gate*) here means the royal *court* (*HALOT*).

## TEXTUAL OUTLINE (2:1–49)

I. Nebuchadnezzar Has a Disturbing Dream and Seeks Its Interpretation. (2:1–13)

*[There are mysteries that intelligence, ingenuity, and investigation will never be able to figure out apart from the gracious revelation of God.]*

    A. Nebuchadnezzar summons his wise men to interpret a disturbing dream. (2:1–3)

    B. Nebuchadnezzar demands what the wise men cannot do. (2:4–13)

II. Daniel and His Friends Humbly Seek the Wisdom and Mercy of God. (2:14–18)

*[God's people are to humbly seek the mercy and wisdom of God.]*

    A. Daniel wisely requests time to find a solution. (2:14–16)

    B. Daniel and his friends pray for wisdom about the king's mystery. (2:17–18)

III. God Graciously Reveals to Daniel What He Needs to Know. (2:19–49)

*[God's people are to trust that God will graciously reveal to them what they need to know in order to be prepared for what will come to pass.]*

    A. Daniel praises and thanks God for the revelation. (2:19–24)

    B. Daniel tells the king his dream and interprets it. (2:25–45)

    C. The king reacts to what Daniel has done. (2:46–49)

## EXPOSITION (2:1–49)

## Nebuchadnezzar Has a Disturbing Dream and Seeks Its Interpretation. (2:1–13)

Theological Point: There are mysteries that intelligence, ingenuity, and investigation will never be able to figure out apart from the gracious revelation of God.

Nebuchadnezzar condemned his wise men to death because they were unable to interpret his dream. People in ancient times paid attention to dreams, and a dream that a king had would have been thought highly significant.

The background information for the episode of Nebuchadnezzar and his dream of a great image occurs in the first three verses of chapter 2. The timing of the dream, Nebuchadnezzar's reaction to it, and his summons to his wise men to interpret it are all narrated in the Hebrew language (2:1–3). The only remaining Hebrew in the first part of the book contains the introduction to the wise men's response in 2:4a.[21] **The change in language to Aramaic at 2:4b thus creates a sense of separation between what was and what is. The Jewish experience is now the Babylonian experience. Daniel and his fellow Jews are now fully immersed in Babylon!**

Nebuchadnezzar is the central figure of this first part of the chapter (2:1–13). The text names him twice in the first verse, and he is referred to as *the king* an additional four times in the next two verses. **The constant repetition has a purpose—Nebuchadnezzar is the center of attention!** He has the dream; he summons the wise men to interpret it; and he controls the direction of the dialogue with the wise men. He also has the last word when he issues the decree to execute all the wise men of Babylon. **His power is absolute and final; no one can oppose him. Against this backdrop of a powerful despot whose actions appear quite arbitrary, the remainder of the chapter shifts the locus of authority to Daniel's God. The eternal God has the real power; Nebuchadnezzar has only received it by divine permission (2:37).** As a result of Daniel's intervention, the king's command was set aside, even after the executioner was prepared to carry out his orders.

*Nebuchadnezzar summons his wise men to interpret a disturbing dream. (2:1–3)*

**2:1.** Being disturbed by his dream, Nebuchadnezzar summons his wise men. Some have supposed that the Hebrew means that Nebuchadnezzar fell back asleep.[22] The unusual *Niphal* form of the verb (נִהְיְתָה [*nihyetah*]), however, is better taken as "and his sleep *was ended* upon him." The context of Nebuchadnezzar's extreme agitation suggests sleeplessness after his dream.[23]

There are obvious similarities between the account of Nebuchadnezzar's dream and Pharaoh's dreams in the time of Joseph (Gen 41:1–45). In both accounts the king had a disturbing dream, "and his spirit was troubled." Nearly identical expressions for the troubled spirit occur in both

---

21. For a more detailed discussion on the use of both Aramaic and Hebrew in Daniel, see Introduction.
22. Steinmann, *Daniel*, 114.
23. Miller, *Daniel*, 77.

accounts, וַתִּתְפָּעֶם רוּחוֹ in Dan 2:1 and וַתִּפָּעֶם רוּחוֹ in Gen 41:8. Pharaoh had his dream two years after restoring his chief cupbearer and hanging the chief baker; Nebuchadnezzar had his dream in his second regnal year. In both stories חַרְטֻמִּים (*soothsayer-priests* or *magicians*) were summoned to interpret the dreams but were unable to do so. In both a Hebrew man came in and interpreted the dream and was consequently rewarded with a high government position. And both Joseph and Daniel acknowledged that it was not by their human ability but only through God that they were able to interpret the dream (Gen 41:16 and Dan 2:27–28). There are also significant differences between the two accounts, and Daniel 2 is hardly a "midrash" on Genesis 41.[24] Aside from the fact that such a view would require taking the account in Daniel as fictional, the nature of the two dreams is entirely different. Pharaoh's dream related only to the continuance of his own kingdom through prudent action advised by Joseph, whereas Daniel's interpretation unveiled future kingdoms that would eventually crumble through divine intervention.

**2:2.** Nebuchadnezzar's dream was so disturbing that he called for his wise men to interpret it. The *wisdom* that they had was not the kind of wisdom spoken of in the book of Proverbs. Instead, it was what is known as *mantic* wisdom. That is, they supposedly had the ability to communicate with the gods through various means of divination. Four categories of wise men are listed, two of which appeared in Dan 1:20 (חַרְטֻמִּים, *soothsayer-priests*, and אַשָּׁפִים, *conjurers*). However, the term *Chaldeans* takes a place of prominence in the narrative of chapter 2, representative of the entire group of wise men throughout the chapter (2:4a, 5, 10; cf. 3:8). **By utilizing this term, the author emphasizes the contrast between Babylonian wisdom and godly wisdom, and, like chapter 1, God's wisdom will prove superior.** Table 2.1 shows the terms for different categories of wise men, giving the Hebrew and/or Aramaic terms and their English translation with a description of their function.

---

24. *Contra* Lacocque, *Book of Daniel*, 36.

| Table 2.1: Terms for Babylonian Wise Men: Aramaic, Hebrew, and English ||||||
|---|---|---|---|---|
| English Term | Hebrew Term | Aramaic Term | Babylonian Cognate | Description |
| Wise Men | NA in Daniel | חַכִּימִין | NA | general term |
| Chaldeans | כַּשְׂדִּים | כַּשְׂדָּאִין | Kal-da-a | general term |
| Soothsayer— Priests | חַרְטֻמִּים | חַרְטֻמִּין | ḫarṭibi (Assyrian) | telling the future, interpret dreams |
| Conjurers | אַשָּׁפִים | אָשְׁפִין | āšipu | warding off evil effects |
| Sorcerers | מְכַשְּׁפִים | NA in Daniel | kaššāpu | warding off evil effects |
| Diviners | NA in Daniel | גָּזְרִין | NA | telling the future |

These wise men were summoned to apply their skills to interpret what was assumed to be a divine message given through the dream, but they also had another function. Since it was believed that a dream like this could cause bad things to happen to the king or to the kingdom, the practitioners were also brought in to ward off any possible evil effects.[25]

**2:3.** Once the Babylonian wise men were standing before the king, he told them that he had a dream and was troubled "to understand" (לָדַעַת) it. The verb translated here *understand* is ambiguous, *to know* being another possible sense. This latter sense is evidently what has led many commentators to think that the king had forgotten his dream and was now asking the wise men to tell him what it was. Josephus states bluntly, "when he arose from his bed, he forgot it."[26] Two factors make it more likely that the king remembered his dream. The first is that the wise men assumed that the king could tell them the dream if he wanted to (v. 5). Second, the king said that he wanted to test the truthfulness of their words by having them tell him the dream before they interpreted it (v. 9). Jerome took an intermediate position. The king had a vague recollection of the dream that could be strengthened by hearing details from the wise men.[27]

---

25. Oppenheim, *Interpretation of Dreams*, 219.
26. Josephus, *A.J.*, 10:195.
27. Jerome, *Commentary on Daniel*, 25; similarly, Steinmann, *Daniel*, 117.

*Nebuchadnezzar demands what wise men cannot do. (2:4–13)*

Why was the king so arbitrary and harsh with the Chaldeans? Rather than simply tell them to recount both the dream and its interpretation he immediately threatened them with execution and ruin if they didn't do just that. In response to their pleading, he accused them of lying and plotting together to "buy time" (2:8–9) by devising some scheme to escape his wrath. He even went so far as to issue a decree to slaughter "all the wise men," and it included Daniel and his friends. They weren't even party to the audience with the king (2:15). **But, as the transition to Aramaic highlights, the Babylonian experience is now the Jewish experience.**

If in fact Nebuchadnezzar did recall at least the main elements of his dream, he probably already had some frightful ideas about what it might mean. He may have sought to have a dream in order to learn about suspected plotting among the Chaldeans.[28] He wanted to be sure that the wise men were capable of giving a true interpretation, so he issued his ultimatums to force them to use all their supposed powers to gain the meaning. If he told them the dream outright, they might resort to mere human reasoning to figure out the parts of the image. And they might use the opportunity to gain some political advantage over Nebuchadnezzar. Perhaps he already had reason to suspect that a plot was afoot. Also, since these dream specialists were expected to dispel any adverse effects of the dream, it was quite important that they really know what the dream meant. If they couldn't share the details of the dream with the king, how would they be able to use their magical powers to ward off impending disaster?

Such reasons are speculative, but from the text itself there appears to be a literary reason. As mentioned previously, it is likely that Nebuchadnezzar's tyrannical and arbitrary wielding of power contrasts with God's power. God alone has the power to "remove kings and raise up kings" (2:21); Nebuchadnezzar's power derives only from God (2:37–38). The mighty king of Babylon had to rely on his diviners' ability to communicate with the gods, but Daniel's God had given the king his dream in order to reveal mysteries of what was to become of Nebuchadnezzar and the kingdom of Babylon.

**2:4.** The Chaldeans requested the king to *tell* them the dream, asking merely for a verbal recounting of his experience. Three different terms are used to communicate the interpretation of the dream to the king,[29] and all

---

28. Deliberately seeking to have a dream is known as *incubation*. A biblical example is Solomon's dream at Gibeon, which he experienced only after sacrificing a thousand burnt offerings on the altar (1 Kgs 3:3–5).

29. The Aramaic forms are: (1) the *Pael* of חוה; (2) the *Haphel* of חוה; and (3) the *Haphel* of ידע. The *Pael* and the *Haphel* are alterations made to an Aramaic verb in

three can be translated *make known*. Some English versions also use *tell* for any of the three. **No matter how they are translated, they imply more than a mere telling of facts. They indicate that the speaker wishes to *inform* or *make known* to someone certain issues that the listener needs to know. Nebuchadnezzar was able to recognize details that the wise men might recount of his dream, but the interpretation was what he was after.**

Everyone in the story to this point, the king and all his wise men, would have assumed that the details of the dream were meant to communicate something to the king from the gods. That is why those called to interpret the dream are associated with various types of magic and divination. They were expected to learn the details of the dream from the gods and then relay those to the king, but to read the king's mind concerning what he had dreamed was not something they would ordinarily do. Thus, they requested the king share what was on his mind so they could then apply their various crafts to determine the divinely intended meaning.

**2:5–6.** Immediately the king threatened the Chaldeans with destruction if they couldn't tell him *both* the dream and its interpretation. The decreed punishment seems unusually cruel, but such cruelty was common in the ancient Near East (2 Kgs 25:7; Jer 29:22) and certainly not unknown even in the modern world. Also, Nebuchadnezzar was quite prepared to bestow gifts and honor on these men if they were able to meet his wishes. In the ancient Near East even telling a dream had a cathartic effect on the dreamer, and the dreamer was expected to do the telling.[30] The king appears to reverse the standard procedure: "I won't tell the dream to you; you tell it to me."

**2:7–9.** The Chaldeans essentially repeated their first request of Nebuchadnezzar. They wanted to hear what the dream was; then they would interpret it. They were careful to continue to show deference to the king, this time addressing him indirectly ("Let the king tell the dream to his servants"). Nebuchadnezzar was obviously peeved to hear them ask the same thing again. He decided with conviction that these specialists in interpreting messages from the gods were not so capable after all. If they couldn't tell him what the dream was, then when it came to the interpretation all they could do was agree on something that was made up. The king hadn't forgotten the dream. If he had, then the wise men could have made up both the dream and its interpretation, and there would have been no reason for them to be so perplexed.

---

order to express certain types of action for that verb. They are roughly equivalent to the *Piel* and the *Hiphil* verb patterns in Hebrew.

30. Oppenheim, *Interpretation of Dreams*, 218–19.

**2:10–11.** The wise men gave two reasons why no one on earth could meet the king's demand. First, it was unprecedented for even a king as powerful as Nebuchadnezzar to ask such a thing. **The second reason is quite telling in relation to the rest of the story. Only gods, who have no direct contact with people, could be expected to reveal what the king was asking.** Unless they heard the message from the lips of the king, they could not be expected to interpret it. In a striking way this admission laid the groundwork for Daniel's accomplishment. They said no one could do it, but Daniel did it. They said only the gods could do it, but that they couldn't be expected to do so because of their distance from mankind; however, Daniel's God revealed both the message and its interpretation to Daniel. The protestations of these Babylonian sages set up the perfect foil against which Daniel and his God came out triumphant.

There is also an irony to the situation that places the Babylonian wise men in a bad light. They claimed to be in communication with the gods through their magical arts, yet they had to admit that they were stumped by the king's demand. If indeed they could communicate with the gods, then why couldn't they simply ask the gods for the answer to the mystery? **An underlying theme of the powerlessness of the gods of the nations comes through clearly.** The gods could not actually speak to wise men any more than the idols that represented the deities (cf. Dan 5:23).

**2:12.** When these Babylonian specialists exposed themselves as frauds, they stirred up Nebuchadnezzar's wrath. He had lost faith in the ability of these experts in divination to truly communicate with the gods.

**2:13.** Whenever Daniel and his three companions are mentioned in the text, the term "wise men" is used rather than *Chaldeans*. The Babylonians considered the Hebrew men in the same category as the rest of the diviners. However, the author of the book literally separates them from the *Chaldeans* to draw attention to the fact that they were different; Daniel and his companions were wise because God had made them wise. They took no part in the ineffective shamanistic shenanigans of the *Chaldeans*. It was through prayer and the graciousness of God, the only revealer of mysteries, that they were able to obtain the answer needed to appease the king (vv. 17–23).

## Daniel and His Friends Humbly Seek the Wisdom and Mercy of God. (2:14–18)

Theological Point: God's people are to humbly seek the mercy and wisdom of God.

Rather than panic, Daniel calmly sought information about the dilemma he and his friends faced. Then he asked for time to find a solution to the underlying cause of their predicament. Finally, he and his friends brought the matter before God, seeking him as the true source of wisdom.

### *Daniel wisely requests time to find a solution. (2:14–16)*

Daniel approached Arioch, the king's executioner, to discover the problem and then requested time to come up with the answer needed to appease the king. From Arioch he learned why the king's anger was so severe. Then he requested some time to discover the interpretation of the dream. In this way Daniel "handled the situation with wisdom and discretion" (NLT). Arioch's titles heighten the tension of the situation. He was the captain of the king's personal bodyguard,[31] a high officer in his service, who had been commissioned to perform the executions.

### *Daniel and his friends pray for wisdom about the king's mystery. (2:17–18)*

As soon as Daniel had informed his friends about the situation, the first item of business was to pray for God's mercy (רַחֲמִין). If they were to escape from their dilemma, it would only be through divine intervention. The king's demand involved a "mystery" or "secret" (רָז) that only God could reveal, something that the Chaldeans had already admitted (2:11). This emphasis on divine mercy and divine revelation of a mystery sets up a theological truth—only the one true God, the God of Daniel, is capable of such a feat. The Babylonian gods were incapable, for if they had been able to reveal the mystery, the Babylonian wise men could have given a proper answer to Nebuchadnezzar. The four young men probably prayed into the night until finally the mystery was revealed to Daniel in a vision. At that point Daniel's first thought was to praise God for the great miracle of this revelation. As

---

31. The Hebrew equivalent for the Aramaic expression occurs in 2 Kgs 25:8.

urgent as the need was to discover the king's mystery, Daniel began where prayer needs to begin—acknowledging and praising God for who he is.[32]

## God Graciously Reveals to Daniel What He Needs to Know. (2:19–49)

Theological Point: God's people are to trust that God will graciously reveal to them what they need to know in order to be prepared for what will come to pass.

After Daniel informed Hananiah, Mishael, and Azariah of the situation and enlisted them to pray, he received a revelation about the mystery through a vision at night. The heart of the episode then follows—a prayer of praise to God. The theology of divine sovereignty that Daniel expressed in this prayer indicates not only the central theme of the chapter but even of the entire book of Daniel. Literarily it is the most prominent part of the chapter, being both a prayer and a poem![33]

### Daniel praises and thanks God for the revelation. (2:19–24)

Daniel uttered two magnificent prayers that are recorded in the book. The first is a hymn of praise and thanksgiving for the answer he received from God about the king's mystery. The second prayer, recorded in chapter 9, is a prayer of confession on behalf of the Jewish people. Daniel carefully crafted his prayer of praise as a poem that has a sense of balance as well as parallelism, the characteristic marks of poetry in the OT.

Daniel initiated his prayer with a desire for God's *name* to be *blessed* (מְבָרַךְ) forever. God's *name* stands for his reputation and his attributes. It is much more than merely a word. The primary way to "bless" God is to praise him for who he is and to thank him for what he has done. Daniel's prayer has both elements. God's "wisdom and power" (חָכְמְתָא וּגְבוּרְתָא, v. 20) both come into play as he oversees the world he has created. **He possesses "wisdom," ensuring that his plans lead to a praiseworthy ending, and he possesses "power," which ensures these plans will come to pass.**

---

32. Cf. Matt 6:9, where the model prayer that Jesus gave his disciples begins with "Our Father in heaven, hallowed be your name" (ESV).

33. Important things in an OT narrative are communicated through poetry. For example, Adam recited his brief poem about the significance of Eve right at the high point of the narrative (Gen 2:23). Prayers also serve to underline the theology found within a narrative (cf. 1 Kgs 8:22–53; Neh 9:5–38; Dan 9:4–19).

## INTERPRETING DANIEL FOR PREACHING AND TEACHING

According to the theology of Daniel's book, true "wisdom" and "power" always originate in God. His "power" and "wisdom" are the themes of verses twenty-one and twenty-two.[34]

**2:21. God has the power to "change the times and the seasons."** The wise men of Babylon could not "buy time," but Daniel, trusting in his God, was able to gain the time he needed to solve the king's mystery. The predictions of "2,300 evening-mornings" (8:14) and the "seventy periods of seven" (9:24), along with various other references to specific periods of time (4:22; 7:25; 12:7, 11, 12), demonstrate God's ability to arrange events with fixed limits of time. And he appoints a time when an end will come for kingdoms and indeed even for the end of the age (8:17, 19; 9:26; 11:27, 35, 40; 12:4, 9, 13).

The two terms that refer to time are זְמָן and עִדָּן. They both refer to general periods of time throughout history. The usual rendering of *times and seasons* is acceptable as long as one thinks of *seasons* as something like the "seasons of life" rather than the four seasons of the year. The idea is that "God has authority over time and history,"[35] a concept which is captured by "the times and the periods" (NASB) or even "The course of world events" (NLT).

God's ability to remove and set up kings also manifests his great power. Who could conceive of a greater power in Daniel's day than that embodied in Nebuchadnezzar, the king of Babylon? As Daniel's interpretation of the king's dream will show, power such as Nebuchadnezzar possessed could come only at the behest of the great God in heaven (2:37–38). And Nebuchadnezzar was only one of many kings who would rule over successive realms, each one under the control of God. This theme reverberates throughout the book of Daniel.[36]

**2:22. The wise men of Babylon were ineffective, because their wisdom had not come from the one true God. Daniel's wisdom, however, was granted to him by God. All "wise men," in fact, attain any wisdom or ability to discern how things really are only as God's gift. Mysteries like the one that the wise men of Babylon declared impossible, and that greatly troubled the mind of the king, were as nothing to the God who can reveal the most obscure mysteries. Places hidden in deep, inaccessible recesses and darkness stand for unattainable knowledge, but God**

---

34. For a survey of how Dan 2:20–23 serves as a key passage throughout the book, see Table 2.2.

35. Péter-Contesse and Ellington, *Handbook on the Book of Daniel*, 46.

36. See Table 2.2 (Daniel 2:20–23 as a Theme Verse) shows how Dan 2:20–23 is echoed throughout the book.

knows all about them. "Light abides with him" (v. 22). He is omniscient and omnipotent.

**2:23.** Daniel concluded his prayer with thanksgiving and praise for what God had done for him. **First, he noted that God had shared with him the "wisdom and power" needed to solve the mystery, using the same two terms that he had initially ascribed to God** (חָכְמְתָא וּגְבוּרְתָא). **Then in two parallel lines he declared that God had "made known" to him the "matter" that troubled the king.** The prayer achieves a fine balance in that the revelation of the request came to Daniel (הוֹדַעְתַּנִי, "you have made known to me"), but the knowledge of the issue was made known to all four men (הוֹדַעְתֶּנָא, "you have made known to us"). Daniel "made known" the reason (מִלְּתָא, the matter) for the sentence of death to his companions, so they all sought God's mercy in prayer. The revelation in the vision of the night then came to Daniel alone, but that revelation let all of them know that God had granted his mercy concerning "the king's matter" (מִלַּת מַלְכָּא).

| Table 2.2: Daniel 2:20–23 as a Theme Verse ||
|---|---|
| Reference | Description |
| 1:2 | The Lord gave Jehoiakim and the temple articles to Nebuchadnezzar. |
| 1:17 | God gave the four Hebrew men knowledge and comprehension. |
| 2:31–45 | The four successive kingdoms illustrate how God "raises up" and "brings down" kings. |
| 3:28 | Nebuchadnezzar praises the God who delivered the three men who disobeyed his order. |
| 4:31–32 (28–29) | Nebuchadnezzar's sovereignty was removed until he would recognize that the Most High rules over the kingdom of men. |
| 4:35 (32) | Nebuchadnezzar confesses that the Most High does whatever he pleases in heaven or on earth. |
| 5:30–31 (5:30—6:1) | The kingdom was transferred by God from Belshazzar to Darius the Mede. |
| 6:26–27 (27–28) | Darius the Mede recognizes that God has a kingdom that endures forever and that he performs miracles in heaven and on earth. |
| 7:9–14 | The Ancient of Days presides over the judgment of the nations and sets up a kingdom that will endure forever. |
| 8:20–26 | More kingdoms will arise, even an arrogant ruler who will war against God, but God will destroy him. His period of dominance will be for only a short period of time. |
| 9:24–27 | All future history for the Jews is laid out in successive periods of time, culminating in the destruction of God's enemies. |

| Table 2.2: Daniel 2:20–23 as a Theme Verse | |
|---|---|
| Reference | Description |
| 10:20—11:1 | Warfare in heaven mirrors the struggle of kingdoms on earth, with God's sovereign will always winning. |
| 11:2-45 | Throughout history kingdoms will rise and fall until God finally destroys the last and most wicked kingdom of all. |
| 12:2 | When God's eternal kingdom arrives, even his followers from the past will be resurrected to populate it. |
| 12:11-13 | God's timing is laid out in advance, even if known only to him. |

**2:24.** Having received the divine revelation, Daniel immediately went to Arioch and sought an audience with the king to declare the interpretation. Most urgently, Daniel requested a stay of execution. He cared about the fate of all the wise men, not only that of himself and his friends.

## Daniel tells the king his dream and interprets it. (2:25–45)

**2:25.** Arioch hastily brought Daniel into Nebuchadnezzar's presence and introduced him as someone from "the exiles of Judah" who would "explain the interpretation to the king." Whether Arioch had confidence that Daniel really could satisfy the king's request is hard to say. Possibly he was risking his own neck by taking Daniel to the king; if Daniel failed, the king's wrath could fall on him.[37]

**2:26-28.** The text moves quickly to the king's questions for Daniel. He asked about his ability to relate both the dream and its interpretation, but Daniel redirected the attention to his God, first reminding the king that the Babylonian wise men had failed to give an answer. Then he stated that the "God in heaven" who "reveals mysteries" was attempting to reveal to the king future events through his dream.

**2:28.** The Aramaic expression בְּאַחֲרִית יוֹמַיָּא (*in the end of the days*) has as its Hebrew counterpart בְּאַחֲרִית הַיָּמִים, which occurs at Daniel 10:14. Here the vision to be explained encompasses history from the present into the distant future, culminates at a certain point where God breaks into history in a striking manner. The translation "in the future" (NLT) is possible in that the Hebrew phrase elsewhere refers simply to the future (Gen 49:1; Num 24:14), but it also occurs in the prophets in the more technical sense of the time when God will establish his kingdom on earth (Isa 2:2; Jer 30:24; 48:47; 49:39; Ezek 38:16; Hos 3:5; Mic 4:1). Whether in any of these passages the terminology itself, as opposed to the broader context, has the

---

37. Steinmann, *Daniel*, 133.

specific sense of "in the latter days" (ESV) is open to interpretation.³⁸ The king probably understood Daniel to mean simply "in future days." Daniel's interpretation reached a point where all of the kingdoms represented by the different materials were destroyed (2:45), but even there he referred simply to "what will happen after this" (מָה דִּי לֶהֱוֵא אַחֲרֵי דְנָה; cf. 2:29). The details of the dream as interpreted by Daniel laid out a sequence of events that from Nebuchadnezzar's perspective were future.

**Daniel used similar language at both the beginning and the end of his recitation of the dream and its interpretation. He prefaced his account of the dream with** אֱלָהּ רַב הוֹדַע לְמַלְכָּא מָה דִּי לֶהֱוֵא אַחֲרֵי דְנָה ("a great God has made known to the king what will happen after this." Then he concluded his interpretation with וּגְלֵא רָזַיָּא הוֹדְעָךְ מָה־דִי לֶהֱוֵא ("and the revealer of mysteries has made known to you what will happen").

Daniel reported the details of the dream in a straightforward manner. **One thing to notice, though, is that except for the head of the image, its parts are described in pairs—chest and arms; belly and thighs; legs and feet. Nebuchadnezzar's kingdom was unified, but the successor kingdoms tended toward more division. Vast empires are difficult to hold together through autocratic rule. The feet and toes represent the most divided elements, and even from Daniel's bare description he gave more detail about the feet than about any other part of the statue. That will be of importance for the interpretation.**

Commentators who deny the historicity of the account are particularly interested in Near Eastern parallels to the dream, hoping to find the source of the author's material. If the chapter describes a real event, then Daniel simply recounted the dream that Nebuchadnezzar actually experienced. Even so, it would still be informative to know something about the background against which the king had his dream. God gave him the dream, as Daniel tells it, to communicate a message, but the message was couched in language and symbols that would at least be familiar to the king.

Persian influence is often posited for Nebuchadnezzar's dream image,³⁹ but Lucas has demonstrated that "there is no compelling evidence of Persian influence on . . . Daniel."⁴⁰ Persian sources would be too late for the time of Nebuchadnezzar. The Greek poet Hesiod, on the other hand, lived a century or two prior to Nebuchadnezzar and wrote of five successive ages, four of which used the identical metals found in the king's dream image.⁴¹

---

38. See Miller, *Daniel*, 89–90.
39. Swain, "Four Monarchies," 10; John Collins, *Daniel*, 166–68.
40. Lucas, "Daniel's Four Empire Scheme," 202.
41. Hesiod, *Works and Days*, 1.109–201.

The different metals relate to different qualities of the people made by the gods, and the fourth race seems out of place with no metallic representation. This myth that Hesiod related was evidently quite widespread and probably well known in the time of Nebuchadnezzar. It could easily have been vague background for the dream that God gave the king to inform him of the future ages of the world.[42]

2:29–30. Daniel introduced his narrative about the dream twice. The first time (vv. 27–28) was in response to the king's question about his ability. In the second introduction (vv. 29–30) Daniel focuses on the reason why Nebuchadnezzar had the dream, namely, for God to lay out future events for him. Daniel then reassures the king that it is not by human wisdom that the mystery was revealed to him. The wisdom that he denied to himself likely referred to the magical practices of divination by which the Babylonian wise men received their information. Instead, he received the solution to the mystery directly from God so that the king could understand the alarming thoughts that went through his mind when he had the dream.

2:31–33. The huge image that the king had seen in his dream was impressively majestic and awesome. From the gleaming gold of its head to the feet composed of iron and clay, it must have startled the king. The metals gold, silver, bronze, and iron also constituted materials used for making idols (Dan 5:4), and the articles that Nebuchadnezzar had taken from the temple at Jerusalem were of gold and silver (Dan 5:2).

2:34–35. As frightening as the image itself must have been, what happened to it was terrifying. The stone "cut out without hands" clearly represented a divine action against the image. It is significant that the entire image crumbled together and completely disappeared when the stone struck the feet. The implication of כַּחֲדָה is that the entire statue disintegrated "all at once." Two long sentences stress the totality of destruction—the wind blew their dust away like chaff on the threshing floor, and not a trace of them was left. Then the stone grew into a great mountain that filled the whole earth. To the Babylonians such a dream would be considered to have terribly ominous import, and it is little wonder that Nebuchadnezzar was terrified.

2:36–45. The details of the dream were of no value unless they had an interpretation. Many reports of dreams and their interpretation from ancient times have been recorded,[43] so the situation depicted in Daniel 2 was

---

42. See Steinmann, *Daniel*, 135.
43. For examples see Oppenheim, *Interpretation of Dreams*.

not uncommon. Daniel proceeded from the top of the image to the bottom, explaining each major part in terms of kingdoms with worldwide scope.[44]

A certain tension occurs in the interpretation between specific kingdoms that are readily identifiable and the scheme of four kingdoms that stands for all the kingdoms of this world, that is, the world system that stands in opposition to the rule of God. Except for the golden head of the image, identified with Nebuchadnezzar himself, none of the other parts receive any explicit definition from the text. **There is a vagueness to the interpretation that allows us to extrapolate the scope of the vision far beyond four kingdoms only.** This becomes clear when we are told that the "stone cut out without human hands" will destroy the total image. The destruction starts with the feet of iron and clay but then extends to all the kingdoms together. Since they succeeded each other, destruction of all of them means that the "stone" will destroy the whole world system that they represent.

**Through this striking dream image God granted Nebuchadnezzar a rare opportunity to see things as they really are. Greatness or glory in this world is purely a gift from God, and the kingdoms of men are progressively deteriorating to the point where he must intervene.** It is not so much that one generation is morally worse than the next. It is more the general truth that as people move away from where God has placed them, giving them an opportunity to glorify him, they lose that greatness and luster that he first gave them. They degenerate to the point of becoming so mixed up with evil that they become ripe for judgment. One kingdom passes into another, and in the end, they are all shown for what they really are—merely chaff (cf. Ps 1:4). Apart from God, as Koheleth ("the Preacher" in Eccl) puts it, life is "vanity of vanities." It is merely a futile chasing after wind.[45]

Nebuchadnezzar saw the image but couldn't understand what he saw. **He needed a Daniel to come and interpret it, and Daniel pointed out to him that everything begins and ends with the "God of heaven." There is no greatness apart from him, and only his kingdom will endure and not be left to another.**

Interpreters debate about how to historicize Daniel, but that is not the most important point of the image and the smiting stone. It is true that Daniel sees a structure and a plan for world history, but that is not the full extent of the message God wanted to convey through Nebuchadnezzar's dream. The dream cuts to the heart of what is real and what is false, a distinction that is sorely needed at a time when for many the

---

44. "Worldwide" means the world as it was known to the ancient Babylonians.
45. See also Longman, *Daniel*, 82–83.

knowledge of science has seemingly eliminated the need for knowledge of God at all. The current kingdoms of the world are part of the feet of the image, the lowest part. And God is preparing to strike it with the "stone cut out without hands." The overall message of the dream is in harmony with the teaching of Jesus of Nazareth: "But seek first the kingdom of God and his righteousness, and all these things will be added to you" (Matt 6:33, ESV). That is the main thrust of the message that Daniel derived, through revelation, from Nebuchadnezzar's dream. In the discussion that follows the historical issues will be detailed, but the broader message to the king should not be lost sight of in the interpretation of the parts of the statue.

**2:36–38.** The clearest interpretation that Daniel made was for the "head of fine gold." It stood for Nebuchadnezzar himself. What has puzzled interpreters is why the head stood for a single monarch, but the other parts of the image referred to entire kingdoms. While it is true that "king" (מֶלֶךְ, *melek*) and "kingdom" (מַלְכוּ, *malku*) are somewhat interchangeable in Daniel and that Nebuchadnezzar could be seen as representative of the Babylonian empire,[46] yet Daniel said rather explicitly: "You are the head of gold" (v. 38).

Seow looks at the מֶלֶךְ/מַלְכוּ issue differently, taking *malku* in the sense of "kingship." Nebuchadnezzar is the first king; then the "kingship" passes successively to the remaining monarchs in the book of Daniel—Belshazzar as the "inferior" king represented by silver, Darius the Mede represented by bronze, and Cyrus represented by iron. "Like the iron that smashes, it will break all these" (2:40), means that Cyrus will conquer both the Babylonians and the Medes. The image of the smiting stone derives from Isa 41:15–16 that has the exiles empowered by God to "thresh" and "winnow" the mountains. The "stone, cut out without hands" then, would stand for people of God who will destroy the nations. The imagery in Daniel also echoes, according to Seow, Gen 12:1–3; Isa 2:1–4; 6:3; 11:9; Mic 4:1; and Ps 22:28–29.[47]

On the one hand, Seow's view has some strengths. It relies solely on additional data within the book of Daniel and fits well with the other biblical passages. On the other hand, it has some major weaknesses. Belshazzar was not historically the immediate successor to Nebuchadnezzar, whereas the text describes "another kingdom/reign after you." Additionally, the term *malku* in verse forty-four must mean "kingdom," not merely "reign" or "kingship." The *malku* "will not be left to another people," implying that people and not merely a king are part of it. The large amount of detail given

---

46. Miller, *Daniel*, 93; Walvoord, *Daniel*, 65.
47. Seow, *Daniel*, 47–48.

to the fourth *malku* also is incompatible with with what the text says about Cyrus. And if "Cyrus the Persian" is another name for "Darius the Mede," as is argued in the Introduction, then the one king could not represent two different reigns.[48]

The key to why the interpretation singled out Nebuchadnezzar lies in his fundamental significance to the transference of royal authority first introduced in Dan 1:1-2. God "gave" Jehoiakim and the temple articles into Nebuchadnezzar's control, and Daniel noted that "the God of heaven" had "given" (יְהַב) to him, as the "head of gold," the regal authority to be "the king of kings." The sequence of world kingdoms that will exist until God breaks into history and sets up his own everlasting kingdom all starts with Nebuchadnezzar himself. It is legitimate to include the entire Babylonian kingdom within the "head of gold," but this monarch's special place in history and in God's economy warrants the extra focus. For two entire verses the text gives detail about his authority and the extent of his realm, all of which "(God) has given into your hand" (v. 38).

It is also important to remember two things as Daniel tells the king what his dream means. First, Daniel did not have direct access to future history other than by divine revelation. And second, Daniel had not yet had the dream vision that is recorded in chapter 7 of the book. It is legitimate to examine history from Nebuchadnezzar to Jesus Christ and even beyond to try to figure out details of the dream, but then those interpretations may go beyond what Daniel actually stated to Nebuchadnezzar.[49] Is it appropriate, for example, to focus on the fact that the image must have had ten toes and relate that somehow to ten kingdoms that existed or will exist simultaneously with their destruction by the smiting stone?[50] Daniel is unconcerned with the number ten here. And while there are striking similarities between the king's dream of the great image and Daniel's vision of the four beasts from the sea where he was more concerned with the number ten (7:7, 20, 24), one cannot automatically assume one-to-one correlations between the two.[51] The "saints of the Most High" (7:22) and the "little horn"

---

48. John Collins discusses and critiques briefly another attempt to think of four kings rather than four kingdoms (*Daniel*, 169).

49. "[I]n the drama of the story the description has to be allowed to remain allusive" (Goldingay, *Daniel*, 58).

50. Walvoord, *Daniel*, 72.

51. A similar criticism can be made of views that interpret the two legs of the image in Nebuchadnezzar's dream as significant when Daniel does not refer to them. For example, Culver (*Daniel and the Latter Days*, 117) refers them to the division of the Roman empire into east (Byzantium) and west (Roman). If the image was to look human

(7:8) don't correspond to any part of the image in Nebuchadnezzar's dream, and the same is true of various other features that are unique to each dream.

On reflection, Nebuchadnezzar's dream was appropriate for a pagan monarch, while Daniel's dream was better suited for a Jewish wise man. In the discussion of Daniel's interpretation, then, it is necessary to look for what would have been significant for Nebuchadnezzar to hear. The main audience for the book, to be sure, is the people of God, both Jewish and Christian, but God communicated something to Nebuchadnezzar in a way that had significance for him. Knowing that he was the head of gold was perhaps a point of pride for Nebuchadnezzar, except that Daniel made it clear that all his royal power and glory came only from the God of heaven. Even so the sequence of metals from most to least valuable and from most malleable to hardest on a great image of which he was the head must have flattered him.

**2:38.** Daniel piled up synonyms in describing the royal authority that God gave to Nebuchadnezzar. This included the power to enforce his will (חִסְנָא וְתָקְפָּא, "the might and the power") as well as the glorious honor (וִיקָרָא, "and the glory") that went along with his position. His realm included territory "wherever people, wild animals, and birds of the sky" live. God had given all these into his power and gave him authority over all of them. The description is to some extent hyperbolic. While Nebuchadnezzar did defeat Pharaoh Necho at Carchemish and various kingdoms in Syria and Judea, he found it necessary to return frequently to the countries to the west of Babylonia and was not able to permanently control Egypt.[52] The point is that whatever sovereign power Nebuchadnezzar had, he wielded it only because the Lord had given it to him.

**2:39.** Nebuchadnezzar's ears must have become attentive also to Daniel's declaration that the second kingdom would be *inferior* (אֲרַע) to him. Various explanations have been proffered. One idea is that it is less powerful or not as extensive.[53] Other suggestions include lack of unity,[54] quality of government,[55] and moral degeneration.[56] Walvoord thought that the

---

it had to have two legs.

52. The fifth Babylonian Chronicle mentions a battle between Nebuchadnezzar and the king of Egypt that ended in a draw (lines 5–7), and it also describes several more incursions by Nebuchadnezzar to "Hattu" (lines 9–24), that is, to various small kingdoms in ancient Syria-Palestine (Grayson, *ABC*, 99–100).

53. Péter-Contesse and Ellington, *Handbook on the Book of Daniel*, 61.

54. Keil, *Ezekiel, Daniel*, 106.

55. Wood, *A Commentary on Daniel*, 68.

56. Miller, *Daniel*, 94.

descending value of the metals pointed to "the degeneration of the human race through the ages," while their ascending strength "suggests increased military might during the times of the Gentiles."[57] It is also possible that *inferior* meant simply *lower* on the image itself, although Daniel did specify that the kingdom was *inferior* to Nebuchadnezzar himself.[58] Each successive kingdom was of lesser quality in that the materials themselves indicated a change in quality. As John Collins puts it, "The progressive decline is required by the symbolism, regardless of historical data.[59] Daniel made no further comment on the nature of the inferiority, but he did stress disunity for the part of the fourth kingdom represented in the feet and toes (v. 41). The inability of iron and clay to mix properly indicated both strength and brittle weakness (v. 42).

Even though Daniel did not identify the various kingdoms that followed Nebuchadnezzar, it is still possible to make some determination of them from history. Historically the kingdom that immediately followed Babylon was Persia, and ancient writers (Josephus, Jerome, Hippolytus) and numerous modern commentators have held that the second kingdom is the Medo-Persian empire.[60] There are indications within the book of Daniel that Media and Persia should be considered a unit. The cryptic *parsîn* in the "handwriting on the wall" (5:25) meant that Belshazzar's "kingdom has been divided and given to the Medes and the Persians" (5:28). Then in chapter 6 there are several references to "the law of the Medes and Persians." When Daniel saw the vision of a ram with two horns (chap. 8) the horns stood for "Media and Persia" (v. 20). Thus, in the book of Daniel the two names always occur together. The only instances in Daniel where they are listed separately are with the titles "Darius the Mede" (5:31; 11:1) and "Cyrus the Persian" (6:28), and there is a good possibility that these two titles refer to the same person. The Greeks often referred to the Persians as Medes, a practice that "evidently dates from the first contact between Greeks in Ionia and Iranians of the west."[61]

---

57. Walvoord, *Daniel*, 66.

58. The OG has "smaller" or "lesser" (ἐλάττων), while Th follows the Aramaic more closely with "inferior" or "weaker" (ἥττων). Many commentators think along similar lines when they make the second kingdom Media (e.g., Hartman and Di Lella: "Media never attained to true world-empire, as did the other three kingdoms" [*Book of Daniel*, 147-48]).

59. John Collins, *Daniel*, 170.

60. Walvoord, *Daniel*; Archer, "Daniel"; Miller, *Daniel*; Steinmann, *Daniel*.

61. Widengren, "Persians," 316.

A rival view is that the second kingdom is Media and Persia is the third.[62] While this interpretation has some ancient support,[63] historically there is virtually no possibility that a Median kingdom followed immediately upon the Babylonian kingdom, and many scholars have been so bold as to accuse the author of Daniel of an historical error in the matter.[64] Some who assign a sixth century BC date to Daniel have thought of a Median kingdom that came to prominence after the death of Nebuchadnezzar,[65] but Dan 5:28 necessitates that the transfer of sovereignty to "the Medes and the Persians" occurred when Belshazzar died at the end of the Neo-Babylonian empire. H. H. Rowley argued that the prophecy to Belshazzar also meant that the kingdom would be "divided," with some of it going to the Medes and some to the Persians.[66] However, "the law of the Medes and the Persians" is referenced under the rule of "Darius the Mede" (6:8[9]).[67]

If the second kingdom is Media-Persia, then the third kingdom must be the Greek kingdom. Alexander the Great conquered the last Persian king, Darius III Codomannus (336–31 BC). Very little is said about this kingdom—only that it "will rule over the whole earth." Alexander, as is well known, died at Babylon of unknown causes shortly after his conquests, and his empire was divided among his generals. Division seems to be a basic characteristic of the statue that Nebuchadnezzar saw in his dream. The Medo-Persian empire, represented by the silver breasts and arms, consisted of two closely related peoples. Now the Greek empire, represented by the bronze belly and thighs, broke into various factions. In the vision that Daniel later received from the angel (chap. 11), he focused on the two main parts of the Greek empire, namely, Egypt to the south of Judah and the vast Seleucid empire that included Syria and Judah to the north. For now, Nebuchadnezzar needed to know only that these other great empires after him would also rule the world.

**2:40–43.** The fourth kingdom received the most detailed interpretation, partly because it represented the last of the kingdoms to flourish

---

62. Montgomery, *Book of Daniel*; John Collins, *Daniel*; Koch, *Daniel 1—4*.

63. In the oldest Syriac manuscripts (sixth and seventh centuries) of Daniel 7, the second beast is identified in a paragraph title as the "Kingdom of the Medes" and the third as the "Kingdom of the Persians." Whether this interpretation extended to Daniel 2 is likely but unknown.

64. Montgomery, *Book of Daniel*, 64–65; H. H. Rowley, *Darius the Mede and the Four World Empires*, 147.

65. Gurney, "Four Kingdoms of Daniel 2 and 7," 41–42; Walton, "Four Kingdoms of Daniel," 30; Pierce, *Daniel*, 41.

66. H. H. Rowley, *Darius the Mede and the Four World Empires*, 148.

67. For further discussion see the Exposition of 6:28 (29).

before God's intervention in history, but also because there was a lesson in it for Nebuchadnezzar ("a great God has informed the king," v. 45). The factor that weakened the fourth kingdom was division, particularly division through improper mixing together of weak and strong elements. Various views have been given of what the intermingling meant.[68] A common view is that it referred to intermarriage for political reasons.[69] According to the view that the fourth kingdom is Greek, the statement would then line up with Dan 11:6, 17. Others see a more general reference to the mixing between ethnic groups, with intermarriage a factor but not necessarily the only factor.[70] Archer saw the "scope" of the verse to refer to "disunity, class struggle, and even civil war."[71] We would suggest that the people who have the strength of iron in them should be those to whom God has given his power and strength, even as he had given power and glory to Nebuchadnezzar. The weak ones are those who do not recognize the true God and act out of their own pride. Mingling these together, either through intermarriage or through some kind of social disunity, would only result in weakening the strong. Nebuchadnezzar would later have a more pointed lesson about this when the Lord gave him a second dream (Dan 4) to motivate him to deal with his own pride. Still later Belshazzar, at the end of the Babylonian dominion, would proudly assert his authority over God by profaning the holy vessels from the Jerusalem temple (Dan 5). As a result, his kingdom was divided and given to a divided nation, the Medes and the Persians. In turn the Medes and the Persians succumbed to the powerful and ruthless Alexander, but when he died at a young age the spoils were divided among his generals and the kingdom was weakened (Dan 8:22).

The final kingdom, in the view of most conservative commentators, represents the Roman power, united at first but later horribly fragmented and virtually undone. The strength of iron could represent almost any of these mighty empires, but Rome was especially fearsome for its powerful armies in the ancient world. It was also a far-flung empire that was weakened by the great diversity of its population and territories. The full scope of what is meant by this kingdom will be treated along with the stone that strikes the image (v. 45).

---

68. The Aramaic in v. 43 is obscure; it is literally "they will mix themselves with the seed/offspring of men but will not stick this with that." The NRSV and the ESV include the issue of intermarriage. The NLT adds a political angle: "forming alliances with each other through intermarriage." Daniel was not that specific in his wording, although intermarriage may be intended.

69. Porteous, *Daniel*, 49; Lacocque, *Book of Daniel*, 52.

70. Keil, *Ezekiel, Daniel*, 109; Walvoord, *Daniel*, 71.

71. Archer, "Daniel," 48.

**2:44–45.** Two key questions confront the reader at the conclusion of Daniel's interpretation of the dream. Who are the "kings" who feature "in the days of those kings"? And what sort of "kingdom" is it that "the God of heaven will raise up"? Modern interpreters are divided in the answers. One idea is that all of the kings of the various kingdoms are meant, with the "kingdom" being the general notion that "the power of God will overcome all the power of human kingdoms."[72] That is certainly a message that the passage conveys, but it also has some specific eschatological details that cannot be glossed over.[73] The details are not as specific as what are spelled out in the second part of Daniel's book, but even so Daniel spoke of a particular moment when God would appear with the "stone cut out from the mountain without hands" in order to destroy all other kingdoms and set up his own.

Most of those who hold to the theory that the fourth kingdom is Greek think of the kings reigning over various Hellenistic kingdoms at the time of Antiochus Epiphanes in the second century BC.[74] At that time, according to the theory, the Jews were expecting God at any moment to break into history and set up his everlasting kingdom that would destroy the kingdoms of their world. That the stone crushed all the parts of the statue (v. 45) is apparently simply a part of the imagery of the dream and not significant for the interpretation.[75]

We have already seen the weakness in the view that the fourth empire is Greek. It is commendable, however, that these critical expositors see that there is some eschatological perspective to the passage. One has to wonder, though, what the alleged readers of the Maccabean era would have thought when the kingdom did not come as the book supposedly predicted. How is it that despite the failure of the author to be accurate on this significant point his book was recognized as authoritative by the Qumran community, by Jesus of Nazareth, and by the early church?

Adherents of the Roman view about the fourth kingdom answer these two questions in two different ways. According to one view, generally in accord with the amillennial or postmillennial perspectives on the Bible,[76]

---

72. Gowan, *Daniel*, 59; see also Wallace, *Message of Daniel*, 58.

73. John Collins, *Daniel*, 174.

74. Montgomery, *Book of Daniel*, 178; Porteous, *Daniel*, 49; Koch, *Daniel 1—4*, 214–16; Pace, *Daniel*, 73–74.

75. Porteous, *Daniel*, 50.

76. The terms *premillennial*, *amillennial*, and *postmillennial* refer to different perspectives on the one-thousand years of reign mentioned in Rev 20:1–20 in respect to Christ's second coming. In simplified language, the *premillennial* perspective thinks of a literal reign of Christ on earth that begins immediately after his second coming.

the stone represents the Messiah, Jesus Christ; and he established the kingdom during his earthly ministry.[77] This kingdom has then continued to grow throughout the present age and will eventually fill the entire earth.[78] This view accounts for the appearance of the stone during the time of the Romans, but it fails to take seriously enough the language of a violent destruction that seems to occur all at once. The other kingdoms are physical realms with kings sitting on their thrones, so one expects that God will replace them with something similar. The stone will "smash and bring to an end all these kingdoms" is language that does not encourage a thought of slow growth. On the one hand, Jesus Christ announced the coming of the kingdom of God, and his expression may spring from Daniel's prophecies.[79] Further, Jesus spoke of the slow growth of the kingdom in the parables of the mustard seed and the hidden leaven (Matt 13:31–33). On the other hand, there is also an eschatological expectation of a kingdom to be established at the end of the age (Matt 13:24–30; 24:14), even with reference to a prophecy in the book of Daniel (Matt 24:15–28). And the book of Revelation also speaks of a future kingdom in terms that are reminiscent of descriptions in Daniel's book (Rev 11:15, 17; 12:10; 20:6; 22:5).

Others who see the fourth kingdom as Roman think that the prophecy refers to the second coming of Christ to establish his kingdom on earth. This view, a *premillennial* or *dispensational* view,[80] fits well with how the kingdom will "smash and bring an end to all these kingdoms" and then endure forever. The main difficulty for this view concerns how to account for the cessation of the Roman empire centuries ago. Many who hold this

---

Christ returns *prior to* the Millennium. The *amillennialist* thinks of a figurative sense of the thousand years that actually applies to the current time when the church is in the world. According to this position the kingdom began with Pentecost and the coming of the Spirit. Through the present age Christ and his saints in heaven reign now and will continue to reign in the eternal state described in Revelation 21. The *postmillennialist* sees a kingdom on earth that is established through the church. As the church grows in number it also influences society to adopt God's ways until finally the whole world is ruled through Christ and his church. Christ returns then to a world that has already been fully prepared by the church's ministry of the gospel.

77. Montgomery notes that the earliest known Jewish interpretations of the smiting stone make it either the Messiah or the Messianic kingdom. Christian interpretations likewise made it either the church itself or the Messiah, "but the strictly Messianic interpretation is earliest and most dominant" (*Daniel*, 191).

78. Jerome, *Commentary on Daniel*, 32; Augustine (see Stevenson and Glerup, *Ezekiel, Daniel*, 170–71); Calvin, *Commentary on Daniel*, 1:180–92; Steinmann, *Daniel*, 139.

79. Wenham, "Kingdom of God and Daniel," 132–34.

80. *Dispensationalism* is a sub-category of the *premillennial* view.

theory would agree that some sort of revived Roman empire is in view,[81] but what about the gap between the end of the Roman empire of history and the revived Roman empire of the end times? A gap doesn't seem likely; all of the other kingdoms succeeded each other directly.[82] It seems that it would be necessary to posit some sort of generic connection between the ancient Roman empire and its future revival, perhaps through European countries that have an historical connection with it.[83]

All attempts to solve the problem of the great distance between the four empires of history and a future empire as a prelude to the end of the age involve a lot of speculation. The number four in Daniel refers to the four points of the compass, in the language of Daniel "the four winds of heaven" (7:2; 8:8;11:4; cf. Jer 49:32, 36; Ezek 37:9; Zech 2:6; Matt 24:31; Mark 13:27; Rev 7:1). These four kingdoms are representative of all the nations of the world that God permits to exercise authority in the "times of the Gentiles" (Luke 21:24). They will all be destroyed by the stone because all of them dominate and flourish only under divine permission (Dan 2:21). Another possibility is that the cutting out of the stone from the mountain signifies the first coming of Christ, while his second coming is symbolized by the stone striking the image. Putting it in the perspective of Daniel and Nebuchadnezzar—the cutting out of the stone from the mountain signifies a decisive point in history at which God will act, and the stone striking the image signifies the eschatological end when God will overwhelm all the kingdoms of this world with his own eternal kingdom.

In summary, the fourth kingdom begins with Rome, and the appearance of Christ marks God's intervention into history through the incarnation. For Nebuchadnezzar it is only significant that the sovereign God will take action during the fourth kingdom. Whether there will be a revival of the Roman empire or a generic connection between it and the destruction of the kingdoms is not clear. Daniel receives further revelation about that in his vision of chapter 7. **The overall message of chapter 2 is that all kingdoms, including Nebuchadnezzar's, have their authority to rule only because Daniel's God gives them that authority.**

---

81. Miller, *Daniel*, 98–99.

82. Cf. Walvoord (*Daniel*, 72): "Daniel's prophecy actually passes over the present age, the period between the first and second comings of Christ . . . ." There are some examples like this, but Walvoord's parallel example of Luke 4:18–19 can easily refer in its entirety to Christ's first coming.

83. Cf. Culver, *Daniel and the Latter Days*, 116; Miller, *Daniel*, 99.

## DREAMS OF GREATNESS

*The king reacts to what Daniel has done. (2:46–49)*

Nebuchadnezzar recognizes the truth of Daniel's interpretation, praises Daniel's God, and rewards Daniel and his three friends. At the conclusion of the interpretation, Nebuchadnezzar immediately showed his gratitude and respect by bowing to him and ordering an offering and incense to be made to him. Then he praised the God of Daniel and his friends and gave Daniel a high government position and many gifts. At Daniel's request he also gave Shadrach, Meshach, and Abednego government positions.

All these reactions seem expected save one. Why did the king seemingly order others to make offerings to Daniel? It is understandable that Nebuchadnezzar might do this, because he thought that Daniel was able to accomplish such a great feat; but he did recognize that it was Daniel's God who had revealed the mystery (v. 47). And one might expect that Daniel would protest if indeed people were trying to worship him. Three times he had emphasized that it wasn't because of his personal abilities but only because of God that he was able to tell the dream and interpret it (2:28, 30, 45). In addition, Daniel emphasized at the start of his interpretation that "the God of heaven" had placed Nebuchadnezzar into his position. **Since Daniel didn't protest the king's actions, it must mean that Nebuchadnezzar really wanted the offerings to be made on behalf of Daniel's God. He had them presented to Daniel because he knew of no other way to show his gratitude to God for revealing the mystery.**[84] Daniel was the only connection he could see to this "great God," so he ordered the offerings to be made to him. Even though Nebuchadnezzar gave orders to present sacrifice and incense to Daniel, when he spoke directly to Daniel (v. 47) he extolled Daniel's God.

This small detail helps to understand where Nebuchadnezzar stood in relation to God. He could name him "God of gods" and "Lord of kings" and "a revealer of mysteries," but he had no personal knowledge of who this God was. He was a pagan king who recognized divine power when he saw it, but he had no way to contact this God except through Daniel. And his seemingly high view of God at this point is belied by the idolatrous image he set up later (chap. 3).[85]

---

84. Jerome, *Commentary on Daniel*, 33.

85. While one might like the Babylonian king to have said "*the* God of gods" and "*the* Lord of kings" (NKJV), implying a monotheistic leaning, that is not what the Aramaic allows.

## SHARPENING THE THEOLOGICAL FOCUS

Chapter 2 unveils for the first time a major theme in Daniel—the schema of four kingdoms that represent God's plan for the ages. These human kingdoms will run their course through history, only to be overwhelmed and destroyed in the end by God's own kingdom. This pattern of four kingdoms, plus God's kingdom as the fifth, will become a major theme in the apocalyptic chapters (7 to 12). That God was able to reveal this plan through Nebuchadnezzar's dream demonstrates his sovereignty over every human kingdom. Nebuchadnezzar was the most powerful man on earth at the time, and God chose to display his wisdom and sovereignty through him. Nebuchadnezzar's powerful kingdom would be followed by another and another and another until such time that God determines to break into history and replace all earthly kingdoms with his own.

God also showed his sovereignty over Nebuchadnezzar (and thereby all rulers who would follow him) through his deliverance of Daniel and his friends. The king in his anger meant to destroy them along with all the wise men of Babylon; God had other plans. His servant Daniel, not the ineffective group of *Chaldeans* at the king's court, would be the vessel through whom God would reveal this mystery of future history. The *Chaldeans* thought they could contact the gods, but those gods were nothing compared to Daniel's God. Only this God could tell the king his dream and reveal its meaning.

In this light it is important to note why the stories of miraculous deliverance in Daniel are told. It is not to make the readers think that they can expect miraculous deliverance just like Daniel and his friends. Instead, it is to showcase God's sovereign power over the rulers of kingdoms. This will be a pattern to observe throughout chapters 2 through 6. The theology does not concern salvation so much as divine sovereignty. Nebuchadnezzar issued an order to execute all the wise men of Babylon, but it was not carried out. The wise men, including Daniel and his three companions, were spared because God revealed the mystery to Daniel, who then revealed it to Nebuchadnezzar. The answer he received then led to deliverance. When we humbly and faithfully serve the Lord, we can trust him to reveal what we need to know in order to accomplish what he wants.

The key emphasis on divine sovereignty in chapter 2 concerns God's ability to reveal mysteries. That ability relates directly to his revelation of future world events found in chapters 7 to 12. Believers can be confident that the future is in God's hands; nothing will take him by surprise. In this respect 2:20–22 serves as a key to the entire book of Daniel. All wisdom and might has its source in God. There is nothing too deep or mysterious or dark for him. He is omniscient and understands everything. And when a new ruler arises over the world scene and another is erased from historical memory, that is only because of God's permission.

## THE FOCUS OF DANIEL 2 FOR TEACHING AND PREACHING

Nebuchadnezzar's dream, the accompanying drama, and the subsequent interpretation by Daniel make for quite a story. But as contemporary audiences hear the story they will naturally wonder about the relevancy and application of such stories in their lives today. To be sure, knowing that God will usher in an everlasting kingdom brings hope.

But the dream story is told in such a way as to highlight something other than the content of the dream.[86] The whole chapter focuses on God as the only true revealer of mysteries. Because he is the one who determines and decrees what will happen, he alone can reveal it. As Daniel notes:

> He gives wisdom to wise men
> and knowledge to those who have understanding.
> He reveals the deep and hidden things (2:21b-22a).

This is an invitation and exhortation for God's people to reject worthless Babylonian wisdom and to humbly seek the Lord's wisdom. And when they do, he will graciously and mercifully reveal to his people what they need to know.

Two reasons emerge in the chapter as to why God may choose to reveal such mysteries. First, to encourage his people. The revelation is about the sweep of history—the establishment of his everlasting kingdom will mean the demise of all earthly kingdoms. Second, God's revelation of this particular mystery at this particular time provides salvation and a future in the king's court for Daniel and his friends. God provides what they need in order to prepare them for what's ahead.

There are two common errors that people will be tempted towards as you begin to apply the message of Daniel 2. The first error would be for people to become passive, tempted to not do anything until they receive a revelation from God. Passivity and slothfulness are never commended in Scripture. A second error would be for people to foolishly think that God will reveal what we need to know in order to accomplish *our* plans. Both errors would be foolish application of biblical truth. The revelation of God has

---

86. That the telling of the dream is only given five of the forty-nine verses reveals that the focus of the chapter lies elsewhere.

always been for the accomplishment of *his* plans, not human ambition. God has given us what we need to know in order to accomplish what he wants. Let us search the Scriptures and fervently pray, with confidence, that God will give us what we need, when we need it, to accomplish what he wants.

## FROM TEXTUAL WORK TO TEACHING

### The Big Idea

- *Exegetical Idea:* Through Nebuchadnezzar's dream and Daniel's interpretation, the God of Heaven reveals the superiority of heavenly wisdom over earthly wisdom, and the sovereign superiority of his heavenly kingdom over all earthly kingdoms.
- *Theological Focus:* God reveals his plans in such a way as to display his superior wisdom and sovereign kingdom.
- *Preaching Idea:* God reveals what we need to know in order to prepare us for what's ahead.

### Outline One: Following the Exegetical Flow

I. The Problem: There are some things we'll never be able to figure out on our own.

   A. Nebuchadnezzar has a troubling dream and doesn't know what it means. (1–3)

   B. None of the Babylonian wise men could reveal the dream or its meaning and so Nebuchadnezzar decrees that all of the wise men, including Daniel and his friends, are to be destroyed. (4–16)

   C. Application—move to relevance: Some things cannot be known apart from the gracious revelation of God.

II. God's people are to humbly seek the mercy and wisdom of God.

   A. Daniel wisely decides to seek a way to present the problem to God.

   B. Daniel and his friends humbly seek the mercy and wisdom of God because only God can reveal the mystery. (17–18)

DREAMS OF GREATNESS

III. God's people can trust that God will graciously guide them and reveal what they need to know in order to be prepared for what will come. (19–49)

   A. God graciously reveals the mystery to Daniel.

   B. Daniel, his companions and the rest of the wise men are spared.

   C. Daniel and his companions are promoted to key positions of leadership.

   D. Application—move to relevance: God graciously reveals what we need to know in order to prepare us for what will come.

      1. God has fully and finally revealed himself in the person and work of Jesus; the mystery of how we meet God is no longer mysterious.

      2. Some examples from Scripture include the mystery of the new people of God, which now includes Jews and gentiles, Peter and Cornelius, and Paul in Acts 18.

      3. God's Word and the mystery of the gospel have been revealed to the church.

      4. Find contemporary examples about missionaries that can be used to illustrate the point.

## Outline Two: Following a Theme

   I. The contrast between the Babylonian gods and Daniel's God

      A. The Babylonian gods are silent and of no help.

      B. Daniel's God is the revealer of mysteries, merciful and gracious.

   II. The contrast between the Babylonian wisemen and Daniel

      A. The Babylonian wisemen appeal to Nebuchadnezzar.

      B. Daniel and his friends appeal to God.

   III. The contrast between Babylonian wisdom and the wisdom of God

      A. Babylonian wisdom will lead to death.

      B. The wisdom of God leads to life.

# Three Men Who Refused to Obey the King of Babylon

## (Daniel 3:1–30)

**Chapter 2 Review:** Daniel 2 centers around Nebuchadnezzar's dream of an image of a man that was destroyed. After the wise men failed to meet Nebuchadnezzar's demand to tell him the dream and its interpretation, Daniel gave the interpretation that God had revealed to him in a dream. The dream informed Nebuchadnezzar that Daniel's God was sovereign over history, a history that will conclude with the full realization of God's kingdom on earth.

**Chapter 3 Summary:** Whereas chapter 2 pits the wisdom of God against the wisdom of the Babylonian court, chapter 3 pits God against the Babylonian gods. By refusing to bow down to a golden image and worship Babylonian gods, Shadrach, Meshach, and Abednego give opportunity for God to demonstrate his sovereign power to deliver, even in a foreign land. God's sovereign power becomes so obvious and undeniable that by the end of the chapter Nebuchadnezzar, the most powerful ruler on earth, declares, "there is no other god who is able to deliver like this."

**Chapter 4 Preview:** God continues to show himself superior to all things Babylonian. In chapter 2 God revealed that his wisdom is superior to the Babylon wise men, and chapter 3 reveals that God is superior to the Babylonian gods. In chapter 4 the theme of God's supremacy continues as he sovereignly humbles the most powerful ruler on earth, Nebuchadnezzar, when he refuses to humble himself.

## THEOLOGICAL FOCUS OF CHAPTER 3

THEOLOGICALLY, DANIEL 3 IS about more than three individuals who refuse to bow down to an idol and are rewarded with a miraculous deliverance from the fire. It presents a challenge between the God of the Jews and the god(s) of the Babylonians. Shadrach, Meshach, and Abednego represent Israel's God, and Nebuchadnezzar represents Babylon's god, possibly Marduk or Bel. A key issue in this chapter concerns the faithfulness of the three men in the face of pressure to worship another god. They remain faithful, despite tremendous cultural pressure, peer pressure, and the threat of death. Because of, and through, this act of faithfulness God shows himself to be sovereign, even over foreign gods in a foreign land. The gods of Babylon are powerless to overcome God's faithful servants.[1]

I. *God's people will, at times, face intense pressure to conform and worship counterfeit gods.*

II. *When God's people refuse to worship counterfeit gods, they will face intense opposition.*

III. *When God's people refuse to surrender to intense opposition, the consequences can be life threatening.*

IV. *God is able to deliver his people and demonstrate his sovereignty.*

## BIG PICTURE (3:1–30)

More than any other chapter in Daniel, the third chapter manifests the stylistic trait of continual repetition of seemingly mundane lists. The seven titles of "all the administrators of the provinces" occur twice (vv. 2 and 3) and another time in an abbreviated form of only four officials (v. 27). "All the administrators" in the first two lists of seven officials occurs at their conclusion, encompassing all of the other officials. A similar thing happens with the list of musical instruments, repeated four times (vv. 5, 7, 10, and 15). The last item in the series is "and all kinds of musical instruments" (וְכֹל זְנֵי זְמָרָא). Various terms for ethnic or national groups make up another list that is repeated three times (vv. 4, 7, and 29), also showing up as the addressees in Nebuchadnezzar's letter (4:1 [3:31]). A fourth list includes three

---

1. See De Bruyn, "Contesting Space," 45: "Utilising spatial markers, the author of Daniel 3 demonstrates to his readers that Elohim indeed has the ability to operate inside the spatial authority (domain) of foreign gods." Further, "In his own manner the author attempts to persuade his readers that Elohim's authority is universal, and not restricted to a particular spatial context."

items of clothing that the men were wearing when cast into the furnace (v. 21), followed by the comprehensive "and their clothing" (וּלְבֻשֵׁיהוֹן). The constant repetition of the names of Shadrach, Meshach, and Abednego is also unique.

Clearly these repetitive lists are intentional and have literary function. The narrator could have been satisfied with simple expressions like "all the administrators of the provinces," "all kinds of musical instruments," "(all) peoples," and "their clothes." And while the combination "Shadrach, Meshach, and Abednego" is sometimes represented by "these men" or a pronoun, the thirteen occurrences of the trio of names outnumber by far all the other repeated items in Daniel 3.[2] Exact knowledge of the kinds of officials or specific musical instruments, while of some interest, contributes very little to the understanding of the text. The narrator had another purpose in mind besides simple information.

The repetition sets up two key contrasts. First, it highlights the solemn, official nature of the proceedings in order to contrast the event with the supreme authority of the God of the Jews. Babylon's complicated authority structure and pompous ceremonialism could not stand up to the firm trust that these three men had in their God. With only a few direct words they challenged Nebuchadnezzar's long-winded decree and actually came out victorious over the king of Babylon. Nebuchadnezzar's face "changed" (אֶשְׁתַּנּוּ) when Shadrach, Meshach, and Abednego challenged him (3:19), but later he was forced to admit that they had "changed" (שַׁנִּיו) the decree of the king through the sacrifice of their bodies (3:28). The king wanted their bodies to burn, but even the very clothes they wore did not burn in the fire (3:27). And the repeated reference to their names highlights their heroic stance. The mighty empire of Babylon, with its great king and numerous officials at various levels, was no match for the faithfulness of Shadrach, Meshach, and Abednego, and their God. The king himself had to bow to God's will and interdict any blasphemous word against him.

Second, the repetition highlights the contrast of these three lone men versus *all* others. *All* the officials of the provinces assembled along with *all* the peoples of the empire. And they *all* fell down and worshiped the image when *all* the musical instruments played. Amidst so many who did everything in unison to the sound of music, there stood Shadrach, Meshach, and Abednego, refusing to bow to the idol. Their act of defiance would have been recognized instantly, and it underlined their determination to remain faithful to their God.

---

2. They receive their Babylonian names, along with Daniel, according to Dan 1:7, and their Hebrew names (Hananiah, Mishael, and Azariah) are used after that only at 2:17.

# THREE MEN WHO REFUSED TO OBEY THE KING OF BABYLON

## TRANSLATION (DANIEL 3:1-30)

1      Nebuchadnezzar the king made an image of gold. Its height was twenty cubits, its width six cubits.³ He erected it in the plain of Dura in the province of Babylon.

2      Nebuchadnezzar the king sent word to assemble the satraps, the prefects, and the governors, the counselors, the chief treasurers, the judges, the magistrates, that is, all the administrators of the provinces,⁴ to come to the dedication⁵ of the image that Nebuchadnezzar the king had erected.

3      Then the satraps, the prefects, and the governors, the counselors, the chief treasurers, the judges, the magistrates—all the administrators of the provinces, assembled for the dedication of the image that Nebuchadnezzar the king had erected. And they stood before the image that Nebuchadnezzar had erected.

4      Then the herald cried aloud:

"You are commanded, O peoples, nations, and languages,

5      when you hear the sound of the horn, the flute, lyre, harp, *psalterion* lyre,⁶ tambour,⁷ and all kinds of musical instruments,⁸

---

3. The OG has *ten cubits* (πηχῶν δώδεκα).

4. It is likely that "all the administrators of the provinces" is intended to summarize all the previous terms (Péter-Contesse and Ellington, *Handbook on the Book of Daniel*, 73).

5. The Aramaic term חֲנֻכָּה (*dedication*) is the basis for the term Hanukkah, the festival that celebrates the rededication of the temple and the altar at Jerusalem under Judas the Maccabee (1 Macc 5:36–59).

6. The פְּסַנְתֵּרִין (*pᵉsanterin*) is generally considered to be borrowed from Greek ψαλτήριον (*psalterion*) as found in the OG and Th. Muraoka (*GELS*) identifies the Greek term as a harp, but Mitchell takes it instead as a second type of lyre ("And the Band Played On," 36–37).

7. סוּמְפֹּנְיָה (*sumponyah*, the *kethiv* at v. 10, is סִיפֹנְיָה) is also a loanword from Greek, either from συμφωνία (*sumphonia*, defined in Muraoka as *concord* or an unknown musical instrument [*GELS*]) or from τύμπανον (*tumpanon*, drum), as claimed by Mitchell ("And the Band Played On," 39). A more detailed explanation for *tumpanon* may be found in Mitchell and Joyce ("Nebuchadnezzar's Orchestra," 26).

8. The rendering "music" for זְמָרָא (ESV) seems odd in a list of instruments. *HALOT* suggests that it might mean either "stringed music" or "musical instruments." The two main lists of government officials (vv. 2a, 3b) end with "and all the administrators of the provinces." Apparently, the last item in the list is a cover term for all the earlier items, and by analogy the same applies to the list of instruments. Compare also "their garments" (וּלְבוּשֵׁיהוֹן) that concludes the list of items the three men were wearing when cast into the furnace (v. 21b).

|   |   |
|---|---|
|   | you must fall down and worship the image of gold that Nebuchadnezzar the king has erected. |
| 6 | And whoever will not fall down and worship, at that moment he will be thrown into the burning fiery furnace." |
| 7 | Therefore, at the time when all the peoples heard the sound of the horn, the flute, lyre, harp, *psalterion* lyre,⁹ and all kinds of musical instruments, all the peoples, nations, and languages fell down (and) worshiped the image of gold that Nebuchadnezzar the king had erected. |
| 8 | Therefore at that time certain Chaldeans came forward and maliciously accused the Jews. |
| 9 | They said to Nebuchadnezzar the king: |
|   | "O king, live forever! |
| 10 | You, O king, have issued a decree that everyone who hears the sound of the horn, the flute, lyre, harp, *psalterion* lyre, tambour, and all kinds of music must fall down and worship the image of gold. |
| 11 | And whoever will not fall down and worship will be thrown into a burning fiery furnace. |
| 12 | There are certain Jews that you have appointed over the administration of the province of Babylon, Shadrach, Meshach, and Abednego. These men have not paid attention to you, O king. They do not serve your gods,¹⁰ and the image of gold that you set up they do not worship." |
| 13 | Then Nebuchadnezzar, furious with rage, commanded to bring Shadrach, Meshach, and Abednego. Then these men were brought before the king. |
| 14 | In response Nebuchadnezzar said to them: |
|   | "Is it true, Shadrach, Meshach, and Abednego?¹¹ You are not serving my gods? And the image of gold that I set up you are not worshiping? |

---

9. The "tambour" (*sumponyah*) is absent from the MT of v. 7. The Vulgate has *symphoniae* as a sixth instrument.

10. The *kethiv* reads the plural, *your gods* (לאלהיך), while the *qere* has the singular, *your god* (לֵאלָהָךְ). See the Exposition.

11. Here the difference between a reconstructed *my god* (לֵאלָהִי) and *my gods* (לֵאלָהַי) lies only in the vowel and not in the letters. The MT, OG, Th, and the Vulgate

| | |
|---|---|
| 15 | Now if you are ready, that at the time that you hear the sound of the horn, the flute, lyre, harp, *psalterion* lyre, tambour, and all kinds of musical instruments you will fall down and worship the image that I have made ... But if you will not worship, at that moment you will be thrown into the burning fiery furnace. And who is a god who is able to rescue you from my hands?" |
| 16 | Shadrach, Meshach, and Abednego responded by saying to the king:[12] |
| | "Nebuchadnezzar, we don't need to give a response about this. |
| 17 | If our God whom we serve is able to deliver us[13] from the burning fiery furnace and from your hand, O king, he will deliver us. |
| 18 | But if not, understand this, O king, that we are not going to serve your gods,[14] and we will not worship the image that you have erected." |
| 19 | Then Nebuchadnezzar was filled with rage, and the countenance of his face changed toward Shadrach, Meshach, and Abednego. |
| 19 | In response he commanded the furnace to be heated seven times more than it was usual to heat it. |
| 20 | And he commanded some strong men from his army to bind Shadrach, Meshach, and Abednego, and to throw them into the burning fiery furnace. |
| 21 | Then these men were bound in their trousers, their coats, their caps, and other items of clothing, and they were thrown into the burning fiery furnace. |
| 22 | Because the king's order was so harsh that the furnace was heated excessively, those men who brought Shadrach, Meshach, and Abednego up to the furnace—the fiery flame killed them. |
| 23 | But those three men—Shadrach, Meshach, and Abednego—fell bound into the burning fiery furnace.[15] |

---

read *my gods*, but the Syriac has the singular.

12. According to the Masoretic accents, the three men addressed Nebuchadnezzar by his name. The OG has τῷ βασιλεῖ Ναβουχοδονοσορ Βασιλεῦ, "to king Nebuchadnezzar, 'King ...'" The Syriac has "to Nebuchadnezzar the king." See the exposition.

13. The translation follows the NRSV, which has the most natural reading of the Aramaic.

14. Here the MT, Th, and Vulgate have the plural (*gods*), while the OG and Syriac have the singular.

15. At this point the OG contains the apocryphal insertions known as "The Prayer

24  Then Nebuchadnezzar the king was astonished and quickly stood up. In response he said to his advisers, "Didn't we throw three men into the furnace of fire bound?" They answered the king, "Certainly, O king."

25  He answered, "Look! I see four men loosed and walking about amid the fire, and they are not harmed. And the appearance of the fourth resembles a divine being."[16]

26  Then Nebuchadnezzar approached the opening of the burning fiery furnace and said, "Shadrach, Meshach, and Abednego, servants of the Most High God, come out!" Then Shadrach, Meshach, and Abednego came out from within the fire.

27  Now the satraps, prefects, and governors, and the king's advisers gathered around and saw those men, that the fire had not overpowered their bodies; the hair of their head wasn't singed; their trousers looked no different; and even the smell of fire had not come on them.

28  Nebuchadnezzar responded by saying,

"Blessed be the God of Shadrach, Meshach, and Abednego! For he sent his angel and rescued his servants who entrusted themselves to him. They violated[17] the word of the king and gave their bodies rather than serve or worship any god except their God.

29  So I issue a decree, that anyone from any people, nation, or language that blasphemes[18] the God of Shadrach, Meshach, and Abednego, shall be dismembered and his house be made into a rubbish heap.

For there is no other god who is able to deliver like this.

30  Then the king promoted Shadrach, Meshach, and Abednego in the province of Babylon.

---

of Azariah and the Song of the Three Young Men." Th has it after v. 24; 1QDan[b] and 4QDan[d] both have enough of the Aramaic text preserved to prove that they did not contain these insertions.

16. Lit., "a son of gods."

17. Lit., *changed* (שַׁנִּיו).

18. The *kethiv* has שלה, evidently related to Akkadian *šillatu* meaning "blasphemy." It fits the context better than the *qere* שָׁלוּ, "negligence" (Paul, "Case Study," 291–92).

THREE MEN WHO REFUSED TO OBEY THE KING OF BABYLON

## TEXTUAL OUTLINE (3:1–30)

I. Nebuchadnezzar Demands All People Worship His God. (3:1–6)

*[God's people will, at times, face intense pressure to conform and worship counterfeit gods.]*

II. Some Chaldeans Accuse Shadrach, Meshach, and Abednego. (3:7–12)

*[When God's people refuse to worship counterfeit gods, they will face intense opposition.]*

III. Shadrach, Meshach, and Abednego Refuse to Worship Nebuchadnezzar's God. (3:13–23)

*[When God's people refuse to surrender to the intense opposition, the consequences can be life threatening.]*

   A. The men appear before Nebuchadnezzar. (3:13–18)

   B. The men fall into the burning fiery furnace. (3:19–23)

IV. God Overrules the King's Decree. (3:24–30)

*[God is able to deliver his people and demonstrate his sovereignty.]*

   A. The fourth man protects God's servants. (3:24–25)

   B. The three men are unharmed. (3:26–27)

   C. Nebuchadnezzar praises the God who delivered his servants. (3:28–29)

   D. Nebuchadnezzar promotes Shadrach, Meshach, and Abednego. (3:30)

## EXPOSITION (3:1–30)

Chapter 3 has four movements. From all the Babylonian officials and people gathered to worship the image Nebuchadnezzar had set up (vv. 1–6), the scene moves to the select group of Chaldeans who accused the three Judeans (vv. 7–12). Then the action shifts to the accused in the presence of the king, who has them thrown into the fiery furnace (vv. 13–23). Subsequently God reverses everything when he rescues the three men. The king then praises the God of Shadrach, Meshach, and Abednego and promotes them in "the province of Babylon" (vv. 26–20).

## Nebuchadnezzar Demands All People Worship His God. (3:1–6)

Theological Point: God's people will, at times, face intense pressure to conform and worship counterfeit gods.

Why Nebuchadnezzar made the image and set it up for officials from the provinces to worship is unknown. The juxtaposition of the incident with his dream image might suggest that the dream gave him the idea to do this. Even so, for the king to demand that everyone, including Jews, worship an image soon after rewarding Daniel and appointing Shadrach, Meshach, and Abednego to their offices seems too abrupt.

Both Greek versions date the incident to Nebuchadnezzar's eighteenth year, some sixteen years following the dream. In that year Nebuchadnezzar laid siege to Jerusalem (Jer 32:1) and also took captive more than 832 people from the city (Jer 52:29). That solves the issue but is suspect since the Masoretic text does not supply any date for the incident.[19]

Shea proposed that the king was demanding a type of "loyalty oath" from his officials in the wake of a rebellion in his tenth year.[20] The occasion could be correlated as well with a trip that Zedekiah, the last king of Judah, made to Babylon in his fourth year (Jer 51:59–64). While the proposal is speculative, Shea has marshaled some impressive evidence in favor of it.[21]

3:1. What sort of image did Nebuchadnezzar make? The arrangement of chapters 2 and 3 might make one think that the king made a statue of himself, and indeed Hippolytus in the early third century so interpreted the text. Others have thought of some Babylonian god, perhaps Marduk or Nebo, that the image was intended to represent.[22] **The text is ambiguous when it first states the construction of the image, but later in the narrative we are told that the offense of the three men included failure to serve Nebuchadnezzar's gods in addition to not worshiping the image (3:12, 14, 18, 28). Someone who embraced the Jewish religion could not in good conscience fall down and worship an image, no matter what god or king it represented.** The view that the image was of Nebuchadnezzar

---

19. One manuscript from Qumran (4QDan^a) contains part of the first line of Dan 3:1, and there does not appear to be room for a date formula.

20. Shea, "Daniel 3," 29–52.

21. At least Shea's proposal gives the chapter a setting that agrees with the general setting found in the text. Many of those who do not attribute historicity to the book of Daniel think that the story was originally attached to the time when Nabonidus, the last king of Babylon and father of Belshazzar, made an image of the god Sin for a temple at Harran, attempting to substitute the worship of Marduk for Sin (John Collins, *Daniel*, 180–81; Beaulieu, "Fiery Furnace in Daniel 3," 275–77).

22. Archer, "Daniel," 50; Goldingay, *Daniel*, 70; Steinmann, *Daniel*, 174.

himself encounters the difficulty that Babylonian kings are not known to have demanded worship of themselves.

The dimensions of the image are puzzling; it was ten times higher than it was wide (ca. ninety feet by nine feet). The text gives little additional information, so it is hard to know if it was supposed to represent a human figure, to include the dimensions of a base,[23] or perhaps even be in the shape of an obelisk. That it was made of gold probably means that it was overlaid with gold. The gold recalls the golden head of the human-like image that Nebuchadnezzar saw in his dream. The same Aramaic term (צְלֵם) is used to define both the dream image and the physical image. Perhaps the king, remembering the image of his dream in which he was only the golden head, decided to make an image completely of gold in the hope that the god it represented would prolong his reign.

The location of the plain of Dura is unknown. According to *HALOT*, the name "Dura" can be related to the Akkadian term *dūru*, meaning a *city-wall* or *a place surrounded by walls*. The reference to the "plain" and to "the province of Babylon" make it unlikely that it referred to a location within the city of Babylon itself.[24]

3:2. The list of officials consists of two groups, the main officials over the kingdom and the lesser and more local officials. The final expression of "all the administrators of the province" incudes all of the previously listed officials. Possibly it also included additional government workers. There is an apparent descending hierarchy from "satraps" to "prefects" and "governors," with the remaining officials representing different types of responsibilities (financial and judicial). Jews who later held the title of *governor* under the Persians were Sheshbazzar (Ezra 5:14), Zerubbabel (Hag 1:1), and Nehemiah (Neh 12:26).

3:4–6. **The herald's proclamation lends a sense of drama to the scene.** Any devout reader on discovering what the herald was saying would immediately realize that a showdown was inevitable. If all "peoples, nations, and languages" had to participate in this ritual, how then could Jews be exempt? The term עַם (*people*) can refer to people in general, but often as here it more specifically denotes an ethnic group. **Jewish people would be included as a group. They viewed themselves with distinctive traits, most significantly as a people who could never bow down and worship an image.** The term אֻמָּה (*nation*) includes the notion of territory. The Jews in Nebuchadnezzar's Babylon were from the nation

---

23. The OG has "ten cubits" (πηχῶν δώδεκα) rather than six for the width of the image.

24. See also Thompson, "Dura (Place)."

of Judah. Whether the Jews spoke Hebrew or Aramaic, at this point they would find themselves included in Nebuchadnezzar's onerous decree that referred also to "languages."

Music has accompanied worship from ancient times, and it seems natural that the playing of an orchestra would signal the need to prostrate oneself in worship before the image. Archaeology and modern study of language have led to more precise definitions of the instruments that were used for the ceremony.

**3:5.** The English versions agree on *horn* for the first musical instrument, a wind instrument perhaps like a shofar or ram's horn. The second instrument is usually termed a *flute* or a *pipe*. The root of the Aramaic term means "to whistle" or "hiss." The third instrument is variously called a *lyre* (ESV), a *zither* (NLT), or a *harp* (NKJV), all three being stringed instruments. The fourth instrument is termed a *trigon* (ESV), *lyre* (NLT), or *sackbut* (KJV, an early type of trombone). Musical references in Greek to this Aramaic term (סַבְּכָא, *sabbᵉka'*) suggest a stringed instrument, and perhaps it was a *harp*. The instruments were small enough to be held while being played. Since the evidence points to a stringed instrument, the *sackbut* doesn't seem likely. The fifth instrument is the פְּסַנְתֵּרִין (*pᵉsanterin*) clearly a Greek loanword (ψαλτηρίου [*psalteriou*] in the Greek versions). Some versions opted for *psaltery* (NASB), another stringed instrument. Mitchell identifies it as a second type of lyre.[25]

Most of the disagreement in the translations centers around the last instrument, the סוּמְפֹּנְיָה (*sumpōnyâ*, another loanword from Greek [συμφωνίας, *sumphonias*]). The KJV has *dulcimer*, a stringed instrument played with hammers, but there is "no evidence for the dulcimer in antiquity."[26] The NKJV picked up on the Greek term and assumed it was no instrument at all: "in symphony with all kinds of music." If the term refers to something like a "symphony of sound," that would help to explain why it is not included at 3:7, although the structure of the Aramaic appears to demand a separate instrument. On the basis of an interchange between the sounds /t/ and /s/ it has been suggested that the Greek term in question is really τυμπανον (*tumpanon*), a type of drum.[27] Another consideration is that a relief from Karatepe (in Turkey) of the eighth century BC shows each of four musicians holding an instrument, one with a handheld drum (tambour), two with two different kinds of lyres, and one with a flute.[28] If

---

25. Mitchell, "And the Band Played On," 36–37.
26. Mitchell, "And the Band Played On," 39.
27. Mitchell, "And the Band Played On," 39.
28. Mitchell, "And the Band Played On," 37.

Mitchell's translations are correct, then all of the instruments in Nebuchadnezzar's orchestra are included in the relief except for the handheld harp.

**3:6. The penalty for failure to comply with the signal to worship the image is striking. According to Jeremiah 29:22, the king of Babylon burned the bodies of Zedekiah and Ahab, two false prophets, with fire, and Babylonian sources record various instances of execution by burning.** Hammurabi's law code (eighteenth century BC) specified death by burning for several offenses, and the Mari archives (ca. 1700 BC) also mention it. Later Babylonian documents describe this form of punishment as well. Beaulieu points out three incidents in which someone was actually thrown into a furnace. Two of the texts even use a word for *furnace* that is cognate with אַתּוּן (*'attun*) in Daniel. The third example is from the Neo-Babylonian period (the era extending from Nebuchadnezzar's father to Nabonidus and Belshazzar). This text "provides the closest known parallel to Daniel 3, not only in the manner of execution but also regarding the context in which it is envisaged, that of a royal order on the correct performance of cultic duties."[29] The element of the fiery furnace, then, fits well into the Babylonian background depicted in Daniel 3.

## Some Chaldeans Accuse Shadrach, Meshach, and Abednego. (3:7–12)

Theological Point: When God's people refuse to worship counterfeit gods, they will face intense opposition.

**God is glorified when the three accused men defy the king.** The danger in arousing the wrath of a king was proverbial (Prov 16:14; 20:2). In the case of chapter 2, Nebuchadnezzar's anger was enflamed because he believed that his own wise men had conspired to interpret his dream to their own advantage. In that situation Daniel wisely sought to seek the interpretation that God would reveal. Then Daniel could interpret the dream for the king and save all of Babylon's wise men in the process of saving his own life.

The case with Shadrach, Meshach, and Abednego was different. This time the king made a demand that was directly contrary to the law of God. Now it became a matter of obedience to God versus obedience to human authority (cf. Acts 5:29). And when they chose to honor God's law, God in turn honored them by delivering them from certain death.

**3:8.** The "Chaldeans" once again surface as the mouthpiece for the group known as "wise men." That they would be the ones to report the

---

29. Beaulieu, "Fiery Furnace in Daniel 3," 281–84.

failure of "the Jews" to obey the command probably stems from jealousy that Daniel the Jew had been appointed "chief administrator over all the wise men of Babylon." Then Daniel promptly petitioned the king to appoint Shadrach, Meshach, and Abednego "over the administration of the province of Babylon." These men, therefore, had close relations with the king and wielded considerable authority, enflaming their accusers with envy and resentment. The idiom that describes the Chaldeans' accusation ("they ate their pieces"—אֲכַלוּ קַרְצֵיהוֹן) indicates a malicious motive. Clearly, they were out to get Shadrach, Meshach, and Abednego.

A rather obvious question arises at this point. Where was Daniel? Why wasn't he part of the accused? Since the text is not forthcoming with an answer all we can do is speculate.[30] Perhaps Daniel may have been in too high a position for the Chaldeans to attempt to go after him, but if so we might still wonder why Daniel didn't come forward in defense of his friends. He may have been away on an important item of business. If the occasion concerned a loyalty oath it may not have been necessary for Daniel to be present at the dedication of the image. The king was already convinced of Daniel's loyalty through the interpretation of his dream.

Even beyond wondering about Daniel, readers could wonder about other Jews in exile in Babylon. Did they bow down to Nebuchadnezzar's image? Details about Daniel and other Jews could have been included in the narrative, and their absence demands a literary explanation in addition to a natural explanation. Probably this gap in the narrative would cause readers to speculate about themselves. As one contemplates where Daniel might have been and about the Jews in Babylon, it encourages one to meditate on what he or she would do in similar circumstances.[31]

One could also wonder about how the three men refused to worship the image. Did they simply remain standing while throngs of people around them bowed down? If so, then surely there were many witnesses besides the Chaldeans. Another possibility is that they absented themselves from the ceremony. The Chaldeans would have had frequent contact with Shadrach, Meshach, and Abednego because of their positions of authority. Their absence would have been quickly noted and reported to the king by this group of wise men. And if the ceremony was intended as a statement of loyalty to the king, then the three were guilty of treason as well as failure to acknowledge the Babylonian gods.

---

30. The absence of Daniel in the narrative speaks to the truth of the story. If an alleged creative editor was including a legendary story loosely attached to other legendary stories, he could easily have included Daniel's name with the others. All four men are referenced together in chapters 1 and 2.

31. See Pace, *Daniel*, 93–94.

**3:9–11.** When the Chaldeans repeat the details about the king's decree, it slows down the action in the story, lending dramatic effect. The Old Greek version spoils this effect by shortening the list of musical instruments to "the trumpet and all kinds of music."

**3:12.** One could wonder why the king didn't already know that as Jews Shadrach, Meshach, and Abednego refused to worship his gods. Surely such a thing had to be common knowledge. Babylonia had plenty of gods, but now Nebuchadnezzar had set up a specific image, possibly even to serve as a test of one's loyalty to the king. For officials to refuse to worship this god would then become a sign of disloyalty or treason.

It is difficult to choose between the reading "god" or "gods" in the text, both of which are a part of the Masoretic text (see note at v. 12). Here it seems to make better sense to equate "your god" with the image that the king had set up. The reading "gods" seems to bring in extraneous information which would already be known to Nebuchadnezzar, although one could argue that the Chaldeans were trying to heap up as much guilt on the men as possible. Following the plural reading, the point could be that Nebuchadnezzar's image was included in the "gods" that the three men refused to worship.

## Shadrach, Meshach, and Abednego Refuse to Worship Nebuchadnezzar's God (3:13–23)

Theological Point: When God's people refuse to surrender to the intense opposition, the consequences can be life threatening.

Daniel's three friends, knowing the dire consequences they must face, continued to refuse to worship Nebuchadnezzar's god.

### *The men appear before Nebuchadnezzar. (3:13–18)*

**3:13.** Nebuchadnezzar was king over a vast realm. Whenever he issued orders, they were carried out immediately. For the men to defy the king's direct order, their very lives were imperiled. Ironically, these defiant men would eventually walk about as free men, released by a higher authority than Nebuchadnezzar. Even Nebuchadnezzar's orders could not be carried out unless God permitted it.

**3:14–15.** Nebuchadnezzar gave opportunity to the three men to change their minds and worship his golden image. Since they would have to do this only when they heard the music, it was not even an immediate demand. They could wait until the next opportunity presented itself. To avoid martyrdom seemed so simple; they had only to bow just once to demonstrate their loyalty. Conformity and compromise can sometimes seem like easy ways out. Extra time that the king so reasonably allowed could give them opportunity to think through some rationalizing way to both please the king and their God at the same time. Perhaps they could have prostrated their bodies but not their spirits, or perhaps it would be better to preserve their own lives than to suffer an agonizing death. Would such reasoning, though, really have pleased God? Not to bow down to a divine image is an absolute command not to be trifled with.

3:15. The alternative to worshiping the image had no extension of time; execution by burning would happen immediately. And Nebuchadnezzar issued a challenge. Who could imagine that any god would have the power to deliver out of his hands? By this challenge Nebuchadnezzar set himself in direct opposition to the God of Shadrach, Meshach, and Abednego.

3:16. The tone of the reply of the three men is difficult to discern from the Aramaic. **The Masoretic phrasing has the men calling the king by his name and with no title, something that is unprecedented in the book of Daniel. When Daniel confronted the arrogance of Belshazzar, he didn't even bother to call the king by name (5:17), but for these men to break with court etiquette and address the king directly by name and no title would seem to show a defiant tone.** Slotki, accepting the Masoretic phrasing, explained that "**by dropping the king's title, the companions implied that he was but a mortal being who had no right to demand of them an act which violated their conscience.**"[32] **These men were prepared to disobey a direct order of the king; in fact, they even stated that they had no need to explain their actions. Whether this is defiance or merely a firm reply is perhaps a matter of semantics.**[33] Would their firm convictions or defiance have led them to break protocol and address the king by his name and not his title, as the Masoretic text implies? We believe so.

It is also possible to phrase the Aramaic differently, yielding: "They said to king Nebuchadnezzar . . . ." In that case the men simply state their case without addressing Nebuchadnezzar by either name or title. The Old Greek translation solved the problem by adding "king" as a direct address:

---

32. Slotki, *Daniel*, 25.

33. Slotki (*Daniel*, 25) denies that their tone was defiant; Miller (*Daniel*, 119) calls their statement "a firm reply."

"They said to king Nebuchadnezzar, 'O king....'" It is best for readers to follow the phrasing of the Masoretic text.

3:17–18. The most difficult translation problem in the chapter arises with verse seventeen and how it relates to verse eighteen. The different possibilities are listed here.

1. If it be [so], our God ... is able to rescue us ...; and He will rescue us.... (NASB; similarly, ESV)

2. If the God we serve exists, then he can rescue us.... (CSB)

3. If our God whom we serve is able to deliver us ..., let him deliver us. (NRSV)

Option one follows the special markers that the Masoretes added to show how to phrase the text, but there is no parallel for taking Aramaic הֵן אִיתַי as "if it be so." The translations that take this route must supply "so" or the like for the rendering to make sense.

Option two recognizes that אִיתַי can predicate existence, but it is doubtful that Nebuchadnezzar and the three men would be debating the existence of any god. As a good polytheist Nebuchadnezzar would have granted the existence of their God; he only doubted that any god could thwart his decree. The exchange concerned ability, not existence.

Option three is really the most natural way to read the Aramaic, although it is better to read "he will deliver us" rather than "let him deliver us." **Most assuredly the men had faith in God's ability to rescue them. That seems clear from their willingness to die for their faith as well as from the tenor of the entire book of Daniel. Their conditional statement is best understood as a direct reply to Nebuchadnezzar's question: "Who is a god who is able to rescue you from my hands?" They answered that if their God is able to rescue them, he would meet the king's challenge.**

**The verb יכל appears twelve times in Daniel,[34] and in every other instance it clearly implies the ability to carry out a task, not the willingness to do it. And Nebuchadnezzar had questioned the *ability* of any god to overturn the power he wielded. The men set up a test through their reply. If their God could meet Nebuchadnezzar's challenge, then he would do it.** Then they left open the possibility that God might not deliver them (*if not*). Were they thereby questioning God's power to deliver them? Or were they perhaps only questioning whether God would be willing to deliver them? Jerome translated and explained: "But if He does not will to do so," in order to "indicate that it will not be a matter of God's inability

---

34. Dan 2:10, 27, 47; 3:17, 29; 4:15, 34; 5:16 (twice); 6:5, 21; 7:21.

but rather of His sovereign will if they do perish."[35] The men stated their "if not" before they entered the furnace. **At that point they did not know what actually would happen. What they did know was that they were going to serve their God, not Nebuchadnezzar's idol. They didn't need to make any reply to the king; their minds were already made up. And even God didn't need to display his power before Nebuchadnezzar; they themselves were a witness to the God who could inspire them with such faith and trust in the face of certain death. No matter the outcome, they would not yield to Nebuchadnezzar's demand.**

*The men fall into the burning fiery furnace. (3:19–23)*

**3:19.** The narrator describes what happened next with terminology that plays on two major concepts in the story. We have heard over and over again about "the image [צְלֵם] of gold" that Nebuchadnezzar set up. Now, when he rages in fury at these men who dared to refuse his order, the text says "the image [צְלֵם] of his face changed." The same term describes both the idol image and the "image" or "countenance" of Nebuchadnezzar. Also, the word for "changed," from the root שנה (sh-n-h) anticipates the king's conclusion after God delivered Shadrach, Meshach, and Abednego: "they *changed* the word of the king." **The king's word was supposed to be inviolable, and he had issued his word concerning the image. Now the men had "changed" or "violated" that word. At first it led to a darkening of Nebuchadnezzar's countenance, but in the end his word changed and he commanded respect for the God of Shadrach, Meshach, and Abednego.**

The detail about making the furnace extra hot contributes to the drama of the scene and reinforces the extreme anger that Nebuchadnezzar felt. No one could survive being thrown into a burning furnace even at its usual temperature. Now these three men were to be thrown into the furnace heated far above that usual setting. In this case the number "seven" is used in its non-literal sense to note something like "as hot as physically possible."

**3:20–23.** The tension continues to rise when strong military men are commanded to bind the men and cast them into the furnace. And not only are the captives bound, but they continue to wear all their items of clothing. If God proved able to rescue the men, he also could rescue what they were wearing. What's more, the flames overpowered the strong men who threw Shadrach, Meshach, and Abednego into the furnace. **This last detail**

---

35. Jerome, *Commentary on Daniel*, 38.

further ratcheted up the tension and shows that Nebuchadnezzar's idol was unable to protect his own men. God would soon protect his three servants, but the image that Nebuchadnezzar had set up could not protect the king's servants. Finally, the three men "fell" into the furnace. If the flames didn't harm them, what about the fall? Every conceivable precaution was taken to make sure that there was no way that any god could intervene on their behalf.

## God Overrules the King's Decree. (3:24–30)

Theological Point: God is able to deliver his people and thereby demonstrate his sovereignty.

God demonstrates his mighty power to rescue his followers and to thoroughly confound Nebuchadnezzar. **The reader finds out what happened to the three men only through the eyes of Nebuchadnezzar and his advisers. Except for the narrator, they are the only voices heard from here to the end of the story.** Only once do Nebuchadnezzar's advisers say anything and then only "Certainly, O king." Nothing further is stated about how the young men responded when God delivered them.[36]

**The last part of the chapter, then, gives Nebuchadnezzar's perspective on the events.** It contains three scenes and a concluding note about Shadrach, Meshach, and Abednego. Nebuchadnezzar initiates the action in each part, but now he acts in an enlightened manner rather than as an arbitrary tyrant. In the first scene he expresses astonishment at what he sees and seeks confirmation of what has happened from his personal advisers (3:24–25). It is in this scene that he makes the remarkable observation that there are *four* men, not three, walking about freely within the furnace. In the second scene Nebuchadnezzar orders the men to come out of the furnace, and only three come out (3:26). It is clear to all assembled that these men were not affected at all by the fire (3:27). In the final scene Nebuchadnezzar praises the God of Shadrach, Meshach, and Abednego and issues a decree that no one is to blaspheme this God (3:28–29). As a capstone to the entire story Nebuchadnezzar promotes the three men that he had previously condemned to death (3:30).

---

36. Their lack of response lies behind the addition found in the Greek, supplying words of praise, confession, and thanksgiving spoken by the three men. While the thoughts in the additions do not have anything theologically objectionable, they distract from the narrative and cannot be considered on the same level of importance as the inspired Aramaic text.

## The fourth man protects God's servants. (3:24–25)

The king felt both amazed and frightened when he saw what happened in the furnace. He immediately had to check with his close personal advisers, probably to assure himself that he wasn't going crazy. The rather laconic reply of the advisers makes them sound like "yes men," but they still play an important role in the next scene as witnesses to the inability of the flames to harm the men.

The most unusual thing that Nebuchadnezzar saw was not that the three men were walking around freely and unharmed within the furnace, but that there was a fourth man in the furnace with them. Nebuchadnezzar thought he looked like "a son of gods" (בַּר־אֱלָהִין), that is, like "a divine being."[37] Later the king referred to him as God's "messenger" or "angel" (מַלְאֲכֵהּ, *his angel* v. 28). This calls to mind Daniel's response from the lions' den, "My God sent his angel (מַלְאֲכֵהּ) and shut the mouth of the lions" (6:23).

Both terms that Nebuchadnezzar used, "divine being" and "angel," were in accord with his own worldview. What, though, of the viewpoint of Daniel or of his Jewish readers? They could have thought either of an angel such as Michael (Dan 10:13, 21; 12:1) or of the Messiah. "The Talmud asserts that it was the archangel Gabriel (Pes. 118a, b)."[38] "The angel of the Lord" could also be a possibility. Many Christian commentators have identified him with Christ himself in pre-incarnate form.[39] Jerome thought that an angel was meant in the story itself but that he "foreshadows our Lord Jesus Christ" as a type. **It is reasonable to look beyond Nebuchadnezzar's perspective to the perspective of the readers, but that also entails an element of theological speculation. What is clear is that the fourth person had to in some way represent the presence of God with the men; God went with them through the trial, either via his angel or via the Son of God himself (cf. Isa 43:2).**

---

37. The translation found in the KJV, "the Son of God," is misleading as well as grammatically incorrect. In Hebrew the term for God (אֱלֹהִים, *ᵉlohim*) that is cognate with the Aramaic term here (אֱלָהִין, *ᵉlahin*) occurs most often in the plural, either as an abstract (*deity*) or as a "plural of majesty." That is not the case in biblical Aramaic, where the plural should normally be taken to mean more than one god, but the expression "son of gods" could mean a divine person.

38. Slotki, *Daniel*, 27.

39. See Borland, *Christ in the Old Testament*.

## THREE MEN WHO REFUSED TO OBEY THE KING OF BABYLON

### The three men are unharmed. (3:26–27)

As Nebuchadnezzar commanded Shadrach, Meshach, and Abednego to come out of the furnace, for the first time he called their God "the Most High God." **Clearly, he realized that there was something special about this God, although he was probably not expressing monotheism. He knew of no other god who could have delivered the three men like this (3:29); in his way of thinking this God must be more powerful than all the others.**

The group of officials that clustered around the king during all these proceedings was a smaller and more intimate group than the totality of officials who had been commanded to fall down and worship the image. The smaller group included only the satraps, prefects, governors, and the king's personal advisers. The term הַדָּבַר (*haddabar, state counselor*) did not occur in the earlier lists of seven officials. The context indicates a high-level personal adviser to the king. Some of the versions obscure this distinction by using *counselors* in both 3:2–3 and 3:24.

The purpose for introducing the officials at this point was to identify them as eyewitnesses. As they gathered around, they could see the evidence. The men and their clothes were fine; they didn't even smell like smoke. But the bonds that had held them were burned, and of course also the soldiers who threw them into the furnace had burned. So here stood the highest officials in the land alongside the king, and they all could see the amazing deliverance that had taken place.

### Nebuchadnezzar praises the God who delivered his servants. (3:28–29)

At the end of chapter 1 Nebuchadnezzar recognized the superior ability of the four youths. After Daniel interpreted his dream, he praised Daniel's God as "God of gods," "Lord of kings," and "revealer of mysteries." The king had seen himself as the golden head of an image, with other kings who would follow him. While the dream revealed that his own kingdom would not be permanent, still his great authority over all living creatures within his vast realm was validated. **In the account of chapter 3 his authority was challenged. There was a limit to what he could order others to do, a limit imposed by the God who delivered his servants from the fiery furnace. Recognizing that the three men had effectively subverted his orders to execute them, he pronounced their God "blessed" (i.e.,** *praiseworthy* **or** *spoken well of***) and proclaimed his ability to rescue greater than any**

**other god.** Realizing now that the Jews could not worship another god besides their own God, he also issued a decree forbidding any blasphemous statements against their God. Nebuchadnezzar's final encounter with the God of the Jews would be more personal, and that episode is recorded in Daniel 4.

**3:28.** Some commentators deny any historical probability to Nebuchadnezzar's statement, especially that he would commend the Jews "for defying the edict of the king." "Defiance" is probably too strong a term for what Nebuchadnezzar said. The Aramaic is literally, "they changed the word of the king." He had just experienced a situation where he issued a command to execute the men, but through divine intervention that command was made of no effect. It makes good sense that he would say that they "violated" the king's word. Otherwise, the plausibility of his statements really depends on the plausibility of the miraculous deliverance.

**3:29.** The threefold reference to "any people, nation, or language" echoes the language of the original decree for people to bow down and worship the golden image (v. 4), except here the terms are all collective singulars rather than plurals. The thought is more of individuals who would belong to any particular group who would defame the God of the Jewish men. Also, the penalty of dismemberment and destruction of the house of the miscreant harks back to Nebuchadnezzar's angry decree against the Babylonian wise men (2:5).

## *Nebuchadnezzar promotes Shadrach, Meshach, and Abednego. (3:30)*

**The fortunes of Shadrach, Meshach, and Abednego were completely reversed. Once condemned to death by the king, they now enjoy his favor.** At Daniel's bidding the king had given them positions of service within the Babylonian province (2:49). Now the king decided on his own to promote them to a higher office. With the brief statement of verse thirty, the text leaves the story of these three men and never returns to them.

## SHARPENING THE THEOLOGICAL FOCUS

The chapter brings to light God's ability to deliver his servants from death for refusing to conform and worship other gods. The first chapter showed God as sovereign over kings and kingdoms, while the second chapter viewed him as the God who reveals mysteries. In chapter three we see that God is sovereignly able to deliver his servants. Shadrach, Meshach, and Abednego recognized that they had no guarantee that God would deliver them. They only knew that there was no way they could worship any other god except God alone. God proved in a stunning way his ability to deliver his people from even the most powerful ruler in the world.

The issue of human uncertainty is also addressed through these three chapters. The political circumstances of God's people are constantly changing because of wars and assassinations and other violent upheavals, but above them all stands the God who is sovereign over the nations (cf. Dan 1:1–2; 2:21). This is a great comfort in uncertain times. There are also occasions when uncertainty abounds with regard to knowledge and actions. The best wisdom that people can muster is not enough to reveal what needs to be known or done, but God is the one who knows all mysteries and can reveal them to his servants (2:20–23). Finally, there is the uncertainty that even the believer has when faced with persecution for his or her faith. What will be the outcome? Can God deliver? Will God deliver? The story of Shadrach, Meshach, and Abednego helps believers to recognize their true identity as sons and daughters of the God who is powerful enough to deliver them in any circumstance. They must never let any power on earth deter them from that certainty. They can know that God will be with them through the fiercest persecution, even as the "fourth man" walked through the flames with the three men. Deliverance is up to him, but his presence in the fiery furnace is always assured. This assurance taught through the story of the three brave men also reassured the readers of Daniel's book that they could rest in God's sovereign care and presence as they faced all the difficulties that are predicted in chapters 7 to 12. God is able to deliver from trouble and will do it if he so wills it. Such assurance enables believers to follow God faithfully. Even if he does not decree deliverance on earth, there will be a resurrection at the end times, as is made plain in Dan 12:2.

The issue of faithfulness also comes into focus from the perspective of God's three servants. Because they were willing to be faithful, not only did God deliver them but he also caused Nebuchadnezzar to reassess what he knew of their God. The main thrust of the story is not so much God's deliverance of his servants, it is his contest with Nebuchadnezzar and his gods. The faithfulness of these men set up this contest between God's sovereign authority and Nebuchadnezzar's royal power. Before Nebuchadnezzar made his confessional statements about the God of the Hebrews, the three men confessed their willingness to go to the death rather than deny their God. If these men had not been faithful, God would not have been glorified by overturning the king's order to execute them by fire; and Nebuchadnezzar would not have been forced to recognize that there was a limit to his power.

## THE FOCUS OF DANIEL 3 FOR PREACHING AND TEACHING

When teaching through narrative material like we encounter in the first half of Daniel, it is tempting to focus on the morality of the men and miss the more important message about God. One way to encourage a theocentric reading and teaching of the text is to make description, rather than prescription, our default understanding. What this means is that in a text like Daniel 3, our first priority is to understand what the text is describing. Once we understand what the text describes, then we can make an informed decision about what the text is trying to accomplish in the life of God's people. Is the text describing what faith looks like? Or is the text describing an event on which to base our faith? Here in Daniel 3 it seems to be both. This story describes what faith looks like—uncompromising; but it also describes an event on which we can base our faith—God rescued Shadrach, Meshach and Abednego from certain death.

Once we understand that the text describes an event on which we can base our faith, then we know that we need to focus on what the text tells us about God. Here in chapter 3 we learn that God is more powerful than the Babylonian gods and their royal representative, Nebuchadnezzar, and he is able to deliver. Because God is able to deliver (what has been described) we know that compromise is unnecessary. God is sovereignly able to deliver us if he so desires. If he doesn't, it is not because he is impotent or because someone else is more powerful.

In reading and teaching narratives like Daniel 3, first look for what the text is saying about God, and only then ask about the implications for Christian living; the morality of a text must flow from the theology of the text.

## FROM TEXTUAL WORK TO TEACHING

### The Big Idea

- *Exegetical Idea:* Through the faithfulness of Shadrach, Meshach and Abednego God demonstrates his unique ability to rescue his people from even the most powerful earthly rulers.
- *Theological Focus:* Through the faithfulness of his people God is able to demonstrate his incomparable ability to rescue them.
- *Preaching Idea:* As our confidence in God grows, our instinct to compromise will diminish.

## THREE MEN WHO REFUSED TO OBEY THE KING OF BABYLON

## Outline One: Following the Exegetical Flow

I. God's people will, at times, face intense pressure to conform and worship counterfeit gods. (3:1–6)

   A. Shadrach, Meshach and Abednego are faced with a choice, conform and worship a golden image or remain faithful to God.

   B. While we may not be forced to physically bow down to images, God's people will constantly face pressure to conform and bow to the cultural gods of the day.

      1. Contemporary gods of cultural mores on sexuality
      2. Contemporary gods of materialism
      3. Contemporary gods of relativism

II. When God's people refuse to conform and worship counterfeit gods, they will face intense opposition. (3:7–12)

   A. Shadrach, Meshach, and Abednego were intensely opposed by Chaldeans in the court.

   B. God's people will face intense opposition from various people.

      1. Coworkers will oppose them.
      2. Family members will oppose them.
      3. Neighbors will oppose them.

III. When God's people refuse to surrender to the intense opposition, the consequences can be life-threatening. (3:13–23)

   A. Shadrach, Meshach and Abednego were thrown into a fiery furnace.

   B. God's people will face consequences ranging from ostracization to loss of job and to even death threats.

IV. God remains with his people and is able to deliver them and demonstrate his sovereignty. (3:24–30)

   A. God was with Shadrach, Meshach and Abednego in the fire and delivered them from the furnace, causing Nebuchadnezzar to acknowledge their God's sovereign ability to deliver.

B. God is with his people and able to deliver them from even the most threatening consequences today.

## Outline Two: Following a Theme

*Introduction:* Set up the story of Daniel 3 by talking about how easy it is to conform to the culture around us and how hard it is to stand up to these pressures. The potential examples are plentiful, and it is best to choose ones that are most relevant to your particular context.

*Body:* Creatively and engagingly tell the story of Daniel 3 in an uninterrupted fashion. Allow the repetition of the story to inform how you build tension in the story and unfold the resolution. Stories are powerful and they rarely need explanatory interruptions.

*Conclusion:* Go back to the examples raised in the introduction that illustrated how easy it is to conform to culture and walk back through those scenarios teaching how those like Shadrach, Meshach and Abednego might handle these situations with the help of an ever-present God.

# A Proud King is Humbled
(Daniel 4:1–37 [3:31—4:34])

**Chapter 3 Review**: By refusing to bow down to a golden image and worship Babylonian gods, Shadrach, Meshach, and Abednego give opportunity for God to demonstrate his sovereign power to deliver, even in a foreign land. God's sovereign power becomes so obvious and undeniable that by the end of the chapter Nebuchadnezzar, the most powerful ruler on earth, declares, "there is no other god who is able to deliver like this."

**Chapter 4 Summary**: Though Daniel 3 concludes with Nebuchadnezzar's confession of God's greatness, chapter 4 reveals that he doesn't yet grasp the power of Israel's God, who is much more than merely a god among the gods. He is the "Most High God." Nebuchadnezzar's pride provides opportunity for yet more revelation of God's sovereignty. God communicates with the king through a frightening dream that Daniel interprets. The dream portends judgment from the "Most High" that is about to happen to the king, and Daniel advises him to renounce his sins by doing what is right and by showing mercy to the poor. Instead, Nebuchadnezzar boasts and his pride activates the promised divine judgment. Only when he recognizes the absolute sovereignty of the "Most High," the "Ever-living One," does his sanity return and he is restored to his kingdom. In his newfound humility he is moved to "praise, exalt, and glorify the King of heaven."

**Chapter 5 Preview**: Chapter 4 sets the stage for chapter 5, which introduces the prideful king Belshazzar, the last of the Chaldean monarchs. Belshazzar's pride leads him to disrespect God by worshiping idols and profanely drinking from the sacred vessels from the temple in

Jerusalem. While Belshazzar is busy partying, a dire message of doom is mediated to him through the sudden appearance of mysterious writing on the wall of his palace. Daniel enters the scene, denounces Belshazzar's rebellious pride, and interprets the writing on the wall—Belshazzar's life and the Chaldean kingdom are both coming to an end.

## THEOLOGICAL FOCUS OF CHAPTER 4

God is powerful enough to humble anyone who proudly thinks he or she is responsible for their own success in life. Truly humble people will come to know God's exclusive sovereignty over the world, repent of their sins, and praise God before others.

  I. *God warns people about the danger of pride.*
 II. *God is powerful enough to humble any who proudly thinks they are responsible for their own success in life.*
III. *Truly humble people will acknowledge God's exclusive sovereignty, repent of their sins, and proclaim God's good works and ways.*

## BIG PICTURE (4:1–37 [3:31—4:34])

**God humbles the proud and powerful so that they will know that he alone is sovereign.** This message advances from chapter 3 in that the faithfulness of Shadrach, Meshach, and Abednego led Nebuchadnezzar to bless their God who delivered them in such a miraculous way. In much the same way, Daniel's faithfulness enabled him to give Nebuchadnezzar advice that would lead to his rescue from the destructive furnace of his own pride.

Daniel 4 (3:31—4:34)[1] is framed as a letter that Nebuchadnezzar sent to his subject nations as a testimonial to what "the Most High" or "the King of Heaven" had done to him. In the opening address Nebuchadnezzar identified himself as the sender and the nations as recipients, then gave a standard greeting of peace (4:1 [3:31]). Following this he stated the purpose

---

1. Through chapter divisions made in the Latin Bible and adopted in printed Hebrew Bibles (which also include the Aramaic portions), the end of chapter 3 in the Aramaic includes the opening part of Nebuchadnezzar's letter. The more ancient scribal division in the Aramaic has a break precisely where English Bibles start a new chapter, namely where Nebuchadnezzar's letter begins. Daniel 3:31–33 in Hebrew Bibles is equivalent to Dan 4:1–3 in English Bibles.

of his letter, to make known **the marvelous things that "the Most High" had done with him** (4:2 [3:32]). He then concluded the opening section of the letter with a two-line poem that recognized **God's mighty wonders and his eternal reign over his kingdom** (4:3 [3:33]). In the body of the letter Nebuchadnezzar laid out all that had happened to him (4:4-36 [4:1-33]), drawing the section to a close with more words of praise to **"the king of heaven"** (4:37 [4:34]).

After Nebuchadnezzar had his dream, he summoned "all the wise men of Babylon" to interpret it for him. Since they were unable to do so, he called for Daniel to interpret. Daniel's entrance (v. 8 [5]) marks the beginning of a new section. This section of the letter lays out the details of the king's dream and its interpretation in three parts: (1) the king's recitation of his dream to Daniel; (2) Daniel's interpretation of the dream; and (3) the fulfillment of the dream. In the dream itself, as reported by the king, the symbols of trees and animals soon dissolved into the interpretation as applied to a human being. Even before Daniel advanced his interpretation it became clear that the man in question was Nebuchadnezzar himself. Repeating each part of the dream, Daniel applied it to the king. In the fulfillment "a voice from heaven" reiterated the king's fate, and then a narrator related what happened to Nebuchadnezzar, following closely the sequence and wording of the dream. **In this way the reader encounters the details of Nebuchadnezzar's fate four different times—twice in the dream itself (vv. 17 [14] and 23 [20]) and twice in its interpretation and fulfillment (vv. 24-25 [21-22] and 31-33 [28-30]). The effect is to heighten the drama of the passage and to underline the importance of what happened to the king. God reduced the most powerful monarch on earth to a raving madman who lived like an animal. The king recovered only when he acknowledged the sovereign power of Daniel's God.**

## TRANSLATION (DANIEL 4:1-37 [3:31—4:34])

1 [3:31][2]   Nebuchadnezzar the king to all the peoples, nations, and languages that live in all the earth, may your peace be multiplied.

2 [3:32]   It seemed good to me to inform you about the signs and wonders that the Most High God has done with me.

3 [3:33]   How great are his signs!

---

2. Nebuchadnezzar's letter begins at 3:31 in the Aramaic, but it becomes 4:1 in English versions. References to the Aramaic text will be placed in parentheses. Otherwise references are to English translations. In the preaching section references will be to English versions only.

                    And how mighty are his miracles!

                    His kingdom is an eternal kingdom,

                    and his rule is with generation after generation.

4 [1]       I, Nebuchadnezzar, was living at ease in my house and flourishing[3] in my palace.

5 [2]       I saw a dream that frightened me, and dream-fantasies while on my bed; and the visions in my head terrified me.

6 [3]       So I ordered to bring in before me all the wise men of Babylon, so that they might make known to me the dream's interpretation.

7 [4]       Then the soothsayer-priests, the conjurers, the Chaldeans, and the diviners came in,[4] and I told them the dream, but they did not make known to me the interpretation.

8 [5]       Finally Daniel came before me, whose name is Belteshazzar after the name of my god, and in whom there is a spirit of the holy gods;[5] and I told him the dream.

9 [6]       "Belteshazzar," [I said], "chief of the soothsayer-priests, I know that a spirit of the holy gods is in you and no mystery is too difficult for you. [Here are] the visions that I saw in my dream; now tell me its interpretation.

10 [7]      Visions were in my head while I was on my bed. While I was seeing dream images, suddenly there was a tree in the middle of the earth. It was very high.

11 [8]      The tree grew large and strong, and it became so high that it reached to heaven and was visible to the end of the whole earth.

12 [9]      Its leaves were beautiful and its fruit abundant, having enough food for all. The animals of the field found shade under it, and the birds of heaven lived in its branches. All living creatures fed from it.

---

   3. The Hebrew cognate of Aramaic רַעֲנַן (*flourishing*) most often describes a tree and is then rendered with *green* or *luxuriant* (e.g., Deut 12:2; 1 Kgs 14:23). This connotation anticipates the dream in which Nebuchadnezzar was depicted as a tree (Slotki, *Daniel-Ezra-Nehemiah*, 30).

   4. For the different categories of wise men, see Table 2.1.

   5. The NKJV, unlike the KJV and nearly every other English version, has "the Spirit of the Holy God," making it appear that Nebuchadnezzar thinks Daniel has the Holy Spirit. That translation represents a mistaken understanding of the Aramaic as well as the cultural background of the passage.

13 [10]  As I continued to observe the visions in my head while on my bed, there came a holy watcher[6] down from heaven.

14 [11]  He cried aloud and said this:

'Chop down the tree and cut off its branches!

Strip off its leaves and scatter its fruit!

Let the animals flee from under it, and the birds from its branches.

15 [12]  Only leave the stump with its roots in the ground, and with a band of iron and bronze [let it be bound] in the grass of the field.

And let him[7] be drenched with the dew of heaven,

and let his portion be with the animals among the plants of the earth.

16 [13]  Let his mind be changed from that of a man, and let him be given the mind of a beast. And let seven periods of time[8] pass by for him.

17 [14]  The decree is by the determination of watchers,

and the decision[9] is by the word of holy ones;[10]

so that[11] the living may know that the Most High is sovereign over the kingdom of men. And he gives it to whomever he wishes. And he can raise up over it the lowliest of men.'[12]

---

6. As shown by the verb נָחִת in the singular ([he] was coming down), עִיר וְקַדִּישׁ (*a watcher and a holy one*) should be taken together for "a holy watcher."

7. A shift from narrative about the "stump" to talking about a person represented by the "stump" appears to start at v. 15b (12b).

8. Aramaic עִדָּן implies a set period of time, not necessarily a year.

9. שְׁאֶלְתָא means *the question*, but here it means the response to the question or a decision (Montgomery, *Book of Daniel*, 237).

10. The first two lines of v. 17 (14) form a poetic couplet, with the complete phrase *holy watchers* divided among the two parts and with the preposition *by* carried over into the second half.

11. The expression עַד־דִּבְרַת דִּי (*so that*) is problematic, because the word עַד (*until*) doesn't seem to have an appropriate sense. The papyri know of a corresponding form עדבר with an assimilation of the *lamed* (ל) to the *daleth* (ד), which could explain the form in the MT (see apparatus to *BHS*).

12. The Hebrew form for *men* is used (אֲנָשִׁים). It differs by only one consonant from the corresponding Aramaic form (אֲנָשִׁין) and could be a scribal mistake (cf. Koch, *Daniel 1–4*, 383).

| 18 [15] | This is the dream that I, king Nebuchadnezzar, saw. Now you, Belteshazzar, tell the interpretation, since all the wise men of my kingdom were not able to inform me of the interpretation; but you can,[13] because a spirit of the holy gods is in you." |
|---|---|
| 19 [16] | Then Daniel, whose name was Belteshazzar, was appalled for a while, and his thoughts disturbed him. |

The king responded[14] by saying,

"Belteshazzar, don't let the dream and the interpretation disturb you."

Belteshazzar responded by saying,

"My lord, would that the dream applied to your enemies, and its interpretation to your foes.

| 20 [17] | As for the tree that you saw, that grew large and strong, and its height reached to heaven so that it was visible to all the earth; |
|---|---|
| 21 [18] | and its leaves were beautiful, and its fruit was abundant so that it had food for all, and the animals of the field lived under it, and the birds of heaven lived in its branches— |
| 22 [19] | it represents you, O king. For you have become great and mighty; and your greatness has increased and reached to heaven; and your dominion reaches to the end of the earth. |
| 23 [20] | And in that the king saw a holy watcher descending from heaven, and he said, |

'Chop down the tree and destroy it;[15] but leave the stump with its roots in the ground,

and let it be bound with a band of iron and bronze in the grass of the field.

---

13. Two different Aramaic verbs are used in Daniel to express the ability to do something, יכל and כהל. In this verse יכל is used of the wise men (who were *not* able) and כהל of Daniel. Both forms occur in the papyri of the Achaemenid (Persian) period and appear to have synonymous meanings and usage (Folmer, *Aramaic Language in the Achaemenid Period*, 634–39). The variation is apparently stylistic.

14. The king is narrating the events in his letter, so one would expect him to say "I responded...."

15. The reference to destruction was added by Daniel; it summarizes the action of stripping off the branches, leaves, and fruit described in v. 14 (11).

## A PROUD KING IS HUMBLED

And let him be drenched with the dew of heaven, and let his portion be with the animals of the field until seven periods of time will pass by for him.'

24 [21]  This is the interpretation, O king.

It is the decree of the Most High that has come upon my lord, the king.

25 [22]  You will be driven away from men, and you will live with the animals of the field. You will be fed with plants like oxen, and you will be drenched with the dew of heaven. Seven periods of time will pass by for you until you realize that the Most High rules over the kingdom of men and gives it to whomever he wishes.

26 [23]  Now since it was said to leave the tree's stump with its roots, your kingdom will continue to be yours once you realize that heaven rules.

27 [24]  Therefore, O king, let my counsel be acceptable to you.

Renounce[16] your sins by doing what is right, and your iniquities by showing mercy to the poor. Perhaps your prosperity will last longer."

28 [25]  All these things happened to Nebuchadnezzar, the king.

29 [26]  At the end of twelve months he was walking about on [the roof of] the royal palace of Babylon.

30 [27]  The king responded [to what he saw] and said,

"Isn't this the great [city of] Babylon, that I myself have built for a royal residence by my mighty power and for my glorious splendor?"

31 [28]  While the word was still in the king's mouth, a voice came from heaven:

"To you it is said, O king Nebuchadnezzar, the kingdom has passed from you.

32 [29]  And you will be driven away from men, and you will live with the animals of the field. You will be fed plants like oxen, and seven periods of time will pass by for you until you realize that

---

16. While *HALOT* recommends *remove, wipe away* for פרק, BDB and others suggest *break off* (Péter-Contesse and Ellington, *Handbook on the Book of Daniel*, 120; Lucas, *Daniel*, 101).

| | |
|---|---|
| | the Most High rules over the kingdom of men and gives it to whomever he wishes." |
| 33 [30] | At that moment the word concerning Nebuchadnezzar was fulfilled. He was driven away from men and ate plants like oxen. His body was drenched with the dew of heaven until his hair grew like eagles' [feathers] and his nails like [the talons of] birds. |
| 34 [31] | "Then at the end of the [appointed] days, I, Nebuchadnezzar, lifted my eyes to heaven, and my reason returned to me. I blessed the Most High and praised and glorified the One who lives forever, him whose rule is an eternal rule and whose kingdom is with generation after generation. |
| 35 [32] | And all who dwell on the earth are accounted as nothing.[17] |
| | He acts according to his pleasure with the host of heaven and with those who dwell on the earth. There is no one who can stay his hand or say to him, 'What have you done?' |
| 36 [33] | At that time my reason returned to me, and for the glory of my kingdom, my majesty and splendor returned to me. Also, my counselors and nobles sought me, and I was reestablished over my kingdom[18] with still more greatness added to me. |
| 37 [34] | Now I, Nebuchadnezzar, praise, exalt, and glorify the King of heaven, |
| | for all his works are right, and his ways are just. |
| | And he is able to humble those who walk in pride. |

## TEXTUAL OUTLINE (4:1–37 [3:31—4:34])

I. Nebuchadnezzar Writes a Letter. (4:1–3 [3:31–33])

II. Nebuchadnezzar Has a Dream about a Tree. (4:4–18 [4:1–15])

*[God warns people about the danger of pride.]*

---

17. The MT has an unusual spelling with *he*, כְּלָה (*as nothing*). Some manuscripts have the more usual כְּלָא (see the note in *BHS*). The rendering "as nothing" is found in Th and the Vulgate.

18. The Aramaic (וְעַל־מַלְכוּתִי הָתְקְנַת) must be corrupt. Literally it reads, "and upon my kingdom it was established." The simplest solution is to read הָתְקְנֵת (*I was established*), but עֲלַי (*to me*) instead of עַל (*upon*) has also been proposed (see note in *BHS*).

A. The wise men of Babylon fail to interpret the dream. (4:4-7 [4:1-4])

B. Nebuchadnezzar tells the dream to Daniel. (4:8-18 [4:5-15])

III. Daniel Interprets the Dream (4:19-28 [4:16-25])

A. Daniel hesitates to tell the interpretation. (4:19 [4:16])

B. Daniel interprets the tree as a symbol for Nebuchadnezzar. (4:20-26 [4:17-23])

C. Daniel advises the king. (4:27 [4:24])

IV. God's Judgment Falls on Nebuchadnezzar. (4:28-33 [4:25-30])

*[God is powerful enough to humble anyone who proudly thinks he or she is responsible for their own success in life.]*

A. Nebuchadnezzar boasts and hears a voice from heaven. (4:28-30 [4:25-27])

B. Nebuchadnezzar is driven away from men. (4:31-33 [4:28-30])

V. Nebuchadnezzar's ordeal ends when he gives glory to God. (4:34-36 [4:31-33])

*[Truly humble people will acknowledge God's exclusive sovereignty, repent of their sins and proclaim God's good works and ways.]*

VI. Nebuchadnezzar Concludes His Letter by Praising the King of Heaven. (4:37 [4:34])

## EXPOSITION (4:1-37 [3:31—4:34])

Reading 4:1-3 (3:31-33) can give a first impression that the paragraph actually does belong with the story of Shadrach, Meshach, and Abednego in chapter 3. The "signs" and "wonders" that Nebuchadnezzar saw could plausibly refer to the miraculous deliverance of the three men, but as the story continues it soon becomes evident that 4:1-3 (3:31-33) are intended as the introduction to a letter that Nebuchadnezzar wrote concerning the events surrounding his dream about the great tree.

The sense of confusion for the reader also stems from the fact that Nebuchadnezzar's letter starts rather abruptly. There is no heading that gives a date or tells the reader that the king wrote a letter. This feeling that the king is still talking about the escape from the furnace and how God nullified his command thus serves as a transition. The experiences with Shadrach, Meshach, and Abednego could be viewed as divine "signs" and "wonders," but once the king begins to narrate his own experience of another dream, the reader concludes that there are going to be more such "signs" and "wonders." The king now recognized the power of the God worshiped by the three Jewish men. Their God could overturn a royal edict. But the king still failed to realize the full extent of God's power over his realm. That new insight is highlighted first thing in this fresh story about Nebuchadnezzar's pride. The letter itself is a sign of Nebuchadnezzar's additional humiliation.

Something unusual from a literary standpoint happens at verse nineteen (v. 16). The conjunction אֱדַיִן (*then*) marks a transition to Daniel's interpretation, but more strikingly the account shifts from Nebuchadnezzar's first-person account to a third person narration. Instead of the expected "I answered and said" as the king's response to Daniel's disturbed state, the text has "the king answered and said." Most of the material in this section (vv. 19-27 [16-24]) contains direct quotation from Daniel, but both Daniel and the king are introduced through a narrative frame—"then Daniel was . . . appalled. . . . The king answered and said." The third person narration continues into the account of how the dream was fulfilled (vv. 28-33 [25-30]), and it is also set off by a division in the Masoretic manuscript between 4:28 (4:25) and 4:29 (4:26). As soon as the story arrives at the point where the king was restored to a normal state, he once again began to relate the events in the first person ("I, Nebuchadnezzar, lifted my eyes to heaven . . ." 4:31).

Why would a letter with the sender telling what happened in the first person ("I") suddenly shift to the third person ("he") and then just as suddenly switch back to the first person? A variety of answers have been given to this question. A few have thought that an editor has inserted the third person material from another source.[19] Most commentators have rejected the view of editorial insertion. A literary or psychological explanation can account for the shift to the third person adequately, especially since the third person section "forms a necessary part of the narrative."[20] Also, an alleged pre-history to the account involves considerable speculation that cannot be supported with solid evidence.

**From a literary perspective, it has been observed that a similar switch in person is not without precedent.**[21] **If Daniel is the main**

---

19. Haag, *Die Errettung Daniels aus der Löwengrube*, 14-25; Henze, *Madness of King Nebuchadnezzar*, 40.
20. John Collins, *Daniel*, 228.
21. Montgomery, *Book of Daniel*, 223; John Collins, *Daniel*, 228.

narrator in the book, then his intrusion into Nebuchadnezzar's account gives a psychological sense of objectivity. Would the king have been entirely objective if he had related everything himself? For that matter, was he even able to remember all the details of his own humiliation? "A madman is prone to make an unreliable narrator."[22] And with respect to the theme of Daniel's book, Nebuchadnezzar's control is relinquished at precisely the point where Daniel begins to declare the interpretation of the dream. This signals "that in reality someone else, the Most High God, is in control both of the world and of Nebuchadnezzar's fate."[23] After he was finally willing to acknowledge God's control, he was also able to return to his own narration and most importantly, to include his words of praise to "the King of Heaven" (Dan 4:37 [4:34]).

## Nebuchadnezzar Writes a Letter. (4:1–3 [3:31–33])

Nebuchadnezzar informs his entire realm of God's dealings with him through a letter. What should one make of this remarkable letter written by the king of a vast empire that stretched across much of the ancient Near East? Is it something that could have really been sent by King Nebuchadnezzar? **The literary form of a letter was part of the humiliation that Nebuchadnezzar experienced. Not only did he go through the process of an insanity imposed by God as punishment for his sinful and prideful behavior, but he also had to proclaim it to all of his subjects throughout his vast empire. The letter acknowledged the absolute sovereignty of Daniel's God.**

Several features of the chapter correspond somewhat to formal features of ancient Aramaic letters. The indication of sender (Nebuchadnezzar) and recipient by the pattern "Sender to [ל] Recipient" occurs also in the letter of the Persian king Artaxerxes to Ezra (Ezra 7:12) and in some later Aramaic letters.[24] The form "to [אל] Recipient (from) Sender" is more common in letters closer in date to the sixth century BC, but in them the sender is usually subordinate to the recipient.[25] There are some letters in Aramaic from the late fifth century BC that are addressed "from Sender to [על] Recipient," and for these the sender has authority over the recipient.[26] Nebuchadnezzar's letter is addressed uniquely to the whole population, making it more

---

22. Fewell, *Circle of Sovereignty*, 75.
23. Lucas, *Daniel*, 104.
24. Fitzmyer, "Notes on Aramaic Epistolography," 211–12.
25. Lindenberger, *Aramaic and Hebrew Letters*, letters 1–3.
26. Lindenberger, *Aramaic and Hebrew Letters*, letters 37–49.

of an open letter or the publication of a royal declaration. At least from its opening line it does have the basic form of a letter.

The greeting with a form of the root שלם (*peace* or *prosperity*) is commonly found in Aramaic letters from the seventh century BC on,[27] although the full form of "your peace be multiplied" occurs only at Dan 6:25 (26) and in later rabbinical texts that are possibly copying the form found in Daniel.[28] Nebuchadnezzar's letter has a close parallel in the letter of the Persian king to Rehum and Shimshai (Ezra 4:17). The first-person narrative form is also usual in letters; additionally it is commonly found in the OT prophets (cf. Isa 8:1; Jer 1:4; Ezek 1:4; Amos 7; Zech 11:4–16) and in Ezra and Nehemiah.

**4:1 (3:31).** Nebuchadnezzar addressed his letter to "all peoples, nations, and languages," using the same combination of terms found throughout the Aramaic portion of the book (Dan 3:4, 7, 31; 5:19; 6:25 [26]; 7:14).[29] An open letter like this from a king to all of his subjects throughout his realm is quite unusual, but the circumstances that called for it were also unusual. For the king to do this was a mark of his newly found humility after he was forced to experience the judgment of God. The letter's theological content probably reflects Daniel's instruction of the king. Perhaps Daniel may even have drafted the letter for the king.[30]

**4:2–3 (3:32–33).** Nebuchadnezzar speaks of "signs" and "wonders" and of God's everlasting kingdom. Later Darius the Mede would also speak of the "signs and wonders" of the living God (Dan 6:27–28). According to Deut 4:34–35 the "signs and wonders" that the Lord did at the events surrounding the exodus from Egypt were designed to show the people "that the Lord is God; there is no other besides him." For Nebuchadnezzar, the revelation was that "the Most High God" does whatever he desires in heaven and on earth (Dan 4:34–35 [4:31–32]). His rule extends over the "kingdom of men," and proud Nebuchadnezzar learned that he ruled only at God's pleasure (4:25 [4:22]).

The Aramaic תְּמַהּ (*wonder*) corresponds to the Hebrew term מוֹפֵת in the phrase "signs and wonders" that occurs frequently throughout the Old Testament and even into the NT in its Greek equivalent.[31] Most often these

---

27. Nearly every Aramaic letter found in Lindenberger (*Aramaic and Hebrew Letters*) has a form of this greeting.

28. Fitzmyer, "Some Notes on Aramaic Epistolography," 215.

29. Cf. 3:29 where the singular of each term is used.

30. Steinmann, *Daniel*, 209.

31. Exod 7:3; Deut 4:34; 6:22; 7:19; 13:1, 2; 26:8; 28:46; 29:3; 34:11; Neh 9:10; Ps 135:9; Isa 8:18; Jer 32:20, 21; Dan 4:2, 3 [3:32, 33]; 6:27 (28); Matt 24:24; Mark 13:22; John 4:48; Acts 2:19, 22, 43; 4:30; 5:12; 6:8; 7:36; 14:3; 15:12; Rom 15:19; 2 Cor 12:12; Heb 2:4. Acts 2:19 quotes Joel 2:30 [3:3] but Joel uses only the term מוֹפְתִים (*wonders*).

miraculous things are done either directly by God or through those who serve him, but it is also possible for them to be done by Satan (2 Thess 2:9) and false prophets (Deut 13:1–3; Matt 24:24; Mark 13:22). In this case God himself performed the signs as a judgment on Nebuchadnezzar, and they were also announced in the dream that Daniel interpreted.

When Nebuchadnezzar recognized the eternal rule of "the Most High God," he referred to God's heavenly reign whereby he had granted him the right to rule over the kingdom of Babylon. That is made clear when Daniel warned the king that God's judgment would fall on him until such time that he would realize that "the Most High rules over the kingdom of men and grants it to whomever he wishes" (4:25 [22]).

Nebuchadnezzar's opening words of praise to God consist of two poetic lines, each divided into two parallel parts. The following layout of 4:3 (22) in woodenly literal form shows the poetic structure. Words linked by a dash represent a single Aramaic word.

| His-signs | how great |
| and-his-wonders | how mighty! |
| His-kingdom (is a) | kingdom-of everlastingness |
| and-his-rule (is) | with generation and-generation |

The first line has complete semantic and grammatical parallelism (*his-signs // his-wonders, great // mighty*), while the second line has parallelism of the main ideas (*kingdom // rule, everlastingness // generation and-generation*) but with different grammatical structures in the two parts. In Hebrew parallelism the second part normally shows some type of advance on the first part, and that is also the case here in the Aramaic. "Wonders" has a stronger connotation of the miraculous than "signs," and "mighty" makes more of an impression than "great." Then the second line moves from a general statement about God's everlasting reign to the more specific rule over each subsequent generation of people.

---

There are no known Hebrew textual traditions that follow the form of the quotation found in Acts, and Luke apparently filled out the parallelism according to the familiar collocation of "signs and wonders."

## Nebuchadnezzar Has a Dream about a Tree. (4:4-18 [4:1-15])

Theological Point: God warns people about the danger of pride.

**Nebuchadnezzar's comfortable ease in his palace contrasts with the frightening dream that he saw on his bed.** It upset him so much that he had to order "all the wise men of Babylon" to come and interpret it for him. His previous dream involved a succession of kingdoms that culminated in a kingdom that God himself would set up. This time his dream dealt more personally with the king himself and his own right to rule. If the golden head of the great human-like image stood for the king of Babylon in all his greatness, the huge tree might also be thought to represent him; but that tree was cut down and destroyed. What might that portend for Nebuchadnezzar?

That Nebuchadnezzar was living a comfortable life and flourishing also was a symptom of something that was wrong. Kings live in luxury in their palaces, but it is not always so easy a life for their subjects. Centuries prior to Nebuchadnezzar the prophet Amos castigated the wealthy who lived a life of ease in Judah and Samaria. While they enjoyed their great banquets, overindulging in food and wine, they failed to recognize the ruined state of their country where there was great suffering among the poor (Amos 6:1-6). The text highlights this emphasis by noting Daniel's advice to the king to demonstrate his repentance "by showing mercy to the poor" (4:27 [4:24). Forgetting to care for the poor was a symptom of Nebuchadnezzar's pride. He had a flourishing life but neglected those who were in need.

It is noteworthy that when the king had his first dream, he refused to tell it to the wise men, insisting instead that they first tell him the dream and only then tell what it meant. In this case he immediately told his wise men what the dream was, but none of them were able to interpret it for him. Since the action of telling someone a dream in ancient Babylonian culture had a cathartic effect,[32] this second dream must have been much more terrifying for Nebuchadnezzar. He couldn't waste any time waiting for someone else to rehearse the details.[33]

*The wise men of Babylon fail to interpret the dream. (4:4-7 [4:1-4])*

**One might wonder why Daniel wasn't part of "all the wise men of Babylon" that the king summoned before him. From a literary perspective the**

32. Oppenheim, *Interpretation of Dreams*, 219.
33. Steinmann, *Daniel*, 232.

separation between the failure of the wise men to explain the dream and Daniel's success heightens Daniel's difference from these Babylonian wise men. He was "the chief of the soothsayer priests," but he did not traffic in their techniques.

There was also a logical reason why Daniel was summoned only after the other wise men failed. In addition to interpreting or decoding the divine message that the dream imparted to Nebuchadnezzar, their job was also to dispel any evil consequences associated with the dream through magical practices.[34] **As a god-fearing Jew, Daniel could not participate in such practices. Just as previously he refused to partake of the king's food, there were divinatory practices involving idolatry that Daniel could not join in. Even though Daniel was a man of great influence, he knew where to draw the line in assimilating to a foreign culture.** Just so today, while Christians may want to have influence in the secular culture, they also need to determine those lines they must refuse to cross. Rather than magically dispelling the consequences foretold in the dream, Daniel recommended instead that Nebuchadnezzar repent (4:27 [4:24]). And knowing that Daniel couldn't participate in the practice of magic, the king summoned him last. Other suggestions are that as the leader, Daniel was summoned only after the lesser practitioners had a chance or that he was not immediately available for the consultation.[35]

From the standpoint of the wise men themselves, they look worse this time than when they were summoned previously to interpret the king's dream. Then they had an excuse for not being up to the task—the king refused to tell them his dream. This time he told them the dream, but they still were not forthcoming with an interpretation. This despite their previous insistence that they could interpret the dream if the king would first relate it to them (2:4, 7). It has also been suggested that the wise men did come up with interpretations, but Nebuchadnezzar could tell that they weren't correct.[36]

## Nebuchadnezzar tells the dream to Daniel (4:8–18 [4:5–15])

After the king introduced Daniel into his narrative, he plunged right into recounting the dream itself, which had four parts. First, there appeared to him a great tree that provided food and shelter to all creatures. Second, a mysterious "holy watcher" came from heaven and commanded that the

---

34. Oppenheim, *Interpretation of Dreams*, 219.

35. The OG simply makes Daniel the only one that the king summoned. The other wise men play no role.

36. Hebbard, *Reading Daniel*, 114.

tree be cut down, scattering all the beasts and birds that relied on it. Third, a stump was to be left in the ground, bound with iron and bronze and exposed to the elements. And fourth, the figure of the stump was exchanged for that of a man whose mind was to be made like that of a beast. All this was to happen for seven periods of time until the man would recognize the absolute authority of "the Most High."

That a tree represented Nebuchadnezzar was an apt image, both culturally and logically. Cultural associations will be treated in the exposition of 4:10 (7). **From a logical standpoint a tree depends for its growth on nourishment that it receives from the soil and moisture that comes from the rain. It may provide shelter and food for many creatures, but it still depends on something else. That is the point of the tree in the dream. It might have been very stately and important, but its growth and nourishment depended on God.** Hence God sent his messengers to cut it down when it began to grow to such heights that it reached into God's heavenly abode. **The inordinate growth of the tree represented Nebuchadnezzar's pride, and its fall to the ground represented how God humbled him.**

**4:8-9 (5-6).** Nebuchadnezzar referred to the one who finally came before him as "Daniel, whose name is Belteshazzar after the name of my god." The name Belteshazzar occurs ten times in the book of Daniel, six of which are in chapter 4. The first time was when Daniel was given his new name (1:7), and the second was when the king questioned Daniel before he interpreted the dream of the great human image (2:26). "Belteshazzar" was later heard on the lips of the queen mother in the time of Belshazzar (5:12), and it wasn't used again until the introduction to Daniel's final vision (10:1). Mostly, then, the Babylonians themselves used this name for Daniel. When Nebuchadnezzar composed his letter to his subjects it was natural for him to give Daniel's Babylonian name.

If the name Belteshazzar means "(The god) protect his life" (see on 1:7), how is it that it was "after the name of my [Nebuchadnezzar's] god"? Even though the god wasn't actually named, the meaning of the name itself assumed that Nebuchadnezzar's god would carry out the desired result, namely the protection of life. The god presumed to be behind the name could have been either Bel Marduk ("Lord Marduk") or Nabu.[37] If, though, Nebuchadnezzar's confession at the end of the letter indicates that he actually adopted Daniel's God, then there could be deliberate ambiguity. Babylonians would assume that he meant a Babylonian god, while Nebuchadnezzar would now know that his God was Daniel's God. **The question**

---

37. See the exposition of Dan 1:1-21 for Shea's proposal ("Bel(te)shazzar," 74-76) that Belteshazzar is a deliberate scribal corruption of Belshazzar ("Bel protect the king").

of exactly how far Nebuchadnezzar advanced toward faith in the one true God is difficult to determine with certainty, but the full force of his praise of "the Most High" who "lives forever" and has a "kingdom" that "endures from generation to generation" (4:34 [31]) at minimum hints at some faith on the part of the king.

A more important question comes to mind. Why did Nebuchadnezzar add the detail about the meaning of the name Belteshazzar? Wouldn't that have been obvious to the Babylonians? Perhaps not if the name of the actual god was assumed; the king clarified here that it was his own personal god who was being invoked. Beyond that, though, Nebuchadnezzar was building up the prestige of Daniel for the recipients of the letter. This man bore a name that called upon Nebuchadnezzar's god to protect life. As an aside, this reference to Nebuchadnezzar's god demonstrates that he still thought of another god than Daniel's God when he wrote this letter.

In the same vein, the king further exalted Daniel when he referred to his spiritual powers. Daniel, according to Nebuchadnezzar, had "a spirit of (the) holy gods in him" (v. 8 [5]). While the English term *holy* typically has connotations of ethical or moral rightness, that is not necessarily the case with the Aramaic here. It could give the idea merely of something separate from the ordinary. Thus, *the holy gods* would mean the gods or divine beings that are separate from mere mortals (cf. Dan 2:11). One could compare how God made the seventh day of the creation week "holy" (Gen 2:3). No implication of ethical holiness was intended then. It was only that God made the day separate from the other days, because that was the day he ceased or rested from his labor of creation.

What did it mean for Daniel (called Belteshazzar here) to be "the chief of the soothsayer priests"? Did he participate in their magical practices that are otherwise forbidden in the Scriptures (Deut 18:10–11; Lev 19:26, 31; 20:6, 27; 1 Sam 28:8–19; Isa 8:19–22; Ezek 22:28; Mal 3:5)? The term חַרְטֹם (*magician* or *soothsayer priest*), whether Aramaic or Hebrew, always refers to non-Israelite practitioners, either Egyptians (Gen 41:8, 24; Exod 7:11, 22; 8:7 [3], 14, 15; 9:11) or Babylonians (Dan 1:20; 2:2, 10, 27; 4:7 [4], 9 [6]; 5:11). Surely a devout Israelite like Daniel would not have practiced their arts in the same way that they did.

**Daniel's practices are clear from his book. He interpreted Nebuchadnezzar's first dream only after he and his friends prayed for the answer (2:18–23), and he let the king know that he didn't obtain his results through any special wisdom of his own. His interpretation came only through "God in heaven" (2:27–30). The "wisdom" of the Babylonian "wise men" consisted of their magical practices, so Daniel explicitly denied that he used such methods. And later he did something that would**

be unexpected for Babylonian wise men—he encouraged the king to repent (4:18 [4:15]).

4:10 (7). The first thing that Nebuchadnezzar saw in his dream was a tree of great height "in the middle of the earth." It kept growing until it reached heaven, and it was visible from the farthest reaches of the earth. Since it was Nebuchadnezzar's dream, it makes sense to look for some background to the imagery in ancient Babylonian and Assyrian sources. Reaching back as far as the neo-Sumerian period (ca. 2100–2000 BC) and continuing into the time of Nebuchadnezzar himself and even later into the Persian period, a stylized image of a tree could represent royal power.[38] Its appearance also in the OT shows how widespread throughout the ancient Near East the motif was. The leaders in Jerusalem were represented as branches of the tops of trees that would be cut off because of apostasy (Isa 10:33), and the Messiah was depicted as "a shoot that will come out of the stump of Jesse" (Isa 11:1). The prophet Ezekiel used the image of the top of a cedar tree to refer first to the captivity of Jehoiachin of Judah and the nobility of Jerusalem (Ezek 17:3–4) and then to the Messiah as growing up from the top of the cedar, plucked by God himself and planted in the ground (Ezek 17:22–24).[39] The closest biblical parallel to Nebuchadnezzar's dream of a gigantic tree is also found in Ezekiel's allegory concerning Assyria (31:3–14). It was higher than any tree and even rivaled "the cedars in the garden of God" (31:8). It also served as shelter for animals and birds (31:6), but because of arrogance it was eventually cut down by other nations (31:10–12). These various parallels to Nebuchadnezzar's dream illustrate that he could have recognized himself in the tree even before Daniel gave him that information, which may explain why he was so anxious about the dream.

Jerome referred to some who taught that since Nebuchadnezzar did not actually rule over the whole earth at this time, the passage was not historical. Jerome took the statement as hyperbolic and argued that the passage was historical.[40] The imagery is contained in a dream, so some exaggeration might be expected, but the dream should be seen as well in light of Nebuchadnezzar's pride and of his earlier dream of the four kingdoms. God had given the king a special position as the holder of kingdom authority after he gave the kingdom of Israel into his hands (1:1–2). **Thus, Nebuchadnezzar's kingdom was representative of all the kingdoms of the world, even if he did not bear literal power over all of them. The king became arrogant and thought that he bore such power in himself. The point of the dream**

---

38. Koch, *Daniel 1–4*, 425.
39. Feinberg, *Prophecy of Ezekiel*, 98.
40. Jerome, *Commentary on Daniel*, 49.

## A PROUD KING IS HUMBLED

**is to let him know that such power as he has is only that which God has granted him.**

4:12 (9). The beauty and bountiful abundance of the tree was a testimony to the greatness of the kingdom that God had granted Nebuchadnezzar. The animals and birds that sought it out reflected how all the peoples of the Babylonian kingdom relied on Nebuchadnezzar for their wellbeing. Human pride can emerge naturally under such circumstances. Leaders who start well often don't finish well because the praise and adulation they receive makes it easy to forget the God from whom all blessings flow.

4:13-14 (10-11). As the king transitioned to the next part of his dream he reiterated that these dream images passed through his head as he lay on his bed. The new and startling image was of an angel, called here "a holy watcher," as it descended from heaven. It brought a divine message that commanded the tree be cut down and stripped of its branches and fruit, with dire consequences for the animals and birds that had sought shelter and nourishment in it.

The term עִיר (*watcher*) for an angelic being is unique to this chapter in Daniel in the OT (4:13 [10], 17 [14], 23 [20]). It appears to mean an angel who is alert or wakeful.[41] In later writings the term refers mostly to fallen angels, although there are some positive references (Jubilees 4:15; 1 Enoch 20:1). At Daniel 3:28 and 6:23 (24) the term is מַלְאַךְ (*angel* or *messenger*), a word cognate with the Hebrew term for *angel*. In those passages the God of the three Jewish men protected them from harm. In Nebuchadnezzar's dream this *watcher* comes to announce judgment. Thus the different terms may indicate different functions. At Daniel 7:10 reference is made to millions of unnamed beings who attend "the Ancient of Days" as he sits on his throne. Two angels are mentioned by name in Daniel, Gabriel (8:16; 9:21) and Michael (10:13, 21; 12:1). Nowhere else in the OT is an angel given a personal name.

4:15 (12). The dream took a strange turn in that the divine message also called for the עִקַּר (*'iqqar*) of the tree to be left in the ground. The etymology and the lexicons suggest that the term has the sense of "root" or "stock" rather than the "stump" of the English versions. *HALOT* posits "main root" or "tap root" for "עִקַּר of its roots." If so, then it is hard to understand what is meant by the "band of iron and bronze" (אֱסוּר דִּי־פַרְזֶל וּנְחָשׁ).

---

41. Lucas (*Daniel*, 110) compares the statement in Ps 121:4 that the Lord as the "keeper of Israel" does not "slumber or sleep" with references in 1 Enoch to "good angels 'who watch' or 'who do not sleep' (20:1; 39:12-13; 71:7): "The class of heavenly beings known as 'Watchers' may have been conceived as those whose activities reflected this particular divine concern to look after and protect humans." Gabriel is included in 1 Enoch 20:1 as one of these angels.

There are some ancient analogies for "putting metal bands on trees," but "the relevance of this evidence to Daniel . . . is very questionable, especially since Daniel speaks of a root (עִקַּר) rather than a stump."[42]

One possibility is that the figure is abandoned here and the "band" refers to something done directly to Nebuchadnezzar. The figure of the tree clearly changes to that of a man at 4:16 (4:13), so possibly the chains refer to those placed on a madman for restraint or protection.[43] The structure of the first part of the verse is against this interpretation. "With bands of iron and bronze" and "in the grass of the field" act as modifiers to the "עִקַּר ['iqqar] of its roots"; no new verb occurs with the modifiers to signal the start of a new clause.

Probably the meaning of עִקַּר should be broadened to include also the stump. This is a reasonable solution in light of the ancient analogies and of the full expression עִקַּר שָׁרְשׁוֹהִי (" 'iqqar of its roots"). Evidence in Assyrian texts regarding a New Year's festival supplies an analogy in "the use of rings or bands of bronze wrapped around the tree [actually a tree trunk stripped bare to represent a source of life] as part of the New Year's liturgy." Since "[t]he aim of the [Babylonian] ritual is to secure and to promote the revival of nature in the New Year,"[44] the "bands" in Nebuchadnezzar's dream likely symbolized a divine intent at restoration. This interpretation of the bands is strengthened in that Daniel explained the "stump of its roots" in relation to the ultimate restoration of Nebuchadnezzar's kingdom (4:26 [23]). The bands were placed around the stump to protect what was left in some way so that eventually the tree could grow back.

The rest of the verse appears to move the dream from that of a tree and its stump to that of a man or a beast wandering in the open fields. A stump could be "drenched with the dew of heaven," but it would be odd to think of it as having a "portion with the animals." Even the term "drenched" (יִצְטַבַּע) is more appropriate for a man or an animal. The text pictures a difficulty rather than the boon that water would be for a tree stump that still has life in it.

**4:16 (13).** For the "mind" or "heart" (לְבַב) to be changed "from" that of a "man" to that of an "animal," the dream must have in view a man.[45] The idea is that as this man wanders about with wild animals and eats grass as they do, he must be acting and thinking like an animal. The detail about the

---

42. Collins, *Daniel*, 226.

43. Theodoret of Cyrus, *Commentary on Daniel*, 119: ". . . having fallen victim to madness, insanity, and mental disease, being deranged in a frenzy and raging against everyone, he had to be kept in chains . . . ."

44. Henze, *Madness of King Nebuchadnezzar*, 89.

45. The physical reference of לְבַב is to the *heart*, as in the KJV, but the modern versions with *mind* capture better the figurative use of the term in its cultural context.

changing of the "heart/mind" is not repeated in either Daniel's interpretation or in the historical note about the fulfillment. The behavior of Nebuchadnezzar in those places speaks for itself—the king acted like a madman.

The "seven times" (שִׁבְעָה עִדָּנִין) that were to pass by for the man in the dream are not defined more closely. Every time the expression occurs in the chapter the same indefinite "times" is used (4:16 [13], 23 [20], 25 [22], 32 [29]). The Old Greek has "seven years" (ἑπτὰ ἔτη), but Theodotion, which normally follows the Masoretic Text closely, has "seven times" (ἑπτὰ καιροί), as does the Vulgate (*septem tempora*). Within the dreams and visions in Daniel references to time are often made in mysterious ways. The term עִדָּן (*time*) was also used in Daniel's prayer of thanksgiving to God for revealing the mystery of Nebuchadnezzar's first dream: "He changes times (עִדָּנַיָּא) and seasons" (2:21). The expression "time, times, and half a time" uses the same term (עִדָּן וְעִדָּנִין וּפְלַג עִדָּן, 7:25) and is generally thought to refer to three and a half years (so *HALOT*). It presumably would take more than seven weeks or seven months to develop the appearance that Nebuchadnezzar eventually assumed.[46] Theodoret of Cyrus took it as seven "seasons" in years with two seasons and thus three and a half years.[47] Seven years seems almost impossibly long for Nebuchadnezzar to have been absent from his throne, if that is what the dream actually meant.

Time limitations are a minor motif throughout Daniel's book. Others include the following:

1. Three years for the youths to be trained under Nebuchadnezzar's plan (1:5)
2. Ten days of testing proposed by Daniel (1:12)
3. Thirty days during which petitions were to be made only to Darius (6:8 [9])
4. "Time, times, and half a time" in Daniel's visions (7:25; 12:7)
5. 2,300 "evening-mornings" in Daniel's vision of the ram and the goat (8:14)
6. Seventy "periods of seven" as derived from Jeremiah's prophecy of seventy years of captivity (9:25–27)
7. 1,290 days in Daniel's final vision (12:11)
8. 1,335 days, which, if waited for and reached, would make a person "blessed" (12:12)

---

46. Wood, *Daniel*, 111.
47. Theodoret of Cyrus, *Commentary on Daniel*, 123.

Also, the "time of the end," indeterminate by human calculations but exactly set by God, recurs throughout the book (8:17, 19; 9:26; 11:27, 35, 40; 12:4, 6, 9, 13).

**4:17 (14).** Since the "decree" that the angelic "watchers" issued has as its purpose "that the living might know that the Most High rules," it is clear that God has to be the ultimate source of the decree. The Aramaic, however, assigns the decision more directly to the "watchers." The OT sometimes mentions a heavenly council presided over by God (1 Kgs 22:19–23; Job 1:6–12; 2:1–6; Ps 82:1). "Evidently, the decree came from this council of watchers, which is understood to be under God's authority."[48] It is also good to keep in mind that this is Nebuchadnezzar, the king, describing what he saw in his dream. In analogy with the human hierarchy, subordinates may make decisions, but only under the authority of the king. Such a perspective highlights God's "exaltedness and transcendent authority."[49] When Daniel interpreted the dream he referred to "the decree of the Most High" (v. 24 [21]). The decree was made so that "the living" (all people) would come to recognize that God is the ultimate ruler over the nations, giving governmental authority to whomever he chooses, even to "the lowliest of men."

In Nebuchadnezzar's first dream the four kingdoms represented successive empires that the Most High would permit to rule. Eventually a kingdom would arrive that would crush all the kingdoms of men, but even before that kingdom arrives Nebuchadnezzar needed to affirm that the Most High is always sovereign over all. **The length of Nebuchadnezzar's rule was irrelevant; God determines the time rulers are permitted to rule, and He sets up kingdoms and tears them down. It was useless for Nebuchadnezzar to set himself up as some kind of final authority.**

**4:18 (15).** Nebuchadnezzar's expression of confidence in Daniel's abilities frames the telling of the dream. He recognized that Daniel could interpret things that were too difficult for the wise men, because he had a divine spirit. By this time Daniel had become more than merely one of the king's wise men or even their "chief." A close relationship had developed between the two men to the extent that Daniel now served as a personal advisor or confidant. The nature of the relationship becomes even more evident in the next section where Daniel was troubled by the negative import of the dream for Nebuchadnezzar and even gives the king personal advice.

---

48. Steinmann, *Daniel*, 237.
49. Goldingay, *Daniel*, 93.

## Daniel Interprets the Dream. (4:19–28 [4:16–25])

Daniel advises Nebuchadnezzar to reform his ways based on his ominous interpretation of the dream. The frame for Daniel's interpretation of the dream consists of his initial reticence to relate the interpretation and his advice to try to avoid the negative effects that the dream portended. The narrative also shifts from Nebuchadnezzar as narrator to an anonymous narrator, as noted previously. **It is perhaps also significant that Daniel is reintroduced as "Daniel, whose name is Belteshazzar." The king himself had made the same introduction when he shifted the focus from the failure of his wise men to Daniel, who had "a spirit of the holy gods" in him. The repetition reinforces the significance of Daniel's presence before the king as the only one who can give the interpretation.** His Babylonian name identifies him as more than merely a captive from Judah; he shares the privileges and prestige of a Babylonian. Nebuchadnezzar's observance of polite protocol in the matter of Daniel's name contrasts with Belshazzar's later condescending address to Daniel: "Are you Daniel who is of the exiles of Judah that my father the king brought from Judah?" (5:13).

Daniel's interpretation consisted of three parts. First, the great tree represented the current reign of Nebuchadnezzar as the most powerful monarch in the world. Second, the commandment to fell the tree stood for God's judgment that would come upon the king. And third, the stump of the tree left in the ground with bands of iron and bronze indicated the promise of a future restoration of Nebuchadnezzar's kingdom once he has learned his lesson. **Actually, the second and third parts are intertwined when both are mentioned together initially (v. 23 [20]), but the interpretation of the stump is not given until after that element of the dream is repeated (v. 26 [23]). In this manner the narrative ties closely together the judgment and the promise, both of which are part of the "decree of the Most High." Also, Daniel highlighted the word of restoration by repeating it twice.** It was part of the decree, but it had special significance for the continuation of Nebuchadnezzar's reign.

### *Daniel hesitates to tell the interpretation. (4:19 [16])*

The king had been frightened, even terrified by the dream (4:5 [2]), now Daniel was appalled and terrified by what he immediately knew the dream meant. He hesitated because he knew how difficult it would be for the king to hear the meaning of his dream. **In light of the experience of Shadrach, Meshach, and Abednego with Nebuchadnezzar, it seems improbable** that he was afraid that the king might punish him for a negative interpretation. Instead, knowing the certainty of God's decree (4:24 [21]), he feared for the future of the king and his subjects. For Nebuchadnezzar to be so incapacitated would indeed be helpful news only for the king's foes. Therefore Daniel wished that the foes would experience the events foretold by the dream rather than Nebuchadnezzar. Daniel's reaction reflected his friendly concern for the king.

## Daniel interprets the tree as a symbol for Nebuchadnezzar. (4:20-26 [4:17-23])

After a nearly verbatim repetition of the elements of the first part of the dream, Daniel applied the image of the tree directly to Nebuchadnezzar. The king had achieved a grand realm that continued to expand. **What Daniel left out may be significant. He didn't give any interpretation regarding the fact that all the animals and birds received nourishment and shelter from the tree. He focused solely on Nebuchadnezzar as the tree that grew to heaven and extended to the far reaches of the earth. Was this perhaps a subtle way of letting the king know that his greatness would be his downfall? That would also be disastrous for the people of the kingdom, but Daniel moved directly from the excessive greatness of the tree to the command to chop it down.**

In light of the angelic decree, one might wonder what would happen to the kingdom. Who would run it? How would the king's condition affect the people? None of that information was relevant to Daniel; the message from God mediated through the dream was for Nebuchadnezzar alone. **The reference to the birds and animals that sheltered in the tree served merely to highlight the greatness and importance of Nebuchadnezzar—a greatness that meant nothing when God decided to humble him.**

Daniel's word to Nebuchadnezzar must have been sobering: "It is the decree of the Most High that has come upon . . . the king." The decree had two parts, however, one part that was bad news for the king, but a second part that contained an element of hope. The bad news was that the king would be driven from men and live and eat among the animals, exposed to the elements. The hopeful word was that everything would be restored to the king once he realized that "heaven rules." That is, he needed to acknowledge that his authority and power were derived from the heavenly realm, ruled over by "the God of heaven." Daniel 1:2 states explicitly that God had given the nation of Judah and its king into the control of Nebuchadnezzar. Now it was important for Nebuchadnezzar himself to come to the same conclusion.

## *Daniel advises the king. (4:27 [24])*

Recognizing that the dream held out the promise of restoration for Nebuchadnezzar, Daniel immediately urged him to repent. Perhaps the king's prosperity could be prolonged. **After all, the Lord is the God who "relents" from bringing judgment when the people repent (Jer 18:8; 26:3, 13; Joel 2:13; Jonah 3:9–10; 4:2). Daniel differed from the other wise men in that he gave the king advice for what to do so as to mitigate the divine decree. The others would have tried to counter it with various magical rituals, but for Daniel it was a matter of morality rather than ritual.** In this he followed in the train of all the prophets of the Lord in the OT. His suggestion actually involved social justice, a common theme in the prophets, in that he advised the king to mend his ways in how he treated the poor.

Aramaic צִדְקָה can be either "correct practice" or "charity."[50] The parallelism with "showing mercy to the poor" has led some[51] to adopt the more specific sense of giving to the poor,[52] but parallel sentences need not overlap in meaning completely. It would be natural in a parallel expression to have a general statement (*doing what is right*) paralleled by a specific example (*showing mercy to the poor*). Nebuchadnezzar could demonstrate the genuineness of his repentance by following Daniel's advice.[53]

Exactly what Daniel urged the king to do to demonstrate his repentance has proved controversial because of the Aramaic terms used. Daniel used the verb פְּרַק in his plea to the king. In later Aramaic that term can mean "to remove" or "wipe away."[54] Hence the NRSV has "atone for." In earlier Aramaic the verb meant *to tear away* or *break off*.[55] From this earlier sense some of the versions have "break off" (KJV, ESV). "Renounce" gives a similar sense but in more natural English. It would be odd for Daniel to use a term like *atone for* in a technical sense. Sacrifices, not good deeds, were the means for making atonement in the OT.

Later Jewish writers were shocked that Daniel would give helpful advice to the Babylonian king who destroyed Jerusalem and the temple. One tradition thought that Daniel was demoted or even suffered the ordeal of

---

50. *HALOT* 5:1963.

51. Collins, *Daniel*, 230.

52. Both Greek versions have ἐλεημοσύναις, *by alms* (cf. the Vulgate, *elemosynis*).

53. Daniel later used the Hebrew cognates צֶדֶק and צְדָקָה in the same sense of just and right behavior (Dan 9:7, 16, 18, 24).

54. *HALOT*.

55. BDB; Koch translates with *zerbreche*, noting that this is an Old Aramaic and Hebrew meaning (*Daniel 1–4*, 385), but Gzella argues that the evidence from Old Aramaic is uncertain, and the meaning should be *redeem* ("פרק *prq*," 611–13).

the lion's den because of his advice. According to another tradition Daniel intended only to help his people who were suffering in exile.[56] The prophet Jeremiah taught that Nebuchadnezzar's actions were actually decreed by the Lord as punishment for the sins of the people (e.g., Jer 25:8–11). Jeremiah even urged Zedekiah, the last king of Judah, to surrender the city to the Babylonians so that it would not be destroyed (Jer 38:17–18). Given that Nebuchadnezzar was the Lord's instrument of judgment, it need not seem so strange that Daniel would give him helpful advice.

Jerome was concerned with the theological issue of how God could withdraw Nebuchadnezzar's punishment once it had been decreed. He appealed to analogies, such as Jonah's preaching to the Ninevites, where in many cases God responded to repentance by withholding judgment for sins. "God is not angered at men but at their sins; and when no sin inheres in a man, God by no means inflicts a punishment which has been commuted."[57]

## God's Judgment Falls on Nebuchadnezzar. (4:28–33 [25–30]).

Theological Point: God is powerful enough to humble anyone who proudly thinks he or she is responsible for their own success in life.

The decreed judgment eventually brings Nebuchadnezzar to his senses. The judgment was not carried out against Nebuchadnezzar until a full year after Daniel interpreted his dream. **Daniel had urged the king to show mercy to the poor to show that he had repented, but the actual judgment fell when the king expressed pride in his own achievements and did not recognize God's sovereignty. The extra time was God's act of mercy in allowing the king time to demonstrate true repentance. The connection between his pride and acts of mercy to the poor is less clear, but it would seem to lie in the fact that much of the poverty in the kingdom was due to an oppressive government. When Nebuchadnezzar gloried in all of his achievements, he failed not only to recognize that the Most High had granted him the right to rule in the first place. He also failed to see that his great wealth and power often came at the expense of the poor. They were oppressed and exploited, while he could look out on all the luxurious wealth of Babylon and claim it as his own. The text does not state this explicitly, but it is implied by the way Daniel's advice is juxtaposed with Nebuchadnezzar's prideful survey of Babylon's greatness.**

---

56. Goldwurm, *Daniel*, 148–49.
57. Jerome, *Commentary on Daniel*, 51–52.

## A PROUD KING IS HUMBLED

The section about Nebuchadnezzar's judgment clearly starts with 4:28 (25), since בֹּלָּא (*all this*) refers to the interpretation that Daniel gave to the dream, not to his advice. Also, the perspective shifts from Daniel's advice to Nebuchadnezzar in the first person to the third person narrator. Verse twenty-eight functions like a paragraph title for what follows. All that the dream portended came on Nebuchadnezzar and happened the way it is described in 4:29-37 (26-34).

### *Nebuchadnezzar boasts and hears a voice from heaven. (4:28-30 [4:25-27])*

Nebuchadnezzar made his prideful comments from the top of the royal palace of Babylon. **The word order of verse twenty-nine (v. 26) stresses the time and the location for the king's stroll. Twelve months gave him sufficient time to demonstrate a changed heart, and the roof of the palace gave him a central vantage point to take in the splendor of the city from his own home.**[58] **The text reminds of another king who walked about on the roof of his palace and thought that he was powerful enough to take another man's wife.** The Aramaic verb that means *walking about*, מְהַלֵּךְ, has a cognate root in the Hebrew that is used in 2 Sam 11:2 to describe how David "walked about" (וַיִּתְהַלֵּךְ) on the roof of his palace when he saw Bathsheba, wife of Uriah the Hittite, and desired her for himself. His act of pride led to God's judgment on his family; now Nebuchadnezzar's prideful boast would also bring judgment from the Most High. **Pride throughout the Bible is one of the main obstacles to a right relationship with God.**[59]

No sooner had the king uttered his prideful words than "a voice from heaven" announced to Nebuchadnezzar what he was about to undergo, repeating the details of the divine decree so that he would make the connection between his dream and what was then happening to him. The only new part of the decree was an ominous pronouncement: "the kingdom has passed from you." Only after the king heard his sentence in full did the judgments actually happen to him.

---

58. Nebuchadnezzar greatly enlarged the city and undertook a series of building projects, including an elaborate palace for himself (Wiseman, *Nebuchadrezzar and Babylon*, 51-56). The so-called "hanging gardens" are problematic historically. See Reade ("Hanging Gardens of Babylon") for a detailed discussion.

59. See Prov 8:13; 16:5, 18; 21:24; Isa 2:17; Hos 13:6; Hab 2:4; Luke 1:51; Jas 4:6; 1 Pet 5:5; 1 John 2:16.

## Nebuchadnezzar is driven away from men. (4:31–33 [4:28–30])

Without further delay God's pronouncement happened. Nebuchadnezzar was driven away from human beings and forced to live and feed like cattle, even taking on a disheveled look with no shelter from the elements. This rather bizarre episode in the life of a great monarch such as Nebuchadnezzar raises some questions. How literally are we supposed to take the description of what happened, and is there any extra-biblical evidence of something like this really happening to Nebuchadnezzar?

Christopher Hays refers to Babylonian and Assyrian materials for analogies to what happened to Nebuchadnezzaar.[60] Divine judgment in these ancient documents is depicted in imagery that refers to various animals and birds. "[D]emons and the dead are frequently portrayed with animal characteristics," but also "the victim can begin to *look like* the dead even before he or she reaches the underworld."[61] Rain and storms also could describe the effect of evil spirits, and in the Bible rain is sometimes connected with suffering as well (Job 24:4–8). Hays notes close parallels with Daniel in the Babylonian "Poem of the Righteous Sufferer" (*Ludlul bel nemeqi*) and in the story of Ahiqar, a tale widely known throughout the ancient Near East (see Tobit 1:21–22; 2:10; 11:18; 14:10).[62] When Ahiqar appeared before the king after he was forced into hiding, he recounted that "the hair of my head had grown down on my shoulders, and my body was foul with the dust, and my nails were grown long like an eagle's."[63]

Hays concludes that the descriptions of Nebuchadnezzar's affliction are not "naturalistic" but "impressionistic, poetic evocations of long traditions of prayer." The images that depict the king living among the animals and taking on animal characteristics "express suffering, lending detail and poignancy to Nebuchadnezzar's condition."[64] While Hays has provided interesting background for the significance of the dream imagery to Nebuchadnezzar, the fulfillment of the divine decree against the king reads like a narrative of real events. Perhaps Nebuchadnezzar wandered close

---

60. Hays, "Chirps From the Dust," 305–25.

61. Hays, "Chirps From the Dust," 318.

62. Fragments of the Ahiqar story, along with various proverbs that sometimes remind of Aesop's fables, were found among the Elephantine papyri in Egypt. These fragments date to about the fifth century BC. Aramaic was probably the original language of the story, and the narrative parts may have originated as early as the seventh century BC (Lindenberger, *Aramaic Proverbs of Ahiqar*, 19–20).

63. Cited by Hays from the Syriac version as found in Conybeare, Harris, and Smith, *The Story of Ahikar from the Syriac, Arabic, Armenian, Ethiopic, Greek and Slavonic Versions*.

64. Hays, "Chirps From the Dust," 324.

enough to Babylon or even somewhere within Babylon that his ministers could feed him vegetables.[65] Many have suggested that he suffered from a mental illness where the sufferer acts like an animal. Harrison gives a detailed description of the malady.[66] **At a minimum the account implies that Nebuchadnezzar would be afflicted with an illness or with demons that would render him a social outcast for a set period of time, at least until he recognized that his own reign over Babylon was only at the behest of the Most High.**

**The concept of demonic influence on Nebuchadnezzar's condition reflects an emphasis later in the book on conflict between God's realm and the demonic realm. That conflict is highlighted in chapter seven by the four beasts that rise from the sea, and by specific reference to spiritual warfare at 10:20—11:1. Daniel's God is sovereign not only over the realm of men and kingdoms, but also over the realm of demonic forces that attempt to control diviners and kings. Even if Nebuchadnezzar's madness is considered a natural disease, the Bible reveals that God has sovereignty over that as well (cf. Job 1:6—2:8 and the numerous references to healing in the New Testament done through casting out demons).**

Is there any extra-biblical evidence of some mental illness or demonic affliction actually happening to Nebuchadnezzar? Critical scholars say that the evidence supports a tradition that originally developed around Nabonidus, the last king of Babylon and the natural father of Belshazzar. Only later was the tradition transferred to Nebuchadnezzar.[67] See the Excursus, "Historical Issues in Daniel 4 and 5," for further discussion.

Eusebius (early fourth century) quoted Abydenus, a Greek historian, who in turn quoted Megasthenes, a Greek geographer:

> [Nebuchadnezzar] went up to his palace, and being possessed by some god or other uttered the following speech: "O men of Babylon, I Nebuchadnezzar here foretell to you the coming calamity ... There will come a Persian mule, aided by the alliance of your own deities, and will bring you into slavery. . . ." He after uttering this prediction had immediately disappeared, and his son Amil-marudocus [Evil-merodach] became king.[68]

This tradition shares several features with the biblical account. Nebuchadnezzar uttered the words from his palace; he disappeared from public view immediately following his pronouncement; and the quotation

---

65. Leupold, *Exposition of Daniel*, 201.
66. Harrison, *Introduction to the Old Testament*, 1115–17.
67. Collins, *Daniel*, 216–18.
68. Eusebius, *Preparation for the Gospel*, 9.41.6.

is framed as first person speech. The reference to Evil-merodach affords a plausible scenario for what happened to the kingdom while Nebuchadnezzar was incapacitated—his son took it over until his sanity was restored.

A fragmentary cuneiform text published in 1975 has a tantalizing reference to Nebuchadnezzar and Evil-merodach.[69] It appears reasonably certain that the line translated "his life appeared of no value to [*him*]" refers to Nebuchadnezzar. Several lines later it refers to someone who "does not show love to son and daughter" and "his attention was not directed towards promoting the welfare of Esagil [*and Babylon*]." Grayson referred these descriptions to Evil-merodach, but Hasel thinks they might "refer to the strange behavior of Nebuchadnezzar during his time of mental incapacity when he neglected his own family, clan, the worship associated with the temple complex Esagila, and the interest of Babylon in general."[70] The poor preservation of the text makes it impossible to determine for certain which monarch was meant.

## Nebuchadnezzar's Ordeal Ends When He Gives Glory to God. (4:34–36 [4:31–33])

Theological Point: Truly humble people will acknowledge God's exclusive sovereignty, repent of their sins, and proclaim God's good works and ways.

Whatever the "seven periods of time" were, once they were completed the king's *understanding* (מַנְדַּע) was restored (v. 34 [31]). There is an interesting interplay between divine sovereignty and free will here. Nebuchadnezzar's lack of human understanding, as evidenced by his behaving like an animal, was not to be restored until he would come to *realize* (תִנְדַּע, with the same root as מַנְדַּע, *understanding*) that "the Most High is sovereign over the kingdom of men." So the end of the madness would not come until Nebuchadnezzar realized something, but at the same time God had decreed it would be for "seven periods of time." And it was "at the end of the (appointed) days," that is, at the end of those "seven periods," that Nebuchadnezzar "lifted [his] eyes to heaven." The text also reinforces what was said in that key passage of 2:21, "He [God] gives . . . *knowledge* [מַנְדַּע] to those who have understanding [יָדְעֵי בִינָה, *knowers of discernment*]." **Before the king could regain enough "understanding" or "knowledge" to confess that God is sovereign, God had to first give him that "understanding." When Nebuchadnezzar humbled himself, God restored his sanity; but even the**

---

69. Grayson, "Tiglath-pileser," 88–89; cf. 2 Kgs 25:27; Jer 52:31.
70. Hasel, "Book of Daniel and Matters of Language," 42.

knowledge to realize God's sovereignty had to come from God himself. It seems like a paradox but is in reality a tension that needs to be held in balance—divine sovereignty over against free will.

Nebuchadnezzar's praise of God occurs in two sections. First, he recounted how he immediately began to praise him when his sanity was restored. Then in the close of the letter, signaled by the adverb כְּעַן (*now*), he reiterated his praise to God in relation to all that had happened to him. He offered his praise to "the Most High," the name of God stated in the king's dream and its interpretation (vv. 17 [14], 24 [21], 25 [22], 32 [29]).

Three synonymous verbs express Nebuchadnezzar's praise. "I blessed" (בָּרְכֵת) refers to praise that is returned to God in gratefulness for all that he has done (cf. Ps 103:1–5). "I praised" (שַׁבְּחֵת) uses a general Aramaic term for ascribing worth and admiration. And "I glorified" (הַדְּרֵת) uses a verb that derives from a noun that means "majesty," "splendor," or "glory." Nebuchadnezzar thereby ascribed majesty to God.

**4:34 (31).** Nebuchadnezzar used two different titles for God in his praise—"the Most High" (עִלָּיָא) and "the Ever-Living One" (חַי עָלְמָא). The latter title can be compared with "the living God" in Hebrew (אֱלֹהִים חַיִּים, אֱלֹהִים חָי, or אֵל חָי, Deut 5:26; 1 Sam 17:26, 36; 2 Kgs 19:16; Ps 42:3 [4]; Isa 37:4, 17; Jer 10:10; 23:36) or "YHWH your God, (who is) from everlasting to everlasting" (Neh 9:5; cf. Ps 41:13 [14]; 45:6 [7]; Isa 40:28; Jer 10:10). **All gods were thought to be immortal, but here the king emphasizes that this God presides over the dominion that lasts forever; he will rule eternally over all.**

**4:35 (32).** Nebuchadnezzar included himself in the statement that "all the inhabitants of the earth are accounted as nothing," reflecting the humiliation that he endured under God's decreed judgment. As a consequence, he recognized that it is God, not man, who runs things both in heaven and on earth. No one can resist his will, something that the king concluded as a result of his experience with the three men who survived the furnace as well as his period of insanity.

**4:36 (33).** God restored Nebuchadnezzar to his former splendor, and by his grace God even added to his greatness. Amazingly, the king's high officials once again sought him out for leadership of the Babylonian kingdom. **In one fell swoop the Most High had both removed Nebuchadnezzar from his power and also restored him to an even greater position.**

## Nebuchadnezzar Concludes His Letter by Praising the King of Heaven. (4:37 [4:34])

Having learned that "heaven rules," Nebuchadnezzar praises the King of Heaven. The letter that the king sent to his subjects was no ordinary letter. **Instead of a concluding section that was standard in letters, this one closes by reiterating praise to God.** Some of the language repeats what was said in the introduction to the letter or in the praise that the king offered immediately after his recovery, but some unique elements are added as well. Now God is "the King of heaven" whose actions are always right and just. God never does anything that could be considered wrong or false. **The term דִּין in the parallel expression can mean "judgment" or "justice." God's ways, like his deeds, always exhibit the quality of "justice" and are therefore "just."** Nebuchadnezzar's confession here harks back to Daniel's earlier advice (4:27 [24]). The king should stop doing things that are unrighteous and do that which is "right" or "just" (צְדָקָה) instead. And he should stop oppressing the poor and show mercy to them. Nebuchadnezzar came to recognize these behaviors as characteristic of "the King of heaven." It would seem that he finally took Daniel's advice. **In his last words in the book of Daniel Nebuchadnezzar expressed the conclusion that had been forced upon him: God "is able to humble those who walk in pride." He now knew that from bitter experience.**

### SHARPENING THE THEOLOGICAL FOCUS

As the book of Daniel opens God manifests his sovereignty over the earth by delivering the king of Judah into the hands of the king of Babylon and by granting superior wisdom and knowledge to Daniel and his three friends. At that point the king recognized that the four youths were superior to even his own wise men, but he remained ignorant of why they had such wisdom. After Daniel interpreted his dream of the great image with four parts, Nebuchadnezzar declared that Daniel's God could reveal mysteries. There are things that are too veiled in mystery for human understanding but that can be known if God chooses to reveal them. Nebuchadnezzar should have seen the transitory nature of all human kingdoms from Daniel's interpretation, but instead he focused on himself as the "head of gold" and erected an image of his own for people to worship. He thought he had the power to set the rules but was forced to recognize that the God of Shadrach, Meshach, and Abednego had the authority to change even "the word of the king." At the point where chapter 4 opens, then, God has demonstrated his sovereign ability to allocate wisdom and understanding, the ability to reveal mysteries, and the ability to overrule the decree of the king.

Chapter 4 brings to a climax the issue of the sovereignty of God when the world's most powerful ruler declares with his own lips that God's sovereign rule is eternal, lasting from generation to generation. That declaration of the king frames the letter that he wrote to all of his subjects throughout his realm (4:3 [3:33] and 4:34 [31]). When Daniel interpreted the king's first dream, he made it clear that "the God of heaven" had given to him "the kingdom, the might, the power, and the glory" (2:37). In his second dream Nebuchadnezzar saw his great power over the world, but he also learned that God would take all of it from him in order to bring him to his knees. Nothing would remain; only the kingdom would be held in reserve by God until Nebuchadnezzar humbled himself and recognized God's sovereignty. He had learned that God could nullify the decree of the most powerful king on earth; now he would learn that God could also remove all that power in an instant. No matter how powerful a person is, that power stems ultimately from God's sovereign will. No one can claim to have attained anything entirely through their own abilities. All abilities and talents are the gift of God. Even the circumstances one finds oneself in have been decreed by the God of heaven. If we don't recognize that now, sooner or later God will humble us. According to both the OT and the NT, "God opposes the proud, but gives grace to the humble" (Jas 4:6 [ESV]; cf. Prov 29:23; Mic 6:8; Matt 11:29; 18:4; Jas 4:10). A humble person is one who acknowledges his or her "own helplessness and utter dependence upon God."[71] From another perspective, humility is knowing who we are in light of who God is. It is letting God be God rather than claiming that prerogative for ourselves.

Another theological emphasis in chapter 4 concerns how God can use his people to minister to others when they are faithful. The first three chapters emphasized the faithfulness of Daniel and his friends. By chapter 4 it is clear that Nebuchadnezzar had a high opinion of Daniel. Their relationship was such that Daniel could proffer advice after hearing the king's disturbing dream. Even though the king eventually disregarded the advice, it is likely that the long relationship the two had was a factor in the king lifting his "eyes to heaven" at the end of his period of madness. Because of Daniel's faithfulness, God was able to use him to have a powerful ministry to Nebuchadnezzar.

Daniel advised the king to "renounce" his sins through justice and mercy to the poor, for he was guilty of obtaining his power through injustice and oppression. Such misuse of power seems inevitable with rulers

---

71. Mendenhall, "Humility," 659.

who obtain absolute power; as Lord Acton astutely noted, absolute power tends to corrupt absolutely. The Scriptures teach consistently that striving for power through corrupt means is opposed by God. The "wisdom" of this world fails where it counts the most—helping people to maintain a right relationship with God. Acting with justice and mercy entails humbling oneself to recognize the rightness of God's ways and then to act in obedience to his requirements. It involves acknowledging that God is always good in whatever he plans to do. After his humiliation, Nebuchadnezzar came to that realization.

Chapter 4, along with the first three chapters, prepares the way for the apocalyptic revelations of chapters 7 to 12. It is through humble service to the Lord that his people will be able to endure and even thrive in the dire circumstances that will overtake them. Chapter 5 will illustrate the same thing but in a negative way. Belshazzar's refusal to humble himself before God led to his downfall. Those who refuse to serve the Lord in humility, will ultimately be humbled. It's true for world leaders and it's true for us. If we don't humble ourselves in the sight of the Lord, he will humble us. Fortunately, Nebuchadnezzar's humiliation caused him to look up to heaven and acknowledge God's preeminence. That action led to his salvation, and the same will be true for all who do likewise today.

## THE FOCUS OF DANIEL 4 FOR PREACHING AND TEACHING

As is the case in every chapter of Daniel, the central theological theme in chapter 4 revolves around the sovereignty of God. The *way* in which God's sovereignty is displayed is through the humiliation of the most powerful earthly ruler. The *reason* for the display is explicitly given three times (vv. 17, 25, 32), "that the living may know that the Most High rules the kingdom of men and gives it to whom he will." Distinguishing between the *way* in which God's sovereignty is communicated, and the *reason* for this particular revelation is important for understanding and teaching this chapter. Generally speaking, God is sovereign over all earthly kingdoms. But we already know that from chapter 1. Chapter 4 deals more specifically with the reason why God chooses to display his sovereignty to Nebuchadnezzar, namely so that people will know that he is exclusively sovereign. He is in a completely different category than earthly kings. God gives the earthly kings their power; they are ultimately under his control. Once people know that God is exclusively sovereign (which is also implied by the name repeatedly used in this chapter, *Most High*) it is a small step to humble and hopeful worship.

Theology that emerges from the text is not simply meant to inform, but also to elicit a response. In this sense, Nebuchadnezzar's humble response and declaration teach us how to respond appropriately to our exclusively sovereign God; "Now I, Nebuchadnezzar, praise, exalt, and glorify the King of Heaven, for all his works are right, and his ways are just. And he is able to humble those who walk in pride" (4:37).

## FROM TEXTUAL WORK TO TEACHING

## The Big Idea

- *Exegetical Idea:* God reduced Nebuchadnezzar, the most powerful monarch on earth, to a raving madman who lives like an animal, so that Nebuchadnezzar would acknowledge the sovereignty of God.
- *Theological Focus:* God humbles the proud and powerful so that people will know that he alone is sovereign.
- *Preaching Idea:* God humbles the proud in order that we know him and exalt him as the Most High.

## Outline One: Following the Exegetical Flow

I. God graciously sends warnings about pride before he sends humiliating judgment. (4:4–27)

  A. God graciously warns Nebuchadnezzar of his pride through a dream and through Daniel.

   1. God's warning comes through a dream and its interpretation.

   2. God's warning comes through Daniel's encouragement.

  B. God graciously warns us in unexpected ways about our pride before he sends humiliating judgement.

   1. God's warnings can come to us through prayer and meditation on Scripture.

   2. God's warnings can come to us through conviction.

   3. God's warnings can come to us through trusted friends.

II. God graciously humbles us when we don't respond to the warnings he sends. (4:28–33)

   A. God graciously humbles Nebuchadnezzar by taking away everything he had.

   B. God will graciously take from us whatever he needs to in order to humble us.

III. God's goal in humbling us is to lead us to a right understanding of who he is, in order to open the door for a relationship with him. (4:1–3; 4:34–37)

   A. Nebuchadnezzar, through God's humbling judgment, comes to understand and acknowledge that God alone is the "Most High" and he rules over all.

      1. He acknowledges God's preeminence.

      2. He repents of his pride.

      3. He proclaims God's good works and ways.

   B. God's humbling judgment will lead us to acknowledge who he is, repent of our pride, and proclaim his goodness.

## Outline Two: Following a Theme

I. We can avoid the sin of pride by remembering who God is, what he has done, and what he will do.

   A. God is the "Most High," "Ever-Living One," whose rule is eternal and his works are just.

   B. God has humbled even the most powerful earthly rulers.

   C. God will ultimately humble all who are proud.

II. We can avoid the sin of pride by helping the poor and the marginalized.

   A. Using what we have to help others will keep us dependent on God.

   B. The more we depend on God the harder it is to be prideful.

## EXCURSUS: NEBUCHADNEZZAR'S THEOLOGY

Words of praise to God (the "Most High") both open and close chapter 4. Certainly, Nebuchadnezzar has grown in his relationship to God when he now praises him for what he has done in his own situation. He no longer thinks only of Daniel's God or the God of Shadrach, Meshach, and Abednego; now he directs his praise directly to God.

Does that mean that Nebuchadnezzar converted to the worship of Israel's God? The Old Greek version of Daniel 4 makes the king's allegiance to "the Most High" very explicit. He confessed that "from now on I will serve him" and spoke of the powerlessness of the gods of the nations to do the things that "the Most High" had done with him. From about the end of the second century BC, then, there was a tradition (Greek) that Nebuchadnezzar committed himself to the worship of Israel's God and denigrated other gods. Also, Nebuchadnezzar's behavior, even in the Aramaic text, contrasts starkly with that of Belshazzar in chapter 5.

Even so the Aramaic text at the end of chapter 4 is more ambiguous than the Greek. Nebuchadnezzar's praise for the God who brought these events upon him is one thing, but nowhere does he renounce other gods. He still thought in terms of many gods when he referred to "a spirit of holy gods" that enabled Daniel to give true interpretations of dreams.

On the one hand, Calvin thought that Nebuchadnezzar was "compelled to give glory to the Most High God" and "so acknowledged the God of Israel as to join inferior deities with him as allies and companions, just as all unbelievers, while admitting one supreme deity, imagine a multitude of others."[72] In his view the king did not "embrace the grace of God," making his humiliation "profitless."[73] On the other hand, the Apology of the Augsburg Confession ". . . takes the view that Nebuchadnezzar was brought to saving faith through the prophetic preaching of Daniel."[74] Wood thinks that "in view of his pagan background" what Nebuchadnezzar did say was "most remarkable" and indicated "a change of heart."[75]

Ultimately God alone judges someone's sincerity in their repentance and the salvific nature of their faith. A more important question than whether Nebuchadnezzar was genuinely converted concerns what the account meant for its Jewish readers and what it has continued to mean through the centuries since. To the Jews who were struggling in exile in various places

---

72. Calvin, *Commentaries on Daniel*, 1:247.
73. Calvin, *Commentaries on Daniel*, 1:304.
74. Steinmann, *Daniel*, 204.
75. Wood, *Daniel*, 127–28.

throughout the ancient Near East, it would have been amazing to read or hear about how their God was directing the king's heart "to wherever he pleases" (Prov 21:1). After all, this powerful monarch was reduced to a wild madman behaving like an animal. And just as suddenly as he had developed his insanity, his sanity was restored after a period determined by God. Even if a king were to become a tyrant such as Antiochus IV Epiphanes, God's people could be confident that he could not do anything outside of the limits that God placed on him. Would a monarch in his anger bring a fiery persecution on God's servants? They could still be confident that God would be present with them through the trial, even as he was present with Shadrach, Meshach, and Abednego in the furnace. Such reassurances of God to those who follow his ways and serve him are universal in scope, reaching beyond the Jews in exile across the ages to those everywhere who have come to know him through faith in his Son, Jesus Christ.

# Belshazzar Is Overthrown
## (Daniel 5:1–31 [6:1])

**Chapter 4 Review:** God communicates with the king through a frightening dream that Daniel interprets. The dream portends judgment from the "Most High" that is about to happen to the king, and Daniel advises him to renounce his sins by doing what is right and by showing mercy to the poor. Instead, Nebuchadnezzar boasts, and his pride activates the promised divine judgment. Only when he recognizes the absolute sovereignty of the "Most High," the "Ever-living One," does his sanity return and he is restored to his kingdom. In his newfound humility he is moved to "praise, exalt, and glorify the King of heaven."

**Chapter 5 Summary:** Chapter 5 introduces the prideful king Belshazzar, the last of the Chaldean monarchs. Belshazzar's pride leads him to disrespect God by worshiping idols and profanely drinking from the sacred vessels from the temple in Jerusalem. While Belshazzar is busy partying, a dire message of doom is mediated to him through the sudden appearance of mysterious writing on the wall of his palace. Daniel enters the scene, denounces Belshazzar's rebellious pride, and interprets the writing on the wall—Belshazzar's life and the Chaldean kingdom are both coming to an end.

**Chapter 6 Preview:** Chapter 5 leads into chapter 6 as Belshazzar is killed on the very night of his banquet, and God transfers kingdom authority from the Chaldean king to Darius the Mede. Darius is friendly towards Daniel and recognizes his wisdom and talent for administration. However, the officials in the new Medo-Persian regime reject Daniel's authority and use his faithfulness to God for their own selfish ends. In these conflicts Daniel continues to serve God faithfully, even when he knows his life is in danger. As a result, Darius the Mede exalts and praises Daniel's God as "the living God" who "endures forever," and the enemies of Daniel experience God's justice.

## THEOLOGICAL FOCUS OF CHAPTER 5

THE THEOLOGICAL FOCUS OF chapter 5 emerges through a series of contrasts. In addition to the more obvious contrasts between the earthly kings Nebuchadnezzar and Belshazzar, and the Chaldean wise men and Daniel, there is a subtle, but more important, contrast between God and Belshazzar. The contrast plays out through what we might call, a "humiliation hoe-down." Who will be ultimately humiliated at this royal party? The showdown begins when Belshazzar tries to humiliate God by bringing out the sacred vessels used in worship in the temple in Jerusalem. He is out to humiliate God by using these holy vessels profanely at his royal party. Immediately, God steps in and the result is utter humiliation for the Chaldean king. What emerges is a portrait of the God of creation who is ultimately in control of even the breaths we take.

I. *God will not be mocked and humiliated, even by kings. (5:1–12)*

II. *God sends warnings, but when they are not heeded, humiliation and judgment follow. (5:13–24)*

III. *God, who holds our very life-breath, will finally judge those who do not humbly honor him. (5:25–31[6:1])*

## BIG PICTURE (5:1–31 [6:1])

Several themes tie together chapters 4 and 5. Most significantly, Nebuchadnezzar and Belshazzar contrast with each other. Nebuchadnezzar had to go through a humiliating experience, but he learned from it to acknowledge the sovereignty of the Most High God. Daniel rebuked Belshazzar, however, because he failed to learn anything from Nebuchadnezzar's experience (5:17–28). Two lengthy back references to chapter 4 occur in chapter 5. The queen mother intruded on Belshazzar's party and reminded him of Nebuchadnezzar's experience with Daniel, a man whose wisdom and ability were so extraordinary that it must have come through divine aid (5:11–12). Then when Daniel was brought in to read and interpret the inscription that the mysterious hand had written on the palace wall, he rebuked the king. After recounting in some detail Nebuchadnezzar's fall from an exalted state to a lowly animal existence that eventually led him to recognize the sovereignty of the Most High God (5:18–21), Daniel told Belshazzar that he had failed to "humble" his "heart" (5:22). Instead, he arrogantly used the sacred vessels for his drinking party and praised worthless idols at the same time (5:23).

The motif of the temple vessels that had been taken from Jerusalem makes a connection between chapter 5 and chapter 1. Nebuchadnezzar had taken the vessels from the temple (1:2), and Belshazzar deliberately sent for them to use for his feast (5:2). In this way the king declared his and Babylon's sovereignty over Judah and its God. Such a direct challenge led to the incident of the inscription written on the wall.

In chapter 1 it was made clear that God had given Judah to Nebuchadnezzar (1:2); here in chapter 5 it will be made clear that God hands the Chaldean kingdom to Darius. The transfer of power also connects chapter 5 with chapter 2. Nebuchadnezzar, as the head of gold and representative of Babylonian power, had to give way to the "chest and arms of silver" that represented the kingdom of the Medes and the Persians. Belshazzar was the unfortunate representative of Babylon who would be held to account for the brazen idolatry (5:4). He is a stark reminder that any earthly kingdom is here for only a brief moment in time; only God's kingdom will last for eternity.

There is a sense in which chapter 5 has an abrupt feel to it. The first four chapters methodically work through highlights of Nebuchadnezzar's reign as it pertains to the Jews and their God. Chapter 5 abruptly covers the last night of the Chaldean kingdom. Some twenty years or more must have transpired between Nebuchadnezzar's restoration and Belshazzar's feast. This gap suggests that the book of Daniel deliberately focuses on the boundaries of the great Babylonian empire, beginning with the transfer of kingdom authority to Nebuchadnezzar and ending with Belshazzar's final night.

In addition to portraying a pattern of succeeding empires, the story of Babylon's decline represents another pattern chronicled in Daniel, an increasing wickedness and rebellion against God. While Nebuchadnezzar seems to move toward the God of Israel, Belshazzar, the last king of the empire, moves farther away from God. In chapter 7 the four beasts that rise from the sea gradually become fiercer and more bizarre until finally there arises the fourth beast that is "terrifying and dreadful and extremely powerful" (7:7). And even from that beast there come various *horns* until finally a *little one* appears on the scene and pulls down the other *horns*. It had human eyes and a mouth "speaking great things" (7:8). When the language transitions from Aramaic to Hebrew in chapter 8, Daniel sees a second vision. This time the vision moves from Medo-Persia to the Greek kingdom founded by Alexander, which itself divides and culminates in Antiochus

IV Epiphanes, a king who would attempt to resist God himself (8:23–25). Finally, even that king will be superseded by a king whose pride and defiance of God will know no bounds (11:36–45).

## TRANSLATION (DANIEL 5:1–31 [6:1])

1   Belshazzar[1] the king put on a great banquet for a thousand of his nobles, and he was drinking wine in the presence of the thousand.

2   Under the influence of the wine Belshazzar commanded to bring the gold and silver vessels that his father Nebuchadnezzar had taken from the temple that is in Jerusalem, so that the king, his nobles, his wives, and his concubines might drink from them.

3   Then they brought the golden vessels that had been taken from the temple, the house of God that is in Jerusalem, and the king, his nobles, his wives, and his concubines drank from them.

4   They drank the wine and praised the gods of gold and silver, bronze, iron, wood, and stone.

5   At that moment the fingers of a human hand appeared and began writing in front of the lampstand on the plaster of the wall of the king's palace. And the king was watching the part of the hand[2] that was writing.

6   Then the king—his face paled,[3] and his thoughts terrified him. The "knots of his loins were untied,"[4] and his knees knocked together.

7   The king cried aloud to bring in the conjurers,[5] the Chaldeans, and the diviners. The king said to the wise men of Babylon, "Any

---

1. The Babylonian form of the name is *Bēl-šarra-uṣur* ("Bel protect the king"). Two spellings occur in the book of Daniel, בֵּלְשַׁאצַּר (5:1, 2, 9, 22, 29) and בֵּלְאשַׁצַּר (5:30; 7:1; 8:1). When the *aleph* became silent some confusion resulted about where it should go in the spelling.

2. Aramaic פַּס יְדָה can mean "palm of the hand," but the palm would not be visible while the hand was writing. פַּס means a *part* or *share* in Egyptian Aramaic (*HALOT*), and "the part of the hand that wrote" in the KJV is hard to improve.

3. Lit., "his face changed on him."

4. There are several opinions about the meaning of the Aramaic here (וְקִטְרֵי חַרְצֵהּ מִשְׁתָּרַיִן). The translation is overly literal to highlight a pun according to which Daniel is able to "untie knots" (5:12, 16). See the Exposition.

5. 4QDan[a] adds חרטמיא (*soothsayer-priests*) to the list, a reading supported by

|   | man who can read this inscription and interpret it for me will be clothed with purple, and a gold chain will be placed around his neck. And he will have authority as the third highest ruler in the kingdom." |
|---|---|
| 8 | Then all the king's wise men came in, but they were not able to read the inscription or to make known the interpretation to the king. |
| 9 | Then Belshazzar the king became very troubled, and his face paled.[6] And his nobles were perplexed. |
| 10 | The queen mother—because of the words of[7] the king and his nobles—she entered the banqueting hall. The queen mother responded by saying: |

"O king, live forever! Don't let your thoughts trouble you. And your face shouldn't pale.[8]

|   |   |
|---|---|
| 11 | There is a man in your kingdom who has a spirit of the holy gods in him. In the days of your father illumination, insight, and wisdom like the wisdom of the gods were found in him. And king Nebuchadnezzar your father—your father the king—made him chief of the soothsayer-priests, conjurers, Chaldeans, and diviners. |
| 12 | (He did this) because an excellent spirit was found in him, in Daniel,[9] to whom the king gave the name Belteshazzar. (It was a spirit of) understanding and insight for interpreting[10] dreams, making known enigmas, and 'untying knots.'[11] |

---

the OG and the *Peshitta*. Th and the Vulgate support the MT.

6. Lit., "his face changed on him."

7. Aramaic מִלָּה, like Hebrew דָּבָר, can mean either a *word*, a *matter*, or a *thing*. The queen may have heard the confused and terrified voices of the king and the nobles, or she may have heard about all the things that were happening (NLT).

8. Lit., "and your face should not be changed."

9. The word order has been rearranged to make the sense clearer in the English (cf. NLT).

10. The MT has a participle, "one who interprets," but the structure of the sentence calls for an infinitive (*the interpreting of*). The infinitive of the simple pattern would have the same consonants but different vowels (מִפְשַׁר).

11. The MT has a participle, "one who unties," but the structure of the sentence calls for an infinitive (*untying knots*). The idiom "untying knots" means "solving difficult problems." See the Exposition.

| | |
|---|---|
| | Now have Daniel summoned, and he will make known the interpretation."¹² |
| 13 | Then Daniel was brought in before the king. The king said to Daniel, |
| | "(So) you're Daniel, who is from the exiles of Judah, whom my father the king brought from Judah? |
| 14 | Now I have heard about you that a divine spirit is in you, and illumination, insight, and extraordinary wisdom are found in you. |
| 15 | Now the wise men and the conjurers were brought before me that they might read this inscription in order to inform me of its interpretation, but they were not able to tell the interpretation of the matter. |
| 16 | And as for me, I have heard about you, that you are able to give interpretations and to 'untie knots.'¹³ Now if you are able to read the inscription and to make known to me its interpretation, you will be clothed with purple and a gold chain around your neck. And you will have authority as the third ruler in the kingdom." |
| 17 | Then Daniel answered and said before the king, |
| | "Keep your gifts and give your presents to someone else. But I will read the inscription for the king and make known to him the interpretation. |
| 18 | As for you,¹⁴ king—the Most High God gave royal authority, greatness, honor, and majesty to Nebuchadnezzar, your father. |
| 19 | And because of the greatness that he gave him all peoples, nations, and languages trembled and feared him. Whomever he wished he killed, and whomever he wished he let live. Whomever he wished he elevated, and whomever he wished he brought low. |

---

12. 4QDanᵃ and 4QDanᵇ appear to add, "and he will read this inscription" as well as interpret it (4QDanᵃ: וכתבא יקרא; 4QDanᵇ: [וכת]בא). It is difficult to tell whether a scribe accidentally omitted or inserted the extra words. The answer has little or no consequence for the meaning of the verse, and Daniel did in fact both read and interpret the inscription (v. 26).

13. See notes on vv. 6 and 12.

14. "You" of this verse should be connected with "but you" of v. 22. Before Daniel reads the inscription, he first lets Belshazzar know how he has failed to measure up to Nebuchadnezzar.

| | |
|---|---|
| 20 | Now when his heart became proud, and his spirit became arrogant so that he acted inappropriately, he was brought down from his royal throne, and his glory was removed from him. |
| 21 | He was driven away from people, and his mind was made like an animal's mind, and he lived with the wild donkeys. He was fed plants like oxen, and his body was drenched with the dew of heaven, until he realized that the Most High God is sovereign in the kingdom of men, and whomever he wishes he sets over it. |
| 22 | But you, his son, Belshazzar—you have not humbled your heart even though you knew all this; |
| 23 | and you have exalted yourself above the Lord of Heaven. And when the vessels of his house were brought before you, you and your nobles, your wives, and your concubines drank wine from them and praised gods of silver, gold, bronze, iron, wood, and stone—gods that do not see or hear or understand. Yet the God in whose power are your life-breath and all your ways you have not glorified. |
| 24 | Therefore the hand was sent from him and this inscription was inscribed. |
| 25 | So this is the inscription that was inscribed: |
| | *mĕnēʾ, mĕnēʾ, tĕqēl,* and[15] *parsîn.*[16] |
| 26 | Now this is the interpretation of the message. |
| | *Mĕnēʾ*: God has counted (the value of) your kingdom and has paid it out.[17] |
| 27 | *Tĕqēl*: you have been weighed in the balances and found deficient.[18] |

---

15. The reading UPHARSIN found in some versions (KJV, NASB) includes the element *and*, represented by the *U*, but that is a connector added by Daniel and not part of the inscription. Daniel didn't refer to it in his interpretation. The third word should be PARSIN.

16. Th reads μανη θεκελ φαρες (*manē thekel phares*). Similarly, the Vulgate: *mane thecel fares*. The Syriac agrees with the MT. The OG has a preface to the chapter in which it gives the inscription as *"mane phares thekel."* The shorter readings fit Daniel's interpretation better, but for that reason they are suspect. See the Exposition.

17. For "has paid it out" (הַשְׁלִמַהּ) see Wolters ("Riddle of the Scales in Daniel 5," 171–72) and *HALOT*.

18. The consonants of *tĕqēl* can also be formed into a verb meaning "you are too light" (Wolters, "Riddle of the Scales in Daniel 5," 173–74; Collins, *Daniel*, 252 [citing also the medieval Jewish commentator Rashi]).

| 28 | *Pĕrēs:*[19] your kingdom has been divided and given to the Medes and Persians.[20] |
|---|---|
| 29 | Then Belshazzar gave a command, and they clothed Daniel in purple and (placed) a gold chain around his neck. And they proclaimed about him that he was to have authority as the third ruler in the kingdom. |
| 30 | That very night Belshazzar the Chaldean king was killed. |
| 31 [6:1] | And Darius the Mede received the kingdom, when he was sixty-two years old.[21] |

## TEXTUAL OUTLINE (5:1–31[6:1])

I. Belshazzar Is Terrified by a Hand that Writes on the Wall. (5:1–9)

*[God will not be mocked, even by kings.]*

II. Daniel Meets with Belshazzar. (5:10–24)

*[God sends warnings, but when they are not heeded, humiliation and judgment follow.]*

III. Daniel Reads and Interprets the Writing. (5:25–31 [6:1])

*[God, who holds our very life-breath, will finally judge those who do not humbly honor him.]*

## EXPOSITION (5:1–31 [6:1])

Important things often happen at banquets. The book of Esther describes several banquets. King Ahasuerus (Xerxes) of Persia put on a lavish feast as a result of which he foolishly deposed Vashti, his queen (Esth 1). After Esther replaced Vashti as queen, Ahasuerus held another banquet in her honor, at which time he granted "remission of taxes" for the provinces of Persia (Esth 2:18). Then Esther prepared two intimate banquets for herself, the king, and Haman. At the first banquet she cleverly enticed Haman into thinking that she wanted to honor him at the second banquet (Esth 5), but instead the second banquet turned out to be his downfall (Esth 7).

---

19. *Pĕrēs* is the singular form of *parsîn*.
20. Or "to Media and Persia." The root consonants of *parsîn* can also mean "Persia."
21. English Bibles make the reference to Darius the Mede v. 31, whereas it is 6:1 in the Aramaic.

Centuries later Herod Antipas was forced by his own pride to have John the Baptist beheaded during another memorable banquet (Mark 6:21–28).

God himself also has great banquets at which there is either terrible judgment or abundant blessing. The prophet Jeremiah spoke of a banquet at which Babylon will drink the wine of God's wrath (Jer 51:39), and the figure of God's wrath as wine that makes the objects of his wrath drunk is also found elsewhere (Isa 51:21–23; Jer 25:15–29; Obad 16; Hab 2:15–16; cf. Rev 19:17–18). On a more hopeful note, eventually God will hold a great banquet on behalf of his people, a banquet that represents the reversal of the curse of death that has been on the earth ever since Adam and Eve sinned in the garden. Isaiah referred to it as a time when the Lord "will swallow up death forever" (Isa 25:8; cf. Isa 26:19).[22] The banquet that Belshazzar held was an occasion for God's judgment, both on Belshazzar, whose pride and arrogance exceeded that of his predecessors, and on the Babylonian kingdom as a whole, which was now ripe for carrying out God's verdict.

**The purpose of the account of Belshazzar in chapter 5 is not to convey historical information, though it is based on factual history; the purpose is to chronicle the passing of kingdom authority from one era to another in line with God's purposes.** First it passed from Jehoiakim of Judah to Nebuchadnezzar of Babylon. **While historically there were four kings between Nebuchadnezzar and Nabonidus, Daniel is interested only in the theological issue of God's rejection of the proud.** Nebuchadnezzar became too proud, and God judged him; but Nebuchadnezzar also came to his senses and was restored to his kingdom. Belshazzar's pride was not reversible; the glory of the Babylonian kingdom ended with him. And from him the new locus of kingdom authority became the Medo-Persian empire.

## Belshazzar Is Terrified by a Hand that Writes on the Wall. (5:1–9)

Theological Point: God will not be mocked, even by kings.

After ordering the sacred vessels to be used at the banquet, Belshazzar panics when mysterious writing appears on the wall. The part of the story that focuses on Belshazzar's actions has three movements. First, he issued an order that the vessels Nebuchadnezzar had taken from the temple in Jerusalem be brought for his guests to use in their revelry. And in that raucous atmosphere they also praised the Babylonian gods. That ushered in the second movement where a human hand suddenly appeared and wrote a

---

22. The NT refers to "the marriage supper of the Lamb" for all those who have been invited (Rev 19:9).

mysterious message on the wall. In the third movement we see Belshazzar's reaction to the supernatural phenomenon. His whole body virtually falls apart because of the fear the apparition stirred up in him, and in his panic he calls for diviners to come and read the writing and interpret it for him.

## *Belshazzar dishonors Daniel's God. (5:1–4)*

**5:1.** For the reader Belshazzar appears quite abruptly.[23] He is "the king," a term applied to him some twenty times in the chapter, and he has a thousand noblemen at the banquet that he prepared. Later the king will be described as a "son" or "successor" to Nebuchadnezzar (5:22), so one can assume that he is king of Babylon and not of some other country. The first time that Nebuchadnezzar appeared in the book he was called "the king of Babylon" (1:1). **Only later in the book will Belshazzar be given that full title (7:1), so why not here? Perhaps it is to enhance the contrast between the two kings.**[24] **Nebuchadnezzar was the great king who built Babylon and reigned for many years, while Belshazzar accomplished nothing more, according to the book of Daniel, than to throw an elaborate party on the very night of his death.** Like Nero, who famously fiddled while Rome burned, Belshazzar diverted his attention from the Persian threat to his country by a wild party.

Belshazzar's real father was Nabonidus, the fourth king of Babylon after Nebuchadnezzar.[25] Because Nabonidus was absent from Babylon for an extended period, Belshazzar took over the duties of running the kingdom while he was gone. Official documents of the time call him "the son of the king" but not "king."

For Daniel, though, it did not matter that in an "official" sense Nabonidus was the "king" while Belshazzar was merely "the son of the king" when Nabonidus was not actually in Babylon. Daniel himself did not even address Belshazzar with the proper greeting of "O king, live forever," but only gave him the title "king" obliquely (vv. 17, 18). The only person who did address Belshazzar with the standard formula was his mother (v. 10). The dating formulas by Belshazzar at 7:1 and 8:1 need not be granted official

---

23. From a historical perspective, though, the night of Belshazzar's banquet had to be more than twenty years after the death of Nebuchadnezzar; cf. the NLT, "Many years later King Belshazzar gave a great feast . . ."

24. Stefanic, "Thematic Links," 124.

25. See Table 0.2: The Neo-Babylonian Kings; also the Excursus: Daniel 5 and History.

status. For the purposes of the book, Daniel received these visions during the time when Belshazzar functioned as king.

**5:2–3. For the Jews in the time of Daniel, and even later, the temple vessels were extremely important.** Since they were returned to the Jews by Cyrus (Ezra 1:8–11), it was important for them to remain sacred until they could be placed into the second temple built in the days of Darius Hystaspes. **Belshazzar's actions were shocking; he was desecrating the one element of holiness that would link the two temples together.**[26]

There is some uncertainty about the significance of the wine at Belshazzar's party. The Aramaic word טְעֵם could mean either *taste, command,* or *influence*.[27] The Greek version known as Theodotion translated with *taste*, and many modern versions have followed this sense as well (KJV, NASB, ESV). The first verse, however, has already indicated that he "was drinking" (שְׁתָה) the wine, so only tasting the wine would not advance the action. Also, Belshazzar's lack of good judgment when he called for the temple vessels is consistent with what too much wine would have facilitated. **A further contrast with Nebuchadnezzar results when we think of the powerful monarch who issued commands as opposed to a pathetic individual who succumbs to the commanding power of too much wine.** "Under the influence of the wine" suits the context best.[28]

Even though too much wine was a factor in Belshazzar's decision to call for the temple vessels, one still wonders why he would do such a bizarre thing. Was he deliberately trying to show disrespect for the God of Israel? It was normal in ancient Mesopotamia for a king to take the gods (idols) of a conquered country to his own capital. Nebuchadnezzar did the equivalent of this; when he conquered Judea, he took various articles from the temple in Jerusalem since there was no image of the Lord for him to take. He treated these items as sacred, however, by putting them in a temple in Babylon (see on 1:2). **Belshazzar, by contrast, used them for a profane purpose, and additionally he used them while acknowledging various gods of his own in the banqueting hall. Daniel interpreted this act as Belshazzar's attempt to exalt himself over the Most High God (5:22–23).** Belshazzar knew that Nebuchadnezzar had conquered the Judeans, so it seems likely that he intended to show that he considered his own gods superior to the Judean God. Such an explanation accounts for the use of the sacred vessels, the simultaneous worship of Babylonian idols, and

---

26. Widder, *Daniel*, 110–11.
27. *HALOT* 5:1885–86.
28. Jerome, *Jerome's Commentary on Daniel*, 56.

**Daniel's condemnation of Belshazzar before he interpreted the writing on the wall.**

The king's wine here also echoes the royal wine that Daniel refused to drink. Daniel's refusal showed his loyalty to his God, while Belshazzar's action of drinking out of vessels sacred to that God indicated his prideful sense of superiority.

Nebuchadnezzar is called the "father" of Belshazzar for the first time in verse two and then five more times throughout the chapter (vv. 11 [3 times], 13, 18). Once Belshazzar is also called Nebuchadnezzar's "son" (v. 22). It is not clear exactly why this relationship is chosen from a historical standpoint. Perhaps Nebuchadnezzar was his grandfather, or perhaps the term "father" means "predecessor" and the term "son" means "successor." **Theologically the relationship illustrates even more the contrast between the two kings. Nebuchadnezzar was wise enough to realize the folly of his pride, but his son, who should have learned from his father, continued in his folly to the day he died.**

Not only the king, but also his nobles, his wives, and his concubines drank from the vessels of gold and silver. The exact status of the two categories of women mentioned is uncertain, but probably the שֵׁגְלָת (*wives*) had a higher status than the לְחֵנָת (*concubines*). These two terms most likely reference "two distinct categories of legitimate spouses that made up the royal harem."[29] The fact that the women attended indicates some special importance for the occasion. One suggestion is that it celebrated Belshazzar's installation as king or as coregent since Nabonidus was away with the army, an installation instigated either by Nabonidus or by Belshazzar himself.[30]

**5:4.** The ancient Babylonians thought that every aspect of life was under the control of the gods, so to worship them at a party would not be exceptional. And if the Persians were "at the gate," so to speak, the Babylonians could also have been praising the gods for previous victories in war and exhorting them to grant them victory over Persia.[31] Except for the "wood" and the "stone," the pattern of metals follows the same sequence as the metallic parts of Nebuchadnezzar's dream image of chapter 2, making another point of contact between the two kings.

---

29. Péter-Contesse and Ellington, *Handbook on the Book of Daniel*, 132.

30. Shea, "Nabonidus, Belshazzar," 140–43.

31. Lucas, "Daniel," 209. The Nabonidus Chronicle refers to various gods found in Babylonian cities that "entered Babylon" (Pritchard, *ANET*³, 306). Since a conqueror would take the gods of the vanquished to his own countries, the king of Babylon brought in these gods to protect them from the Persians (Beaulieu, *Reign of Nabonidus*, 223).

Nebuchadnezzar set up his own golden image for people to worship, but ultimately, he was forced to admit that the God of Shadrach, Meshach, and Abednego had the power to counter his command (3:28). Then he decreed that no one was to blaspheme this God (3:29). Belshazzar violated Nebuchadnezzar's decree and blasphemed the same God who had delivered the three young men.

*Daniel's God sends a message that shocks Belshazzar to the core. (5:5–7)*

**5:5.** At the very time that Belshazzar and his guests were drinking from the vessels and praising the idols, the king saw a strange event unfold. Nebuchadnezzar had received his messages from God through dreams that required Daniel's interpretation. Now there was a written message, but a message so cryptic that it also would require interpretation. **The images in a dream are only available for the interpreter to decipher when the dreamer tells them. Or in the case of Nebuchadnezzar's first dream, Daniel was enabled by God to recite even the dream itself. Writing is something that everyone can see, and it has a more permanent and settled feel to it. Daniel could warn Nebuchadnezzar to try to counteract, or at least delay, the effects of the dream about the great tree, but here was Belshazzar's fate and the fate of the Babylonian kingdom written on the palace wall and illuminated by a light so that all could see it.**

**5:6.** Nebuchadnezzar had been "troubled" (2:1), "astonished" (3:24), "frightened" (4:2), and "terrified" (4:2) by the things he had seen, but he never lost his composure publicly in such a complete manner as Belshazzar. First, all the color drained out of Belshazzar's face. **The term translated** *face* **here is** זִיו**, and it is also used of the** *splendor* **of Nebuchadnezzar's royal authority (4:36 [33]). It signifies** *brightness* **or** *luster,* **and applied to the face it refers to a bright or ruddy complexion that would indicate health. Not only did Belshazzar's bright face lose its color; his frightened reaction before the nobles also caused him to lose the splendor that a king should always display before his subjects.**

Next Belshazzar's "thoughts terrified him." Seeing the hand writing on the palace wall raised all sorts of alarming scenarios for him. The terror of the moment must have been visible in his eyes as the thousand nobles looked on. Of interest is that the only other place where we read about a face becoming pale in conjunction with terrifying thoughts is in the account of Daniel's first vision (7:28). Daniel himself had the same experience in reaction to his vision, but his reaction occurred in private and he "kept the matter" to himself (7:28). And according to the heading for the vision of chapter 7, Daniel had his vision "in the first year of Belshazzar king of Babylon," whereas Belshazzar's banquet occurred on the last day of his reign. **Daniel reacted to troubling prophecies about the future of the world, whereas Belshazzar had a near physical collapse thinking about what the sight he was viewing might portend for his own future.** As Steinmann puts it, "The difference [between Daniel's reaction and Belshazzar's] . . . is that Daniel knows the gracious God of Israel, whereas Belshazzar only knows God's wrath."[32]

What happened next to Belshazzar is not clear. The NASB gives a literal rendering of the Aramaic: "his hip joints loosened" (cf. KJV). That doesn't convey a concrete picture of what happened, and the ESV has "his limbs gave way."[33] The ensuing statement about his knees knocking together, though, might preclude that he had collapsed. Rashi (eleventh century Jewish commentator) thought of several belts or fasteners that loosened,[34] presumably meaning that his clothes opened or fell off and exposed the king.[35] More recently it has been proposed that the reference is to the sphincter muscles of the bladder and anus, causing the king to lose control of his bodily functions.[36] **With any of these explanations it was a very embarrassing situation for the king. The knocking together of the knees emphasizes the extreme physiological reactions that the king had to what he saw. It would be safe to say that God himself, through the device of such a shocking experience, humiliated Belshazzar in response to his defiant act.**[37]

5:7. Belshazzar did not issue an order for the wise men to come as Nebuchadnezzar had done (1:3; 2:2, 12; 3:2, 19, 29; 4:3). Instead, he screamed in panic for the interpreters to come, at the same time promising them a great reward for reading and interpreting the inscription. He had not yet regained his composure.

All three of the rewards relate to governing authority. The purple clothing signified royal authority or a high social status. Only the very rich could afford to acquire clothing colored by the purple dye used.[38] The gold

---

32. Steinmann, *Daniel*, 274.

33. Th reads similar to the NASB (καὶ οἱ σύνδεσμοι τῆς ὀσφύος αὐτοῦ διελύοντο, "and the joints of his loins were giving way" [NETS]), while the OG omits it.

34. Goldwurm, *Daniel*, 161.

35. Pace, *Daniel*, 167.

36. Wolters, "Untying the King's Knots," 117–20.

37. Such a scene of humiliation in the face of pride calls to mind Haman's humiliation before Mordecai (Esth 6).

38. Péter-Contesse and Ellington, *Handbook on the Book of Daniel*, 136. Cf. Jdg

chain for the neck compares to the one that the Pharaoh gave to Joseph (Gen 41:42), and it was a sign of respect and authority.[39]

The Aramaic term תַּלְתִּי has the literal meaning *third*, and it has been interpreted in various ways. Some think that it has lost the sense of *third* and now represents only some kind of official.[40] The Old Greek version has "authority over the third part of the kingdom." This conception of the office would support those who see in the term a *triumvir*, that is, three people of equal authority.[41] Others take it as the one who would rule as the third in authority over the kingdom (cf. ESV). This would comport well with Belshazzar as second in command after Nabonidus, leaving the third spot for the one to receive the reward. Daniel does receive this honor but from Darius the Mede after Belshazzar is killed (6:2 [3]).

*The wise men fail to read or interpret the writing. (5:8–9)*

As on previous occasions, the Babylonian wise men are unable to do what the king asks them to do. Once again, they failed to give an interpretation of the divine message the king had received.

**5:8.** The wise men of Babylon had their most difficult task when Nebuchadnezzar demanded that they tell him both his dream and its interpretation (2:5). Their next task was easier, because Nebuchadnezzar first told them the dream and then asked them to interpret it (4:7 [4]). **This final task should have been the easiest of all. They only needed to read the writing and then interpret it; they still failed. They couldn't even read the inscription, let alone interpret it. Their constant failure highlights Daniel's success, which of course was possible only because "God had given" to Daniel and his companions "understanding and comprehension in every kind of scribal skill and wisdom"** (1:17).

Various explanations have been given as to why the wise men failed. Perhaps they were unable to read a text without vowels in the absence of an appropriate context,[42] especially if the words were not divided from each other.[43] Or the text may have been coded somehow, reading backwards, from top to bottom, or following some type of coded alphabet.[44] Or perhaps

---

8:26; Esth 8:15; Prov 31:22; Song 7:5 [6]; Jer 10:9; Ezek 23:6; Mark 15:17; Acts 16:14.
   39. The term הַמְנִיכָה (*qere*) is a Persian loanword meaning a *necklace* (*HALOT*).
   40. Goldingay, *Daniel*, 101; Montgomery, *Book of Daniel*, 256.
   41. Wood, *Daniel*, 138.
   42. Goldingay, *Daniel*, 109.
   43. Wolters, "Riddle of the Scales in Daniel 5," 158.
   44. Goldwurm, *Daniel*, 163.

it was in an unusual script.[45] It is not impossible that these sages were afraid to read and interpret the writing. Since it bore a dire message for Belshazzar, they may have feared that the king might kill the messengers. **Whatever the reason, despite their years of training as specialists in divination and scribal skills, they were unable to read three simple words that Daniel easily recited and interpreted. And when Daniel did read and interpret it, he received the reward, showing that at least the king was convinced that Daniel had read it properly.**

5:9. The failure of the wise men to even read the inscription only added to Belshazzar's consternation. His physical manifestations of fear increased, leading to a sense of helplessness on the part of the nobles present at the banquet. Seemingly there was nothing to be done, at least not until the queen mother entered the banquet hall after hearing all the commotion.

## Daniel Meets with Belshazzar. (5:10–24)

Theological Point: God sends warnings; when they are not heeded, humiliation and judgment follow.

Belshazzar receives a double warning: first from his mother and then from Daniel.

### The Queen Mother advises Belshazzar to summon Daniel. (5:10–12)

The queen mother asserts that Daniel could interpret the writing and urges Belshazzar to summon him.

5:10. The Aramaic word מַלְכְּתָא means "the queen," but there is virtual unanimity among interpreters that she must have been the queen mother rather than Belshazzar's wife. Since she only appeared in response to the turmoil at the banquet, she was not part of the "wives and concubines" who were guests. It is unlikely that Belshazzar would have excluded his favorite wife from the banquet, and her tone when she spoke to the king contained sage words of advice. She was more like an adviser to the king than an intimate companion.[46] Also, she had thorough knowledge of the relationship

---

45. Keil, *Ezekiel, Daniel*, 185.

46. The queen mother played a significant role in ancient Israel (cf. 1 Kgs 1:11, 26; 14:21; 15:2, 13; 22:42, 52; 2 Kgs 8:26; 10:13; 11:1–3; 12:1 [2]; 14:2; 15:2, 33; 18:2; 21:1, 19; 22:1; 23:31, 36; 24:8, 12, 18). For her role in other areas of the ancient Near East see Montgomery, *Book of Daniel*, 258.

between Nebuchadnezzar and Daniel, being from an older generation than Belshazzar. As an older person who had considerably more wisdom than the king, she immediately brought a sense of calmness to the room.

The queen mother could not have been the famous mother of Nabonidus, Adadguppi, known through an inscription commissioned by Nabonidus.[47] She died in the ninth year of Nabonidus, some eight years before the events of Daniel 5.[48] Most likely the mother of Belshazzar was Nitocris, a daughter (or widow?) of Nebuchadnezzar who presumably married Nabonidus. Or the queen mother could have been some other daughter of Nebuchadnezzar that Nabonidus married.[49]

**5:11-12.** In the account of Nebuchadnezzar's first dream, Daniel needed Arioch to obtain an audience with the king (2:15). Daniel's amazing abilities on that occasion so impressed Nebuchadnezzar that he made him the head of all the wise men of Babylon (2:48). By the time the king had his second and more frightening dream, Daniel needed no introduction. Nebuchadnezzar had perfect confidence that Daniel would interpret his dream for him (4:9 [6]). **That the queen mother had to inform or remind Belshazzar about Daniel shows that Daniel had lost some prominence in the king's court. Belshazzar's failure to utilize the services of such a helpful adviser places him in the unenviable company of kings like Rehoboam, who rejected the wisdom of his older advisers (1 Kgs 12:1-19), and Jehoiakim, who thought he could avert the effects of Jeremiah's prophecies by burning them (Jer 36).**

The queen mother summarized Daniel's qualifications as a wise man, using language that was also found in Nebuchadnezzar's letter. Daniel had, according to her, "a spirit of the holy gods" and even "wisdom that was like the wisdom of gods." As she piled up synonyms in praise of Daniel's abilities, she also mentioned that he was one skilled at "solving difficult problems" (מְשָׁרֵא קִטְרִין). The expression is literally "untying knots," and it makes a literary connection to the physical reaction that Belshazzar had upon watching the hand that wrote on the wall: "The knots of his loins were untied" (5:6). Later the king also referred to Daniel's abilities "to untie knots" (5:16). It hardly seems likely that such an unusual expression could occur three times in the same story without some significance to it. It lends an element of humor as a *double*

---

47. It is published and discussed in Gadd, "Harran Inscriptions," 35-92; a translation may be found in Pritchard, *ANET*[3], 560-62. It is clear from this inscription that Nabonidus was not the biological son of Nebuchadnezzar. If Nebuchadnezzar was Belshazzar's grandfather, it would have to be through the wife of Nabonidus.

48. Grayson, *ABC*, 107.

49. See also the Exposition on 5:2.

*entendre*,[50] **but more than that it also pits the foolishness of men against the wisdom of God. Belshazzar defied Daniel's God, but Daniel, through the power of his God, had the ability to solve the mystery that had so humiliated the king.** After all, the queen mother twice ascribed Daniel's powers to the "gods." The astute reader, who knows that the book is placed within the broader canon of Scripture, realizes that it is not "gods" but "God" who gave Daniel this power. Nebuchadnezzar came to recognize that "the King of heaven" is able "to humble" the proud (4:37 [34]); now Belshazzar had been humbled by God, and what happened when Daniel came before Belshazzar would reveal whether the king was also humbled in spirit.

The queen mother further dignified Daniel by indicating that Nebuchadnezzar had assigned him the name Belteshazzar, and she expressed confidence in his ability: "have Daniel summoned, and he will make known the interpretation."

### *Daniel is summoned before Belshazzar. (5:13–24)*

Daniel rebukes Belshazzar for his failure to learn from Nebuchadnezzar's humiliation. The text does not state that Belshazzar summoned Daniel, and the reader is left with the impression that it was at the word of the queen mother that he was brought before the king. Daniel could have read the inscription and given its interpretation immediately. Instead, he first told the king why the hand had come to write the inscription, and that gave some context for its interpretation. That was ultimately why the wise men were unable to even read the inscription; they lacked the proper context for it and hence could make no sense of it. Daniel, though, understood fully why this had happened to the king, and he had to explain it to him first before the words could be read and interpreted.

**5:13–16.** Daniel was "brought in" even as the king had commanded to "bring in" the temple vessels (v. 2). The use of the same verb in both cases highlights the similarity. The vessels represented the God to whom they were dedicated, and Daniel spoke before the king as the one who represented God.

When the king met Daniel face to face, he managed to disrespect him in several ways. The first words he spoke to Daniel put him in a subservient light. He was one of the Judean exiles brought from Judah by "my father the king." By this time Daniel had been established as a wise man and was also in his late seventies or eighties. He deserved more respect than to be immediately reminded of his humble background. Contrast Belshazzar's

---

50. Wolters, "Untying the King's Knots," 121.

rudeness with Nebuchadnezzar's respectful address when Daniel came before him to interpret the dream about the tree: "Belteshazzar, chief of the soothsayer priests" (4:9 [6]).

As Belshazzar continued, he spoke only of what he had "heard" about Daniel, merely echoing the language of the queen mother. Nebuchadnezzar, like the queen mother, expressed confidence in Daniel's abilities: "I know that a spirit of the holy gods is in you and no mystery is too difficult for you." **After Belshazzar recounted the failure of his wise men, a group that no longer included Daniel, the king again spoke rather skeptically. Still, he could only mention what he had heard, and he had some doubt about Daniel's ability. "If you are able," he said condescendingly (v. 16). At least the king still held before Daniel the promise of the reward, but judging from Daniel's response the king's tone of voice may have been grudging or resentful. Reading between the lines, perhaps Belshazzar thought something like the following: "I am the king of Babylon, yet here I have to rely on the supposed abilities of this exile from a country that my father conquered."**

5:17. Without giving the customary respectful greeting, "O king, live forever," Daniel immediately refused the gifts and asserted that he would read and interpret the inscription anyway. This contrasted with how Daniel expressed such discomfort before giving Nebuchadnezzar the bad news. He had been silent for a brief period and had to be coaxed by Nebuchadnezzar to interpret the dream (4:19 [16]). **Belshazzar's lack of confidence in Daniel and his lowly opinion of him was met by Daniel's boldness and marked displeasure with the king. Belshazzar had acted the fool when he spoke to Daniel, and Daniel responded by sharply rebuking him.**

5:18-21. Before Daniel read and interpreted the inscription, he first called Belshazzar to task for not learning anything from the experience of his "father" Nebuchadnezzar. He began his recitation "you, king." Then he immediately switched to talking about Nebuchadnezzar and only resumed his address to Belshazzar directly at verse twenty-two. The unusual structure has the effect of adding further emphasis to the vexation that Daniel felt.

Since the Most High God had granted to Nebuchadnezzar all his power and authority, the implication is that no less would be true of Belshazzar. The God he had dared to challenge is the very God who had raised him up to his position of authority (cf. 2:21).

Nebuchadnezzar, Daniel said, had the power of life and death over anyone in his kingdom. His arbitrary decree to condemn to death all the wise men of Babylon illustrated that well enough (2:5, 12). Such seemingly unlimited power, however, led to excessive pride that God ultimately judged. Nebuchadnezzar, the most powerful person on earth, was nothing compared to the omnipotent God of heaven. Therefore, Nebuchadnezzar was driven away from people and made to live like an animal until he would realize that God's will is above that of any king.

5:22–24. Daniel confronted Belshazzar directly—the king had not learned anything from Nebuchadnezzar's experience. **Belshazzar was aware of what had happened; he couldn't plead ignorance. Despite his knowledge he committed the sacrilegious act against God, even praising his idols while drinking out of the holy vessels from God's temple in Jerusalem. Daniel was quick to take this opportunity to criticize the Babylonian idols. They were lifeless images with no power whatsoever. Daniel's God is different. He controlled not only the course of Belshazzar's life but even his very breath.** The term for "breath" is Aramaic but cognate with the Hebrew term used in Gen 2:7 of the "breath of life" breathed into Adam. Daniel likely alludes to this event with his reference to the God who has power over Belshazzar's *life-breath* (נְשָׁמָה). Such was the God that the king had refused to glorify; such was the God who had sent the hand to write on the wall.

## Daniel Reads and Interprets the Writing. (5:25–31)

Theological Point: God, who holds our very life-breath, will
finally judge those who do not humbly honor him.

Now that Daniel had laid the proper background for the interpretation he could at last turn to the words and their meaning. The Aramaic text merely tells us how Daniel *read* the inscription. It does not inform us about what Daniel actually *saw* on the wall. Although he may have seen simply the Aramaic consonants, other possibilities such as some kind of code or strange script have been proposed but are less likely (see on 5:8). The vowels that go with the letters were added by the Masoretes in the Middle Ages, but they added them on the basis of an ancient reading tradition. When Daniel read the letters he had to supply vowels with them in order to vocalize them as words, namely "*mene, mene, teqel, parsin.*"[51]

A curiosity often noted is that Daniel interpreted *mene* only once, and when he interpreted *parsin*, a plural word, he introduced his interpretation with *peres*, the singular. The normal procedure would have been to state the entire inscription first and then repeat each word in it with its

---

51. Possibly *upharsin*, but that would make no difference for the interpretation; the /u/ merely means *and*.

interpretation. In this case the way the interpretation is stated doesn't quite match the initial reading.

Some have thought that in the process of transmission the original text had been copied incorrectly. According to this view a scribe would have written *mene* twice by accident, and the plural of *peres* would have been introduced to match the two interpretations that Daniel gives to it. The reading that results, "*mene, teqel, peres*," has some textual support,[52] but it is difficult to understand how the changes found in the Masoretic Text could have been introduced when they made an apparent discrepancy between the reading and the interpretation. It is best, then, to interpret according to the received text (MT).[53]

Even though the English versions are mostly in close agreement with each other, scholars who have done detailed studies of the passage have presented different interpretations. The ESV is representative of most of the English versions:

> *Mene*: God has numbered the days of your kingdom and brought it to an end.
>
> *Tekel*: You have been weighed in the balance and found wanting.
>
> *Peres*: Your kingdom is divided and given to the Medes and Persians.

In this traditional interpretation each term has two ways in which it is explained or interpreted. The following table, based on the ESV, makes this plain:

| Table 5.1: The Traditional Interpretation of the Writing on the Wall | | |
|---|---|---|
| Aramaic Word | Interpretation | Assessment |
| מְנֵא *mene* | numbered | brought it to an end |
| תְּקֵל *teqel* | weighed | found wanting |
| פְּרֵס *peres* | divided | given to the Medes and Persians |

---

52. Th reads μανη θεκελ φαρες (*mane thekel phares*). Similarly, the Vulgate: *mane thecel fares*. The Syriac agrees with the MT. The OG has a preface to the chapter in which it gives the inscription as "*mane phares thekel*." The shorter readings fit Daniel's interpretation better, but for that reason they are suspect.

53. Steinmann (*Daniel*, 280-81) proposed that the duplication of *měnēʾ* and the pluralizing of *pěrēs* was due to Daniel's oral reading rather than to the inscription itself (cf. Wolters, "Riddle of the Scales in Daniel 5," 157).

The traditional interpretation raises several problems.[54] First, what exactly was "numbered?" The phrase "the days of" must be added. According to Wolters, "the verb *měnāh* by itself never has this specific meaning elsewhere [i.e., the *numbering* of days]; it simply means 'to count or reckon.'"[55] Second, while it is easy to connect "found wanting" and "Persians" with the terms *teqel* and *peres*, respectively, it is not so easy to relate "brought to an end" with *mene*. And third, the meaning "divided" (*peres*) requires some caution. Since it was the Medes and the Persians united under Cyrus who conquered Babylon, it does not mean that a separate Median kingdom and a separate Persian kingdom each received a share. Instead, *peres* should be taken in the sense of *destroyed* by cutting in two or *broken in pieces*.[56] That is, the Babylonian kingdom is broken up and given to the Medo-Persian empire.[57]

Wolters seems to have arrived at a correct view of the central figure of the riddle—a balance scale. The "scales" (מֹאזַנְיָא) are at the center of Daniel's interpretation. There is general agreement among current scholars that Daniel read each term as a unit of weight, something that would fit well with the theme of scales. That is:

*mene* = a mina (sixty shekels)

*teqel* = a shekel

*peres* = a half mina, or a half shekel; *parsîn* = two half minas/shekels

All the interpretations that Daniel gave can be tied into the image of the balance scales. *Mene* means that God has "counted" (מְנָה [*menah*]) the silver to be placed on the scales to counterbalance Belshazzar's kingdom.[58] Then he "paid it out" (הַשְׁלְמָה) to complete his part of the transaction, handing over the money to another nation.[59] *Teqel* means that on Belshazzar's side of the scale he has been "weighed" (תְּקִילְתָּה [*teqiltah*], "you have been weighed") but found "deficient" (חַסִּיר).[60] *Peres* signifies that Belshazzar's kingdom has been "divided" (פְּרִיסַת [*perisat*]) by God and given to the Medes and Persians.[61]

---

54. Much of our interpretation depends on, or has been stimulated by, Wolters ("Riddle of the Scales in Daniel 5").

55. Wolters, "Riddle of the Scales in Daniel 5," 165.

56. Keil, *Ezekiel, Daniel*, 189.

57. Wolters ("Riddle of the Scales in Daniel 5," 170) rendered *assessed*, but the lexical evidence for that meaning is weak.

58. Wolters, "Riddle of the Scales in Daniel 5," 165.

59. Wolters, "Riddle of the Scales in Daniel 5," 172; cf. Isa 43:3; Ezek 29:20.

60. An interpretation based on reading the consonants of *těqēl* as תְּקַל [*tiqqal*], "you are too light" (Wolters, "Riddle of the Scales in Daniel 5," 173–74).

61. פְּרַס [*paras*]; cf. Farsi, the Persian language.

Daniel interpreted the inscription in a manner, then, that both referred to God's assessment of Belshazzar's kingdom and to the outcome of that assessment. The shekel (*těqēl*) occurred in the middle because of the potential for the root to refer to "weighing" on scales, the main idea of what the inscription was all about.[62] The plural form of *pĕrēs* had also the two-fold interpretation of the destruction of the kingdom and the Persian enemy that would receive it. Cyrus had already conquered the Medes, so the forces of Media and Persia were under Persian control.

The duplication of *mĕnē'* in the inscription is the hardest to explain, and most commentators ignore it. Daniel did not refer to it directly. If it is accepted as part of the original text, the best idea is to interpret the first *mĕnē'* as a passive participle, "counted," followed by the three monetary terms. Thus Goldingay: "Counted at a mina, a shekel, and two halves."[63]

**5:29.** When Daniel refused the rewards, he showed his displeasure with the king. It's likely that he also wanted the guests at the party to know that his interpretation was not motivated by the desire for reward. Now that he had given the interpretation, and a disastrous interpretation for the king at that, he no longer needed to be concerned that his statements would be misinterpreted.[64] Also, Belshazzar had little choice but to give the rewards since he had promised them in front of so many guests.[65] One could wonder too if Daniel would have any choice but to receive the honors when the king commanded them.

**5:30.** Belshazzar is called "the Chaldean king," not the king of Babylon. The term "Chaldean" in the book of Daniel nearly always refers to a category of wise men who were summoned by the king to solve a mystery for him. Its use as an ethnic term, as here, is rare in Daniel. In 2:4 it refers to the language spoken by Chaldeans, and in 3:8 it might refer to Daniel's accusers as ethnically Chaldean. Then 9:1 refers to "Darius, the son of Ahasuerus, of the seed of the Medes, who was made king over the kingdom of the Chaldeans." Nebuchadnezzar is not called a Chaldean in the book of Daniel, making another contrast with Belshazzar, but in Ezra 5:12 he is called "Nebuchadnezzar, the king of Babylon, the Chaldean." Otherwise, the

---

62. The scale imagery may relate as well to the fact that Babylon fell "immediately after the annual morning rising of the constellation Libra." Libra is represented by scales, and Daniel's interpretation showed that "Libra is not a great god of heaven with power over the fate of nations, but rather an instrument in the hand of Daniel's God, who uses it to weigh the nations against His standards, and to punish them if they do not measure up" (Wolters, "Riddle of the Scales in Daniel 5," 177).

63. Goldingay, *Daniel*, 100, 102.

64. Wood, *Daniel*, 145.

65. Archer, "Daniel," 75.

ethnic designation is never applied to Nebuchadnezzar directly. When Nebuchadnezzar is first mentioned in Daniel he is "Nebuchadnezzar, the king of Babylon" (Dan 1:1). The title "king of Babylon" had a more universal sense. The Neo-Babylonian empire was essentially Chaldean, but Chaldeans were only a part of it. Belshazzar is called "the king of Babylon" in the introduction to Daniel's vision recorded in chapter 7, but at the end of his reign, even at the end of the kingdom of Babylon, he is merely "the Chaldean king." That may seem a trivial distinction, but for the ancients, titles and names were considered important. Nebuchadnezzar was the great king of Babylon, but Belshazzar was merely the Chaldean king. The kingdom of Babylon had truly come to an end.

The subtle hand of God in the narrative is seen in the reference to Belshazzar's fate. The passive קְטִיל (*he was killed*) combined with the immediate execution of God's will, as expressed through the writing on the wall, stresses the divine judgment.

5:31 [6:1]. The last two verses of the chapter depict the transfer of the kingdom authority from Belshazzar to Darius the Mede. Darius "received" (קַבֵּל) "the kingdom," which refers to the transfer of royal authority. Commentators are divided over the meaning of קַבֵּל (*received*). Does it mean that he took over or *acquired* the kingdom?[66] Or did he *receive* it from Cyrus[67] or from God?[68] **Any one of these three interpretations is possible, but the emphasis of the whole book of Daniel on God's sovereign control of kings and kingdoms tips the scale in favor of the last view mentioned. Darius received the kingdom according to the will of God, even as God had given Jerusalem into Nebuchadnezzar's power.**

In the Aramaic manuscript the notation about Darius receiving the kingdom follows a major section divider, and the verse is accordingly counted as 6:1. English translations, recognizing that the verse brings to a satisfactory conclusion the fate of Belshazzar, make it 5:31. The verse is transitional and effectively bridges the stories of Belshazzar and Darius the Mede.

## SHARPENING THE THEOLOGICAL FOCUS

With so much time passing between Nebuchadnezzar and Belshazzar, there must have been a long period of relative inactivity for Daniel. We know that under Belshazzar he didn't have any regular contact with the monarch. However, despite Daniel's absence from center stage in kingdom affairs, his

---

66. Goldingay, *Daniel*, 102.
67. Leupold, *Daniel*, 239; Whitcomb, *Daniel*, 39–40.
68. Steinmann, *Daniel*, 289; Seow, *Daniel*, 84.

reputation remained intact. The implication is that Daniel continued to be faithful to his God even though things were not going as well as they had under Nebuchadnezzar. It took the queen mother's detailed reminder for Belshazzar to send for Daniel. She was influenced by Daniel's reputation, and the same must have been true for many others. Daniel didn't become despondent or blame God when his circumstances changed; he continued to be faithful and to influence others around him. Even Belshazzar knew enough about Daniel to reward him when he read and interpreted the mysterious writing. For Belshazzar it was too late; his fate was certain. In his faithfulness Daniel fearlessly reprimanded the king and then delivered the message that came from the writing on the wall.

A prominent theme of the chapter, as evidenced by the intentional contrasting of Nebuchadnezzar and Belshazzar, spotlights God as one who humbles those who refuse to humble themselves. This whole episode is humiliating for Belshazzar. In a drunken condition he saw something that terrified him in front of all his invited guests. Then his own wise men, again in front of all the guests, were unable to unravel the mystery of the writing on the wall. Finally, his own mother had to come and give him the only sensible advice of the evening—summon Daniel. Daniel then put his finger on the problem—the king had exalted himself "above the Lord of Heaven" when he brought in the sacred vessels from the Jerusalem temple for common use at the party and proceeded to praise mere idols. His pride was his downfall. The Lord of Heaven himself had sent the message of doom. The story of Belshazzar makes a fitting illustration of Dan 2:21, "He removes kings and he raises up kings." The Lord removed Belshazzar and raised up Darius the Mede.

Another prominent theme in the chapter revolves around the temple vessels. These items were considered sacred even by Nebuchadnezzar, who placed them "in the treasury of his god" (Dan 1:2), yet Belshazzar brought them out for common use at a party that included excessive drinking and idolatrous rites. The vessels were set apart because of their use in the worship of God, but the king truly offended God by actions that struck at his holiness. In the ancient Hebrew culture, distinctions between clean and unclean or sacred and profane were a crucial part of everyday life. And the worship of God could not be mixed in any way with the worship of idols. For Belshazzar to do what he did with the vessels violated the boundary between sacred and profane so completely that God had to humble this proud king. His kingdom could endure no longer.

The idolatry performed with the temple vessels introduces the theme of God as Creator, the first time in Daniel that this theme arises. Belshazzar praised gods of mere human craftsmanship but refused to glorify "the God in whose power are your life-breath and all your ways" (5:23). This was a perfect example of Paul's statement that people have "exchanged the glory of the incorruptible God for an image in the form of corruptible mankind, of birds, four-footed animals, and crawling creatures" (Rom 1:23, NASB).

This theme of God as Creator sets the stage for the future, as forecast in chapters 7 to 12. The Creator has absolute control over everything—all the kingdoms of the world, and he even determines the life and death of individuals. In short, he is sovereign over all creation and all life therein. Nebuchadnezzar and Darius the Mede acknowledged that sovereignty, but Belshazzar refused. And in so doing he crossed a line that meant he must suffer God's judgment, a fate also decreed for all the proud rulers described in Daniel 7—12.

Daniel noted in his prayer that God's name should "be blessed forever and ever" (2:20), a thought that was reinforced by Nebuchadnezzar (4:34 [31]) and Darius the Mede (6:26 [27]). Blessing God's name implies worship, and true worship must always maintain God's holiness. He holds accountable those who would treat him commonly or with contempt. While believers today have direct access to God's presence through the work of Jesus Christ on the cross, holiness through faithful trust in Christ is still required (Heb 10:19–25). And God still holds accountable those who treat as common "the blood of the covenant by which they were sanctified" (Heb 10:29 NRSV).

## THE FOCUS OF DANIEL 5 FOR PREACHING AND TEACHING

By referring to God as the one "in whose power are your life-breath and all your ways," Daniel is referring to God as the sovereign Creator. This stands in contrast to the lifeless gods that Belshazzar worshiped, "gods of silver and gold, of bronze, iron, wood and stone." That God would be referenced, for the first time in Daniel, as the sovereign Creator here in chapter 5 is of great significance. Up to this point in the story, God has been proving himself sovereign over against a particular king, Nebuchadnezzar. Here in chapter 5, the point is made that God is not merely sovereign over a particular king. As Creator of all, he is sovereign over the transition of one kingdom to another. The writing on the wall specifically makes the point that it's not just Belshazzar that will come to an end; his *kingdom* will end (vv. 26 and 28). As Creator, God is the author of history. Literally, the point is made as well. Belshazzar suddenly appears, as if out of nowhere, to begin the chapter (v. 1), and just as suddenly, he disappears. "That very night Belshazzar the

Chaldean king was killed. And Darius the Mede received *the kingdom...*" (vv. 30–31).

That God is the sovereign Creator has implications for our personal lives as well, not only for kingdoms. As the Creator, he is the author of life—each and every individual life. Because of this, each and every individual is accountable to God. Whether we are a king or a pauper, an executive or an assistant, a parent or a child, we owe everything to God—our heartbeat, our breath, our abilities and our successes are all ultimately under God's control.

## FROM TEXTUAL WORK TO TEACHING

### The Big Idea

- *Exegetical Idea:* God, the sovereign Creator, judges Belshazzar by handing Babylon over to Darius the Mede because, unlike Nebuchadnezzar, he does not honor God.
- *Theological Focus:* God, the creator and sustainer of life, will judge those who do not honor him.
- *Preaching Idea:* Take heart, what the author of life writes will come to pass.

### Outline One: Following the Exegetical Flow

I. God will not be mocked, even by kings. (5:1–9)

  A. Belshazzar tries to humiliate God by using temple vessels profanely at a party.

  B. God responds to Belshazzar with writing on the wall.

  C. When we mock God, we can expect a response from God.

  1. Examples of how we mock God.

  2. Examples of how God may respond to being mocked.

II. God sends warnings, but when they are not heeded, humiliation and judgment follow. (5:10–23)

  A. Belshazzar failed to learn from the warning God sent through the life of Nebuchadnezzar.

B. God warns us through the judgments that fall on others.

III. God, who holds our very life-breath, will finally judge those who lift their hearts against God and do not humbly honor him. (5:24–31)

   A. God judges Belshazzar by taking his kingdom and his life.

   B. God's judgment will come if we do not humbly honor him.

## Outline Two: Following a Theme

I. The contrast between Nebuchadnezzar and Belshazzar highlights the contrast between humbly responding to God and proudly responding to God.

   A. Nebuchadnezzar responded to God humbly and was restored; Belshazzar responded pridefully and was removed from the throne and killed.

   B. Nebuchadnezzar respects and looks to God's servant, Daniel; Belshazzar treats Daniel with condescension.

   C. Nebuchadnezzar led people to worship God; Belshazzar led people to dishonor God and to worship idols through the profane use of the temple vessels.

   D. Do our lives and leadership lead people to, or away from, God?

II. The contrast between Daniel and the Chaldean wise men highlights the superiority of God's wisdom.

   A. The Chaldean wise men, who looked to idols, had no clue as to what was happening.

   B. Daniel, who looked to God, knew exactly what was happening.

   C. Are we looking to God or to idols to discern what is really happening?

III. The contrast between the earthly king, Belshazzar, and the Most High God reveals who is ultimately worthy of honor.

   A. Belshazzar's kingdom and life end in death.

   B. God is ultimately in control, even over life and death.

## EXCURSUS: HISTORICAL ISSUES IN DANIEL 4 AND 5

Some problematic elements occur in Daniel 5 concerning Babylonian history (see Table 0.2). From contemporary and other historical sources it is known that Nebuchadnezzar's son Evil-Merodach reigned for two years after his father's death in 562 BC.[69] Neriglissar came to the throne next and reigned until 556 BC.[70] He was followed by his son Labashi-Marduk, who was assassinated after only a few months in a conspiracy that included Nabonidus and his son Belshazzar.[71] In the third or fourth year of his reign Nabonidus left for a stay of ten years in Arabia and entrusted the kingdom to Belshazzar. Upon his return to Babylon, he resumed the duties of king and reigned another few years until 539 BC when Cyrus of Persia conquered Babylon.[72] Why, then, was Belshazzar called the "king" when the last king of Babylon was Nabonidus? And why was Nebuchadnezzar referred to as Belshazzar's "father" when Nabonidus was his biological father?

Many scholars have assumed that the book of Daniel got the wrong name in chapters 4 and 5. Instead of Nebuchadnezzar, it was Nabonidus who abandoned Babylon for a period of time (Dan 4) and who was literally the father of Belshazzar (Dan 5). The theory is that a legend about Nabonidus was later transferred to Nebuchadnezzar, since he was the more well-known figure.[73]

A key component in defending the accuracy of the book of Daniel occurs here in chapter 5. It is quite amazing that Daniel's book is aware of the figure of Belshazzar at all. None of the ancient extra-biblical sources reported anything about Belshazzar—not even his name. Outside of the Bible we know about him only through the contemporary cuneiform tablets which were not deciphered until the late nineteenth century.[74] The only exception is sources that had access to the book of Daniel. Herodotus, the Greek historian of the fifth century BC, spoke of two kings named Nabonidus, one the son of the other. Thus, he knew of Belshazzar but not by name. Berossus, a contemporary of Alexander the Great and a Babylonian priest

---

69. Also known as Amel-Marduk, his name means "man of Marduk." He is mentioned twice in the Bible in parallel passages (2 Kgs 25:27; Jer 52:31).

70. Possibly Neriglissar is the Nergal-Sharezer of Jer 39:3 and 13; he was not the king at that time but a Babylonian official.

71. Beaulieu, *Reign of Nabonidus*, 95–98.

72. Beaulieu bases this on detailed analysis of documents contemporary with or shortly after Nabonidus (*Reign of Nabonidus*, 149–60).

73. Hartman and Di Lella, *Book of Daniel*, 178–79, 186; Beaulieu, "Nabonidus and the Neo-Babylonian Empire," 978–79.

74. Dougherty, *Nabonidus and Belshazzar*.

who wrote in Greek, did not mention Belshazzar. Josephus must have obtained his information about Belshazzar from the book of Daniel, because he noted that after "Labosordachos" (Labashi-Marduk) died, "Baltasarēs, who was called Naboandēlos by the Babylonians," took the throne.[75] That is, Josephus assumed that the Belshazzar of the book of Daniel was the same as Nabonidus of the other sources that he consulted. Hippolytus (third century) in his commentary on Daniel thought that Belshazzar was the brother of Evil-Merodach.[76] Jerome (late fourth and early fifth centuries) thought that Belshazzar was the biological son of Labashi-Marduk.[77] Keil, who commented on Daniel prior to the modern decipherment of the cuneiform sources, was clearly confused about how to fit Belshazzar into Babylonian history. After much convoluted discussion he finally identified him with Evil-Merodach.[78] By way of contrast, the modern reading of the cuneiform tablets confirmed that there was an individual named Belshazzar who in some sense was ruling in Babylon while his father, Nabonidus, was in Arabia. So for nearly two thousand and five hundred years the book of Daniel recorded accurate history that no one else got right.

The Greek historian Xenophon (fourth century BC) knew of a tradition that the king of Babylon was killed when the city was captured,[79] while Berossus indicated that Nabonidus was captured at Borsippa and exiled to Carmania by Cyrus.[80] It is possible to reconcile these two accounts if we assume that the "king of Babylon" mentioned by Xenophon was none other than Belshazzar. "Xenophon would agree on this point with the Book of Daniel."[81] These two significant points of agreement between the book of Daniel and the ancient cuneiform and historical sources ought to give one pause before attributing historical errors to Daniel's book.

From cuneiform sources we also know that Nabonidus left Babylon to fight against the Persians, who invaded from the north. According to the Nabonidus Chronicle, when Sippar fell, Nabonidus fled and did not get back to Babylon until after it fell to Cyrus.[82] Although there is no direct extra-biblical evidence, it is likely that Belshazzar was entrusted with the

---

75. Josephus, *A.J.*, 10:231.
76. "Hippolytus," 147.
77. Jerome, *Commentary on Daniel*, 55.
78. Keil, *Ezekiel, Daniel*, 162–76.
79. Xenophon, *Cyropaedia*, 7:5:29–30 (Henderson LCL).
80. Burstein, *Babyloniaca of Berussus*, 28.
81. Beaulieu, *Reign of Nabonidus*, 231.
82. Grayson, *ABC*, 7:13–16.

affairs of the kingdom while Nabonidus fought with the Persians. That would explain why Belshazzar is so often called *king* in Daniel 5.[83]

A document from the Qumran scrolls known as *The Prayer of Nabonidus* (*PN*) further complicates discussion about the historicity of Daniel 5. The text is fragmentary, but enough of the writing remains to reconstruct the basic details of the story. Nabonidus, writing in the first person, says that he suffered from a bad skin disease that God decreed for him. But God forgave his sins and healed him. For seven years, Nabonidus claimed, he had his skin disease while he was worshiping his gods of silver, gold, [bronze, iron], wood, stone, and clay.[84] A Jewish diviner then urged him to give in writing praise and honor to "the name of [the Most High G]od."

Many scholars have reasoned that the *PN* is an earlier version of an alleged legend regarding the madness of Nebuchadnezzar (Dan 4). They point out similarities with the account of Nebuchadnezzar's affliction as well as with Daniel's dealings with Belshazzar.[85] The starting assumption for those scholars who argue that the *PN* served as a source for Daniel 4 is that the account of Nebuchadnezzar's troubles is only a legendary tale.

Exactly how similar or different are Daniel 5 and *PN*? There are some important differences. First, the kings were different: Nebuchadnezzar and Belshazzar in Daniel and Nabonidus in *PN*. Second, the maladies are different: Nebuchadnezzar's apparent insanity or demonic oppression and Nabonidus's skin ailment. Third, Daniel warned Nebuchadnezzar *before* God judged him, whereas the Jewish diviner told Nabonidus to give God glory *after* God had healed him. Fourth, Nabonidus confessed his worship of false gods for seven years, while Nebuchadnezzar's pride led to his humiliation before God restored him. The major similarities include the seven periods of time (Daniel) or seven years (*PN*), the decree of God against a sinful Babylonian king, and a declaration of praise to God after the healing or restoration.

There are further connections. Nabonidus was "struck by the decree of G[o]d," whereas in Nebuchadnezzar's dream the "decree" about him was by the "determination of holy watchers" (Dan 4:17 [14]). Nabonidus professed to worshiping "gods of silver and gold, [bronze, iron], wood, stone, clay." These idols were the same gods that Belshazzar worshiped at his banquet (Dan 5:4).[86] A Jewish "diviner" either "forgave" Nabonidus's sin or suggested to him that he should write a decree praising the God who forgave

---

83. Shea, "Nabonidus, Belshazzar," 141–42.
84. Gaps due to damage are shown in square brackets.
85. VanderKam, *Dead Sea Scrolls Today*, 177–78.
86. Idols made of *clay* are not mentioned in Daniel 5.

his sin. The term for "diviner" in Daniel (2:27; 4:7 [4]; 5:7) refers to a category of Nebuchadnezzar's or Belshazzar's wise men who could not solve the mystery of the respective king. Belshazzar's mother encouraged him to consult Daniel, whom "Nebuchadnezzar your father appointed chief of the magicians, conjurers, Chaldeans, and diviners" (Dan 5:11). Otherwise, Daniel is never called a "diviner."

Nabonidus was the biological father of Belshazzar, but the Queen Mother called Nebuchadnezzar Belshazzar's father. The consensus of the medieval period was that Belshazzar was Evil-Merodach's son, based on Jer 27:7.[87] In the absence of additional information that was a reasonable guess, but the evidence of texts in Babylonian cuneiform that were contemporary with Belshazzar and Nabonidus confirms their relationship. If one interprets Jer 27:7 literally, then it could refer to EvilMerodach, the son of Nebuchadnezzar, and to Belshazzar if he was in fact the grandson of Nebuchadnezzar.[88]

Dougherty reasoned that a statement in Herodotus showed that Nabonidus was married to Nitocris, a daughter of Nebuchadnezzar by an Egyptian princess, and that Belshazzar was therefore the grandson of Nebuchadnezzar.[89] As Aramaic בַּר can mean *grandson* as well as *son*, a literal meaning can be given to Belshazzar's relationship to Nebuchadnezzar as his grandson. Likewise, אַב (father) sometimes means *grandfather* or *ancestor*. Some have questioned the accuracy of Herodotus in the matter and opt for a second explanation, namely that אַב means *predecessor* and בַּר means *successor*.[90] That the queen mother referred to Belshazzar's "father" three times (v. 11) makes the explanation that Belshazzar was Nebuchadnezzar's grandson more likely. There is no clear extra-biblical evidence, however, to support that relationship.

The name Nabonidus does not occur anywhere in the Bible or related writings, and even ancient historians such as Herodotus and Xenophon gave confusing information about Nabonidus. Also, they knew nothing of Belshazzar. With so little known about Nabonidus and Belshazzar, why is so much attention paid to them in the book of Daniel and in the *PN*?

For Daniel, the Babylonian kingdom had a significant part in the scheme of four world powers that would rule until the everlasting kingdom of God overtook them. Belshazzar's presence at the final banquet was significant for the encounter that Daniel had with him. Since Nabonidus was

---

87. Goldwurm, *Daniel*, 156; cf. Jerome, *Commentary on Daniel*, 55.
88. Feinberg, "Jeremiah," 544; cf. Lundbom, *Jeremiah 21–36*, 316.
89. Dougherty, *Nabonidus and Belshazzar*, 39–66.
90. Steinmann, *Daniel*, 261–63.

off fighting the Persians, Belshazzar represented the last sitting monarch of the Babylonian kingdom.

Possibly there is an Idumean/Nabatean background to the *PN*. It is probable that Nabonidus destroyed the kingdom of Edom in the sixth century BC and replaced the king with a Babylonian governor.[91] Traditions of this king who decimated Edom even as Nebuchadnezzar decimated Judah could have survived among the Idumeans or Nabateans. The assimilation to elements from the book of Daniel could then have occurred among the Jewish population in Arabia and Edom at that time. Complicating the issue is that in the *PN*, Tema in Arabia is spelled as *Teman*, the location of a region in the south of Edom. Steinmann gives another view of the relationship between Daniel 4 and *PN*. He sees the *PN* as composed to supplement the historical gap between Nebuchadnezzar and Belshazzar, with the *PN* drawing on several chapters of Daniel but especially chapters 4 and 5.[92]

In conclusion, there is a relationship between the *Prayer of Nabonidus* and Daniel's account of Nebuchadnezzar and Belshazzar, but that relationship went from Daniel to the *PN*. Daniel's account is older by anyone's dating of the book, and it sticks more closely to images of illness found in the Ancient Near East. Viewing the *Prayer* as more ancient than Daniel entails a questionable assumption of the transfer of legendary characteristics of a lesser-known figure to a more well-known figure. And that assumption does not account for the differences between the *PN* and Daniel 4.

---

91. Bartlett, "Edom," 2:293.

92. Steinmann, *Daniel*, 227; Steinmann (*Daniel*, 215–28) has an extended discussion of *PN*, including his own translation from the Aramaic.

# Daniel in the Lion's Den
(Daniel 6:1–28 [6:2–29])

**Chapter 5 Review**: Chapter 5 introduces the prideful king Belshazzar, the last of the Chaldean monarchs. Belshazzar's pride leads him to disrespect God by worshiping idols and profanely drinking from the sacred Jerusalem temple vessels. While Belshazzar is busy partying, a dire message of doom is mediated to him through the sudden appearance of a mysterious writing on the wall of his palace. Daniel enters the scene, denounces Belshazzar's rebellious pride and interprets the writing on the wall; Belshazzar's life and the Chaldean kingdom both come to an abrupt end.

**Chapter 6 Summary**: Chapter 5 leads into 6 as God transfers kingdom authority from the Chaldean king, Belshazzar, to Darius the Mede. Darius has a friendly attitude towards Daniel and recognizes his wisdom and talent for kingdom administration. However, the officials in the new Medo-Persian regime oppose Daniel and try to use his faithfulness to God to eliminate him. In these conflicts Daniel continues to serve God faithfully, even when he knows his life is on the line. As a result of Daniel's faithfulness and God's deliverance, Darius the Mede exalts and praises Daniel's God as "the living God" who "endures forever," and the enemies of Daniel experience God's retributive justice.

**Chapter 7 Preview**: Chapter 7 marks a major genre shift in Daniel, from historical narrative to apocalyptic revelation. The first six chapters assure God's people that God *was* in control of all that had transpired from the fall of Jerusalem to the fall of Babylon. The next six chapters provide assurance that God *is* in control of all that will happen in the future. Chapter 7 sets the stage for the rest of the book by specifically highlighting God's sovereignty over history, portraying him as Lord over time. The nations come and go, but the Ancient of Days has determined when they come and when they go. And all earthly kingdoms will end at the appointed time of the inauguration of God's everlasting kingdom.

## THEOLOGICAL FOCUS OF CHAPTER 6

CHAPTER 6 FOCUSES ON Daniel's conflict with officials in the new Medo-Persian regime. These conflicts set up a battle, not so much between Daniel and his enemies, though Daniel is certainly involved, but between Daniel's God and Daniel's enemies. It appears as though these enemies have the upper hand when Daniel falls into their trap. However, as the story comes to a climactic close, it becomes clear that God (and Daniel) will be the victor. The narrator deftly makes the theological points of the story through the words of another foreign king, this time Darius the Mede, who proclaims Daniel's God as "the living God" who "endures forever" and Daniel as the faithful servant of God "whom [he] serve[s] *constantly*" (6:16, 20). From these two theological points emerges a theological thrust for the teaching of chapter 6: God exalts over their enemies those who are faithful to him.

   I. *God's faithful servants can expect to face intense opposition when they are successful. (6:1–15 [2–16])*

   II. *God exalts over their enemies those who remain faithful to him. (6:16–24 [17–25])*

   III. *When others observe the faithfulness of God's people, it encourages them to praise and glorify God. (6:25–27 [26–28])*

## BIG PICTURE (6:1–28 [6:2–29])

As elsewhere in Daniel's book, much of the artistry of the writing centers around repetition of key terms, or at least of their roots put into various forms. This also means that different meanings of the forms are brought out in such a way that it is difficult to discern in translation.[1] The first of these roots to occur in chapter 6 is קום, with a basic sense of *to arise* or *to get up*. In the causative form (*Haphel*) it means *to appoint* or *to establish*. A noun

---

1. See Goldingay, *Daniel*, 125.

derived from the same root means an *ordinance*, and a related adjective has the sense *enduring*. Its distribution in chapter 6 is as follows:

| 6:2 (3)   | Darius *appointed* one hundred and twenty satraps. |
|-----------|----------------------------------------------------|
| 6:3 (4)   | Darius desired to *appoint* Daniel over the whole kingdom. |
| 6:7 (8)   | The officials asked Darius to *establish* an ordinance. |
| 6:8 (9)   | The officials asked Darius to *establish* a prohibition. |
| 6:15 (16) | An ordinance that the king *establishes* cannot be changed. |
| 6:19 (20) | The king *arose* at the break of dawn. |
| 6:26 (27) | God *endures* forever. |

From this distribution it is evident that the text stresses that the actions of the king may appear permanent, but they are not. The king's *appointees*, except Daniel, were punished with death, and his supposedly unchangeable *ordinance* was changed by God. And God in turn lives and *endures* forever.

Then there is the root בעה (*to seek, ask, petition*). It forms the basis for the test of Daniel's faith.

| 6:4 (5)   | The officials *sought* to find a pretext against Daniel. |
|-----------|----------------------------------------------------------|
| 6:7 (8)   | Anyone who would *ask a petition* of any god or man . . . . |
| 6:11 (12) | Daniel was *petitioning* his God. |
| 6:12 (13) | Anyone who would *petition* any god or man . . . . |
| 6:13 (14) | Daniel *asks* his *petition* three times a day. |

Because of the king's decree, put in place at the prodding of the jealous court officials, *prayer* or *petition* was forbidden. Yet Daniel continued to *pray* and to *petition* God. That was the religious pretext that the officials were *seeking*. God honored Daniel's faithfulness in *prayer* by delivering him from the lions.

Another word play is the contrast made between the *law* (דָּת) of God and the "*law* of the Medes and Persians." When the administrators and satraps sought a pretext against Daniel, they realized it would have to be with regard to "the *law* of his God" (6:5 [6]). When they proceeded to set up a situation that would require Daniel to break that law, they had to make it airtight. The king himself could not change their *law*, but God did in fact change it by rescuing Daniel (6:27 [28]). God's rule is greater than any earthly rule.

Additionally, the term for *find* (root שכח) occurs eight times in the chapter, making it another key motif. The verb also serves as a link between chapters 5 and 6 (see 5:11, 12, 14, 27).

# DANIEL IN THE LION'S DEN

| 6:4 (5) | The officials sought to *find* a pretext but couldn't find one. |
|---|---|
| 6:4 (5) | No negligence or corruption was *found* in Daniel. |
| 6:5 (6) | They wouldn't *find* any pretext . . . unless they *found* . . . . |
| 6:11 (12) | They *found* Daniel . . . . |
| 6:22 (23) | Daniel was *found* innocent. |
| 6:23 (24) | Daniel was *found* free of harm. |

The officials *found* what they wanted, a pretext by which to get rid of Daniel. God, however, *found* Daniel to be innocent and allowed no harm from the lions to *be found* on him. Thus, in the end the officials were thwarted by what they *found*. Daniel's faithfulness to his God was *found* to be more significant than any pretext they might have *found*.

Finally, the term *harm* (root חבל) plays a prominent role near the end of the account.

| 6:22 (23) | The lions did not *harm* Daniel. |
|---|---|
| 6:22 (23) | Daniel did no *harm* to the king. |
| 6:23 (24) | Daniel was found free of *harm*. |
| 6:26 (27) | God's kingdom will never *be destroyed* [lit., *be harmed*]. |

The lions quickly crushed Daniel's accusers and their families but spared Daniel from any *harm*. This was because in his faithful service to God Daniel had not *harmed* the king in any way, and consequently God would not allow any *harm* to come to him. Since God's kingdom can never *be destroyed* (i.e., *violently harmed*) Daniel, as a servant of God, also enjoyed protection from *harm*.

## TRANSLATION (DANIEL 6:1-28 [6:2-29])

6:1 [2][2]    It seemed good to Darius to appoint one hundred and twenty[3] satraps over the kingdom who would be throughout the kingdom.

2 [3]    And (he appointed) three administrators over them, Daniel being one of them, that these satraps might give a report to them so that the king would not suffer loss.

---

2. In the Aramaic chapter 6 begins with the statement that "Darius received the kingdom," whereas in English versions, chapter 6 begins with Darius setting up one hundred and twenty satraps. See footnote 2 on p, 127.

3. The OG reads "127 satraps"; cf. Esth 1:1; Th agrees with the MT.

3 [4]   Then this Daniel distinguished himself above all the administrators and satraps, because he had an extraordinary spirit. And the king planned to appoint him over the entire kingdom.

4 [5]   Then the administrators and the satraps sought to find a pretext against Daniel from the standpoint of kingdom issues. But they could not find any pretext or corruption, because he was faithful, and no negligence or corruption could be found in him.

5 [6]   Then these men said, "We cannot find any pretext against this Daniel unless we find something against him through the law[4] of his God."

6 [7]   Then these administrators and satraps came in a crowd[5] to the king and said as follows:

"King Darius, live forever!

7 [8]   All the administrators of the kingdom, the prefects, satraps, treasurers, and governors, have agreed that the king should establish an ordinance and enforce[6] a prohibition—that anyone who asks a petition of any god or man for thirty days except from you, O king, shall be thrown into a pit[7] of lions.

8 [9]   Now, O king, establish the prohibition and put it in writing, so that it may not be revoked."

9 [10]  Therefore, Darius the king signed the written prohibition.

10 [11] Now when Daniel knew that the document had been signed, he went to his house, which had windows in its roof chamber opened toward Jerusalem, and three times a day he knelt on his knees and prayed and offered thanks[8] before his God, just as he had been doing previously.

11 [12] Then those men came in a crowd and found Daniel petitioning and pleading for mercy before his God.

---

4. The term for *law* is not the familiar Hebrew term *Torah* (תּוֹרָה) but דָּת (*dāth*), a Persian loanword that substituted in Aramaic for the Hebrew term.

5. *HALOT*, "רגשׁ," 5:1979; Gzella says that here it means that the officials exerted *pressure* on the king, "רגשׁ," *TDOT*, 16:704.

6. Based on Assyrian parallels, Paul ("Daniel 12:9," 110) argued that לְתַקָּפָה should mean *to make a document legally binding and valid*.

7. The traditional "*den* of lions" (גֹּב אַרְיָתָא) might make one think of a natural place where lions stay. The context indicates a *pit* dug out large enough to hold some captured lions.

8. Or "praise." See Gzella, "ידי," *TDOT*, 16:332–34.

12 [13]    Then they approached the king and spoke about the king's prohibition.⁹

"Didn't you sign a prohibition that anyone who would ask a petition of any god or man for thirty days except from you, O king, would be thrown into a pit of lions?"

The king responded,

"Certainly, the matter is according to the law of the Medes and Persians that cannot be revoked."

13 [14]    Then they responded to the king,

"Daniel, who is from the exiles of Judah, he has not paid attention to you or to your prohibition that you signed. Three times a day he asks his petition."

14 [15]    Now when the king heard the matter, he was very displeased, and he determined to rescue Daniel. Even to the setting of the sun he made every effort to deliver him.

15 [16]    Then those men came in a crowd to the king and said to the king,

"Understand, O king, that it is a law of the Medes and Persians that any ordinance that the king establishes cannot be changed."

16 [17]    Then the king gave the order, and they brought Daniel and threw him into the pit of lions. The king said to Daniel,

"Your God, whom you serve constantly, will rescue¹⁰ you."

17 [18]    Then a stone was brought and placed over the mouth of the pit. And the king sealed it with his signet ring and with the signet rings of his nobles, so that what was planned about Daniel could not be changed.

---

9. The OG, Th, and the *Peshitta* all omit any equivalent for עַל־אֱסָר (*about the prohibition*) and read the second occurrence of מַלְכָּא as a vocative. 4QDan^b supports the MT.

10. The *nun* that occurs between the verb and the pronoun object in יְשֵׁיזְבִנָּךְ makes it unlikely that it means "May he rescue you" rather than "He will rescue you" (see Rosenthal, *Grammar of Biblical Aramaic*, 55).

18 [19]  Then the king went to his palace and spent the night without eating. He had no entertainment[11] brought before him, and he couldn't sleep.[12]

19 [20]  Then at the first light of dawn the king arose and hurried to the pit of lions.

20 [21]  And when the king approached the pit. he cried out to Daniel with an anguished voice saying,[13]

"Your God whom you serve constantly—has he been able to rescue you from the lions?"

21 [22]  Then Daniel spoke with the king:

"O king, live forever!

22 [23]  My God sent his angel, and he shut the mouths of the lions. They didn't harm me, because I was found innocent before him. Also, O king, I have not done anything to harm you."

23 [24]  Then the king was very pleased, and he issued an order to bring Daniel out of the pit. Then Daniel was brought out of the pit, and he was found to be completely free of harm, for he had trusted in his God.

24 [25]  Then the king issued an order, and they brought those men who had maliciously accused[14] Daniel and threw them into the pit of lions, along with their children and their wives. They had not reached the bottom of the pit before the lions overpowered them and crushed all their bones.

25 [26]  Then Darius the king wrote:

"To all peoples, nations, and languages, that dwell throughout the whole land,[15] Peace be multiplied to you.

26 [27]  I issue a decree that throughout my royal dominion people are to tremble and fear before Daniel's God.

---

11. The Aramaic term דַּחֲוָה (pl. דַּחֲוָן) is unique to this verse and has never been explained adequately. Th has ἐδέσματα, a term for *food*. The Vulgate and the *Peshitta* follow Th. Some rabbinic sources translated with *table*, others with *happiness* or *music* (Goldwurm, *Daniel*, 188).

12. Lit., "and his sleep fled from him."

13. The MT is redundant, adding "the king answered and said," which is simplified in OG to "saying" but omitted in Th.

14. See the translation note on Dan 3:8b.

15. Even allowing for hyperbole, the context for כָּל־אַרְעָא should be the whole land of Persia, not the whole earth. The Persian empire at the time still did not include Egypt.

# DANIEL IN THE LION'S DEN

> For he is the living God and endures forever.
>
> His kingdom will never be destroyed, and his dominion will never end.[16]

27 He rescues and delivers and performs signs and wonders in heaven and on the earth. He[17] has rescued Daniel from the lions."

28 [29] Now this Daniel prospered in the reign of Darius, even in the reign of Cyrus the Persian.[18]

## TEXTUAL OUTLINE (6:1–28 [6:2–29])

I. Daniel Has a Conflict with the Officials of the Kingdom. (6:1–15 [2–16])

*[God's faithful servants can expect to face intense opposition when they are successful.]*

  A. Darius appoints Daniel over the other officials. (6:1–5 [2–6])

  B. The officials set a trap for Daniel. (6:6–10 [7–11])

  C. The officials accuse Daniel before Darius. (6:11–15 [12–16]

II. Daniel Is Thrown into the Pit of Lions. (6:16–24 [17–25])

*[God exalts over their enemies those who remain faithful to him.]*

III. Darius Exalts and Praises Daniel's God. (6:25–27 [26–28])

*[When others observe the faithfulness of God's people, it encourages them to praise and glorify God.]*

## EXPOSITION (6:1–28 [2–29])

The first six chapters of Daniel deal with the Jewish people in exile. These chapters illustrate how it was possible for individual Jews to rise to high government positions even in exile, but they also deal with challenges of living by faith in an environment that in certain ways was hostile to their faith. The challenge in chapter 1 concerned how to avoid total assimilation

---

16. Lit., "(will be) unto the end."

17. Aramaic דִּי apparently relates to "Daniel's God" in v. 26.

18. The OG has: "And the king Darius was gathered to his fathers, and Cyrus the Persian received his kingdom."

to the foreign culture. Accepting a new name was one thing, but identifying with the king's control through consuming his food and drink was another. Daniel demonstrated that it was possible to maintain a diet of God's choosing when it seemed like that wouldn't be possible. Even though Daniel and his companions came through the Babylonian educational system with the highest marks, it was their God who granted them the wisdom and insight that far exceeded any knowledge that the Babylonians could teach them.

Daniel's exceptional wisdom was put to the test when Nebuchadnezzar had his dream of the great image (chap. 2). Daniel and his companions found themselves under the decree of death, not because of anything they had done personally, but because of what the other wise men had failed to do. In this case Daniel brought the seemingly impossible mystery of the king's dream and its interpretation before God in prayer, soliciting his companions to join him in that prayer. In this way Daniel was able to deliver himself and his friends as well as all the wise men of Babylon. And in the process, he prophetically foresaw how God's will would unfold through the ages.

Being required to bow down to Nebuchadnezzar's image (chap. 3) also exceeded the bounds of what faithful Jews could do. They could not worship any god except the God of heaven, the Most High God. In this case they had to be prepared to lay down their lives in order to remain loyal to God alone.

Because of his evident wisdom Daniel eventually found himself to be one of Nebuchadnezzar's most trusted advisors (chap. 4). The king had developed confidence in Daniel's abilities and when lesser wise men were unable to interpret his dream, he brought his troubled thoughts to Daniel. When Daniel himself was disturbed about the content of the dream, the king told him to not hesitate to give him the interpretation. As a result, Daniel was able to give Nebuchadnezzar spiritual advice, and that advice was likely the catalyst that enabled the king to escape his own exile from society and testify to the greatness of "the Most High."

Daniel moved from advice to prophetic critique under the last king of Babylon (ch. 5). Despite God's clear warning through what had happened to Nebuchadnezzar, Belshazzar remained stubbornly prideful. With great boldness Daniel rebuked Belshazzar for his pride and revealed the ominous omen of the writing on the wall, something none of the other wise men neither could do or dared to do.

The bold faithfulness of Daniel is on display in chapter 6 when he continues to pray to God in spite of the king's decree not to do it. This unyielding faithfulness becomes an opportunity for the other court officials to get rid of Daniel once and for all. However, as the story unfolds, it becomes clear that the cunning genius of the court officials is no match for the sovereignty of God and the faithfulness of his servant, Daniel.

## Daniel Has a Conflict with the Officials of the Kingdom. (6:1–15 [2–16])

Theological Point: God's faithful servants can expect to face intense opposition when they are successful.

The first section of Daniel 6 (vv. 1–15 [2–16]) includes the background of the administrative division of the new kingdom and how Daniel came into conflict with the administrators because of his faithfulness to God. The second division (vv. 16 –24 [17–25]) tells how God delivered Daniel from the den of lions. The third section (vv. 25–28 [18–29]) shows how Darius the Mede glorified Daniel's God after he reversed the decree of the king that could not be reversed according to "the law of the Medes and the Persians." The chapter ends with a note about Daniel's successful service in the reign of Darius the Mede, who was also Cyrus the Persian. The two titles emphasize the success of Daniel in the united kingdom of Medo-Persia.

### Darius appoints Daniel over the other officials. (6:1–5 [2–6])

The officials of the kingdom plot against Daniel because of their jealousy at how rapidly he became their leader.

**6:1–2 (2–3).** The first two verses give necessary background information for the reader to understand what happened to Daniel after Babylon fell to the Medes and the Persians. Darius set up a two-tiered organizational structure with three administrators who had responsibility for the one hundred and twenty satraps or lower officials. Some of these satraps may have had duties on a lesser level than a provincial governor. Verses six and seven (7 and 8) imply that the term אֲחַשְׁדַּרְפְּנַיָּא (*satraps*) included various lower-level officials. That would also help to explain why there were as many as one hundred and twenty satraps.[19]

Daniel was one of the three top officials, so Darius must have heard of his capabilities and given him this position. It is known that Cyrus let other

---

19. Herodotus reported that the later Darius Hystaspes (not Darius the Mede) divided Persia into twenty "satrapies" (3:89). Stolper ("Governor of Babylon," 291) mentions a Babylonian text that refers to "the possibility of a lawsuit before 'king, *aḥšadrapanu* [Babylonian for *satrap*], or judge,'" offering evidence that the term for satrap "may indicate a class of offices rather than a particular rank."

Babylonian officials continue with a position in the Persian government. Even Nabonidus was apparently given a governorship of one of the provinces, and Cyrus allowed a certain Nabû-aḫḫê-bulliṭ, who had been governor of Babylon under Nabonidus, to remain in his office.[20] Hence it should not seem unusual that Daniel also was retained as a government official. **It is interesting too that Belshazzar had promised as a reward a position as "third ruler in the kingdom," and under Darius Daniel became one of three top administrators.**

**6:3 (4). Eventually Daniel "distinguished himself" above the other two leaders by virtue of his extraordinary abilities. His "excellent spirit"** (רוּחַ יַתִּירָא) **was very early interpreted by the Old Greek as a "holy spirit"** (πνεῦμα ἅγιον), **but the idea is more that Daniel had unusual wisdom.** Elsewhere the book of Daniel notes that God "gave" such capabilities to Daniel and his friends (1:17; cf. 2:21), and Daniel so surpassed the other wise men in the kingdom that Nebuchadnezzar thought he must have "a spirit of the holy gods" (4:8–9 [5–6], 18 [15]; cf. 5:11).

**6:4–5 (5–6). When Daniel's outstanding performance led the king to consider appointing him the top leader in the kingdom, the trouble started.** The other two administrators, in conjunction with some of the additional leaders,[21] began to look for some charge that would force the king to either demote Daniel or perhaps even oust him from leadership altogether. Jealousy would seem a natural factor, and ethnic issues may also have played a role. When the group later accused Daniel before the king, they used only his Hebrew name and noted that he was "from the exiles of Judah." They thought of him only as some upstart from a captive people that certainly did not deserve to have a position of authority over them. Daniel proved to be impeccable in the way he carried out his duties, and not being able to find anything to accuse him of, they plotted to trip him up through a religious scruple. And therein lies the basis for what happened next.

*The officials set a trap for Daniel. (6:6–10 [7–11])*

**6:6–7 (7–8). The jealous officials devised a clever scheme whereby they would get the king to issue a religious law that would entrap Daniel.**

---

20. Nicolò, *Prosopographie neubabylonischer Beamten*, 61.

21. The Aramaic doesn't specify how many of the officials were involved. If the author wanted to emphasize that all were involved, he could have inserted "all." With no need to emphasize a specific number, he merely stated the groups involved. Logic would dictate that they were officials in close contact with Daniel.

What's more, it would have to be a law that even the king himself couldn't revoke once it was passed. After all, it was the king who desired to make Daniel the main ruler. Their plan would backfire if he rescinded the law when they tried to trap Daniel by it.

The content of the proposed law is not entirely clear. It was stated as an injunction against anyone making a request of any "god or man for thirty days" except of the king. **The mention of "god" makes it clear that the law had a religious aim; the instigators were trying to find an occasion against Daniel "in the law of his God" (v. 5 [6]). The religious nature of the law ought to color how to interpret "or man" that was included in the prohibition. It evidently referred to priests who would mediate between people and a god. It did not mean that no one could make any request at all from anyone except the king.**[22] The decree called for Darius to make himself the sole mediator. He was not going to personally grant the requests; instead, he would intervene on behalf of the petitioner to the god. It is not necessary, therefore, to think with some commentators that the king was being made a god or semi-divine himself.[23]

The prohibition that the officials suggested would have been fraught with political implications. It is doubtful that anyone would have expected it to apply to the common person. Some sort of loyalty test has been suggested,[24] and that well may have been its purpose.[25]

Here the verb הַרְגִּשׁוּ (*came in a crowd*) indicates more than a mere arrival to the king, for which there were other more common possibilities. The point appears to be that a large group of officials came in what appeared to be an excited mob. They were eager to carry out their plan and hoped to impress the king with their numbers. The term doesn't need to imply that the group was disorderly when they met the king. They wanted to pressure him and therefore would have put on a more organized front. The point of the text is that they were convinced that their plan would get rid of Daniel, and they pounced on it eagerly.

The officials were attempting to deceive the king into thinking that the leaders of virtually the entire country had agreed on their plan. They failed to disclose, of course, that Daniel was not part of it, and the text

---

22. Contra R. D. Wilson, *Book of Daniel*, 313.
23. Baldwin, *Daniel*, 128; John Collins, *Daniel*, 267.
24. Miller, *Daniel*, 180-81.
25. Walton ("Decree of Darius," 285-86) speculates that the conspirators asked Darius to take "a stand for the worship of Ahura Mazda according to the pure teachings of Zarathuštra." Only Medes and Persians would be expected to participate, not other peoples in the kingdom, and not even Daniel himself. Daniel would be brought into it, however, because he was "a high Persian official."

had said nothing previously of anyone other than satraps and the small, select group of high officials.

**6:7 (8).** The government bureaucrats were also anxious for the king to make the law completely binding. They wanted him to establish their idea as a firm law and to enforce it with his royal authority. Their proposed law was meant to flatter the king as well.[26]

**6:8 (9).** It seems odd that there would be a law so binding that it couldn't be revoked even by the king. Is this so unusual that it should be considered implausible?[27] Many commentators have noted a possible parallel with a passage from Diodorus of Sicily, who wrote that Darius III regretted having ordered the execution of a certain Charidemus.[28] In this case, however, the king was unable to undo an execution *after* the fact. The officials wanted to be sure that the king could not undo an order of execution *before* it was carried out. The only real parallel to the comment about the irrevocable nature of "the law of the Medes and the Persians" currently known is in the book of Esther (1:19; 8:8). **The text of Daniel emphasizes, though, that the officials requested a special type of law. It had to be an edict of the king himself, and he had to sign it. And possibly the thought is even that the unalterable status of the law was an unusual provision, a clause that required skill to draft.**[29] **As such it adds to the tension in the narrative.**

**6:10 (11). The text implies that Daniel not only knew of the prohibition but also deliberately disobeyed it. It was his usual custom to pray, but it was "when he knew" that he went to his house to worship and pray. When a law directly contradicts what God requires one to do, it is not wrong to disobey it.** That should only happen, though, when it is clear that the law violates what God would require, as in the case of Peter and John before the Sanhedrin (Acts 4:18–20).

In his customary times of prayer Daniel knelt and faced Jerusalem. While a special time, place, and posture in prayer is not always necessary, there is benefit and encouragement toward such practices found elsewhere in Scripture. For example, Ps 55:17 (18) mentions prayer at "evening, morning, and noon"; 1 Kgs 8:29–30, 35 encourages prayer facing the temple in Jerusalem; and 1 Kgs 8:54 refers to prayer while kneeling and with hands "spread out toward heaven."

---

26. Wood, *Daniel*, 160.

27. Collins, *Daniel*, 268.

28. Diodorus of Sicily was a Greek historian of the first century BC. The reference is to book 17.30.4–7; see Montgomery, *Book of Daniel*, 270; Steinmann, *Daniel*, 316.

29. Paul ("Daniel 1–6," 57–58) finds an Assyrian background to the expression לְתַקָּפָה אֱסָר, meaning "'to ratify'—i.e., to make a document legally binding."

Prayer was an essential part of Daniel's life. In a time of emergency Daniel prayed and enlisted the additional prayers of his friends (2:17–18); when he was burdened by the unrighteousness of his people, he prayed prayers of confession and repentance (9:3). **Daniel would have thought it unthinkable to abandon his prayers for thirty days, particularly at a time when he saw what the other leaders were planning against him.**

The term for Daniel's prayer, מְצַלֵּא, was often used in ancient Aramaic for prayers on behalf of the king.[30] The term's only other use in the Bible occurs in a decree issued by Cyrus in the first year of his reign. By it the king allowed the Jews to rebuild their temple in Jerusalem with government funds, so that the priests could offer sacrifices and "pray for the life of the king and his son" (Ezra 6:10). **The text doesn't tell us what petitions Daniel might have made, but since the prohibition concerned petitionary prayer** (יִבְעֵה בָעוּ, "he will ask a request"), **it is quite possible that Daniel included prayers for the king (cf. 1 Tim 2:1–2). When the jealous leaders finally caught Daniel, they found him "petitioning [בָּעֵא] and pleading for mercy" [מִתְחַנֵּן]** (6:11 [12]).

## The officials accuse Daniel of ignoring the king's decree (6:11–15 [12–16])

**6:11–13 (12–14). The officials accused Daniel before the king of failure to obey the decree. The text pictures an eager mob of men, and when they arrive at Daniel's house, they catch him in the act of prayer. Taking their accusation to the king, they put him in a bind. Darius had no desire to execute Daniel, but he could not ignore the evidence of all the witnesses.**

First, the officials persuaded the king to agree to sign the prohibition; then they surprised him with the news that Daniel was guilty of ignoring it. **When the king delayed carrying out the sentence that was demanded, the men once again "came in a crowd" and reminded him that he could not set aside an edict that was according to "the law of the Medes and Persians." There was no way out, and Daniel's seemingly hopeless fate set up another occasion for God to do the impossible. The king of the mightiest empire in the ancient world could not find any way to deliver Daniel, but God would find a way to overrule even "the law of the Medes and Persians."**

**6:13 (14). When the accusers referred to Daniel by his Hebrew name and called him a Judean exile, they showed their contempt for him. They thought of him as a lowly foreigner, and perhaps they even**

---

30. For an example see Cowley, *Aramaic Papyri*, 112 (text no. 30, lines 15, 26).

exhibited some anti-Semitism. They certainly didn't want him to be in a position of authority over them.

6:14 (15). The narrator used two verbs for the king's attempt to "rescue" Daniel, שֵׁיזִב and נְצַל. Both verbs mean to *rescue* or *deliver*. The former term is a loanword from Babylonian,[31] and its synonym is native Aramaic. Later the king used the Babylonian term to express his confidence that Daniel's God would "rescue" him from the lions (6:16 [17]). Then he used it again when he inquired whether God had indeed "rescued" him (6:20 [21]). Finally, he used both terms together in his written praise to all the peoples of the kingdom, "He *rescues* and *delivers* . . . for he *rescued* Daniel" (6:27 [28]). In this way the text highlights God's ability to rescue and deliver in contrast to the king's inability.

The contrast between Darius's authority and God's authority is heightened further by the king's remarkable effort to save Daniel. His determination (שָׂם בָּל, *he set mind*) to do something for Daniel (מִשְׁתַּדַּר, *exerting himself*) led him to think of nothing else until sunset. And even then, he spent a sleepless night after Daniel was thrown to the lions (6:18 [19]).

6:15 (16). By their speech the accusers show themselves to be enemies not only of Daniel but also of the king. They neglected to use the standard greeting for the monarch, "O king, live forever." Then they spoke to him with a direct command, "Understand, O king . . . ." Proper respect would have required an indirect address, "Let the king understand . . . ." At this point these rebellious officials had the upper hand, but the trouble they caused the king and Daniel turned on them later after God delivered his prophet; they themselves would be mauled by the lions.

## Daniel Is Thrown into the Pit of Lions. (6:16–24 [17–25])

Theological Point: God exalts over their enemies
those who remain faithful to him.

Daniel faces the lions, but they are restrained from overpowering him. Ultimately, the king had to concede defeat and order Daniel to be thrown into the pit of lions. Even so, he encouraged Daniel with a statement of confidence in the ability of his God to deliver him from the lions, and he anxiously awaited the first light of the morning to determine his friend's fate.

---

31. The *shin* (שׁ) used to form the causative of the root is characteristic of Babylonian.

If Daniel were to be delivered, it would have to be the work of his God. There was no escape from the pit with the lions; the seal of the king and of each of his nobles assured that no one could tamper with the stone placed over the entrance.

Miraculously, Daniel was delivered from the lions, and he and the king had a joyous reunion. **God delivered him, Daniel claimed, because he was really an innocent man. He was pure regarding the law of God, and he had not done anything harmful to the king. It was Daniel's accusers who had harmed the king by tricking him into signing the injunction, and in an act of retributive justice they were themselves thrown to the lions along with their families.**

**6:16 (17). The context requires that the king's words to Daniel should be taken as encouragement.** He had tried desperately to avoid having to condemn Daniel to the lions; when Daniel was in the pit with the lions, all he could do was assure Daniel that his God would deliver him. The king had observed Daniel's constant devotion to his God, and he had likely heard of the miraculous deliverance of Shadrach, Meshach, and Abednego from the flames. **Darius did show some trepidation by his actions after the pit was sealed, but his expression of confidence to reassure a condemned man doesn't necessarily mean that he himself had complete confidence in his words.**

Mesopotamian kings "kept lions in cages or pits from the Ur III period [ca. 2100–2000 BC] on."[32] The pit must have been large enough at the bottom to contain more than one lion but small enough at the top to place a stone over its mouth.[33] Perhaps the statement is hyperbolic, but the reference to the lions overpowering the officials before they reached the bottom (6:24 [25]) would indicate a vertical shaft into which one would be "thrown." It is not necessary to think of all the officials and their families cast into the pit at once. They could have suffered their fate one at a time.[34]

Lions figure in many biblical settings. The Mediterranean lion, now extinct, was plentiful in OT times and often a dangerous animal for humans (1 Kgs 13:24; 20:36; 2 Kgs 17:25-26). The lion also became a frequent metaphor in the Bible for ferocity (Num 23:24; Deut 33:20; Prov 30:30), strength

---

32. Oppenheim, *Ancient Mesopotamia*, 46; see also Keil, *Ezekiel, Daniel*, 216.

33. In the parallel story found in "Bel and the Dragon" there were seven lions.

34. Toorn ("In the Lions' Den," 632) cites an Assyrian letter from the time of Sennacherib (late eighth to early seventh century BC) that mentions "the lion's pit," but as a metaphor for the writer's former colleagues who worked against him. He thinks a similar metaphor lies behind the lions in Dan 6 ("In the Lions' Den," 638). That speculation aside, the cited text demonstrates that there were pits for lions in a time frame close to Daniel. The metaphor must have developed from real knowledge of lions.

(2 Sam 1:23), danger (Gen 49:9), and even judgment from the Lord (Jer 2:15; 4:7; 50:17; Amos 3:8; 5:19). Jesus Christ is symbolized like a lion for his regal bearing and fierceness in judgment (Rev 5:5), and the devil is like a lion because of the dangerous way that he entices into sin and then destroys the sinner (1 Pet 5:8).

6:17 (18). The "sealing" of the pit was done with signet rings impressed into wet clay and placed around the edges of the stone. Miller thinks of clay applied to chains attached to the stone in such a way that any attempt to remove them would break the seal. Each ring would have its own unique design and/or inscription to represent its owner.[35] Contextually, the "nobles" with their signet rings must represent the officials who accused Daniel. None of the parties involved in the execution of Daniel would be able to alter "the law of the Medes and Persians." The Aramaic term for the officials (רַבְרְבָנִין, lit. *great ones*) indicates their status as important figures at the royal court, whose authority was represented by their rings. The same term for *nobles* is also used of Nebuchadnezzar's officials at Daniel 4:36 (33); 5:1, 2, 3, 9, 10, 23.

6:18 (19). By his actions the king showed his concern for Daniel. He refused to eat or to be entertained, and he spent a sleepless night. *Sleep* figures prominently in Daniel. Nebuchadnezzar had his dreams while asleep, and Daniel had visions at night (2:19; 7:1), when people would normally be asleep. Then when Daniel first encountered Gabriel, he fell into a "deep sleep" (8:18), something that also happened when he heard the voice of the majestic person who appeared to him at the start of his final vision (10:9). Finally, the dead at the great judgment are called "those who sleep in the dusty ground" (12:2). From the biblical perspective, God works while people sleep (1 Kgs 3:5; Ps 127:2). He reveals himself and his plans through dreams and visions during sleep (cf. Job 4:13; 33:15–16), and he awakens sleepers to new life (Pss 17:15; 139:18; Isa 26:19; John 11:11; Rom 6:4; Eph 5:14). Darius the Mede was unable to sleep because of his anxiety about Daniel, but at the break of the new day he would come to a fuller understanding of Daniel's God.

6:19–22 (20–23). The king, knowing that if Daniel survived the night, he could free him, rushed to the pit at the earliest sign of light. Anxiously he called out to see if his friend had survived. **For the second time he referred to Daniel as one who served his God "continually." That continual service could not be interrupted by the king's decree, but the king recognized that there was something special about Daniel's God. He was "the living God," and the king hoped that he had been able to deliver Daniel**

---

35. Miller, *Daniel*, 185–86.

from the lions. This was quite a contrast from Nebuchadnezzar before his humiliation. He could hardly imagine that any god existed who could deliver anyone from his powerful grasp (3:15).

Several factors point to 6:19-22 (20-23) as the literary height or "peak" of the narrative of chapter 6. The reader experiences maximum tension when the king gets up in the early light of the day and rushes off to see what has happened to Daniel. At verse nineteen (v. 20), Aramaic שְׁפַרְפָּר (*dawn*), which for biblical Aramaic occurs only in this verse, is reinforced by another term used only here, נָגְהּ (*brightness*). It is used synonymously for *daybreak*. Then verse twenty (v. 21) contains the only example in biblical Aramaic of an infinitive governed by the preposition כ used for a *when* clause ("when he approached the pit"). In the next verse the text says that Daniel "spoke with" (מַלִּל עִם) the king. This is the first time in the book that someone's response is not introduced by the stock phrase, "answered and said." In fact, it is the only time in the book that this Aramaic verb for *speak* and the preposition עִם (*with*) is used to introduce a quotation. These factors of dramatic tension, unusual vocabulary, and unusual grammar combine to make this section (vv. 19-22 [20-23]) a "zone of turbulence" that characterizes the "peak" episode of a narrative discourse.[36] The reader knows that this interaction between Daniel and the king is highly significant for the story.

6:21 (22). It may seem strange that Daniel's first words to the king would be the phrase demanded by court etiquette, "O king, live forever." He had not addressed Belshazzar this way, and he knew he had nothing to fear from Darius. Nevertheless, there are several important reasons for his deference. First, it showed Daniel's complete composure in the situation, a calmness that contrasted with the anxiety that the king felt. Literarily it also relieves the tension of the reader, who realizes that not only did Daniel survive the lions, but he also will maintain a good relationship with the king. Despite what the king had done, Daniel was still loyal to him. Second, Daniel would have noticed that the king referred to "the living God," and his reply indicated his wish that the God who ever lives would grant length of life to the king. Like Joseph, who saw God's hand in the events that had been precipitated by his brothers (Gen 45:5-9; 50:20), so also Daniel's trust in his God enabled him to overcome any ill feelings toward the king. **Part of wisdom is being able to see the world through God's perspective. Daniel does not get involved in petty jealousy or in efforts to outdo others. And God's broader perspectives**

---

36. We have applied Longacre's description of a "peak" episode (*Grammar of Discourse*, 38) to Dan 6:19-22 (20-23).

are always for good in regard to his chosen ones, even if they may not always seem good at the time (cf. Rom 8:28).

The accusers had failed to use the appropriate courtly language when they stormed in to demand that the king send Daniel to the lions. **Daniel now recognized his own innocence before the king as well as his need to remain a loyal servant. He was able to serve both his God and the king faithfully, even though he had to choose faithfulness to God when a conflict arose.**

6:23 (24). At first, the king had been "very displeased" (6:14 [15]) upon hearing the accusations against Daniel. Now he was "very pleased" to hear Daniel speak in his own defense.

6:24 (25). It may seem odd that the families were also punished along with the plotters. Such an action was prohibited in the Mosaic law (Deut 24:16).[37] The text points to the arbitrary ruthlessness of autocratic rulers, as already seen in Nebuchadnezzar's decree to execute all the wise men of Babylon and in his attempt to put Shadrach, Meshach, and Abednego to death.

## Darius Exalts and Praises Daniel's God. (6:25–27 [26–28])

Theological Point: When others observe the faithfulness of God's people, it encourages them to praise and glorify God.

**The king praises "the living God." Darius was so impressed by how God had delivered Daniel that he issued a written decree to be sent throughout the kingdom that people were to fear and respect Daniel's God.** He concluded his message with his own words of praise for "the living God," and he sounded a familiar theme in the book of Daniel: "[God's] kingdom will never be destroyed, and his dominion will never end." **This is one of the strongest statements in the book about the uniqueness of Daniel's God.** Darius here echoes Nebuchadnezzar's praise but expresses it positively rather than negatively.[38] The gods of the nations were only lifeless idols (Dan 5:23), but the God that Daniel served ever lives (cf. 4:34 [31]).

6:25 (26). The book of Daniel refers to "peoples, nations, and languages" numerous times (also 3:4, 7, 29; 4:1 (3:31); 5:19; 7:14) and it is striking that both Nebuchadnezzar (chapter 4) and Darius the Mede wrote

---

37. That Achan's family was stoned along with him is a special case because of the "ban" (חֵרֶם), with the things that Achan retrieved from Jericho being things devoted to destruction (Josh 7:15). Possibly Achan's family was aware of what he had done.

38. Baldwin, *Daniel*, 131.

out their praise for Daniel's God in a letter to all their subjects. Writing lends more permanence to words than speaking, and it was important for the words from the lips of pagan kings to become a permanent record for future generations. They preserve words of enduring praise for the one true and exalted God who is sovereign over all peoples of the earth.

6:26-27 (27-28). Like Nebuchadnezzar's words of praise to God, Darius's praise takes a poetic form, marked notably by parallelism. Remarkably, Darius referred to Daniel's God as "living" and "enduring forever." Elsewhere in Scripture God is referred to by the title "living God."[39] Daniel must have given a powerful witness to Darius about his God, even as he had admonished Nebuchadnezzar to repent from his evil ways (Dan 4:27 [24]). **God had desired Israel to be a witness among the nations,[40] and Daniel and his companions were good examples of bearing witness to God even under threat of persecution.**

## Conclusion to Daniel's Service to the King (6:28 [29])

A concluding comment marks the boundary between Daniel's service to the king and his personal visions. Daniel 1:21 marked the beginning of the narrative about his service to kings, concluding with the first year of Cyrus. The last verse in chapter 6 draws to a close Daniel's service to kings. Both verses are thus literary markers to show the boundaries of chapters 2 to 6. Nowhere in the book is there any specific statement that Cyrus or the Persians received the kingdom. The Old Greek supplies such a statement, but that was probably because the translator interpreted the Aramaic to mean that there were two kingdoms, one under Darius the Mede and the other under Cyrus the Persian. Indeed, most translators and interpreters have taken the text to refer to two separate kings if not two kingdoms.

God "gave" the king of Judah and the temple vessels to Nebuchadnezzar, and Darius the Mede "received" the kingdom (5:31 [6:1]). And in both chapters 5 and 6 we read of "the Medes and Persians" together as though they are a unified kingdom. After being "assessed," Belshazzar's kingdom was to be "given to the Medes and Persians" (5:28). Also, in a later vision of Daniel a ram with two horns represented "the kings of Media and Persia" (8:20). Given these facts it is at least plausible to read 6:28 (29) as "in the

---

39. 1 Sam 17:26, 36; 2 Kgs 19:16; Pss 42:2 (3); 84:2; Isa 37:17; Jer 10:10; 23:36; Hos 1:10; Matt 16:16; 26:63; Acts 14:15; Rom 9:26; 2 Cor 3:3; 1 Thess 1:9; 1 Tim 4:10; Heb 3:12; 10:31; 12:22; Rev 7:2.

40. Deut 28:9-10; Pss 22:27-28 (28-29); 86:9; Isa 49:6; Jer 4:1-2; see Wright, *Mission of God*, 222-43.

reign of Darius, *even* in the reign of Cyrus the Persian," thereby equating Darius and Cyrus as the same person. Commentators who have followed this interpretation include Baldwin, Lucas, and Steinmann. Miller lists it as a possible alternative to the view that it represents two different kings.[41]

**Verse three (4) and verse twenty-eight (29) refer to "this Daniel." The demonstrative pronoun emphasizes to the reader that it is the same Daniel in the new kingdom of Darius who was previously laboring in the Babylonian administration.** Perhaps the force of the demonstrative could be brought out by "this same Daniel." The repetition at the beginning and end of the chapter helps to set it off as a coherent unit.

## SHARPENING THE THEOLOGICAL FOCUS

Each of the first six chapters of the book of Daniel resonates with the theme that God's kingdom is everlasting in contrast to the temporary duration of merely human kingdoms. In chapter 1 God appears as the one who chooses to transfer kingdom sovereignty from Jehoiakim to Nebuchadnezzar. In chapter 2 God's kingdom smashes like a stone all the realms portrayed in Nebuchadnezzar's image. In chapter 3 Nebuchadnezzar is forced to recognize that God can deliver his servants even from the king's hand, and in chapter 4 Nebuchadnezzar praises the God whose kingdom endures forever. Then in chapter 5 God removes sovereignty from Belshazzar and gives it to the Medes and the Persians. Finally, Darius the Mede, in chapter 6, speaks of a kingdom that "will never be destroyed" and a dominion that "will never end."

This motif of God's eternal reign continues into the second part of the book and serves to tie together both halves. In Daniel's vision of chapter 7 the "one like a son of man" receives "an everlasting dominion that will never pass away." Then Daniel is told in the vision of chapter 8 that a king who would dare to challenge the "Highest Commander" will be "broken without (human) power" (8:25). The "seventy weeks" prophecy of chapter 9 introduces a time of "everlasting righteousness" (9:24), to be ushered in by the destruction of "one who desolates" (9:27). Chapters 10 and 11 need to be read together, and they culminate in the destruction of a king who will once again seek to exalt himself over "all gods," and especially over "the God of gods" (11:36, 45). Finally, at the end of the book a resurrection is predicted (12:2). "The living God" will summon the dead to life, assigning

---

41. Baldwin, *Daniel*, 132; Lucas, *Daniel*, 145; Steinmann, *Daniel*, 313; Miller, *Daniel*, 189.

some to "everlasting contempt" but others to "everlasting life." God's future kingdom will truly be a kingdom of life and endless days.

Another major theological theme of chapter 6 is that God exalts over their enemies those who are faithful to him. Twice Darius the Mede himself said that Daniel served his God "constantly" (vv. 16 [17], 20 [21]). Daniel's faithfulness in prayer despite the king's interdiction formed the basis for that description. An important aspect of faithfulness is knowing where to draw the line. For Daniel the line was crossed when the king prohibited prayer to any God except through him as mediator. Daniel's habitual prayer life is seen throughout the book (2:18-23; 9:3-19; 10:2-3 [mourning and fasting implied prayer as an accompaniment]), and he could not put it on hold even for a king. Moreover, it would not be proper to pray directly to the king or to use him as an intermediary between himself and God. Theologically that could not work. Another aspect of faithfulness is being prepared to suffer the consequences of obedience to God, even bodily harm or death. Daniel knew that the prescribed punishment was death by the lions, and it is likely that he also knew that the law had been crafted to entrap him. Knowing that, he continued his usual practice of praying three times a day.

Faithfulness makes sense for the believer, because in the end God will triumph. It is interesting that on the one hand Shadrach, Meshach, and Abednego affirmed their faith that God could deliver them from the fiery furnace. They were determined not to bow down to the image (3:17-18). On the other hand, Daniel's faithfulness was so obvious to Darius the Mede that the king himself stated his belief that God would rescue Daniel from the lions (6:16 [17]). After the rescue, Darius proclaimed that God's kingdom will last forever (6:26 [27]). When others see the work of God in his faithful servants, even some of their enemies may decide to become God's servant as well. And in this way God will exalt his servants over their enemies.

Chapters 5 and 6 prepare the way for the coming apocalyptic chapters of the book by focusing on judgment for those who refuse to submit to God. In chapter 5 Belshazzar's prideful and profane use of the temple vessels led to the written decree of his demise, while in chapter 6 the enemies of Daniel fell into their own trap. They plotted to have Daniel devoured by the lions, but in the end the lions devoured them. In chapter 7 (v. 11; cf. 9:27; 11:45) we read of a king who will be destroyed at the great judgment because of his boastful words. He will attempt to change sacred times and seasons, but only the Ancient of Days can control time (Dan 7:25; cf. 2:21).

Daniel 6 parallels chapter 3 in several ways. In each chapter some of the king's officials accuse faithful servants of Israel's God of disobeying the king's decree. Even the same idiom was used for making the accusation, literally "to eat the pieces of."[42] In both chapters the faithful are condemned to death but are then delivered by God. And in both chapters an angel or a messenger sent by God intervened to prevent any harm to God's servants. Nebuchadnezzar saw a fourth man in the furnace with the three men, a man whom the king thought was like "a divine being" (lit., "a son of gods") and whom the king later called God's "angel" (3:25, 28). Likewise, Daniel told Darius that God "sent his angel and he shut the lions' mouths" (6:22 [23]).

The book of Daniel shows what happens when God's servants are faithful to him—God is honored and praised. Nebuchadnezzar and Darius both recognized the majesty and power of the God of the Jews who could perform such great wonders through his servants. The first six chapters of the book reveal what faithfulness to God looks like in a foreign and pagan culture, and they reveal how God receives glory through his people when they remain true to their faith in such a context. As the Lord Jesus Christ would later say, "Let your light shine before others, so that they may see your good works and give glory to your Father who is in heaven" (Matt 5:16 ESV).

## THE FOCUS OF DANIEL 6 FOR PREACHING AND TEACHING

While there are many similarities, chapter 6 is not a repeat of chapter 3; it offers something new and adds to what has previously been taught. This buildup is important because too often God's people live under the impression that once they get through "the fire" life will get easier. Chapter 6 is a reminder that life is relentless. Get past one problem (e.g., Nebuchadnezzar) and another problem will emerge (e.g., saboteurs).

As the closing story of the first half of Daniel, chapter 6 fittingly ties together two primary themes. First, it spotlights the sovereignty of God and the everlasting nature of his kingdom. Second, chapter 6 highlights the importance of faithfulness on the part of God's people. It's easy to think of God's sovereignty and human faithfulness in either/or terms: "If God is sovereign, then our faithfulness really doesn't matter." Through Daniel, and his friends, it becomes clear that this is simply not the case. God works in and through the faithfulness of his people in order to carry out his plans. This is an important truth that serves to close out the historical narratives and transition into the apocalyptic section of Daniel; God is in control, and the faithfulness of his people makes a difference. This is brought to the forefront in chapter 6 through the words of Darius. Twice, in reference to Daniel,

---

42. אֲכַל קַרְצִין; 3:8 and 6:24 [25]

he says, "Your God, whom *you serve constantly*" (6:16, 20). Daniel didn't suddenly seek faithfulness when trouble came. He was characterized by a faithfulness that was evident to all, friends and enemies alike. The officials knew that this is how they could trap him, and Darius knew that this is why God would save him. Chapter 6 reveals that the inevitability of God's sovereign deliverance is motivation for faithfulness.

## FROM TEXTUAL WORK TO TEACHING

### The Big Idea

- *Exegetical Idea:* God exalts innocence over guilt and justice over malice by giving to Daniel's enemies what they had plotted for him.
- *Theological Focus:* God exalts over their enemies those who are faithful to him.
- *Preaching Idea:* We don't always know how or when, but God will ultimately vindicate those who honor him.

### Outline One: Following the Exegetical Flow

I. God's faithful servants can expect to face intense opposition when they are successful. (6:1–15)

    A. Daniel is successful in Darius's court and appointed to a top spot. (1–5)

    B. The other officials set a trap and when Daniel falls into it, they report him to the king. (6–15)

    C. When God's faithful servants are successful, they can expect to face intense opposition.

        1. Jealous coworkers will maliciously oppose advancement.

        2. Spiteful "friends" and "family" can even prove to be enemies.

II. God exalts over their enemies those who remain faithful to him. (6:16–24)

    A. Daniel is thrown into the pit of lions and leaves unscathed.

B. Daniel's enemies are thrown into the pit of lions and destroyed.

   C. God exalts us over our enemies when we remain faithful to him.

      1. Sometimes we see this happen in life (over jealous coworkers, etc.).

      2. Sometimes this won't happen until eternity.

III. When others observe the faithfulness of God's people, it points them to God. (6:25–27)

   A. Darius exalts and praises Daniel's God.

   B. Others will see our faithfulness and they will praise and glorify God.

      1. Others will see how we respond to the jealous coworkers, and they may praise and glorify God.

      2. Even if we are not vindicated in this life, remaining faithful unto death will point others to the God we serve.

## Outline Two: Following a Theme

Another way to approach this chapter for preaching/teaching would be to structure the sermon/lesson around the word plays in the chapter. Set them up in such a way as to draw out the tension and this will bring a fresh perspective to a familiar story.

### Whose Appointments Matter Most?

- 6:1—Darius *appointed* one hundred and twenty satraps.
- 6:3—Darius desired to *appoint* Daniel over the whole kingdom.
- 6:7—The officials asked Darius to *establish* an *ordinance*.
- 6:8—The officials asked Darius to *establish* a prohibition.
- 6:15—An *ordinance* that the king *establishes* cannot be changed.
- 6:19—The king *arose* at the break of dawn.
- **6:26—God *endures* forever.**

## What Are We Seeking?

- 6:4—The officials *sought* to find a pretext against Daniel.
- 6:7—Anyone who would *ask* a *petition* of any god or man . . .
- 6:11—**Daniel was *petitioning* his God.**
- 6:12—Anyone who would *petition* any god or man . . .
- 6:13—Daniel *asks for* his *petition* three times a day.

## What Will People Find When They Look into Our Lives?

- 6:4—The officials sought *to find* a pretext but couldn't *find* one.
- 6:4—No negligence or corruption *was found* in Daniel.
- 6:5—They wouldn't *find* any pretext . . . unless they *found* . . .
- 6:11—They *found* Daniel . . . .
- 6:22—**Daniel *was found* innocent.**
- 6:23—Daniel *was found* free of harm.

# Vision of Beasts and Kingdoms
(Daniel 7:1–28)

**Chapter 6 Review**: Daniel 6 opens with Darius the Mede organizing the kingdom. However, the Masoretes were right to make 5:31 the first verse of the chapter (6:1 in the Hebrew Bible). Darius received the kingdom from the Lord. God gave the kingdom to Nebuchadnezzar, and now Darius the Mede receives it. As the chapter continues, it focuses on Daniel's faithfulness to his God despite conflicts with the new kingdom officials. As a result, Darius the Mede exalts and praises Daniel's God and the antagonists experience God's retributive justice.

**Chapter 7 Summary:** Chapter 7 marks a major genre shift in Daniel, from historical narrative to apocalyptic revelation. The first six chapters assure God's people that God *was* in control of all that had transpired from the fall of Jerusalem to the fall of Babylon. The next six chapters provide assurance that God *is* in control of all that will happen in the future. Chapter 7 sets the stage for the rest of the book by specifically highlighting God's sovereignty over history, portraying him as Lord over time. The Ancient of Days has determined the ending date of all earthly kingdoms and the inaugural date of his everlasting kingdom. In this vision Daniel is transported into the heavens and learns the interpretation from an angel.

**Chapter 8 Preview**: For the first time, Daniel 8 leaves the realm of Babylonia and centers Daniel's vision in Susa, an important city in Elam (i.e., Persia). Conflict between kingdoms is symbolized by a fierce fight between a ram with two uneven horns and a male goat with a "conspicuous horn." These worldwide conflicts will culminate with a ruler who will fight against God's people and even challenge God. His time will be limited, however, and God will overcome him.

## THEOLOGICAL FOCUS OF CHAPTER 7

EVEN THOUGH THE KINGDOMS of this world will continually challenge the authority of God, their destiny is firmly in the hands of the Ancient of Days, who has fixed the time for their judgment. His servants will undergo tremendous persecution and testing, but the time will come for the people of God to be delivered and to enter his kingdom that will never end.

I. The kingdoms of this world will continually challenge the authority of God. (7:1–8)

II. The destiny of the world's kingdoms and peoples are firmly in the hands of the Ancient of Days, who has fixed the time for their judgment. (7:9–14)

III. God's servants will undergo tremendous persecution and testing. (7:15–21)

IV. The time will come for God's servants to be delivered and to enter his kingdom that will never end. (7:22–28)

## BIG PICTURE (7:1–28)

Chapter 7 tells of Daniel's first dream vision and the angel's interpretation of it. It gives a broad, universal outline of the course of history, with only the final earthly kingdom receiving any detailed treatment. As such it makes a transition from the narrative stories to the apocalyptic chapters. Though the stories were miraculous and included dreams, they dealt with events as they happened on the ground in the Babylonian and Medo-Persian realms. With chapter 7 readers are immediately transferred to the heavenly realm. It is still Daniel who sees the elements of the vision, but now an angel serves as the interpreter. The vision of chapter 7 prepares readers for the additional details that will emerge in chapters 8 to 12. Chapter 7 functions, then, as an introduction to the rest of the book.

In relation to the rise and fall of empires, the book of Daniel has a cyclical view of history, but with an end in sight. While Nebuchadnezzar's dream of a human image in chapter 2 has some similarities to Daniel's vision in chapter 7, Daniel's vision broadens out to heavenly realities. It looks to the future to see what will become of world kingdoms. History will continue to repeat itself as empires rise and fall, but the pattern is temporary because history is ultimately linear, culminating in the establishment of God's eternal kingdom.

The four kingdoms of chapter 7 are symbolized by beasts that emerge from a "great sea." That "great sea" represents a chaos that is saturated with evil. These kingdoms are thus hostile to God and his purposes, and they arise through war and conquest. When the Ancient of Days judges the four beasts, he is bringing order out of the chaos of the "great sea." It is like a new act of creation (Isa 65:17; 66:22; 2 Pet 3:13; Rev 21:1), even as God brought order out of the chaos when he created the heavens and the earth (Gen 1).[1] The first three kingdoms, less developed in their opposition to God, received a reprieve as long as they did not attempt to assert their own authority. The final kingdom was destroyed for its overreaching pride and violent opposition to God and his people. With the people of God, who are ruled by the "one like a son of man," there arises a new fixed, eternal order. No longer will there be any need to remove a king or to set a limit to the time that the kingdom will endure. It will indeed constitute a new heaven and a new earth.

## TRANSLATION (DANIEL 7:1–28)

1    In the first year of Belshazzar king of Babylon, Daniel had a dream with visions in his head as he lay on his bed. Then he wrote down the dream.

The beginning[2] of what he said:

2    Daniel stated,[3]

"I saw in my vision of the night, and there were the four winds of heaven[4] stirring up the Great Sea. And four large beasts were rising from the sea, different from each other.

---

1. The concept of *chaos* for the language of Gen 1:2 (תֹהוּ וָבֹהוּ [*tōhû wābōhû*] and "darkness over the surface of the deep [תְּהוֹם]") has fallen out of favor recently (Mathews, *Genesis 1—11:26*, 143), but there are still those who see a "polemic against the common mythology" of "a Canaanite dragon myth" (Konkel, "בֹּהוּ," 1:608). As such, the function of *tōhû* "is to indicate chaos in contrast to the order of creation" (Konkel, "בֹּהוּ," 1:607).

2. Or a *summary*. The phrase is omitted in Th, and it may be missing in 4QDan[b] (see discussion in *DJD* 16, 204).

3. Literally, "answered and said."

4. The idiom "four winds of heaven" means "winds from every direction" (*HALOT* 3:1198).

| | |
|---|---|
| 4 | The first was like a lion, and it had wings of an eagle. I kept watch until its wings were plucked off, and it was raised up from the ground and made to stand on two feet like a human. And a human heart was given to it. |
| 5 | Then there was another beast, a second one resembling a bear. It was raised up to one side, and three ribs were in its mouth between its teeth.

It was told as follows: 'Arise, devour much flesh.' |
| 6 | After this I looked and there was another beast that was like a leopard. It had four wings of a bird on its back, and the beast had four heads; and authority to rule was given to it. |
| 7 | After this I saw in the visions of the night, and there was a fourth beast—terrifying and dreadful and extremely powerful. It had great iron teeth with which it devoured and crushed, and the remains of its prey it trampled with its feet. It was different from all the beasts that were before it, and it had ten horns. |
| 8 | As I was contemplating the horns another horn, a little one, rose among them, and three of the first horns were pulled out before it. There were eyes like human eyes in this horn and a mouth speaking arrogant things. |
| 9 | As I watched, thrones were put in place, and the Ancient of Days sat down.

His clothing was white like snow, and the hair of his head was like pure wool.

His throne was flames of fire; its wheels were burning fire. |
| 10 | A river of fire was flowing and coming out from his presence.

A thousand thousand were serving him, and ten thousand times ten thousand were standing before him.

The court convened, and books were opened. |
| 11 | As I watched, then, because of the sound of the arrogant things that the horn was speaking, I kept watching until the beast was killed, and its body was destroyed and consigned to the burning fire. |
| 12 | And as for the rest of the beasts, their authority to rule was taken away. |

|     | And they were granted a lengthening of their life for a time and a season. |
| --- | --- |
| 13  | As I watched in the visions of the night, then there came with the clouds of heaven one like a son of man.[5] |
|     | He came to the Ancient of Days and was presented before him. |
| 14  | And he was given authority to rule, and honor, and a kingdom, that all peoples, nations, and languages should serve him. |
|     | His dominion is an everlasting dominion that will never pass away, and his kingdom is one that will never be destroyed. |
| 15  | As for me, Daniel, my spirit was distressed within my body,[6] and the visions in my head disturbed me. |
| 16  | I approached one of those standing by and asked him the true meaning about all this, and he told me that he would make known to me the interpretation of these things. |
| 17  | 'These four great beasts are four kings[7] that will rise from the earth. |
| 18  | But the holy ones of the Most High will receive the kingdom, and they will possess the kingdom forever, even forever and ever.' |
| 19  | Then I wanted to know the true meaning about the fourth beast that was different from all of them, very fearsome, with iron teeth, and with claws of bronze. It was devouring (and) crushing and trampling with its feet what was left. |

---

5. The expression בַּר אֱנָשׁ is literally "a son of man" but means "a human being" or "a man" (*HALOT*). He looks like "a human being" as opposed to the four beasts. We have retained the literal translation so that the reader is alerted to this important usage of the phrase. See further discussion under Exposition.

6. Lit., "within (its) sheath." Aramaic נִדְנֶה (*sheath*) is attested in 1QapGen ar 2:10 as נדנהא (*[my soul within] its sheath*) and in Hebrew נְדָנָהּ (*its sheath*, 1 Chron. 21:27). With a slight change of the vowel points of the MT, the form in Dan 7:15 could also be *its sheath* (נִדְנָהּ). The similarity of the line from the *Genesis Apocryphon* to the concept in Daniel is striking.

7. Both the OG and Th, as well as the Vulgate, have "kingdoms" (βασιλεῖαι), while the *Peshitta* has "kings." By changing one letter of the Aramaic text the word would be "kingdoms" (*mlkwn* instead of *mlkyn*), and in some manuscripts of the DSS the letters *waw* and *yodh* are difficult to distinguish. The reading in the Greek and Vulgate could also be an interpretation of the Aramaic.

## VISION OF BEASTS AND KINGDOMS

20    Also (I wanted to know) about the ten horns that were on its head and (about) another (horn) that came up and three (horns) fell before it.

And that horn also had eyes and a mouth speaking boastful things, and its appearance was greater than the others.

21    As I watched, that horn waged war with the holy ones and prevailed against them,

22    until the Ancient of Days came and the judgment was rendered in favor of the holy ones of the Most High. For the time had arrived for the holy ones to take possession of the kingdom.

23    Here is what he said: 'As for the fourth beast, a fourth kingdom will be on the earth that will differ from all the kingdoms. And it will devour the whole earth and trample it and crush it.

24    As for the ten horns, from that kingdom ten kings will arise. Then another will arise after them, and he will differ from the previous ones and will bring down three kings.

25    He will also speak words against the Most High and will wear down the holy ones of the Most High. He will intend to change set times and law. And the holy ones will be given[8] into his power for a time, times, and half a time.

26    But the court will convene, and his dominion will be taken away in order to annihilate and to destroy him to the end.

27    Then the sovereignty and the dominion and the greatness of the kingdoms under the whole heaven will be given to the people of the holy ones of the Most High.

His kingdom is an everlasting kingdom, and all the ruling powers will serve and obey him.'"[9]

28    To here is the end of the matter.

"As for me, Daniel, my thoughts greatly troubled me, and my face turned pale. But I pondered the matter in my mind."

---

8. The Aramaic has "and they will be given...."

9. The ESV (*their kingdoms...obey them*) refers the singular pronouns on מַלְכוּתֵהּ and לֵהּ to "the holy ones of the Most High" viewed as a collective whole. Th supports the reading *his kingdom* and *obey him*, which accords best with the verbs for "serving" and "obeying."

## TEXTUAL OUTLINE (7:1–28)

I. Four Beasts Rise from the Great Sea. (7:1–8)

*[The kingdoms of this world will continually challenge the authority of God.]*

II. The Ancient of Days Convenes Court. (7:9–14)

*[The destiny of the world's kingdoms and peoples are firmly in the hands of the Ancient of Days, who has fixed the time for their judgment.]*

III. The Saints of the Most High Will Suffer Defeat. (7:15–21)

*[God's servants will undergo tremendous persecution and testing.]*

IV. The Saints of the Most High Will Be Delivered and Enter His Everlasting Kingdom. (7:22–28)

*[The time will come for God's servants to be delivered and to enter his kingdom that will never end.]*

## EXPOSITION (7:1–28)

### Four Beasts Rise from the Great Sea. (7:1–8)

Theological Point: The kingdoms of this world will continually challenge the authority of God.

In the first eight verses the time of the vision is established, and the four ferocious beasts are introduced. In this section the action takes place on the earth, with the wind stirring up "the Great Sea." The rest of the vision takes place in the heavenly realm. **Each of the four beasts has some unusual feature that indicates something of its inner nature. People would naturally be terrified of such animals. Who would want to meet a lion or a bear or a leopard in an open field? And these creatures have other features that make them more fearsome.** The lion at first has wings that are then removed, but at the same time it is given human powers of reasoning. The bear has the remnants of devoured prey in its mouth and is being urged to consume more prey. The leopard has wings that make it swift and four heads that would surely terrify anyone who saw it.

**The fourth beast, though, is exceptionally frightful and powerful. Its nondescript appearance only adds to the stark terror that it instills by**

crushing and devouring with its iron-like teeth and trampling with its feet whatever is left of its prey.

Daniel's eyes do not focus for long on the fourth animal; he soon turns to observe its ten horns and what happens with them. Finally, Daniel sees the rise of a "little" horn that oversees the defeat of three horns and that has eyes and a mouth that speaks boastfully. **Despite its size this horn frightens, not because of its potential to devour and crush but because of what it is able to see and speak.**

From the earthly realm the action shifts to heaven, where the Ancient of Days convenes a heavenly court and judgment is pronounced for the beasts. In this manner the narrative reveals God's ultimate decision concerning the fate of the nations. Once the beasts reach the end of their time in history, the way is prepared for the "one like a son of man" to arrive and receive the kingdom. That scene is taken up in the next part of the vision.

7:1a. The setting for Daniel's vision is in the first year of Belshazzar,[10] a date that places it chronologically prior to Daniel 5. The date should be about 553 or 552 BC, when Nabonidus left for Arabia.[11] Daniel saw this vision, then, near the beginning of the reign of the Chaldean king, whose foolishness and weakness contrasted with Nebuchadnezzar's strength and wisdom (chap. 4). **The vision takes a negative view of these beasts that rise out of the sea, a place notorious in the Bible as an environment that contained creatures hostile to God and that he brought into subjection** (cf. Job 26:12; Ps 89:9-10 [10-11]; Isa 27:1). Daniel saw this vision, then, during the reign of a king who did not acknowledge and praise the greatness of Daniel's God.

7:1b. The text parallels "dream" and "visions" in an interesting way. Daniel was lying on his bed and the term *dream* occurs twice, but what he saw was "visions in his head." Even as Nebuchadnezzar experienced dreams that needed to be interpreted, so Daniel also had a dream and saw various images that would call for interpretation. That interpretation would come not from a human interpreter but from a heavenly figure that Daniel saw within the dream. The visual images and their interpretation occurred in the same night, and all of it happened within Daniel's "head."[12] **It is likely**

---

10. The extant Babylonian texts give regnal dates only by the reign of Nabonidus, not by the reign of Belshazzar; but those texts are economic, not literary. From Daniel's perspective Belshazzar began his reign when Nabonidus left for Arabia and placed Belshazzar in charge.

11. Beaulieu, *Reign of Nabonidus*, 159.

12. It is unlikely that Daniel thought in terms of images within the brain as moderns would. The "head" is mentioned because the eyes are in the head, and even in a

the element of interpretation within the dream itself that gives it the label "vision." It is a "vision" because of its revelatory nature; God here reveals significant aspects about the future through these dream images.[13]

**7:1c.** When Daniel awoke, he recorded his dream in writing. There are two variant translations of the last phrase of the verse, depending on how the Aramaic word רֵאשׁ is interpreted. Its basic sense is *head*, and in an extended sense it can be either *main content* or *beginning*. Since 7:28 refers to the "end" of the account, some commentators have taken רֵאשׁ to refer to its *beginning*.[14] Archer objects that the term would more likely have been רֵאשִׁית,[15] but *HALOT* notes a usage of רֵאשׁ in the Aramaic papyri where it means *beginning*. The idea of a marker of the beginning of the vision makes good sense in the overall structure of the book. The strictly visionary part of the book begins with Daniel's vision, and the Aramaic portion of the book ends with that same vision (7:28).

**7:2.** In Hebrew the phrase הַיָּם הַגָּדוֹל ("the Great Sea") **normally refers to the Mediterranean Sea (e.g., Num 34:6, 7; Josh 1:4; 9:1; Ezek 47:10), but here the Aramaic phrase,** יַמָּא רַבָּא ("the Great Sea"), **is more of a metaphor than a geographical location. Like the beasts that represent kingdoms, so the "Great Sea" represents their origin from an environment that is hostile to God.**[16] **The OT sometimes alludes to (but does not validate) an ancient creation myth in order to describe poetically the Lord's sovereign control over all creation (Job 7:12; 9:8; 26:12–13; Pss 74:13; 89:9–10 [10–11]), or to describe his victory over the Egyptians at the parting of the Red Sea (Ps 106:9; Isa 50:2; 51:9–10; Hab 3:8, 15), or some other judgment against the nations (Nah 1:4; Isa 27:1; Ezek 32:2). Also, the nations** *roar* **like the** *roaring* **of the seas (Isa 17:12–14; Jer 6:23). According to the book of Revelation, John saw a "beast rising out of the sea" (Rev 13:1), a clear allusion to Daniel 7: 2. And in the "new heaven and new earth" the sea is no longer present.**[17]

Three of the animals that Daniel saw—a lion or lioness, a leopard, and a bear—occur together in Hos 13:7–8, but there they stand for the ferocity

---

dream, as the ancients thought, one would see by means of the eyes.

13. For further discussion on the distinction between *vision* and *dream* see Naudé ("חזה," 2:58–59).

14. Montgomery, *Book of Daniel*, 284; Goldingay, *Daniel*, 144

15. Archer, "Daniel," 85; HALOT, "רֵאשׁ," 5:1975.

16. See Gardner, "Decoding Daniel," 412–15

17. Given how the Scriptures refer to the great hostility of the sea and its monstrous creatures, it seems reasonable that the lack of a sea describes figuratively the absence of evil.

of God's judgment against Israel. Here they represent entities that rise from the hostile sea.[18]

7:4. For Nebuchadnezzar's dream of the great statue the first element, the head of gold, stands for Nebuchadnezzar and his kingdom of Babylon. Daniel made that explicit in his interpretation (2:37-38). Then the next element, the chest and arms of silver, is stated to be "after" Nebuchadnezzar and "inferior" to him (2:39). **For Daniel's vision of the four beasts, however, the angel gave an interpretation that was more mysterious. The four beasts were "four kings" (i.e., "kingdoms") that would arise "from the earth" (7:17). The fourth kingdom was described in much greater detail than the other three, but none of them was identified explicitly with any particular earthly kingdom. This indefiniteness makes the interpretation more typological in nature.**

The indeterminate nature of the symbolism of the four beasts is important to keep in mind. There are specific historical kingdoms that can fit the descriptions, but the features for comparison are not clear enough to garner unanimity among expositors. Jewish and Christian interpreters have had various views about the historical referents of the beasts since the early centuries of the Christian era.[19] The text stresses that when the fourth kingdom is destroyed, the "saints of the Most High" will possess ruling authority forever (vv. 26-27). Whether the fourth kingdom is Greek or Roman, the challenge remains that many kingdoms have come and gone since those empires flourished. **Daniel's vision makes the theological point that all the kingdoms of this world have their ruling authority only from the Most High, and for all of them their time is limited. The kingdom represented by the fourth beast will surpass all in terror and horror, but because "heaven rules" (Dan 4:26 [23]) even that kingdom will be no match for the Almighty God.**

The first kingdom in Daniel's vision is normally identified with Babylon. The vision took place during the reign of Belshazzar, king at the time that Babylon fell, and it would make sense for the first beast that Daniel saw to represent a kingdom contemporary with him. The prophet Jeremiah portrayed the Babylonian threat to Judah metaphorically as a lion (Jer 4:7; 50:17), and Ezekiel pictured it as an eagle (Ezek 17:3, 12; cf. Deut 28:49; Jer 49:22; Lam 4:19; Hab 1:8).

---

18. There is considerable debate about the possibility of a Babylonian background to the vision of chapter 7. John Collins ("Stirring up the Great Sea") argues in favor of it, while Ferch ("Daniel 7 and Ugarit") takes an opposing view. Since Daniel had his vision while in Babylon, some Babylonian background is likely.

19. See the Excursus on "Daniel 7 in the Syrian Christian Tradition."

Many interpreters also apply at least some of what happens to the beast directly to Nebuchadnezzar. Steinmann, for example, takes the winged lion to represent "the rapid expansion of the Neo-Babylonian Empire under Nabopolassar [Nebuchadnezzar's father] and Nebuchadnezzar."[20] The removal of the wings then indicated a slowing of the expansion during Nebuchadnezzar's reign, and "the humanizing of this beast represents the lessening ferocity of the Babylonian Empire under its later kings."[21] Saadia Gaon (tenth century) took the eagle's wings as representative of Nebuchadnezzar's hair that grew like eagles' feathers and his nails like birds' claws. Then when his wings were removed and he was stood up on his feet and given a human heart, it meant that Nebuchadnezzar had been restored to his state as a normal human and had intelligence to think like a human (Dan 4:31–34 [28–31]).[22] Many moderns have followed a similar line of interpretation to Gaon's, although not necessarily attaching the same significance to the wings as reminiscent of Nebuchadnezzar's long hair.[23]

While it seems clear that the winged lion represents Babylon in some way, it is not so clear that the references elsewhere in Scripture to Babylon attacking like a lion or an eagle must be the source of the imagery here. What Daniel saw was a creature that looked like a lion that had the wings of an eagle; nowhere in the other Scriptures cited is there such a combination of images. There is also reason to doubt that the imagery referred to Nebuchadnezzar. The timing of the vision was during the last king of Babylon; Nebuchadnezzar had been dead already for many years. There must be some theological significance to the timing. Belshazzar's reign was hardly as stellar as Nebuchadnezzar's reign. There is no hint of a golden era like when Nebuchadnezzar made Babylon the center of a thriving kingdom. Even though a reference back to Nebuchadnezzar as representative of the entire duration of the Babylonian kingdom would not be impossible, the vision has such a forward looking perspective that a back reference is unlikely. The angel spoke of four kings or kingdoms that "*will arise from the earth*" (7:17). At the time of the vision during the reign of Belshazzar, the Medo-Persian realm had already come on the scene and was poised to take over Babylon, but Belshazzar still had some years of reign ahead of him.

To understand why Daniel sees the lion with wings it helps to examine what sort of images he would have seen on a regular basis. Winged lions

---

20. Steinmann, *Daniel*, 343.
21. Steinmann, *Daniel*, 343.
22. Goldwurm, *Daniel*, 196.
23. Wood, *Daniel*, 182; Walvoord, *Daniel*, 153–54; Miller, *Daniel*, 197.

are known from Assyrian cylinder seals.[24] The main processional street at Babylon was also lined with walls that had some one hundred and twenty lions made from enameled bricks.[25] Gods were often depicted with wings in Assyrian and Babylonian iconography, and winged bulls with human heads served as guardians to Assyrian palaces (ninth to eighth centuries BC). Lions with wings are also depicted on various media from the early second millennium to the seventh century BC.[26] **The kind of animals that Daniel saw, then, could represent not only earthly kingdoms but also beings that from the Babylonian point of view represented the realm of the gods.**[27] **For Daniel they represented forces that were opposed to God but that would eventually be judged. And again, that they arose from the Great Sea is indicative of their opposition to God.**[28] **The "prince of the kingdom of Persia" stood against the angelic messenger sent in response to Daniel's prayer (10:13). In a similar manner these beasts in Daniel's first vision represent demonic forces that were present in each kingdom as well as the human king who was directed by them. The demonic forces, however, were tamed by God's forces.** The lion was stripped of its wings and made to stand like a man, and its human heart replaced its lion-like ferocity.[29] Worschech compares the first beast to Assyrian-Babylonian depictions of a man who is covered with a lion pelt with the head of the lion intact and who stands erect.[30] The Babylonian empire, represented by

---

24. Porada has pictures from Assyrian seals ("Why Cylinder Seals?", 580–81), and Lucas provides a picture of a winged lion on the palace of Darius Hystaspes ("Daniel," 548).

25. Pritchard (*ANEP*, 762) has a picture with discussion.

26. Strommenger, *5000 Years of the Art of Mesopotamia*, plates 159, 187, 192, 198, 220, 226; see also Pace, *Daniel*, 230.

27. Lucas (*Daniel*, 170–71) thinks of Mesopotamian omens that describe the birth of strangely shaped animals as background for the beasts in Daniel's vision. He rejects the argument from Babylonian iconography because bears "are rarely depicted" and only lived in the mountainous areas of Iran (168). That is a weak argument. As his source mentions, bears were at least known (Noth, "History in Old Testament Apocalyptic," 211). Moreover, a bear is depicted on a lyre from Ur (ANEP, no. 192), and Sennacherib referred to tying up a Babylonian king at Nineveh "like a bear" (CAD, D:17). With all the education that Daniel had at the Babylonian court, he must have seen at some time a depiction of a bear.

28. "Daniel's original audience would likely have understood that the vision Daniel reported is one where the authority of God is challenged by chaotic beasts, which readers are told are symbolic of human empires and their kings (7:17)" (Barnes, "Theological Interpretation," 312).

29. See Pace, *Daniel*, 232–33; Steinmann, *Daniel*, 343.

30. Worschech, "Der assyrisch-babylonische Löwenmensch," 330–32.

this lion-like figure, was both ruthless in its conquests[31] and benevolent in its treatment of captives (Daniel and his companions; Jehoiachin [2 Kgs 25:27–30]). **For Jewish captives this would have meant that behind the fearful Babylonian metaphor of a lion that pointed to the realm of gods and demons there was only a very human and earthly kingdom that was within God's power to control. That would highlight the major theme of Daniel that God's kingdom triumphs over all the kingdoms of man.**

7:5. The second beast represents a major dividing line among interpreters of Daniel. Some take it to refer to the kingdom of the Medes, while others think of the Medo-Persian empire. The most important argument in favor of Media is that Daniel refers to "Darius the Mede" (5:31; chap. 6; 9:1; 11:1) and to "Cyrus the Persian" (6:28 [27]; cf. 1:21 and 10:1), seemingly showing that the Medes preceded the Babylonian kingdom. Cyrus and Darius the Mede, as we have argued in the Introduction, are likely different titles for the same person, making it possible to attach either title to the Medo-Persian empire.[32] Those who take the fourth kingdom as Greece assume that the bear must by default represent an independent Median kingdom.[33]

Many interpreters agree that the bear symbolizes the kingdom that conquered Babylon.[34] That conquest is ascribed to Media by Isaiah (13:17) and Jeremiah (51:11), but the role of Cyrus is also clear from Isaiah's prophecies (44:28; 45:1). The reference to the bear "raised up to one side" most naturally indicates that one side of the bear was higher than the other, and this in turn could easily refer to the Medo-Persian empire, with Persia as the more dominant element.[35] A similar idea is conveyed in the vision of chapter 8 by the ram with two horns, one higher than the other and arising at a later time (Dan 8:3). Historically, Media arose first but was then conquered by Cyrus and incorporated into the Persian empire prior to his conquest of Babylon. The Medes and the Persians were thus unified when they attacked Babylon but were nonetheless composed of two peoples, one of which was more powerful and significant. The vision of the bear thereby brings together the predictions of the fall of Babylon made by both Isaiah and Jeremiah.[36]

---

31. "The ravenous appetite of Babylon, the devastator of the Kingdom of Judah, is strongly stressed in the prophets (Jer 5:15ff; Hab 2:5)" (Hartman and Di Lella, *Book of Daniel*, 212).

32. See also Colless, "Cyrus the Persian and Darius the Mede."

33. E.g., Goldingay, *Daniel*, 162; Seow, *Daniel*, 103.

34. E.g., Keil, *Ezekiel, Daniel*, 225; Walvoord, *Daniel*, 155; Steinmann, *Daniel*, 344.

35. Keil, *Ezekiel, Daniel*, 225; Wood, *Daniel*, 183.

36. See Gardner, "Decoding Daniel," 228–30; other ideas are that the bear was raised up on its hind legs, poised to attack (Baldwin, *Daniel*, 139), that the one side

Why should a bear rather than some other animal symbolize the Medo-Persian empire? A Jewish interpretation points to the fact that the Persians were benevolent rulers, and the bear in the vision had to be commanded to eat meat (conquer Babylon), contrary to its nature.[37] The bear is known, however, to sometimes eat meat (1 Sam 17:34), and the three ribs in its mouth when the command was given to "eat much flesh" most naturally represent an animal in process of being devoured or already devoured. Another suggestion is that the bear as an astrological symbol represented the nations from the far north that were to attack Babylon, according to Isa 13:5 when compared with Job 38:32-33.[38] For Keil the bear is "[n]ext to the lion . . . the strongest among animals."[39] **The context appears to demand a symbol of a ferocious and powerful nation that had a rapacious appetite for conquest, something that fits Medo-Persia well despite its apparent overall benevolence to the Jews (Dan 8:4; 11:2).**[40]

The three ribs in the bear's mouth have been interpreted in a variety of ways. One view refers to three Babylonian kings known from Scripture—Nebuchadnezzar, Evil-Merodach, and Belshazzar.[41] Jerome, who interpreted Aramaic עִלְעִין as "rows" rather than "ribs," referred to "the three kingdoms of the Babylonians, the Medes, and the Persians, all of which were reduced to a single realm."[42] Perhaps the ribs refer to conquests already made, while the unidentified voice urges the kingdom to further conquest. Keil identified the three conquests with Lydia and Babylon under Cyrus, and Egypt under Cyrus's son Cambyses.[43] **From a theological standpoint, the voice that commands the bear to "eat much flesh" represents divine control of the situation. Three nations have already been conquered, but God wills it to conquer more.**

**7:6.** The number *four* figures prominently with the third beast—four wings and four heads. The four heads especially make one think that the nature of the kingdom itself is fourfold, and the only ancient kingdom that fits such a description is Greece, following the death of Alexander the Great.

---

represented Darius the Mede (Hartman and Di Lella, *Book of Daniel*, 212-13), or that the phrase represents some kind of deformity in the bear (Seow, *Daniel*, 103).

37. Goldwurm, *Daniel*, 197-98.

38. Gardner, "Decoding Daniel," 229. The "Bear" constellation of Job 38:32 is עַיִשׁ in Hebrew, different from the normal term for "bear," דֹּב, in both Hebrew and Aramaic.

39. Keil, *Ezekiel, Daniel*, 224.

40. Note also how easily Xerxes (Ahasuerus) was persuaded by Haman to allow him to exterminate all Jews in the Persian empire (Esther 3).

41. Lacocque, *Book of Daniel*, 140.

42. Jerome, *Commentary on Daniel*, 74.

43. Keil, *Ezekiel, Daniel*, 226.

He would be represented by the leopard, and the four heads would stand for the division of his empire. The leopard is known for its speed and ferocity, apt characteristics to represent Alexander's rapid and ruthless conquest of the known world. Those who relate the leopard to Persia are unable to find such a specific referent for the number four.[44] **An important statement is that "authority to rule was given to it." As the rule of kings changed from one type to another, it was always God who transferred ruling power.**

7:7. **The fourth beast, as the text says, is "different" from all the others. Its special nature is shown by the amount of detail devoted to describing it and also by its treatment at the heavenly judgment scene. The others were stripped of their ruling authority but also granted an extension of their lives, while the fourth beast was summarily killed and destroyed (7:11–12).** And aside from a reference to its horns and imposing size and ferocity, the fourth beast was not named. An elephant has been suggested, but that is speculation that goes beyond what the text indicates.[45] Also, it is based on the interpretation that the fourth beast represents the Greek kingdom.[46]

Those who identify the fourth beast with Greece have been hard pressed to identify the ten horns. Goldingay lists six different views about who the predecessors were to Antiochus IV, allegedly the referent for the "little horn." He concludes that confidence in the matter is "impossible."[47] The angel interprets these ten horns as arising from the fourth kingdom itself (7:24). Then another horn would arise and "bring down three kings." **The horns here stand for individual kings; the additional horn is the one who would "wear out" the "saints of the Most High," at the same time speaking "words" against "the Most High" (7:25).** In the later vision of the ram with two horns (8:3), though, the horns stood for the two parts of the Medo-Persian empire ("the kings of Media and Persia," 8:20).[48] The single horn on the goat that attacked the ram had its referent in the "first king" of Greece, but then the four horns that replaced it were to be "four kingdoms"

---

44. John Collins (*Daniel*, 298) notes the four Persian kings of Dan 11:2 but thinks the number more generally represents the four corners of the earth, making Persia a universal empire. Dan 11:2 mentions "four more" Persian kings, so there were at least five according to that passage. Universality could apply even more to the Greek empire of Alexander.

45. Goldingay, *Daniel*, 163; Blasius, "Antiochus IV and Ptolemaic Triad," 523.

46. See Hanhart, "Daniel's Vision in the Night," 576.

47. Goldingay, *Daniel*, 179–80.

48. The ancient versions (Greek, Syriac, and Latin) took the two horns to represent "the king of Media and Persia."

(8:21–22). In several other places in the OT the horn of an animal stands for military power or strength.⁴⁹

In John's heavenly vision, recorded in the book of Revelation, he saw both a "dragon" (Rev 12:3) and a "beast" (Rev 13:1; 17:3, 7) with seven heads and ten horns, and the horns were "ten kings who have not yet received a kingdom" but who would receive "authority as kings" with "the beast" (Rev 17:12). John's vision thus expands on Daniel's and sets its timing at the end of the age. As such it is not possible to identify the ten kings, because they have not yet come on the scene. Will they rule over some form of a revived Roman empire?⁵⁰ Perhaps, but **the text stresses only that Daniel's fourth kingdom would be different from all the others.** Historically the Roman empire followed the Greek kingdom, and that is the basis for the view of a revived Roman empire in the future. The nondescript nature of the fourth beast, however, should caution the interpreter against assuming too much regarding such a specific identification. The four kingdoms arose from the "great sea" as "the four winds of heaven" stirred it up. **While Rome could complete the sequence as the fourth, the "little horn" on the fourth beast also represents the culmination of all human rule that is against God, an antipathy that will be focused in the horns** (see also the Excursus: "Daniel 7 and Revelation 17").

Readers who are used to thinking of the fourth kingdom as Rome may be surprised to realize that there is no direct reference to Rome in the rest of the book of Daniel.⁵¹ The interpretation proper takes place in two parts. First, the angel states that the four beasts stand for four kings or kingdoms that will arise on the earth, after which "the holy ones of the Most High" will receive a lasting kingdom (7:18). In the second part, Daniel asks for more information about the fourth beast, adding some details not previously mentioned (7:19–22). Then the angel interprets each element that Daniel asked about: the fourth beast, the ten horns, the judgment, and how "the holy ones of the Most High" will receive God's kingdom (7:23–27).

From a historical perspective, chapter 8 moves from Medo-Persia to Alexander the Great and culminates with the Greek king Antiochus IV Epiphanes. Chapter 9 leaves behind the scheme of four world powers in favor of the seventy weeks. The crucifixion of the Messiah and the destruction of Jerusalem and the temple (9:26) are the only events that can be placed within the Roman period. Then chapters 10 and most of 11, like chapter 8,

---

49. See Deut 33:17; 1 Sam 2:1, 10; Pss 18:2 (3); 75:4–5 (5–6), 10 (11); Jer 48:25; Ezek 34:21; Mic 4:13; Zech 1:18–21 (2:1–4).

50. Wood, *Daniel*, 187, 200.

51. The only indirect reference is to the "commander" (קָצִין) of 11:18, who was probably a Roman.

deal with Medo-Persia, Alexander the Great, and the conflict in the later Greek period between the Seleucids (kings of the North or Syria) and the Ptolemies (kings of the South or Egypt). Only with 11:36—12:1 does the time frame leap forward to the final conflict between the Antichrist and "Michael the great prince." In some respects, the third kingdom lives on through history as the Greco-Roman civilization, and the fourth kingdom might turn out to surprise everyone.[52] It could be a revived Roman empire, but that is not certain from the text.[53] Gabriel's revelation of the seventy "weeks" of Daniel 9, as will be argued, contains a gap. Those periods of sevens deal more specifically with God's work among the Jews, which has not been completed, but paused as he works through the church.[54] The fourth beast relates more generally to world power that will come to an end when God's kingdom is established.

**7:8.** Daniel focused intently on the horns, among which was a "little" horn that arose and brought down three others. Here the text says only that the three horns were "uprooted" before it, but the angelic interpretation clarifies the hostile action of the little horn (v. 24). Daniel also supplemented his description of the little horn at verse twenty-one. It waged war with the "holy ones" and prevailed against them.

**For being a "little" horn this one was quite aggressive and powerful, and one could wonder why it should be described as "little." It was "little" but it also spoke "arrogant things," and the contrast is significant. Even though the horn tried to make itself sound big as it railed against God, in his eyes it was simply "little." That was also an encouragement to "the holy ones." The horn might wage war with them and prevail for a season, but its doom was certain. However mighty it might seem to God's people, it was only a small matter for their God to destroy it.** "Behold, the nations are like a drop from a bucket, and are accounted as the dust on the scales" (Isa 40:15 ESV).

The horn also had "eyes like human eyes," a feature that would look grotesque on an animal horn. God has many "eyes" that enable him to see all that goes on in the world (Prov 15:3; Ezek 1:18; 10:12; Zech 3:9; 4:10; Rev

---

52. See Stephen Cook, *Apocalyptic Literature*, 51.

53. Steinmann (*Daniel*, 57) worries about the gap that dispensationalists assume lies between the fourth beast (Rome) and "the ten-nation confederacy and the rise of the Antichrist." While this is not the place to discuss the pre-millennial view of a literal earthly kingdom versus the amillennial view that the kingdom represents the church, Miller (*Daniel*, 202–3) speaks not of a "gap" but of "a confederation of kings (kingdoms or nations) that emanate from the old Roman Empire." He also cites two amillennialists, Young (*Prophecy of Daniel*, 149) and Leupold (*Daniel*, 323), who also see or at least suggest continuity from Rome to the current nations of Europe.

54. See Saucy, *Progressive Dispensationalism*, 246–63

4:6, 8; 5:6), and perhaps the eyes on the horn make it seem more menacing, with a complex system for gathering information on people. **As "human" eyes, though, their ability is greatly limited compared to God's eyes, which give him omniscience.** From another vantage point, "eyes" can be an indication of pride when they are "haughty" (Prov 6:17; Isa 5:15) or when they focus completely on the achievements of the one who has them (Prov 12:15; 26:12; 28:11; Isa 5:21). Prov 6:17 possibly includes all three elements ascribed to the horn—"haughty eyes," "a lying tongue" (the boastful mouth), and "hands that shed innocent blood" (the attack on the "holy ones of the Most High," vv. 21, 25). An earlier king of Assyria had "haughtily raised" his eyes and voice against "the Holy One of Israel" (Isa 37:23).[55]

## The Ancient of Days Convenes Court. (7:9–14)

Theological Point: The destiny of the world's kingdoms and peoples are firmly in the hands of the Ancient of Days, who has fixed the time for their judgment.

The scene shifts suddenly to a courtroom in heaven, with the Ancient of Days presiding. **The multitude of attending angels, as well as the fiery throne, add to the glory and importance of the Ancient of Days. His court is the highest possible place of justice; no one can appeal to any higher authority.** The fourth beast is the first to receive its sentence—death by burning. The others appear to have something like probation—stripped of ruling authority but granted an extension of life. **All this sets the scene for the entrance of the "one like a son of man" to receive kingdom authority.**

7:9–10. The title "Ancient of Days" for God is unique to Daniel.[56] It refers to his eternal existence and fits well with the book's emphasis on issues of time.[57] While the beasts represent kingdoms whose time is limited by God; the kingdom of God will endure forever even as he endures forever. The Ancient of Days is the God "who changes the times and the seasons" (Dan 2:21); he created time itself.

---

55. Goldingay, *Daniel*, 164; see the exposition of 7:25 for further discussion.

56. Some have compared the epithet with the title "father of years" (*ab šnm*) given to the god El in the Ugaritic texts. For the Ugaritic references see Simon Parker, *Ugaritic Narrative Poetry*, 92, 116, 127, 149). Ferch ("Daniel 7 and Ugarit") argues vigorously against any Ugaritic connection.

57. Smith and Wegner, "עתק (6980)," *NIDOTTE* 3:569.

The garments "white as snow" worn by the Ancient of Days refer to his moral purity. White snow elsewhere indicates such purity (Ps 51:7 [9]; Isa 1:18), and no one is purer than God, in whom "there is no darkness at all" (1 John 1:5). The white hair parallels poetically the white garments. "Pure wool," coming from a white sheep, would also have a brilliant whiteness to it. Pure white hair could also be a sign of advanced age, although in the OT that is normally indicated by gray hair (Prov 20:29).[58] **Here the parallelism makes an advance on the thought of purity. The clothes that the Ancient of Days wears symbolize his purity, and even the hair on his head displays his moral perfection.**

After the brief description of the clothing and hair of the Ancient of Days, Daniel described his throne. Several features are common to this throne and the one that Ezekiel saw when in Babylonia (Ezek 1).[59] The element of fire is common to both, and both had wheels. Both also supported a depiction of God in some way. Ezekiel saw something that looked like a human form surrounded by a gleaming radiance (1:26–27), while Daniel saw the Ancient of Days in a brilliant white splendor. Ezekiel saw creatures that bore the throne; Daniel saw myriads of attendants standing before the Ancient of Days. Isaiah also had a vision of the Lord seated on a throne with seraphs attending him (Isa 6:1–3). **All three images depict God's authority as the King over all, who is served by heavenly angels, and in each there is also an element of judgment.** Isaiah was given a mission to proclaim judgment to a stubborn people (6:10–13), and Ezekiel would later see "the glory of the Lord" depart from the temple and Jerusalem, a sign that the Lord was about to destroy the idolaters along with the temple and the city (10:1–18). Now Daniel saw in his vision that judgment would fall on the kingdoms of the world.

The fiery river proceeding from the throne reminds readers of the water that proceeded from the temple in Ezekiel's vision (Ezek 47:1–5; cf. Rev 22:1–2), but the reference to fire here speaks of judgment rather than life (Ps 97:3; Isa 66:16; Ezek 38:22; Joel 2:3; Heb 10:27; 2 Pet 3:7). The fire could also point to God's glory (Exod 24:17; Deut 5:24; Zech 2:5 [9]).

---

58. The white buds of the almond tree appear to be a metaphor for old age in Eccl 12:5.

59. One shouldn't expect all such descriptions to be exactly the same. Since "no one has ever seen or can see" God (1 Tim 6:16 ESV), any image that involves him must be only suggestive. Ezekiel distanced himself from any thought that his vision was a realistic portrait of God: "That was the appearance of the likeness of the glory of God" (1:28). Each prophet sees images that point to theological realities about God (cf. Exod 33:18—34:8).

The Ancient of Days "sat down" first. Then the others for whom the thrones had been placed were seated in order to convene the tribunal. The scene could be compared to a divine council as depicted in Job 1:6–12, Ps 82, and 1 Kgs 22:19–23. The "books" that were opened when the court "sat" revealed the deeds of people (cf. Rev 20:12). Scripture depicts various "books" in heaven in which records are kept, very much like an earthly king would keep records or "chronicles" of the events of his reign (cf. 2 Kgs 1:18; 1 Chr 27:24; Esth 2:23; 10:2). In these books are recorded the believer's tears (Ps 56:8 [9]), the names of the righteous (Ps 69:28 [29]; Dan 12:1 [cf. Mal 3:16]; Phil 4:3; Rev 3:5; 13:8; 17:8; 20:15; 21:27), the deeds of the righteous (Neh 13:14; cf. Mal 3:16), and things ordained or decreed (Ps 139:16; Dan 10:21).

7:11–12. Aramaic חָזֵה הֲוֵית ("as I looked," or, "I kept watching") occurs twice in verse eleven. At the onset of the verse, it separates the judgment of the beasts from the description of the court. The Old Greek omits the second occurrence of the phrase, leading some to treat it as secondary (*BHS*). **The repetition, however, causes the reader to focus on the killing of the fourth beast. The same phrase at the start of verse thirteen signals the arrival of "one like a son of man" to receive the everlasting kingdom.**

**The contrast between the fourth beast and the first three is heightened by the major difference in their judgments—death and destruction versus removal of authority but prolonging of life.** The crimes of the fourth beast, especially those of the "little horn" that originated from the beast, were against the whole world and even against the Most High and his "holy ones" (7:23–25). Hence the beast deserved the death sentence. Walvoord finds "an obvious parallel to Rev 19:20 where the beast and the false prophet are cast alive into the lake of fire burning with brimstone at the time of the second coming of Christ."[60]

The other beasts were merely successive earthly kingdoms;[61] but if so, why were they granted additional life? One view is that the successive "empires were to some extent continued in their successors; that is, Gentile power shifted as to rulership but continued more or less in the same pattern."[62] Steinmann finds a parallel in Matt 13:24–43, "where God does not immediately root out the weeds, but allows them to continue until the judgment."[63] Archer thought of the citizens of the earlier kingdoms as "re-

---

60. Walvoord, *Daniel*, 165.

61. A few interpreters think of kingdoms contemporary with each other rather than successive (Hanhart, "Daniel's Vision in the Night"; Fröhlich, *Historical Consciousness*, 74–75.

62. Walvoord, *Daniel*, 166; see also Wood, *Daniel*, 191; Miller, *Daniel*, 206.

63. Steinmann, *Daniel*, 355.

served for a day of judgment by the returning Christ."[64] Other commentators look for a literary reason to explain the extra life given to the first three kingdoms. "The fourth beast was *different* from the others and so was dealt with differently, as its greater offences deserved."[65]

Some biblical passages indicate that in a future kingdom, nations that had oppressed the people of Israel will become their servants (Isa 14:1–2; 49:22–23; 60:10–12; Amos 9:12; Obad 21).[66] Perhaps the kingdoms given renewed life after their sovereignty has been taken away symbolize the remnants of such nations that will enter into the kingdom and have some role as servants.[67]

**If the first three kingdoms are illustrative of various kingdoms that rise and fall throughout history, the fourth kingdom would then be the final kingdom in the eschatological end time. The three are allowed to continue their normal course, but the fourth will be destroyed and replaced with the everlasting kingdom of the Ancient of Days.**

7:13–14. The "one like a son of man" enters the scene and is presented before the Ancient of Days. The Aramaic כְּבַר אֱנָשׁ is literally "like a son of man." The NRSV represents the idiom most accurately with "one like a human being," but it loses the sense of how the term came to be used later by Jesus (esp. Matt 26:64; Mark 13:26; 14:62; Luke 21:27; 22:69).[68] **Daniel saw a human figure, but what or who that figure represented is a separate issue.** Unlike "(the) Ancient of Days," the Aramaic term "son of man" is not a specific title in the book of Daniel but a descriptor, like the term "man" (אָדָם) on the throne in Ezek 1:26.

This third major scene in Daniel's vision (vv. 13–14) is clearly the high point of the vision. An extra-long introductory formula prefaces it: "as I watched in the visions of the night." **While the first scene began with beasts rising from the sea, now we see a human figure coming with "the clouds of heaven." As he is presented to the Ancient of Days, readers' minds are taken back to the judgment scene. The other nations were judged, we now see, so that this one might come and rule over an eternal kingdom. And familiar refrains that have been heard throughout the book strike the ears:**

---

64. Archer, "Daniel," 89.

65. Lucas, *Daniel*, 183; see also Pace, *Daniel*, 244–45.

66. See Lucas, *Daniel*, 183.

67. See Heaton, *Book of Daniel*, 181.

68. Buth posits that Jesus may have preached in Hebrew but referred to himself by the Aramaic title from Daniel 7 ("Semitic Background," 186–89).

- "peoples, nations, and languages" (3:4, 7, 29, 31 [4:1]; 5:19; 6:26)
- "his dominion is an everlasting dominion" (4:31; cf. 6:27)
- "his kingdom will never be destroyed" (2:44; 4:34 [31]; 6:26 [27])

A strong word, פלח (to serve), is applied to the service that the nations render to the human figure. Everywhere else that the term occurs in Daniel it refers to service rendered to God or to a god (3:14, 17, 18, 28; 6:16 [17], 20 [21]; 7:27).[69] It would seem, then, that the nations will "serve" the "one like a son of man" as though he were God. The angel later applies similar language to the Most High: "His kingdom is an everlasting kingdom, and all the ruling powers will serve [יִפְלְחוּן] and obey him" (v. 27).

7:13. Who is this "one like a son of man"? Surprisingly, the interpreting angel does not give any specific interpretation about him. Largely for that reason, some have viewed him as merely a figurative representation for "the people of the holy ones of the Most High" (7:27).[70] These "people of the Most High" will receive "the sovereignty and the dominion and the greatness of (the) kingdoms under the whole heaven," even as the "one like a son of man" received "authority to rule and honor and a kingdom" (v. 14). Since they both received the same thing, so goes the argument, they must also be the same thing. In other words, when the angel says that "the people of the holy ones of the Most High" will receive the kingdom, he is interpreting that part of Daniel's vision that refers to the "one like a son of man." Additionally, it is noted that the human figure from heaven contrasts with the beasts from the sea. Even as they were figurative of Gentile kingdoms, so the human figure represents God's people who will receive his kingdom.[71]

While the representative view has some support from the text, there are additional considerations that point instead to an individual person who is described as "one like a son of man" (i.e., a human being). First, the angel calls the beasts "four kings" that will arise. Each beast is represented by a king who also possesses a kingdom. If each of the "kings" has behind him a demon who plays a role in the affairs of each successive kingdom, then the "one like a son of man" should be a heavenly figure who will rule over "the people of the holy ones of the Most High."

---

69. The OG has λατρεύουσα αὐτῷ (*serving him*), and the verb λατρεύω signifies to perform religious service (Muraoka, *GELS*).

70. Montgomery, *Book of Daniel*, 323; Hartman and Di Lella, *Book of Daniel*, 218-19; Casey, *Son of Man*, 24-29.

71. See Montgomery, *Book of Daniel*, 317-24; Hartman and Di Lella, *Book of Daniel*, 94-102; Casey, *Solution to the 'Son of Man' Problem*, 85, 114.

According to John Collins, a human being in a visionary experience normally represents an angel.[72] Daniel also sees men in his later visions who represent heavenly figures (8:15; 9:21; 10:5, 18; 12:6, 7). Collins concludes that the human figure of Daniel 7 represents the angel Michael, the "prince" of Israel.[73] It should be noted, though, that the "man" referenced in 10:5 might be a theophany. Some similarity with the human figure of Ezek 1:26 should also be noted. For Ezekiel this human-like figure must represent Yahweh. Ezekiel's entire vision represents "the appearance of the form of the glory of Yahweh" (v. 27). In a similar way, Daniel's figure is "like a human being" but has divine characteristics. He comes "with the clouds of heaven" and receives universal honor from the nations.[74] And while Isa 6:1 uses the term *Lord* (אֲדֹנָי) rather than a term for *man*, it is likely that Isaiah saw a human figure seated like a king on his throne.

Daniel 10:5-6, as we will argue, is described in terms that indicate deity, and a similar issue arises with the "one like a son of man." The service rendered this human figure by the nations is stated in terms of religious service offered to God (7:14), and at 7:27 it is the Most High whom the nations serve or worship (יְפַלְחוּן, "*they will serve*").

**Whether the "son of man" is viewed here as representative of God's people who will inherit the eternal kingdom or of a heavenly person who represents the Lord himself, a messianic interpretation is still called for. The deity of the Messiah can be seen in Pss 2:7; 110:1; Isa 9:6 (5); and Zech 12:10 and 13:7. Daniel actually used the term "anointed one" (מָשִׁיחַ) twice (9:25, 26) with reference to the Messiah, and the concept of an eternal kingdom brought about through God's intervention in history demands a ruler who would be the Messiah.** Amos, probably the earliest of the writing prophets, quotes the Lord: "In that day I will raise up the fallen shelter of David" (Amos 9:11) at a future time when "I will restore the fortunes of my people Israel" (Amos 9:14). It will be a time when Israel will be "planted" on their land and "never again be uprooted" from it (Amos 9:15). Micah prophesied the coming of a ruler from Judah whose "origins are from of old, from ancient days" (Mic 5:2 [1]). The post-exilic prophet Zechariah foresaw a king who will come to Jerusalem, riding in triumph on a donkey and whose kingdom will be "from the river to the ends of the earth" (Zech 9:9-10). The NT authors portray Jesus of Nazareth as referring

---

72. John Collins, *Daniel*, 306. The first beast (v. 4) and the "little" horn (v. 8) both had some characteristics described as like a man, but only as part of the beast imagery.

73. John Collins, *Daniel*, 310; cf. Dan 10:13, 21)

74. Groningen, *Messianic Revelation*, 814-15.

to himself as the "son of man,"[75] and at least some of Jesus's statements must reflect Daniel's vision.[76]

**7:14.** The language of verse fourteen offers strong support for taking the "one like a son of man" as a divine figure. The Aramaic verb פלח (*p-l-ch*) has been rendered as *serve* (ESV); or *obey* (NLT). Within the context of biblical Aramaic, nine of the ten instances occur in the book of Daniel (3:12, 14, 17, 18, 28; 6:16 [17], 20 [21]; 7:14, 27). Aside from 7:14 the term always refers to service of God or of an idol. At 3:18 and 3:28 פלח is used together with the verb סגד (*s-g-d*), which is a stronger term for *worship*. In Ezra 7:24 (also in Aramaic) the participle of פלח is used to refer to temple servants. Rosenthal's Aramaic grammar glosses פלח with *to serve, to worship*.[77]

The first part of verse fourteen describes what the "**one like a son of man**" will be given—ruling authority (שָׁלְטָן), honor (יְקָר), and a kingdom (מַלְכוּ). The second part says that all nations will פלח him. That most likely means that they will *worship* him. The people of God cannot be worshiped; only God can receive worship. The last part of the verse then describes the authority and the kingdom given to the "one like a son of man" as eternal—"an eternal authority that will not pass away and a kingdom that will not be destroyed." Such statements apply most naturally to God, but from the structure of the context they must apply to the "one like a son of man." This "one like a son of man" will be presented to the Ancient of Days," much like the Lord established his *anointed one* as *king* on his holy mountain, proclaiming to him: "You are my Son; today I have begotten you (Ps 2:7)."[78]

---

75. Matt 13:41; 16:27–28; 19:28; 24:27–30, 37–39; 25:31; 26:63–64; Mark 8:29–31, 38; 13:26; 14:61–62; Luke 9:26; 12:40; 17:22–30; 18:8; 21:27; 22:69; John 1:51; 3:13; 5:27; 6:62; 13:31; cf. Acts 7:56; Rev 1:13; 12:10; 20:4.

76. For further discussion see Walvoord ("Biblical Kingdoms") and Saucy (*Progressive Dispensationalism*, esp. chaps. 9—12). For a discussion of whether the "Ancient of Days" represents God the Father while the "one like a son of man" represents God the Son, or whether both represent "the Divine Christ," see Royer, "Ancient of Days."

77. Rosenthal, *Grammar of Biblical Aramaic*, 93.

78. Steinmann, *Daniel*, 359–60.

## The Saints of the Most High Will Suffer Defeat. (7:15–21)

Theological Point: God's servants will undergo
tremendous persecution and testing.

When what Daniel saw began to trouble him, he sought help to understand the vision from one of the angels standing by. The angel agreed to interpret it for him, and from that point on Daniel still experienced the vision but only in conversation with the angel. Daniel's questions and the angel's answers centered around certain details of the vision; but not all the details were discussed, and Daniel even introduced some new elements that had not been mentioned before.

The interpretation given by the angel flows from the threefold structure of the vision itself. First, the angel gave a general summary of the four beasts and of the culmination when "the holy ones of the Most High" would receive the kingdom (vv. 16b–18). The section is bounded on the one side by Daniel's distress at what he saw and his request for interpretation (vv. 15–16a), and on the other side by the term *then* (אֱדַיִן, v. 19) that leads into the second part, Daniel's request for more detailed information regarding the fourth beast. He wondered about its ten horns, and the additional horn that "waged war with the holy ones" and even overcame them. The victory lasted only until the Ancient of Days arrived and judgment was given in favor of "the holy ones of the Most High," after which they were able to take possession of the kingdom.

The third part of the angel's interpretation consists of his response to each individual point that Daniel had raised. The fourth beast represented a fourth kingdom that will be different from all the others in terms of its terrifying effects on the earth. The ten horns represent ten kings that will arise from the fourth kingdom, followed by another that is different from all the others. This one, after defeating three kings, will speak against the Most High, "wear down" (יְבַלֵּא) the "holy ones of the Most High," and plan to change "set times and law" (זִמְנִין וְדָת). **The wicked king's time will be limited, however, to "a time, times, and half a time," after which he will be removed from power and destroyed. This will take place to give the ruling authority to "the people of the holy ones of the Most High" in God's kingdom that will never come to an end.**

When the end of both the vision and its interpretation is reached, the text explicitly marks the boundary—"to here is the end of the matter" (עַד־כָּה סוֹפָא דִי־מִלְּתָא). Daniel then adds a notation about his reaction of alarm to the vision and how he committed it to memory.

If one asks why the interpreting angel left so many details of the vision unexplained, the answer is twofold. On the one hand, it may be that some details have been left for others to interpret. On the other hand, perhaps the lack of detail is so that the message will have more universal appeal. That is, less specificity would lead to a generalized interpretation that any generation could apply to itself. For example, Jesus' comment that even he does not know the day or hour of his coming (Matt 24:36; Mark 13:32) leaves open the possibility for the reader to assume that it could happen at any moment. In a similar way, the angel gave Daniel a bare outline of human history that covers the span from Daniel's own day to the day when "the people of the holy ones of the Most High" will possess the everlasting kingdom. Even the additional detail regarding the final king of the fourth kingdom is not enough for a clear picture of who he will be. He will differ from all the others in ferocity and in defiance of the Most High God, to the point of changing laws and times set by God. Where and when he will arise remain a mystery known only to God.

7:15. Daniel found the vision greatly upsetting, and he used a rare expression to describe what he felt. Literally, it is "my spirit . . . was distressed within (its) sheath." The picture is of his *spirit* contained inside his body,[79] and it was *distressed*. He felt in his body some kind of internal turmoil. He emphasized his intense emotion by adding a further reference to himself: "My spirit, I Daniel, was distressed within (its) sheath." In English one has to say something like "as for me, Daniel, my spirit was distressed within my body." Theodotion's Greek translation has, "My spirit shuddered in my bodily condition, I Daniel." Daniel gave a parallel expression to further describe his condition: "And the visions in my head disturbed me."

While the vision began on a dark note, with strange animals that had unusual characteristics, it concluded with a reference to an everlasting kingdom that appeared after all the beasts had received their judgment. So why should the vision have been so disturbing to Daniel? After all, it carried the positive inference that God's side will win in the end. The terrifying element of the vision, however, consisted in the thought that the world would be controlled by all these monstrous creatures until the time for their judgment arrived. Daniel looked down the ages of history and saw the earth in the grip of demonic forces represented by a lion, a bear, and a leopard. And all these dangerous animals would be overcome by a beast too terrible even to name. Sometimes a pleasant dream might suddenly turn into a nightmare; other times the nightmare

---

79. This verse offers evidence for the view that the soul is a separate entity from the body, whether one takes the view of dichotomy (body and soul/spirit) or trichotomy (body, soul, and spirit).

might end on a glorious note. Either way the dream could leave one shaken and frightened about the implications. For Daniel the implications were terrifying to contemplate.

7:16. Daniel sought relief from his terror by seeking out someone who could explain the dream vision to him. He approached an angel, apparently one of the myriads who were attending the Ancient of Days, and asked for insight into the *true meaning* (יַצִּיבָא) of the vision. When Daniel had to interpret Nebuchadnezzar's vision, he and his companions prayed; and God revealed both the details of the vision and its interpretation. Here Daniel had his own dream vision and, still within the vision, requested the interpretation.

7:17. The general interpretation of the four beasts is quite simple—they represent four "kings" who "will rise from the earth." These "kings" stand for rulers of kingdoms. The angel who interpreted the vision called the fourth beast a "fourth kingdom" that will differ from "all the kingdoms." Each king represents a kingdom, and like the four beasts, they will follow one after the other.

An important clue to thinking that the kingdoms are successive is the broader context of chapter 7 within the whole book of Daniel. In chapter 2, Nebuchadnezzar's dream image represented successive kingdoms, and Daniel's second vision in chapter 8 deals with the transition from Persian rule to Greek rule. Then when Daniel asked for more detail about the fourth beast in chapter 7, the angel interpreted the various horns as a succession of kings that would culminate in a king who would differ from the previous monarchs and in fact bring down three of them. Throughout the book one reads of a "realm" or "sovereign authority" that God transmits from one kingdom to another. Reiterating the key verse of the book at 2:21, God "removes kings and sets up kings." He delivered the kingdom authority to Nebuchadnezzar, transferring it from Judah to Babylon (1:2). Hence Nebuchadnezzar, "the king of kings," was "the head of gold" in his own dream vision (2:37). After him "another kingdom" would arise and "a third kingdom" that would exercise authority over "the whole earth" (2:39). And following the fourth kingdom God's own kingdom would arise, smashing all worldly powers and enduring forever (2:44–45). Later Nebuchadnezzar (4:34–37 [31–34]), and still later Darius the Mede (6:26–27 [27–28]), acknowledged that God's authority is sovereign over all other authorities. Belshazzar refused to acknowledge that to his own peril (5:22–30). In chapter 8 we read that history flows from the Persian kings through Alexander and finally to Antiochus Epiphanes. Then in chapters 9 to 12 Daniel records the future from the return from Babylonian exile to the rise and fall

## VISION OF BEASTS AND KINGDOMS

of Antichrist and the triumph of the people of God at the end of the age (9:25-27; 11:2—12:11).

7:18. The key question for verse eighteen concerns the identity of "the holy ones of the Most High." Are they angels, that is, heavenly beings?[80] Or are they God's people?[81] Or are they both angels and people?[82] It is argued in favor of the view that they are angels that when the plural adjective that means *holy* is used as a noun (קְדֹשִׁים) in the OT, it usually refers to angels. Collins lists Job 5:1; 15:15; Ps 89:5 (6), 7 (8); Prov 30:3[83]; and Zech 14:5 as certain examples where קְדֹשִׁים means angels and Exod 15:11 and Deut 33:3[84] as "probable" examples.[85] Exodus 15:11 in the Hebrew means, "Who is like you in *holiness*," but in the Greek (LXX) it is "Who is like you among the *holy ones*," with *holy ones* in parallel with *gods*." The verse then gives further description of God: "Awesome in praises, doing wonders." The MT makes good sense and does not need any emendation. "Holy ones" in Zech 14:5 at first glance seems to be clear, but it is also possible that it could include both angels and resurrected righteous ones (cf. Dan 12:2-3; 1 Thess 4:13-17).[86] "Holy ones" in Pss 16:3 and 34:9 (10) most likely refer to people.

Even though *holy* in Leviticus functions as an adjective rather than a noun, it is relevant to the argument that no less than six times the people of Israel are admonished to be *holy* (קְדֹשִׁים) even as the Lord is *holy* (11:44, 45; 19:2; 20:7, 26; 21:6; so also, Num 15:40; cf. Num 16:3). It would not be unusual, then, to refer to the righteous in Israel as "the holy ones of the Most High."

The strongest argument given by Collins concerns the use of "holy ones" for angels in other passages in Daniel.[87] Usage in the context of the book should be more decisive than usage elsewhere. The argument is mitigated, though, by the context of chapter 7 in contrast to the context of the other chapters in Daniel. Only in Daniel 7 are the *holy ones* said to receive

---

80. John Collins, *Daniel*, 313–17; cf. Gowan, *Daniel*, 112.

81. Hasel, "Saints of the Most High," 190–92; Poythress, "Holy Ones of the Most High," 208–13.

82. Seow, *Daniel*, 110–11.

83. Prov 30:3 most likely uses קְדֹשִׁים as a title for Yahweh, *i.e., the Holy One*, as in Prov 9:10; see Waltke, *Proverbs 15—31*, 456.

84. Deut 33:3 is notoriously difficult and possibly the text has suffered corruption. The presence of "peoples" (עַמִּים) suggests that "holy ones" also refers to people. Probably the verse places "peoples," understood as the people of Israel, in apposition with "his holy ones" (see ESV, NLT). Cf. Craige, *Deuteronomy*, 393.

85. John Collins, *Daniel*, 314.

86. Charles Feinberg, *God Remembers*, 197; Conrad, *Zechariah*, 193.

87. John Collins, *Daniel*, 317–18.

the *kingdom*. The kingdom is reserved for the righteous who trust in the Lord; the angels are already part of the heavenly realm.[88]

**In conclusion, then, "the holy ones of the Most High" should be the righteous who trust in the Most High, not angels. People will inherit the kingdom of God (Matt 5:10; Mark 10:14; 14:25; Luke 6:20; 13:29); the (good) angels already attend on God in heaven, as Dan 7:10 indicates. Daniel 7:27 speaks of the kingdom "given to the people of the holy ones of the Most High," identifying the *people* with *the holy ones*.**[89]

Two different terms in the Aramaic portions of Daniel are rendered "the Most High." Both come from the same root letters, but one form is singular (עִלָּיָא), while the other (עֶלְיוֹנִין) has been borrowed from Hebrew but given an Aramaic plural.[90] When the term derived from Hebrew is employed in Daniel 7, it is always plural and always associated with "the holy ones" (vv. 18, 22, 25, 27). The Aramaic singular occurs only once (7:25), where it refers only to *the Most High* and not in association with others. Apparently, when speaking of the people who serve the Most High God, the Hebrew form was borrowed into Aramaic and pluralized. Perhaps that was due to analogy with the Hebrew plural form that means *God*,[91] or possibly because of attraction to the plural form of *holy ones*. Whether the Hebrew or the Aramaic form was used, the referent was the same—the Most High God.

**7:19.** In the visual part of the chapter Daniel focused his attention on the horns of the beast (v. 8); now when receiving the interpretation orally he inquired particularly about the fourth beast. And he adds to his previous description more detail about that beast. It had "iron teeth" and "claws of bronze" by which it "devoured" and "crushed" and "trampled." Iron and bronze occur often in the OT in the context of war or hostility (Job 20:24; 40:18; 41:27 [19]). These metals pertain to the fourth and third kingdoms in Nebuchadnezzar's dream (2:35, 45). They also comprised the "band" that held the taproot of the tree that was cut down (4:23 [20]), symbolizing the preservation of Nebuchadnezzar's kingdom (4:26 [23]); and they were the

---

88. So Brekelmans, "Saints of the Most High," 326–29.

89. עַם (*people*) should be analyzed as a noun in construct with קַדִּישֵׁי עֶלְיוֹנִין (*holy ones of the Most High*) in an appositional relationship—*people who are holy ones of the Most High*. John Collins (*Daniel*, 322) took it as "the people pertaining to or under the protection of the holy ones," based on comparison with the "angelic prince" of chs. 10–12, who fights for God's people. While the interpretation is possible grammatically, the verse states that the kingdom will be given to the people; and that is what v. 18 states about "the holy ones."

90. Rosenthal, *Grammar of Biblical Aramaic*, 57.

91. Hartman and Di Lella, *Book of Daniel*, 207.

substance of some of the idols worshiped by Belshazzar (5:4, 23). **Iron and bronze, then, are symbols of strength and might but also of world powers that in their idolatry stand against the Lord.** The Lord can make use of such weapons against the wicked, but, as the interpreting angel makes plain, the armies of the fourth world empire will have powerful weapons of war to crush all their enemies (Dan 7:23).

**7:20.** As Daniel questioned the angel further about the horns on the fourth beast, he summarized what he had seen in his vision. He thus stressed through repetition the importance of this part of the vision. The struggle among the horns finally led to the triumph of a single horn that had eyes and "a mouth speaking arrogant things" (v. 8). The ten horns, according to the angel (v. 24), represent ten kings that will arise from the fourth kingdom, with another king who "will bring down three kings." And the latter king's arrogant words will be "against the Most High" (v. 25).

**7:21.** At this point Daniel introduced another new element into the vision that was important enough to warrant an additional "as I watched" (חָזֵה הֲוֵית). Now there is talk of a war "with the holy ones" in which the final horn "prevailed against them" (וְיָכְלָה לְהוֹן). In other words, the final king "will wear down the holy ones of the Most High" (v. 25).

## The Saints of the Most High Will Be Delivered and Enter His Everlasting Kingdom. (7:22–28)

Theological Point: The time will come for God's servants to be delivered and to enter his kingdom that will never end.

**7:22.** Daniel summarized the final events of his vision in verse twenty-two. The Ancient of Days came and gave a judgment in favor of "the holy ones of the Most High," at which point the time had arrived for "the holy ones" to take possession of the kingdom. One could ask why the angel chose to pass over the "one like a son of man." Is it because that figure stands for "the holy ones of the Most High"? Hardly. "The holy ones" were overcome by the horn, while the "one like a son of man" came "with the clouds of heaven" once the judgment had been passed and the fourth beast had been destroyed. He came from heaven and was presented before the Ancient of Days to receive the kingdom, meaning that he was the heavenly representative of the "holy ones." Even as each kingdom was governed by earthly kings, so "the holy ones of the Most High" will have as their ruler this "one like a son of man," a king with a heavenly origin.

**7:23–24.** The angel picked two of Daniel's questions and answered them in succinct style that became a model for later commentaries. The style in literal form is as follows: "The fourth beast—a fourth kingdom . . . ." The style continues into verse twenty-four, with the answer to another of Daniel's questions: "And the ten horns—from that kingdom ten kings will arise."[92] The general details of the interpretation follow naturally from the vision itself. **The fourth beast represents a fourth kingdom, and its horns stand for various kings. Also, the fact that the fourth beast differed so much from the other beasts led to a corresponding interpretation that the fourth kingdom would "differ from all the kingdoms." And just as the fourth beast devoured, crushed, and trampled (v. 19), so the fourth kingdom would do the same to all other realms on earth.** The angel continued the interpretation with reference to the ten horns of the beast and the one that came up last with three horns falling before it. **All this represents a succession of ten kings. The last three and another king that will follow the ten will engage in a war, with the three brought down by the final king. While it would be interesting to know who these kings will be, the history of fruitless speculation should warn the interpreter against building a hypothesis on very little evidence.**

**7:25.** As the angel continues to explain the "little" horn, he turns to its mouth and its human-like eyes. **The eyes may underline the prideful words and actions, but they also relate to the king's schemes to alter "times and law."** Some take "times" to refer to set times for religious festivals such as Passover or Easter.[93] More likely they refer generally to the times that God has ordained to accomplish his purposes.[94] Daniel stressed elsewhere that only God controls time (2:21), and his law is superior to "the law of the Medes and Persians" that even the king could not change (6:4 [5], 7 [8], 11 [12], 16 [15], 27 [26]). If indeed the eyes on the horn represent the king's own ideas about his intelligence, even to the point of thinking himself to know everything, then that would explain his plan to change the set times (זִמְנִין) and law that God has established. To work against God in such a way would be folly, and God himself will set a limit

---

92. This procedure is reminiscent of the commentaries from Qumran (*pesharim*) on certain biblical passages, most notably on Habakkuk 1—2. There, however, the term פשרו (*its interpretation*) was inserted between the portion of Scripture quoted and the interpretation given by the author (see e.g., Vermes, *The Complete Dead Sea Scrolls in English*, 478–85). Since the book of Daniel was popular at Qumran it is likely that the general format here, and in Dan 5:25–28, provided a model for the writers at Qumran.

93. *HALOT*, "זְמָן," 5:1966; Péter-Contesse and Ellington, *Handbook on the Book of Daniel*, 199; Miller, *Daniel*, 214.

94. Keil, *Ezekiel, Daniel*, 241; Goldingay, *Daniel*, 180–81.

## VISION OF BEASTS AND KINGDOMS

of "a time, times, and half a time." Up to that limit established by God the king will be able to "wear down" the "holy ones," but no longer than that.

The expression "time, times, and half a time" is not clear. It is usually taken to mean three and a half years based on other calculations within the book of Daniel. The Hebrew equivalent at Dan 12:7 apparently relates to the 1290 days and 1335 days of 12:11–12, although neither figure would match precisely three and a half years. If the "weeks" of Daniel 9:25–27 mean periods of seven years each, then the division of the final week in half would also result in three and a half years. **It is worth pointing out, though, that no specific unit of time is mentioned for either the seventy "weeks" (i.e., periods of seven) or the "time, times, and half a time." Like the seventy "weeks," these three times and a half can be viewed as figurative for the persecution of God's people. The last of the seventy "weeks" represents the end times, and the last earthly king will rule as a cruel tyrant. The people of God will suffer tremendous persecution, but only for half of the week will he have power over the people.**

Revelation 11:2 refers to forty-two months or three and a half years when Jerusalem will be trampled by the nations, clearly an allusion to Dan 7:25 and 12:7. Revelation 11:3 assigns 1260 days to the time when God's "two witnesses" will prophesy. Forty-two months of thirty days each amount to 1260 days.[95] It is uncertain, though, whether the book of Revelation is attempting to calculate the length of time for Daniel's expression, or if it is alluding to Daniel as a rhetorical device to make a point about something else.

Since the term for "times" is not in the dual in either the Aramaic or the Hebrew expression, the interpretation as "two years" or even "two periods of time" is uncertain. In any event, it is important to leave the translation as vague—*time, times, and half a time*.

**7:26.** The interpreting angel made the obvious connection between the heavenly court scene and God's future judgment of the king (the little horn). The expression "to the end" (עַד־סוֹפָא) likely means that the king's dominion will be removed and destroyed forever.[96]

**7:27. All the kingdoms of this world, all authority and power, will be handed over to "the holy ones of the Most High." God's everlasting kingdom will then be theirs forever, and all dominions everywhere will worship and serve him** (cf. Isa 45:23; 1 Cor 15:24–28; Phil 2:9–11).

---

95. See Walvoord, *Daniel*, 176.

96. See Dan 6:26 [27] for a clear temporal usage of "to the end"; see also BDB and *HALOT*, "סוֹף," 5:1938. Some versions take it instead as complete destruction (NRSV, "totally"; NLT, "completely").

Is it the Most High who will receive the service/worship and obedience? Or is it "the people of the Most High"? Since the pronoun is singular in the Aramaic (לֵהּ, lit. *him*) it might seem that the service must be rendered to the Most High. The problem lies with the Aramaic term for *people* (עַם). In English it reads as a plural and hence a plural pronoun (*them*) would be demanded, but in Aramaic it can be treated as a collective singular. That is, a singular pronoun could refer to it, thinking of the people as a unitary group, and *people* could then be the antecedent of the possessive pronouns.[97] Even so, the terms *serve/worship* and *obey* (see on 7:14) imply, from the perspective of Daniel's worldview, actions that only God can receive.

**7:28. Daniel's troubled feelings after such a triumphant conclusion to his vision might seem surprising, but he surely realized that before the triumph there must first be the agonizing persecution of his people. Words like "wear down the holy ones" and "given into the hand" of the wicked king of the end times were difficult to take.** Like Jeremiah, the "weeping prophet," Daniel knew that his people faced some incredibly difficult times. Believers, with great joy, can look forward to the day when Christ will return and establish his kingdom. But in the meantime, they have a share in "the sufferings of Christ" (1 Pet 4:13; cf. 2 Cor 1:5).[98]

## SHARPENING THE THEOLOGICAL FOCUS

The vision of chapter 7 is the only one of Daniel's own visions recorded in Aramaic. Chapters 8 to 12 narrate his additional visions in the Hebrew language. This begs the "why" question. Why is chapter 7 linguistically connected to the narratives about Daniel and his friends at the king's court, but through genre (a vision) to the remaining chapters in the book? To state the question this way highlights the observation that chapter 7 is transitional. The language ties it with the first half of the book, while the visionary content anticipates what follows in the second half. There are other lines of connection as well.

The most obvious connection to the first half of Daniel is Nebuchadnezzar's dream of the image of four parts, also in Aramaic. The four beasts of Daniel's vision correspond to the four segments of the image in

---

97. Cf. the NRSVu, "their kingdom shall be an everlasting kingdom, and all dominions shall serve and obey them."

98. The NT gives additional revelation regarding what appears to be two phases to the return of Christ. The first phase is the "rapture" of the church (1 Thess 4:17), while those remaining on the earth undergo unprecedented tribulation. Much debate surrounds this issue that is beyond the scope of this commentary.

Nebuchadnezzar's dream. The horns on the fourth beast correspond roughly to the extra detail given about the feet and toes of the king's dream (2:41).[99] And the judgment scene presided over by the Ancient of Days reflects the stone cut out of a mountain without human hands that struck the image and destroyed it. When that stone grew into a great mountain that filled the whole earth, it was a precursor to the "one like a son of man" who received an everlasting kingdom and authority over all the peoples of the earth.[100]

There are also significant differences between the two dream visions, chief among them that the heavenly scene of judgment that Daniel saw was lacking in Nebuchadnezzar's dream. Daniel's vision provides a wealth of detail about the horns and their relation to each other, whereas Nebuchadnezzar's dream about the legs and feet of iron and clay has significantly less detail. Additionally, the perspective of how the dreams were experienced and interpreted differs. According to chapter 2, the sovereign God gave Nebuchadnezzar a dream so that he could reveal to him "what will be" (2:29). Daniel was then called in to tell and interpret the king's dream. In chapter 7 Daniel himself has the dream, and the interpreter is an angel. Even in this different perspective, however, there is also similarity. Daniel had a vision the night before he spoke to the king, and that vision revealed the king's dream and its interpretation. In both Nebuchadnezzar's dream and Daniel's vision there are different symbols that speak to similar content, thereby emphasizing the scheme of four world kingdoms followed by God's kingdom arriving with judgment and hope for a new kingdom that will last forever.

Additionally, Daniel 7 serves as a climax to the first part of the book. Daniel's own vision underlines the truth of Nebuchadnezzar's dream, and the appearance of the Ancient of Days in his glorious splendor among myriads of attending angels makes the apex of Babylonian glory seem dull in comparison. The glory of Nebuchadnezzar gave way eventually to the decadence of Belshazzar, but the heavenly reign of the Ancient of Days and the kingdom he bestows on the one "like a son of man" will never dim in its brilliant luster.

The vision of chapter 7 covers the full sweep of history, from Babylon to the its culmination in the eternal kingdom. The remainder of the book (chs. 8 to 12) also culminates in the kingdom, but the details concern mostly the Medo-Persian and Greek kingdoms, with only a brief allusion devoted to the Roman empire and what follows it. In those details about Medo-Persian and Greek rule we see how various world events intersect with the

---

99. Feet would have toes, but the reading "toes" at 2:41 has some doubt; see note on the translation of 2:41.

100. See also Seow, *Daniel*, 109.

Jews, whether in the diaspora or in their land of Judah, thus a transition back into Hebrew.

While chapters 7 to 12 have the theme of kingdoms that rise and fall, they also move beyond that theme when they culminate in a wicked world ruler.[101] A climax is reached at chapter 12 with the resurrection of the righteous, the judgment of the wicked, and an exhortation to wait patiently for the arrival of God's everlasting kingdom. Chapters 1 to 6 showed the transitions of kingdom rule from Jehoiakim of Judah to Nebuchadnezzar and Belshazzar of Babylon to Darius/Cyrus of the Medo-Persian kingdom. Chapter 7 recapitulates the full sweep of Gentile realms until their final judgment. In this way, Daniel 8—11 parallels Daniel 1—7, filling in details about additional world rulers and their fate.

A key theological feature of Daniel's vision of the four beasts is the focus on heavenly activity that is otherwise behind the scenes of world history. God appears as the Ancient of Days in great splendor and glory and sets up a court to judge the beasts (kingdoms). The kings or kingdoms represented by the beasts remain on the earth, but all the action is directed from heaven. As Nebuchadnezzar had to admit, "heaven rules" (4:26 [23]).

## THE FOCUS OF DANIEL 7 FOR PREACHING AND TEACHING

We have noted that chapter 7 functions as an introduction, a transition, and a summary. As you preach/teach it, you will want to touch on all three. However, the point of your teaching should not be to articulate how chapter 7 functions as an introduction to the rest of Daniel, or a transition from historical narrative written primarily in Aramaic to apocalyptic prose written primarily in Hebrew, or how it serves as a summary of world history. **While these are all true and important to understand, they point to something greater. They point to the unique and majestic revelation of God as the *Ancient of Days* who is sovereign over time and has set a date to inaugurate his everlasting kingdom through "one like a son of man." This is the message that brings perspective to God's people. It was meant to encourage the Jews living in exile and, even more so, it should encourage those who now know the identity of the divine Son of Man and what he has accomplished in history.**

When transitioning to the apocalyptic chapters of Daniel, one needs to prayerfully consider how much detail to cover from the visions. As a general rule, explain whatever details are necessary for the listeners to see how

---

101. This coming world ruler is symbolized by a "beast" in Rev 11—20.

the central truth emerges from the text. In this chapter, do not feel the need to identify specific empires and rulers with the kingdoms/beasts. Rather, use historical kingdoms to illustrate the point that Gentile kingdoms will rise and fall and this is all part of God's plan.

It is helpful to note that chapter 7 unfolds like a drama in three acts. In the first act, four huge and fantastic beasts rise out of the sea, and the spotlight settles on the action that takes place with the horns of the fourth beast. The second scene opens with a heavenly courtroom. After the Ancient of Days convenes the court, the four beasts are judged and receive their sentences. Then in the third act "one like a son of man" approaches the Ancient of Days and receives authority to rule over the nations in a kingdom that will never end. These three acts reveal the trajectory of world history up to its consummation in God's kingdom.

When the angel interprets the three scenes, he doesn't deal with all their features. And, as already stated, some new details are introduced that were part of what Daniel saw but were hidden from the readers' eyes until after the "play" was over. The effect is that some mystery remains about certain details, while other aspects receive greater clarity. One can speculate about those elements of the vision that receive no interpretation, but certainty cannot be attained from the text itself. It may simply be that some parts of the vision (e.g., the "three ribs" of 7:5) were mentioned only to add vividness to the scene, which can also inform the preaching/teaching of chapter 7.

The vagueness of the text contrasts starkly with the efforts of preachers and teachers through the ages to render specific identities. However, "there is no objective basis provided in Dan 7 to link the four beasts with specific historical kingdoms."[102] And though the kingdoms can't be nailed down, the mysterious "one like a son of man" can be, and was, on a cross. Reading Daniel in light of the rest of Scripture makes it clear that Jesus is the one seated by the Ancient of Days. And while there is a natural curiosity to know more details than just the identity of the "one like a son of man," something more significant is conveyed through the silence of the text. The message it conveys is quite simple—Gentile kingdoms will rise and fall; that is all part of God's plan. At the end of the ages, however, God himself will bring in a kingdom that will supplant all others and continue forever.

---

102. Goswell, "Visions of Daniel," 138.

## FROM TEXTUAL WORK TO TEACHING

### The Big Idea

- *Exegetical Idea:* Through Daniel's vision of the four beasts God reveals himself as sovereign over time and empires, and he declares that he will one day give his people an everlasting kingdom through a divine son of man.
- *Theological Focus:* God is sovereign over time and has determined the ending date of all earthly kingdoms and the inaugural date of his everlasting kingdom.
- *Preaching Idea:* When things on earth look bleak, take a look from heaven's perspective.

### Outline One: Following the Exegetical Flow

I. The kingdoms of this world will continually challenge the authority of God. (7:1–8)

  A. Biblical examples of kingdoms that challenged the authority of God.

  B. Historical examples of kingdoms that challenged the authority of God.

  C. Contemporary examples of "kingdoms" that challenge the authority of God.

II. The destiny of the world's kingdoms and peoples are firmly in the hands of the Ancient of Days, who has fixed the time for their judgment. (7:9–14)

  A. Biblical examples of kingdoms falling.

  B. Historical examples of kingdoms falling.

  C. Encouragement that the contemporary "kingdoms" that challenge the authority of God will fall.

III. God's servants will undergo tremendous persecution and testing. (7:15–21)

  A. Examples of the persecution Israel faced in the OT.

>    B. Examples of the persecution the church faced in the NT and throughout church history.
>
>    C. Examples of the persecution Christians are facing around the world today.
>
> IV. The time will come for God's servants to be delivered and to enter his kingdom that will never end. (7:22–28)
>
>    A. God, the Ancient of Days, has inaugurated his kingdom through the work of "one like a son of man," Jesus the Christ, who now sits at his right hand in the heavenlies.
>
>    B. One day this kingdom will be fully realized on earth as it is in heaven.

## Outline Two: Following a Theme

*Introduction:* Introduce listeners to the genre of apocalyptic literature through a story that reveals what we wouldn't know unless someone reveals it to us. Work towards the point that we are naturally uncomfortable not knowing; we want things explained to us. However, "being in the know" can be difficult.

*Part 1:* In this section of the sermon focus on how being "in the know" can take a toll. Being "in the know" shook Daniel to his core; his vision was terrifying. Focus on the terrifying portions of Daniel's vision/interpretation and emphasize the effects they had on Daniel.

- Relevance: The terrifying portions of Daniel's vision are scary for us as well. There is still persecution ahead for God's people, we share in the sufferings of Christ.

*Part 2:* In this section transition to the comforting side of being "in the know." Knowing a favorable outcome is certain offers something to focus on through the defeats.

- Daniel's vision gives a glimpse of what will happen when the Ancient of Days holds court: the wicked are judged, the Son of Man is enthroned, and God's people are victorious.
- Because Christ has been raised from the dead, he is enthroned, the wicked will be judged, and God's people will be victorious.

*Conclusion:* While it's good to be "in the know," it's better *to know the One who knows.*

## EXCURSUS: DANIEL 7 AND 8 IN THE SYRIAN CHRISTIAN TRADITION

Historical headings were inserted into the ancient Syriac translation known as the *Peshitta*. These headings are found in the oldest manuscripts, dating to the sixth and seventh centuries. Here are how the headings are laid out:

- To 7:4: "The Kingdom of the Babylonians"
- To 7:5: "The Kingdom of the Medes"
- To 7:6: "The Kingdom of the Persians"
- To 7:7: "The Kingdom of the Greeks"
- To 7:8b: "Antiochus"
- To 7:21: "Antiochus"
- To 8:20: "Darius the Mede"
- To 8:21: "Alexander"

These headings indicate that the translator (or glossator) thought that the fourth kingdom was Greece and that the "little horn" represented Antiochus (IV). This represents an alternative Christian tradition to the Roman view found in Jerome and other early Christian writers, including Hippolytus and Theodoret of Cyr. These writers identified the third beast with Greece and the fourth with Rome.[103] The Syrian tradition is also reflected in the writings of Ephrem the Syrian of the fourth century. He equated the third kingdom with Persia, the fourth with Greece, and the "little horn" with Antiochus.[104] This early Syrian tradition for interpreting Daniel 7 has been carried on by those who approach Daniel through a historical critical lens, as well as by a few evangelical writers.[105] The earliest Jewish interpretations viewed the second beast as Medo-Persia and the fourth as Rome.[106]

---

103. See the relevant quotations in Stevenson and Glerup, *ACCSOT* 13: 224–25.

104. Stevenson and Glerup, *ACCSOT* 13: 224, 226, 243.

105. Gurney, "The four kingdoms of Daniel 2 and 7"; Walton, "Four Kingdoms of Daniel"; Pierce, *Daniel.*

106. For Jewish views see Goldwurm (*Daniel*, 196–201) and Braverman (*Jerome's Commentary on Daniel*, 90–94).

It would be incorrect, though, to think of a common Syrian tradition that thought of the fourth kingdom as Greece. Aphrahat, the earliest Syrian Christian writer known to have commented on Daniel (*Fifth Demonstration*, AD 337), thought "that the second beast of Dan 7 represents Medo-Persia and the little horn Antiochus Epiphanes ...," but he identified the fourth beast as Rome.[107] John Chrysostom (AD 347—ca. 407) took the fourth beast as Rome, and Theodoret (AD 393f—ca. 466) took the Roman view of the fourth beast and also identified the "little horn" as the Antichrist.[108]

## EXCURSUS: DANIEL 7 AND REVELATION 17

Some allusions to Daniel's vision of the four beasts from the Great Sea may be found in Revelation 17, especially 17:8, 12. John saw a "beast" with seven heads and ten horns (v. 3), calling to mind both the fourth beast that Daniel saw that had ten horns (7:7) and the third beast that had four heads (7:6). John's beast "was and is not and is about to ascend from the Abyss" (17:8). The "Abyss" (ἄβυσσος) probably alludes to the "Great Sea" from which Daniel's four beasts arose (7:2). The Greek term is used in the Septuagint to translate תְּהוֹם ([the] *deep*), which often implies the deep waters of the sea (Gen 1:2; 7:11; 8:2; Pss 33:7; 77:16 [17]; 104:6; 107:26; 135:6; Job 38:16; Jonah 2:5 [6]; Isa 51:10; Ezek 26:19). Even as for Daniel the different beasts represented the demonic forces behind the nations in their opposition to God, so the Abyss stood for the abode of demons (Luke 8:31; Rev 9:11; 11:7; 20:1-3). Both Daniel and John saw that the beast will wage war against the faithful in a future world kingdom. Then God will win the victory so that the saints may inherit an everlasting kingdom. For Daniel, the "little horn" was the king who defeated in battle "the holy ones" only to be judged by the Ancient of Days (Dan 7:21-22), while for John it was the last of the kings represented by the seven heads and seven mountains (Rev 17:11).

Of interest is how elements of Daniel's vision were blended into the elements of John's vision. The beast that John saw had the seven "mountains" (ὄρη) that represented seven "kings" or "kingdoms," and these in turn correspond to the four beasts that Daniel saw in his vision. Even as interpreters have struggled to identify Daniel's beasts, so they have wrestled with the interpretation of the seven "mountains." Are they to be taken more figuratively to represent the fullness of evil in the beast?[109] Or should they be connected to specific empires? The most popular form of the latter view

---

107. Ferch, "Porphyry," 141.
108. Ferch, "Porphyry," 143.
109. Alan Johnson, "Revelation," 560.

refers to the five "fallen" kingdoms as Egypt, Assyria, Babylon, Persia, and Greece/Seleucid. Then the one that in verse ten "is" would be Rome, and the one that "has not yet come" would be the future kingdom of the Antichrist.[110] Knowing how much John was influenced by Daniel, it might be better to consider the five "that have fallen" to be Babylon, Medo-Persia, Greece under Alexander, Egypt under the Ptolemies, and Syria under the Seleucids. Those could correspond with Daniel's first three beasts.

Daniel's fourth beast would have its counterpart in John's vision in both the king (kingdom) who "is" and the one who "has not yet come." That is, Rome was ruling in John's time, and in the future the Antichrist will arise as leader of the seventh kingdom, making an "eighth" (Rev 17:11). Thomas explains that the beast ". . . is king over an eighth kingdom because his reign following his ascent from the abyss will be far more dynamic and dominant than before."[111] In other words, according to this view there will be two phases to the reign of the Antichrist, as "one of the seven kings before his supposed demise and resurrection [Rev 13:3] and **an eighth** king afterwards during the second phase of his rule."[112]

While these interpretations may be correct, it is difficult to demonstrate with confidence their validity. Be that as it may, an important point for the discussion about Daniel 7 concerns how the beast of Revelation 17 is said to be "of the seven" (ἐκ τῶν ἑπτά). It shares its identity with all the kingdoms of this world. In a similar fashion, as argued in the exposition, the fourth beast of Daniel 7 need not be limited to Rome. It represents more simply the ultimate human kingdom that stands against God. As sovereign rule in the human sense passed from one people to another, there were not necessarily sharp boundary lines between them. That is how the smiting stone in Nebuchadnezzar's dream crushed the various parts of the image "all at once" (Dan 2:35) and why the four beasts in Daniel's vision all participate together in the judgment. There is some pertinence to deciding which historical kingdoms are represented, but in the final analysis the theological message brings to the fore the ultimate sovereignty of the Ancient of Days, of the Lord of lords and the King of kings (Rev 17:14).[113]

---

110. Thomas, *Revelation 8—22*, 297; Easley, *Revelation*, 310–11; MacArthur, *Revelation 12—22*, 169.

111. Thomas, *Revelation*, 299.

112. MacArthur, *Revelation 12—22*, 169 (emphasis his).

113. For a more detailed study of how the book of Revelation interprets Daniel, see "Interpretations of Daniel in the Apocalypse" in Hamilton, *With the Clouds of Heaven*, 201–20.

# The Ram and the Male Goat
(Daniel 8:1–27)

**Chapter 7 Review**: Chapter 7 marked a major genre shift in Daniel, from historical narrative to apocalyptic revelation. The first six chapters assured God's people that God *was* in control of all that had transpired from the fall of Jerusalem to the fall of Babylon. The next six chapters provide assurance that God *is* in control of all that will happen in the future. Chapter 7 set the stage for the rest of the book by specifically highlighting God's sovereignty over history, portraying him as Lord over time. The Ancient of Days has determined the ending date of all earthly kingdoms and the inaugural date of his everlasting kingdom.

**Chapter 8 Summary**: The vision of chapter 8 (in Hebrew), like that of chapter 7 (in Aramaic), is structured around animals that stand for kingdoms, and the horns on one of the animals represent further political developments from the kingdom it represents. The vision has a scheme of four kingdoms but develops the theme differently than the four empires found in chapter 7. Chapter 7's broad sweep of world history focuses on spiritual or demonic forces that receive divine judgment, while chapter 8 moves to more earthly political powers.

**Chapter 9 Preview**: Whereas chapters 7 and 8 begin with visions given to Daniel, chapter 9 interrupts the pattern and begins with Daniel contemplating the word of the Lord given to Jeremiah. In response to God's word, Daniel prays for forgiveness for himself and his people. Gabriel interrupts his prayer with a vision of seventy weeks that will consummate all history.

## THEOLOGICAL FOCUS OF CHAPTER 8

GOD WARNS HIS PEOPLE that until he establishes his kingdom, his people will face periods of persecution, but the persecution will not last, and the persecutors will be destroyed. He is sovereign over the persecutors and their persecutions.

I. *Until God establishes his kingdom, his people will face periods of persecution.*

II. *God is sovereign over those who persecute his people and the extent of the persecution.*

   A. *The persecution will not last.*

   B. *The persecutors will be destroyed.*

## BIG PICTURE (8:1–27)

Daniel had the vision of chapter 8 during the reign of Belshazzar, the king of Babylon, but the vision opens in Susa, the main capital of the Persian empire. The timing of the vision situates the Babylonian empire in a state of decline and the Medo-Persian empire in a state of ascendancy. This partially explains why Babylon has no place in the vision, which focuses prophetically on the period of history that extended from Persian rule to Greek rule just before the beginning of Roman rule. This historical setting foreshadows the advent of the new age when Messiah's kingdom will supplant all other kingdoms,[1] but in the meantime the Jewish people would continue to be dominated by foreign powers. Initially the shift from Babylon to Medo-Persia bodes well for the people because Cyrus allowed the Jews to return to their land. However, though they were back in the land, they weren't independent; they remained under the control of foreign rulers who did not recognize their God. Under the Greek kingdoms that followed the conquest of Alexander things got worse, until eventually they found themselves under the tyrannical rule of a fierce king who was determined to turn them away from the worship of God as laid out by the Torah of Moses.

---

1. See also Isa 2:1–4; Joel 3:17–21 [4:17–21]; Amos 9:11–12; Obad 21; Zeph 3:14–20; Zech 8:20–23; 14:3–11.

# THE RAM AND THE MALE GOAT

## TRANSLATION (DANIEL 8:1-27)

1   In the third year of the reign of Belshazzar the king a vision appeared to me, Daniel, after the one that appeared to me at first.

2   So I looked in the vision, and when I looked,² then I was in the fortress town of Susa, which is in the province of Elam. Now when I saw the vision, I was beside the canal of the Ulai river.³

3   Then I raised my eyes and saw, and there was a certain ram standing in front of the canal. And it had two horns, and the horns were high. And one of the horns was higher than the other, and the higher one was rising up last.

4   I saw the ram butting to the west, to the north, and to the south.⁴ And none of the animals were able to stand before him, there being no one to deliver them from its power. And it was doing whatever it wanted and becoming great.

5   While I was pondering, there was a male goat coming from the west over the surface of all the earth without touching the ground.

    As for this goat, a prominent⁵ horn was in its forehead.

6   Then it approached the ram with the two horns that I had seen standing in front of the canal, and it charged it with furious force.

7   Then I saw it as it reached the ram, and it became enraged at it and struck the ram and shattered both of its horns. There being

---

2. Th begins the verse with "I was in Susa." This makes Susa Daniel's physical location rather than his location in the vision as in the MT. The OG could go either way.

3. The OG has "at the gate Olam" and also has "gate" (πύλη) every time the MT has "canal" (אוּבַל). Th transliterates the Hebrew for "canal" as *Oubal* and omits the name "Ulai." The Vg (*portam*) and the Syriac (*'abbul, gate*) agree with the OG. Hartman and Di Lella (*Book of Daniel*, 224) accept this variant, explaining that the Hebrew should derive from Akkadian *abullu*, "city gate." For the translation "the canal of the Ulai (river)" see Finkelstein ("Mesopotamia," 89).

4. The OG and 4QDanᵃ add an eastward direction. It being common knowledge that the Persian empire extended to India (cf. Esth 1:1), the lack of a reference to the east seems strange. Hence the MT has the more difficult reading. Collins (*Daniel*, 330) thinks that the eastward direction dropped out of the text by "mechanical error." After a thorough discussion, Pace (*Old Greek Translation of Daniel 7—12*, 104-8) opts for the MT.

5. A term meaning *prominent* is not in the best manuscripts of Th. The OG has "one horn," possibly reading אֶחָד (*one*) instead of חָזוּת (*prominent*), adopted by the NRSV (*a horn*).

| | |
|---|---|
| | no strength left in the ram to stand before it, [the goat] threw it to the ground and trampled it. And there was no one to deliver the ram from its power. |
| 8 | Now the male goat grew exceedingly great, but at the height of its power the large horn was broken. Then four prominent [horns][6] rose in its place to the four winds of heaven. |
| 9 | And from one of them there came out a little horn,[7] and it grew very much toward the south, the east, and the beautiful [land].[8] |
| 10 | Then it grew right up to the army of heaven, and it cast some of the army and some of the stars to the ground and trampled them.[9] |
| 11 | Even up to the Commander of the army he magnified himself; and from [the Commander] the regular service was removed, and the foundation of his sanctuary was cast down. |
| 12 | And an army[10] will be set [by the horn] against the regular service by a transgression.[11] And it will cast truth to the ground, and it will succeed in what it does. |
| 13 | Then I heard a holy one speaking, and one holy one said to another one that was speaking: |
| | "How long will it be—the vision, the regular service, and setting in place the transgression that desolates, [and] both holiness and an army [subjected to] trampling?"[12] |
| 14 | And he said to him:[13] |

---

6. Hebrew חָזוּת אַרְבַּע; Th and the Vulgate lack an equivalent for חָזוּת, and the OG has "four others" (ἕτερα τέσσαρα), possibly from a reading אחרות ארבע (BHS).

7. Lit., "a horn from smallness" (קֶרֶן־אַחַת מִצְּעִירָה).

8. The Hebrew is difficult. Either וְאֶל־הַצְּבִי ("and to the beauty") is a gloss (Montgomery, *Daniel*, 332–33) or the term אֶרֶץ (*land*) somehow fell out of the text. The other occurrences of צְבִי (*beauty*) in Daniel modify either אֶרֶץ (*land* 11:16, 41; cf. Jer 3:19) or הַר (*mountain*, 11:45).

9. Cf. 2 Macc 9:10.

10. The translation assumes that the *army* (צָבָא) of v. 12 is different than the *army* of vv. 10 and 11. See the exposition.

11. Or "And an army will be given against the regular service in a transgression." The transgression could be by those who provide the horn with the army.

12. Or "(and) a giving over (to the horn of) both the sanctuary and the (heavenly) army?" For the translation proposed here see the exposition.

13. Reading with the OG, Th, Peshitta, and the Vg; the MT has לִי (*to me*).

"For 2,300 evening-mornings; then holiness[14] will be restored."

15  When I, Daniel, had seen the vision, I sought for understanding. And there before me was someone who looked like a man.

16  Then I heard a human voice between the [banks of the] Ulai calling aloud:

"Gabriel, explain the vision to this one."

17  Then he came beside where I was standing, and when he came I was terrified and fell on my face. Then he said to me, "Understand, son of man, that the vision is for an appointed end time."

18  And when he spoke with me, I fainted[15] with my face on the ground. Then he touched me and stood me upright.

19  Then he said, "I am here to make known to you what will happen later in the time of wrath. For [the vision] pertains to the appointed time of the end.

20  The ram that you saw that had two horns: It is the kings of Media and Persia.

21  And the male goat: It is the king of Greece.

And the large horn that was between its forehead: That is the first king.

22  And the broken horn in whose place four stood up:

Four kingdoms will arise[16] from [his] nation but not with his power.

23  And in the latter part of their reign, when the transgressors have reached full measure, a fierce and devious[17] king will arise.

24  And his power will increase (but not by his own power), and he will cause terrible destruction.[18] He will destroy mighty ones and a holy people.

25  And by his cunning he will even make a deceitful scheme prosper through his power. And he will think himself great. Without

---

14. Or *the sanctuary*.

15. The noun תַּרְדֵּמָה, cognate with the verb נִרְדַּם, can refer to a deep sleep, a state in which a person can receive revelation from God (Gen 15:12; Job 4:13; 33:15).

16. For analogs to יַעֲמֹדְנָה instead of the expected תַּעֲמֹדְנָה see Gen 30:38 and 1 Sam 6:12 (GKC 47k).

17. Lit., *one understanding ambiguous sayings*.

18. Lit., "he will destroy wondrously" ("fearful destruction," NRSVue).

26   warning he will destroy many. He will even stand against the Highest Commander, but he will be broken without [human] power.

26   And the vision of the evenings and the mornings that was spoken is true.

Now as for you, close the vision because it is yet for many days (in the future)."

27   And as for me, Daniel, I was exhausted[19] and sick for days.

Then I got up and did the king's business, but I was overcome with horror because of the vision; and there was no one to give me insight.

# TEXTUAL OUTLINE (8:1–27)

I. Daniel Sees a Ram and a Male Goat. (8:1–14)

*[Until God establishes his kingdom, his people will face periods of persecution.]*

  A. A ram with two horns appears and attacks other animals. (8:1–4)

  B. A male goat with one horn subdues the ram. (8:5–8)

  C. A little horn becomes great and powerful. (8:9–12)

II. Two Angels Speak of 2300 Evening-Mornings. (8:13–14)

III. Gabriel Explains the Vision to Daniel, (8:15–27)

*[God is sovereign over those who persecute his people and the extent of the persecution]*

---

19. The Hebrew, נִהְיֵיתִי, is unclear. The *Niphal* of הָיָה can mean *to happen* (Exod 11:6) or possibly *to have gone*, which seems to be the sense of נִהְיְתָה in Dan 2:1 ("his sleep *had gone* from him"). Here it would mean that Daniel was "spent" or "undone." *BHS* recommends deleting the word in 8:27 due to its similar shape with the following word, וְנֶחֱלֵיתִי ("and I was sick"). The OG has no equivalent for נִהְיֵיתִי.

## EXPOSITION (8:1-27)

## Daniel Sees a Ram and a Male Goat. (8:1-12)

Theological Point: Until God establishes his kingdom,
his people will face periods of persecution.

Daniel sees a ram and a male goat in combat, four horns and a little horn that arise from the goat, and two angels in conversation about the timing of the destructiveness of the little horn. Certain key phrases demarcate the four main elements of the vision of the ram and the male goat. Daniel saw the *ram* when "I lifted my eyes." That phrase also introduces the later vision of the man dressed in linen (10:5). The *male goat* came on the scene when Daniel "was pondering" (מֵבִין, 8:5) what he had just seen. His musing marks a pause in the action prior to the appearance of the new animal. The *little horn* is the third major participant, and it came on the scene "from one of [the horns]" (8:9). The mysterious statement about the "2,300 evening-mornings" is the fourth main element of the vision, and it is marked by an auditory experience. Daniel heard two heavenly beings speaking to each other about the vision and its duration (8:13-14). The move from seeing to hearing helps to resolve some of the tension when the small horn struggles against the armies of heaven and even God himself.

From the perspective of discourse analysis, the four parts of the vision can be called four "scenes," with the "peak" of the discourse taking place in the third scene.[20] Several changes in the grammar of the passage isolate the peak, and they will be discussed when dealing with the third scene. Suffice it to say that the peak occurs when the horn dares to challenge the heavenly hosts and even the "Captain of the host" (God) himself (8:10-12). The final scene is a "post-peak" episode that brings a sense of closure. While it introduces the additional mystery of the 2,300 evening-mornings, it nevertheless reduces the tension by setting a time limit on the actions of the horn.

After Daniel saw the vision, the angel Gabriel came and interpreted it for him. Gabriel did not make specific historical identifications of people in his interpretation, but it is possible for moderns to make some from the history of events between Daniel's time and the era of Antiochus IV. The basic interpretation of the vision applies to that period of history—future

---

20. Longacre (*Grammar of Discourse*, 37) defines the "peak" of a narrative as "any episode-like unit set apart by special surface structure features and corresponding to the climax or denouement in the notional structure." "Plot" and "climax" are *notional* ideas about a narrative in that they are discerned by a literary rather than a linguistic analysis. "Peak" corresponds roughly to "climax" but has linguistic indicators.

to Daniel but past to all who have come after Antiochus. Any application to events still future would have to be through a typological pattern.

Even though the vision concerns only Media-Persia and Greece, it still presents a scheme of four different realms. The kings of Media-Persia (the ram with two horns) are followed by a powerful Greek king (the male goat, representing Alexander the Great), who in turn is followed by the division into four parts after his death, and finally by the "fierce and devious king" (Antiochus IV). And those four parts are themselves described as "four kingdoms" (v. 22). This emphasis on the number four combines with some other features to intimate future history to its endpoint. Indeed, Gabriel's opening comment (v. 19) refers to "later in the time of wrath" and to "the appointed time of the end." Then the king who arises in "the time of the end" will take his warfare, according to the vision, to the heavenly hosts and its Commander. The mysterious time expression of 2,300 "evening-mornings" can be compared with the seventieth "week" of Dan 9:27, with the "time, times, and half a time" of Dan 7:25 and 12:7, and with the 1,290 days and 1,335 days of Dan 12:12–13. It is also significant that the "little horn" that Daniel saw in his first vision (7:8, 11, 20–21, 24–25) has certain resemblances to the "little horn" of 8:9, even if they have different referents.

Some interpreters have applied 8:10–14 and the corresponding interpretation in 8:23–26 to the final Antichrist at the end of the age, without denying that it also refers to Antiochus IV Epiphanes.[21] This would involve an interpretive principle of "double fulfillment."[22]

### *A ram with two horns appears and attacks other animals. (8:1–4)*

**8:1–2.** Daniel had a vision at the time when Babylonian power was about to be eclipsed by the Medes and the Persians. There are two ways that the vision is located in time—it occurred in Belshazzar's third year, and it happened after the previous vision (chap. 7). These notations of time also help to locate the vision in relation to the rest of the book. Daniel had his vision of the four beasts in Belshazzar's first year (7:1), and both that vision and the vision of chapter 8 must have occurred prior to Belshazzar's last night as ruler of Babylon (chap. 5). **Clearly, the organization of the book of Daniel is both chronological and topical. Chapters 1 to 6 are chronological**

---

21. Luck, *Daniel*, 96–97; Phillips, *Book of Daniel*, 147–49.

22. Blomberg defines "double fulfillment" as a situation where a "prophetic author consciously looked for a relatively immediate referent and for a longer-term eschatological fulfillment" ("OT Prophetic Fulfillment in Matthew," 19)

## THE RAM AND THE MALE GOAT

regarding the accounts of Daniel and his friends at the king's court, and chapters 7 to 12 are chronological with respect to Daniel's own visions.

Assuming that Belshazzar's third year was about 550 BC, that was also around the time that Cyrus defeated Astyages and thereby conquered the Medes.[23] The significance of the year is that it is the point at which the Medo-Persian kingdom was formed.

The geographic notation given in the vision raises an issue of interpretation. Was Daniel physically in Susa by the Ulai river when he saw the vision?[24] Or did the scene in the vision appear to him elsewhere? The Hebrew seems clear that the location at Susa was a part of the vision. A river is a significant element in two of Daniel's visions, here (also 8:16) and when he was beside "the great river, that is the Tigris" (10:4). As the final vision of chapter 12 drew to a close, Daniel saw two angelic figures standing on opposite banks of "the river" (12:5–7), presumably also the Tigris, although the Hebrew name (יְאֹר) normally means the Nile.

Susa was one of the capitals of the Persian Empire (also Persepolis), and the vision begins with the realm of Medo-Persia, not with Babylon as in the prior vision of chapter 7. **The ram with two horns represented the Medo-Persian empire, and Susa in the vision was a sign that the Babylonian kingdom would pass off the scene with Belshazzar's reign.**

**8:3.** The first animal that Daniel saw was a certain ram with two horns. Nowhere else in Scripture does a ram symbolize a kingdom, but animal horns frequently stand for a powerful country (Jer 48:25; Mic 4:13; Zech 1:18–21 [2:1–4]).[25] **The one animal emphasizes unity, while the two horns show that it consists of two parts.** The angel Gabriel will later tell Daniel that the horns stand for the kings of Media and Persia (8:20).[26] The reference to the uneven size of the horns, with the higher horn coming up last, presumably refers to Persia's conquest of and dominance over Media, although that interpretation is not proffered by Gabriel. Compare also the bear raised up to one side in Dan 7:5. **The horns are described as "high" and "higher."** From the perspective of an observer *longer* horns on a ram would appear *higher*, so they could be thought of as *long* and *longer*, but *high* has a metaphorical connotation of *pride* or *haughtiness* (1 Sam 2:3;

---

23. Young, "Cyrus," I:1231; Waters, "Cyrus and the Achaemenids," 92.

24. Jerome, *Commentary on Daniel*, 83; Goldwurm, *Daniel*, 215 [citing Gersonides]; see Josephus, *A.J.*, 10:264.

25. Cf. the similes in Jer 51:40 and the language of *rams* and *male goats* for different parts of Israel in Ezek 34:17.

26. Animal horns also symbolize power and might in the OT (Zech 1:18–19 [2:1–2]).

Ps 101:5; Prov 16:5; Eccl 7:8; Isa 5:15). This is a ram that will think to conquer the world, but will in the end be overthrown.

**The ram stands in front of the river that is located near Susa, but the geography creates some dissonance with the timing in the third year of Belshazzar. Babylon is not represented in this vision, even though it still exists as a world kingdom. Belshazzar is not given any positive treatment in the book of Daniel.** In his pride and disregard for the God of Judah, he drank wine from sacred vessels and praised mere idols at the same time (5:4). His reign was overshadowed by the queen mother; she provided the only wise counsel at the final banquet the night that the kingdom passed to Media-Persia. And her contribution was only to suggest that Belshazzar summon Daniel to interpret the handwriting on the wall (5:10–12). The glory days of Nebuchadnezzar had long since passed, and Belshazzar was "found deficient" (5:27). In Daniel's second vision Belshazzar is passed over as though he counted for nothing. For Daniel, Nebuchadnezzar *was* the Babylonian kingdom; no other king of Babylon equaled him.

8:4. With a repetition of "I saw," Daniel's attention turned from the appearance of the ram to its actions against other animals, which must represent various nations or peoples. Since the ram represents Media-Persia, its thrusts would include the conquest of Babylonia to the west, Asia-Minor to the north, and Egypt to the south. It might seem strange that the eastern direction was not mentioned, since the Persian kings also penetrated to India (Esth 1:1). The rest of the book of Daniel shows no interest in India or other points east of Media-Persia, so in his vision the ram only strikes at those nations in the specific areas governed by the Greeks and by the kings of the north (Seleucids) and the kings of the south (the Ptolemies of Egypt).

**Nothing could stop the ram's progress until the male goat came on the scene. Until then no one was powerful enough to rescue any other animal from the ram, and the ram did whatever it pleased and kept growing in power.** The ram, representing Media-Persia, grew in its power as its empire expanded.

## *A male goat with one horn subdues the ram. (8:5–8)*

The sudden appearance of a male goat coming from the west finally presented a challenge to the ram.[27] Rather than two horns, the goat strangely had only one "prominent horn." When the goat came, it crossed over all the land without touching the ground, signifying a great distance traversed

---

27. The Hebrew for *male goat* is literally "a male goat of the female goats," language that suggests prominent ancestry.

swiftly. Gabriel clearly interpreted the goat to represent Greece (יָוָן, 8:21), and the prominent horn was by inference Alexander the Great. History teaches that Alexander soundly defeated Darius III of Persia at the Battle of Issus in 333 BC.[28]

**8:5-7. The struggle between the male goat and the ram is drawn out through highly dramatic imagery. The verbs become increasingly intense: the goat** *came* **to the ram; then it** *ran* **at it in** *great fury;*[29] **it** *reached* **the ram and became** *enraged* **at it; and finally, it "struck the ram and shattered its two horns."** The ram that once overcame every animal such that "none could deliver from its power" (8:4) now faced the same fate. It was powerless before the goat and "none could deliver the ram from its power" (8:7). So goes the history of the world. A nation rises but then eventually falls before another; it is a cycle that will never end until God himself breaks it.

8:8. Just as swiftly as the male goat overcame the ram, his horn was broken off. We are not told how the horn was broken, but applying the vision to Alexander, it must have been a result of his fatal illness in Babylon in 323 BC as he was preparing to conquer Arabia. Soon after the horn was broken, four more horns took its place. These horns share the same "prominence" or "distinction" as their source, and evidently refer to the four main divisions of Alexander's empire. Gabriel interpreted them as "four kingdoms from [his] nation" (8:22). "To the four winds of heaven" reprises the corresponding Aramaic phrase for the geographical distribution of the four beasts that Daniel saw in his first vision (7:2). In Daniel's final vision he will hear also of four Persian kings (11:2). **While it is possible to point to specific kings or kingdoms to correspond to the four, the repetition of the number four throughout the book (see also 2:37-40) lends a sense of completeness to the history of the nations from the time of Nebuchadnezzar to the time when God steps into history and sets up his own kingdom. One after another the kingdoms rise and fall until finally God will set up the kingdom that will never be removed.** Here, specifically, the new division into four parts sets the scene for the rise of another horn.

## *A little horn becomes great and powerful. (8:9-12)*

The rise of the "little horn" brings the reader to the most significant part of the vision. **Previously the battles were furious but involved only the struggle between animals. In the present scene with the little horn the**

---

28. Dandamaev, *History of the Achaemenid Empire*, 319-23.
29. בַּחֲמַת כֹּחוֹ ("in the fury of its power").

battle turns cosmic, spreading to the angelic army of heaven and even to "the Commander of the host," that is, to God himself. Moreover, the horn succeeds in "trampling" some of the heavenly army and some of "the stars."[30] Then the ruler behind the "horn," utilizing his own "army," removes the "regular offering" from "the Commander of the host" and casts down "the foundation of his sanctuary." Daniel and his readers would have found this part of the vision exceptionally frightful. Relief and resolution come in the announcement of the 2,300 "evening-mornings" (vv. 13–14); the battle may be fierce but it will soon be over (cf. Matt 24:22; Mark 13:20). Until then the picture is bleak and depressing.

**The horn, and the tyrant it represents, take center stage in this part of the vision, and the entire scene forms the linguistic peak or the literary climax of the vision report.** Several elements mark this high point for the reader. First, the location shifts from earth to heaven, raising the level of tension. After growing powerful in three directions, the horn then becomes powerful enough to challenge the heavenly army, even to the point of casting some of its soldiers to the ground and trampling on them. Second, the horn becomes so brazen that it dares to challenge the Commander of the host of heaven. Third, at that point even the figure of the horn is dropped and the person it represents comes to the forefront—*he*, not *it*, boasts against the Commander. Fourth, in the final verse of the scene (v. 12) the language moves from figures in a vision to a prophetic description of what the ruler will do to fulfill the vision. It is as if Daniel shifts from the time within the vision itself to the real time that is outside of the vision. **All four of these devices—moving the scene to heaven, having the horn confront the Commander, changing the pronoun referent to speak directly of a king rather than a horn, and moving from vision time to real future time—help the reader to know that Daniel's narration of his vision experience has reached its peak.**

8:9. The Hebrew does not make explicit where the "little horn" comes from. Is it from among the four "prominent" horns or from one of the "four winds of heaven"? Hassler argues that a geographical origin is called for by comparison with how both the ram and the goat come from a geographical location. In this way he can say that the "little horn" does not come from the third kingdom and therefore cannot be Antiochus IV.[31] A "horn," though, should be attached to an animal, even if the animal is not described (as in

---

30. Shepherd (*Daniel*, 94–95) speculates that overcoming the heavenly lights stands for banning the festivals of worship whose "appointed times" (מוֹעֲדִים) were governed by the luminaries in the sky (Gen 1:14 and Lev 23:2).

31. Hassler, "Little Horn," 35–36; see also Doukhan, *Daniel*, 28; Pröbstle, "Daniel 8:9–14," 119–26.

Zech 1:18 [2:1]). The reader is more likely to expect the horn to come from the animal with the four horns than to follow a literary "pattern" (as Hassler suggests) that consists of two examples. That expectation is reflected in virtually every commentary from ancient times to the present.[32] **If the "little horn" comes from one of the four horns that came from the male goat whose horn was shattered, then it must represent Antiochus IV.**

The "little horn" came out from one of the four horns of the previous scene, then, and extended its power "to the south, to the east, and to the beautiful (land)." At this point Daniel's eyes began to focus on the horn's actions against Judea, "the beautiful (land)." Apparently, this "beautiful (land)" also represents the western thrust of the small horn.[33]

The horn's actions mirror to some extent the actions of the ram and of the goat in the previous scenes. The ram butted in three directions, and the horn "grew great" in three directions. The goat threw the ram to the ground and trampled it after breaking its horns, and the horn "cast some of the host and some of the stars to the ground and trampled them" (v. 10). **Antiochus IV Epiphanes, according to the vision, would act like he was one of the mighty kings of Persia (the ram) or even like Alexander the Great (the prominent horn on the goat); but, as Gabriel was quick to inform Daniel, "not with his [Alexander's] power" (8:22).**

Daniel's vision of chapter 7 lays out the general course of world history, culminating with the "little" horn that represents the Antichrist, who appears soon before God judges the kingdoms of this world and replaces them with his own eternal kingdom. Then in the vision of chapter 8, the more immediate future of the world kingdoms is brought into view. For the first time names are attached to the kingdoms that follow upon the heels of Babylon. The ram with two horns, says Gabriel, represents "the kings of Media and Persia" (8:20), and the male goat represents "the king of Greece" (8:21).

Despite the similarity in language, the "little horn" of 7:8 does not seem to be the same as the "little horn" of 8:9. The former emerged out of the long history of the fourth beast, while the latter emerges from one of the additional four horns of the male goat. It makes sense to connect this little horn of 8:9 with a Greek ruler. The angel interprets at 8:23: "And in the latter part of their reign [i.e., the reign of the four kingdoms represented by the four horns that appeared on the ram after the single horn was broken] ... a fierce and devious king will arise." Here it is directly stated that the king

---

32. Among others, Ephrem the Syrian (Stevenson and Glerup, *ACCSOT*, 13:251); Jerome, *Commentary on Daniel*, 85; Walvoord, *Daniel*, 185; Steinmann, *Daniel*, 389-90.

33. See footnote 8, p. 266.

represented by the "little horn" appeared during the time of the four horns on the male goat.

**All this is not to say that there is no similarity between the "little horn" of chapter 7 and the "little horn" of chapter 8. The actions of the latter horn make one think of "the great dragon . . ., that ancient serpent called the devil, or Satan," who will also challenge God's army, led by Michael the archangel (Rev 12:7–9). The immediate historical referent is Antiochus, but he stands for every tyrant throughout history who sets himself up against God, including the final Antichrist.**

8:10. When the little horn "grew up to the host of heaven," it began to participate in a cosmic struggle. The "host of heaven" comprises "the sun and the moon and the stars" (Deut 4:19), but it can also signify the angelic army that attends the Lord (1 Kgs 22:19; 2 Chr 18:18; Neh 9:6; Isa 6:1–3). The "stars" also apparently refer to angelic beings. Other examples of "stars" as angels can be found in the Bible. The "stars fought from heaven" against Sisera (Judg 5:20), and "the morning stars sang together" while "all the sons of God shouted for joy" when God created the earth (Job 38:7). Later, the Apostle John saw "seven stars" that were identified as "the angels of the seven churches" (Rev 1:20).

It seems incredible that the horn could actually "cast down to the ground some of the host and some of the stars and trample them." How could anyone fight against angels and defeat some of them? The answer lies in the distinction between the *vision* that Daniel saw, and the *interpretation* given by Gabriel. In his interpretation Gabriel spoke of the "holy people" (עַם־קְדֹשִׁים, 8:24) that a certain king would destroy (8:23), indicating that the fulfillment of the vision concerned people rather than angels. This has been explained in one of two ways. Either the angels in the vision stood for the people of God,[34] or the angels represented the cosmic dimension of the struggle of Antiochus against the people of God.[35] The tribes of Israel can also be called "the hosts of Yahweh" (Exod 12:41; cf. 7:4). **The angels and stars as the "host of heaven," then, most likely correspond to the Jews, who are "holy ones" because of their status as the chosen people.**[36] **At the same time, various clues throughout the book point to struggles in the heavens that correspond in some ways to struggles on earth.** Here are several examples: The four "beasts" of chapter 7 that rise out of "the great sea" are beasts that represent demonic forces arrayed against God (7:4). The angel Gabriel came to Daniel only when he began

---

34. Walvoord, *Daniel*, 185; Archer, "Daniel," 99; Steinmann, *Daniel*, 402.
35. Goldingay, *Daniel*, 209–10; Lucas, *Daniel*, 215.
36. Keil, *Ezekiel, Daniel*, 297.

to pray (9:23), demonstrating the interplay between human concerns and angelic missions. After Daniel had fasted and prayed for three weeks, he saw the vision of "a man clothed in fine linen" (10:5). The angel, who appeared next, referred to a struggle with "the prince of the kingdom of Persia" that had lasted for three weeks (10:13). And the same angel (Gabriel?) had also helped "Michael your prince" ever "since the first year of Darius the Mede" (10:21—11:1). The struggles that Daniel and Darius experienced were matched by angelic struggles in heaven on their behalf. **The question is not *either* that the "hosts" of heaven represented the Jewish people *or* that they stood for struggles taking place in the realm of heaven. *Both* are true. Spiritual struggles stand behind the struggles that take place on earth. Human tyrants are motivated by demonic forces (Eph 6:12).**

**8:11.** The movement of the struggle from "the host of heaven" to "the Commander of the host" increases the tension. In this case, though, "to the Commander of the host" comes first in the clause. The verb shifts from the *Qal* of גדל (*become great*) in 8:10 to the *Hiphil*, implying not merely growth, but also "to show oneself great" or "to boast." The title שַׂר צָבָא was common for the commander of an army. Sisera was the "commander" of Jabin's army (Judg 4:2), and Abner was the "commander" of Saul's army (1 Sam 14:50). Since the army of heaven is depicted here, its "Commander" must be a heavenly figure. Most identify the "Commander of the host" with the Lord himself.[37] It was not enough that the horn thought to challenge the army of heaven; he even dared to boast before God himself. The divine figure in the vision is identified as the "highest Commander" ("Commander of commanders") in the angelic interpretation (8:25), and in the vision the "regular service" (תָּמִיד, *tamid*) is removed from the Commander. In other words, the sacrifices and other services offered on a regular basis to the Lord were removed from the Lord.[38]

Given that Joshua encountered a figure who was called "the Commander of Yahweh's host" shortly before the battle for Jericho (Josh 5:14, 15), one might question whether the Commander in Daniel's vision was the Lord or some figure such as the archangel Michael.[39] In Dan 10:13 Michael is called "one of the chief commanders," but in 8:11 it is "*the* Commander of the host" and therefore not Michael. Probably the person that Joshua

---

37. Jerome, *Commentary on Daniel*, 85; Keil, *Ezekiel, Daniel*, 297; Montgomery, *Daniel*, 335; Miller, *Daniel*, 226.

38. Cf. John Collins, *Daniel*, 333.

39. Lacocque, *Book of Daniel*, 162; Pröbstle, "Daniel 8:9–4," 180-83; Ibn Ezra, a Jewish writer of the twelfth century, referenced in Goldwurm, *Daniel*, 224.

encountered was the angel of Yahweh, who in many places is barely distinguished from Yahweh himself (Gen 16:10; Exod 3:2–4; Judg 2:1).[40]

Up to now, the focus has been on the *horn* (קֶרֶן), in Hebrew a feminine noun. Consequently, the pronoun references to this horn are with feminine forms: "*it* grew very much"; "*it* cast (down)"; and "*it* trampled them" (v. 10). **At the start of verse eleven, however, it is "*he* acted arrogantly," a signal for a more direct reference to the "king" (8:23) who stands behind the horn. The figure of the horn resolves into its referent exactly at the moment of the human encounter with the divine.** The remainder of the verbs in the verse revert to the feminine form, and once again the horn (or possibly the "army") is in view as the actor. When Gabriel interprets the vision, he states that "he [the king] will succeed when he acts" (וְהִצְלִיחַ וְעָשָׂה, 8:24). The same thing is stated of the "horn" at the end of verse twelve, only with the verbs in reverse order and in feminine forms: וְעָשְׂתָה וְהִצְלִיחָה ("and it will act and succeed").

Two opinions have been expressed about the word הַתָּמִיד (*the continual* or *the regular*). The term often occurs as an adverb meaning *continually* (Exod 25:30; Pss 16:8; 25:15), but it may also have the sense of something done *regularly* (Exod 29:38; 30:8; 2 Sam 9:10; 2 Kgs 4:9; 1 Chr 16:6). The word could also refer to a specific kind of burnt offering that was offered "regularly" every day, once in the morning and once in the evening (Exod 29:38–42; Num 28:15; Ezra 3:5). Outside of Daniel the term הַתָּמִיד (*the tāmîd*, "the continual") occurs only to modify something else. Neh 10:34 mentions מִנְחַת הַתָּמִיד ("the perpetual grain offering") and עוֹלַת הַתָּמִיד ("the perpetual burnt offering"; cf. Num 28:10). Also, there was "the continual bread" (לֶחֶם הַתָּמִיד, Num 4:7). Within Daniel "the continual" occurs four times without modifying anything else (8:11, 12, 13; 11:31). Since a similar usage is found in the Mishnah and in the Talmud as a technical term implying the more specific "regular burnt offering" sacrificed twice a day, many have claimed that the same usage occurs in the book of Daniel.[41] The NRSV has in all four instances of הַתָּמִיד in Daniel, "the regular burnt offering." That the more specific usage of הַתָּמִיד (*the tāmîd*) is meant in the book of Daniel is doubtful,[42] even though many conservative commentators and the modern versions have taken it that way.[43] **The context speaks of the temple**

---

40. Many have identified the angel of Yahweh with a pre-incarnate appearance of Christ, a distinct possibility for "the Commander of the host" in Daniel's vision (Steinmann, *Daniel*, 402–3).

41. Montgomery, *Daniel*, 336; Lust, "Cult and Sacrifice in Daniel," 672–73.

42. The use of the definite article may represent its function as reference to a general category, *i.e.*, "sacrifices or other acts of worship done regularly."

43. E.g., Baldwin, *Daniel*, 157; Archer, "Daniel," 100; Miller, *Daniel*, 227.

and the תָּמִיד, and it would be odd to restrict the latter term to one particular type of sacrifice when temple worship included much more.[44] The book of First Maccabees refers to an edict of Antiochus Epiphanes (the referent behind the "horn") that prohibited "burnt offerings and sacrifices and drink offerings in the sanctuary" (1 Macc 1:45 NRSV), showing that the fulfillment of Daniel 8:11 was more comprehensive than merely a cancellation of "the regular burnt offering."[45] Pröbstle made a comprehensive study of the use of תָּמִיד in Daniel, concluding that it refers to "the continual worship and service of Yhwh," whether conducted by the priests or by any worshiper. He parallels the term with the reference to Daniel's "constant" worship of his God in 6:17 and 6:21.[46]

Since the *Hiphil* of the root שׁלך normally means *to throw down*, and since there is no record that Antiochus IV Epiphanes destroyed the temple, how is it said that the temple (מְכוֹן מִקְדָּשׁוֹ "the place of his sanctuary") "was thrown down" (הֻשְׁלַךְ)? The *HALOT* explains that the verb here means "to be violated." John Collins refers to "the desecration of the altar,"[47] but that seems unlikely, in that the Hebrew has מִקְדָּשׁוֹ ("his sanctuary"). The explanation in *HALOT* is better. **The temple was thoroughly violated or desecrated by Antiochus. The forceful verb adds to the vividness of the vision.**

8:12. Some translations render in the past tense everything mentioned in verse twelve, while others frame the same events in the future. It is possible to give a reasonable explanation for the apparent future reference. It may be that verse twelve already begins to explain the meaning of the vision even prior to the angelic interpretation. After all, the "regular service" of the Lord and his "sanctuary" are elements from the real world rather than from the symbolic world. Gabriel's exposition (vv. 20–26) focuses on the *king* represented by the *horn*, but he talks about the actions of the king only in general terms (except for his confrontation with the "Highest Commander," v. 25). **Here Daniel speaks of what *will* happen concerning the worship of the Lord, anticipating the revelation of what the vision means. This also would help to identify the peak or climax of the vision. Daniel describes real elements within the vision, not symbols, that will undergo the events that he sees. It is as if he shifts from the time within the vision itself to the real time that is outside of the vision (cf. 7:14).**

---

44. "הַתָּמִיד is everything in the worship of God which is not used merely temporarily, but is permanent, as the daily sacrifice, the setting forth of the shew-bread, and the like" (Keil, *Ezekiel, Daniel*, 298).

45. Young, *Daniel*, 172; Goldingay, *Daniel*, 211.

46. Pröbstle, "Daniel 8:9–14," 206–32.

47. *HALOT*, "שׁלך," 4:1530; John Collins, *Daniel*, 334.

The term צָבָא (*army* or *host*) in verse twelve has two grammatical problems—it lacks a definite article, and it is normally treated as a masculine noun. Here it apparently functions as a feminine noun.[48] At Daniel 10:1 צָבָא is clearly treated as masculine, but there it means "conflict" or "struggle." Possibly there is a textual issue that would explain the use of a feminine verb in 8:12. That צָבָא is without the article favors the view that it means "an army" rather than "(the) host (of heaven)."[49]

Is this "army" on God's side or on the side of the "horn"? It makes most sense in the context to understand it as an army that will be controlled by the king represented by the "horn." Most translations render עַל־הַתָּמִיד with something like "together with the daily sacrifice." That is, both the *host* and the regular service will experience the same fate. The structure of the Hebrew, though, precludes taking the preposition as *together with*.[50] The preposition עַל with "the regular service" as its object works best in the sense of *over*,[51] in which case the "army" of verse twelve is different from the "host of heaven" in verses ten and eleven. It appears, then, that the grammar of the passage favors taking the second occurrence of צָבָא as "an army" that exerts power *over* the "regular service."[52] Naturally, it would be understood that the hostile "army" would be under the command of the *king* that the *horn* represents. Seow thinks that God permitted the king to come with an army against the temple, even as he *gave* Jehoiakim into the power of Nebuchadnezzar (Dan 1:2).[53] The parallel is interesting in that the same verb נָתַן (*to give*) occurs in both places, but the overall context of 8:9–12 concerns the success of the horn/king against God as the "Commander of

---

48. Isa 40:2 is often taken as a parallel for treating צבא as feminine, מָלְאָה צְבָאָהּ ("her warfare has been fulfilled"), but that passage is not free of problems. 1QIsa[a] reads מלא, and others have proposed to read the verb as a *Piel* ("she has fulfilled her warfare"). The reading of the Isaiah scroll could be an assimilation to the usual grammar, and the *Qal* form of the MT makes for a better parallel with the following clause ("her iniquity is pardoned" [ESV]).

49. Keil (*Ezekiel, Daniel*, 300) argues that the indefinite noun indicates that "only one part of" the host, the part "cast down" according to v. 10, is in view. His argument has been followed by Young (*Daniel*, 172) and Wood (*Daniel*, 216). Pröbstle rightly argues that there is no grammatical precedent for taking an indefinite noun in this manner ("Daniel 8:9–14," 266).

50. Pröbstle gives two linguistic reasons. First, when two items are joined by the preposition עַל they should be "part of the same semantic group," whereas *the army* involves people while *the regular service* involves activities. Second, "when two entities are combined by עַל, they almost always appear next to each other." Here the terms are separated by the verb ("Daniel 8:9–14," 276–49).

51. Goldingay, *Daniel*, 197.

52. So also, Seow, *Daniel*, 124.

53. Seow, *Daniel*, 124.

the host." Hence, it would be odd for God as Commander to dispatch an army against "the regular service," when in fact the horn had removed that service from God. It must be the royal power behind the "horn" that sets the "army" against the "regular service." **Part of the tension of the vision is that while God has been shown as sovereign in previous visions, at this point it appears that perhaps the horn might be gaining the upper hand. The tension is relieved only when a time limit for the horn's seeming victory is established through a divine decree (8:13–14).**

The referent for פֶּשַׁע (v. 12) is also unclear. It could refer to the *transgression* of the people or to the *transgression* of the king and his troops. Verse thirteen refers to "the transgression that devastates," so it would be more consistent with the context to make the king and his army the transgressors.[54]

**There is virtual unanimity that the "truth" that the horn flings to the ground refers to the Law of Moses or perhaps to the Scriptures that were extant in Daniel's day.**[55] Antiochus tried to nullify the requirements of the Torah in order to replace Jewish religious practices with pagan practices (cf. 1 Macc 1:41–61).

## Two Angels Speak of 2300 Evening-Mornings. (8:13–14)

After the frightening conclusion to the previous scene, the present section introduces an element of hope. **The mysterious king represented by the horn will successfully overthrow the people of God and the temple with its sacrifices, but the horrible times will have a limited duration. Eventually, God will restore the nation.**

8:13–14. Daniel comments when the new scene opens: "Then I heard a holy one speaking." Each time Daniel identifies himself in this way a new scene or topic begins to unfold. This scene has some specific ways in which it brings the vision to its conclusion. A conversation between two angels has a drawn-out description of the two participants in the dialog, underlining the solemnity of the occasion and increasing the tension as the reader tries to imagine what will be said. The speech of the first angel is unusual grammatically. Rather than complete clauses, the angel phrases the question through isolated words that recall the key details of the vision. A woodenly literal translation of the question is as follows: "How long the vision, the

---

54. Walvoord, *Daniel*, 188; Hartman and Di Lella, *Book of Daniel*, 226; for the view that the term refers to Israel's transgression see Archer ("Daniel," 100) and Miller (*Daniel*, 227).

55. See Archer, "Daniel," 101; Miller, *Daniel*, 228.

regular and the transgression (that) devastates, giving, and holiness, and an army trampling?" The reply of the second angel is cryptic. A specific time limit is given but is expressed in a form that is hard to interpret the exact time meant, namely "2,300 evening-mornings."

**8:13.** The term קָדוֹשׁ (*holy one*) for an angel is attested in Dan 7:18. At Dan 4:10, the "watcher," clearly an angel, is equated with "a holy one" (קַדִּישׁ in Aramaic). In the context of 8:13, the natural expectation is that the conversation about how long the vision will apply would be discussed by angelic figures (cf. Zech 1:12).

"How long the vision?" (עַד־מָתַי הֶחָזוֹן) refers to the length of time for the disastrous events within the fourth scene, events that are enumerated one by one in the rest of the verse. First, the term הַתָּמִיד ("the regular") reminds the reader of how regular worship had been "removed" from the "the highest Commander" (8:11). The sacrifices and attendant rituals were associated with the presence of the Lord. The removal of these acts of worship would be disastrous to the temple cult (cf. Joel 1:9), cutting the people off from access to the Lord.

In addition to the removal of sacrifices and other elements of worship from the temple, the people will be confronted with "the transgression that desolates." According to verse twelve, the hostile army "will be set against the regular service by transgression." Since a form of the same verb for *set* (נָתַן) occurs in verse thirteen (תֵּת), it makes sense to construe it with the term for *transgression*. The versions mostly relate the infinitive תֵּת in verse thirteen to what follows, but even though an infinitive clause with the object placed before the infinitive is rare,[56] it makes better sense to take the object as what precedes: "and setting in place the transgression that desolates." Both Greek versions support this rendering: "and the sin of devastation which has been assigned." Also, a comparison with Dan 11:31 and 12:11 shows that the verb נתן (*give* or *set*) governs as its object in both cases "the abomination that devastates." The instance in 12:11 is even governed by the infinitive of נתן. These parallels, then, provide evidence that the infinitive in 8:13 should be taken with *the transgression that devastates*.

**8:14.** The angel replies to the question "how long?" with one of the most enigmatic statements in the entire book of Daniel. The period will

---

56. Pröbstle ("Daniel 8:9–14," 354–58) discusses the issue of the object preceding the infinitive, rare in biblical Hebrew but more common in biblical Aramaic. Carmignac ("Aramaïsme biblique et Qumränien") places the phenomenon of an object complement prior to the governing infinitive within the context of Semitic, adducing examples from Akkadian, Ethiopic, various dialects of Aramaic, and biblical Hebrew. We would add two possible Aramaic examples from Qumran: 1) חכמתא למאלף (*to learn wisdom*; 4Q213 [Levi[a] ar]); and 2) להתבה לגבר כות[י] (*to return the Cuthean man*; 4Q550c [4QPrEsther[d] ar]).

be "2,300 evening-mornings." The angel did not say "2,300 evenings *and* mornings"; the two terms for the components of a day are placed side by side with no intervening conjunction. The two main views are that it means either 2,300 *days* or it means 1,150 *days*. The former meaning is based on an interpretation of "evening-morning" as a single day, following the pattern found in Genesis 1. The oldest evidence for this interpretation is from the Greek versions: "until evening and morning, 2,300 days." It was also supported by Jerome in his commentary.[57]

The figure of 1,150 days assumes that "the regular service" (הַתָּמִיד) refers to the morning and evening sacrifices. Because the sacrifice would be offered twice a day, 2,300 of them would be offered in a span of 1,150 days.[58] If הַתָּמִיד does not refer to the daily burnt offerings sacrificed each morning and evening, then the figure of 1,150 days cannot be accepted. If, however, הַתָּמִיד does refer to those daily offerings, then either opinion about the 2,300 "evening-mornings" is possible. That is, one could think of one תָּמִיד (*regular offering*) as comprising both the evening and the morning sacrifices, so that it would still take 2,300 days to complete them.[59]

Granted that an "evening-morning" could be a unique way to refer to a "day," the question still arises why that should be so in the context of Daniel 8. In other words, why did the angel choose such unusual terminology to refer to a day? Why not simply say "2,300 days" or "1,150 days"? The view that it refers to the two parts of the תָּמִיד (evening and morning) would supply an explanation,[60] but as explained previously, it is unlikely that the term הַתָּמִיד ("the continual") refers specifically to the "regular burnt offering." The Hebrew expression may include that offering, but it probably refers to all the "regular service" conducted in the temple.

Theodoret of Cyrus (fifth century) thought that the "evening" referred "to the beginning of the calamities," and "morning" spoke of the end of those times.[61] This is unsatisfying; it would be better to find something that relates to the temple worship that is prominent in the context. Aaron was instructed to keep a lamp outside the veil in the tent of meeting burning "continually" (תָּמִיד) "from evening to morning" (Lev 24:3). Also, when the tabernacle was erected, a cloud covered it in the morning, but "in the evening" and "until morning" it had the appearance of fire (Num 9:15).

57. Jerome, *Commentary on Daniel*, 86.

58. Montgomery, *Daniel*, 343; Archer, "Daniel," 103; John Collins, *Daniel*, 336.

59. Schwantes, "*Ereb Bōqer* of Dan 8:14"; Goldingay, *Daniel*, 213.

60. Although, as Schwantes points out, "the language of the ritual always designates the morning sacrifice before the one of the evening, without exception" ("*Ereb Bōqer* of Dan 8:14," 381).

61. Theodoret of Cyrus, *Commentary on Daniel*, 215.

Such descriptions are instructive but still don't get to the heart of how a day is comprised of an evening and a morning.

Perhaps the reason for the expression "evening-morning" relates to the language of Passover, the ritual that celebrated God's deliverance of his people from slavery in Egypt. The first Passover meal was eaten in the evening, and the liberating exodus took place in the morning (Exod 12:6–10, 22; Deut 16:6). In the intervening period the Lord was at work on behalf of his people, striking down at midnight "all the firstborn in the land of Egypt" (Exod 12:29). Later, Moses and Aaron instructed the people: "In the evening you shall know that it was the Lord who brought you out of the land of Egypt, and in the morning, you shall see the glory of the Lord" (Exod 16:6–7a). They said this concerning the supply of quail in the evening and manna in the morning, both examples of God's graciousness to Israel despite the complaints of the people.

Looking elsewhere in the book of Daniel for clues to the expression "evening-morning" or "the evening and the morning" (8:26), it is striking that when Gabriel came to Daniel with the message about the "seventy weeks" (9:24–27), it was "about the time of the evening offering" (9:21).[62] **Like the message of the 2,300 "evening-mornings," the message of the "seventy weeks" concerned some troubling times for God's people, but times that were under his control. The thought, then, would be that the horrible events of the rule of Antiochus IV (the "little horn") that appeared to be a defeat for the Lord were really under the Lord's control after all. The times of Antiochus were in the hands of the Lord, and he would deliver his people even as he delivered them from slavery in Egypt.**

If the 2,300 "evening-mornings" make up that many days, when do they begin and when do they end? The end took place most probably in 164 BC, the year that the temple was cleansed and restored under Judas the Maccabee (1 Macc 4:36–59) and when Antiochus IV died from an illness (1 Macc 6:8–16; 2 Macc. 9).[63] It is more difficult to calculate the time when the era began. The usual response is that it began with the murder of Onias III, as recorded in 2 Macc 4:30–34.[64] Onias had been the High Priest until Antiochus IV came to power. At that time Onias's brother, Jason, bought an

---

62. The term for "evening offering" is מִנְחַת עֶרֶב and not עֹלַת תָּמִיד. One might have expected the latter phrase or similar if הַתָּמִיד in Daniel 8 referred to the morning and evening sacrifices.

63. 1 Macc 6:16 implies that Antiochus died in 163 BC, whereas 2 Macc 9 and 10 imply that he died prior to the cleansing of the temple. Gera and Horowitz ("Antiochus IV," 249–50) present evidence from a Babylonian astronomical text that Antiochus expired shortly before the cleansing of the temple in 164 BC.

64. Walvoord. *Daniel*, 190; Seow, *Daniel*, 125.

appointment to the office from the new king (2 Macc 4:7–10). Sometime later, Menelaus acquired the office from Antiochus by outbidding Jason (2 Macc 4:23–24), and it was Menelaus who arranged for Onias to be killed, according to the story in Second Maccabees, because Onias had exposed a plot by Menelaus to steal some of the gold vessels from the temple to pay off his debt to Antiochus. From that point on "many acts of sacrilege" were committed in Jerusalem, leading up to Antiochus's plundering the temple and suppressing the practice of Judaism (1 Macc 1:20–64; 2 Macc 4:39—7:42). It is possible, however, that Onias was not murdered. **Regardless, somewhere around 170 BC Antiochus began to intensify his persecution, and that intensification marks the most likely starting point for the 2,300 days.**

Since קֹדֶשׁ usually means *holiness* and מִקְדָּשׁ occurred earlier for the "sanctuary" (8:11), it seems unlikely that קֹדֶשׁ means "sanctuary" in 8:13, even though most of the English versions so render it.[65] The more general sense would imply something like "restored to a proper state of holiness."

## Gabriel Explains the Vision to Daniel. (8:15–27)

Theological Point: God is sovereign over those who persecute his people and the extent of the persecution.

Daniel "sought for understanding" of the vision, and in response a figure who looked like a man stood before him. Before this "man" began to interpret the vision, though, Daniel fainted from his awestruck terror at what was happening. The "man," who was identified as Gabriel, raised Daniel up, and told him that the vision pertained to an "appointed end." Then he proceeded to single out various parts of the vision and explain what they meant.

### Introduction to the Interpretation (8:15–19)

Some five verses introduce Gabriel's detailed interpretation. **This lengthy prelude to the interpretation serves three functions. First, it highlights the mystery in the vision—*even* Daniel must reflect on it and requires further revelation to explain it. Second, it emphasizes the awesome nature of the vision. A prominent angel like Gabriel comes to explain it, and Daniel faints into a deep sleep when he encounters Gabriel. This leads the reader to expect the revelation to be freighted with divine splendor. If Daniel could not maintain his composure when Gabriel**

---

65. NASB, "the holy place"; NLT, "the Temple."

showed up, how could any human being not be in absolute awe during such an angelic visitation? Third, the introduction turns the reader's attention to the "appointed time of the end."

**8:15.** When Daniel tried to understand the vision, he was immediately confronted by a heavenly figure who looked like a man. The term for *man* here is גֶּבֶר, and it is the only time it occurs in the Hebrew part of the book of Daniel. This compares with eight occurrences of אִישׁ, the usual Hebrew term for *man*, and four of אָדָם, a generic term that means *human being*. Since Gabriel is summoned by a "human voice" to interpret the vision for Daniel, it is likely that Gabriel is also the "man" that Daniel saw.[66] The name "Gabriel" means "man of God,"[67] with "man" a form of גֶּבֶר.

**8:16.** After he saw Gabriel, Daniel heard a "human voice" (קוֹל־אָדָם) command Gabriel to explain the vision to him. The source of the "voice" is a mystery, and whoever it is must rank higher than Gabriel. The Hebrew term for "human" here is אָדָם, and it occurs only four times in Daniel (8:16, 17; 10:16, 18). Twice it is an element in the (Hebrew) phrase "son of man" (8:17; 10:16) and emphasizes human frailty and mortality. Daniel himself was addressed as "son of man" in 8:17. The "voice" must be either the voice of God expressed in human language,[68] or less likely, the voice of a leading angel such as Michael.[69] Probably the same figure is present in the vision of 10:5–7 and 12:7.

Why does the "voice" come from "between Ulai" (בֵּין אוּלָי)? Finkelstein suggests that it refers to an area between two tributaries of the Ulai, based on an idiom from Old Persian.[70] **The mention of the Ulai brings the reader back to the beginning of the vision (8:2) and into the territory of Media-Persia as represented by the ram with two horns. If the speaker is God himself, speaking with a human voice so that Daniel could understand, then he spoke to stress that he was in control of the situation from the start. The 2,300 "evening-mornings" represent the time limit that God imposed on Antiochus IV; now he exercises his sovereign power**

---

66. Miller (*Daniel*, 231) thinks that the גֶּבֶר (*man*) is actually God and also the source of the "voice," because Daniel did not fear angels (7:16) or Gabriel (9:21–23.). Daniel fainted from fear, though, only after Gabriel was already speaking with him.

67. The element –*i* in "Gabriel" is most likely an archaic ending attached to the construct state of a noun; cf. "Abdiel" (*servant of El*, 1 Chron. 5:15). Other suggestions for the name "Gabriel" are "God has shown himself strong" (Baldwin, *Daniel*, 158) and "God is my hero/warrior" (Collins, *Daniel*, 336).

68. Walvoord, *Daniel*, 191; Lucas, *Daniel*, 219.

69. John Collins, *Daniel*, 336; Smith-Christopher, "Book of Daniel," 114; Jerome mentions a Jewish tradition that Michael was the one who commanded Gabriel (*Commentary on Daniel*, 88).

70. Finkelstein, "Mesopotamia," 89.

over Media-Persia and commands Gabriel to convey the interpretation to Daniel.

**8:17–19.** Gabriel laid out the general time frame of the vision for Daniel before interpreting the details. The events of the vision are "for the time of the end" (v. 17b) and "for the time appointed for the end" (v. 19c); they will happen "at the end of [the time of] wrath" (v. 19b). It is difficult to determine the referent for this "time of the end." At least three different views have been proffered. For some commentators the "end" refers to the "end" that immediately precedes the establishment of God's kingdom on earth.[71] For others the "end" here can refer only to the ending of the life of Antiochus IV.[72] A mediating view thinks of either a double fulfillment of the vision or a typological interpretation that connects the time of Antiochus to the end of the age.[73]

Gabriel referred the "time of the end" specifically to "the vision," so it is difficult to see how that time can refer to anything beyond the period of Antiochus unless it be through typology. **There is nothing in Gabriel's interpretation of the vision that necessitates a double fulfillment or somehow takes the vision beyond Antiochus. And the "wrath" or "indignation" that he mentions fits naturally with the persecution that the Jewish people endured under that tyrant. The vision pertained to the time that began with the kings of Media-Persia and continued until the end of the tribulations that the Jews suffered under Antiochus IV.**[74]

Wood sees a partial fulfillment of the vision in the time of Antiochus but "complete fulfillment" in the Antichrist.[75] As Archer points out, "the future dealings of Antichrist can only be conjectured or surmised,"[76] so it is better to leave Antiochus at this point as merely a "type" or "foreshadowing" of Antichrist rather than a partial fulfillment of the vision. After a lengthy discussion, Walvoord commended the view that "... regards the entire chapter as historically fulfilled in Antiochus, but to varying degrees foreshadowing typically the future world ruler who would dominate the situation at the end of the times of the Gentiles."[77]

**Daniel kept hearing in his visions that the message is for a certain "time of the end"** (8:17, 19; 9:26; 11:27, 35, 40; 12:4, 6, 9, 13). There

---

71. Hassler, "Little Horn," 37.
72. Gowan, *Daniel*, 122; Pace, *Daniel*, 275.
73. Walvoord, *Daniel*, 195–96; Sprinkle, *Daniel*, 216.
74. See also Miller, *Daniel*, 233.
75. Wood, *Daniel*, 222–24.
76. Archer, "Daniel," 106.
77. Walvoord, *Daniel*, 196.

appear to be two of these "ends." One period ends with the age of Antiochus IV, while the other culminates with the second advent of the Messiah. Daniel sees both periods and the events that precede them closely in time. He also sees the first advent of the Messiah but in a more veiled form (9:25–26).

### The Elements of the Vision Interpreted (8:20–26)

**Gabriel identifies each of the main elements of the vision succinctly, until he comes to the "insolent" or "fierce" king who is also "skilled in intrigue." At that point he begins to go into more detail, and that corresponds with the vision itself, where the major focus is on the "little horn." Clearly, Gabriel identifies that "horn" with the "fierce and devious king" (v. 23).**

Surprisingly, Gabriel did not interpret the revelation about the 2,300 "evening-mornings." He simply affirmed that "it is true" or "reliable" (8:26). After that affirmation, Gabriel told Daniel to make the vision secure by recording it in writing and storing it in a safe place. **Then the vision will be available for the people of God in the future when they need it for encouragement.**

8:20. The ram with its two horns refers to "the kings of Media and Persia."[78] Everywhere in Daniel "Media and Persia" is considered a political unity, and that is underscored by the reference to a single animal with two horns. Elsewhere in the book we encounter "Darius the Mede" and "three more kings" of Persia (11:1–2). The fact that the ram represents "kings" means that it must refer to the kings of Media and Persia considered as a group. The last king would be Darius III (336–31 BC), who was overthrown by the "large horn" on the "male goat."

8:21–22. The "large horn" must be identified with Alexander the Great. He conquered Darius III and was "the first king" of Greece. Technically, Alexander's father, Philip of Macedon, was first, but the vision was given in terms of one vast kingdom or empire overtaking another. In that sense, Alexander's realm far surpassed that of his father, and he truly was the first king of the extensive empire that he conquered.

Since "the male goat" refers to "the king of Greece," how does the goat differ from "the large horn"? Apparently, the animal itself refers

---

78. The OG, Th, the Vulgate, and the Syriac all translated מַלְכֵי ("kings of") as a singular ("king"). The oldest Syriac manuscripts supply some historical notations for chapters 7 and 8, identifying "the king of Media and Persia" to be "Darius the Mede." The change to the singular is most likely secondary, based on a desire to identify a specific king.

to the royal leadership of Greece, while the horns represent specific kings. Thus "the king of Greece" is virtually equivalent to "the kingdom of Greece"; but there is a subtle difference, in that "king" is used of the office, and "the large horn" was the first to fill that position. The four additional horns represent four leaders who will arise from their positions in relation to Greece, but when they consolidate their territory, they will form four separate kingdoms.

Great turmoil followed the death of Alexander the Great in 323 BC, with a struggle between his various generals for political succession.[79] These generals are commonly known as the *diadochi* (*successors*), but it is difficult to pin down exactly which ones might be meant by the four horns. The only name that is common to virtually all lists is Ptolemy I, who seized Egypt and eventually attempted to seize Palestine as well.[80]

Two clues from the text help to sort out what the fourfold division of Alexander's empire entailed. First, v. eight indicates that the "four (horns)" arose "to the four winds of heaven," indicating the four directions of the compass. Second, the interpretation (v. 23) refers to "four kingdoms," not to four kings. **It is not necessary to find specific kings who would correspond to the horns.** After several wars between the generals, four kingdoms arose: Macedonia (west), Egypt (south), Syria and Babylonia (east), and Thrace and Asia Minor (north).[81] These kingdoms came from Alexander's realm, but they did not have the same "power" (כֹּחַ) because of disunity and the fragmentation of his empire.

**8:23-25.** Gabriel does not identify which element of the vision he interprets next, but it is obvious that his words must apply to the "little horn." That was the element in the vision after the four horns, and his description easily fits its details as given in verses nine to twelve. Nearly all interpreters agree that Antiochus IV Epiphanes matches historically the "fierce and devious king" described here by Gabriel.

**8:23a.** The timing of the appearance of Antiochus is described in two ways. It was "in the latter period of their reign" (בְּאַחֲרִית מַלְכוּתָם) and

---

79. For details see Walbank, *Hellenistic World*, 46–59.

80. Jerome (*Commentary on Daniel*, 85) lists: Philip Aridaeus of Macedonia; Antigonus of Asia Minor; Seleucus Nicanor of Syria, Babylonia, and "all the kingdoms of the East"; and Ptolemy of Egypt. Walvoord (*Daniel*, 184) and Wood (*Daniel*, 211) list: Cassander of Macedonia and Greece; Lysimachus of Thrace, Bithynia, and most of Asia Minor; Seleucus of Syria and Babylonia; and Ptolemy of Egypt. Hartman and Di Lella (*Book of Daniel*, 235) assign Asia Minor and northern Syria to Antigonus, but otherwise have the same list as Walvoord and Wood.

81. Josephus (*A.J.* 12:2) identifies five areas: Asia (Antigonus); Babylon "and the nations thereabouts" (Seleucus); Hellespont (Lysimachus); Macedon (Cassander); and Egypt (Ptolemy).

"when the transgressors have reached full measure" (כְּהָתֵם הַפֹּשְׁעִים). Nearly 150 years passed between the death of Alexander and the start of the reign of Antiochus (175 BC). The "transgressors" or "rebels" (8:23) are often identified with Jews who sided with Antiochus IV's attempt to Hellenize Judea and Jerusalem, thus turning away from God's law.[82] If our exegesis of 8:12 is correct, however, the term more likely refers to the transgressions of the foreign power against the Lord and his people.[83] It is also possible that the term includes both the Seleucids and Jewish sympathizers, but the point is that rebellion against God can only go on for a time that is determined by him. After that the judgment must come (cf. Gen 15:16).

**8:23b.** Antiochus is called עַז־פָּנִים, literally, "strong of face." Similar expressions occur in Deut 28:50; Prov 7:13; and 21:29. These passages give the idea of bold or brazen action, and that appears to be the sense here. **Antiochus IV will step forward boldly and without shame to carry out his wicked schemes against God's people.**

This bold or fierce king will also be "devious." There is an idiom here that ties in with something that was said of Daniel himself. "Devious" could be rendered with "understand riddles" (מֵבִין חִידוֹת), but "riddles" in the sense of dark sayings or words with hidden meaning. Daniel himself was someone who could "explain riddles" (אַחֲוָיַת אֲחִידָן) and "solve difficult problems" (literally, "untie knots," מְשָׁרֵא קִטְרִין). **The Aramaic term for "riddles" used in Dan 5:12 is cognate with the Hebrew term used here. The subtle message is that Daniel's wisdom came from God and was therefore used for a good purpose, whereas Antiochus relied on his own wisdom and even placed himself in opposition to God.**

**8:24.** Like other kings before him, Antiochus became quite powerful and used that power absolutely. He caused "unheard of disaster," destroying "mighty ones" and the "holy people." **He achieved his great success seemingly by his own cunning and pride, and he even appeared to overcome God himself. His success was short-lived. When he dared to stand against the "Highest Commander" he was "broken without (human) power."**[84] **That is, he did not die by violence but through an act of God.** The exact circumstances of his death are uncertain, but it involved some type of illness.

---

82. Miller, *Daniel*, 234; Steinmann, *Daniel*, 415.

83. See also Seow, *Daniel*, 130.

84. יָד (*hand*) often refers to control or power. "Without a hand" means without human assistance (*HALOT*), both in Hebrew (2 Sam 23:6; Job 34:20) and in Aramaic (Dan 2:34).

8:26. The only statement that Gabriel made about the 2,300 evening-mornings was that the vision "is true" (אֱמֶת). What might that mean in relation to the vision as a whole and to Daniel's other visions? Before answering this question, we will first consider Gabriel's instructions to Daniel: "close (סְתֹם) the vision because it is yet for many days (in the future)." The verb סתם is used of "stopping up" water springs (2 Kgs 3:19), and the *Niphal* pattern can refer to gaps in a wall that have been blocked (Neh 4:1). Gabriel told Daniel, then, to "seal up" or "close" the vision.[85] In Dan 12:4 the command סְתֹם is paralleled by חֲתֹם (*seal*), so סְתֹם there should refer to something done to the document. In that sense, "close" or "shut" seems to catch the meaning of what Daniel was commanded to do. In 8:26 the reference is to the "vision," not to "the book" as in 12:4. Nevertheless, Daniel still needs to record the vision, so the action need not be that different. Daniel is to "close" the words of the vision into a written document. There it will be preserved for any of "the wise" (הַמַּשְׂכִּילִים) who will learn from it in the future (Dan 11:33, 35; 12:3, 10). **So, it is not so much about keeping the vision a secret as it is preserving it for future readers, but those future readers will not understand it unless they are spiritually attuned to hear it. That is why Gabriel emphasized that the vision was "true." Antiochus and his army would "cast truth to the ground," but God's truth as recorded by Daniel would endure.** "The grass withers, the flower fades; but the word of our God will stand forever" (Isa 40:8).

## Daniel's Reaction to the Vision and Its Interpretation (8:27)

As with each of Daniel's visions, he had a strong reaction when the vision concluded. Suffering from exhaustion,[86] he became physically ill for a few days. When he finally was able to get up and return to his work, he was still troubled by the ramifications of his vision, but there was no one who could give him any further explanation. He had some general conception of how the prophecy would be fulfilled, but he longed to have more explanation about some of the details.

---

85. For various interpretations see Archer, "Daniel," 105; Miller, *Daniel*, 236; Steinmann, *Daniel*, 417.

86. The Hebrew, נִהְיֵיתִי, is unclear. The *Niphal* of הָיָה can mean *to happen* (Exod 11:6) or possibly *to have gone*, which seems to be the sense of נִהְיְתָה in Dan 2:1 ("his sleep *had gone* from him"). Here it would then mean that Daniel was "spent" or "undone."

## SHARPENING THE THEOLOGICAL FOCUS

While the vision of the four beasts from the sea (chap. 7) broadly surveyed all of history from Babylon up to its consummation in God's eternal kingdom, the vision of chapter 8 focuses on the period from the Medo-Persian empire to the Greek empire established by Alexander and then passed down through his generals and their descendants to Antiochus IV Epiphanes. This is a period of history with great relevance to Daniel and his readers. It encompasses the fortunes of the Jews under the more benevolent Persians but then culminates in a severe persecution against faithful Jews in the time of Antiochus. During the Persian period many Jews returned to their homeland, rebuilt the temple in Jerusalem, and even completed the walls surrounding Jerusalem. Judaism as it emerged after the destruction of the temple in AD 70 had deep roots within the period of the Greeks and Romans. It is difficult to overemphasize the significance of the persecution under Antiochus and the subsequent cleansing of the temple under the Maccabees for the depth of these roots. During the time of the Maccabees and following, the main Jewish groups found in the first century BC and the first century AD came into existence—the Sadducees, the Pharisees, and the Essenes. From the standpoint of Gentile kingdoms, Daniel's visions become even more detailed with the first part of chapter 11. Then the second part of chapter 11 to chapter 12 provides additional details about the transition from the kingdoms of this world to God's kingdom that will never end.

The universal message of Daniel 8 is that God is still in control even when it seems like he isn't. That Daniel sees in his vision details about coming events indicates that these events are already completely within the Lord's command. Only God can know the future. More than that, even though the tyrant will be able to remove the temple service from the Lord and pollute the temple itself, God already has in mind a time limit for such wickedness. Even as chapter 7 depicted the Most High as Lord of time, so also chapter 8 demonstrates that the times are in his hands.

The question of how the all-powerful God can allow evil to flourish is a common theme in the OT. One psalmist wondered why the Lord seems hidden in times of trouble (Ps 10:1), and others asked "how long" before the Lord would judge the wicked (Pss 13:1 [2]; 35:17; 74:10; 94:3). The prophet Habakkuk echoed the cry when he saw wickedness and violence among his own countrymen (Hab 1:2). Daniel contributes to the issue by speaking of a time of the "end" and by expressions like "2,300 evening-mornings" (8:14) or "seventy periods of seven" (9:24). **The answer to the question "how long" refers to God's timing. He knows the "end," and he has determined the timing of the course of history. When the faithful understand this, they** are then able to endure to the end. They can wait patiently even if grave times lie in their future (cf. Hab 3:16–19). Daniel's vision of the ram, the he-goat, and the "little horn" gives a firm basis for confident faith.

The vision of chapter 8 also points to the tension of the relationship between God's faithful people and the kingdoms of this world. On the one hand, the Jews were able to flourish to some extent under the protective hand of the Persians and the Hellenism that followed in the wake of Alexander's conquests. On the other hand, they were at the mercy of powerful rulers who, at times, became tyrants. Eventually, the wrath of Antiochus nearly destroyed the religious purity of the Jewish people. Only the grace of God prevented an even greater catastrophe than the horrific persecution the faithful experienced at that time. It has always been so. In the time of the Apostle John there were martyrs who cried "how long" before they would receive justice (Rev 6:10), and in the current day there are reports that the number of martyrs has dramatically increased as Christianity continues to spread globally.[87]

The truth of God's word also finds emphasis in chapter 8. The "little horn" tried to overturn the truth of the Law of Moses, but the statement about the "2,300 evening-mornings" was absolutely reliable in the face of this threat. For a little while the "horn" might cause the regular service in the house of God to cease, but it was helpless against the period of time decreed by God. This reminds as well of Nebuchadnezzar's decree against Shadrach, Meshach, and Abednego, a decree that God countered by delivering them from the furnace. Or there was the time when Daniel's enemies at court had a decree signed by the king such that even the king could not repeal it, but God frustrated it. God's word stands firm against every attempt to destroy it.

## THE FOCUS OF DANIEL 8 FOR PREACHING AND TEACHING

Daniel's vision in chapter 8 covers several hundred years of history. During those years, God's people would experience good times, like a return to their homeland under the helpful hand of an unlikely "servant of the Lord," Cyrus. They would also experience bad times, the worst being the persecution of a maniacal ruler, Antiochus IV Epiphanes. Though it specifically deals with particular points in history, the theology of chapter 8 is timeless. Until God destroys the last earthly opposition and establishes his kingdom, God's people will experience varying degrees of support and persecution.

87. Ministries such as *Voice of the Martyrs* and *Christian History Institute* continue to track and report the persecution of Christians around the world.

Our hopes will never be ultimately fulfilled by earthly powers; only our sovereign God can put all wrongs to right.

While earthly opposition frames the message of chapter 8, the underlying cause of the opposition is what undergirds the theology of Daniel's vision. Six times in chapter 8 *gadal* (גדל) is used to describe the earthly powers;[88] once for Persia (v. 4), once for Greece (v. 8) and four times for Antiochus IV Epiphanes (vss. 9, 10, 11, 25). The final appearance of the word is key to understanding the theological thrust and will help to build a sermon/teaching that flows from the text. The first five times the word appears, in the vision itself, it is simply descriptive. "Great" describes the nature of the animals/empires. The fact that it is only used once to describe "the ram" and "the goat," and then three consecutive times to describe the "little horn," indicates emphasis. The stage is set; this "little horn" is some kind of great! The word is not used again until the end of the interpretation of Daniel's vision when it says, "And he will think himself great" (v. 25). Like Nebuchadnezzar and Belshazzar before him, and like all earthly leaders who will oppose God after him, Antiochus IV Epiphanes is struck with the disease of conceit; and like all the others, he will be humbled.

Because it is apocalyptic in style, Daniel 8 has seen its fair share of nuanced and speculative interpretation. In order to avoid fruitless speculation and engage in powerful preaching/teaching, one needs to follow where the text goes. Three things will help to keep the teaching on track.

First, realize that chapter 8 is focused more on the question of "How long?" than on the question of, "Why?" In chapter 2 (v. 21) God "changes times and seasons; he removes kings and sets up kings." In chapter 7 God is the *Ancient of Days* and, therefore, sovereign over time. Chapter 8, building on what has already been revealed, teaches that because God is sovereign over time, he knows when events will happen and how long they will last. Chapter 8 reveals that God's people can expect to encounter a period of great persecution; a period that will only last as long as God has determined. The suffering will end.

Second, chapter 8 is specific with regard to future empires, and this specificity is meant to prepare and encourage God's people. Daniel 1 to Daniel 6 are historical narratives—they tell about what happened. They teach that God was always in control of what had happened. Chapter 7 served as a transition and introduction to the apocalyptic chapters of Daniel. But it was a broad view of the future. In contrast, chapter 8 is quite specific. It tells what is going to happen (though it is now in the past, it was in the future for

---

88. Goldingay (*Daniel*, 205, 217) and Greidanus (*Daniel*, 256–57) also point to the repetition of key words in this chapter as important for discerning the theology of the text.

Daniel and for everyone else who heard it over the next four centuries). The apocalyptic vision of chapter 8 prepares God's people for what's to come by giving them a preview; if they know what's coming, it can strengthen faith rather than extinguish faith when what was predicted comes to pass. For those who have lived since the reign of Antiochus IV Epiphanes, knowing that God revealed what actually happened, increases confidence in God's Word as a reliable map as we seek to find the way of faithfulness.

Finally, because Daniel 8 is specific with regard to the empires, and because there is virtual certainty that the final ruler mentioned is Antiochus IV Epiphanes, it is important to become familiar with this period of Jewish history.[89] It was absolutely brutal to be an observant Jew during this reign of terror. Daniel's vision needed to be specific so that the people were prepared for what they were going to face.

## FROM TEXTUAL WORK TO TEACHING

### The Big Idea

- *Exegetical Idea:* Through Daniel's vision, God warns Israel that they will endure a period of severe persecution and he assures them that the days of persecution will be limited and the persecutor will be destroyed.

- *Theological Focus:* God warns his people that until he establishes his kingdom, his people will face periods of severe persecution, but the persecution will not last and the persecutors will be destroyed.

- *Preaching Idea:* God warns us of persecution so that we will be motivated to persevere.

### Outline One: Following the Exegetical Flow

I. Until God fully and finally establishes his kingdom, his people will face periods of persecution.

    A. The Jewish people will continue to face periods of persecution.

        1. They will face persecution under the reign of the Medo-Persian empire.

---

89. Reading 1 and 2 Maccabees can be helpful in this regard. The Apocrypha can be found in the NRSV.

2. They will face persecution under the reign of the Greek empire.

3. They will face persecution under the reign of Antiochus IV Epiphanes.

B. God's people will continue to face periods of persecution.

1. Historical examples from the early church through the twentieth century

2. Contemporary examples

II. God is sovereign over those who persecute his people and the extent of the persecution they inflict.

A. The persecution will not last longer than God has decreed.

1. The periods of persecution in chapter 8 came to the end that God decreed.

2. The periods of persecution in church history have ended at God's decree.

3. The persecution Christians face today will come to an end.

B. The persecutors of God's people will be destroyed.

1. The persecutors in chapter 8 were all destroyed.

2. The persecutors of the church through the ages have been, or will be, destroyed.

## Outline Two: Following a Theme

In a *New York Times* Opinion piece, Piers Brendon writes, "The past is a map, not a compass. It charts human experience, stops at the present and gives no clear sense of direction. History does not repeat itself nor. . . does it proceed in rhythms or cycles. Events buck trends. Everything. . . is subject to the vicissitudes of fortune."[90] The book of Daniel would beg to differ. Daniel 8 is both a map and a compass.

- As a map, Daniel 8 charts the experience of God's people through suffering.

---

90. Brendon, "Like Rome Before the Fall? Not Yet."

- The experience of persecution by evil regimes.
- The experience of "bad guys" winning.
- The experience of "good guys" having to sacrifice, even their lives.
- The experience of God's deliverance (Exod 12, Isa 40, the death of Antiochus IV Epiphanes).

- As a compass, Daniel 8 gives a clear sense of direction through suffering.

  - Daniel was faithful about the king's business, even when the king didn't recognize his talents and work. (This vision comes during Daniel's years of relative anonymity in Belshazzar's court.)
  - God's people have endured suffering through the centuries and there are stories after stories of their faithfulness and perseverance because they knew it was going to come to an end according to God's decree.

The history of God's people through suffering serves as a map and a compass for God's people until Jesus returns.

# Prophecy of Seventy Weeks
## (Daniel 9:1–27)

**Chapter 8 Review**: The vision of chapter 8 (in Hebrew), like that of chapter 7 (in Aramaic), is structured around animals that stand for kingdoms, and the horns on one of the animals represent further political developments from the kingdom it represents. The vision has a scheme of four kingdoms but develops the theme differently than the four empires found in chapter 7. Chapter 7's broad sweep of world history focuses on spiritual or demonic forces that receive divine judgment, while chapter 8 moves to more earthly political powers. Daniel's vision of a conflict between a ram and a male goat symbolized the future history of the Gentiles, moving from the Medo-Persian empire to the Greeks, and from Alexander to Antiochus.

**Chapter 9 Summary**: When Daniel prayed a prayer of confession and pled for forgiveness for the people and himself, the Lord sent a message by Gabriel. His message laid out a future for the people of Israel that would include both a promise of hope through the coming of the Messiah and of coming struggles that would be devastating for them. The conclusion of their history, though, would end with the destruction of their enemies and a restored relationship with Yahweh.

**Chapter 10 Preview**: After Daniel's thorough preparation for spiritual battle, he receives a vision of God that assures him of divine presence through tremendous physical and spiritual struggles that are to come.

PROPHECY OF SEVENTY WEEKS

## THEOLOGICAL FOCUS OF CHAPTER 9

THE PRESENCE OF GOD with his people is palpable throughout both Daniel's prayer and Gabriel's message of the seventy weeks. In the prayer Daniel confessed that the Lord had kept his part of the covenant responsibilities. The dire circumstances in which the people now found themselves was because they had not kept their part of the covenant, but that did not mean that the Lord had abandoned them. Daniel had hope that the Lord would listen to his prayer and show them mercy in accordance with his nature as a merciful God. And the Lord did respond to Daniel's prayer with an immediacy that underlined his eagerness to renew his dealings with his people.

The seventy weeks represented a long stretch of time into the future for Daniel, but its purpose would be for renewal of the Lord's presence among his people. The sin problem will be taken care of and even eradicated, all the prophecies of old will be fulfilled, righteousness will prevail forever, and God's presence in the most holy place among his people will be restored (cf. Rev 21:1–3).

I. *The Lord reveals his will for his people through his prophetic word. (9:1–3)*

II. *God, who is merciful in nature, hears the prayers of his people and reconciles them to himself when they confess their sins and plead for forgiveness. (9:4–19)*

III. *While God's people are incapable of complete faithfulness, his plan makes a way for all to experience his mercy. (9:20–27)*

## BIG PICTURE (9:1–27)

Chapter 9 has three major sections. The first part contains Daniel's meditation on a prophecy of Jeremiah, prefaced by an extended heading (9:1–3). Based on his meditation, Daniel then prayed a prayer of corporate confession and plea for forgiveness (9:4–19). Before he even finished his prayer, the Lord responded by sending the angel Gabriel with a message (9:20–27). That message from the Lord developed further a prophecy that Jeremiah had made of seventy years for the nations to serve Babylon, after which Babylon itself would be punished (Jer 25:11–12). Moreover, the Lord had promised through Jeremiah that after those seventy years he would bring his people back to their land. But he also noted a condition for full restoration of the relationship between himself and his people. They would need to "pray" and "seek" Yahweh wholeheartedly (Jer 29:10–14). That is the burden of Daniel's prayer—he poured out his heart to the Lord, imploring him to forgive the sins of the people that they had committed in Babylon and other places of exile. He was seeking the Lord wholeheartedly through his prayer of confession and supplication, and he believed he was confessing sins on behalf of all his fellow Jews who were in exile.

Responding to Daniel's prayer, Gabriel gives him a revelation from God, but it occurs in mysterious references to "seventy weeks." The message has two parts. The first part explains the purpose for the decreed "seventy weeks," and the second part lays out the historical flow of those "weeks." How one interprets the purpose for these weeks determines how one understands the events they prophesy. Their general context concerns the Jewish people ("your people") and Jerusalem ("your holy city").

## TRANSLATION OF DANIEL 9:1–27

1–2   In the first year of Darius, son of Ahasuerus,[1] of Median descent, who was made king over the Chaldeans—in the first year of his reign, I, Daniel, understood from the written documents,[2] the number of years, according to Yahweh's word to Jeremiah the prophet, (needed) to complete the devastations of Jerusalem, namely, seventy years.

3   Then I set my face toward the Lord God, seeking him in prayer and pleading for mercy, with fasting, sackcloth, and ashes.

4   I prayed to Yahweh my God and confessed, saying,

"Ah Lord, the great and awesome God, who keeps the covenant and faithful love toward those who love him and keep his commandments,

5   we have sinned and done wrong.

We have become guilty and rebelled and turned away from your commandments and rules.

6   We have not listened to your servants, the prophets, who spoke in your name to our kings, our officials, and our ancestors, and to all the people of the land.

7   You, O Lord, are in the right, but we are in deep shame even to this very day, (we)—the men of Judah, the inhabitants of

---

1. OG Ξέρξου (Xerxes); Th Ασυήρου (Asuerou).
2. Or, *from the letters* (cf. Jer 25:13; 29:1).

| | Jerusalem, and all Israelites who are near or far in all the lands where you have exiled them because of the disloyalty they have shown to you. |
|---|---|
| 8 | Yahweh, we have deep shame, including our kings, our officials, and our ancestors, because we have sinned against you. |
| 9 | But the Lord our God has mercy and forgiveness, even though we have rebelled against him. |
| 10 | And we have not obeyed[3] Yahweh our God by walking in his teachings[4] that he set before us through his servants the prophets. |
| 11 | Indeed, all Israel has transgressed your Torah and turned aside, not obeying you.[5] |
| | So, the curse solemnly sworn[6] came upon us, what was written in the Torah of Moses, God's servant, for we sinned against you. |
| 12 | So (God) confirmed his words that he spoke against us and against our rulers who ruled us, bringing upon us a great disaster. (It was a disaster) that has not been done under the whole heavens in the same way that it was done in Jerusalem. |
| 13 | All this disaster[7] that has come upon us is exactly what was written in the Torah of Moses,[8] yet we did not seek the favor of Yahweh our God by turning from our iniquities or gaining insight into your truth. |
| 14 | So Yahweh was intent on[9] the disaster and brought it upon us. For Yahweh our God is just in whatever he has done, but we did not obey him.[10] |

---

3. Lit., "we have not listened to the voice of."

4. בְּתוֹרֹתָיו (bᵉtorotayw); "teachings" is better than "laws" (HALOT).

5. Lit., "by not listening to your voice."

6. Lit., "the curse and the oath"; this should be taken as a *hendiadys* for a curse sworn with a solemn oath (Péter-Contesse and Ellington, *Handbook on the Book of Daniel*, 241).

7. The particle אֵת marks the phrase as the subject of the passive participle כָּתוּב (*written*). For this rare use of the particle see Waltke and O'Connor (*Introduction to Biblical Hebrew Syntax*, par. 10.3.2, p. 182).

8. The translation reverses the order of the Hebrew for clarity.

9. וַיִּשְׁקֹד (*wayyishqod*); the verb stresses that Yahweh took care to see that justice was done (cf. Jer 1:12; 5:6; 31:28; 44:27).

10. Lit., "we did not listen to his voice."

| 15 | So now, Lord our God, who brought your people out of the land of Egypt by a mighty hand and made for yourself a name that is renowned to this day—we have sinned, we have acted wickedly. |
|---|---|
| 16 | Lord, in full accord with your righteous ways may your anger and wrath turn away from your city Jerusalem, your holy hill. For because of our sins and the iniquities of our ancestors, Jerusalem and your people have become an object of scorn to all who surround us. |
| 17 | So now, our God, listen to the prayer of your servant and to his pleadings. May your face shine upon your desolated sanctuary for your[11] sake, Lord. |
| 18 | Incline your ear, my God, and listen. Open your eyes and see our devastating plight and the city that is called by your name. For it is not because of our righteous behavior that we are casting our pleas before you, but because of your great mercy. |
| 19 | O Lord, listen! |
| | O Lord, forgive! |
| | O Lord, pay attention and act; don't delay! |
| | Do this[12] for your own sake, my God, because your city and your people are called by your name. |
| 20 | While I was still speaking and praying, confessing my sin and the sin of my people Israel, and casting my plea before Yahweh my God on behalf of the holy mountain of my God— |
| 21 | while I was still speaking in prayer, the man Gabriel, whom I had seen in the earlier vision, having been sent forth in flight,[13] reached me about the time of the evening sacrifice. |
| 22 | And he gave insight[14] and spoke with me and said, |

---

11. The MT does not have "your"; it has been supplied from context, as in Th; OG has "for the sake of your servants."

12. "Do this" added for clarity.

13. Lit., "in swift flight" (ESV). Alternatively, it may refer to Daniel's "extreme weariness" (NASB). While Hebrew יעף otherwise always means *be weary*, it is likely here a variant of עוף, which means *to fly*. The ancient versions are unanimous in making the text refer to Gabriel's swift arrival.

14. The OG and the Syriac *Peshitta* (cf. NRSV) read *and he came* (for וַיָּבֹא). The MT has וַיָּבֶן ("and he gave insight"), which makes sense but is unexpected prior to the verb for speaking. The Hebrew should be retained.

"Daniel, now I have come forth to give you understanding and insight.

23  When you first began to plead, a message went forth, and I have come to tell (it to you), for you are highly esteemed.[15] Consider this message and gain insight into the vision.

24  Seventy weeks[16] have been determined concerning your people and your holy city,

> to complete[17] transgression,
>
> to put an end[18] to sin,[19]
>
> to atone for iniquity,
>
> to bring in everlasting righteousness,
>
> to seal vision and prophecy,[20]
>
> and to anoint a most holy.

25  So know and understand—from the pronouncement of a word to restore and rebuild Jerusalem unto Messiah the Prince, there will be seven weeks and sixty-two weeks.[21]

It will be rebuilt with streets and trench, and it will happen in troubled times.

26  And after the sixty-two weeks the Messiah will be cut off and have nothing.

---

15. The plural form of the noun (חֲמוּדוֹת) indicates intensity.

16. Hebrew שָׁבֻעִים literally means "periods of seven." The translation "weeks" has become traditional.

17. The form כַּלֵּא is from a variant of the root כלה (*HALOT*). "Restrain" could be read from the same Hebrew consonants (Young, *Prophecy of Daniel*, 198; Payne, "Goal of Daniel's Seventy Weeks," 98–104).

18. The *kethiv* has ולחתם "and to seal up," whereas the *qere* has וּלְהָתֵם "and to bring to an end." The *qere* makes more sense as applied to *sins*, and the *kethiv* was probably influenced by the same word later in the verse. Modern versions are virtually unanimous in following the *qere*.

19. The *kethiv* has the plural (*sins*); the *qere* has the singular.

20. Lit., "prophet"; the parallel with "vision" and the use with "seal" point to the message rather than the person of the prophet. The NLT assumes a hendiadys, "the prophetic vision."

21. The Masoretic accents indicate a full stop between "seven weeks" and "sixty-two weeks"; see the exposition.

The army[22] of a leader who is to come will destroy[23] the city and the sanctuary, and its end[24] will come in an overwhelming manner. Until the end of the war, a great desolation[25] is determined.

27   Then he will make a firm covenant with the many for one week. And in the middle of that week, he will abolish sacrifice and offering. And on a desecrated place[26] he will make desolate, until a complete destruction that has been decreed will be poured out upon the one who desolates."

# TEXTUAL OUTLINE (9:1–27)

I. Daniel Meditates on God's Promise to Jeremiah to Restore Jerusalem (9:1–3)

*[The Lord reveals his will for his people through his prophetic word.]*

II. Daniel Confesses the Sins of God's People and Pleads for Mercy. (9:4–19)

*[God, who is merciful in nature, hears the prayers of his people and reconciles them to himself when they confess their sins and plead for forgiveness.]*

III. Gabriel Brings a Word that Reveals God's Plan to Take Care of His People's Faithlessness. (9:20–27)

*[While God's people are incapable of complete faithfulness, his plan makes a way for all to experience his mercy.]*

   A. Gabriel arrives in the middle of Daniel's plea for mercy. (9:20–23)

---

22. Or "people."

23. One Hebrew manuscript, Th, and the Syriac translate *with* instead of *army/people of*, reading עִם instead of עַם, a reading that also requires changing the *Hiphil* יַשְׁחִית (*he will destroy*) to a *Niphal* (*he will be destroyed*). The emended text would then mean that the *leader* will be destroyed *along with* the city and the temple, not the one who destroys them. Steinmann supports reading the preposition as "with" (*Daniel*, 447); Montgomery makes a cogent defense of the MT (*Book of Daniel*, 384).

24. Or "his end."

25. The plural שֹׁמֵמוֹת is intensive.

26. The translation assumes that כְּנַף (normally *wing*) refers to the temple in some way (see Exposition).

B. Gabriel unveils God's plan in a prophecy of seventy weeks (9:24–27)

1. God's plan will deal with the people's lack of faithfulness. (9:24)

2. God's plan is laid out historically in the framework of seventy weeks. (9:25–27)

# EXPOSITION (9:1–27)

## Daniel Meditates on God's Promise to Jeremiah to Restore Jerusalem. (9:1–3)

Theological Point: The Lord reveals his will for his people through his prophetic word.

**As Daniel prepares to pray, he expects a new work of God.** Jeremiah proclaimed a period of seventy years for the sovereignty of Babylon (Jer 25:11–12; 29:10–14). Now God was transferring that world power to a new king of Median descent, a sign that he was ready to do something fresh for the Jews. Like Naomi, who heard in Moab that Yahweh had turned his attention to his people by giving them bread (Ruth 1:6), **Daniel now realized from his study of the prophecy of Jeremiah that the time was ripe for Yahweh to return his people to their land. He also realized that renewed blessing could not happen if the people maintained their stubborn ways of rebellion against Yahweh.** So, he prayed and confessed the sins of his people and fasted in sackcloth and ashes.

9:1. An extended heading prefaces Daniel's meditation. It is significant that God sent his revelatory response to Daniel's prayer through Gabriel in the first year of Darius. Since Jeremiah spoke of seventy years for the nations to serve Babylon, after which it would be punished (Jer 25:11–12), the first year of Darius would then be the first year after the demise of Babylon's kingdom (538 or 539 BC).

The Lord made Darius king over the Chaldeans (Babylonians) after he conquered them (5:27, 31 [6:1]). The transition in the book to Cyrus the Persian (6:28 [29]) or the king of Persia (10:1) proceeds without any reference to a conquest of the Medes or of any transference of the kingdom from the Medes to the Persians. Instead, when both terms are used, they are viewed as a unity (5:27; 6:8 [9], 12 [13], 15 [16]; 8:20). The realm of Darius of Median descent was also the realm of Cyrus the Persian, and it is likely that Cyrus and Darius are alternate names for the same person.[27]

**9:2–3.** Daniel "observed" or "perceived" (בִּינֹתִי) that Jeremiah had prophesied a period of seventy years "for the fulfilling of the desolations of Jerusalem." **Since that period must have begun with Nebuchadnezzar's accession to the throne in 605 BC and ended with the return of the exiles to Jerusalem in 538 or 537 BC, Daniel recognized that the time for a change in the fortunes of his people was at hand. He also knew that the people were still not ready spiritually to fulfill the condition of Jeremiah's prophecy. They needed to "seek" the Lord "with all" their "heart" (Jer 29:13), and that need formed the basis for Daniel's prayer. He was seeking the Lord with all his heart on behalf of the entire nation.**

The reference to written documents (סְפָרִים), in the form of scrolls or letters,[28] is remarkable—also that a prophecy of Jeremiah was included among them. How did Daniel have access to them? After all, Jeremiah was himself an older contemporary of Daniel, and he eventually went to Egypt, not Babylon (Jer 43:5–7). One form of Jeremiah's prophecy of the seventy years of Babylonian sovereignty was in a letter (סֵפֶר) that he sent to the exiles in Babylon (Jer 29:1–10). That letter may be the particular focus of Daniel's study, given that it refers to the need to repent before the Lord can perform his gracious work.[29] The letter in question was perhaps part of a broader collection of materials brought to Babylon by some of the exiles.[30]

**For the first time in his book Daniel used the term *Yahweh* when he referred to "the word of Yahweh to Jeremiah." This name for God occurs eight times in Daniel 9 (vv. 2, 4, 8, 10, 13, 14 [twice], 20) and nowhere else in the book. As a personal name, *Yahweh* stresses God's intimate relationship with his people. The usage here is appropriate in that the chapter deals with personal family matters between God and his people, issues that are not treated elsewhere in the book.** Moreover, the use of *Yahweh* may reflect the fact that Jeremiah's oracle in his letter to the captives began with "Thus says *Yahweh* of Hosts, the God of Israel" (Jer 29:4).[31]

**9:3.** Daniel faced Jerusalem to plead with "the Lord God." **The name אֲדֹנָי (*Lord*) occurs eleven times in Daniel, once in the first chapter (v. 2) and the other ten times in the prayer of chapter 9 (vv. 3, 4, 7, 9, 15, 16,**

---

27. See Exposition of 6:28 [29].

28. "Books" are technically pages with writing on both sides that are placed between covers, a technology not invented until the late first or early second century AD.

29. Gerald Wilson, "Prayer of Daniel 9," 95–96.

30. Wood, *Daniel*, 232–33.

31. Gerald Wilson, "The Prayer of Daniel 9," 94.

17, 19 [3 times]). The three terms *fasting, sackcloth,* and *ashes* occurs together also in Isa 58:5 and Esth 4:3. The combination implies that Daniel was in great mourning while making his prayer.

## Daniel Confesses the Sins of God's People and Pleads for Mercy. (9:4–19)

Theological Point: God, who is merciful in nature, hears the prayer of his people and reconciles them to himself when they confess their sins and plead for forgiveness.

**Daniel recognized that Israel's sinfulness led to the exile and the destruction that the Lord himself had decreed, but he refused to attribute any injustice or malice to God. More than once he stressed that the Lord is righteous, merciful, and forgiving, despite the rebelliousness of Israel (vv. 7, 9). True confession of sin acknowledges not only the sin but also the rightness of any consequences that have come from God. Forgiveness for sin does not entail the eradication of consequences.**

In making his confession Daniel used eight different verbs to describe the people's sin, being careful to always include himself.

- "We have sinned" (חָטָאנוּ, v. 5).
- "We have done wrong" (עָוִינוּ, v. 5).
- "We have acted wickedly" (הִרְשַׁעְנוּ, v. 5).
- "We have rebelled" (מָרָדְנוּ, vv. 5, 9).
- "(We have) turned away" (סוֹר, v. 5).[32]
- "We have not listened/obeyed" (לֹא שָׁמַעְנוּ, vv. 6, 10).
- "(All Israel) have been disloyal to you" (מָעֲלוּ־בָךְ, v. 7).
- "(All Israel) have transgressed" (עָבְרוּ, v. 11).

In addition, Daniel stated how ashamed the people were for their behavior (vv. 7, 8), how they had failed to seek Yahweh's favor through repentance, and how they had failed to gain insight into his truth when they suffered consequences (v. 13).

When Daniel was ready to make his urgent plea, he first reminded the Lord that it was he who had brought the people out of the land of Egypt,

---

32. The Hebrew infinitive absolute marks the end of a series of verbs, a phenomenon that occurs elsewhere (e.g. Gen 41:43; Deut 14:21; Esth 2:3; 9:1).

thereby making a "name" for himself (v. 15). Daniel reflects on how Moses pleaded with the Lord not to destroy Israel; otherwise, he would ruin his reputation among the nations (Exod 32:9–12). Daniel based his plea on how the Lord's action would conform to his "righteous acts" (v. 16). In the past God had delivered his people who were in covenant relationship with him; now Daniel was pleading for a new deliverance for Jerusalem based on that same covenant and based on God's righteousness.

**9:4. Daniel's prayer is replete with scriptural language.**[33] **In addition to Jeremiah's letters, he was familiar with Deuteronomy and other parts of Scripture.** This can be seen most clearly from his address to the Lord in the opening of his prayer. "The great and awesome God" is almost identical to "the great, mighty, and awesome God" in Deut 10:17. In both passages the term for *God* is the less common אֵל rather than אֱלֹהִים, which is more than ten times more frequent. Then "who keeps the covenant and acts faithfully towards those who love him and keep his commandments" is found verbatim in Deut 7:9. These phrases show up in prayers from the time of Ezra and Nehemiah as well (Neh 1:5; 9:32) and could be considered part of "the liturgical idiom."[34] Ezra's own prayer and "confession" also has much in common with Daniel's (Ezra 9:6–15). Daniel's prayer has additional echoes in Ps 79 and in Solomon's prayer at the dedication of the temple in Jerusalem (1 Kgs 8:23–53). "A person saturated with such books as Exodus, Deuteronomy, Psalms, Jeremiah, and Ezekiel could spontaneously incorporate words or phrases from these sources into his prayers."[35]

**9:5.** Daniel had a striking solidarity with his fellow Israelites. "*We* have sinned," he confesses, even though everywhere else in the book he appears as a blameless man. He had been only a youth when taken captive by Nebuchadnezzar, but even then, he "resolved that he would not defile himself with the king's provisions or with the wine that he drank" (1:8). When jealousy drove his colleagues to try to trap him through his loyal service to God, even they knew that he would not deviate from that loyalty (6:4–5 [5–6]). **So why did he include himself in the sins of his people?**

**For one, he recognized that before the presence of Yahweh, the Most High God, he as a mere mortal could not claim perfect innocence or righteousness (cf. Isa 6:5; Rom 3:23). He also identified thoroughly with his countrymen. That identification is evident from the whole tenor of his prayer, but it also stands out in his visions.** He saw "the people of the saints of the Most High" inheriting their eternal kingdom (7:27). The

---

33. Venter, "Daniel 9: A Penitential Prayer," 34.
34. Newman, *Praying by the Book*, 81.
35. Rosscup, "Prayer Relating to Prophecy in Daniel 9," 50.

constant back and forth between the king of the north and the king of the south in chapter 11 relates to the Jewish people caught in the middle. And he saw beforehand the victory of his people when "Michael the great prince" will fight for them (12:1). Daniel was a faithful Jew, and he identified closely with his fellow Jews even in their need to repent.

**9:6.** The expression "your servants, the prophets" occurs also in 2 Kgs 9:7; 17:13; Ezra 9:11; Jer 25:4; 35:15; and Zech 1:6. Here Daniel brings into focus the message that God's judgment came because the people refused to listen to the prophets. In this case, the prophets were warning of consequences for failing to obey God rather than forecasting the future. His requirements were not burdensome; they were designed to allow his people to flourish and to attain their full potential as human beings. Nonetheless, the people went their own way and suffered greatly because of it.

**9:7.** The expression "shame of face" (בֹּשֶׁת הַפָּנִים) occurs elsewhere only in 2 Chr in reference to Sennacherib's return to Assyria after Yahweh's angel destroyed his army (2 Chr 32:21), but the concept of *shame* was common in the OT. In the garden the man and the woman were "not ashamed" before they disobeyed God's command (Gen 2:25), but after they ate the forbidden fruit, they tried to hide from God and cover their nakedness that was now shameful (Gen 3:9–13, 21). Shame accompanied defeat by an enemy (e.g., Ps 6:10; Zech 10:5), and that was certainly the case with Daniel's generation that had lived through defeat under the Babylonians (Jer 51:51). More to the point, though, is the shame that the people experienced because they rejected the Lord and his commandments (Isa 1:29; Jer 2:26; 7:19; Ezek 16:27, 52, 54, 61, 63; Hos 4:18; 10:6). When it is difficult to show one's face, it is a sign of deeply felt shame.

The term מַעַל signifies *disloyalty* or *faithlessness*. The root occurs as a noun or a verb with some frequency throughout the OT. In Dan 9:7 the noun and the verb occur together. Even Moses and Aaron were not allowed to enter the promised land because they "broke faith" (מְעַלְתֶּם) with the Lord at Meribah-kadesh (Deut 32:51).

**9:9.** The word for *forgiveness* (סְלִיחָה) is rare in the noun form, found only twice elsewhere. The noun in the singular occurs in Ps 130:4, but Neh 9:17, like Dan 9:9, has it in the abstract plural form. The verb סָלַח (*to forgive*), though, is more common in Scripture, occurring also at Dan 9:19. Further similarity between God's dealings with Moses and Daniel's prayer is shown through an incident recorded in Num 14. After a particularly egregious rebellion of the Israelites against the Lord, Yahweh threatened to destroy the people and make a greater nation out of Moses. Moses then pled with Yahweh based on what other nations might say if he slaughtered the people in the wilderness. After reminding God of his merciful nature and the need to punish iniquity, Moses pled for forgiveness: "Please *forgive* [סְלַח] the iniquity of this people according to the greatness of your steadfast love" (Num 14:19). In response the Lord said, "I have *forgiven* [סָלַחְתִּי] according to your word" (Num 14:20). Daniel hoped that the Lord would likewise remember his covenant with his people and have compassion on them.[36]

**9:11.** "The curse solemnly sworn" (הָאָלָה וְהַשְּׁבֻעָה) references those places in the Torah where the Lord threatened punishment for disobedience to his commands (Lev 26:14–39; Num 33:55–56; Deut 28:15–68; 29:19–28; 32:19–35).

**9:12.** The "great disaster" (רָעָה גְדֹלָה) refers to the occasions between 605 and 586 BC when the Babylonians took the people of Judah captive and the consequent destruction of Jerusalem and the temple.

**9:13.** The prophetic pattern of judgment from the Lord that failed to bring about the intended repentance can also be found in Lev 26:14–39 and Amos 4:6–11.

**9:14. That "Yahweh kept watch over the disaster" signifies that he had to ensure that his word was fulfilled.** It does not help a child if a parent makes empty threats; such threats would not be worthy of Yahweh. Justice required him to act against his people when they refused to obey him.

**9:15.** The central act of the Lord in the OT was when he brought his people out of Egypt. The plagues that forced Pharaoh's hand initiated it, and the miraculous crossing of the Red Sea (Exod 7–15) consummated it. Then the Lord continued to show his mighty power and grace by caring for the people through their wilderness wanderings. All these things did not escape the notice of the surrounding nations, who greatly feared the name of Yahweh (cf. Josh 2:8–11).

**9:16.** In his message Gabriel spotlighted the central concerns of Daniel's prayer—Jerusalem, the temple, and Daniel's people. When Nehemiah heard of the awful condition of Jerusalem, including how it was "an object of scorn," he mourned, fasted, and prayed a similar prayer of national confession, pleading passionately for the Lord to hear his prayer (Neh 1:3–11). Daniel used the same term (חֶרְפָּה) to describe how Jerusalem was "an object of scorn" in his day. By reminding the Lord of the disgraceful condition of his holy city and his people, Daniel hoped to move him to action.

Because the term for *righteousness* is plural, צִדְקֹתֶךָ is best rendered "your righteous acts," as in most modern versions. The "righteous acts of Yahweh" refer elsewhere to occasions when he delivered his people (Judg 5:11; 1 Sam 12:7; Mic 6:5), but what was the basis for calling these deeds "righteous"? **Two strands of argument meet here in verse sixteen. First,**

---

36. Rosscup, "Prayer Relating to Prophecy in Daniel 9," 64–65.

Daniel recognized that God himself is the standard for determining what is righteous (v. 7). And second, Yahweh is the God who keeps his covenant and is jealous for his name (cf. v. 18). Yet now the people are in great distress. Their neighbors heap scorn on them, and Jerusalem and the temple stand desolate. They need Yahweh to once again deliver them.

**9:17–18. Daniel piled up verbs as he pleaded with the Lord to take notice of the desolate condition of Jerusalem and the people.** "Listen" (שְׁמַע) opens the plea but then increases in intensity to "incline your ear" (אָזְנְךָ... הַטֵּה) and "open your eyes" (פְּקַחה עֵינֶיךָ) and "see" (רְאֵה).

**9:17.** God shining his face on his people recalls the blessing that Aaron and the priests were to bestow upon the people (Num 6:25). The same language occurs in several psalms (Pss 31:16 [17]; 67:1 [2]; 80:3 [4], 7 [8], 19 [20]; 119:135). The full effect of the idiom is hard to capture. Daniel 2:22 notes that "light abides" with God. Here Daniel asks for the light that illumines God's face to send out rays that would fall upon "your desolated sanctuary," restoring it to its full glory. Daniel desires to see the glory of the Lord once again fill the sanctuary (cf. Exod 40:34, 35; 1 Kgs 8:11; 2 Chr 5:14; Ezek 43:5; 44:4; Hag 2:7).

**9:19.** Daniel repeats in staccato fashion his plea for the Lord to listen and respond without delay. One can imagine that at this point Daniel was on his knees with his face to the ground, with weeping in his voice. This remarkable prayer is rightly considered one of the greatest prayers in the Bible, ranking alongside the prayers of Moses, Solomon, Ezra, and Nehemiah. In the NT it is eclipsed only by the prayer that Jesus Christ prayed for his disciples on the night that he was betrayed (John 17).

## Gabriel Brings a Word that Reveals God's Plan to Take Care of His People's Faithlessness. (9:20–27)

Theological Point: While God's people are incapable of complete faithfulness, his plan makes a way for all to experience his mercy.

Verses twenty to twenty-seven divide neatly into two parts—Gabriel's arrival with a message from the Lord (vv. 20–23) and the message itself (vv. 24–27). Nearly as much space is devoted to Gabriel's arrival as to his message. Several important facts stand out as preliminary to the prophecy. First, Gabriel came to respond to the prayer. When he arrived, he even intruded on Daniel's prayer. And God had sent Gabriel on his way at the very moment that Daniel began to pray. Gabriel came to give Daniel insight or understanding. Second, Gabriel was the same angel that Daniel had seen in his previous vision of the ram and the male goat (chap. 8). That vision also included a prophecy involving a period of time, the "2,300 evening-mornings" (8:14). Third, Gabriel presented himself to Daniel "about the time of the evening sacrifice." Fourth, Gabriel came because Daniel was "highly esteemed." Finally, Gabriel instructed Daniel to consider carefully what the revelation meant.

In the vision of chapter 8, Gabriel made his first appearance (if he wasn't the unnamed interpreting angel of chapter 7), and it was after that vision that Daniel lacked someone "to give me insight" (8:27). Now Gabriel appeared to give Daniel insight. Perhaps Daniel was studying Jeremiah's letter(s) precisely because he desired some insight into the vision he had already received. And the shift from the Babylonian kingdom to the Medo-Persian kingdom made him even more eager to understand God's plan for the future. The vision of chapter 8 did not even concern Babylon; it dealt only with Persia and Greece. The fulfillment of the prophecy of chapter 9 begins sometime in the Persian era. There is, therefore, a close connection between chapters 8 and 9, a connection only strengthened by their common language of Hebrew.

*Gabriel arrives in the middle of Daniel's plea for mercy. (9:20–23)*

God sometimes interrupts the activities of people, even when those activities involve something spiritual. Abraham's servant, sent to obtain a bride for Isaac, was in the middle of his prayer for guidance when Rebekah, the chosen bride, appeared before him (Gen 24:15). In the parable of the prodigal son the father began to run to his son even before the son could arrive and give the speech he had rehearsed (Luke 15:20). When Peter preached the gospel to the crowd assembled in Cornelius's house, the Holy Spirit "fell upon all who heard the word" while Peter was still speaking (Acts 11:15). **When Gabriel came to Daniel, it was while he was still pleading with God for mercy. That is told twice for emphasis (9:20, 21). Gabriel was sent at the start of Daniel's prayer and came in great haste with God's message. This message was so important that Daniel had to be interrupted in the middle of his prayer. Interruptions like this illustrate how intent God the Father is on responding to the prayers of his people** (cf. Matt 7:7–11).

9:20. The focus of Daniel's prayer was not merely a plea for forgiveness; he was also concerned for God's "holy mountain." That mountain included the temple mount, where the Lord used to dwell in the midst of his people (Ps 99:9; Isa 56:7), and it included as well Jerusalem, the holy city (Ps 87:1 [2]; Dan 9:16). Eventually, this mountain will become the focal point for Israel and for all peoples on earth to worship the Lord (Isa 2:1–3; Ezek 20:40; Mic 4:1–2). The people needed to become holy to worship at God's holy mountain (Zeph 3:11).

**9:21.** For the name *Gabriel* see the Exposition at 8:15–16.[37] After hearing Gabriel's explanation of the vision of the ram and the male goat (8:15–26), Daniel was so perplexed that he fell ill for some days (8:27). Try as he might, he was unable to penetrate the mystery, and he was concerned about the violence and destruction that the vision entailed. His concern came to a head as he studied Jeremiah's prophecy and made his impassioned plea on behalf of his people. Now Gabriel came again with a new message so that Daniel might have "successful understanding," as Hess renders לְהַשְׂכִּילְךָ בִינָה in verse twenty-two.[38] In chapter 8 Gabriel only interpreted the vision that Daniel had seen (8:16); now he came with "supernatural insight that comes directly from God."[39]

**That Gabriel arrived "about the time of the evening sacrifice" further highlights Daniel's concern with forgiveness and with the restoration of the "holy mountain." The temple had been destroyed for nearly half a century, so there was no evening sacrifice offered there. Yet Daniel retained the memory of those daily sacrifices and longed to see them restored.** He normally prayed three times a day, but in his house facing Jerusalem in lieu of the temple (Dan 6:10 [11]). One of those three prayers was likely at the time that the evening sacrifice would have been offered if the temple were still standing. Right at the moment when the remembrance of the evening sacrifice was in Daniel's mind, Gabriel arrived.[40]

Also, the "evening sacrifice" connects the vision of chapter 8 with chapter 9. The "2,300 evening-mornings" of 8:14 were a sign of God's graciousness to his people Israel. Now Gabriel arrived with a message concerning God's plans for his people, plans that would culminate in a glorious new "morning" when there would be everlasting righteousness in the kingdom.

**9:23.** Phillips lists three reasons why Gabriel came to Daniel. He came to clear up Daniel's perplexity concerning his study of Jeremiah's prophecy; he came because of Daniel's prayer; and he came because of who Daniel was—a man "highly esteemed" by God.[41] The Lord had a fresh message

---

37. That Gabriel is called "the man" means only that he appeared to be a man, not that he had a human nature. Angels are called *men* elsewhere in the Bible because of how they appeared (Gen 18:2; 19:1, 10, 12; Mark 16:4; Luke 24:4).

38. Hess, "Seventy Sevens," 316.

39. Hess, "Seventy Sevens," 316.

40. In the NT prayer is sometimes viewed as incense that accompanies a sacrifice (Rev 5:8; 8:3, 4).

41. Phillips, *Book of Daniel*, 162.

for his people, a message that was developed from Jeremiah's prophecy but that would extend beyond it. It was also a message that was related to Daniel's prayer. Gabriel was sent because this great man of God was pouring out his heart in prayer. The answer to the prayer was not simple; it would require additional study and special wisdom from God.[42] Daniel was up to the challenge. He was "highly esteemed" and also one of the "wise ones" (מַשְׂכִּילִים) who would "lead many to righteousness" through the writings that he preserved (Dan 12:3).

Gabriel brought the "message" (דָּבָר) that "went forth" when Daniel began to pray. Some interpret Hebrew דָּבָר as "a command," linking it with the "word" (דָּבָר) or "command" that signals the start of the seventy "weeks" (9:25; *NLT*). Others think that Gabriel is bringing an "answer" to Daniel's prayer (*CSB*). Since it is likely that דָּבָר refers to the full content of Gabriel's message, "command" does not seem appropriate.[43] And "answer" assumes too much. Gabriel comes with something that relates to Daniel's study of Jeremiah, but it will be new and different from Jeremiah's prophecy. Only indirectly will it provide an "answer" to Daniel's prayer for forgiveness.

In two places an angel called Daniel "highly esteemed" (also 10:11). Because of his faithfulness throughout his long and distinguished career, the Lord considered him worthy to receive visions that pointed to significant events in Israel's future. Through his passionate intercession for his people Daniel was something of a second Moses, who also had pleaded for the preservation of the people when the Lord prepared to destroy them (Exod 32:7–14). Even the argument that Daniel used in his prayer resembled the pleading of Moses. Both prophets desired to protect the Lord's reputation before the nations; they both appealed to the covenant; and they both referred to the Lord's act of bringing the people out of Egypt.

The noun מַרְאֶה occurs ten times in Daniel, five times in the sense *appearance* (1:4, 13; 8:15; 10:6, 18) and five times as *vision* (8:16, 26, 27; 9:23; 10:1). By its parallel with *the message* that Gabriel brought to tell to Daniel, it must be a *revelation*.[44] Goldwurm identifies the term מַרְאֶה with the *vision* of chapter 8.[45] While there are connections between chapters 8 and 9, the parallelism in 9:23 between "consider the message" (בִּין בַּדָּבָר) and "gain insight into the vision" (הָבֵן בַּמַּרְאֶה) supports instead a reference to Gabriel's revelatory message to Daniel that evening.

---

42. Baldwin, *Daniel*, 167.
43. The OG has πρόσταγμα (command).
44. Miller, *Daniel*, 252.
45. Goldwurm, *Daniel*, 258.

## PROPHECY OF SEVENTY WEEKS

*Gabriel unveils God's plan in a prophecy of seventy weeks. (9:24-27)*

Gabriel's message of the "seventy weeks"[46] is notorious for its difficult challenges and numerous competing interpretations. Already in the early fifth century Jerome hesitated to choose between the "opinions of the great teachers of the Church," deciding instead to "simply repeat the view of each, and leave it to the reader's judgment as to whose explanation ought to be followed."[47] Likewise, Hill simply lists a variety of interpretations, with some brief interaction with each one. In the end, he is content to simply list ways in which the theology of Dan 9:25-27 agrees with the theology of the whole book.[48] That the message was delivered by the angel Gabriel shows its great significance. Its importance was further enhanced when Jesus referred to it in his discourse to the disciples on the Mount of Olives (Matt 24:15; Mark 13:14). Even though the message is difficult to interpret, it is nonetheless important to wade through the issues to a reasonable conclusion. We will do more here than simply report the views of others, but the reader should keep in mind that various "men of greatest learning" have "expressed [their] views according to the capacity of [their] own genius."[49] Dogmatism is difficult when uncertainties abound, and uncertainty sometimes breeds dogmatism.

In developing the interpretation two factors should be held in tension. One factor concerns what Daniel and his initial readers understood from Gabriel's words. For them these words were mysterious and needed spiritual discernment to interpret them (cf. Dan 12:10). The other factor concerns what can be learned from looking back at these predictions. Jesus of Nazareth, the Messiah, has come, lived as a man on the earth, was crucified and buried, was resurrected, and ascended to heaven, as reported in Acts 1:9-11 and 1 Cor 15:3-8. As the central event of all of history it would seem peculiar if a prophecy that laid out future history did not include some word concerning this first coming of the Messiah. How clear that would have been even to Daniel is debatable, but from a post-New Testament vantage point some of the mysterious aspects of Gabriel's message seem clearer. Nevertheless, it is still a mystery that has not been revealed in its fulness. Vagueness and mystery are features of the whole book of Daniel, and even Daniel himself needed angelic interpretation.

---

46. For simplicity we will designate the "seventy periods of seven" with the more common "seventy weeks."
47. Jerome, *Commentary on Daniel*, 95.
48. Hill, "Daniel," 170-75.
49. Jerome, *Commentary on Daniel*, 95.

## God's plan will deal with the people's lack of faithfulness. (9:24)

The "seventy weeks" that Gabriel announced had a specific purpose that is expressed through verbs that refer to consummation—*to bring to completion*;[50] *to put an end to*; *to atone for*; *to bring in*; *to seal*; and *to anoint*. These six purpose clauses in verse twenty-four delineate what will happen either during or at the end of the seventy weeks. They can be divided further into two sets of three purposes each.

1. The first set concerns sin.

   A. "To bring to completion transgression [הַפֶּשַׁע]."

   B. "To put an end to sins [חַטָּאוֹת]."

   C. "To atone for iniquity [עָוֹן]."

2. The second set concerns the state of the nation after the sin problem has been resolved.

   A. "To bring in everlasting righteousness."

   B. "To seal up prophetic visions."

   C. "To anoint a most holy."[51]

**All these references to completion lend an eschatological significance to the seventy weeks. The period in question will consummate the old order of things in preparation for the new order, made possible by *atonement*, and inaugurated by the *anointing*.**

Since Daniel had entreated the Lord to forgive the sins of the people, it makes sense that "bringing to an end transgression," "an end to sins," and "atonement for iniquity" relate generally to the national sins mentioned in the prayer.[52] The NLT makes this explicit by adding *their* before each term for sin. Even so, the language of the prophecy bursts the bounds of Daniel's prayer and applies to *transgressions*, *sins*, and *iniquity* generally (see Isa 2:2–4; Zech 8:20–23). If the new order is in fact God's everlasting kingdom, then there will be no more unrighteousness (cf. Isa 11:9). Or at least it will be a rule where any lawless actions will be dealt with immediately.

---

50. "The piel form [of כלא] in Dnl. 9:24 speaks of the apocalyptic end of Israel's sin" ("כלא," *TDOT* 7:145).

51. *Anointing* inaugurates the new function or ministry of the person or thing anointed.

52. See Lucas, *Daniel*, 241–42, for a refutation of the view that the sins mentioned here are not those of the Jews but of the enemies of the Jews.

While the three terms, *transgression* (פֶּשַׁע), *sin* (חַטָּאת), and *iniquity* (עָוֹן), are synonyms for actions that are an affront to God, they look at those actions from different perspectives. **Transgression is a strong negative term that here refers to deliberate acts of rebellion against the covenant with Yahweh.** It is Israel's "covenant treachery."[53] Hebrew חַטָּאת is first used of God's warning to Cain that "sin is crouching at the door, eager to control you" (Gen 4:7, NLT). Next, it is used of the *sin* of Sodom and Gomorrah (Gen 18:20). Joseph's brothers used the term together with *transgression* when they begged Joseph to forgive them (Gen 50:17). Much later the Lord declared through the prophet Isaiah that Israel made plans and alliances that were contrary to his will, thereby "adding *sin* to *sin*." **Sin thus appears to be a general term for mistreating others or acting contrary to God's will.** The term *iniquity* is often used in conjunction with *sin* (Exod 34:9; Deut 19:15; 1 Sam 20:1; Job 10:6; Neh 9:2; Isa 59:2; Hos 4:8; Ps 65:3 [4]; Prov 5:22; Dan 9:16), and in addition to Daniel 9:24 there are five passages where *transgression, sin,* and *iniquity* are used together (Lev 16:21; Job 13:23; Ps 32:5; Isa 59:12; Ezek 21:24 [29]). **This piling up of synonyms for sin lends emphasis to the message. Sin has abounded in God's people of the covenant, but it will all be brought to an end and atoned for.**

Gabriel's prophecy to Daniel is remarkable for its failure to mention explicitly God's eternal kingdom. Nevertheless, "everlasting righteousness" refers to the kingdom of God obliquely. In his prayer Daniel confessed that God was morally right to bring the people into their position of shame (9:7) and to deal with them in wrath (9:16). That moral rightness is expressed by the term צְדָקָה (*righteousness* or *justice*). The cognate term צֶדֶק in 9:24 has a more general sense of everything being *right* in God's kingdom. **There will be no injustice or anything at all that would disturb the well-being of the community that forms this kingdom.**

That "vision and prophecy" will be "sealed" can point either to the certainty that they will be fulfilled or to the fact that there will be no need for them in the period of "everlasting righteousness" (cf. Zech 13:2-6; 1 Cor 13:8). Both ideas may be in mind. The *sealing* will authenticate all past prophetic visions as they find their ultimate fulfillment in the eschatological age, and it will also thereby bring the era of prophecy to its final close.[54]

The *anointing* of a "most holy" has been referred to the Messiah as the Anointed One,[55] and that would agree with the two references to the Messiah in verses twenty-five and twenty-six. More likely, though, it refers to the

---

53. Carpenter and Grisanti, "פֶּשַׁע," 3:708.
54. "חָתַם," *TDOT* 5:269.
55. Steinmann, *Daniel*, 466-67.

"most holy place" within the temple in Jerusalem, where God dwelled. The Hebrew קֹדֶשׁ קָדָשִׁים is literally "holy of holies" and can refer to a particular part of the temple or tabernacle (Exod 26:33; 1 Kgs 8:6; Ezek 45:3), the temple mount (Ezek 43:12), various structures within the tabernacle (Exod 30:29), various offerings (Exod 30:36; Lev 2:3; 6:10), and even to Aaron as the High Priest (1 Chron 23:13). The prophecy, like that of chapter 8, is most concerned about the fate of the temple, because that sanctuary represents the presence of God. Also, it might be noted, the Messiah is by definition already anointed and would not need to be anointed again. From another perspective, does it make any difference whether the "most holy" refers to a place or to a person? God dwells with his people in the person of the Messiah; and in the new Jerusalem there will be no need for a temple, "because the Lord God Almighty and the Lamb are its temple" (Rev 21:22). Even so, the primary referent of the "most holy" should be to a restored temple.

## GOD'S PLAN IS LAID OUT HISTORICALLY IN THE FRAMEWORK OF THE SEVENTY WEEKS. (9:25–27)

Several questions arise when considering the chronological framework for the "seventy weeks" (שָׁבֻעִים שִׁבְעִים). These questions are interdependent—the answer to one question will influence the answer to another. Here we list six crucial questions for the interpretation of Gabriel's word from God.

1. What is meant by the term שָׁבֻעִים, commonly translated *weeks*?
2. At what point in history did the seventy weeks start?
3. What is the end point of the seventy weeks?
4. How should verse twenty-five be structured?
5. Are the weeks continuous or is there a gap?
6. What are the events of the final week?

**What is meant by the term שָׁבֻעִים (*heptads* or *weeks*)?** There are three main possibilities.

1. A single *week* consists of seven years.
2. A single *week* means a sabbatical year.
3. Reference to the *weeks* is a symbolic way to represent the working of God in the history of the Jews.

Time for ancient Israel was divided into periods of seven, starting from the week that ended with the Sabbath. Every seventh year was a *sabbatical year* when the fields were to lie fallow (Lev 25:2–7). Then the fiftieth year after seven *sabbatical years* would be a Year of *Jubilee* (יוֹבֵל), with the forgiveness of debts and the return of land that had been sold (Lev 25:8–55). The counting of the years to a Year of Jubilee included the previous Year of Jubilee as the first of the next forty-nine years.[56]

Taking *seventy weeks* as a period of seventy times seven years is based on Daniel's meditation on Jeremiah's prophecy of the seventy years (שִׁבְעִים שָׁנָה) that Israel would be in captivity in Babylon, after which Yahweh would judge the Babylonians (Jer 25:11–12) and restore his people (Jer 29:10). According to one version of this view, Gabriel's word to Daniel reinterprets Jeremiah's prophecy.[57] What Jeremiah saw as seventy years is now seen as seventy times seventy years. It is theologically suspect, though, to take God's original promise and modify it this way. Others see not a reinterpretation of Jeremiah, but an additional prophecy in terms that expand the seventy years far into the future because of the spiritual failure of God's people.[58]

If, with most ancient and modern commentators, the seventy weeks are taken to refer to four hundred and ninety years, a question arises about how the years are calculated. The ancient Babylonians followed a combination lunar and solar calendar. A year of twelve lunar months would fall about eleven days short of a solar year, but an intercalary system was devised to keep the calendar in sync with the solar year.[59] Ancient Israel followed a lunar calendar of three hundred and fifty-four days per year,[60] with an extra month (second Adar) inserted occasionally to keep pace with the solar year.[61]

The Jewish community at Qumran followed a solar calendar of three hundred and sixty-four days, making important festivals fall on the same day of the week every year. It consisted of twelve months of thirty days each with an extra day added at the end of each quarter.[62]

Some have posited that a year based on twelve months with thirty days each should be used in calculating Daniel's seventy weeks.[63] Julius Africanus (third century) was apparently the first to calculate Daniel's

---

56. Kim, "The Jubilee," 149.
57. Hartman and Di Lella, *Book of Daniel*, 247; Pace, *Daniel*, 297–98.
58. Miller, *Daniel*, 257–58.
59. Finegan, *Handbook of Biblical Chronology*, 26–27.
60. See Sir 43:6–7.
61. Finegan, *Handbook of Biblical Chronology*, 31–32.
62. Beckwith, *Calendar and Chronology*, 219.
63. Anderson, *The Coming Prince*, 75; Walvoord, *Daniel*, 220.

seventy weeks on the basis of a lunar year.[64] Support is found in the book of Revelation where Daniel's phrase "time, times, and half a time" (Dan 7:25; 12:7) is alluded to with 1260 days (Rev 12:6, 14) and possibly forty-two months (Rev 11:2; 13:5). While a single year could be calculated this way, is that how all four hundred and ninety years would have been calculated? It seems likely that over a course of so many years intercalation to synchronize the lunar year with a solar year must have occurred,[65] particularly if some relation to sabbatical and Jubilee years is meant.

According to Wacholder, ancient Jewish interpretation, in contrast to medieval Jewish interpretation, explained each of Daniel's *weeks* as a sabbatical year.[66] This was based on a "calendar of sabbatical cycles," such that "each seven-year period had its fixed place in a series, precise in beginning and end."[67] He attempts to correlate Daniel's seventy weeks with cycles of sabbatical years by assuming that they began at the time that Jeremiah uttered his prophecy. He also assumes that the first week ended with Zerubbabel (*the anointed prince*). Additionally, "Daniel seems to insist that the time of the exile was to be counted as part of the sixty-two cycles, the period of Jerusalem's rebuilding."[68] One problem with taking the weeks as sabbatical years is that the Jews were apparently not able to calculate them during the exile and only resumed the count during the time of Ezra and Nehemiah.[69] In the final analysis, Wacholder's calculations support many of the same conclusions of critical scholars who date the final form of the book around 165 BC.[70]

Many biblical scholars have taken a more symbolic view of Daniel's seventy weeks, seeing them not as units of time but as a way to divide up history.[71] While the message of Gabriel to Daniel has a similar structure to years of Jubilee, Gabriel does not mention any unit of time, leaving it to the reader to decide whether the numbers refer to days, months, years, or something else. Daniel's use appears to be based also on "the threat of sevenfold punishment in Lev 26:18, 21, 24, 28."[72] The number seven is used figuratively elsewhere in Daniel 3:19 and possibly in 4:16 (13) and 7:25 (half

---

64. Knowles, "Interpretation of the Seventy Weeks," 156.
65. Archer, "Daniel," 115.
66. Wacholder, "Chronomessianism," 202–4.
67. Wacholder, "Chronomessianism," 203.
68. Wacholder, "Chronomessianism," 205.
69. Rodger Young, "*Seder Olam* and the Sabbaticals," 255.
70. Wacholder, "Chronomessianism," 207.
71. Steinmann, *Daniel*, 452–53.
72. Baldwin, *Daniel*, 168; see also Lucas, *Daniel*, 241; Collins, *Daniel*, 352.

of seven).[73] Since the Israelites marked time by sevens, the prophecy concerning Israel's future would naturally be told in periods of seven, even as the history of the Gentile nations was told in terms of four in light of the four points of the compass (see Dan 7:2). The nations settled throughout the world, whereas Israel had a special location chosen by God and sanctified by him through the holiness of the Sabbath, of the sabbatical year, and of the Year of Jubilee. There is thus a sense of holy mystery to Daniel's "seventy weeks."[74]

What would an Israelite from the ancient Near East think about Gabriel's message of seventy weeks? Moderns think of numbers as representing a specific count, but for the ancients, numbers sometimes were used for rhetorical effect. For example, Klein observes that while the troop figures in 2 Chr for the first four kings of Judah are impossibly large, they have a rhetorical purpose. Jehoshaphat, the most consistently righteous of the four kings, had a total of one million, one hundred and sixty thousand troops (2 Chr 17:14–18). His father, Asa (2 Chr 14–16), also a righteous king and even a reformer, made the mistake of relying on the king of Aram rather than on the Lord when Baasha of Israel invaded Judah. The "seer," Hanani, chastised Asa for this, and Asa put him in stocks and brutally oppressed some of the people at the same time (2 Chr 16:7–10). Asa's troops numbered five hundred and eighty thousand (2 Chr 14:8) or exactly half the size of Jehoshaphat's troops. And if the figures for Rehoboam (one hundred and eighty thousand; 2 Chr 11:1), Abijah (four hundred thousand; 2 Chr 13:3), and Asa are added together, the total also equals the total for Jehoshaphat.[75] Klein concludes: "The numerical design and sequence of the military forces of the first four Judean kings was calculated to reflect the rise of Judah's military power after the division of the kingdoms."[76] It also reflected something of the faithfulness to the Lord of each of the kings. While this type of rhetoric seems strange to moderns, hyperbolic troop and casualty figures were common in the annals of the ancient Near East.

**The seventy weeks found in Daniel 9 cry out for a symbolic or rhetorical interpretation. They are stated in a way that does not make for an easy calculation of the time involved. Their starting point is unclear, as well as the end point.** And then there is Jeremiah's prophecy of seventy years (25:11–12; 29:10–14) that Daniel was contemplating when

---

73. Steinmann, *Daniel*, 452.

74. Collins, *Daniel*, 352–53, notes that dividing history into periods is characteristic of apocalyptic works that narrate history as though it were prophecy. While we do not consider Daniel to have *ex eventu* prophecy, it still has characteristics of apocalyptic.

75. Klein, "Chronicler's Code," 6–11.

76. Klein, "Chronicler's Code," 11.

he confessed the sins of his people. That figure represented completion for Babylon's kingdom and Israel's exile. But precision is lacking about when that period started and when it ended. The figure is an approximation, possibly based on a typical lifespan of seventy years (Ps 90:10).[77] The Chronicler interprets Jeremiah's seventy years as ten sabbatical years (2 Chr 36:21). For Zechariah the period of seventy years had become a fixed way of referring to Jerusalem's suffering under the Babylonians, regardless of exactly when that period began (Zech 1:12; 7:5).

**If the seventy weeks are symbolic or rhetorical, what do they symbolize? What is their message?** *Seven* symbolizes completion or perfection, so *seventy times seven* would mean the ultimate completion, the ultimate perfection.[78] **In other words, the *seventy weeks* refer to the consummation of the age, the eschatological end.** Points within the total period can be marked, such as the coming of the Messiah and his death or the time for the restoration of Jerusalem. These points are symbolized by the divisions in the seventy weeks. There are seven weeks for rebuilding, and sixty-two additional weeks until the Messiah comes. Then the last week brings the current age to a close. By this view the seventieth week is the longest, but its status as the last week prior to the tenth Jubilee or the end of the age could account for its indeterminate length. Or as we will argue, there could be a transitional period of indeterminate length that moves the action from the end of the sixty-nine weeks to the seventieth week.

**At What Point in History Did the Seventy Weeks Start?** Since Daniel felt compelled to pray while studying Jeremiah's prophecy, many have connected the *word* or *decree* (דָּבָר) with which the seventy weeks would begin to Jeremiah's prophecy (Jer 29:10). That would put the start at about 594 BC[79] or 605 BC.[80] The main difficulty with this view is that the word to Daniel would then be reinterpreting Jeremiah's prophecy, not giving a new prophecy based on the failure of Israel to repent. If the word to Daniel reaches all the way back to the prophecy delivered to Jeremiah, then it is taking God's original word and reshaping it to fit a new situation. God, however, "does not make promises and then go back on His word."[81] Scripture is clear that Jeremiah's prophecy was fulfilled (2 Chr 36:22–23; Ezra 1:1–4). It makes more sense to assume that the prophecy to Daniel builds on the

---

77. Bright, *Jeremiah*, 160; cf. Charles Feinberg, "Jeremiah," 532.

78. Cf. Matt 18:21–22, where Jesus speaks of no limit on how often one should forgive a brother or sister in terms of either *seventy plus seven* or *seventy times seven*.

79. Hartman and Di Lella, *Book of Daniel*, 250–51.

80. Pierce, *Daniel*, 160.

81. Paul Feinberg, "Daniel 9:24–27," 190.

number *seventy* given to Jeremiah and then gives a new *word* or *pronouncement*. Jeremiah focused more on a period of exile and devastation than a time of restoration and rebuilding for Judah and Jerusalem.

When Gabriel came to Daniel, he told him that when he first began to pray, "a word went forth and I have come to tell (it to you)" (v. 23). Then he noted that the prophecy would commence "from the going forth of a word to restore and rebuild Jerusalem" (v. 25). Does this mean that the countdown of the seventy weeks had already begun when Daniel fell to his knees in prayer? Some have supposed that such is the case, based on the similarity in wording and the assumption that the "word" in both cases must be a pronouncement from God rather than from an earthly monarch.[82] What went forth from God, however, was the message that Gabriel brought. And that message spoke of a time that would begin with a pronouncement concerning Jerusalem's restoration. There is no necessary connection between the two points. Gabriel emphasized both that God was eager to respond to Daniel's prayer and that the message he sent would begin to take effect when a "word" or "decree" was issued. While the seventy weeks had already been determined by God (v. 24), the boundaries of the time were contained within the message itself.[83]

Closely related to the view that the "word" of Daniel at verses twenty-three and twenty-five are the same is the view that the "word" meant the decree of Cyrus.[84] It is also possible to think of a word from God that was inaugurated by Cyrus."[85] It is often objected to this view that Cyrus issued a decree concerning the rebuilding of the temple, not the city of Jerusalem.[86] It is true that the two citations of Cyrus's decree in Scripture mention only the temple and not the rebuilding of the city (2 Chr 36:23; Ezra 1:2). According to Isa 44:28, however, the Lord said about Cyrus, "He will say of Jerusalem, 'Let it be rebuilt,' and of the temple, 'Let its foundations be laid'" (cf. Isa 45:13).[87] The decree of Cyrus is a viable option for the onset of the seventy weeks, especially if one assumes they have a figurative or rhetorical sense.[88]

---

82. Steinmann, *Daniel*, 470.

83. See Keil, *Ezekiel, Daniel*, 351.

84. Calvin, *Prophet Daniel*, 212; Keil, *Ezekiel, Daniel*, 352; Edward Young, *Prophecy of Daniel*, 202–3.

85. Steinmann, *Daniel*, 470.

86. Walvoord, *Daniel*, 225; Archer, "Daniel," 114; Miller, *Daniel*, 262–63.

87. Hoehner ("Chronological Aspects," 52–53) attempts to counter the force of the Isaiah reference by assuming that the decree in Daniel must refer to "a complete restoration" rather than "a partial rebuilding." The "decree" says nothing that specific, only "from the issuing of a word/decree to restore and to rebuild Jerusalem."

88. See also Sprinkle, *Daniel*, 268.

Two additional starting points have been suggested, both falling within the reign of the Persian king Artaxerxes I (465–425 BC). In the seventh year of his reign, he commissioned Ezra to return from Babylon to Jerusalem to establish the "law of God" in Judah and Jerusalem. The "decree" (Aramaic טְעֵם) called for sacrifices to be made on behalf of the king and for all needful expenses to be covered by "all the treasurers in the province Beyond the River" (Ezra 7:21, ESV).[89] Ezra was also given authority to "appoint magistrates and judges who may judge all the people in the province Beyond the River, all such as know the laws of your God" (Ezra 7:25 ESV). This decree given to Ezra, then, while not specifically mentioning building activity, could still fall under the general topic of the restoration of Jerusalem. The date was 458 BC.

Later still, in the twentieth year of the reign of Artaxerxes (445 BC), Nehemiah, the king's cupbearer, requested permission to return to Jerusalem to "rebuild it" (וְאֶבְנֶנָּה, Neh 2:5). The king then gave "letters" to Nehemiah authorizing him to acquire materials for building the city wall. Africanus (late second to third century) was the first known commentator to suggest this date for the onset of Daniel's seventy weeks.[90] The following table shows the various possible starting points for the "word" or "decree" of Dan 9:25.

| Table 9.1 Suggested Starting Points for Daniel's Prophecy of Seventy Weeks | |
|---|---|
| Jeremiah's Prophecy of 70 Years | 605 or 594 BC |
| Cyrus the Great's Decree | 539 or 538 BC |
| Ezra's Return Under Artaxerxes I | 458 BC |
| Nehemiah's Return Under Artaxerxes I | 445 BC |

The reign of Artaxerxes seems too late in history for the start of the seventy weeks. From the first year of Darius (539 BC) to Ezra's return would be about eighty years, and it would be nearly ninety-five years to Nehemiah's return. Surely, though, Daniel expected the message that Gabriel brought to apply soon if not immediately. There is no indication that he would not be able to see the initiation of the prophecy in his lifetime. Gabriel told Daniel to "consider the message and gain insight into the vision," but he would be dead for well over fifty years when the message was activated according to either view that ties it to Artaxerxes. The decree of Cyrus has the prophecy

---

89. Ezra 4:8—6:18 and 7:12–26, like Dan 2:4b–7:28, were originally composed in Aramaic.

90. Quoted by Jerome, *Commentary on Daniel*, 96.

of Isaiah and the date given in Dan 9:1 that favor it as the start of Gabriel's word from God.

**What Is the End Point of the Seventy Weeks?** Gabriel's remarks about the purpose of the seventy weeks (9:24) show that they will result in conditions characteristic of the eschatological kingdom. Only when the seventy weeks come to an end will all unrighteousness be eradicated, and will Jerusalem and the people of Israel be prepared for God's presence among them. The termination of the seventy weeks, then, must be where Daniel's book consistently places the coming of God's everlasting kingdom—when God judges the kingdoms of this world and brings them to an end (Dan 2:44; 7:9-12). It will not work to conclude the seventy weeks with the death of Antiochus about 163 BC,[91] or with the destruction of Jerusalem in AD 70,[92] or with "the beginning of the New Testament era."[93] Those historical events did not lead to the far-reaching results that were envisioned for the seventy periods of seven. Sin continued and prophecies remained unfulfilled. Atonement was made possible through the sacrifice of Christ on the cross, but its full appropriation by the Jewish people awaits the end of the present age (Rom 11:25-27).

**How Should Verse Twenty-Five Be Structured?** Interpreters have chosen one of two possible structures for verse twenty-five:

1. seven weeks from the word/decree to restore Jerusalem to an anointed one, a leader; sixty-two weeks to restore Jerusalem.

2. seven weeks and sixty-two weeks from the word/decree to restore Jerusalem to an anointed one, a leader; Jerusalem is rebuilt in the first seven weeks.

The first structure follows the division of the verse according to the Tiberian Masoretes.[94] If it is correct, the restoration of Jerusalem would have occurred during the additional sixty-two weeks.[95] This structure became fixed within Judaism.[96] It also became a prominent interpretation

---

91. John Collins, *Daniel*, 357.

92. Knowles, "Interpretation of the Seventy Weeks," 143–52, ascribes this view to Clement of Alexandria, Tertullian, and Origin.

93. Groningen, *Messianic Revelation*, 835.

94. An *atnach* makes a major break between "seven weeks" and "and sixty and two weeks."

95. Montgomery, *Commentary on the Book of Daniel*, 378–80; Seow, *Daniel*, 148–49; Pace, *Daniel*, 300–301.

96. See Goldwurm, *Daniel*, 261–63.

among the early church fathers.[97] While the Masoretic system for dividing a verse into logical parts is normally helpful, it is not on the same level of authority as the words themselves. The Masoretes preserved a tradition for chanting the text in the synagogue. The chanting tradition was older than the Masoretes, but it is uncertain how much older.

The second structure combines the first seven weeks with the sixty-two weeks to make a total of sixty-nine weeks until the coming of *Messiah the Prince*. Then the restoration of Jerusalem would occur during the first week.[98] *Theodotion*, an early Greek translation, grouped the seven weeks and the sixty-two weeks together, giving the second interpretation ancient evidence as well. Since the main division of verse twenty-five has been understood two different ways in both ancient and modern times, the Masoretic division represents only one of the two traditions.

The text mentions two events, the coming of "Messiah (the) Prince" (or, *an anointed one, a prince*) and the rebuilding of Jerusalem. Since it also divides the numbers into two parts, *seven weeks* and *sixty-two weeks*, it might seem obvious to apportion each event to one of the two numbers.[99] Because the *word* or *decree* concerns the rebuilding of Jerusalem, however, it is most natural to think of that as the first event, with the coming of the Messiah later. And if the rebuilding of Jerusalem comes first, then its mention after the reference to the sixty-two weeks means that "the seven weeks and sixty-two weeks" should be joined as a unit.

Is it normal Hebrew grammar, though, to divide sixty-nine weeks into *seven weeks and sixty-two weeks*? If a full sixty-nine weeks until the Messiah were meant, why wasn't the number *sixty-nine* used? The text emphasizes periods of seven, so obtaining another period of seven would be motivation to break up the number into *seven and sixty-two*. That would also imitate a pattern used when counting numbers in the decimal system. For example, the nine hundred and sixty-nine years of Methuselah in the Hebrew are literally "nine and sixty years and nine hundred years" (Gen 5:27). And finally, as mentioned, the seven-week period can be assigned to the rebuilding of Jerusalem.

**To summarize, it is best to group the "seven and sixty-two weeks" together, with some emphasis placed on the rebuilding of Jerusalem during the first seven weeks. This structure has the advantage of taking the two major events and placing one, the rebuilding of Jerusalem, at the**

---

97. See Knowles, "Seventy Weeks of Daniel," 136–60; McComiskey, "Seventy 'Weeks' of Daniel," 30–35.

98. Walvoord, *Daniel*, 227–28; Archer, "Daniel," 113–16; Miller, *Daniel*, 262–66.

99. John Collins, *Daniel*, 355.

**start of the period, and the other, the coming of the Messiah, at its conclusion.** Since the period of weeks begins "from" the issuing of the decree to rebuild Jerusalem, the rebuilding referenced at the end of verse twenty-five should have started soon after the decree was issued. Hence it would occupy the first seven weeks.

The key event, aside from the rebuilding of Jerusalem, is the appearance of "an anointed one, a leader" or "Messiah, (the) Prince." The Hebrew term מָשִׁיחַ (*anointed one* or *Messiah*) occurs in 9:25 and again in 9:26. The first time it is combined with נָגִיד (*leader* or *Prince*), but the second time it occurs by itself. In the last part of verse twenty-six, though, there is another reference to a נָגִיד. The question here concerns how many individuals are meant—one, two, or three?

A prophet could be anointed with (olive) oil (1 Kgs 19:16); also, a high priest was anointed (Exod 28:41; Lev 7:36; 16:32; Num 35:25). The overwhelming references to an *anointed one* in the Old Testament, though, are to a king (e.g., 1 Sam 16:13; 1 Kgs 1:34; 19:15; Ps 2:2; Isa 45:1; Lam 4:20). Also, the coming Servant of the Lord would be anointed and carry out the functions of a king (Isa 61:1).[100]

The term נָגִיד (*leader* or *prince*) is also used frequently of the king (e.g., 1 Sam 9:16; 2 Sam 5:2; 1 Kgs 1:35; 14:7; 2 Kgs 20:5; 2 Chr 11:22). Additionally, it was used of tribal leaders (1 Chr 12:28; 27:16; 2 Chr 19:11; 35:8), rulers in general (1 Chr 5:2; Job 31:37; Ps 76:12; Prov 28:16), military or administrative officers (1 Chr 13:1; 2 Chr 11:11; 28:7; 32:21; Job 29:10), and an official in charge of the temple or its affairs (2 Chr 35:8; Neh 11:11). In 2 Chr 31:13 a certain Azariah is said to be the נָגִיד (*supervisor*) "of the house of God" (also 1 Chr 9:11). He is probably the same individual called "the high priest" (הַכֹּהֵן הָרֹאשׁ) in 2 Chr 31:10. A similar situation pertains to Seraiah (Neh 11:11; cf. 2 Kgs 25:18 and Jer 52:24). In the case of Azariah and Seraiah the term נָגִיד refers more to their supervisory function over the house of God than to their priestly role. נָגִיד refers to a priest, then, only to stress his supervision of the temple. The term נָגִיד occurs appositionally with מָשִׁיחַ only in Dan 9:25, and it occurs by itself only in Dan 9:26 and 11:22.

The strictly etymological sense of מָשִׁיחַ נָגִיד (*māšîᵃḥ nāgîd*) yields *anointed (one), a leader*, but if both terms are titles referring to a specific person, the reading would be *(the) Anointed One, (the) Ruler*. A ruler or king is prominent or at least an important figure in nearly every chapter of Daniel, so the general thrust of the book also suggests a ruler figure in 9:25, 26.[101]

---

100. Jesus claimed that he fulfilled Isa 61:1 (Luke 4:18–21).

101. Contrary to those who think of Joshua the High Priest during the late sixth century (Montgomery, *Book of Daniel*; John Collins, *Daniel*, 355).

It has been suggested that the individual mentioned in verse twenty-five is either Cyrus, king of Persia,[102] or Zerubbabel, who would have been king if Judah were still an independent country.[103] The choice of Cyrus would assume that the period of seventy weeks began with Jeremiah's prophecy, while Zerubbabel (or Joshua) would assume a starting point from Daniel's prophecy itself, that is, from the first year of Darius/Cyrus. If the person in question appears at the end of sixty-nine weeks, then the choice narrows to an anointed leader who appeared sometime from the first century BC to the first century AD, if the sixty-nine weeks total at least 483 to about 560 years. Whether one takes the start of the sixty-nine weeks from Cyrus or from Artaxerxes, מָשִׁיחַ נָגִיד (*masih nagid*) would still be *Messiah the Prince*. And that the Messiah is said to be *cut off* or killed adds to the possibility that the Messiah is Jesus of Nazareth.

Some commentators have countered that the Davidic Messiah is not a subject of interest in the book of Daniel. "The decisive objection against the messianic interpretation [of the *son of man* in Dan 7] is that nowhere in the book do we find either support for or interest in the Davidic monarchy."[104] For Montgomery the prophecy of Daniel 9 concerns "the maintenance of the [temple] cult" rather than "the legitimate royal line."[105] Is it true that one should so quickly dismiss a messianic import to the prophecy? Is it possible instead that this expected leader was the Messiah,[106] namely Jesus Christ, as the church has traditionally held?

Daniel's book pits the kingship of earthly rulers against the kingship of God. Proud Nebuchadnezzar is humbled until he recognizes that "heaven [i.e., God] rules," and Belshazzar is removed from power because he failed to learn this lesson. Darius the Mede treated Daniel with great favor, but "the law of the Medes and the Persians," which even he could not overturn, was in fact overturned by God. The "stone" that struck and destroyed Nebuchadnezzar's image was cut from a mountain "without hands." In other words, it represented divine judgment. And divine judgment against the four beasts is prominent in Daniel's vision of chapter 7. Then, in the vision of the ram and the goat (chap. 8), the future ruler who challenges God and

---

102. Goldwurm, *Daniel*, 262; Towner, *Daniel*, 143; cf. Isa 45:1.

103. Knowles, "Seventy Weeks of Daniel," 159; Goldingay, *Daniel*, 261; Seow, *Daniel*, 148.

104. John Collins, *Daniel*, 309.

105. Montgomery, *Book of Daniel*, 379.

106. *HALOT* (2:645) considers מָשִׁיחַ as "Messiah" for 1 Sam 2:10; Ps 2:2; and Dan 9:25, "but not an eschatological saviour . . . ." Oswalt, on the other hand, identifies Dan 9:25, 26 as the only "two unambiguous references" in the OT to the eschatological Messiah ("משח," 2:1126).

his armies is "broken without a hand," an evident allusion to Daniel 2:45. Near the close of the book Daniel sees numerous kings rise and fall and clash with each other, only to be followed by "the king" who "will magnify himself above every god" and speak "against (the) God of gods" (11:36). Terrified by rumors, this most prideful king of all will "come to his end with no one to help him" (11:44-45). God's sovereignty is unmatched by any ruler, no matter how powerful in earthly terms.

While Daniel does not think in terms of the restoration of the Davidic dynasty like, for example, Isaiah (9:6-7 [9:5-6]; 11:1) or Amos (9:11), he still sees a ruler for God's future kingdom that will displace all the kingdoms of this world. The "one like a son of man" receives the kingdom (Dan 7:13-14). Daniel's view of the coming divine kingship could be compared to Zechariah's concluding prophecies (esp. 9:9-10; 11:7-14; 13:7; 14:1-9) in which he envisions God's kingship expressed through a ruler, without specifying that it is a Davidic ruler. Also, the "Servant of the Lord" in Isaiah 52:13—53:12 was applied to Jesus as the Messiah in the NT, but Davidic kingship is not at the forefront of this way of looking at the ministry of the Messiah.[107] **All this to say that the "anointed one, prince" could refer to the Messiah even if his Davidic lineage is not in view. Since the OT knows of more than one way to describe the expected Messiah, the lack of Davidic material in Daniel hardly eliminates the messianic potential of Daniel's** *Messiah, the Prince.*

According to verse twenty-six, the מָשִׁיחַ (Messiah) is said to be "cut off" (יִכָּרֵת) and to "have nothing" (וְאֵין לוֹ). The term for *cut off* implies the death of this person (cf. Gen 9:11; Exod 9:15; Deut 12:29; Obad 1:9; Nah 1:15 [2:1]; Zech 13:8).[108] Those who see the reach of the prophecy no farther in history than the Maccabean period generally identify the one who is killed with Onias III, a high priest allegedly murdered about 171 BC (2 Macc 4:33-38).[109] Josephus mentions conflicting traditions about Onias III, one in which he was not murdered but fled to Egypt and founded a temple at Leontopolis,[110] and another that refers to his death, but not his murder, attributing the building of the temple at Leontopolis to Onias III's young son (Onias IV).[111]

---

107. France, *Jesus and the Old Testament*, 110-28.

108. Th has ἐξολεθρευθήσεται, *be destroyed utterly* or *perish utterly*, while the OG has ἀποσταθήσεται, *be deposed*. The Syriac has *nqṭl, be killed*; the Vulgate has *occidetur, be killed*.

109. John Collins, *Daniel*, 356.

110. Josephus, *J.W.* 1:31-33; 7:423-32; See Parente, "Onias III," and Joan Taylor, "A Second Temple in Egypt."

111. Josephus, *A.J.* 12:387-88; 13:62-73.

Christian writers have traditionally seen the death of Jesus of Nazareth on the cross in the statement that "the Messiah will be cut off and have nothing."[112] According to this interpretation, "and have nothing" would refer to his apparent defeat at the cross. It was expected that he would usher in the kingdom and reign as its king; instead, he died a criminal's death and seemed to have nothing to show for his ministry.

Daniel's reference to "the army [or *people*, עַם] of a leader who is to come" has led to multiple interpretations. For some this *leader/prince* is the same as *Messiah the Prince* in verse twenty-five.[113] The strength of this view is the use of the same term נָגִיד (*leader* or *prince*) in both places, albeit without the appositional relationship with מָשִׁיחַ (*Messiah*) in verse twenty-six. The statement that the army or people of this coming *leader* will "destroy the city and the sanctuary" poses a problem for taking the *leader* as the Messiah. Either the Jewish people would have to be responsible for the destruction, or "the ministry, atoning death, and resurrection of Christ . . . rendered the temple obsolete, requiring its destruction."[114] Either explanation seems forced.

Most commentators understand the *leader* or *prince* of verse twenty-six to differ from the *leader* of verse twenty-five. Those who posit a second century BC date for Daniel's book usually take the second *leader* to be Antiochus IV.[115] As Baldwin pointed out, the problem with this view is that Antiochus "destroyed neither the Temple nor the city of Jerusalem, though undoubtedly much damage was done (1 Macc 1:31, 38)."[116] For most of those who view the passage as genuinely prophetic, the second figure is either a Roman emperor (Vespasian or Titus) or the Antichrist.[117] Josephus wrote that "our country [Judea] should be made desolate" by the Romans, alluding to Dan 9:26.[118] Tertullian apparently connected the destructive events with both the death of Christ and with Vespasian.[119] Clement of Alexandria (late second to early third century), applied the passage specifically to Vespasian, the father of the Titus who destroyed Jerusalem in AD

---

112. Jerome, *Commentary on Daniel*, 94; Calvin, *Commentaries on Daniel*, 2:221; NLT.

113. Steinmann, *Daniel*, 448, 474.

114. Steinmann, *Daniel*, 447–48, 474.

115. John Collins, *Daniel*, 357.

116. Baldwin, *Daniel*, 171.

117. E.g., Keil, *Ezekiel, Daniel*, 362; Wood, *Commentary on Daniel*, 256; Miller, *Daniel*, 268.

118. Josephus, *A.J.*, 10:276; see Montgomery, *Book of Daniel*, 396–97.

119. Knowles, "Seventy Weeks of Daniel," 148.

70.[120] A Jewish scholar from the late eleventh century (Rashi) applied the prophecy to "the legions of Vespasian and Titus."[121] Calvin suggested the leader to be a Roman emperor, and more recent interpreters who follow this line of thinking include, among others, Edward Young, and Archer.[122]

**Are the Weeks Continuous or Is there a Gap?** As for the question of any hiatus or gap in the sequence of the seventy weeks, there may be an indefinite period of transition between the sixty-ninth week and the seventieth week.[123] The most important reason is that verse twenty-six includes events that occurred "after [אַחֲרֵי] the sixty-two weeks," but verse twenty-seven mentions different events that will occur during the seventieth week. Most importantly, there is a *firm covenant* that encompasses the entire last or seventieth week (v. 27). It seems that the one who "makes firm a covenant" (v. 27) must be different than the "coming leader" of verse twenty-six. According to Laato, "v. 27 stands isolated in its present context. There is no person in 24–26 to whom the reference 'he' in 27 is made."[124] Laato goes on to argue that 9:24–26 is based on an earlier tradition than 9:27. While that conclusion would unnecessarily question the unity of the chapter, it supports the idea of a gap or hiatus between 9:25–26 and 9:27. The proposed transition maintains the threefold structure of the weeks—one week and sixty-two weeks (9:25), and one final week (9:27). During the transition the Messiah is "cut off" and "the army [or people] of the coming ruler will destroy [יַשְׁחִית] the city (Jerusalem) and the sanctuary," with "great desolation." Another view sees the gap between verses twenty-five and twenty-six. Miller, for example, explains that it is "the people of the coming prince" who destroy the city and sanctuary in verse twenty-six, not the "coming prince" himself.[125] Miller calls this a "literal" interpretation, but it does not seem like a natural interpretation. "The army [or people] of the coming prince" would more naturally apply to a leader who interacts with the people at the same time. This would then mean that the destruction of Jerusalem and the temple under the leadership of the "coming prince" must also be that which occurred in the first century.[126] The hiatus can be explained by the way in which both the first and second comings of the Messiah are blended

---

120. Knowles, "Seventy Weeks of Daniel," 142–43.
121. Goldwurm, *Daniel*, 264.
122. Calvin, *Commentaries on Daniel*, 2:204–14; Edward Young, *Prophecy of Daniel*, 207; Archer, "Daniel," 116.
123. See Walvoord, *Daniel*, 231.
124. Laato, "Seventy Yearweeks," 221.
125. Miller, *Daniel*, 268.
126. See Walvoord, *Daniel*, 231.

in many messianic prophecies (Isa 9:6–7 [5–6]; 11:1–10; Jer 31:31–34; Joel 2:28–32 [3:1–5]; Zech 6:11–15; 9:9–10).[127]

**What Are the Events of the Final Week?** The chronological issues regarding verses twenty-six and twenty-seven are complex. On the one hand, most of the events of verse twenty-six have happened already. The Messiah was cut off, and the army (or, people) of "the coming leader" destroyed Jerusalem and the temple. But what of the statement that "until the end of the war desolations are determined"? The line concerns issues that continue to this day (cf. Matt 24:6–8). On the other hand, the events of verse twenty-seven lie in the future, and we would argue, in the eschatological future. This leader is most likely the Antichrist. At some point during the final week a new ruler will make an agreement with "the many" (לָרַבִּים), that is, the Jewish people in their land. This group of people is evidently the same group mentioned three times elsewhere in Daniel (cf. 11:33, 39; 12:3). In short, the coming wicked ruler, the Antichrist, will make an agreement with the Jewish people (cf. Dan 9:24).[128] The details of that agreement are not spelled out, but presumably it will be a peace agreement that will be in force for at least a short time.

Rather abruptly the ruler will abolish sacrifices and offerings in the middle of this final week. That sacrifices and offerings will be made implies that the temple will be rebuilt in Jerusalem, something that could well be part of the *covenant* made with *the many*. As will be explicated further, the *wing* most likely refers to the altar or the temple. What should be a holy place will become a place of abominable things because of the ruler who "will make desolate." That is, in place of the sacrifices required by the law of Moses, something abominable to God will be offered on the altar or at the temple. Antiochus Epiphanes did something like this, but the precise act was viewed diversely. Josephus referred to a pagan altar and the sacrifice of a pig, while Jerome spoke of a statue of Jupiter Olympus and a statue of Antiochus himself placed in the temple.[129] Jerome went on to say, however, that "these things took place in a preliminary way as a mere type of the Antichrist, who is destined to seat himself in the Temple of God, and make himself out to be as God."[130] It is fair to say that the destruction of the temple by Nebuchadnezzar, its desecration by Antiochus, and later its destruction by Titus, were typical of what foreign rulers of Jerusalem have done to the temple. The behavior of these past rulers is a paradigm or template for what

---

127. See Paul Feinberg, "Study of Daniel 9:24–27," 212–13.
128. Walvoord, *Daniel*, 234.
129. Josephus, *A.J.* 12:253; cf. 1 Macc 4:43; *Jerome's Commentary on Daniel*, 134.
130. *Jerome's Commentary on Daniel*, 134.

the ruler of the future will do. This idea of patterns of events or actions in history that repeat over and over will become more evident in chapter 11 of Daniel.

The conclusion to the entire prophecy refers to the complete destruction of "the one who desolates," that is, of the ruler who exercises his authority during the final week. Elsewhere in Scripture this period is associated with intense persecution of the Jewish people (Amos 9:9; Zeph 1:14–18; Zech 14:1–2; Mal 4:1 [3:19]; Matt 24:15–28).

**9:27.** The term for making a covenant is unusual. The root גבר in the *Hiphil* pattern occurs elsewhere only at Ps 12:4 (5), where it refers to gaining the upper hand through the tongue.[131] Some see the Messiah as the subject of the verb and reason that the idea is not to *make* a covenant but to *confirm* a covenant already in existence.[132] The more common view, though, is that the verb implies "forcing an agreement by means of superior strength."[133] It is likely that the unusual verb implies something that lies outside of the normal sense of God's covenant with Israel/Judah.

A different interpretation is taken by those who see Christ as the one who *confirms* the covenant and who makes the sacrifices and offerings cease, a strong tradition in the history of the church.[134] More recently this position has been advocated by Steinmann.[135] He then applies his interpretation "typologically" to Christ's destruction of "the false religion and worship promoted by the Antichrist (2 Thess 2:1–12; Rev 13:11–18)" at the end of the seventieth week.[136] Sacrifices at the temple were not stopped until it was destroyed by the Romans in AD 70. At best, one could say with Steinmann's interpretation that the efficacy of the sacrifices ceased with Christ's sacrificial death, but that is not apparent from the wording of the text.

Daniel 9:27 has some challenges for the translator and interpreter. Table 9.2 (Renderings of Dan 9:27b) should help to at least clarify the issues. Two Hebrew phrases are placed at the head of each column, and the translations given in various versions may then be read across the rows.

---

131. NLT, "We will lie to our hearts' content." Another view is that the phrase means "to make difficult the covenant" or even "to break it" (see *HALOT*, "גבר," 1:175).

132. Young, *Prophecy of Daniel*, 209; Steinmann, *Daniel*, 448, 475.

133. Baldwin, *Daniel*, 171.

134. Ephrem the Syrian (fourth century) as quoted in Stevenson and Glerup, *Ezekiel, Daniel*, 269; Calvin, *Commentary on Daniel*, 226–27.

135. Steinmann, *Daniel*, 474–76.

136. Steinmann, *Daniel*, 476.

| Table 9.2: Renderings of Daniel 9:27b ||| 
|---|---|---|
| Version | Hebrew Phrase 1 | Hebrew Phrase 2 |
| | וְעַל כְּנַף שִׁקּוּצִים מְשֹׁמֵם | וְעַד־כָּלָה וְנֶחֱרָצָה תִּתַּךְ עַל־שֹׁמֵם |
| KJV | And for the overspreading of abominations he shall make it desolate, | even until the consummation, and that determined shall be poured out on the desolate. |
| NKJV | And on the wing of abominations shall be one who makes desolate, | even until the consummation, which is determined, is poured out on the desolate. |
| NASB | And on the wing of abominations *will come* the one who makes desolate, | until a complete destruction, one that is decreed, gushes forth on the one who makes desolate. |
| ESV | And on the wing of abominations shall come one who makes desolate, | until the decreed end is poured out on the desolator. |
| NRSVue | And in their place[137] shall be a desolating sacrilege | until the decreed end is poured out upon the desolator. |
| CSB | And the abomination of desolation will be on a wing of the temple | until the decreed destruction is poured out on the desolator. |
| NLT | And as a climax to all his terrible deeds, he will set up a sacrilegious object that causes desecration, | until the fate decreed for this defiler is finally poured out on him. |

The ESV, NKJV, NASB, and CSB are formally equivalent to the Hebrew, but their rendering of כְּנַף as *wing* is opaque for an English reader. What exactly is "the wing of abominations"? The NRSVue and NLT are more idiomatic and have translations for כְּנַף that refer to some sacrilegious object. *Abominations* translates שִׁקּוּצִים, usually in reference to idols as *detestable* or *abominable* things (Deut 29:17 [16]; 1 Kgs 11:5, 7; Jer 7:30; Ezek 5:11; 11:21; 20:7) but also applied to other things or practices considered detestable to the worship of Yahweh (Isa 66:3; Jer 13:27; Zech 9:7). While the term here has a plural form (as in "abominations"), the singular is found in the parallel passages in Dan 11:31 and 12:11 (cf. Matt 24:15; Mark 13:14).

The two Greek versions refer to the temple, and the association of כְּנַף (*wing*) with the temple in Jerusalem has been made in several ways. Perhaps it refers to the pinnacle of the temple or to the top of its porch.[138] If כְּנַף (*wing*) is thought of as a place in or on the temple or the temple itself (by metonymy), then "the כְּנַף [*wing of*] abominations" would refer to the place where the

---

137. The reading is based apparently on a textual emendation (see BHS).
138. Montgomery, *Book of Daniel*, 387.

abominations are practiced. In some passages the Lord's protective "wing" is also associated with the tabernacle or temple (Pss 36:7–8 [8–9]; 61:4 [5]). Gabriel's message to Daniel would be that some idol or other detestable thing would replace the reassuring presence of the Lord in his temple.

A different approach to the "wing of abominations" was taken by the KJV, which interpreted the כָּנָף to be an "overspreading" of various abominations by the wicked ruler. Finally, the NLT's "as a climax" is apparently based on the reference כָּנָף sometimes has to extremities (Job 37:3; 38:13; Isa 11:12; 24:16), albeit the connection is obscure.

The structure of the Hebrew best supports taking מְשֹׁמֵם as "one who makes desolate," but the parallel passages in Daniel (11:31; 12:11) and the Gospels (Matt 24:15; Mark 13:14) are better taken as "the abomination that makes desolate." The translations are more unified with respect to the second Hebrew phrase, but with two differences. First, some versions refer to "destruction" or "complete destruction," while others have the softer "end" or "consummation." The word in question, כָּלָה, stems from a root that means *be finished* or *be complete*, but the noun form is nearly always used for *complete destruction*.[139] The only possible exception is an adverbial use where it signifies *completely* or *altogether* (Gen 18:21; Exod 11:1). While "end" is plausible from the etymology, usage favors "complete destruction." A second issue concerns whether to take שֹׁמֵם at the end of the verse as "desolator" or as "desolate." In this case usage favors "desolate" (2 Sam 13:20; Isa 49:8, 19; 54:1; 61:4; Lam 1:4, 13, 16; 3:11; Ezek 36:4; Dan 9:18, 26), but the context strongly supports "desolator."[140] The KJV and the NKJV have "desolate," but what does it mean that the determined consummation will be poured out on the "desolate"? The "desolate" should be the people of Israel, but there is high expectation from the context that the wicked ruler will be destroyed. The people of Israel have already been through enough "desolations" (v. 26). With such a strong dissonance between usage and context, one suspects that there might be some textual corruption.[141] Or perhaps "desolate one" refers to the wicked ruler himself. Preordained destruction will be poured out on this one who is "desolate" of all help or resources.[142] In that case, both "desolater" and "desolate" would refer to the same person.

---

139. BDB; *HALOT*.

140. The *Qal* participle is expected to mean *desolate*, whereas *desolator* should be the *Polel* participle, as in the first instance of the root שׁמם in the verse. The Greek versions support the MT with something like *desolation* (ἐρήμωσιν). See also the Exposition on Dan 8:13.

141. The *Polel* participle (מְשֹׁמֵם) has already occurred in the verse (phrase 1 in the table), and a *mem* could have dropped out of the second instance.

142. Goldingay, *Daniel*, 263.

## SHARPENING THE THEOLOGICAL FOCUS

Wrestling through the detailed exposition of the prophecy of the seventy weeks, it has occurred to us that the passage has more mystery to it than we had previously realized. Certain things that are often described as "obvious" are not so obvious after all. Anyone who approaches this text must come with humility. As a prophecy, its full meaning will become evident only after its complete fulfillment at the end of the age. There are, though, some certainties that come from this text if one keeps in mind that it is a revelation from God.

### The Problem of Sin in the Prayer and in the Prophecy.

Some have denied that the prophecy of the seventy weeks deals with the sin problem that Daniel raised in his prayer.[143] "The events that verses 24–27 promise emerge from God's sovereign will; they are not a response to Israel's sin or Daniel's confession at all."[144] The main issue is that while in Daniel's visions "the primary sin is that of the gentile king, and the course of history is arranged in advance," in his prayer "Israel is punished for its own sin and appeals to God for mercy."[145] The seventy "weeks" have been *determined* (נֶחְתַּךְ) for accomplishing all of God's purposes right down to the end of the age (v. 24). And his purposes include "troubled times" (v. 25) and further destruction of Jerusalem (v. 26). In the prayer, however, Daniel pleads for the Lord to forgive the sins of his people and to turn away from his wrath and restore Jerusalem. There appears to be tension between God's will that is determined and Daniel's prayer for immediate restoration. The tension is further heightened when Gabriel calls Daniel "highly esteemed" (v. 23). How could the Lord delay for so long a positive response to the fervent prayer of such a righteous man (cf. Jas 5:16)?

The differences between the prayer and the revelation may be evident, but they are not contradictions. Pre-determined history does not have to mean that people are not responsible for their actions. Jeremiah 29:12–13, which follows a reference to the seventy years of Babylonian sovereignty, calls on the people to pray and seek the Lord wholeheartedly. Daniel did that throughout his life at the Babylonian court and in his penitential prayer. The interface between the determined future for Babylon and the

---

143. Some have even suggested that the prayer and the prophecy must stem from two different authors (Lacocque, *Book of Daniel*, 178–79; Hartman and Di Lella, *Book of Daniel*, 245–46).

144. Goldingay, *Daniel*, 259.

145. Collins, *Daniel*, 359.

plea for God's people to seek him wholeheartedly shows up in Daniel 9 as well. The prayer lays out a pattern for how God's people are to respond during the long period of history that has been laid out before them. The glorious promises of 9:24 will come about, but believers must wait patiently for the Lord's complete plan to unfold (Dan 12:12–13). They can be confident in the knowledge that there is a limit to the course of world history during which there is so much distress (9:25). And they can rest assured that in the end the "one who devastates" will meet with complete destruction from the Lord (9:27).

Daniel was familiar with more Scripture than merely Jeremiah. He understood from the book of Deuteronomy that the Lord would keep his covenant with "those who love him and keep his commandments" (Deut 7:9). And he also understood that Israel had not been faithful to keep the commandments or even to love the Lord. That was the dilemma that he brought before the Lord. Israel's unfaithfulness meant that the Lord was right to have brought the exile upon the nation. Even exile had not taught the people to seek the Lord (9:13). All Daniel could do, therefore, was to confess the sins of his people and on their behalf throw himself on the Lord's mercy. A cry for salvation now is not incongruent with a reply to wait patiently for the Lord's good timing.

## Prayer in the Life of the Believer

The theology of prayer is advanced through Daniel's prayers. It includes praise and declaration of who God is (Dan 2:20–23). He is the one who can understand what is mysterious to us, and he is the source of all wisdom. Prayer also is a discipline that should be done on a regular basis (Dan 6:11–12). Prayer sometimes is urgent, requiring extraordinary measures such as fasting and other signs of earnestness (Dan 9:3). Prayers are often linked together with the study of Scripture (Dan 9:2), and they need to include earnest repentance and confession of sin (Dan 9:4–19).

While believers today should not expect new revelations mediated through an angel, they should wait upon God for the answer to fervent prayers that accompany careful study of and meditation on the Scriptures. Believers throughout history have testified to "hearing" from God during such times. They would not necessarily speak of auditory or visual experiences, but nevertheless they believed strongly that they had received a firm answer to what they requested from the Lord.

## God's Control of History

The revelation that Gabriel brought to Daniel continues the theme of the periodization of history but focuses it away from the nations in general and toward Judah in particular. The four-kingdom scheme relates to the division of the world into four parts (Dan 7:2), whereas the people of Israel thought in terms of sevens—the Sabbath day, the Sabbath year (Exod 23:11; Lev 25:4; Deut 15:12), and the year of Jubilee that occurred after seven Sabbath years (Lev 25:8–11).

**The first six chapters of the book demonstrate how God has been in control of human affairs in the past. Chapters 7 to 12 deal with his control of the present and of the future. In the present moment, according to the scheme of the seventy weeks, any reader can be assured that God is working out his sovereign purposes for their ultimate good. And even when dire things happen to his people, they can be confident that history is moving toward a great climax when good will triumph over evil. Jerusalem will fall again, and the Jews will suffer horrible persecution; but God is in control of that too. The persecutor will be destroyed in the end.** Even though nothing explicit is said about the coming of the kingdom, Daniel is reassured at the beginning of Gabriel's message that history is moving toward the goal of a new era of everlasting righteousness. All the glorious prophecies of old will come to fruition, atonement for all will be provided, and iniquity will be rooted out of the kingdom for good.

## The Messiah

One of the certainties of the prophecy of the seventy weeks relates to the Messiah. Evangelical commentators of all stripes are nearly unanimous that the passage predicts the coming and death of the Messiah, identified as Jesus of Nazareth. Whether the "weeks" are taken as figurative or as literal periods of seven years each, there is agreement that they extend to the Roman period when Jesus ministered. Studies like those of Sir Robert Anderson are overly optimistic about an exact chronology of the first sixty-nine weeks, but even those who, like Steinmann, reason that "[t]he 'seventy weeks' in Daniel should be understood as having only symbolical import" still interpret the weeks in a messianic way.[146] The "stone" in Nebuchadnezzar's dream that struck the image gave a hint of some work of God that would break into history. In Daniel's first vision the "one like a son of man" represents the ruler of the kingdom of God. Here in Daniel 9, there is a glimpse of the

---

146. Robert Anderson, *Coming Prince*; Steinmann, *Daniel*, 453.

earthly ministry and death of the Messiah. Chapter 12 references a future resurrection of the dead, but that could only be possible because Jesus Christ represents the "first fruits" of the resurrection (1 Cor 15:20–23).

## The Role of Scripture

Daniel 9 also illustrates the significant role of Scripture in the life of God's people. Most obviously, Daniel was meditating on the prophecy of Jeremiah when he fell to his knees and began to confess and beseech the Lord on behalf of the community of exiles. Jeremiah's prophecy may have been included with a letter he sent to the exiles, or possibly an edition of the book of Jeremiah was available to Daniel.[147] Either way, Daniel believed Jeremiah to be a true prophet and was pondering the implications of his prophecy concerning the seventy years before God would do a new work among his people Israel.

Less obvious to the casual reader—Daniel's prayer was saturated with echoes of the Pentateuch. Twice he mentioned "the law of Moses" (vv. 11, 13). Moses appealed to the Lord based on the exodus from Egypt. If the Israelites then perished in the wilderness, the Egyptians would mock the Lord. On that basis he pleaded with the Lord to turn away from his burning anger against the people. Moreover, he also brought up the covenant that the Lord had made with the fathers (Exod 32:11–14). In a similar way Daniel referenced the covenant (v. 4), the exodus from Egypt (v. 15), and the Lord's "name that endures to this day" (v. 15). When he noted that God "confirmed the words that he spoke against us" (v. 12), he alluded to the curses found in several places in the books of Moses (Lev 26; Num 33:55–56; Deut 28:15–68; 29:19–28; 32:5–38). Some other phrases occur in Daniel's prayer that come right out of the law of Moses. For example:

- *the great and awesome God* (9:4; Deut 7:21; 10:17)
- *those who love him and keep his commandments* (9:4; Deut 7:9)
- *who (you) brought your people out of the land of Egypt* (9:15; cf. Exod 3:10, 12; 18:1; 32:11; Deut 9:12, 26; 29:25)

Daniel's prayer, so steeped in Scripture, was part of a long trajectory of penitential prayer that began with Solomon (1 Kgs 8:22–53) and continued with Daniel and Ezra after the return from exile (Ezra 9:5–15; Neh 9:5–37).

147. From the time of the Septuagint two editions of Jeremiah were in circulation. One edition is found in the MT, while the other was the otherwise unknown Hebrew edition from which the translator of the Septuagint worked (Archer, "Septuagint and Massoretic Text," 139–50; Hays, "Jeremiah and Inerrancy," 133–49).

From a negative standpoint, Daniel realized that the people had failed to *gain insight* from God's *truth* (9:13). The people were aware of the law of Moses and of prophets such as Hosea, Amos, and Isaiah, but they had not allowed the truth of divine revelation to penetrate their hearts. In other words, Scripture as it has been given through the prophets of old should give insight to those who study it. Failure to let that truth change the heart makes the study worthless (cf. Jas 1:23–25). Scripture has the power to give wisdom and discernment to those who meditate on it and study it carefully, but only as its readers act upon what the Spirit of God tells them through the words on the page (cf. Heb 4:12).

## Personal and Corporate Responsibility

A notable aspect of Daniel's prayer concerns how he identified with his fellow Jews. He includes himself in everything that he confesses. "*We* have sinned and done wrong." "*We* have not listened . . . ." "*We* are in deep shame even to this very day." The narrative part of the book portrays Daniel as righteous in all he does, and in the visionary part an angel greets him with "highly esteemed" three times (9:23; 10:11, 19). Why should Daniel identify so strongly with the sins that the nation committed? The answer relates to the sense of community solidarity that Daniel had. His fellow Israelites, sinful though they might be, were under the covenant that God made with Abraham and the fathers. If sin was in the camp, then he was part of that camp.[148] Daniel recognized that as a leader in the community of exiles, he had a responsibility to confess the sins of the people. He could not detach himself from that community and be thankful that he wasn't personally guilty of their sins. He chose to plead for mercy on behalf of the community, himself included. He longed for deliverance from exile, but only as it would be a deliverance for all the people of God. The final answer to his prayer would be when all the "saints of the Most High" receive the kingdom of God that will never pass away.

## THE FOCUS OF DANIEL 9 FOR PREACHING AND TEACHING

Daniel, his role in history, and most of his communication with God, is unique. God rarely works through people in the way that he worked

---

148. Cf. Achan, who brought all Israel under the *ban* because of his secret sin (Josh 7:1–21).

through Daniel. However, in chapter 9—at least until Daniel's vision—we encounter a man who is meant to be a model for God's people for all time. Three things are worth noting, which in turn should help with the transition from theology to teaching/sermon. First, note Daniel's engagement with Scripture. The changing of the empires led Daniel to wonder about God's plans and the future of his people. Where does Daniel begin his search for understanding? He begins with the word of the Lord revealed through the prophet Jeremiah. This is all the more impressive and instructive when you consider the wisdom, insight, and visions God had already granted to Daniel. Here, it is the written word of God that moves Daniel. This leads into the second focus of chapter 9. Through his study of the Scriptures, Daniel is led to seek the Lord through prayer. People often think of prayer and Scripture as two different ways of communicating with God. Throughout chapter 9 prayer and Scripture are woven together. Scripture spurs him to pray and his prayer is based on Scripture. Third, pay attention to the corporate identity Daniel assumes in his prayer. To this point in the book, he has been a model of faithfulness and excellence. If anyone had the right to pray for the sins of "those people," it was Daniel. He was taken captive as a youth, not yet old enough to be blamed for what happened, and yet here he is identifying himself with the people of God and all of their failures. In addition to faithfulness and excellence, Daniel is a model of humility, much like Moses (see Exposition). Finally, as you work through chapter 9, you will also notice that God's presence is particularly important to the thrust of the chapter. Though Jerusalem is in shambles and the dwelling place of God has been destroyed, God is near enough that Daniel can seek him in prayer, and the answer to the prayer includes God once again dwelling with his people.

As previously mentioned, it is easy to get bogged down in the interpretive details of Daniel's vision. While they are not irrelevant, and it is not wasted effort to examine all of the options and come to a conclusion, the details of Daniel's vision are not what you want to make the bulk of your sermon. Rather, it is better to spend time explaining what will be germane to the thrust of the sermon, namely that we can hope in Yahweh, a personal God, who does not forget his promises, his people, or his future plans to dwell among them. In order to drive this home, explain how both God and Daniel are uniquely portrayed in this chapter. First, focus on the portrait of God that emerges. Throughout the commentary we have noted the unique revelations of God and his sovereignty that emerge in each chapter. Here, it is the unique and personal name of God that is revealed. Not only is it revealed, it is used eight times (vv. 2, 4, 8, 10, 13, 14 [twice], 20). More than any other chapter in Daniel, God is portrayed personally and familiarly here in chapter 9. It is no accident that God is revealed as personal and familiar in the midst of Daniel's penitential prayer. God's people need to know, and be continually reminded, that God is concerned about them and is committed to caring for them, even when they've sinned. Even when his people forsake the covenant, God is the great covenant keeper. The name Yahweh is a perpetual reminder of his faithfulness. In addition to the portrayal of God in chapter 9, point out how Daniel is portrayed; he is a man saturated in Scripture. The chapter begins when he references the word of the Lord to Jeremiah. Daniel's prayer is dripping with Scriptural references. Besides Jeremiah, twice he explicitly references "the law of Moses," and he also alludes to many other passages (see Exposition and Theological Focus for the specific references). In short, Daniel is a man who is familiar with God's Word. And rather than this knowledge puffing him up, it breaks his heart and leads him to seek the Lord on behalf of his people.

God responds to his prayers with news that the tough times will continue long into the future. But there is hope. God has not, nor will he ever, forget the promises he has made to his people. Yahweh entered into a covenant with his people, and one day every single promise that God has made will be fulfilled. Sins will be atoned for, injustice will be wiped away, and righteousness will be everlasting. Most significantly, God, whose dwelling place seems distant and desolate, will return to dwell among his people. While many aspects of God's promises are yet to be fulfilled, some have already been fulfilled through the work of Jesus the Christ. Sin has been dealt with through his atoning death; God has proven that nothing will keep him from covenant faithfulness, not even if it costs him the death of his son. That's how far Yahweh will go to right the wrongs of his people. Now we await the second coming of Jesus, when he will establish for all time his kingdom in all its fullness. It's the day Daniel longed for and it's the day we continue to hope for even still.

By pointing out the covenant faithfulness of Yahweh and the promise of fulfillment highlighted in chapter 9, people will leave with a sense of hope. People should not leave a sermon on Daniel 9 with a wishy-washy sense that maybe they can expect God to act on their behalf. No! Rather, they should leave with certainty that God has acted on their behalf, through Jesus, and that they can grow in certainty and hope by devoting themselves to seeking the Lord through the study of Scripture and prayer. Just as Daniel was inspired to seek the Lord in response to his study of Jeremiah, we should be stirred to seek the Lord in response to our study of Daniel. "Hope deferred makes the heart sick; but a desire fulfilled is a tree of life" (Prov 13:12 ESV). Help your people to see that God is our greatest desire and He is delighted to fulfill this desire.

PROPHECY OF SEVENTY WEEKS

## FROM TEXTUAL WORK TO TEACHING

## The Big Idea

- *Exegetical Idea:* In the writings of the prophet Jeremiah, Daniel perceives that the time of the desolations of Jerusalem may be nearing an end and so he obediently prays to Yahweh for forgiveness and the restoration of Jerusalem; in response Yahweh reveals that at the end of seventy weeks sin will be eradicated, righteousness will prevail, prophecies will be fulfilled and God will dwell among his people.
- *Theological Focus:* In Scripture, God's people find hope because Yahweh is faithful to his promises (for blessing and cursing), forgiving to his people, and certain to fulfill his decrees.
- *Preaching Idea:* Hope in Yahweh, who does not forget his promises, his people or the future he has with them.

## Outline One: Following the Exegetical Flow

I. The Lord reveals his will for his people through his prophetic word. (9:1–3)

   A. Daniel meditates on God's promise to Jeremiah to restore Jerusalem.

   B. We need to be looking to God's Word to learn, and hope in, his promises.

II. God, who is merciful in nature, hears the prayer of his people and reconciles them to himself when they confess their sins and plead for forgiveness. (9:4–19)

   A. Daniel confesses the sins of God's people and pleads for mercy, based on God's merciful nature.

      1. Daniel's prayer of confession (9:4–14)

      2. Daniel's plea for mercy (9:15–19)

   B. We need to regularly confess and pray for God's forgiveness, and trust in God's mercy.

      1. Pray corporate and individual prayers of confession

2. Be assured of God's mercy as revealed in Scripture

III. While God's people are incapable of complete faithfulness, his plan makes a way for all to experience his mercy. (9:20–27)

   A. Gabriel brings a word that reveals God's plan to take care of his people's lack of faithfulness.

   1. Gabriel arrives in response to Daniel's prayer.
   2. Gabriel reveals God's plan to forgive and restore.

   B. God has made a way for us to experience his mercy through Christ, and one day his people will be fully and finally restored for all of eternity.

## Outline Two: Following a Theme

*Key Theme:* Confession is powerful, and forgiveness is healing.

Daniel 9 lends itself to a worship service focused on corporate prayer. Too often God's people are characterized by factions within the church and an "us versus them" mentality towards those outside the church. Daniel's prayer can serve as a powerful example of how to pray as one of God's people, for God's people. As people enter the service consider giving them time to write down a particular sin they would like to anonymously confess. Collect the prayers and then pray through them using first person plural pronouns. For example, "Lord, we confess that we . . ." Once you have prayed through the list of sins and corporately confessed them, read Dan 9:24, "Seventy weeks are decreed about your people and your holy city, to finish the transgression, to put an end to sin, and to atone for iniquity, to bring in everlasting righteousness, to seal both vision and prophet, and to anoint a most holy place" (ESV).

Then point your people to the atoning work of Christ and the hope we have in his second coming—the ultimate fulfillment of Daniel's vision. An effective way to do this would be to work through the significance of the words Daniel uses to capture the essence of sin in this passage:

- "We have sinned" (חָטָאנוּ, v. 5)
- "We have done wrong" (עָוִינוּ, v. 5)
- "We have acted wickedly" (הִרְשַׁעְנוּ, v. 5)
- "We have rebelled" (מָרָדְנוּ, vv. 5, 9)

- "(We have) turned away" (סוֹר, v. 5)
- "We have not listened/obeyed" (לֹא שָׁמַעְנוּ, vv. 6, 10)
- "(All Israel) have been disloyal to you" (מָעֲלוּ־בָךְ, v. 7)
- "(All Israel) have transgressed" (עָבְרוּ, v. 11)

In addition to explaining the meaning of the words, give examples of each from the life of Israel and the life of the church. Focusing on both corporate and individual examples will drive home the point that we are *all* guilty and *all* can be forgiven.

## EXCURSUS: JEREMIAH'S PROPHECY OF SEVENTY YEARS

Jeremiah prophesied about a period of seventy years in two places (25:11–12; 29:10–14). Other passages that deal with the figure, besides Daniel 9, include 2 Chr 36:21; Zech 1:12; and 7:5. The Chronicler interpreted Jeremiah's seventy years as ten sabbatical years, while according to Zechariah's vision the angel of Yahweh wondered aloud how much longer than seventy years Jerusalem and Judah would have to suffer (1:12). This assumes that the seventy years were already completed. Later, Zechariah's word from Yahweh spoke of how for seventy years the people had been fasting and mourning to commemorate the fall of Jerusalem (7:5; 586 or 587 BC). For Zechariah, then, the period of seventy years had become a fixed way of referring to Jerusalem's suffering under the Babylonians, regardless of exactly when that period began.

Commentators disagree about both the precision of Jeremiah's prophecy and its application. Charles Feinberg notes that many scholars, whether conservative or liberal, think the figure is an approximation, possibly based on a typical lifespan of seventy years (Ps 90:10). He also mentions two attempts at a precise calculation,[149] but both must treat the text of Jeremiah in an arbitrary manner. One calculation is from Nebuchadnezzar's first year in 605 BC (Jer 25:1) to 536 BC, when Zerubbabel and Joshua led a contingency of Jews back to the land (Ezra 2). Another option is from 586 BC, when the temple was destroyed by the Babylonians to the year 516 BC, when the second temple was completed (Ezra 7:15). Jeremiah treats the seventy years as the duration of Babylonian rule, which ended in 539 BC, when Cyrus conquered Babylon. The prophet spoke more about the conquest and devastation of Babylon than about the return of Judeans to the land. Moreover,

---

149. Charles Feinberg, "Jeremiah," 532.

it is not certain that the year of the first return from Babylon was 536 BC. The return could have been any time after Babylon's fall; Jeremiah prophesied only that the Lord would "visit" his people and bring them back to the land "when seventy years have been completed [for Babylon]" (Jer 29:10). Nevertheless, the text of Jeremiah 25:1–12 is best taken with the standard view that it refers to the time from Nebuchadnezzar to Cyrus, amounting to sixty-six or sixty-seven years.[150] The figure of seventy years must be either a round number or a general reference to a life span.

It is Jeremiah's second prophecy about Babylon's seventy-year duration (29:10–14) that provided the impetus for Daniel's prayer. The Lord sent his answer (*word*) through the angel Gabriel. Because of Daniel's "highly esteemed" status before the Lord, the Lord was now making an additional promise to set a time frame for bringing in "everlasting righteousness" and attendant blessings. Daniel was not reinterpreting Jeremiah's prophecy of seventy years;[151] he was focusing on the promise of restoration that was conditioned on total obedience.[152] The new prophetic word would include not seventy years, but seventy periods of seven years. The seven-year period calls to mind the sabbatical year (Exod 23:10–11; Lev 25:3–5), and the Jubilee year would fall after seven sabbatical years. Then the whole period of four hundred and ninety years could represent ten Jubilee years (Lev 25:10–24).[153] This allusion to the seven-year cycles that God had prescribed for Israel emphasizes the focus on the Jews. Gentile history has four periods of indeterminate length, but Jewish history can be summed up in their constant celebration of God's blessings as seen in the weekly Sabbath, in the Sabbath year, and in the Jubilee year.[154] Even though there is the chronological cycle that could total four hundred and ninety years, the figures in an apocalyptic book like Daniel are not meant for literal calculations of time. Instead, the continuous cycle of sabbath, sabbatical year, and Jubilee year speaks of God's continuing work through his people that will eventually come to an eschatological end.

---

150. But cf. Lundbom, *Jeremiah 21—36*, 249–50.

151. *Contra* John Collins, *Daniel*, 352–53.

152. See Bergsma, "Persian Period as Penitential Era," 54–57.

153. While there is some difference of opinion it is best to take the fiftieth year, the Jubilee year, as the first year counted toward the next Jubilee (Bergsma, *Jubilee*, 88–91). That way ten Jubilee years would actually be four hundred and ninety years, with the next Jubilee starting the following year.

154. Steinmann (*Daniel*, 452–53) argues against the sabbatical year/Jubilee issue, reasoning instead that the "week" is not meant to be taken literally. It reflects the creation week of Gen. 1:1—2:4 and emphasizes the concept of re-creation that God has planned for Israel.

## EXCURSUS: NAMES FOR GOD IN THE BOOK OF DANIEL

A variety of names for God occur in the book of Daniel. The general term for *deity* is *Elōhîm* (אֱלֹהִים) in Hebrew and *Elāh* (אֱלָהּ) in Aramaic. *Elōhîm* also refers most frequently to Israel's God, the one and only God, the God who created all things. As a form that is technically plural, *Elōhîm* may refer to the "gods" of the nations or to Israel's "God." In Daniel it is found with this latter sense most often in chapter 9 (vv. 3, 4, 9, 10, 11, 13, 14, 15, 17, 18, 19, 20 [twice]) but also in 1:9, 17; 10:12; and 11:32. It refers to a "god" or "gods" in 11:8 and 11:37. The Hebrew term *Elōah* (אֱלוֹהַּ) also denotes in 11:37–39 any "god" that the "king" of the end times will not worship, or of the "god of fortresses" that he will honor.

When Daniel and the kings he served conversed about God, their ideas about him differed significantly. Nebuchadnezzar and Belshazzar were polytheists, and Darius the Mede (Cyrus) may have worshiped Ahura Mazda, a god about whom very little is known.[155] When Daniel mentions his God to Nebuchadnezzar, the king thought of him as one of the gods, even if he was led to proclaim him "God of gods and Lord of kings" (2:47), or even "the Most High" and "him who lives forever" (4:34 [31]). When Daniel conveyed something about God to Nebuchadnezzar, he did not start by correcting his theology. Instead, he told the king that his God was "a God in heaven who reveals mysteries" (2:28) or "a great God." Daniel left it up to God to convince Nebuchadnezzar that the God of the Jews was the only true God.

The expression "God of heaven" in Daniel occurs only in chapter 2 and always on the lips of Daniel or of Daniel as narrator (vv. 18, 19, 37, 44). Nebuchadnezzar called Shadrach, Meshach, and Abednego "servants of the Most High God" (3:26), a title that he also accorded to God after his period of insanity (4:2 [3:32]). The terminology "Most High" (עִלָּאָה)[156] without the addition of "God" also occurs within the content and explanation of Nebuchadnezzar's dream (4:17 [14]), 24–25 [21–22]; cf. 5:18, 21), in the "voice from heaven" (4:31 [28]), and in the king's worship of "the Most High" (4:34 [31]). When Daniel has his vision, he also hears of "the Most High," but the Aramaic occurs both in a uniquely plural form (עֶלְיוֹנִין, 7:18, 22, 27) and in the standard singular form (עִלָּאָה, 7:25).[157]

God's personal name *Yahweh* occurs about six thousand and eight hundred times in the Hebrew Bible, yet it is not attested in biblical Aramaic,

---

155. See Waters, "Cyrus and the Achaemenids," 99.

156. The *qere*; the *kethiv* is עליא. This *kethiv/qere* situation pertains to all forms of the adjective that are singular.

157. See the Exposition of 7:18 for further discussion.

and it is relatively rare in the book of Daniel. This name that English versions normally represent with *the Lord*, is present in the book of Daniel only in chapter 9 (vv. 2, 4, 8, 10, 13, 14 [twice], 20). Eventually a tradition developed that replaced the name *Yahweh* with the term *Adōnāy* (אֲדֹנָי) in public reading of the Hebrew text. The term *Adōnāy* (*the Lord* in English) occurs in the Hebrew of Dan 1:2 and ten additional times in chapter 9 (vv. 3, 4, 7, 9, 15, 16, 17, 19 [three times]). Two unique names for God in Daniel are the *Ancient of Days* (7:9, 13, 22) and the *Commander of the host* (or *army*; 8:11).

# Prelude to the Final Revelation
(Daniel 10:1—11:1)

**Chapter 9 Review**: Daniel's prayer of confession shows the strong connection between the study of Scripture and prayer. In response to his prayer the angel Gabriel brings a message about the future of Jerusalem, the temple, and the Jewish people.

**Chapter 10 Summary**: God honored the spiritual disciplines that Daniel practiced by sending an angel with a significant revelation, showing that disciplines in some way move God to action. It was Daniel's faithful heart that was significant. The disciplines were merely outward expressions of his heart.

**Chapter 11 Preview**: After a brief peek into the Persian period, chapter eleven focuses on a time when the Jews in Jerusalem and Judea would be caught between a struggle for dominance of Egypt and Syria-Palestine by powerful rulers. That era would climax with the autocratic rule of Antiochus IV Epiphanes, who would in turn be a type or a model of the world leader in the end of the age.

## THEOLOGICAL FOCUS OF CHAPTER 10:1—11:1

As THE FAITHFUL ACTIVELY seek God's direction, disciplines of abstinence can be combined with the engaging disciplines of prayer and Bible study, to make themselves more receptive to the leading of the Lord. As the faithful struggle in these disciplines, they can break through spiritual warfare and hear from the Lord.

I. *The faithful actively seek God's direction.*

II. *The faithful can be more receptive to the Lord's leading through disciplines of abstinence combined with the disciplines of prayer and Bible study.*

III. *As the faithful struggle in spiritual disciplines, they can break through spiritual warfare and hear from the Lord.*

## BIG PICTURE (10:1—11:1)

Chapter 10 serves as a prologue to Daniel's final vision. After a spiritual preparation of three weeks, Daniel sees a man who has a glorious appearance, the sight of whom causes him to faint into a deep sleep with his face to the ground. Then another figure touches Daniel and speaks to him,[1] raising him to a standing position. This angelic figure explains why he was unable to reach Daniel during his twenty-one days of mourning and self-denial. He had been struggling against the Prince of Persia, and could get to Daniel only when Michael, a "chief Prince," arrived to help him. Daniel still could not speak, but another touch, this time on his lips, enabled him to speak of his lack of strength, leading to an additional touch that strengthened him. The angel then reassured Daniel and explained that he would need to return to the struggle with the Prince of Persia, but first he would reveal to him what is in the "Book of Truth." Once the Prince of Persia was taken care of, the angel said, the Prince of Greece would come.

## TRANSLATION (DANIEL 10:1—11:1)

1a   In the third year of Cyrus king of Persia, a message was revealed to Daniel, who was named Belteshazzar. And the message is true and concerns a great conflict. He understood the message and had understanding in the vision.

2    In those days, I, Daniel, was in mourning for three full weeks.[2]

3    I did not eat any fancy food, and meat and wine did not enter my mouth. Nor did I anoint my body with any oil until three full weeks had passed.

---

1. Some think the one who touches and speaks with Daniel is the same as the first figure.

2. Lit., "three weeks, days." The addition of *days* (יָמִין) indicates that these are standard *weeks* of seven *days* each, in contrast to the *weeks* of 9:24–27.

## PRELUDE TO THE FINAL REVELATION

| | |
|---|---|
| 4 | Then on the twenty-fourth day of the first month, when I was beside the Great River (the Tigris).³ |
| 5 | Then I looked up and saw there a man clothed in fine linen, with his waist girded with gold of Uphaz.⁴ |
| 6 | His body was like topaz, and his face had the appearance of lightning. His eyes were like torches of fire, and his arms and legs gleamed like polished bronze. When he spoke,⁵ it was like the sound of a multitude of people. |
| 7 | Now I, Daniel, I alone, saw the vision, but the men who were with me did not see the vision. Nevertheless, great fear fell upon them, and they fled and hid. |
| 8a | So I was left all alone when I saw this great vision. |
| 8b | No strength remained in me, and the color of my face turned deathly pale.⁶ I could not retain any strength. |
| 9 | Then I heard the sound of him speaking,⁷ and when I heard the sound of him speaking, I fainted with my face to the ground. |
| 10 | Then there was a hand that touched me, and it set me trembling on my knees and the palms of my hands. |
| 11a | And he said to me, |
| | "Daniel, highly esteemed one, understand the words that I speak to you, and stand upright. For now I have been sent to you." |
| 11b | When he spoke this word with me, I stood up trembling. |
| 12 | Then he said to me, |
| | "Don't be afraid, Daniel, for from the first day that you determined to understand and to afflict yourself before your God, your words were heard. And I have come because of your words. |

---

3. The *Great River* normally means the Euphrates, which is the reading of the Syriac Peshitta (prt).

4. פָּז (*pāz*) means *pure gold* or *refined gold*, so possibly the element א (*û*) was written for ו (*û*), which means *and*. Then בְּכֶתֶם אוּפָז would mean "with gold and pure gold," meaning "very fine gold" (Montgomery, *Book of Daniel*, 408); *from Uphaz* in Jer 10:9 makes a place name more likely.

5. Lit., "the sound of his words."

6. Lit., "My complexion was turned on me to destruction"; see *HALOT* for הוֹד as *complexion*.

7. Lit., *the sound of his words*.

| | |
|---|---|
| 13 | But the prince[8] of the kingdom of Persia was standing against me twenty-one days. Then Michael, one of the chief princes, came to help me, since I had been left[9] there with the kings of Persia.[10] |
| 14 | Now I have come to explain to you what will happen to your people in the end of the days, for the vision is still for the days ahead." |
| 15 | Now when he spoke with me about these matters, I turned my face to the ground and was speechless. |
| 16 | Then there appeared someone who looked like a mortal man,[11] who touched my lips. Then I opened my mouth and spoke and said to the one standing before me, |
| | "My master, because of the vision my pains have come upon me and I have not retained any strength. |
| 17 | So how can my master's servant then speak with my master, since now I have no strength to stand and there is no breath left in me." |
| 18 | Then the one who looked like a human being touched me again and strengthened me. |
| 19a | Then he said, |
| | "Don't be afraid, highly esteemed one. Peace be to you. Be strong; yes, be strong." |
| 19b | And when he spoke with me, I was strengthened. So, I said, |
| | "Let my master speak, for you have strengthened me." |
| 20 | Then he said, |
| | "Do you know why I have come to you? Now I must go back to fight with the prince of Persia, and when I leave, then the prince of Greece will come. |
| 21a | However, I will tell you what is inscribed in the Book of Truth. |
| 21b | Now there is no one who will stand firmly with me against these princes, except Michael your prince. |

8. 4QDan<sup>c</sup> reads שרי (*princes of*).

9. The OG and Th, "and I left him there." See the exposition.

10. The OG has "the commander of the king of the Persians," while Th has "the ruler of the kingdom of the Persians." Jerome read the singular "king." See the Exposition.

11. Lit., "like the appearance of the sons of mankind."

11:1     And as for me, I stood[12] to strengthen and to be a protection for him[13] in the first year of Darius the Mede."[14]

## TEXTUAL OUTLINE (10:1—11:1)

I. Daniel Mourns for Three Weeks to Prepare for Further Revelation. (10:1–3)

*[The faithful actively seek God's direction]*

II. Daniel Has a Vision of a Glorious Man. (10:4–9)

*[The faithful can be more receptive to the Lord's leading through disciplines of abstinence combined with the disciplines of prayer and Bible study.]*

III. Daniel Talks with an Angel. (10:10—11:1)

*[As the faithful struggle in spiritual disciplines, they can break through spiritual warfare and hear from the Lord.]*

## EXPOSITION (10:1—11:1)

### Daniel Mourns for Three Weeks to Prepare for Further Revelation. (10:1–3)

Theological Point: The faithful actively seek God's direction.

Daniel's final vision has two introductions. First, a narrator (or Daniel in a narrative mode) indicates the timing of the vision, Daniel's great struggle to receive it, and that he understood it (v. 1). Second, Daniel himself describes his spiritual preparation to receive the vision. He mourned, fasted, and refrained from treating his body with lotion or oil for a period of three full weeks (vv. 2–3).

Daniel's three weeks of mourning is prefaced by a reference to a "message" (דָּבָר) that Daniel will receive through revelation. The message,

---

12. The MT has עָמְדִי (*my standing*), while 4QDan[c] has עמדתי (*I stood*).

13. We have reversed the Hebrew word order to clarify that the angel helped Michael, not Darius. See Péter-Contesse and Ellington, *Handbook on the Book of Daniel*, 277–78; they also discuss various textual issues with the verse.

14. Both Greek versions read Κύρου (Cyrus) in place of "Darius the Mede." Pace argues that this represents the original reading (*Old Greek Translation of Daniel 7—12*, 120).

though, concerns not what is included in chapter 10, but instead what is included in chapters 11 and 12. Chapter 10 is about Daniel's preparation for that message he will receive in chapter 11. Chapter 10 includes a theophany that assures Daniel of God's presence among his people, and an angel speaks with Daniel to give him insight into the spiritual warfare taking place in heaven.

**10:1a.** By the third year of Cyrus (ca. 536 BC), the king had already issued his decree allowing the Jews to return to their land (2 Chr 36:22–23; Ezra 1:1–4), and the first return under Sheshbazzar, Zerubbabel, and Joshua had likely taken place (Ezra 1:5—2:2). Daniel, being a very old man, stayed behind and sought another vision that would give more insight into what he had already received from the Lord. Perhaps when he heard word from Judah about the successful return of the exiles, he began his fast of three weeks to show his support for his kinsmen. In any case, **this *third* year of Cyrus promised to usher in a new era in the history of the temple. That the work ultimately stopped for many years was disappointing, but Daniel's final vision would assure the remnant that returned that their God was still working on behalf of his people.**

**10:1b.** While for other visions Daniel was left perplexed and wondering, for this vision he "understood" and "had insight." That Daniel "understood the matter" implies that he wasn't struggling to comprehend it, as he had with Jeremiah's prophecy (9:2). The *vision* that he was now about to receive gave him the discernment that he so longed to obtain. As always, understanding and insight come from God (Dan 2:21). The final chapters of the book still contain much mystery, and to the extent that Daniel did understand the vision, he preserved it for posterity (cf. 12:4). Though even at the very end of the book, he still expressed some lack of understanding (12:7).

It is difficult to know how to render צָבָא; it is an additional description of the "matter" (דָּבָר) or message that "was revealed" to Daniel, but without any indication of how it describes that message. The term most commonly refers to military troops (cf. Dan 8:12, 13) or to a military campaign. The latter sense is represented in the versions by "conflict" or "war" (NLT). A *war* is also a *conflict*, but does the *conflict* refer to the struggle among the angels who represent various nations (10:13—11:1)? Or does it refer to the struggle that Daniel endured to receive the message?[15] Or perhaps it means the wars that are described in chapter 11? Since the verse concerns the "message" that "was revealed" to Daniel, the "conflict" likely refers to the wars and struggles that are described in 11:2—12:3. It is not impossible,

---

15. Péter-Contesse and Ellington, *Handbook on the Book of Daniel*, 262.

PRELUDE TO THE FINAL REVELATION

though, that the "conflict" refers both to the heavenly struggle and to the wars on earth. That would agree with both heavenly and earthly conflicts described throughout chapters 7 to 12.

The KJV and the NKJV took a different route altogether—"the time appointed was long." The Jewish commentator Rashi (eleventh and early twelfth century) understood צָבָא to mean *time*,[16] an interpretation followed by Calvin.[17] The KJV translators followed this tradition. Neither BDB nor HALOT, however, list *time* as a meaning for צָבָא. The rendering *time* is not justified based on the semantic and contextual evidence.

Daniel's Babylonian name, Belteshazzar, is used here. It is found nine times in the first five chapters that come from the Babylonian period, but this instance is unique for the Medo-Persian period. Perhaps the name emphasizes that Daniel did not return to Judah with his fellow exiles. Being an old man and still having an administrative post in Babylon, he stayed behind while many of his fellow captives followed Zerubbabel and Joshua the high priest to Judah (Ezra 1:5—2:70).

10:2-3. To prepare for further revelation Daniel mourned and fasted from rich food and luxury. He thereby indicated not only his deep sense of the sinfulness of the nation (cf. 9:4–19), but also his distress upon hearing of further troubles for his people and Jerusalem (cf. 9:25-27). **Daniel's three weeks of fasting is matched by the twenty-one days that the angel had to struggle with "the prince of the kingdom of Persia" (10:13). Daniel's discipline in refraining from pleasurable activities corresponds to the spiritual struggle taking place in heaven.**

10:3. Daniel abstained from fine food, meat, and wine, a diet like the one he followed when he and his companions were being educated for service to Nebuchadnezzar. The king's table included meat and wine, but Daniel purposed to eat only vegetables and to drink water rather than wine (1:8–12).

*Oil* (שֶׁמֶן) probably refers to olive oil, a common commodity in the ancient Near East, used for cooking (Ezek 16:13), medicine (Isa 1:6; Mark 6:13; Jas 5:14), as a cosmetic (Ps 104:15), and for anointing leaders (1 Sam 10:1). A gracious host might pour oil on the head of a guest, something considered refreshing and symbolic of joyful acceptance (Pss 23:5; 133:2; Luke 7:46). Not using oil on one's body was considered a sign of mourning and often accompanied fasting (2 Sam 12:15–20; 14:2; Isa 61:3; Matt 6:16–18).

---

16. Goldwurm, *Daniel*, 268.
17. Calvin, *Commentary on Daniel*, 2:233.

## Daniel Has a Vision of a Glorious Man. (10:4–9)

Theological Point: The faithful can be more receptive to the Lord's leading through disciplines of abstinence combined with the disciplines of prayer and Bible study.[18]

10:4. The twenty-fourth day of the first month implies that Daniel began his fast on the third or fourth day of the month (24 less 21). Since the Persian year, like the Babylonian, began in the month of Nisan,[19] Daniel's reference to the first month should also be to Nisan (March/April). The fast lasted a full three weeks or twenty-one days, and during the vision, the angel shared with Daniel that he had resisted "the prince of the kingdom of Persia" for twenty-one days. **The correspondence between the number of days implies that the angel was able to bring his message to Daniel immediately after the three weeks of fasting.**

Since the Passover lamb was slaughtered on the fourteenth of Nisan (Exod 12:6), Daniel's fast from Nisan 4 to Nisan 24 must have lasted right through Passover (cf. Esth 3:12 and 4:16). Daniel would not have celebrated Passover in exile, since he didn't have access to the temple and the altar for sacrifices.[20] Perhaps knowing that it was the time for Passover encouraged Daniel to carry out his fast. It was a time to mourn the loss of the temple and the inability of the people to conduct sacrifices.

The *twenty-fourth* of the month was a propitious day for receiving a vision or for mourning and fasting. Haggai received his prophetic revelations on the *twenty-fourth* day of the sixth and ninth months, respectively (Hag 1:15; 2:10, 18, 20), and Zechariah heard the Lord's word on the *twenty-fourth* of the eleventh month (Zech 1:7). Still later, the exiles who returned fasted and mourned for their sins on the *twenty-fourth* of the seventh month (Neh 9:1–2).

"The Great River" elsewhere in Scripture refers to the Euphrates (Gen 15:18; Deut 1:7; Josh 1:4; Rev 9:14; 16:12), but here it is the Tigris. The only other biblical reference to the Tigris is found in Gen 2:14, where it was one of the four branches or headwaters that originated from the river that

---

18. See Willard (*Spirit of the Disciplines*) for the division of spiritual disciplines into those of abstinence and those of study.

19. Finegan, *Handbook of Biblical Chronology*, 26.

20. Ibn Ezra thought that *the first month* could not have been Nisan, because Daniel must have at least consumed *matzah* and the four cups of wine at Passover (Goldwurm, *Daniel*, 270–71). It cannot be assumed that celebrating Passover apart from the sacrificial lamb was a custom prior to the fall of Jerusalem in AD 70 (see Bokser, "Unleavened Bread and Passover," 762–64).

## PRELUDE TO THE FINAL REVELATION

flowed from the garden of Eden. In modern times the Tigris River is located about fifty miles east of Babylon (in Iraq). That the text so explicitly identifies the river where the vision took place shows that it has some importance, although it is difficult to determine why it was significant. Since Daniel was now associated with Persia rather than Babylon, perhaps a river closer to the Persian capital than the Euphrates was an appropriate place to receive his vision.[21]

10:5-6. The *man* with a glorious appearance that Daniel saw in his vision resembles the figure that Ezekiel saw by the river Chebar (Ezek 1:26-28). In both cases a human-like figure had a bright glow from exceedingly luminous substances—sapphire, fine linen, gold, topaz, lightning, and fire. The vision caused Daniel and his companions to react in terror.

Did Daniel perhaps see a vision of Gabriel?[22] When Daniel previously encountered Gabriel, he did not lose his strength, turn deathly pale, and faint at the sound of his voice. He did become frightened and fell on his face the first time he saw him (8:16-17), but the second time no bodily reaction is recorded (Dan 9:21). Gabriel came only as a messenger, whereas here the *man* appears more like a warrior,[23] and the text emphasizes his glorious appearance (see v. 6). Gabriel only interprets visions or brings a word from God. He is not himself the subject of a vision (cf. Luke 1:19, 26).

**Since Gabriel or some other angel does not seem to fit the vision that Daniel saw, he may have seen the Lord himself.**[24] **If this appearance is indeed a theophany, then the figure would be either the Angel of Yahweh or some other figure who had only the appearance of a man. Perhaps it was a Christophany (a pre-incarnate appearance of Christ). Just as the vision of the Lord in his glory assured Ezekiel of God's presence and power despite the fall of Jerusalem to the Babylonians, so also Daniel received assurance of God's continuing presence with his people. Such assurance was needed after the prophecy of chapter 9, which foretold great distress for the nation.** And chapter 11 will go on to fill in details of the coming fearful conflicts.

There are also parallels with the vision of the "one like a son of man" that the Apostle John saw, including his terrified reaction (Rev 1:12-20). John clearly saw Jesus Christ, and this vision of Christ had eyes "like a flame of fire," feet "like fine bronze when it has been refined in a furnace," and a

---

21. Lebram, *Das Buch Daniel*, 114.
22. John Collins, *Daniel*, 373.
23. Steinmann, *Daniel*, 408.
24. Hippolytus, *ACCSOT*, 13:272; Walvoord, *Daniel*, 243; Lacocque, *Book of Daniel*, 206; Miller, *Daniel*, 281-82; Steinmann, *Daniel*, 498, 500.

voice "like the sound of many waters" (Rev 1:14–15). The similarity with Daniel's vision is remarkable in these three features. Another figure in John's vision, a "mighty angel" (Rev 10:1), also has similarities with Daniel's "man." He has "a great voice like a roaring lion"; his legs "are like pillars of fire"; and his face is "like the sun" (Rev 10:1, 3).[25] Remarkably, the "mighty angel" in John's vision "raised his right hand to heaven and swore by him who lives forever and ever . . . , 'There will be no more delay!'" (Rev 10:5–6). In this case the angel's actions resemble what the "man clothed in linen" does according to Dan 12:7. The figure in both Daniel and in John takes an oath "by him who lives forever," and the oath concerns the timing of the end. Clearly John's "mighty angel" is modeled after Daniel's "man clothed in linen."[26]

Some connect the *hand* that touched Daniel (v. 10) and the *voice* that subsequently spoke to him with the glorious figure that caused him to fall into a faint. If so, then it is unlikely that the person in the vision represented God himself, for later he noted how "the prince of the kingdom of Persia" was able to hold him at bay for twenty-one days (v. 13). **Since the figure that Daniel first saw has so many features that point to a vision of God himself, but later conversation makes one think more of an angel, the simplest solution is to posit two different figures. What Daniel** *saw* **rendered him unconscious; what then** *touched* **him was the hand of an angel sent with a divine message.** Lacocque thinks that the second figure, to be identified with Gabriel, appears only at verse sixteen.[27] The "man," according to Lacocque, is described in verse six in a "theophany-like" manner.[28] A "theophany" seems, then, the best description for the first figure that Daniel saw, but the appearance of the angel (Gabriel?) should begin at verse ten, since verse eleven goes on to describe the figure as telling Daniel that he is going to give him the message; and he reiterates the same thing in more detail in verse twenty-one.

**10:7.** Curiously, people were with Daniel when he first glimpsed the *man* who had such brilliance. They react in terror and leave Daniel all alone. Then Daniel's initial reaction is to faint. No details are given about his companions. Were they all on a journey? Were they aware that Danial was mourning and fasting? Did they participate in the same type of rituals? **Lacking any specific details, the reason for including them in the account must be literary. They help to affirm the** *truth* **or** *reliability* **that**

---

25. Despite the title "strong angel," Beale identifies this figure as "the divine Angel of the Lord" known from the OT, who is also to be identified with Jesus Christ (*Book of Revelation*, 522–26).

26. Collins, *Daniel*, 399; Steinmann, *Daniel*, 569.

27. Lacocque, *Book of Daniel*, 206.

28. Lacocque, *Book of Daniel*, 206.

is so often stated about the message that Daniel is about to receive. The term אֱמֶת (*truth, faithfulness, true*) occurs in Daniel 10:1 to affirm that the *message* Daniel is about the receive is *true*. At the end of the chapter (10:21), the angel tells Daniel, "I will tell you what is inscribed in the Book of Truth [כְּתָב אֱמֶת]" (cf. 11:2). The men with Daniel serve as witnesses but not participants. Daniel is alone when he experiences the vision, but these witnesses can testify that he had a numinous experience.[29]

10:8–9. Daniel's encounter with the man of glorious appearance left him exhausted. And when he heard the man speak, he fainted. The noun תַּרְדֵּמָה, cognate with the verb נִרְדָּם, can refer to a deep sleep, a state in which a person can receive revelation from God (Gen 15:12; Job 4:13; 33:15). It is likely that Daniel fell into a trance-like state so he could receive the revelation.

## Daniel Talks with the Angel. (10:10—11:1)

Theological Point: As the faithful struggle in spiritual disciplines,
they can break through spiritual warfare and hear from the Lord.

After Daniel saw the theophany, an angel came to minister to him, bringing a difficult message. When Daniel fainted because of his terror at seeing the glorious man and hearing his voice, an unnamed angel appeared and touched him three times. He did this to prepare Daniel to receive a message from God's Book of Truth. After the first touch, Daniel could only get up on his hands and knees. Once the angel touched his lips, Daniel spoke only of his extreme weakness and inability to stand up. When Daniel received the third touch, his strength was renewed and he asked the angel to give the message.

Preliminary to the main message found in chapters 11 and 12, the angel described a spiritual struggle with forces that represented Persia and Greece. **The struggle was so powerful that both the angel speaking with Daniel and Michael, the angel assigned to protect God's people Israel, had to work together to overcome their opponent. Daniel's struggle, marked by mourning and fasting for his people, thus mirrored the angelic struggle with forces hostile to God.**

10:10. Daniel said only that "a hand" touched him; any other details about the person involved are not given. Additionally, the use of the particle הִנֵּה (*behold*) indicates the start of a new part of his vision. Putting these two

---

29. Paul's encounter with Jesus on the road to Damascus has some similarities with Daniel's experience (Acts 9:1–7).

facts together, it makes good sense to see a different figure behind the *hand* than the glorious image that Daniel saw at first.

**Daniel's gradual recovery from his unconscious state—first *trembling* on his hands and knees—stresses the intensity of his encounter with the "man clothed in fine linen." That intensity also points to the likelihood that what Daniel saw at first was a theophany.**

**10:11.** The angelic figure noted that he had been *sent* to Daniel. Gabriel had such a mission to Daniel previously (8:16; 9:21). If this angel were Gabriel, one might expect that the text would name him. Perhaps, though, since he was named twice before, the reader is expected to know that this person also must be Gabriel. For Daniel as "highly esteemed" see on Daniel 9:23.

**10:12.** The angel made an interesting theological observation when he connected Daniel's spiritual exercises to his commission to Daniel with a message. **Prayer is a two-way activity. The one who prays speaks to God, but he or she can also hear from God through the Scriptures or through a time of silent listening. The text reassures that God responds to his people when they pray and fast.** Some other examples from Scripture of people who received a message from God when they sought him earnestly include Abraham's intercession for Lot and his family (Gen 18:22–32), Abraham's servant when he sought a bride for Isaac (Gen 24:12–27), Hezekiah's prayer regarding Sennacherib's incursion into Judah (2 Kgs 19:15–34), and the complaints of the prophets Jeremiah and Habakkuk about the prospering of the wicked ( Jer 12:1–15; Hab 1:2—2:20).

**10:13.** The mysterious "prince of the kingdom of Persia," according to Jerome, "was the angel to whose charge Persia was committed, in accordance with what we read in Deuteronomy [32:8]: 'When the Most High divided the nations and distributed the children of Adam abroad, then He established the bounds of the nations according to the number of the angels of God.'"[30] The concept of a divine council lies behind this idea of nations having angels assigned to them by God. These angels may be either good (Michael assigned to Israel) or evil, the evil ones being demons. Scriptural support for the idea of a divine assembly (in addition to the reading of Deut 32:8 in the LXX) includes Job 1:6 (Satan was among *"the sons of God"* who "came to present themselves to Yahweh"); Ps 29:1 (*the sons of the gods* [בְּנֵי אֵלִים] are admonished to "ascribe glory and strength to Yahweh"); Ps 82:1 (where עֲדַת אֵל is "probably . . . a fixed formula for 'divine assembly' or

---

30. Jerome, *Commentary on Daniel*, 114. Here Jerome follows the reading of the LXX, while in the Vulgate he followed the Hebrew text that has "sons of Israel" (בְּנֵי יִשְׂרָאֵל) rather than "angels of God." See Heiser ("Deuteronomy 32:8," 52–74) for an argument that the LXX represents a more original text than the MT.

'divine council.'"³¹ The judgment scene in Daniel 7 assumes a divine council, with thrones set up for judgment of the four beasts. The struggle between the nations and God's people (the Jews) is mirrored by the struggles in heaven among angelic or demonic representatives of those nations and Michael, the angel assigned to the Jews.³²

Even though a few have identified this *prince* with Cambyses (the son of Cyrus), or even Cyrus himself,³³ the text is clear that he was a supernatural being who was struggling with an angel for many days. And even that angel required the combining of forces with Michael. Since Persia was the most powerful kingdom at the time of Cyrus, it has even been thought that this prince might have been Satan himself.³⁴

It is only the book of Daniel in the OT that mentions Michael by name.³⁵ Michael, called a "chief prince," is titled an *archangel* (ἀρχάγγελος) in Jude 9. He also appears as the leader of heavenly warriors in Rev 12:7. The only other use of the term *archangel* is in 1 Thess 4:16. There the *archangel* makes the *shout* (and blows the trumpet?) at the rapture when "the dead in Christ will rise first." At Dan 12:1, Michael is said to be the protector of Israel, and at 10:21 he is "your prince," with *your* being a plural form, thus including not only Daniel but also his people.

That Michael was summoned to the aid of the angel who spoke with Daniel indicates great spiritual conflict with "the prince of the kingdom of Persia." The exact nature of this conflict cannot be identified with certainty. One suggestion refers it to the opposition the Jews faced when they first attempted to rebuild the temple in Jerusalem (Ezra 4:1–5).³⁶ Jerome speculated that the prince of Persia was "enumerating the sins of the Jewish people as a ground for their justly being kept in captivity and as proof that they ought not to be released."³⁷ **What stands out most clearly from the text is that the angel had a message for Daniel concerning what would happen to Daniel's people "in the end of the days" (v. 14), but the "prince**

---

31. Tate, *Psalms 51–100*, 329.

32. Ephesians 6:12 gives a NT perspective on this struggle. See also Seow, *Daniel*, 160.

33. Calvin, *Commentaries on Daniel*, 2:252; Shea, "Wrestling," 255.

34. Miller, *Daniel*, 284.

35. Many have speculated about the identity of Michael. For references to him in other Jewish apocalyptic literature see Watson, "Michael (Angel)," 1:811. For discussion among the reformers about whether he should be identified with Jesus Christ, see Carl Beckwith, *Ezekiel, Daniel*, 385–87.

36. Calvin, *Commentaries on Daniel*, 2:252; Keil, *Ezekiel, Daniel*, 416–17; Edward Young, *Prophecy of Daniel*, 227.

37. Jerome, *Commentary on Daniel*, 114.

of the kingdom of Persia" prevented that from happening during the entire time that Daniel was fasting and praying. The stranglehold was broken only when Michael arrived on the scene to help. The Hebrew verb נוֹתַרְתִּי (*I was left*) implies that the angel who spoke with Daniel was the last one remaining after others had to leave or even retreat. At that point Michael arrived with help, freeing him to go to Daniel with his message from the Lord.[38]

The "kings of Persia" were probably multiple demonic powers that were attempting to influence the affairs of Persia, although some think instead of the concurrent and subsequent kings of that country.[39]

**10:14.** Here the term *vision* (חָזוֹן) refers to the oral message that the angel has for Daniel, not images that he would see.

**10:16.** The angelic figure who touched Daniel's lips resembled an ordinary mortal (כִּדְמוּת בְּנֵי אָדָם, "as the likeness of the sons of men"). He was not the glorious, shining *man* (אִישׁ) that Daniel saw at the beginning of his vision. He is not to be identified with the "one like a son of man" of 7:13, nor with the Messiah.[40] In verse eighteen the same angel is also said to be "like the appearance of a human being" (כְּמַרְאֵה אָדָם). He was most likely the same angel who touched Daniel when he was unconscious and who needed the archangel Michael to come to his aid against the prince of Persia. Now he came to touch Daniel's lips so that he could speak clearly.

**10:16b–19.** When Daniel confessed his lack of strength, the angel touched him a third time, infusing him with new strength. These three touches have a progression to them. The first touch brought Daniel back to consciousness; the second enabled him to speak; and the third gave him strength to receive the vision. The significance of these touches for the book possibly relates to Daniel's praise of God in 2:20–23. God is completely sovereign over all wisdom and knowledge; only he can reveal deep truths. Perhaps because of his long fast, Daniel was unable to even retain consciousness in the presence of the theophany; the form of a *man* in dazzling brightness thoroughly overwhelmed him. And the prophetic message that the angel now bore required supernatural infusion of ability and strength. "Wisdom and power" were needed (2:20, 23), and the angel communicated them through his touches.

**10:20a.** In the Hebrew language a question prefaced with the interrogative particle is normally rhetorical, and indeed the angel has already

---

38. Lucas (*Daniel*, 259) interprets the Hebrew to mean "I was no longer needed there," a doubtful rendering.

39. Keil, *Ezekiel, Daniel*, 429; Montgomery, *Daniel*, 412; Slotki, *Daniel–Ezra–Nehemiah*, 83; Wood, *Daniel*, 274.

40. *Contra* Steinmann, *Daniel*, 493, 504.

## PRELUDE TO THE FINAL REVELATION

told Daniel the purpose of his coming (v. 14). Resolving the rhetoric, the meaning is: "Surely you know why I have come to you." He had come to help Daniel understand what will happen to the Jewish people "in the end of the days" (v. 14).

**10:20b.** The intent of the last part of verse twenty is difficult to discern from the grammar alone; the context must determine the correct view. When the angel refers to a going forth or leaving, does he mean when he leaves Daniel? Or is it when he leaves "the prince of Persia"? Most likely the tense of the participle יוֹצֵא (*going out*) is governed by the imperfect אָשׁוּב (*I will return*), meaning the angel will leave when he has finished the battle with the Persian prince.[41] After that "the prince of Greece" will come to take up the spiritual battle afresh. More dynamic in its translation, the NRSV gives the basic idea: "and when I am through with him, the prince of Greece will come."

**10:21—11:1.** Written documents contained in heaven are mentioned three more times in Daniel. At 7:10 there are the "books" that form the basis for judgment against the nations. The four "beasts" that Daniel saw in his vision represent the nations from the four corners of the world (cf. Rev 20:12). Then at 12:1 there is a "book" that contains the names of all those among the Jews who will be delivered in the time of a future period of great tribulation. **The *Book of Truth* here refers to a written document that contains the events that the angel will reveal to Daniel, events that have been decreed for a future time.** In the NT there is reference to a "book of life" (also "the Lamb's book of life") that contains the names of all those who have been chosen by God for salvation (Phil 4:3; Rev 3:5; 13:8; 17:8; 20:12, 15; 21:27). Other OT passages also refer to a book with the names of those recorded for salvation (Exod 32:32-33; Ps 69:28 [29]; Isa 4:3; Mal 3:16). **Some think these books should be distinguished from each other,[42] but we see no reason why they could not all be considered a metaphor for "the eternal and inviolable decree of God himself."[43] God's decree would encompass judgments for the guilty, salvation for the elect, and his plan for the unfolding of the history of the world.**

The angel anticipated additional conflict with the demonic forces that represented nations arrayed against God's people. That is clear from the presence of Michael, Israel's protector, in the conflict. The angel who continued to reveal to Daniel the truth inscribed in the book saw his own role to be a help for Michael in the battle.

---

41. Similarly, John Collins, *Daniel*, 376.
42. John Collins, *Daniel*, 376; Steinmann, *Daniel*, 505.
43. Calvin, *Commentaries on Daniel*, 2:265.

## SHARPENING THE THEOLOGICAL FOCUS

Daniel's prayer of confession in chapter 9 shows the strong connection between the study of Scripture and prayer. Chapter 10 gives insight into the connection between fasting and hearing from God. Willard has divided the "spiritual disciplines" into "disciplines of engagement" and "disciplines of abstinence."[44] Prayer and the study of Scripture constitute "engagement" with God in a direct way, while fasting, "mourning" and not "anointing the body with oil" are "disciplines of abstinence." Although it would have been a luxury for some, the daily application of oil on the body was a normal practice for the ancients (cf. Matt 6:17). And to go into "mourning" indicated withdrawal from the normal activities and contacts of everyday life. Daniel's disciplines moved God to action; he responded to them by the vision of the glorious-appearing man and the angel who came with the message. The disciplines were not a magical way to move God, God responded because it was Daniel, his faithful servant, who abstained. It was Daniel's faithful heart that was significant. The disciplines were merely outward expressions of a sincere heart seeking God.

Daniel was engaged in the same, or similar, spiritual disciplines of abstinence when he had his revelation of the seventy weeks. Sackcloth and ashes were a sign of mourning (9:3), and it is not likely that he anointed his body with oil at that time either. The difference in chapter 10 is the duration of Daniel's abstinence, further details about the food and drink not consumed, and the comment about not anointing himself. Of interest is that there is no mention of prayer in 10:3, though it is difficult to imagine that Daniel didn't engage in earnest prayer during those three weeks. By deemphasizing Daniel's efforts to understand through study of Scripture and prayer, God's sovereign decision to communicate with his "highly esteemed" servant stands out. Withdrawal from the pleasures of life put Daniel in a posture to experience God in a fresh way. This time he saw a vision of God himself, not only of an angel. And the glory of that encounter prepared him for the revelation of what was contained in the Book of Truth (10:21).

A discipline of abstinence, especially abstinence from something luxurious or comfortable, removes the "noise" of reliance on one's own abilities and resources, making way for the voice of God to be heard more clearly. As the faithful seek God's direction, even as Daniel sought more understanding, disciplines of abstinence can be combined with the engaging disciplines of prayer and Bible study to make oneself more receptive to God's leading.

---

44. Willard, *Spirit of the Disciplines*, 158.

The spiritual disciplines are not only for developing one's personal relationship with the Lord. They are also important "weapons" whereby the faithful believer engages in the spiritual warfare that goes on behind the scenes of ordinary life. God dispatched Gabriel with a message for Daniel the very moment he began to pray while studying the prophecy of Jeremiah (9:23). Then during the entire three weeks that he fasted and mourned, Gabriel (or some other angel) struggled with the Prince of Persia (10:3 and 13). It would not have been easy for Daniel to abstain from the foods he was used to, or to abandon the normal care for his body, but as he did a corresponding struggle was happening in the spiritual realm. Daniel was "highly esteemed" because, as a righteous man who was willing to give up his personal comfort in order to draw near to his God, he in some mysterious way was aiding angels with their struggles against the forces of darkness. Fasting, in particular, is a discipline that often accompanies prayer at critical moments in history. Nehemiah fasted, prayed, and mourned "for days" when he heard of Jerusalem's wretched condition (Neh 1:4). God then stirred the heart of the king of Persia to allow Nehemiah to travel to Jerusalem and rebuild it (Neh 2:6). Previously, the same king had allowed Ezra to go to Jerusalem to reinstitute the Law of Moses at the temple, "because the hand of Yahweh his God was upon him" (Ezra 7:6). The king even supplied Ezra with a letter that granted him safe passage and the material needs to make offerings (Ezra 7:11–28). At the river Ahava, Ezra, and those who travelled with him, "fasted and requested" God to protect them in the journey (Ezra 8:21–23). At a critical time, when a locust plague threatened to overwhelm the small community in Jerusalem, the prophet Joel told the people to return to the Lord "with fasting and with weeping and with mourning" (Joel 2:12). And there was Esther, who asked the Jews to fast for three days before she entered to the king when their lives were threatened by Haman's decree (Esth 4:16). Prayer is not mentioned in the book of Esther, but it is unthinkable that fasting was not accompanied by crying out to God for deliverance. All of these instances of fasting and mourning, including Daniel's, were intended to move the Lord to act on behalf of his people. And he did.

Another theological insight from chapter 10 relates to God's sovereign oversight of history. As terror-inspiring as the theophany that Daniel experienced was, it also vouchsafed that God would continue to reign supreme over all that would happen in history. In the vision of the Ancient of Days there were "books" that were opened from which the beasts were judged (7:10). Now the angel speaks of the Book of Truth (10:21) which will reveal the unfolding of history to its end. Something written down implies permanence and inviolability, and *truth* (אֱמֶת) from the Hebrew perspective implies reliability as well. To God, all world events are as inscribed in a book (cf. Ps 139:16); nothing ever surprises him. Humans, mere mortals, view the future as unknown and sometimes even frightening. The angel communicated to Daniel a different perspective. There is no need for God's faithful ones to fear the future.

## THE FOCUS OF DANIEL 10 FOR PREACHING AND TEACHING

In the literary flow of the book, chapter 10 functions as an introduction to Daniel's final vision. However, because important theological implications emerge in this chapter, it is worthwhile to preach/teach chapter 10 on its own. Two key preaching themes emerge in this transitional chapter. First, the passage beautifully ties together two key themes that have been present throughout the book: Daniel's faithfulness and Daniel's need to depend on God. With regard to Daniel's faithfulness, note how he is described in this lengthy introduction to the final vision of the book.

- Daniel faithfully sought the Lord: "In those days, I, Daniel, was in mourning for three full weeks. I did not eat any fancy food, and meat and wine did not enter my mouth. Nor did I anoint my body with any oil until three full weeks had passed." (10:2–3)
- Everyone but Daniel fled the scene because of fear; he faithfully remained. (10:7)
- He is referred to twice as the "highly esteemed one." (10:11, 19)
- Angels were sent to him because he had "determined to understand." (10:12)
- To him alone is going to be revealed "what is inscribed in the book of truth." (10:21)

With regard to Daniel's need to depend on God, notice how the text highlights Daniel's insufficiencies.

- Daniel is unable to understand and make sense of how God is working out his plans and so he seeks the Lord for understanding. (10:2–3)
- When God responds via theophany, Daniel is unable to stand in his presence and he passes out. (10:8–9)
- It takes the touch of an angel sent by God to wake Daniel up. (10:10)

- It takes another touch of the angel for Daniel to even have the strength to speak. (10:16)
- It takes yet another touch of the angel to strengthen Daniel so that he could speak and eventually have enough strength to hear his final vision. (10:18–19)

While God is always the main point, Daniel is portrayed as a model of faithfulness throughout the book, and he is consistently recognized for that faithfulness. As the book works toward its conclusion, beginning here in chapter 10, the text specifically recognizes and praises Daniel's life of faithfulness, and insofar as Daniel is faithful, he can serve as a model for God's people to emulate as they seek to live faithfully.

A second key theme that emerges from this chapter that lends itself to a preaching point is the necessity and function of spiritual disciplines. While spiritual disciplines are present throughout the book, here in chapter 10 there is an explicit link between what Daniel is doing on earth and what angels are doing in the spiritual realm. In other words, spiritual disciplines win spiritual battles and believers need to be engaged.

## FROM TEXTUAL WORK TO TEACHING

### The Big Idea

- *Exegetical Idea:* God responds to Daniel's humble and earnest quest for understanding by appearing to him and by sending an angel to strengthen and prepare Daniel to hear his final vision.
- *Theological Focus:* God responds to the humble and earnest seeking of his people in a way that strengthens and prepares his people for what is to come.
- *Preaching Idea:* When God's people humbly and earnestly seek God, he shows up.

### Outline One: Following the Exegetical Flow

I. The faithful actively seek God's direction.

  A. Daniel mourns for three weeks to prepare for further revelation. (10:1–3)

B. Faithfulness includes actively seeking God's direction.

II. The faithful can be more receptive to the Lord's leading through disciplines of abstinence combined with the disciplines of prayer and Bible study.

    A. Daniel has a vision of a glorious man. (10:4–9)

    B. As we faithfully seek God through disciplines of abstinence and engagement we can expect God to show up.

III. As the faithful struggle in spiritual disciplines, they can break through spiritual warfare and hear from the Lord.

    A. Daniel learns that his spiritual disciplines are not only a means to seek the Lord, they are spiritual warfare. (10:10—11:1)

    B. As we practice spiritual disciplines, we are not only seeking the Lord, we are fighting spiritual battles.

## Outline Two: Following a Theme

The way in which chapter 10 weaves together Daniel's faithfulness and Daniel's dependence provides a snapshot of the Christian life. In addition to the specifics highlighted in this chapter, preaching/teaching on this theme allows one to go back and highlight aspects of Daniel's faithfulness and dependence throughout the book. Because this chapter leads into the final and ultimate conflict, it is an appropriate time to paint a fuller portrait of faithfulness, which includes dependence.

*Introduction:* Highlight the way in which the chapter describes Daniel as "the highly esteemed one" and what God is doing because Daniel is "highly esteemed."

*Body of the Sermon:*

- God esteems the faithfulness of his people.

  - Daniel is highly esteemed because of his faithfulness (give examples from chapter 10 and from other passages in Daniel).
  - God esteems the faithfulness of his people today (give examples from the lives of people in your congregation).

- God esteems the dependence of his people.
  - Daniel is highly esteemed because of his dependence (give examples from chapter 10 and from other passages in Daniel).
  - God esteems the dependence of his people today (give examples of what dependence looks like for God's people today).

# Prophetic History

(11:2—12:2)

**Chapter 10 Review**: Chapter 10 serves as a dramatic introduction to the final prophetic message given to Daniel, but it is also transitional, in that it serves as an introduction to Dan 11:2—12:2. It highlights Daniel's spiritual discipline in preparation for the message and ensures God's presence through all of the trials that the Jewish people will face.

**Chapter 11 Summary**: Daniel 11:2—12:2 extends from the Persian period to the final wicked king, that is, the Antichrist. His defeat will usher in God's eternal kingdom as the archangel Michael fights on behalf of the Jews, and everything culminates in a great resurrection of the righteous and the unrighteous.

**Chapter 12 Preview**: Daniel 12:3–13 will tie together the visions of chapters 8 and 10–11. God will reward Daniel's faithfulness and the faithfulness of all who have acted wisely by following God. Much time will pass before the final eschatological end, and the wicked will increase their folly, while the wise will come to understand the wisdom of God's plan.

## THEOLOGICAL FOCUS OF CHAPTER 11:2—12:2

GOD'S PEOPLE WILL FACE hardship in the present age. Their faithfulness will be tested, but they can endure as they remember that God will reward their faithfulness.

I. *God's people will face domination and hardship as earthly kingdoms fight for power. (11:2–35)*

II. *The faithfulness of God's people will be ultimately tested under the reign of the Antichrist. (11:36–45)*

III. *God's people can endure as they remember that they will be delivered and that resurrection is coming. (12:1–2)*

## BIG PICTURE (11:2—12:2)

Chapter 11:1—12:2 spans all history from the Persian period to the resurrection of the dead. In only one verse (11:2) four Persian kings are covered. Though there were more kings between Cyrus/Darius and Alexander the Great (11:3), Daniel prefers to outline Gentile history in terms of four. Alexander's empire was divided into four parts, and the focus then shifts to the southern area of Egypt and the northern part of Syria-Palestine. Here too, there are four parts: southern hegemony over Judah; northern hegemony over Judah; persecution under Antiochus IV; and the King in the time of the end of the age. A continual conflict occurs between the king of the South and the king of the North. Judah and the Jews (Daniel's people) were caught in the crossfire between these kingdoms, as the kings fought for control of the region that included Judah and Jerusalem. Daniel's sweep of history homes in on the reign of Antiochus IV Epiphanes as king of the North. He tries to destroy the system of sacrifice that was set up by the Torah, and he persecutes those who try to uphold it. Antiochus serves as a type or pattern for a future king, the Antichrist, who will arise at the time determined by God. When the tremendous struggle reaches a peak, Michael, the great Prince and guardian angel of Israel, will arise and deliver the persecuted people from their unprecedented distress. Then the resurrection will take place, resulting in a final separation between the righteous and the unrighteous.

In the period spanning from the Persian kings to Antiochus IV, the Jews will suffer much. They will continue to live under the domination of foreign autocratic rulers, experiencing first hand the uncertainties of life in the crosshairs of warring rulers. The external strife they face will include burdensome taxation and the conscription of sons to fight in the armies of foreign rulers. The internal strife, particularly in the time of Antiochus IV, will include conflict with brothers and sisters who choose obedience to Antiochus IV rather than obedience to Torah.

Since all these events are prophesied beforehand, it is clear that God is still in control. And those who continue to trust in him will get their names written in the Book of Life. Their faithfulness through great suffering will be rewarded when they become part of the great assembly of the righteous who will rise from the dead. Justice will triumph when their persecutors will rise to a destiny of everlasting shame.

## TRANSLATION (11:2—12:2)

| | |
|---|---|
| 11:2a | Now I will tell you the truth.[1] |
| 2b | There are three more kings who will arise for Persia,[2] |
| 2c | and the fourth will amass greater riches than all of them.[3] And when he is powerful through his wealth, the entire kingdom will stir up the kingdom of Greece.[4] |
| 3 | Then a mighty king will arise and rule with great authority, acting as he pleases.[5] |
| 4 | But when he has risen, his kingdom will break up and be divided to the four winds of heaven, but it will not be divided to his posterity, and it will not be like the ruling authority with which he ruled, for his kingdom will be uprooted and be for others besides these. |
| 5a | Then the king of the South will become strong,[6] |
| 5b | but one of his officers will prevail against him,[7] and he will rule his realm with great authority. |
| 6a | After some years they will form an alliance.[8] |

---

1. The first verse of chapter 11 should be included with chapter 10. It continues the angel's message concerning the struggle with "the Prince of Persia" and "the Prince of Greece."

2. The proposed identity of the various kings mentioned throughout the chapter will be discussed in the Exposition, but the conclusions will be found in footnotes to the translation for the convenience of the reader. Here the three kings are probably Cambyses, Bardiya/Gaumata, and Darius Hystaspes (not Darius the Mede).

3. Probably Xerxes, the king of Persia known as Ahasuerus in the book of Esther.

4. *BHS* suggests a textual emendation for the difficult Hebrew, but 4QDan$^c$ supports the MT.

5. Alexander the Great; see 1 Macc 1:1–4.

6. Ptolemy I Soter, the ruler of Egypt, is the first "king of the South."

7. Seleucus I Nicator, who eventually ruled a vast empire that included Babylon and Syria as well as more eastern lands, is the first individual who could be called "the king of the North." See Whitehorn, "Seleucus (Person)," *ABD* 5:1076–77.

8. The reference here must be to later kings, namely Ptolemy II Philadelphus and Antiochus II Theos.

| | |
|---|---|
| 6b | The daughter of the king of the South will go to the king of the North to make an agreement,[9] but she will not hold on to a position of power, and his power will not endure. She will be given over, along with her attendants, her father, and the one who supported her in those times. |
| 7 | Then one will arise in his place from a shoot of her roots,[10] and he will engage the army and enter the fortress of the king of the North.[11] And he will act against them and prevail. |
| 8a | He will also bring captive to Egypt their gods, along with their molten images and their precious articles of silver and gold. |
| 8b | Then he will stay away from the king of the North for some years. |
| 9 | Then he [the king of the North][12] will enter the realm of the king of the South[13] but return to his own country. |
| 10 | Then his sons[14] will prepare for war, gathering a multitude of great armies. It will keep coming and pass through like a flood, and it[15] will again wage war as far as his fortress.[16] |
| 11a | Then the king of the South will become enraged,[17] and he will go forth and fight with him, with the king of the North.[18] |
| 11b | He will raise up a great multitude,[19] but that multitude will be delivered into his power.[20] |

9. Berenice, the daughter of Ptolemy II, married Antiochus II to form an alliance.

10. מִנֵּצֶר שָׁרָשֶׁיהָ; cf. Isa 11:1 נֵצֶר מִשָּׁרָשָׁיו ("a shoot from his roots"). The reference should be to Berenice's brother, Ptolemy III Euergetes.

11. Seleucus II Callinicus.

12. Seleucus II Callinicus.

13. Ptolemy III Euergetes.

14. Following the *qere*; the *kethiv* reads ובנו, "his son," as in the OG. The sons are Seleucus III Ceraunus and Antiochus III the Great. Seleucus III was murdered, and Antiochus III carried out the campaign.

15. The *qere* has the singular; the *kethiv* reads ויתגרו, "and they will wage war." Alternatively, the subject of the verb may be Antiochus III the Great.

16. I.e., the fortress of Ptolemy IV Philopater.

17. Ptolemy IV Philopator.

18. Antiochus III. The reference is evidently to the battle of Raphia (ca. twenty miles southwest of Gaza) at which Antiochus suffered a great defeat. This gave Ptolemy control over Coele-Syria, which included Palestine.

19. The subject of the verb is Antiochus III.

20. I.e., the power of Ptolemy IV Philopater.

| 12 | When the multitude is carried away, he will become arrogant,[21] and he will cast down myriads but will not prevail.[22] |
|---|---|
| 13a | Then the king of the North will again[23] raise up a multitude greater than previously. |
| 13b | And at the end of some years,[24] he will keep coming with a great army and with much equipment. |
| 14 | And in those times many will stand against the king of the South,[25] and violent ones from your people will lift themselves up to cause a vision to stand, but they will stumble. |
| 15a | Then the king of the North[26] will come and build up a siege ramp and capture a well-fortified city.[27] |
| 15b | The forces of the south will not be able to stand; even his choicest troops will be unable to stand. |
| 16a | The one who comes against him will do as he pleases, and no one will stand in his way. |
| 16b | He will take (his) position in the glorious land, with destruction in his power. |
| 17 | Then he will determine to enter the strongholds of his entire kingdom,[28] and he will make an agreement with him. He will give him a woman[29] [in marriage] to destroy it [the kingdom];[30] but it [his plan] will not hold up, and it will not come about for him. |

---

21. Antiochus III.
22. Antiochus III defeated Ptolemy V at Paneas.
23. The verb שׁוּב is used adverbially here to mean "again."
24. Lit., "at the end of the times, years." *BHS* suggests that either הָעִתִּים (*the times*) or שָׁנִים (*years*) is a gloss.
25. Ptolemy V Epiphanes.
26. Antiochus III.
27. Probably Sidon, a Phoenician city; see Seow, *Daniel*, 174.
28. Or, "to come with the might of his whole kingdom." See the Exposition.
29. The MT has וּבַת הַנָּשִׁים (lit., "and the daughter of women," while 4QDanᶜ has [ת]וּב אנשים ("and a daughter of men"). The OG has "a daughter of a man," a reading also found in the Syriac *Peshitta*. Th agrees with the MT. Similarity between the consonants *he* and *aleph* could account for the Qumran variant. The "daughter" is Cleopatra; see Seow, *Daniel*, 174.
30. 4QDanᶜ has להשחיתו, "to destroy him," also supported by the OG in Papyrus 967. Collins (*Daniel*, 365) accepts it as the best reading.

## PROPHETIC HISTORY

18a    Then he will turn[31] his attention to the coastlands and capture many,

18b    but a commander will put a stop to his taunting of him,[32] so that he will not be able to return his taunt to him.

19a    Then he will turn his face to the strongholds of his own land,

19b    but he will stumble and fall and not be found.

20     Then there will arise in his place one who sends an oppressor/tax collector for royal splendor,[33] but in a short while[34] he will be broken, but not in anger or in battle.

21     Then in his place there will arise a contemptible person.[35] He was not given royal majesty, but without warning he will come and seize the kingdom through intrigues.

22     And forces will be utterly overwhelmed before him, and they will be broken, along with the prince of the covenant.[36]

23     After an alliance is made with him, he will act deceitfully and will grow stronger[37] with only a small number in a nation.

24     Without warning he will also enter the richest parts of the province and do what his ancestors or even his distant ancestors[38] had not done. He will distribute plunder, booty, and goods to them, devising his schemes against fortified cities, but only for a limited time.[39]

---

31. The idea of turning the face, using the *Hiphil* of the verb שׁוּב is rare (1 Kgs 2:16, 20; Ezek 14:6), so one should read וַיָּשֶׁב with the *kethiv*. The *qere* (וְיָשֵׂם) replaces the rare construction with a more common one; plus it occurred in v. 17 as well. Th and the Peshitta support the *kethiv*; the OG supports the *qere*.

32. The *commander* is evidently Scipio, the Roman commander who defeated Antiochus III at Magnesia (Collins, *Daniel*, 381).

33. The successor to Antiochus III was Seleucus IV Philopater, and the *oppressor* or *tax collector* was a certain Heliodorus (see 2 Macc. 3:7).

34. וּבְיָמִים אֲחָדִים is literally "and in a few days."

35. Antiochus IV Epiphanes.

36. Many take the "prince" to be the High Priest Onias III (e.g., Steinmann, *Daniel*, 526); another possibility is an adopted son of Antiochus IV.

37. Lit. "he will arise and become mighty" (וְעָלָה וְעָצַם). The verb עָלָה can sometimes have the sense of *increasing* (cf. 1 Kgs 22:35; *HALOT*).

38. Lit., "his fathers or the fathers of his fathers."

39. וְעַד־עֵת ("and up to a time"). BHS suggests deleting the phrase because of dittography with וְיָעֵר ("he will stir up") in the following verse, but Th, Peshitta, and Vg support the MT.

| 25a | Then he will stir up his strength and his courage against the king of the South with a great army.[40] |
|---|---|
| 25b | And the king of the South will wage war with an exceedingly large army, but he will not stand, for plots will be devised against him. |
| 26 | His closest advisers[41] will ruin him, and his army will be swept away, and many will be killed. |
| 27 | As for the two kings, their minds will be bent on evil. They will speak lies at one table; but it will not succeed, because the end is still for an appointed time. |
| 28 | Then he will return to his country with great possessions, and his mind will be set against the holy covenant.[42] He will act and return to his country. |
| 29 | At the appointed time he will again enter the south, but this latter time will not be like the former time. |
| 30 | Ships of the Kittim will come against him,[43] intimidating him. So he will turn back and act in rage against the holy covenant. He will turn back and pay attention to[44] those who forsake the holy covenant. |
| 31 | Armed forces from him will take their position, profane the temple fortress, remove the regular service,[45] and set in place the abomination that devastates. |
| 32 | Those who act wickedly toward the covenant he will corrupt by smooth words, but the people that know their[46] God will act courageously.[47] |

---

40. Ptolemy VI Philomator.
41. Lit. "and those who eat his food."
42. Possibly this refers to an attack on the temple in Jerusalem (cf. 1 Macc 1:20–24).
43. Most identify the Kittim here with the Romans.
44. Or, "he will again pay attention to . . . ," taking וְשָׁב (*and he will turn back*) as an adverbial modifier.
45. For תָּמִיד as "regular service" see the Exposition on Daniel 8:12.
46. The singular suffix on אֱלֹהָיו (*his God*) refers collectively to the Jews.
47. For the *Hiphil* of חזק, *HALOT* has "show oneself courageous." The two actions, "show themselves courageous and act" can then be a *hendiadys*, "act courageously."

## PROPHETIC HISTORY

33  Those who are wise among the people[48] will make the many understand, but they will fall by sword, flame, captivity, and plundering for some time.[49]

34  When they fall, they will receive a little help, but many will join up with them with false motives.

35  Some of the wise will fall to refine, purge, and purify them until the time of the end, for it remains[50] for the appointed time.

36  And the King will act according to his will and exalt himself and magnify himself above every god. He will speak dreadful things against the God of gods. He will prosper until the period of wrath is finished, for it has been determined and accomplished.

37  He will not pay attention to the gods of his ancestors, nor will he pay attention to the desire of women or to any god; for he will magnify himself above all of them.

38  He will honor on his cult stand the god of fortresses, even a god that his fathers did not know he will honor with gold, silver, precious stones, and costly things.

39a  He will attack the strongest fortresses accompanied by a foreign god.

39b  Whoever recognizes [him] he will greatly honor, giving them authority over many and distributing the land for a price.

40  Then in the time of the end, the king of the South will wage war with him, and the king of the North will storm against him with chariots, horsemen, and many ships. He will enter countries and sweep through them like a flood.

41a  Then he will enter the glorious land, and tens of thousands[51] will fall.

41b  Yet these will escape from his power—Edom and Moab and the main part of the Ammonites.

42  He will stretch out his hand against the countries, and as for the land of Egypt, it will not escape.

---

48. מַשְׂכִּילֵי עָם (maśkîlê ʿām).

49. See Péter-Contesse and Ellington on יָמִים (days) (*Handbook on the Book of Daniel*, 312).

50. Lit., "for still [עוֹד] for the appointed time."

51. Or "many countries."

| 43 | He will gain control of the hidden treasures of gold and silver, even of all the riches of Egypt, with Libyans and Cushites[52] in his train. |
|---|---|
| 44 | Then rumors from the east and from the west will terrify him, and he will go forth in great rage to destroy and annihilate many. |
| 45 | He will pitch his royal tents between the seas and the glorious holy mountain, where he will come to his end with no one to help him. |
| 12:1a | Now at that time Michael the great Prince will stand, he who stands watch over the sons of your people. |
| 1b | There will be a time of distress, such as has not happened from when a nation[53] came to be until that time. |
| 1c | At that time your people will be delivered, everyone whose name is written in the book. |
| 2 | Many of those who sleep in the dusty ground will awaken, some to life everlasting, and others to shame and everlasting contempt. |

## TEXTUAL OUTLINE (11:2—12:2)

 I. The Jewish People Will Suffer under Foreign Domination. (11:2–35)

 *[God's people will face domination and hardship as earthly kingdoms fight for power.]*

    A. Three Persian kings will arise, and a fourth. (11:2)

    B. The time for the kingdom of Greece will come. (11:3–35)

        1. A mighty king and his realm (11:3–4)

        2. The rise of the king of the South and the king of the North (11:5–6)

        3. Southern domination of the North (11:7–12)

        4. Northern domination of the South (11:13–19)

        5. Oppression of God's people (11:20–35)

---

52. "Cush" (כּוּשׁ) is often rendered "Ethiopia," following the LXX. It did not include the territory of modern Ethiopia but roughly much of modern Sudan as well as modern Egypt south of the Aswan dam.

53. Possibly *nation*, refers to Israel in particular.

II. The Jews Will Be Ultimately Tested by the King at the Time of the End. (11:36–45)

*[The faithfulness of God's people will be ultimately tested under the reign of the Antichrist.]*

    A. The religious character of the king (11:36–39)

    B. The military exploits of the king (11:40–43)

    C. The downfall of the king (11:44–45)

III. Michael Will Deliver the Jews, and a Resurrection Will Happen. (12:1–2)

*[God's people can endure as they remember they will be delivered and resurrection is coming.]*

## EXPOSITION (11:2—12:2)

## The Jewish People Will Suffer Under Foreign Domination. (11:2–31)

Theological Point: God's people will face domination and hardship as earthly kingdoms fight for power.

Daniel's foretelling of history is structured around various Gentile kings: four kings of Persia (11:2); a mighty king whose vast realm will be "divided to the four winds of heaven" (11:3–4); various kings of the north and of the south (11:5–35); and "the king" who "will magnify himself above every god" (11:36–45). Whereas the message of the seventy weeks concluded with the destruction of the last earthly ruler at the end of the final seven years (9:27), the prophecy that unfolds from "the Book of Truth" (10:21) continues further to Michael's deliverance of the people from a time of great distress (12:1) and the resurrection of some to everlasting life and others to everlasting shame (12:2).

    A transition is marked at 11:2 by וְעַתָּה (*and now*), and from that point on the rest of the chapter details various Persian and Greek kings who will come on the scene between Cyrus and Antiochus Epiphanes. At 11:36 another transition occurs,[54] moving to "the king" who will appear at the future time of the end. The horrible conditions that developed under Antiochus will be intensified with that future king. Then chapter 12 brings

---

54. The transition is marked by a *waw* with a perfect (וְעָשָׂה, "and [he] will do") and the introduction of "the king" (הַמֶּלֶךְ).

the reader to "Michael, the great prince," who will fight on behalf of Daniel's people. **At 12:1 the phrase וּבָעֵת הַהִיא ("and at that time") signals the additional change of topic, but the reference back to "that time" synchronizes the appearance of Michael with "the king" of 11:36–45. The text moves, then, from the Persian and Greek period (11:2–35) to the final consummation of history and the resurrection of the dead (11:36—12:2).**

The detail given to the prediction of future events may seem unusual in this prophetic discourse. **Why was it important to predict the battles of all these kings, sometimes in vivid detail? First**, it is important to note that it is not possible to identify these kings from the book of Daniel itself; one can do that only after the fact. Now that the history of the period between Alexander the Great and Antiochus IV Epiphanes has been studied through ancient sources, it is possible to identify most, if not all, of the kings mentioned with historical figures. Even so, many details remain obscure, as is evident from various interpretations that modern historians have given to them. **Second**, the period in question (from the Persians to Antiochus IV) was of extreme importance to the Jewish people. It represented a time when various foreign nations ruled the land of Israel. Daniel 1–5 saw the Jews living in exile in Babylon, chapter 6 marked a transition to the Medo-Persians who allowed the Jews to return to their land, and chapters 8–11 fleshed out the political forces that raged around the Jews who had returned. **Third**, the period of foreign domination from Persia to Greece fits within the broader scheme of God's plan for his people that extends all the way to the resurrection of the just and the unjust. Chapter 7, which stands in the middle of the book, gave an overview of the entire period of foreign rule from Babylon to the final appearance of God's kingdom on earth. Daniel 11:36—12:13 then gives more detail concerning the future time of the end when all the kingdoms of men will be overcome by God's kingdom. Daniel 11:2–35 then fills in significant historical details prior to the messianic kingdom. **Fourth**, prophets who ministered prior to the fall of Nineveh in 722 BC, or the destruction of Jerusalem in 586 BC, also sometimes predicted these events with vivid details. Thus Nahum foresaw chaos within Nineveh at its last battle (esp. Nah 2–3), and Jeremiah predicted that the Babylonians would completely destroy Judah and its inhabitants, even naming Nebuchadnezzar as the conqueror and setting a limit on Babylonian rule at seventy years (e.g., Jer. 25).

We do not know how widely accessible Daniel's prophecies would have been to those Jews living under the Persians or the Greeks, but surely, they would have been a source of encouragement to any who could read them. Readers would discern that God had not given up on his people Israel. We do know that Daniel's book was known in the time of the Maccabees

(1 Macc 2:60) and that it was popular with the people who lived at Qumran and with Jesus and the writers of the NT (see the Introduction). And we know of a tradition recorded by Josephus[55] that when Alexander the Great entered Jerusalem he was shown Daniel's prophecy that a Greek king would destroy the Persian empire.[56]

### *Three Persian kings will arise, and a fourth. (11:2)*

"Three more kings of Persia" could be taken two ways, depending on the interpretation of "Darius the Mede" in 11:1. If Darius is another name for Cyrus, then the text must mean three kings following Cyrus. If Darius was a separate ruler from Cyrus, then Cyrus must be one of the "three more." Both the Old Greek and Theodotion have "Cyrus" instead of "Darius the Mede," although "Darius the Mede" is supported by a reading from the Dead Sea Scrolls.[57] The text also mentions a "fourth" ruler, and even assuming that Cyrus is not part of the three, more than four kings followed Cyrus the Great. The challenge, then, is to figure out which four kings are meant. What follows is a comprehensive list of the kings of the Persian empire.[58]

- Cyrus the Great (539–530 BC)
- Cambyses (530–522 BC)[59]
- (Pseudo-)Smerdis/Bardiya/Gaumata (522 BC)[60]

55. Josephus, *A.J.*, 11:337, cf. Dan 8:20–21; 11:3.

56. Speculation that the "Magi" of Matt 2:1, 7, 12, 16 may have descended from the wise men that Daniel worked with in Babylon could explain the tradition of the coming birth of a king of the Jews (MacArthur, *Matthew 1—7*, 27-28; Ferrari-D'Occhieppo, "Star of the Magi," 47). The history of the Magi is shrouded in mystery, and Maalouf (*Arabs*, 193-218) argued that they came from Arabia rather than Persia.

57. 4QDan<sup>c</sup>; Pace (*Old Greek Translation of Daniel 7—12*, 120) thinks the Greek reading is more original, but others consider the phrase or even the entire verse to be a gloss (Hartman and Di Lella, *Book of Daniel*, 285–86).

58. Compiled from Dandamaev, *History of the Achaemenid Empire*, 349–54.

59. Cambyses, the son of Cyrus, was made king of Babylon in 538 BC. He also conquered Egypt and was made king of that country.

60. Bardiya was the son of Cyrus the Great of Persia. According to both Herodotus, who rendered Bardiya's name as "Smerdis," and Darius's account in his inscription at Bisitun, Bardiya was murdered by his brother, Cambyses, but was later impersonated by Gaumata, a Magian, who was able to seize the throne when Cambyses died in 522 BC. The usurper reigned for eight months before he was slain by Darius Hystaspes and other Persian nobles suspicious of his origin (Yamauchi, *Persia and the Bible*, 138–140). Many historians consider that Darius invented the story of Gaumata to justify his actions (Olmstead, *History of the Persian Empire*, 109–11; Dandamaev, *History of the Achaemenid Empire*, 91; Allen, *Persian Empire*, 42).

- Darius I Hystaspes (522–486 BC)
- Xerxes (486–465 BC)[61]
- Artaxerxes I Longimanus (465–424 BC)[62]
- Xerxes II (424 BC)
- Sekyndianos (also spelled Sogdianos; 424–423 BC)
- Darius II Nothus (423–404 BC)[63]
- Artaxerxes II Mnemon (404–359 BC)
- Artaxerxes III Ochus (359–338 BC)
- Arses (338–336 BC)
- Darius III Codomannus (336–330 BC)[64]

Why does Daniel mention only four additional kings after Cyrus when there were twelve?[65] Collins, following Montgomery, thinks of the four Persian kings that are named in the Bible, namely Cyrus, Darius, Xerxes, and Artaxerxes.[66] According to Montgomery, "that the Jewish tradition had any memory of Xerxes' wars with Greece it is absurd to conceive."[67] Laato, to the contrary, observes that "Dan 11:2 fits in well with the historical situation at the beginning of the fifth century when the Persians attacked the Greeks at Marathon (490 BC), Thermopylai (480 BC), Salamis (480 BC) and Plataiai (479 BC)."[68] It may be "absurd" that an alleged Maccabean period author might not know this, but how then did such an author know about Belshazzar? Montgomery himself observes that outside of cuneiform documents contemporary with Belshazzar, that Babylonian king "had entirely disappeared from history except for the reff. in Dan." and sources that

---

61. Xerxes is most likely the Ahasuerus of the book of Esther.

62. Artaxerxes I was the king under whom Ezra and Nehemiah came to Judah.

63. Darius II is probably "Darius the Persian" mentioned in Neh 12:22 (Breneman, *Nehemiah, Esther*, 262), although Darius I is also a possible candidate (Williamson, *Nehemiah*, 364–65).

64. Alexander the Great conquered Darius III.

65. Jerome (*Commentary on Daniel*, 119) refers to Darius III as "the fourteenth king of the Persians after Cyrus," evidently counting both the real Bardiya and the alleged pseudo-Smerdis.

66. Collins, *Daniel*, 377; Montgomery, *Book of Daniel*, 423.

67. Montgomery, *Book of Daniel*, 423; cf. Laato, "Seventy Yearweeks," 212.

68. Laato, "Seventy Yearweeks," 215. To be fair, Laato thinks of an old tradition that lies behind Dan 11:2, not Daniel himself. But the point is that there is no reason to think that the author of Dan 11 has made a mistake.

were dependent on Daniel.⁶⁹ A real person named Daniel living in the sixth century BC, however, could be expected to know about Belshazzar and the early days of the Medo-Persian empire.

Goldingay and Baldwin take the numbers in verse two as a "graduated numerical saying." Other examples are found in Proverbs 30 and in Amos 1—2.⁷⁰ Thus, "the phrase may denote the Achaemenids as a whole," with the great wealth of the fourth representing the "accumulated wealth of the last Persian king."⁷¹ While Goldingay takes Greece as the object of the hostility, Baldwin posits that the text means that "Persian wealth will eventually invite attack from all, even the kingdom of Greece."⁷² The text, though, says that it is not wealth, but the king who had acquired power through his wealth who "will stir up all."

The majority view about what the fourth king does can be represented by the ESV: "He shall stir up all against the kingdom of Greece."⁷³ Baldwin objects that "against" is not in the text,⁷⁴ but Keil points out Exod 9:29, and 33, where the direct object marker אֶת indicates "the accusative as the object of the movement." Literally, "he will stir up the all toward the kingdom of Greece."⁷⁵

**As is apparent by now, it is difficult to decide how to render verse two correctly. The most likely view is the majority view, taking Xerxes as the fourth king. He was the one who amassed "great riches" and "stirred up" his army against the "kingdom of Greece."** Then the other three kings must come between Cyrus and Xerxes. Since Daniel's vision is dated to "the third year of Cyrus the king of Persia" (10:1), "three more kings" (עוֹד שְׁלֹשָׁה מְלָכִים) must refer to his successors.⁷⁶ Jerome named these kings as follows: Cambyses the son of Cyrus, Smerdis the Magian, and Darius. The fourth king he identified as Xerxes.⁷⁷ The reason why the remaining kings of Persia were not mentioned, according to Jerome, is because "the Spirit of prophecy was not concerned about preserving historical detail but in summarizing

---

69. Montgomery, *Book of Daniel*, 67.
70. Goldingay, *Daniel*, 294–95; Baldwin, *Daniel*, 185.
71. Goldingay, *Daniel*, 295.
72. Baldwin, *Daniel*, 185.
73. See Keil, *Ezekiel, Daniel*, 431; Miller, *Daniel*, 291.
74. Baldwin, *Daniel*, 185.
75. Keil, *Ezekiel, Daniel*, 431.
76. Some take the adverb עוֹד in the sense of "still" or "yet" and include Cyrus in the count (e.g., Porteous, *Daniel*, 158), but since Dan 10:1 makes it clear that Cyrus was already king, it is best to understand עוֹד as "more."
77. Jerome, *Commentary on Daniel*, 118–19.

only the most important matters."[78] It is important to note that for Daniel, history was constantly divided into four parts—the four main parts of Nebuchadnezzar's dream image (chap. 2), the four beasts (chap. 7), and the fourfold division of Alexander's empire (8:22; 11:4). True to form, Daniel notes only four Persian rulers, with the fourth representing the ruler who first aroused the wrath of the Greeks.

**Why was it important for Daniel to record this additional period of Persian rule? Aside from the pattern of four it would appear to be the issues of wealth and power in the Persian empire. God knew of the wealth and power that would be concentrated in Xerxes, leading him to lust for more by attacking the Greeks. Eventually the Greeks would be the downfall of the Persians, highlighting again Daniel's recognition that God "removes kings and raises up kings" (2:21).**

*The time for the kingdom of Greece will come, (11:3–35)*

The angel proceeded to relate to Daniel events that would extend from the time of Cyrus (10:1) to a "contemptible" tyrant who would be a usurper (11:21). This latter ruler is given the most coverage in the chapter, some fifteen verses (vv. 21–35).[79] Historically this person is known as Antiochus IV Epiphanes (175–164 BC).

**The historical details of Daniel's text can be filled in through ancient historians.[80] But it is important to remember that even though the predictions given through Daniel have been corroborated by history, the purpose of the passage is not to give a detailed history from Cyrus to Antiochus IV to the Antichrist. Only certain events with a theological purpose are selected for this revelation. They aim to demonstrate the futility of human struggles to gain power in the face of the sovereignty of God. They also deal with events that would impact the Jews, whether scattered in exile or living in Judea.**

---

78. Jerome, *Commentary on Daniel*, 119.

79. A common view among historical critics is that the verses about this king of the North, namely Antiochus IV Epiphanes, extend to the end of the chapter. The view that 11:36–45 deals with a king of the future who will have worldwide dominion will be defended and explicated in the next sectioon.

80. There is general agreement about the history of the period covered by Daniel 11:2–35, and more detail than what is presented here can be found in John Collins (*Daniel*). For modern works that discuss the history of the period see Walbank (*The Hellenistic World*), Grainger (*Seleukos Nikator*), and volumes six and seven of *CAH*. For information on ancient sources, including inscriptions and papyri, see Walbank (*The Hellenistic World*, 13–28). Translations of many of the pertinent sources may be found in Austin (*Hellenistic World*).

The first critical point was the rise of Alexander the Great, who defeated the Persians (11:3). Daniel 11:13 marks another critical point, with a new campaign that Ptolemy IV waged against Antiochus III. Ptolemy was able to repulse the advances of Antiochus into Palestine through a major victory at the battle of Raphia, southwest of Gaza. At that time many Jews also turned against Ptolemy (Dan 11:14). Despite this turn of events, Antiochus III was still able to regain control over Palestine. So it was that Seleucus IV, who succeeded Antiochus III, was able to send Heliodorus, the *oppressor* or *tax collector* of 11:20, through the land to increase the royal coffers by seizing treasures from the temple in Jerusalem (2 Macc 3). With the death of Seleucus IV the stage was set for Antiochus IV Epiphanes to wrest control of the north and to eventually interfere oppressively in the affairs of Judea and Jerusalem (11:21–35).

**Two general principles will help to interpret 11:3–35. First, abrupt shifts occur when moving from one king or realm to another.** For example, without prior historical knowledge it would seem most natural that the "king of the North" and the "king of the South" mentioned in verse five would be the same kings mentioned in verse six. The only contextual clue that they might be different is the phrase "after some years." From historical sources it appears that "the king of the North" in verse five would be Seleucus I Nicator, while in verse six he would be his grandson, Antiochus II Theos. Similarly, the earlier "king of the South" would be Ptolemy I Soter, while the later one, who gave his daughter in marriage, would be Ptolemy II Philadelphus. Daniel concerns himself here more with relations between the north and the south than with singling out particular kings, even as he focused on only a portion of the Persian empire that had special significance. The different kings of the North and the kings of the South are footnoted in the translation for Daniel 11:3–35.

**A second general principle for interpreting Daniel 11—the entire prophecy concerns world events that happen *in relation to Judah*.** If the four Persian kings are in fact monarchs from Cyrus to Xerxes, these are kings that played a special role in the restoration of the Jews to their land in Judea. When Alexander the Great amassed his vast empire, Judea became a significant part of it. And when Alexander's empire divided "to the four winds of heaven," the most important parts for Judea were Coele-Syria to the north and Egypt to the south, hence "the king of the North" and "the king of the South." The territory known as Coele-Syria, which included Samaria and Judea, was of major importance because it encompassed the heartland of the Jews.[81] Egypt was also significant because of the large number of

---

81. The realm of the Seleucid kings (of the North) included also Babylonia and Persia.

Jews that eventually settled in Alexandria. Israel is sometimes referred to as "the land between," always the crossing place for armies marching north or south.

## A MIGHTY KING AND HIS REALM (11:3–4)

**11:3–4.** The reference to Alexander the Great seems obvious in 11:3–4. He was the only king known to history who conquered a vast realm but whose empire was then divided "to the four winds of heaven." No sooner had Alexander conquered his vast empire than his death led to a division of the realm, not among his sons but among his commanders. For an interpretation of the division of Alexander's kingdom into four parts see the Exposition on 8:21–22.

A key to the importance of Alexander for Daniel's preview of history lies in the statement that "he will act as he pleases" (וְעָשָׂה כִרְצוֹנוֹ). The term רָצוֹן means *what is pleasing to someone* or *will*,[82] and it occurs four times in Daniel. In 8:4 it referred to the Persian empire symbolized by the ram that "was doing whatever it wanted." The other three instances are all in chapter eleven and refer to Antiochus III in his campaign against Egypt (11:16) and to the yet future ruler who will also "do as he pleases" and "exalt himself and magnify himself above every god" (11:36). Outside of the book of Daniel, the term also designates the will of God (Ps 40:8 [9]; 103:21; 143:10; Ezra 10:11).[83] **Daniel envisions a great clash of wills that will culminate in God's will enforced over all the earth. History has known many mighty tyrants and despots, but they have always been, and will always be, subject to God's will.**

## THE RISE OF THE KING OF THE SOUTH AND THE KING OF THE NORTH (11:5–6)

**11:5–6.** After the division of Alexander's kingdom, the revelation to Daniel narrows to two areas of special interest to the Jews in Judea—Egypt to their south and Syria to their north. Daniel revealed what history later recorded—the struggle between these two realms, with the Jews who had returned from exile caught in between. For Daniel the leader of Egypt became "the

---

82. *HALOT* 3:1282.

83. The participle of the Aramaic verb צְבָה (*to desire, wish for*) refers to God's *will* or *desire* in Dan 4:17 (14), 25 (22), 32 (29), 35 (32); 5:21.

king of the South," while the leader of Syria became "the king of the North." How these two realms developed is the topic of verses five and six.

The breakup of Alexander's empire was not a simple affair. His successors are known as the *Diadochi*, and there were several wars between various factions before the dust settled and kings were firmly in place over their realms.

Ptolemy I Soter was one of the main commanders at Babylon when Alexander died, and almost immediately he became satrap of Egypt. Later he tried to annex portions of southern Syria and Phoenicia. Near the end of the fourth century BC, he declared himself king—the first "king of the South." He is noted for making Alexandria the new capital of Egypt, a city that eventually had a large Jewish population, either from migration or exile.

Seleucus I Nicator, one of Alexander's officers, became the satrap of Babylon in 320 or 321 BC.[84] Eventually he was forced to flee to Egypt because of struggles among the *Diadochi*. There he served Ptolemy I, who eventually helped him to regain Babylon. After returning to Babylon, Seleucus declared himself a king and expanded his territory to India in the east and to Syria and large parts of Asia Minor in the west.[85] He was the first "king of the North" and had a vast realm.

Passing over some period of conflict between north and south, an attempt at alliance through marriage is singled out in verse six. Jerome identified the parties involved as Antiochus II Theos, the grandson of Seleucus I, and Berenice, the daughter of Ptolemy II Philadephus. Jerome continued his account, noting that Antiochus was already married to Laodice but promised to elevate Berenice to the position of "royal consort." Laodice then poisoned him. Berenice bore a son to Antiochus, but Laodice had him put aside in favor of Seleucus Callinicus as the heir to succeed Antiochus. Eventually Berenice and her son were both murdered by Antiochus II, and a new war broke out between Antiochus and Ptolemy III.[86]

**What was there about this incident that warranted its revelation to Daniel? The events seem especially depraved—intrigue, adultery, and murder. They remind us of "politics as usual," but they also hauntingly call to mind the incident of David and Bathsheba. The first son of their**

---

84. *Babylonian Chronicle 10* states that "the satrap of Akkad entered Babylon" in October or November of a year immediately prior to "the fifth year of Philip" (III of Macedon). Seleucus is named the satrap for that fifth year (Grayson, *ABC*, 115–16). Grainger (*Seleukos Nikator*, 32) has Seleucus become the satrap in 320 BC, but Whitehorne ("Seleucus," 1077) places the event in 321 BC.

85. For a detailed discussion of Seleucus I's rise to power see Grainger (*Seleukos Nikator*, 24–113).

86. Jerome, *Commentary on Daniel*, 121–22.

union died, and eventually their son Solomon did succeed to the throne. In the case of Antiochus and Berenice everything failed. Perhaps the coup that Laodice effected by getting her son to succeed to the throne instead of Berenice's son was a key factor in singling out this incident. It reaffirms the truth that Daniel emphasizes throughout the book—kings rise and fall at God's command. No matter how clever men might make their schemes, they must all bow to the fact that "heaven rules" (Dan 4:23).

### Southern domination of the North (11:7–12)

In verses seven to twelve the text emphasizes the great armies that would be amassed. It was a strategy that would ultimately prove ineffective to help either the northern or the southern king. The king of the North was defeated, and while the king of the South proudly exulted in his victory, he was unable to press his advantage. **In this way the prophecy emphasizes the futility of massive troop buildups. Also, the text demonstrates the inability of the false gods of the nations to bring any advantage to those who possessed them.** Ptolemy brought gods from the north to Egypt, but that did not prevent further attacks from the north or ultimately the shift of power from south to north.

11:7–9. The new king in Egypt was Berenice's brother, Ptolemy III Euergetes, "a shoot of her roots." The king of the North that he attacked was Seleucus II Callinicus, the son of Antiochus II Theos, who came to power by his mother Laodice. **The most striking thing about Ptolemy's successful attack was how he took Syrian idols and other articles of gold and silver to Egypt, a detail reminiscent of Nebuchadnezzar's capture of temple articles from Jerusalem (Dan 1:2).** Jerome says that Ptolemy brought two thousand and five hundred idols to Egypt, gods that had previously been taken to Persia by Cambyses when he conquered Egypt. Verses eight and nine summarize further activity between these two kings as a stalemate.[87]

11:10. The sons of Seleucus II were Seleucus III Ceraunus, the eldest, and Antiochus III the Great. According to Jerome, they "assembled an army against Ptolemy [IV] Philopator and took up arms." Seleucus III, however, was killed in Phrygia, so the army summoned Antiochus III the Great "from Babylon to assume the throne." Antiochus then advanced with the armies, waging war all the way to Ptolemy's fortress in Egypt.[88]

---

87. Jerome, *Commentary on Daniel*, 123.
88. Jerome, *Commentary on Daniel*, 123.

11:11-12. Ptolemy followed up with a counterattack, a battle that took place "near the town of Raphia at the gateway of Egypt."[89] Raphia is about twenty miles southwest of Gaza and a "strategic location on the frontier between Palestine and Egypt."[90] The huge army that Antiochus raised was "delivered into his power."

Ptolemy did not gain much from his great victory. He strengthened his control of southern Syria, Phoenicia, and Judea, and then returned to Egypt.[91] Assuming that verse twelve refers to Ptolemy, he would cast down myriads in his attempt to quash an internal rebellion in Egypt after the battle of Raphia.[92]

## Northern Domination of the South (11:13-19)

The next section of the prophecy focuses on Antiochus III the Great. Despite his defeat at the hands of Ptolemy IV, Antiochus was able to regroup, and this time gain a great victory. The importance of this new battle for Daniel and his people lay, however, in the participation of some Jews in the conflict. They would attempt to fulfill a prophetic vision (v. 14), but they would be unsuccessful. Furthermore, Antiochus would at long last wrest control of Judea ("the beautiful land," v. 16) from Ptolemy V, a momentous event. As if the shift in control of Judea from Egypt to Syria were not enough, Antiochus III also attempted to take over all of Egypt. Only the intervention of Scipio, the Roman commander, put a stop to Antiochus's ambitions. His failure was noted in verse nineteen: "He will stumble and fall and not be found." **These world-shaking events for the Jews in Judea and in Egypt were laid out through God's message to Daniel centuries before they happened.**

11:13-16. The new reference to the king of the North in verse thirteen still stands for Antiochus III. Ptolemy IV was kept busy with internal rebellion until his death, and Antiochus was able to amass another army, this time even larger than before. His attack was probably occasioned by the death of Ptolemy and the accession of his young son, Ptolemy V.[93] The battle referred to in these verses concerns a great conflict in 200 BC that culminated at Paneas, north of the Sea of Galilee at one of the headwaters of the Jordan River. The Egyptian forces were led by Scopus, Ptolemy's general,

---

89. Jerome, *Commentary on Daniel*, 124.
90. Keck, "Raphia," 622.
91. *CAH* 7:730-31.
92. Whitehorne, "Ptolemy (Person)," 543.
93. Ptolemy V was honored by the Egyptian priests in the famous Rosetta Stone.

and after their defeat Scopus fled to Sidon, the "well-fortified city" that Antiochus then besieged (v. 15). After Scopus surrendered to Antiochus III, the king of the North had control of Judea and Philistia as far south as Gaza.[94]

**11:14.** The "many (who) will stand against the king of the South" likely refers to the internal uprisings in Egypt during the early reign of Ptolemy V. A certain Agathoclea ruled the kingdom on behalf of the boy king. Jerome explains that "so great was the dissoluteness and arrogancy of Agathoclea, that those provinces which had previously been subjected to Egypt rose up in rebellion, and even Egypt itself was troubled with seditions."[95]

It is difficult to determine who are meant by the "violent ones from your people." They "will lift themselves up to cause a vision to stand, but they will stumble." Who are they? "What is the "vision"? And how did they "stumble"? Commentators are not unified in their answers. The earliest interpretation is found in the Old Greek. The translator read the word for "sons of" as "he will rebuild" (ἀνοιλοδομήσει), interpreting that "the king of Egypt" (Ptolemy) would rebuild the ruins of Daniel's people and attempt to fulfill the prophecy. Even so, the people would "stumble." In other words, it was expected that the kingdom could have been restored through Ptolemy, but that the effort was thwarted when Judea fell into the hands of Antiochus III instead.

Jerome relates the passage to the occasion when Onias the High Priest fled to Egypt with "a large number of Jews," where Ptolemy granted them permission to build a temple in Heliopolis. Onias thought he and his followers were fulfilling the prophecy found in Isa 19:19 about an altar of the Lord in Egypt, but their sin was "to offer blood-sacrifices to God in another place than what He had commanded."[96] Consequently, their city and temple were eventually destroyed. Jerome makes it sound as though the event described would be contemporary with the invasion by Antiochus III ("in those times"), but the migration of Onias III or his son to Egypt occurred only some years later.[97] Jerome's interpretation cannot be correct.

The term פָּרִיץ refers to thieves (Jer 7:11) or to those whose ways are violent (Ps 17:4; Ezek 18:10). Montgomery, based on Jerome, took it in a religious sense to mean those who broke God's law, noting that "the sense

---

94. Jerome, *Commentary on Daniel*, 126. Paneas is known in the NT as Caesarea Philippi and was the location for Peter's confession of Jesus as the Messiah (Matt 16:16).

95. Jerome, *Commentary on Daniel*, 125.

96. Jerome, *Commentary on Daniel*, 125.

97. Josephus has conflicting accounts of the event, with one account attributing the founding of the temple in Egypt to a son of Onias III (*A.J.* 12:237–388; 13:61–68, 383–88) and the other to Onias III himself (*J.W.* 1:31–33; 7:420–436).

'violent' must not be pressed."[98] Others prefer the nuance of "violence" or "robbers," and that is how it is defined in *HALOT*.[99]

The structure of the Hebrew indicates a contrast here. A huge force will stand against the king of the South, *but* these violent ones of Daniel's people "will lift themselves up" (יִנַּשְׂאוּ) to "cause a vision to stand." The use of the *Hithpael* verb emphasizes the independent action of the Jews over against the massive troops assembled by Antiochus.[100] It would seem, then, that the Hebrew better supports taking the "violent ones" as opponents of Antiochus rather than of Ptolemy. Goldingay also views them as opposing Antiochus, since they were defeated (וְנִכְשָׁלוּ, "they will stumble"), but Antiochus was victorious.[101] Others see these violent ones joining Antiochus III against Ptolemy, largely on the basis of Josephus, who notes that the Jews "readily joined his [Antiochus III] forces in besieging the garrison which had been left by Scopas in the citadel of Jerusalem."[102] To take the latter view one has to assume either that Scopas retaliated against the Jews in a campaign prior to his defeat at Paneas,[103] or that the "stumbling" involved the persecution under Antiochus IV.[104]

The Old Greek translator thought of the "vision" as the prophecy of Amos 9:11, which refers to "raising up" the "fallen booth of David."[105] What about the "vision" that Daniel's people tried "to raise up"? Another thought is that the vision pertains to Daniel's prophecy itself, either this prophecy in Daniel 11,[106] or more generally, to all of Daniel's prophecies.[107] According to another view, the people tried prematurely to bring about the final kingdom of the Lord.[108] Goldingay thinks of the "vision" mentioned in Ezek 7:26. The violent ones referenced in Daniel's vision would "unconsciously fulfill" the vision that Ezekiel described.[109] It's not impossible that the vision refers to the altar and a pillar dedicated to Yahweh in the land of Egypt (Isa 19:19),

---

98. Montgomery, *Book of Daniel*, 439–40.

99. Walvoord, *Daniel*, 262; Archer, "Daniel," 132; Miller, *Daniel*, 295.

100. The *taw* of the *Hithpael* has assimilated. Possibly, the *Niphal* could be read instead (*BHS*). Either way the action would be reflexive or reciprocal.

101. Goldingay, *Daniel*, 297.

102. Josephus, *A.J.* 12:133. See Zöckler, "Daniel Theologically and Homiletically Expounded," 244.

103. Porteous, *Daniel*, 163; Seow, *Daniel*, 174.

104. John Collins, *Daniel*, 380.

105. John Collins, *Daniel*, 380.

106. Archer, "Daniel," 132.

107. Wood, *Daniel*, 290.

108. Keil, *Ezekiel, Daniel*, 439–40.

109. Goldingay, *Daniel*, 298.

especially if the rebels were pro-Egyptian. The way the Hebrew of Daniel is phrased, it sounds as though these "violent ones" looked to a "prophet" among them who would "raise up" a vision for them. Tweaking Goldingay's view some, we could say that **when the people take matters into their own hands, one of their number will claim to have a prophecy concerning their success, but they will be defeated.**

11:15–16. After Scopas, Ptolemy's general, was overwhelmed at Paneas, he fled to Sidon, and that is evidently the "city of fortifications" that Antiochus III would capture. Scopas's "forces" (זְרֹעוֹת, lit. "arms") and "choicest troops" (עַם מִבְחָרָיו) will be unable to hold out, forcing Scopas to surrender. Nothing would stand in the way of Antiochus (v. 16), and he would then gain control of "the beautiful land," that is, Judea.

**The reference to "the beautiful land" brings out the main point of this section of Daniel's prophecy, namely, what will happen to Judea when Daniel's people live there. For many years it will be under the control of the various kings of Egypt, but then that control will shift to the Seleucid kingdom ("the king of the North"). And even though Antiochus III was largely benevolent toward the Jews, that momentous event will set the scene for the rise of Antiochus IV, a Seleucid king so cruel that he even became a type or foreshadowing of the future Antichrist.**

11:17. Verse seventeen refers to a plot by Antiochus III to conquer Egypt through diplomacy. The agreement that he concluded with Ptolemy V included a marriage between Cleopatra, Antiochus's daughter, and Ptolemy.[110] It is not entirely clear whether לָבוֹא בְּתֹקֶף כָּל־מַלְכוּתוֹ means that Antiochus planned "*to come* with the might of his whole kingdom" or "*to enter* into the strongholds of his [Ptolemy's] whole kingdom." The verb בּוֹא with the preposition בְּ often means "to enter into" something (e.g., Gen 31:33; Exod 8:3 [7:28]; Deut 23:25; Josh 2:18; Judg 7:17), but the combination can also mean "to come with" (2 Kgs 5:9; 2 Chr 22:1; 24:24). Either way, the sense is that Antiochus intended to follow up the peace negotiations with an invasion of Egypt. If he had succeeded in conquering Egypt, he would have brought under his control virtually all the realm that Alexander the Great had conquered. The prophecy, however, predicts the failure of this effort, an outcome confirmed by history. According to Jerome, Cleopatra sided with her husband and the plot fell through.[111]

11:18. Antiochus's plans for controlling Egypt having been thwarted, he turned his attention to the coastlands. Jerome claimed that Antiochus

---

110. Cleopatra was a common royal name, and this Cleopatra was not the one made famous through Shakespeare's *Antony and Cleopatra*.

111. Jerome, *Commentary on Daniel*, 127.

seized the islands of Rhodes, Samos, Colophon, Phocea, "and many other islands" in Asia Minor.[112] Even that action was thwarted, however, by a "commander" (קָצִין, cf. Josh 10:24; Judg 11:6, 11). Polybius noted that Antiochus, after being defeated in a naval battle, was given a list of terms by the Roman general Scipio.[113] Antiochus, who had once proudly taunted his enemies, was now humiliated by the terms of his agreement with Rome.

**11:19.** There was nowhere else for Antiochus to turn except to his own strongholds. This meant his territory on "the other side of the Taurus range."[114] There "he took refuge in Apamia and Susa and advanced to the easternmost cities of his realm." Finally, says Jerome, "during a war against the Elymaeans [Elamites] he was destroyed together with his entire army."[115]

**Daniel's rather detailed prophecy regarding Antiochus III lays out the rise and fall of one of the greatest of the Seleucid kings. He vastly expanded his realm and nearly conquered the known world. It was only the strength of Egypt and the might of Rome that was able to stop him. His greatest accomplishment from the standpoint of the Jewish people was that he wrested control of "the beautiful land" from the Ptolemies of Egypt.**

### Oppression of God's People (11:20-35)

Seleucus IV Philopator succeeded to the throne of his father Antiochus the Great in 187 BC. He reigned until 175 BC, but the only interest the book of Daniel shows in him concerns his minister Heliodorus, the "oppressor" or "tax collector" (נוֹגֵשׂ) who collected for "royal glory." Seleucus "inherited his father's great debts."[116] Thus it was necessary for him to obtain funds through taxation in order to sustain his "royal splendor."

Antiochus IV Epiphanes was the "contemptible" king who replaced his older brother Seleucus IV in 175 BC. The historian Polybius stated of him: "Antiochus surnamed Epiphanes ['(god) manifest'] gained the name of Epimanes ['madman'] by his conduct."[117] The book of 1 Macc called him "a sinful root" from the descendants of Alexander's generals (1:10).[118] The

---

112. Jerome, *Commentary on Daniel*, 127.
113. Polybius, *Histories*, 5:21.13–115.
114. Jerome, *Commentary on Daniel*, 128.
115. Jerome, *Commentary on Daniel*, 128.
116. Lucas, *Daniel*, 282.
117. Polybius, *Histories*, V:26.1.
118. English translations from the Apocrypha are from the NRSV unless otherwise indicated.

prophecy given to Daniel concerning the period of the Ptolemies of Egypt and the Seleucids of Syria comes to a climax in Antiochus Epiphanes, but we will also argue that at verse thirty-six the topic shifts to a king who, though patterned after the model of Antiochus, is an even more wicked and powerful king of the future, who will terrorize the world.

Jerome took all of chapter 11 from verse twenty-one to apply "prophetically" to "the Antichrist who is to arise in the end of time."[119] At the same time, he also saw Antiochus "as a type of the Antichrist, and those things which happened to him in a preliminary way are to be completely fulfilled in the case of the Antichrist."[120] While it is true that general features about Antiochus as described in verses twenty-one to thirty-five can also apply to the coming Antichrist, there are details about the career of Antiochus IV that will not necessarily be duplicated by the Antichrist. Revelation 13 focuses on the "haughty and blasphemous words" that the "beast" that will rise from the sea will speak. It uses metaphorical language to describe the Antichrist there, but Revelation has no interest in such detail about his career as we see in Daniel. **Even though the language is somewhat vague, Daniel's prophecy can be clearly traced in the historical career of Antiochus Epiphanes. Daniel 11:36 and following, however, just as clearly move to details that have not yet found fulfillment in history. It is safer, therefore, to think that Antiochus exhibited basic characteristics of the future Antichrist, not that the course of his career paralleled in detail the Antichrist. Daniel 11:36–45 gives more detail concerning the person of the Antichrist.**

11:20. It is most natural to read the object for the verb "send" as a series of nouns in relation to each other: נוֹגֵשׂ הֶדֶר מַלְכוּת ("a tax collector of glory of royal dominion"). If so, then the funds collected are to be for the "royal splendor" of Seleucus. Since Seleucus reigned for more than ten years, why does the text say that he would "be broken" after a short time? The Old Greek interprets that his demise would occur "in (the) final days" (ἐν ἡμέραις ἐσχάταις) of his reign. Theodotion translated it "in those days" (ἐν ταῖς ἡμέραις). **Possibly the text refers to the short time during which the murder of Seleucus was carried out, but it may be simply that his reign was predicted to be short and uneventful. Hence "a short while" may be hyperbolic to emphasize his insignificance.**

11:21–24. Antiochus IV assumed the throne through political scheming. The description of how his intrigues unfolded will follow largely Mørkholm's biography of Antiochus IV. After Heliodorus assassinated Seleucus IV,

---

119. Jerome, *Commentary on Daniel*, 129.
120. Jerome, *Commentary on Daniel*, 129.

he proclaimed the young son of Seleucus king, also named Antiochus. Many years prior to that event Antiochus IV, the brother of Seleucus, had been held in Rome as a hostage after their father, Antiochus III, had been forced by the Romans to agree to a treaty that stipulated huge sums of money to be paid in installments over many years. Evidently sending his son to Rome as a hostage was also part of the agreement. Eventually the Romans summoned Demetrius, the oldest son of Seleucus IV, to replace his uncle Antiochus (IV) as hostage. Thereupon Antiochus went to Athens, and while he was there, news arrived of the death of his brother Seleucus. At that point Eumenes II of Pergamum and his brother Attalus helped Antiochus take back the kingdom of Syria from Heliodorus. Exactly what happened to Heliodorus is uncertain, but Antiochus IV then ruled as co-regent with the young son of Seleucus for five years, after which Antiochus had him put to death.[121]

Daniel's prophecy anticipated the unusual way in which Antiochus IV Epiphanes obtained his throne. Being out of the country at the time that Seleucus died, he had to appear suddenly and take royal authority "through intrigues." The "overwhelming forces" mentioned in verse twenty-two are most likely the ones that Antiochus had to overcome with the help of his allies from Pergamum.[122] Archer and Miller refer the struggle with these forces to an Egyptian campaign,[123] but there is no reference here to the "king of the South." Collins prefers to see a more general reference to the king's standard mode of operation,[124] but verse twenty-three appears to continue the narrative about the king's rise to power: "He will grow strong with only a small number in a nation." That is, from a small number of supporters he will gradually gain complete control, perhaps a reference to the time when he became the sole ruler. The "alliance" of verse twenty-three likely refers to the help from Pergamum as well as those in his own nation that support him.[125]

---

121. A Babylonian king list from the Hellenistic era supplies the information, although it has to be interpreted. The list calls the young Antiochus the "son" of Antiochus, but it makes more sense that he was actually the son of Seleucus and the nephew of Antiochus. Seleucus was married to a Cleopatra who was his own sister. Probably Antiochus IV adopted his young nephew as his own son. The list states explicitly that the son was put to death "at the command of Antiochus." Diodorus Siculus (first century BC) and John of Antioch (seventh century) confirm some of this information (Mørkholm, *Antiochus IV*, 42–45). For the king list see Sachs and Wiseman ("Babylonian King List," 202–12).

122. Seow, *Daniel*, 176; Steinmann, *Daniel*, 525.

123. Archer, "Daniel," 136; Miller, *Daniel*, 299.

124. John Collins, *Daniel*, 382.

125. Wood (*Daniel*, 295–96), Walvoord (*Daniel*, 266), and Archer ("Daniel," 137) think of an alliance with Egypt, but none is known from history.

**11:22.** Verse twenty-two makes an obscure reference to "the prince of the covenant," who "will be broken." Some have thought of an ally who was betrayed, possibly Ptolemy of Egypt.[126] We have already noted that it is unlikely that Ptolemy would be referred to by anything other than the "king of the South." By far the most popular view is that this "prince of the covenant" refers to the murder of, or at least to the deposing of, the Jewish high priest, Onias III.[127] The murder of Onias is described in 2 Macc 4:30–34. Some conflicting material from Josephus indicates that Onias III was not murdered,[128] in which case the "prince of the covenant" may have been the young child nephew of Antiochus IV, who was in line for the throne and was killed by Antiochus IV. Whether Onias was murdered or not, Antiochus's nephew seems like a plausible possibility. The nephew would have been in line for the throne, and verse twenty-two tells about Antiochus's quick and forceful rise to power. The term *covenant* need not refer to the "holy covenant" (11:28, 30); for 9:27 and 11:22 it is at least possible that בְּרִית refers to a strictly human agreement (cf. Gen 21:27; 2 Sam 3:13; Amos 1:9; Obad 7; Ezra 10:3).[129]

**11:24.** Antiochus IV followed a general policy of acquiring "prestige and influence for himself and his kingdom throughout the Greek world" through monetary gifts.[130] According to 1 Macc 3:30 he was more lavish in his gifts than previous kings had been, and he exhausted his financial resources. That made it necessary for him to take unusual steps to enrich his treasuries. **The statement that he surpassed his predecessors presumably refers to the degree to which he exceeded them in his evil schemes and intentions. Anticipating what comes next, the text notes that the king's schemes will have a time limit. Not for long would this monstrous tyrant have free reign to carry out his plans.**

**11:25–28.** The "king of the South" would now be Ptolemy VI Philometor, the son of Cleopatra I, Antiochus's own sister. From history we know that Ptolemy's forces made the initial advance into Syrian territory about 170 BC, but Antiochus had prepared well for such an encounter.[131] The prophecy notes that it would be the king of the South who would "wage war" with his "exceedingly large army," and Antiochus would prepare

---

126. Miller, *Daniel*, 299.

127. John Collins says a reference to the murder of Onias in Daniel 11:22 "is universally accepted by modern scholars" (*Daniel*, 382); see Walvoord, *Daniel*, 265; Steinmann, *Daniel*, 526.

128. Josephus, *J.W.* 1:31–33; *contra A.J.* 13:62–73.

129. *Contra* Steinmann, *Daniel*, 526.

130. Mørkholm, *Antiochus IV*, 62.

131. Mørkholm, *Antiochus IV*, 73–74.

against such an advance with his own "great army." A resounding defeat was predicted for the king of the South, and Antiochus did win a decisive victory over the Egyptians at Mount Casius on the shore of the Mediterranean Sea, east of Pelusium.[132]

Antiochus did not follow up on his victory but "showed a prudent mildness against the vanquished enemy," probably an indication of his political ambitions to eventually extend his territory over Egypt.[133] He concluded an armistice after the battle and was willing to make peace due to the difficulties of an invasion of Egypt when the Nile was in flood and because he wanted "to make a favourable impression on the Egyptian army."[134] Eventually Antiochus reconciled with his nephew Ptolemy and took on the role of the younger man's tutor. It was apparently at this time that the two kings sat down at "one table" and spoke lies to each other. Antiochus was intent on eventually ruling Egypt himself, while Ptolemy had hopes of regaining control of Alexandria. The lies seem like standard political procedure, but telling them at a table set with food represented treachery of the worst kind. It violated standard oriental ethics of hospitality.[135]

Ptolemy, in the meantime, had "established a new government, appointing Cleopatra II, the sister of Philometor, and his brother, the younger Ptolemy, joint rulers."[136] Even though Antiochus laid siege to Alexandria, he was unable to take it. As the prophecy has it, "an end of the appointed time is still to come." Hebrew קֵץ here refers to the "end" of a period of time ultimately in the mind of God. **As was pointed out in the discussion on Dan 8:17, the prophecies revealed to Daniel apparently concern two "ends." One of them finds its climax during the persecution of the Jews under Antiochus, while the other one culminates with the second coming of Christ. The current passage focuses on the former time, although some reference to the final end before the second coming of Christ may not be entirely absent. At any rate, the prophecy stresses here that Antiochus's failure to press his advantage over Egypt relates to the fact that his appointed end had not yet arrived.** It will only arrive when Antiochus throws Judah and Jerusalem into turmoil with great persecution and many martyrdoms, presumably lasting until the king's death. Archer referred the "end" here to the end of Antiochus's campaign, elucidated by the reference

---

132. Mørkholm, *Antiochus IV*, 73–75.
133. Mørkholm, *Antiochus IV*, 74.
134. Mørkholm, *Antiochus IV*, 74.
135. Montgomery, *Book of Daniel*, 454.
136. Mørkholm, *Antiochus IV*, 85.

to his return to Syria in verse twenty-eight.[137] That seems unlikely in light of the combination with עוֹד, "still" or "yet," and מוֹעֵד, an "appointed time." It must be God who would appoint it.

**11:28.** When Antiochus returned to his capital city of Antioch in Syria, he took with him "great possessions." He apparently increased these possessions by plundering the temple of God in Jerusalem (1 Macc 1:20–24). As Daniel put it, "his mind will be set against the holy covenant."

**11:29–35.** The term מוֹעֵד (*appointed time*) frames the final section about Antiochus Epiphanes. It opens with a statement that these events will happen when the מוֹעֵד has arrived, and it closes with the statement that there is a מוֹעֵד that is yet to come (v. 35). The expression is fraught with tension. Now the prophecy will deal with a great agony that the Jews had to suffer under Antiochus. He will unleash his fury on them, bringing out the worst and the best of the people of Judea. Some will cooperate with the evil ruler and make it possible for him to carry out his plan to Hellenize the Jews, but others will go through a refining process that will result in loss of property, loss of homeland, and, for many, even loss of life. **The מוֹעֵד, however, also had an element of hope for the Jews. The time, difficult as it would be, was appointed by God. Everything was in his control; the faithful need not worry about this time when the world will seem to crash around them. The God who is sovereign over history itself knows all about it well in advance and has a purpose—he desires only to refine and purify his people. Better things were yet to come. The "one like a son of man" was yet to receive the kingdom, and the fallen were yet to rise in resurrection.**

**11:28–30.** When Antiochus realized that Ptolemy Philometor had rejoined forces with the people in control of Alexandria, he renewed his war with Egypt. The real power in the ancient world currently was neither the Syrians under Antiochus nor the Egyptians under Ptolemy; it was Rome. And it was Roman representatives, not an army, who confronted Antiochus when he was about to take Alexandria. Virtually everyone agrees that the "ships from Kittim" (צִיִּים כִּתִּים) refers to the Romans. The interpretation is found as early as the Old Greek translation of Daniel, which has Ῥωμαῖοι ("Romans"), omitting the term for "ships."[138] The term Kittim referred originally to Cyprus but came to apply to any of the coastlands of the Mediterranean Sea.[139] The prophecy in Daniel does not give a direct reference to the Romans, but history showed the specific fulfillment. According to Polybius, the Roman commander Popilius gave Antiochus a letter that ordered him

---

137. Archer, "Daniel," 138.
138. Cf. the Vulgate: *trieres et Romani* (*ships and Romans*).
139. BDB, s.v. כִּתִּים.

to cease the hostilities immediately. Antiochus wanted to discuss it with his advisors first, but Popilius drew a circle around Antiochus with a stick and told him that he must stay inside the circle until he had made his decision. Antiochus wisely decided to withdraw.[140]

The prophecy stated that the "ships from Kittim" would intimidate the king, alluding to a pronouncement given by Balaam in the time of Moses (Num 24:24). Steinmann notes that Balaam had predicted not only the action of the Kittim against Assyria and the Hebrew people, but also the eventual destruction of the Kittim people. And since Balaam's prophecy of "a star from Jacob" and "a scepter from Israel" can be taken as messianic, the implication in Daniel is that "the Messiah foreseen by Balaam will come shortly thereafter (in the era of the Kittim, the Roman era)."[141] Steinmann's conclusion is possible, but the difficulties interpreters have with the Balaam oracles lend some uncertainty to that conclusion.[142] First Macc 1:1 infers that the Kittim are Greeks. Thus the term can be used of more than one group of people.

Having been thoroughly intimidated by the arrival of the Roman fleet, Antiochus would then return to Syria. Then in a rage (זָעַם) he would take action "against the holy covenant" and turn to "those who forsake the holy covenant." The verb בִּין (*to pay attention to*) here indicates that Antiochus would listen to those who had forsaken their God, taking their advice about how to handle the Jewish situation.

**11:31.** Antiochus's troops profaned the temple in Jerusalem, here called "the sanctuary, the fortress" (הַמִּקְדָּשׁ הַמָּעוֹז). The phrase may refer to the entire temple or to some part of it that was especially fortified.[143] The troops would remove, according to the prophecy, "the regular service" (הַתָּמִיד) and install "the abomination that devastates" (הַשִּׁקּוּץ מְשׁוֹמֵם). Exactly what the Hebrew meant is not clear. The phrase occurs in slightly different forms in Daniel 8:13 (הַפֶּשַׁע שֹׁמֵם, "the transgression that devastates"), in 9:27 (וְעַל כְּנַף שִׁקּוּצִים מְשֹׁמֵם, "and on a desecrated place he will make desolate"), and in 12:11 (שִׁקּוּץ שֹׁמֵם, "a devastating abomination").[144] Matthew 24:15 and Mark 13:14 follow the form found in the Old Greek when they quote Jesus' sermon to his disciples concerning the future of the temple—τὸ βδέλυγμα

---

140. Polybius, *Histories*, VI:29.7.
141. Steinmann, *Daniel*, 529.
142. Ashley, *Numbers*, 509–10.
143. See Montgomery, *Book of Daniel*, 457.
144. In 8:13 and 12:11 the root שמם occurs in the *Qal* pattern, while here (11:31) and in 9:27 it is in the *Polel* pattern. Most see a similar denotation despite the varying forms, although some suggest textual corruption as well (cf. *HALOT*).

τῆς ἐρημώσεως ("the abomination of the devastation").[145] The Greek phrase (without the article) also occurs in 1 Macc 1:54: "he [Antiochus] erected an abomination of devastation on the altar." Most likely Daniel's prophecy refers to the altar of burnt offering on which unclean sacrifices were offered, possibly pigs (1 Macc 1:47). Jerome referred to some who mentioned "an image of Jupiter Olympus in the Temple at Jerusalem, and also statues of Antiochus himself."[146] Perhaps Jerome was thinking of 2 Macc 6:2, which refers to calling the temple in Jerusalem "the temple of Olympian Zeus." Jupiter is the Roman equivalent for Zeus. Since "the abomination that devastates" replaced "the regular service," an altar with sacrifices seems more likely than a statue. The passage in 2 Macc doesn't have to imply anything more than that Antiochus dedicated the temple to Olympian Zeus.[147]

**11:32-34.** It is well known that Antiochus did not carry out his actions against orthodox Judaism unilaterally; he had cooperation from more liberal Jews within the nation (cf. 1 Macc 1:43, 52). **These would be those who "act wickedly toward the covenant" (11:32), and they undoubtedly included many of the important religious and political leaders. The "smooth words" (חֲלַקּוֹת) by which they were corrupted refer to subtle lies or flattery (Ps 12:3 [4]; Prov 26:28).**

**Despite the capitulation of some there would also be many who would continue faithful to God and "act courageously."** The prophecy probably doesn't mean the Maccabees at this point, who took to armed resistance, for verse thirty-three emphasizes those who are faithful to the point of martyrdom. The Maccabees may be meant by the "little help" of verse thirty-four, those who "will join up with them [the faithful] insincerely."[148] **Daniel appears to maintain a non-violent posture throughout his book. His three companions spoke boldly but also trusted in their God to deliver them from Nebuchadnezzar's fiery furnace (3:16-18). Likewise "those who are wise among the people" (מַשְׂכִּילֵי עָם) will teach (יָבִינוּ) others how to maintain their faith in a time of great persecution.**

**11:35.** The key teaching of verses twenty to thirty-five comes with verse thirty-five. God has a purpose in mind; he desires "to refine, purge, and purify" his people until the end of this era of persecution. Armed

---

145. The Greek texts of Daniel lack the article. Th has "destroyed" (ἠφανισμένον) instead of "devastated."

146. Jerome, *Commentary on Daniel*, 134.

147. Many commentators since Nestle ("Zu Daniel," 248) assume that the שִׁקּוּץ שֹׁמֵם refers through a play on words to the Phoenician god "Baal-shamem" (e.g., Montgomery, *Book of Daniel*, 388; Collins, *Daniel*, 357; Lucas, *Daniel*, 245). Lust ("Cult and Sacrifice in Daniel," 675-77) gives strong arguments against this idea.

148. The term חֲלַקְלַקּוֹת (*insincerely*) is a variant form of חֲלַקּוֹת (*smooth words*).

resistance would be taking matters into their own hands; instead, they will wait patiently for the appointed time to come to its end.

Those who remain faithful to God in the face of persecution are called *the wise* (הַמַּשְׂכִּילִים, *hammaskilim*). They are wise, but theirs is a special kind of wisdom. They have *insight* into the ways and purposes of God. They can remain faithful because they understand the difference between the empty promises of political leaders and the true rewards of serving God. They will have an inheritance in the kingdom of God that will last forever.

## The Jews Will Be Ultimately Tested by the King at the Time of the End. (11:36–45)

Theological Point: The Faithfulness of God's People Will Be Decisively Tested Under the Reign of the Antichrist.

A break in thought occurs at verse thirty-six, but there is still continuity with the discussion about Antiochus IV. The end of Antiochus himself has not been revealed, but the language about tyranny that has been prevalent throughout the section intensifies into the rise of a monstrous tyrant who sets himself up in total opposition to God. **Daniel describes this one as the ultimate foe of God, using language that goes far beyond what history allows for Antiochus IV. For those who think that the author of the book wrote in the second century BC, disguising his historical report in the language of prophecy, it is at this point that the alleged author attempted genuine prophecy but failed to get things right. That is a move that is unworthy of inspired Scripture. False prophecy does not emanate from God (Deut 18:20–22; Jer 14:13–14; 28:9). It makes more sense to seek a reason consonant with God's purposes for the shift in mood at verse thirty-six.**

Throughout history tyrants have come and gone. That is a major theme of the book of Daniel: God "removes kings and sets up kings" (Dan 2:21). No tyrant can abide forever. Sooner or later he or she departs from the scene and is replaced by someone else. **Verse thirty-five left the reader pondering the way that the righteous suffer for their faith, wondering when God will act on their behalf. They must be satisfied with the word that "it remains for the appointed time." It is comforting, though, because it reveals that God is in control of the time; he has appointed it.** Then the message shifts to "the time of the end" (v. 40), the time when the fiercest tyrant of all will seemingly dominate the faithful with absolute power. As always, the faithful need to wait for the end, but the full flowering of wickedness will signal the absolute end to all the kingdoms of men. **The persecution of the faithful will be severe, but Michael will fight for God's people, and those faithful who have fallen in the past will be raised to new life so they can enjoy the eternal kingdom that God has prepared for them (12:2).**

**Some structural details of verses thirty-six to thirty-nine show that the section marks a break with the discussion about Antiochus and moves on to the ruler of the end times. First, the conjunction** *waw* (*and*) **joined with a verb in the perfect and followed by the subject tends to mark a new section (Dan 11:3, 7, 13, 20, 21).** This pattern occurs in verse 36, with "according to his will" between the verb (*and he will do*) and its subject (*the King*). **Second, a new title is used here for the first time, "the King."** Elsewhere Antiochus IV had been referred to as "a contemptible person," a usurper (v. 21), and one who acts "deceitfully" (v. 23). **Third, in other places the prophecy jumps from one king to another without warning**, most notably at 11:6 where the "king of the South" must be Ptolemy II, not Ptolemy I as in verse five, and at 11:11, where "the king of the South" is now Ptolemy IV, not Ptolemy III as in 11:7–9. **Fourth, a parallel is made between this new king and Alexander the Great.** The sentence "he will do as he pleases" is said of both rulers (vv. 3 and 36). The wording appears also in 11:16, but there the parallel with 11:36 is not as close as at 11:3.[149] At any rate, the parallelism between Alexander the Great and this new "king" takes the rhetoric to a new level. **Fifth, "the time of the end"** (עֵת קֵץ) **at the close of verse thirty-five is picked up again in verse forty and reiterated in 12:4, 9.**[150]

Even as a reference to the "time of the end" marked the close of the previous section dealing with Antiochus Epiphanes, so within 11:36–45 another reference to that same "time of the end" divides between its two main parts at verse forty. The first part details how this proud king will do whatever he pleases, not allowing any god or even the "God of gods" to stand in his way (11:36–39). Curiously, though, he will honor a god who will accompany him into battle. The identity of that god will be discussed later.

**The King will be wildly successful in his endeavors, but the text repeats twice that God will put a limit on his accomplishments. The King may "speak wondrous things against the God of gods," but an end to his indignations has been predetermined (v. 36).** The second part (11:40–45)

---

149. וְיַעַשׂ הַבָּא אֵלָיו כִּרְצוֹנוֹ ("and he will do, the one who comes against him, according to his will").

150. Steinmann, *Daniel*, 539.

details the king's accomplishments, but also the end of this fiercest foe of God's people.

## The religious character of the King (11:36–39)

The coming king will be filled with pride, doing whatever he pleases and placing himself "above every god." He will even "speak wondrous things against the God of gods." That is, he will say blasphemous things about the God of Israel, Daniel's own God. God's people will be astounded that he would dare to utter such things against the God who is above all gods. This future king must be identical to the "little horn" that Daniel saw in his first vision (7:8). This horn will utter boastful words (7:8, 11, 20) and will "wage war with the saints" (7:21). The angel who interpreted that vision for Daniel also said that "he will speak words against the Most High" (7:25).

**11:37a.** The prophecy elaborates on the king's unholy pride by stating that he will have no regard for "the gods of his ancestors." This is an especially difficult claim for those who think that the text continues to deal with Antiochus Epiphanes. Mørkholm refuted any idea that Antiochus replaced the worship of Zeus with Apollo.[151] Collins calls the phrase "problematic" and explains it as "deliberate polemical distortion" to make Antiochus look as bad as possible.[152] While hyperbole is not unknown in the writings of the Hebrew prophets, it is possible to recognize it as a rhetorical device where it occurs. It seems simpler to assume that the text is not speaking any longer of Antiochus; it has moved on to another figure who is yet to come. And that figure will have no regard for any of the gods that his ancestors had worshiped.

One conservative line of interpretation translates אֱלֹהֵי אֲבֹתָיו as "the God of his fathers," as in the KJV and NKJV. If the text refers to the God of Israel, then the ancestors of the coming king would necessarily be Jewish.[153] It is doubtful, however, that this rendering is correct. In its favor is the fact that אֱלֹהִים always means *God* when paired elsewhere with the term אָבוֹת (*ancestors* or *fathers*). Nevertheless, **the context makes it clear in those other places that Israel's God is meant. In the near context of 11:37, an unambiguous singular, either אֵל or אֱלֹהַּ, is used for *God* or *god*.**[154] **Add to this that the Greek tradition uniformly has the plural "gods of his**

---

151. Mørkholm, *Antiochus IV*, 131; cf. Goldingay, *Daniel*, 304.
152. Collins, *Daniel*, 387.
153. Gaebelein, *Prophet Daniel*, 188; Charles Feinberg, *Daniel*, 174–75.
154. See also Walvoord, *Daniel*, 273–74; Wood, *Daniel*, 306; Archer, "Daniel," 144–45.

fathers." Based on this passage there is little reason to think that the coming king will be Jewish.

**11:37b.** The "desire of women" (חֶמְדַּת נָשִׁים, v. 37) has perplexed many interpreters. The expression can mean either that the women are desired, or that they are the ones who desire. Sandwiched between "the gods of his ancestors" and "any god," it likely refers to some deity known as "the desire of women." It is unlikely that it means the king's desire for women,[155] or that it points to the Messiah that Jewish women desired to birth.[156] Many commentators have thought of the god Tammuz (also known as Adonis among the Greeks) in light of Ezek 8:14,[157] but reference to such a specific god among very general references also seems unlikely. It would presuppose the view that Antiochus is still under discussion in verse thirty-seven. We would suggest two possibilities. For one, it might add to the all-inclusiveness of the statement. The king will not pay attention to the gods of his ancestors, to any god that even women would desire, or to any god at all. Or it might refer to a goddess—the king will not worship any god at all whether male or female.

**11:38a.** It is interesting that the king will not only exalt himself above every god and reject the gods of his ancestors; he will also honor the "god of fortresses." How is it that this "god of fortresses" is not included in the expression "above every god"? According to one explanation, the "god of fortresses" is not literally a god but only a manifestation of the king's trust in his own military might.[158] He will set this "god" on a pedestal by amassing his military forces and relying on them and his own military prowess to accomplish his goals. The vast amount of plunder that he garners from his expeditions will then be his "offerings" to honor this "god." This will indeed be a "foreign god" (v. 39), in that for a human leader to trust completely in himself and not rely on any other god would be a foreign idea.[159]

Another explanation holds that the king will in fact have a god that he will honor that others have not recognized. Since he will be a god that has not been worshiped previously, it is not possible to identify him with any known god from the ancient Near East. Therefore, he would not be included in "every god" of verse thirty-six. Charles Feinberg and Gaebelein

---

155. Jerome, *Commentary on Daniel*, 464–65; Archer, "Daniel," 144.
156. Gaebelein, *Prophet Daniel*, 188; Charles Feinberg, *Daniel*, 175.
157. Montgomery, *Book of Daniel*, 461–62; John Collins, *Daniel*, 387.
158. Edward Young, *Prophecy of Daniel*, 249; Walvoord, *Daniel*, 275–76; Steinmann, *Daniel*, 543.
159. Keil, *Ezekiel, Daniel*, 465–66.

connect this unknown god with the beast of Rev 13:1–10,[160] who represents the "head of the revived Roman empire."[161] The "king" of Dan 11:36–45 would then be the Antichrist of Revelation 13:11–17. According to the latter passage he will make "the earth and its inhabitants worship the first beast, whose mortal wound was healed" (Rev 13:12, ESV). It seems more likely, however, that the first beast of Rev 13:1–8 represents the Antichrist described in both Daniel 7 and 11. Phillips thinks that the Antichrist's god will be Satan himself.[162]

**Whoever the king's god is, the king will overcome mighty strongholds and gain the power to distribute land to all who recognize his authority. The Revelation of John apparently picks up on these deeds and expounds on them in his description of Rev 13:1–8.**

## *The military exploits of the King (11:40–43)*

The angel who delivered the prophecy to Daniel reinforced the time reference—it is "in the time of the end." The terminology changes again in this section from "the King" to "the king of the North" and "the king of the South," raising the question whether "the king of the North" is the same person as "the King" of the previous section or someone else. Walvoord and Sprinkle suppose that "the King" is the Antichrist who was then attacked by both the king of the North and the king of the South.[163] Sprinkle notes that seeing three kings rather than two "allows one more readily to identify the king [not identified as of the North or the South] here with the little horn figure of Daniel 7."[164]

It may help to consider why such cryptic language has been used throughout chapter 11 rather than something more specific, like "the king of Syria" and "the king of Egypt." The directions are given from the standpoint of Judah and Jerusalem; they stand in the middle of all this back-and-forth warfare. The historical fulfillment for 11:5–35 involved Syria and Egypt, but for the present passage (11:40–43) it is not necessarily true that the same countries would be involved. Some commentators have tried to identify specific countries according to their own contemporary situation, only to have that situation change to something entirely different. A Russian ruler

---

160. Charles Feinberg, *Daniel*, 176; Gaebelein, *Prophet Daniel*, 188.
161. Charles Feinberg, *Daniel*, 176.
162. Phillips, *Book of Daniel*, 210.
163. Walvoord, *Daniel*, 277; Sprinkle, *Daniel*, 327.
164. Sprinkle, *Daniel*, 327.

has been suggested, for example,[165] but since the fall of Communist Russia in the late twentieth century that does not seem as pertinent.[166] Comparison with Ezekiel 38–39 could be helpful except that there are many conflicting opinions about it. Wood equated the battle described by Ezekiel with the battle in Dan 11:40–43, whereas Walvoord thought that the battle described in Daniel occurred later than that in Ezekiel.[167] Archer wisely cautioned that it is better to stay with the details as they are found in Daniel rather than to bring in issues from elsewhere.[168] Block associates the nations mentioned in Ezekiel with areas in western Asia Minor.[169] **As with all of the prophecies given in Daniel 11, exact historical identification is not possible until the events have already happened. The details are vague enough that they could be applied to many different scenarios, but they are also specific enough that once they have been fulfilled, it will be clear what was meant. The purpose for the prophecy was not to write history in advance but to give broad outlines of where the future was headed.**

To return to the original question about the relationship between "the king" and "the king of the North," it seems simplest to equate them as the same individual.[170] If "the king" were a third party attacked by both north and south, then some more specific identification would be expected. Jerome also equated the king of the North with Antichrist, noting as well that Porphyry continued to identify him with Antiochus.[171]

"The king of the North," also known as "the king," must be the ruler over some area that can be described as "north." The area of Syria seems too restricted, but exactly what is meant by the "north" is still unclear. Directions in the OT are often based on practical considerations rather than strict geography. Since Judah and Jerusalem were normally invaded from the north, even Babylon, more east than north, could be considered a northern invader (Jer 1:14; 6:22). The invader could have his capital as close as Damascus or as far away as Rome or Moscow. Since the fourth empire of chapters 2 and 7 was possibly Roman, Rome could be in view. Even so, the

---

165. Wood, *Daniel*, 308–9.

166. The נְשִׂיא רֹאשׁ in Ezek (38:2, 3; 39:1), taken as "the prince of Rosh" by NASB 1995 and the NKJV is better translated as "chief prince" (Block, *Ezekiel 25—48*, 434-35). Virtually all other English translations have "chief prince," including the NASB 2020 and the KJV. Even if "Rosh" is adopted, as in the LXX, that doesn't necessarily mean that it refers to Russia (see Block, *Ezekiel 25—48*, 434-35).

167. Wood, *Daniel*, 309; Walvoord, *Daniel*, 277–78.

168. Archer, "Daniel," 147.

169. Block, *Ezekiel 25–48*, 436.

170. Archer, "Daniel," 147; Miller, *Daniel*, 309–10.

171. Jerome, *Commentary on Daniel*, 139.

nebulous nature of the fourth empire, having in some fashion continued even until the present day, would seem to point to other possibilities.

The king of the South would apparently still refer to Egypt or at least to some country in that general region, since plunder from Egypt, Libya, and Cush are mentioned in verse forty-three. It is the southern kingdom or coalition that will initiate the conflict, but the king of the North will defeat that kingdom with overwhelming force. Those commentators who refer these verses to the end times generally understand that the instruments of war that are mentioned are those that would be familiar to Daniel's original readers; however, more modern equivalents will actually be used.[172]

The "glorious land" (אֶרֶץ הַצְּבִי) refers to the land of Judah. Various OT prophecies mention an invasion of Judah in the end times (Isa 29:1–8; Ezek 38–39; Joel 3:1–2 [4:1–2]; Zech 12; 14:1–5; Mal 4:1 [3:19]), but their relationship to the invasion described in Dan 11:41 is uncertain. Charles Feinberg equates the battle described in Zechariah 12 and 14 with Armageddon (Rev 16:16).[173] Walvoord places the battle between the kings of the north and south later than the battle mentioned in Ezekiel 38—39. He argues that the attack mentioned in Ezekiel comes when Israel is at peace (Ezek 38:8, 11, 14) and therefore should be "when Israel is in covenant relationship with the Roman ruler and protected from attack." The conflict that Daniel references, on the other hand, occurs in "the period of world rule."[174] Miller agrees with Whitcomb and Wood that both Ezekiel and Daniel depict the same battle that will take place in the middle of the tribulation period,[175] because "two separate conflicts within such a short period of time (approximately three years) on the massive scale described in Ezek 38–39 and Dan 11:40–45 seems a virtual impossibility."[176]

Why should Edom, Moab, and the Ammonites "escape from his [the king of the North's] power" (11:41)? A more basic question concerns the referent for these nations in a time when they no longer exist as such. They comprise modern day Jordan but were viewed by Daniel under their more ancient identities. The reason why the king of the North should bypass them is unclear. Perhaps their geographical position east of the Jordan River will not fall within the line of march. Such an explanation could be implied by the reference to a rapid attack: "He will enter countries and sweep through

---

172. Wood, *Daniel*, 310; Archer, "Daniel," 147.
173. Charles Feinberg, *Daniel*, 172.
174. Walvoord, *Daniel*, 277–78.
175. Miller, *Daniel*, 310–11; Whitcomb, *Daniel*, 161; Wood, *Daniel*, 311.
176. Miller, *Daniel*, 310.

them like a flood" (v. 40). Jerome thought that the Antichrist would bypass them because "the saints are to flee thither to the deserts."[177]

### *The downfall of the King (11:44–45)*

The king will perish while encamped "between the seas at the glorious holy mountain" (בֵּין יַמִּים לְהַר־צְבִי־קֹדֶשׁ). The "seas" are the Mediterranean and the Dead Sea, with Jerusalem due east of the northern end of the Dead Sea. The mountain would then be the temple mount. It is quite certain that Antiochus Epiphanes met his end in a different way. According to 1 Macc 6:1–16, he died in Persia upon hearing the news that the Jews had routed his armies and taken back the temple in Jerusalem. The king in these verses cannot be equated with Antiochus. It is uncertain what rumors will lure the king to Jerusalem, but he will go there with murderous intent. There he will meet his doom with no one to help him. His final destination is the lake of fire (Rev 19:20), a fate that he will share with those who will be resurrected "to shame and everlasting contempt" (Dan 12:2).

## Michael Will Deliver the Jews, and the Resurrection Will Happen. (12:1–2)

Theological Point: God's people can endure as they remember they will be delivered, and a resurrection will happen.

The time frame of 12:1–2 overlaps with 11:36–45. Both describe a period of great persecution against the Jews, but the latter passage brings into focus "the king," while the present passage focuses on the deliverance of God's people. **The king or Antichrist will rise and fall, but those who are "wise" in the ways of God will rise never to fall again. Even those who have fallen in the past will be brought back to life to inherit the everlasting kingdom. Michael, "the great prince," will participate in delivering the redeemed Jews from their unprecedented "time of distress."**

While it is important to determine the meaning of an OT text in its own context before considering data from the NT, much of the book of Revelation covers the same timeframe as what is prophesied in Daniel. Particularly for chapter 12 of Daniel it will be helpful to look at Revelation 12—20 for additional details that will help to unlock some of the mystery of Daniel's vision.

177. Jerome, *Commentary on Daniel*, 140.

**12:1a–b.** Michael will arise to fight against the forces of the Antichrist in the great tribulation that the Jews will experience at the time of the end. Revelation 12:7–9 depicts a battle that takes place in heaven between Michael and his angels and the "dragon" or Satan himself. After Satan is cast down to earth, he then begins to persecute "the woman," who represents the Jewish people (Rev 12:13). She is hidden in "the wilderness" and protected by the elements from further harm (Rev 12:17).[178]

**12:1c.** The future distress for the Jews under the Antichrist is mentioned in Dan 7:25; 9:26–27; and 11:41. Elsewhere in Scripture this period of tribulation is referenced in Zeph 1:14–18; Zech 11:15–16; 14:1–2; Mal 4:1; Matt 24:15–22; Mark 13:14–20; Luke 21:20–24; 1 Thess 5:2–3; and Rev 13:7. For a discussion about the "book" containing the names of people who are to be delivered, see the Exposition of 10:21.

**12:2a.** It has been noted often that Dan 12:2 is the clearest reference to a resurrection of the dead in the Old Testament.[179] It is also sometimes considered to be the only such reference;[180] but while the doctrine of the resurrection in the OT is somewhat sketchy in comparison to the teaching of the NT, it can be found elsewhere in the OT.

A few commentators have attempted to think of a metaphorical rather than a literal resurrection. This was apparently Porphyry's solution, who took the reference to apply to "guardians of the Law, who had been, as it were, slumbering in the dust of the earth . . . ."[181] In this way he could apply the passage to the Maccabean period even though a general resurrection did not happen then. In more recent times, some conservatives have also given a non-literal interpretation to the passage.[182] They consider the resurrection figurative "of the national revival of Israel in that day," appealing to Isaiah 26 and Ezekiel 37 for analogous metaphorical uses of resurrection imagery.[183] While the "dry bones" of Ezek 37:4 are typically applied to Israel in the return from exile,[184] Isa 26:19 is more controversial with regard to a real or a figurative resurrection. Sawyer calls this passage "a reference to the resurrection of the dead which no-one but a Sadducee, ancient or modern,

---

178. For further discussion about Michael, see the Exposition of 10:13.

179. Walvoord, *Daniel*, 285; Steinmann, *Daniel*, 560; Pace, *Daniel*, 337; hesitantly, Goldingay, *Daniel*, 306–8.

180. See John Collins, *Daniel*, 394–95.

181. Jerome, *Commentary on Daniel*, 146–47.

182. Gaebelein, *Prophet Daniel*, 200; Ironside, *Daniel the Prophet*, 231.

183. Gaebelein, *Prophet Daniel*, 200.

184. Even if the reference is only to a "resurrection" of the nation, Ezek 37 still illustrates the concept of the dead coming back to life.

could possibly misconstrue...."[185] Motyer sees that "the terms of [Isa 26:19] go beyond the figurative to the literal and declare a full resurrection, including the resurrection of the body. Within the progressive revelation of the OT only Dan 12:2 is comparable."[186] That is, the "resurrection" in Isa refers to the Lord's promise to provide salvation for "all peoples" and to ultimately "swallow up death forever" (Isa 25:6–7). Daniel enlarges on that promise by noting that bodily resurrection will mean everlasting life for some and everlasting abhorrence for others. Daniel 12:2 also shares some vocabulary with Isa 26:19. *Awaken* occurs as an imperative in Isa (הָקִיצוּ) and an imperfect in Dan (יָקִיצוּ), and *dust* (עָפָר) is mentioned in both verses. Moreover, the two passages share "the explicit contextual setting of apocalyptic eschatology."[187]

That it is "many" (רַבִּים) who will be resurrected has occasioned much controversy. Augustine thought that the term was used instead of *all*. He compared the meaning of Abraham's name, "father of many nations," with the covenant promise that "all the nations of the earth" will receive a blessing through Abraham's descendants.[188] His example lacks force in that "many nations" in Abraham's name does not mean the same thing as "all nations" in the covenant. Theodoret of Cyrus also argued that *many* meant *everyone*, but he based his view on the Apostle Paul's statement that "many died through one person's fall" (Rom 5:15).[189] He grounded the argument on Greek usage, though, rather than Hebrew usage. Steinmann also sees *many* as an alternative expression for *all*, but he provides a more pertinent example in Isa 2:2–3, where "all the nations" and "many peoples" have a parallel relationship.[190] While this shows that it is possible for רַבִּים to imply the same as *all*, it by no means proves the case for Dan 12:2. Here there was no need for a parallel term, so if Daniel meant *all*, why did he choose the term *many*? Based on a broader investigation of how רַבִּים is used grammatically, Hasel demonstrates that a partitive usage is meant in Daniel. That is, it must mean *many* selected from the group in question, as in Esth 8:17 (cf. 2 Chr 30:18).[191] Keil argues that while the *many* refers explicitly to Daniel's people Israel, implicitly it means "all peoples who belong to God's kingdom

---

185. Sawyer, "Hebrew Words for the Resurrection," 234.
186. Motyer, *Prophecy of Isaiah*, 219.
187. Hasel, "Resurrection," 276.
188. Augustine, ACCS 13:304.
189. Theodoret of Cyrus, *Commentary on Daniel*, 319.
190. Steinmann, *Daniel*, 560.
191. Hasel, "Resurrection," 279.

of the New Covenant founded by Christ."[192] Edward Young follows the same line of thought:

> We may paraphrase: "At the time of this persecution many shall fall, but thy people, who are written in the book, shall be delivered. Likewise, from the numbers of those who are asleep in the grave many (i.e., those who died during the tribulation) shall arise. Of these, some shall arise to life and some to reproach." The words, of course, do not exclude the general resurrection, but rather imply it. Their emphasis, however, is upon the resurrection of those who died during the period of great distress.[193]

Not everyone thinks that Daniel's wording implies a general resurrection. Maimonides (twelfth century) thought that only the righteous would be rewarded by resurrection.[194] For Saadiah Gaon (tenth century) only the righteous will live; unbelievers who died without repentance will remain in the grave.[195] His view is also followed by some modern scholars.[196]

The way the Hebrew is constructed, it is clear that the same event of resurrection will happen to both groups but with different outcomes. Here is a literal rendering of the Hebrew:

> And many of those that sleep (in) the ground of dust will awaken,
> these to life everlasting
> and these to shame, to contempt everlasting.

Close parallels to this construction may be found in 2 Sam 2:13 and Ps 20:8 (9; cf. 1 Kgs 10:19, 20; Zech 5:3). The *awakening*, according to the grammar of the Hebrew, should happen to both groups. One group will "awaken to life everlasting," while the other will "awaken" to "shame" and "contempt everlasting." An explanation for the term *many* cannot be sought in restricting the *awakening* to only the first group.

**The best solution to how to interpret *many* lies in seeing different times for the resurrection of the two groups. The wicked will not be raised to everlasting shame and contempt until after the righteous are raised to everlasting life. The righteous will be raised first. It is also possible that the prophecy delivered to Daniel focuses on those martyred**

---

192. Keil, *Ezekiel, Daniel*, 481–83.
193. Edward Young, *Prophecy of Daniel*, 256.
194. Goldwurm, *Daniel*, 321.
195. Goldwurm, *Daniel*, 320.
196. Culver, *Daniel and the Last Days*, 175; Hartman and Di Lella, *Book of Daniel*, 308; Hasel, "Resurrection," 279; Spronk, *Beatific Afterlife*, 340–41; Péter-Contesse and Ellington, *Handbook on the Book of Daniel*, 324; Smith-Christopher, "Book of Daniel," 148.

during the reign of the Antichrist and those responsible for their deaths. This would also account for the collective focus of the prophecy ("your people"). Daniel's *people* will escape, whether through the help offered by Michael or through resurrection from the dead. And justice will be served by the judgment of all of the enemies of the Jews. This would also involve resurrection at two different times, for the enemies of the Jews would be resurrected to "everlasting shame" only at the time when the rest of the wicked dead enter into that condition. In this view the rest of the dead, whether righteous or wicked, are simply not covered by this particular prophecy.

The Hebrew phrase חַיֵּי עוֹלָם ("life everlasting") is unique to Dan 12:2, but the concept occurs elsewhere. In the book of Proverbs חַיִּים (*life*) by itself often refers to relationship with God, particularly when it is symbolized by the "tree of life" (Prov 3:18; 11:30; 13:12; 15:4) or the "fountain of life" (Prov 14:27; 16:22). "In sum, 'life' in the majority of Proverbs texts refers to abundant life in fellowship with God, a living relationship that is never envisioned as ending in clinical death in contrast to the wicked's eternal death (see 2:22–23)."[197] In Prov 12:28 the term *life* is paralleled by *immortality* (אַל־מָוֶת), and in Ps 16:11 the "path of life" (אֹרַח חַיִּים) is further explained as "fullness of joy" in God's presence and "eternal pleasures" at his "right hand." According to Ps 73:24 there is an *afterward* when God will receive the psalmist to himself. *Life* could sometimes refer, then, to an abundant life that consists in a relationship with God that will never end.[198]

The term דִּרְאוֹן (*abhorrence* or *contempt*) occurs only here and in Isa 66:24. The similarity between the two passages points to a relationship between them. The wicked dead, whose *contempt* will last forever, appear in both verses. Isaiah's prophecy uses the imagery of an undying infestation of worms and an unquenchable fire to stress the eternal nature of the fate of the wicked.

---

197. Waltke, *Proverbs 15—31*, 105.
198. See also Johnston, *Shades of Sheol*, 200–206.

| Table 11.1: The Kings of the North and the Kings of the South ||| 
|---|---|---|
| Reference | King of the North | King of the South |
| 11:5 | Seleucus I Nicator<br>312/311–281 BC | Ptolemy I Soter<br>323–282 BC |
| 11:6 | Antiochus II Theos[199]<br>261–246 BC | Ptolemy II Philadelphus<br>282–246 BC |
| 11:7 | Seleucus II Callinicus<br>246–225 BC | Ptolemy III Euergetes<br>246–222 BC |
| 11:8 | Seleucus II | Ptolemy III |
| 11:9 | Seleucus II | Ptolemy III |
| 11:10 | Seleucus III Soter<br>225–223 BC<br>Antiochus III the Great<br>223–187 BC | Ptolemy IV Philopator<br>222–204 BC |
| 11:11–12 | Antiochus III | Ptolemy IV |
| 11:13 | Antiochus III | Ptolemy IV |
| 11:14 | Antiochus III | Ptolemy V Epiphanes<br>204–180 BC |
| 11:15–16 | Antiochus III | Ptolemy V |
| 11:17 | Antiochus III | Ptolemy V |
| 11:18–19 | Antiochus III | Ptolemy V |
| 11:20 | Seleucus IV Philopator<br>187–175 BC | |
| 11:21–24 | Antiochus IV Epiphanes<br>175–164 BC | |
| 11:25–26 | Antiochus IV | Ptolemy VI Philometor<br>180–145 BC |
| 11:27 | Antiochus IV | Ptolemy VI |
| 11:28 | Antiochus IV | |
| 11:29–30b | Antiochus IV | Ptolemy VI |
| 11:30c–31 | Antiochus IV | |
| 11:32–34 | Antiochus IV | |
| 11:35 | Antiochus IV | |
| 11:40 | The Antichrist | Uncertain |

199. Coregent with his father, Antiochus I, from 268 BC.

## SHARPENING THE THEOLOGICAL FOCUS

When discerning what Dan 11:2—12:2 teaches about God, it is important to remember two things. First, the introduction to the vision found in chapter 10 reveals that everything that is predicted to happen reflects spiritual warfare between the forces of God and evil forces that lie behind what is happening on earth. Second, the people of God in this passage, the Jews, are caught in the middle of all the world-changing events that are described. With Cyrus they were allowed to return to their land, but many, like Daniel, stayed behind in Babylonia and Persia. Despite much opposition, those who did return were eventually able to establish themselves in Judah, rebuilding Jerusalem and the temple.[200] There they experienced the continual marching of troops through their land, the forces of Egypt or Syria passing through to engage each other in battle. The people had no real independence, as political control of Judah passed from Persia to Alexander to Egypt and to Syria. They were at the mercy of their overlords.

None of these things, according to Daniel, escaped the attention of the God of the Jews, the God who had made a holy covenant with them. He was aware of the course of history and had determined in advance its end. The faithful could have hope that God's forces were destined to win the ultimate victory over the kingdoms of this world. And they could know that if they endured, even to the point of death, resurrection to everlasting life was in their future.

In chapters 11 and 12, and indeed in the entire book of Daniel, God was laying out a prototype of human history that will in many ways repeat itself until the resurrection. Tyrannical rulers arise again and again, often inflicting suffering on the people of God. These rulers fall, giving relief to the afflicted, but before long other rulers arise. For believers, obedient faithfulness is what is required. They may not be able to discern all that God is doing on earth, but they can still know that in the end God triumphs. And that is enough to endure any persecution, even martyrdom.

According to the book of Daniel, the faithful servants of God are marked by wisdom, and that becomes particularly clear in chapters 11 and 12. The "wise ones" (מַשְׂכִּילִים, *maskilim*), who "make many understand" how to serve God will themselves suffer most severely at the hand of tyrants (11:33). These same "wise ones" will resurrect to eternal life and "shine like the brightness of the sky" and "like the stars forever and ever" (12:3). Daniel himself is the quintessential "wise one," imbued with understanding and insight by God himself (1:17, 20; 5:11, 14; 9:22). All of the court stories in

---

200. See Ezra, Neh, Hag, Zech, and Mal.

some way demonstrate the superior wisdom of Daniel and his three companions, superior precisely because they were "servants of the Most High God" (3:26). Daniel attributed all his wisdom to God (2:23, 30). Believers gain wisdom as they learn from God through his Word, through his Spirit, and through serving him. Wisdom like the wisdom of Daniel and his companions is available to all who will seek it through a personal relationship with Jesus Christ (1 Cor 1:24; Eph 3:8–11).

As has been repeatedly noted, the book of Daniel brings out the sovereignty of God in every chapter. Chapter 11 focuses attention on his omniscience by demonstrating his ability to predict future events in rather startling detail. As stated previously, though, the purpose of the chapter is not to give a detailed history from Cyrus to Antiochus IV. The selection of events had a theological purpose, namely, to demonstrate the futility of human struggles to gain power in the face of the sovereignty of God. Thereby the chapter also highlights the omnipotence of God.

## THE FOCUS OF DANIEL 11 FOR PREACHING AND TEACHING

As the narrative moves to the vision itself in chapter 11, notice how God's sovereignty over the details of history and the futility of earthly leaders and kingdoms is emphasized through the description of their demise.

- "But when he has risen his kingdom will break up and be divided..." (v. 4)
- "But she will not hold on to a position of power...she will be given over..." (v. 6)
- "But [he will] return to his own country." (v. 9)
- "But that multitude will be delivered into his power..." (v. 11)
- "But [he] will not prevail." (v. 12)
- "But they will stumble." (v. 14)
- "But it [his plan] will not hold up, and it will not come about for him." (v. 17)
- "But a commander will put a stop to his taunting of him..." (v. 18)
- "But he will stumble and fall and not be found." (v. 19)
- "But in a short while he will be broken, but not in anger or in battle." (v. 20)

The earthly battles rage, and eventually reach a crescendo with Antiochus IV (vss. 21–35), who attacks God himself and severely persecutes God's people. But even he is not the worst that God's people will have to face. The climax of this last vision is the ascent of a "king of the north" who is greater and more evil than even Antiochus, the Antichrist. This king will appear in the final days to persecute God's people, but, as has been proven time and time again in Daniel, God will sovereignly deliver his people, even raising them from the dead. He will fully and finally exalt them in his glorious and everlasting kingdom (12:1–3).

This final vision ties together several key themes that have been present throughout the book: God's sovereignty, the fruit of faithfulness, and the rise and fall of kingdoms. With regard to God's sovereignty, the details of history recorded in Daniel's final vision emphasize that God has ordained what will happen in the "book of truth." God doesn't just know generally what is going to happen, he knows specifically what, and when, things are going to happen. The evil empires that cycle through history are not surprising to God. The world leaders and systems who stand stubbornly opposed to God's rule and his people are not thwarting God's plans. Rather, they are a part of God's plans. They rise to power and are dethroned not by the whims of history, but by the governing hand of God. We don't have to wonder if their end will come, for God has already determined when their end will come.

Because God is sovereign and because he will one day, fully and finally, impose his rule and kingdom on earth, God's people can be hope-filled and faithful. God's sovereignty is meant to encourage us toward faithfulness. Because God is sovereign, we can trust that he will fully and finally vindicate the faithful. Throughout the book God has graciously responded to, and rewarded, Daniel's faithfulness. This is highlighted in chapter 10, as God graciously responds to Daniel's prayers for understanding. Even more, here at the end of the vision, God explicitly reveals that, like he has done for Daniel, he will respond and reward our faithfulness, too. One day God will deliver "everyone whose (name) is written in the book" and "awaken [them]. . .to life everlasting."

Until the appointed time, the battles and persecutions will continue. Of this we can be sure. And while much of Daniel has focused on the rise and fall of earthly kingdoms and on earthly wars, here in chapters 10 and 11, the curtain is pulled back and we are confronted with the truth that these earthly battles are only a small part of a great war being waged in the spiritual realm. This should motivate God's people to seek God's wisdom so that we can faithfully navigate life in the crosshairs of those who oppose God.

PROPHETIC HISTORY

## FROM TEXTUAL WORK TO TEACHING

## The Big Idea

- *Exegetical Idea:* God gives Daniel a final vision, which reveals the rise and fall of future kingdoms, the ongoing persecution of God's people, and their ultimate hope of resurrection and exaltation as it has been ordained in the book of truth.
- *Theological Focus:* Earthly kingdoms will continue to rise and fall and rebel against God and persecute his people until God destroys the final rebellious leader, the Antichrist, and delivers his people from persecution, raises them from the dead and exalts them in his eternal kingdom.
- *Preaching Idea:* Be encouraged and wise for one day God will fully and finally eradicate evil and vindicate his people.

## Outline One: Following the Exegetical Flow

I. God's people will face domination and hardship as earthly kingdoms fight for power. (11:2–31)

    A. God's people have historically faced domination and hardship; it's nothing new.

        1. Under the Persian empire (11:2)

        2. Under the empire of Greece (11:3–35)

    B. For much of church history God's people have faced domination and hardship, and the "Gates of Hell" have yet to prevail.

II. The faithfulness of God's people will be ultimately tested under the reign of the Antichrist. (11:36–45)

    A. God's people will continue to face great hardship.

    B. Knowing that the domination and hardship imposed by the Antichrist is part of God's plan will help God's people to endure.

III. God's people can endure as they remember they will be delivered and resurrection is coming. (12:1–2)

    A. The "time of distress" will come to an end and everyone whose name is written in the book of life will be delivered.

B. There will be a resurrection, some to everlasting life, and others to everlasting condemnation.

## Outline Two: Following a Theme

In addition to specific revelation about future rulers and empires that God's people would/will have to endure, chapter 11 portrays discernable patterns. It portrays the pattern of sins characteristic of those who oppose God; it portrays the persistent conflict that God's people will face; and it portrays the faithfulness of God's response. Focusing on these patterns can bring a cohesive structure to the sermon and help listeners to not get lost in the details.

- Patterns of sin characteristic of those who oppose God and his people:
  - Lust for power and wealth
  - Idolatry
  - The chase for military might
- Persistent clashes that God's people will face:
  - God's people will be caught in the crossfire between warring nations.
  - God's people will be blamed for the failures of world leaders.
  - God's people will have to deal with the internal corruption stirred up by those who aren't faithful.
  - God's people will face the temptation to take matters into their own hands and not wait on God's timing.
- God's faithful response
  - He will bring an end to every single kingdom that opposes him.
  - He will finally judge all those who opposed him and his people.
  - He will vindicate and reward those who wisely followed him.

# Waiting Patiently for God to Act
(Daniel 12:3–13)

**Chapter 11 Review**: Daniel 11:2—12:2 subtly demonstrates God's sovereignty over history through predicting historical details before they occur. The prophesied events start with the transition from Judah under Persian rule to the consequences of Alexander the Great's conquest of the ancient world. The focus shifts to conflicts between the South (Egypt and the Ptolemies) and the North (Coele-Syria and the Seleucids), with Judah caught in the middle. The prophetic history climaxes with the rule of the Seleucid king Antiochus IV Epiphanes. His wicked treatment of the Jews who remained faithful to the Torah set a pattern that will apply to the final ruler at the end of the age, the Antichrist.

**Chapter 12 Summary**: Daniel 12:3–13 acts as the denouement to the climax of Dan 11:2—12:2. Those who have acted wisely will be rewarded with everlasting glory; the wicked will be assigned to everlasting shame. Daniel's questions cannot be answered, but God's kingdom will come and the faithful must wait patiently for it.

## THEOLOGICAL FOCUS OF CHAPTER 12:3–13

ONLY THOSE WHO DILIGENTLY seek God's wisdom will find it and have great reward in the kingdom of God. Those who trust in God need to remain faithful and wait diligently for the eschatological end.

I. *Only those who diligently seek God's wisdom will find it, and those who do will have great reward in the kingdom of God. (12:3-4)*

II. *Those who trust in God need to remain faithful and wait for him to act, regardless of the circumstances, for the eschatological end. (12:5-13)*

## BIG PICTURE (12:3-13)

After conclusive remarks regarding the "wise" and Daniel in 12:2, Daniel surprisingly received another revelation. He sees two heavenly figures ask a third figure how long it would be until the end of these eschatological events. Upon hearing the answer to that question Daniel queried further about the outcome of these events. The angel responded not with an answer to his question, but with a final charge to be faithful to the end of his life and to look forward to his future resurrection and inheritance. Whereas the charge to Daniel in verse four concerns sealing the *book*, in verse thirteen it concerns Daniel himself.

The last eleven verses of Daniel function as an epilog that ties together various elements of Daniel's visions, which is prompted by his interest in the timing of the events at the end of the age. Like the disciples of Jesus who inquired about the *when* of his return, but could not be told (Acts 1:6), once Daniel heard about the resurrection and the fate of the righteous and the unrighteous, he was informed that any more specific information was unavailable. The words of the book had to be carefully preserved until the *end* would finally arrive. People would try to understand the book, but only the "wise" would be able to understand it. Spiritual discernment is required to learn wisdom from God's Word.

## TRANSLATION (DANIEL 12:3-13)

3   Then the wise ones will shine like the brightness of the sky,

   and those who lead many to righteousness like the stars forever and ever.

4   Now as for you, Daniel, close these words by sealing the book until the time of the end. Many will rush about that knowledge may increase.

## WAITING PATIENTLY FOR GOD TO ACT

5     Then I saw, I Daniel, and look, there were two others standing there, one at this side of the bank of the river[1] and one at the other side of the riverbank.

6     Then (one of them) said[2] to the man clothed in linen who was above the waters of the river, "How long to the end of these astonishing events?"

7a     Then I heard the man clothed in linen who was above the waters of the river when he raised his right hand and his left hand toward heaven and swore by him who lives forever that (it will be),

7b     "For a time, times, and half (a time).

7c     When the shattering of the power of the holy people is complete, all these (things) will be finished."

8     Now I myself heard, but I did not understand. Then I said, "My lord, what will be the outcome of these things?"

9     Then he said, "Go, Daniel. For these matters are closed up and sealed until the time of the end.

10     Many will be purified, cleansed, and refined, but the wicked will continue to act wickedly. None of the wicked will understand, but the wise will understand.

11     Now from the time when the regular service is removed to the setting in place of a devastating abomination[3] (there will be) 1290 days.

12     Any who wait and reach 1,335 days will be worthy of congratulations.[4]

13     And as for you, continue to the end. You will rest, and you will rise to your allotted portion at the end of the days.[5]

---

1. While הַיְאֹר normally refers to the Nile, in this case it should be the Tigris on the basis of Daniel 10:4.

2. The OG has "I said" (εἶπαν); the Syriac *Peshitta* has "and they said."

3. The *Qal* form of the verb should have the stative sense of *desolation*. The *abomination* will be a *desolation* for the people of Israel.

4. We translate אַשְׁרֵי as "worthy of congratulations" in order to capture the sense that this is something to live up to, "an ideal to emulate," as Leslie Allen puts it (*Psalms 101–150*, 242).

5. *The days* (הַיָּמִין) is a blended form, having a Hebrew definite article (*the*) and the vowel *ā* rather than *ô* but an Aramaic plural ending, much like the book of Daniel, which consists of both Hebrew and Aramaic portions.

## TEXTUAL OUTLINE (12:3–13)

I. The Wise Will Be Greatly Rewarded in God's Kingdom. (12:3–4)

*[Only those who diligently seek God's wisdom will find it and those who do will have great reward in the kingdom of God.]*

   A. The wise will shine gloriously in the kingdom of God. (12:3)

   B. The foolish will not understand the message of Daniel. (12:4)

II. The Man Clothed in Linen Reviews Details about the Eschatological End and Encourages Daniel to Continue in Faithfulness. (12:5–13)

*[Those who trust in God need to remain faithful and wait for him to act, regardless of the circumstances, for the eschatological end.]*

   A. The man clothed in linen reveals the timing of the eschatological end. (12:5–7)

   B. Daniel asks for further explanation. (12:8)

   C. The man clothed in linen reveals what the end times will entail. (12:9–12)

   D. Daniel is told to continue in faithfulness awaiting his allotted portion. (12:13)

## EXPOSITION (12:3–13)

### The Wise Will be Greatly Rewarded in God's Kingdom. (12:3–4)

Theological Point: Only those who diligently seek God's wisdom will find it and those who do will have great reward in the kingdom of God.

*The wise will shine gloriously in the kingdom of God. (12:3)*

**12:3. In stunning language the angel reveals the glorious future of those who faithfully seek and follow God's ways.** The poetry is classic for its use of parallelism and sense of balance, as the following layout shows. (A dash is used to join English words that are a single word in the Hebrew.)

| and-the-wise-ones | | will-shine | like-the-shining-of | the sky |
| and-those-who-lead-to-righteousness | the-many | like-the-stars | | forever and-ever |

**Remembering that it is God who "gives wisdom [חָכְמָה] to wise men and knowledge to those who have understanding" (Dan 2:21), it is clear that "the wise ones" who will receive such honor are those who have been faithful to him.** The term מַשְׂכִּלִים (*maśkilîm, wise ones*) is a special type of wisdom that refers to *insight* or *understanding, wisdom* being the more general term. *Maśkilîm* occurs five times in the book of Daniel (1:4; 11:33, 35; 12:3, 10). When Nebuchadnezzar first issued his call for youths to be trained in the Babylonian ways, one quality he demanded was that they be *maśkilîm* (1:4). He thought only of special skill in tasks that required wisdom and insight, but Daniel and his friends were already *maśkilîm* in the unique sense of those whose *wisdom* or *insight* derived from their God. They first demonstrated that *skillful insight* when Daniel suggested the test of ten days to see if their diet of vegetables would obtain superior results to Nebuchadnezzar's provision of fine foods and wine. **Similarly, in chapters 11 and 12 the *maśkilîm* are those who continue in the ways of God despite persecution and even martyrdom. Their wisdom is in their insight into the truth. The *maśkilîm* also teach others the way of faithfulness to the Lord (11:33) and are therefore called "those who lead many to righteousness." In contrast to the wicked, who face everlasting shame at their resurrection, these *maśkilîm* will be rewarded with honor that compares with the bright stars in the sky.**[6] They have not only acted according to the righteousness of God, but they have also faithfully encouraged others to abandon wickedness and follow God.

Isaiah's "Servant of Yahweh" would also *act wisely* (יַשְׂכִּיל) and be *highly exalted* (Isa 52:13), and it may be that the *maśkilîm* in Daniel are purposely identified with this Servant.[7] Spronk meant his remarks to equate the Servant of the Lord in Isa 52:13 with the *maśkilîm* in Daniel, but Sprock's idea does not have to exclude that the Servant in Isa was an individual. The Servant of the Lord is the *wise one* (מַשְׂכִּיל) *par excellence.*

*The foolish will not understand the message of Daniel, because it is hidden from them. (12:4)*

**12:4.** One point of view concerning סְתֹם (*seal, close*) is that Daniel was commanded to keep the book *secret*, hidden away from view. Those who take the

---

6. Miller, *Daniel*, 319–20.
7. Sprock, *Beatific Afterlife*, 341.

prophetic standpoint of the book as a literary fiction think that the secrecy went along with that fiction. Since they allege the book was written in the second century BC, its claim to having been issued by a prophet in the sixth century BC would be bolstered by stating that it had been kept hidden in the intervening period.[8] It takes a lie to support a lie, but that hardly seems worthy of a book so widely accepted and cherished in ancient times as Daniel.

Others have thought that during the reign of Cyrus, the prophecy was not understood, but that as time progressed ever closer to the eschatological end it would be increasingly understood. Thus, it was hidden from the original readers but now is much clearer because of proximity to the end of the age.[9] Its main target audience would then be those living in the age of the Antichrist and the great tribulation.[10] Baldwin takes a similar view but in a "metaphorical" sense. The issue is "spiritual stupor," much like the situation described in Isa 29:9–11. The prophecy of judgment that Isaiah delivered became "like words of a sealed book." The people could not understand because of their spiritual blindness.[11] A similar explanation lies behind the parables that Jesus taught (Matt 13:14–15). "[M]uch that was of value was hidden except to those who wanted it sufficiently to give all in exchange for it (Matt 13:44, 45)."[12]

Under Baldwin's view, the spiritual blindness would have to continue to the point marked by *the end* (cf. Gen 15:16). This is also the force in Dan 11:35; those who have insight (the *maśkîlîm*) into the truth of the Lord will continue to experience refinement through persecution and even martyrdom *as far as* or *until the time of the end*. That parallel use lends support for Baldwin's view. **The book is not so much kept secret until the generation that lives during the end, as it is withheld from those who are not part of the *maśkîlîm*, those who lack spiritual insight.** Such a view avoids the difficulty that a part of God's revelation was not really intended, at least in its full force, for the generation that received it. This is particularly true if the statement is meant to apply to Daniel's entire book and not merely to the prophecies found in chapters seven to twelve.[13]

Another view is that Daniel was to *preserve* the book so that the faithful could learn from it in generations to come. The *sealing* of the document,

---

8. Porteous, *Daniel*, 171; John Collins, *Daniel*, 399.
9. Walvoord, *Daniel*, 291.
10. Miller, *Daniel*, 321.
11. Baldwin, *Daniel*, 206.
12. Baldwin, *Daniel*, 206; the twelfth century Jewish scholar Ibn Ezra thought that "none but the worthy" should see Daniel's book (Goldwurm, *Daniel*, 323).
13. See Keil, *Ezekiel, Daniel*, 320–21.

then, would not refer to making it obscure or inaccessible, but affirming its truth as God's word.[14] This view is not mutually exclusive with the view that the book was for the *maśkîlîm* but not for those who reject the Lord.

That people are said to *rush about* (יְשֹׁטְטוּ) refers to intense effort to look for something.[15] In two places in the OT it refers to the *eyes of Yahweh* that search throughout the earth, looking to see what might have some relevance for the people of Israel (2 Chron 16:9; Zech 4:10). God told the prophet Jeremiah to rove through the streets of Jerusalem in search of a man of integrity (Jer 5:1). Amos, a prophet of Israel in the eighth century BC, spoke of a time when the people of Israel will "run to and fro" in a fruitless search for "the word of Yahweh" (Amos 8:12). It is probably this last image that inspired Daniel's. From his day to the end of the age many people will be in a mad rush to obtain knowledge of things that will always elude them unless they turn to the Lord.[16] The *knowledge* people seek can be found in the prophecies of Daniel, but only the *wise* (*maśkîlîm*), that is, those who have insight, will find it. Those who rush about seeking knowledge need to have their eyes opened by the God who "gives wisdom to wise men and knowledge to those who have understanding" (Dan 2:21). With eyes to see they may simply meditate on Daniel's words, not *rush to and fro* in a vain effort to obtain knowledge.

## The Man Clothed in Linen Reviews Details About the Eschatological End and Encourages Daniel to Continue in Faithfulness. (12:5–13)

Theological Point: Those who trust in God need to remain faithful and wait for him to act, regardless of the circumstances, for the eschatological end.

### *The man clothed in linen reveals details of the eschatological end. (12:5–7)*

**12:5.** According to chapter 10 there was an angel, probably Gabriel, who "touched" Daniel and came in response to his "words" in prayer to

---

14. Miller, *Daniel*, 320–21.

15. Dan 12:4 uses the *Polel* of שׁוט, which contributes to the sense of intensity or urgency in the roaming. The *Qal* pattern can also be used of wandering about in search of something (Num 11:8; 2 Sam 24:2, 8), and it is used to describe Satan wandering through the earth as though on patrol (Job 2:2).

16. Montgomery, *Daniel*, 473–74.

communicate "the truth" to him from "the book of truth" (10:21). The "two others" mentioned in 12:5 were likely the same two angels ("holy ones") who engaged in a dialog regarding the 2,300 evening-mornings in Daniel's vision of the ram and the male goat (8:14). That same vision also included a canal (אוּבָל), the Ulai (8:2, 16). In this final vision a river or stream (יְאֹר) also plays an important part. The angels shout to each other from opposite banks of the river, and "the man clothed in linen" stands above the water (v.6). And Daniel was standing beside "the great river, that is the Tigris," when the "man clothed in linen" first appeared to him (10:4-5). **With so much attention on a river in these visions, the river must have some important purpose. It marks the geographical position, if all three terms for the waterway refer to the same river or stream.**[17] **Yet it must have some symbolic value as well. The river that is described in Ezekiel 47 was a source of renewal for the Dead Sea, as well as life for fish and trees. "The river of the water of life" mentioned in Rev 22:1 is modeled after the river in Ezekiel. It flows "from the throne of God and of the Lamb," and it waters "the tree of life" that has leaves "for the healing of the nations" (Rev 22:2). The imagery also borrows from Ps 1:3, which likens the righteous person to "a tree planted by streams of water." Perhaps the revelation that takes place in the setting of a river points to the hope for a renewal of the people of Israel that will lead to new life from God.** Judgment and great tribulation will come upon the people, but enduring hope lies at the end of all the troubles.

12:6-7. The "man clothed in linen" was "above the waters" because of his higher rank. Since he is defined by the article (*the* man), he should be the same "man clothed in linen" seen at the beginning of the previous vision (10:5). If he was indeed an appearance of God in human form (a theophany), then it seems unusual that he would look to heaven and swear by God ("him who lives forever"). However, if he is "the angel of Yahweh" or Christ in his pre-incarnate form (a Christophany),[18] then it would make sense for him to take such an oath. There were times when God swore an oath by himself (Gen 22:16; Isa 45:23; Jer 22:5; 49:13; cf. Heb 6:13). Most notable is the occasion when Yahweh swore, according to the song of Moses, to avenge his enemies and the enemies of his servants (Deut 32:40-43).[19] It would not seem so strange, then, that Yahweh's personal representative, his *angel* who is closely identified with him or even his Son, would raise both hands

---

17. Cf. Seow, *Daniel*, 192.

18. For discussion of a possible Christophany in the book of Daniel, see Hamilton, *With the Clouds of Heaven*, 144-54.

19. See Collins, *Daniel*, 399; Steinmann, *Daniel*, 569.

to swear a solemn oath by "the one who lives forever." For further discussion about the identity of the "man clothed in linen," see the Exposition on 10:5–6.

**12:7.** For the expression "time, times, and half (a time)" see the Exposition of Daniel 7:25. It has the same force in both visions. That is, it refers to the time when the "king" or "little horn" (Antichrist) will persecute the people, a persecution that will last until he has completely overwhelmed "the holy people." **At the conclusion of the allotted time, Michael will fight a great spiritual battle on their behalf (cf. Rev 12:7–10); the resurrection will occur; and the process of setting up God's everlasting kingdom will begin.**

*Daniel asks for further explanation. (12:8)*

**12:8.** Daniel's reactions to each of his visions indicate that he had less than a thorough understanding of how God's plans would specifically unfold. At the end of his first vision, he was "greatly troubled" and continued to ponder what he had experienced (7:28). The second vision exhausted him and made him physically sick because of his horror and his lack of further insight (8:27). Two years after the revelation of the "seventy weeks" Daniel was engaged in a prolonged mournful fast, seeking further understanding (10:1–3; cf. 9:1). And after receiving the instructions to seal his book, Daniel still needed more help to understand what was going to happen and when it would happen (12:5–7). **After all of this, Daniel still did not fully understand. Despite experiencing visions and revelations, this prophet who was "greatly esteemed" (9:23; 10:11, 19) needed additional insight into heavenly mysteries. How odd it is that many modern interpreters of Daniel's book seem confident that they have a firm understanding of it. The prophet's own experience should give interpreters a certain cautious humility about their explanations.**

*The man clothed in linen reveals what the end times will entail. (12:9–12)*

**12:9.** The answer to Daniel's question has two parts. First, he is reassured; he can't really expect to understand everything. The matters in his book are to be preserved and sealed until the time of the end. **Daniel will not live to see this end, but in light of it he needs to continue in faithfulness to his God, realizing that there will always be wicked people who will never understand, and righteous people who will. They will understand what Daniel already knows—faithfulness to God in the face of any and**

every circumstance will eventually be vindicated. One should not allow the flourishing of evil kingdoms to drive them to despair. God is in control and will bring down one kingdom and raise up another. In the end his kingdom will come, and those who have suffered persecution and even martyrdom have a glorious hope for the future. Resurrection day is coming; God's eternal kingdom will someday spread through the whole earth (cf. Ps 72:8; Isa 11:9; Mic 5:4 [3]; Zech 9:10).

**12:10.** The term יִתְבָּרֲרוּ is mostly rendered "be purified," as in the NIV. It signifies the removal of impurities from the *wise*. Since the *Hithpael* pattern of the verb is normally reflexive, the ESV has "purify themselves." That misses the implication, however, that the NLT makes plain—the purification will happen "by these trials." **The text refers to a refining process accomplished through persecution, not a self-initiated action.** The *Hithpael* can have a passive meaning as well as its usual reflexive sense.[20]

**12:11–12.** Verses eleven and twelve are among the most enigmatic in the book. Their intent is obviously to give some feel for the timing of the events of the end, but how the 1,290 days and the 1,335 days relate to the "time, times, and half (a time)" mentioned in verse seven is not so clear. Gunkel thought that the two calculations were glosses added when previous calculations failed during the time of the Maccabees. Gunkel's idea was followed by Montgomery and Collins.[21] Porteous accepted that the book was composed in the second century BC, but he failed to see "how urgent corrections, such as these would be, could have been added to a book that had just been issued, even though in a limited number of copies."[22] He thought instead that "these mysterious calculations" bore witness to the faith of those who lived through the Maccabean persecutions.[23] Indeed, it is difficult to envision how a book could have fresh calculations added to it soon after its composition and still maintain an alleged fiction of authorship in the sixth century BC.

Some medieval Jewish interpreters interpreted the 1,290 *days* as *years*, yielding the number of years from the time when temple sacrifice ceased until the Messiah would come. Then forty-five additional years would be added for a time when the Messiah would be hidden. Nachmanides (thirteenth century) opined that it was 1,290 years to Messiah ben Ephraim who would die in the war of Gog and Magog, only to be followed by "the Messiah

---

20. Waltke, *Introduction to Biblical Hebrew Syntax*, 431 (par. 26.3).
21. Gunkel, *Creation and Chaos*, 350; Montgomery, *Daniel*, 477; Collins, *Daniel*, 401.
22. Porteous, *Daniel*, 172.
23. Porteous, *Daniel*, 172.

of the seed of David" forty-five years later.[24] There is no evidence to equate the word *days* in Daniel with *years*, and the calculations have long since been disproved by history.

Baldwin interpreted the sixty-nine-and-a-half weeks of Daniel 9 to symbolize that "the end is not yet," since it fell short of the full seventy weeks. Then the 1,290 days completed the seventy weeks and the persecution. The 1,335 days indicated the "need to persevere a little longer." The symbolism is then in "the emphasis on endurance to the end," as in Jesus' teaching.[25] What Baldwin presents is an appropriate application of the passage, but as an interpretation it fails to do justice to the specificity of these numbers.

Steinmann presents a more nuanced symbolic view. Assigning the removal of the "continual offering" and the setting up of the "detested thing of desolation" to the time of Antiochus IV, he makes the 1,290 and the "three and a half times" or 1,260 days (42 months x 30 days) both extend to the period of the second advent of Christ. The larger figure of 1,290 days (one symbolic month longer) is because it began prior to "the birth of Jesus and the church age."[26] That is, according to his view, the 1,290 days began with Antiochus IV desecrating the temple in 167 BC, while the 1,260 days ("time, times, and half a time") begins with the birth of Christ and ends with his second coming. Then the 1,335 days represent the time from Daniel himself in 536 BC to the return of Christ. While Steinmann carefully reasons through each step, his solution fails to engender confidence in that he builds hypothesis upon hypothesis.

We can agree with Jerome that the time frame needs to be that of the future Antichrist (Daniel's "little horn" and "the king") rather than the Maccabean period or the current church age.[27] Then the 1,290 days could be either a more specific calculation than the three-and-a-half years,[28] or an extra month for judging the nations (Matt 25:31–46) beyond the 1,260 days represented by calculating twelve months of thirty days each.[29] In either case the 1,335 days could then represent the additional time required to establish the messianic kingdom on earth. While this may be plausible, one can agree with Jerome that "the reason for the forty-five days of inaction after the

---

24. Goldwurm, *Daniel*, 328–30.
25. Baldwin, *Daniel*, 210.
26. Steinmann, *Daniel*, 575–76.
27. Jerome, *Commentary on Daniel*, 150.
28. Jerome, *Commentary on Daniel*, 150; Archer, "Daniel," 156.
29. Walvoord, *Daniel*, 294–96; Wood, *Daniel*, 327–28.

slaying of the Antichrist is a matter which rests in the knowledge of God."[30] After all, even Daniel himself was not given any additional clarification.

*Daniel is told to continue, awaiting his allotted portion. (12:13)*

The final charge to Daniel implies that he will not see the consummation that was revealed to him. **He will, however, rise from the dead in the future to receive his allotted portion in God's kingdom. As one of the precious "saints of the Most High" he will inherit the "everlasting kingdom" (7:27). His book would remain to bless its readers through many ages, but Daniel needs to continue faithful to his God through the rest of his life. He can be assured that he will receive his reward in the eschatological end.**

If Daniel first "rests" in death and then later "stands" in his "allotted portion," there is a strong sense that he will join those who will rise from the dead (12:2). The verb עָמַד (stand) usually means *stand in place*, but it can sometimes include the action of getting into that position (Dan 10:11) or of getting up from a seated or prone position (Neh 8:5). The specifics of how this will play out is of secondary importance. The more important issue is the promise that Daniel will stand in his *allotted portion* (גּוֹרָל). At the beginning of the book, Daniel was taken into exile, he was removed from the Promised Land. The book ends with a promise of return, he will forever be in his Promised Land for all of eternity. This is no small anticlimactic ending to the book. It echoes the promises made to Israel, first fulfilled under Joshua's leadership. When Israel entered the land and was given their inheritance (Josh 14–21) Joshua painstakingly records each tribes allotment (גּוֹרָל). The book of Daniel ends with a promise of a full and final return from exile that will be enjoyed for all of eternity.

## SHARPENING THE THEOLOGICAL FOCUS

In Daniel 1, the introduction to the book, God is portrayed as sovereign over the worst period in Israel's history to date—the fall of Jerusalem. The text forces God's people to wrestle with the truth that God is in control, even while his city, his temple, and his people are plundered. Here in chapter 12, the conclusion to the book, God is portrayed as sovereign over a period yet to come, one that will be far worse for God's people than even the fall of Jerusalem. What is this knowledge of God's sovereignty supposed to do in

---

30. Jerome, *Commentary on Daniel*, 151.

the life of God's people? The same thing it has done throughout the book, inspire faithfulness. Just as God has sovereignly delivered Daniel, Shadrach, Meshach and Abednego, he will one day deliver all of his people, even those who have died in spite of, and because of, their faithfulness.

As well as inspiring faithfulness, the concluding words of Daniel remind us that helplessness is not hopelessness. Though God's people will be rendered helpless with regard to turning back the approaching tsunami of evil, we are not hopeless. It is not on us to defeat evil. It is on us to remain faithful to the end. Our hope is not in our ability to help God, our hope is in his promise of resurrection and fulfillment. One day he will raise us to our destined allotment. Because of this, like Daniel, we can trust.

In light of this, Daniel 12 reminds God's people that they can, and should, wait patiently for the eschatological end. The way of wisdom is always to remain faithful and to wait patiently for God's perfect timing. An encouraging example of faithful waiting that overlaps with Daniel's life is the extended context of Isa 40:30–31. "They who wait for the Lord," says Isaiah, "shall renew their strength" (ESV). When Israelites did things in their own strength, they grew weary and failed, but God's plan finally succeeded in the later years of Daniel's life. The Lord sent his people safely back to Judah and even arranged for the Persians to support them financially (Ezra 7–8; Neh 2:1–9). God's prosperity of his people, in a physical sense, may not be realized in this life, persecution and devastation may befall believers. However, there is promise of a great blessing in the end, "Blessed are any who wait and reach the 1,335 days" (Dan 12:12), and that blessing includes the promised allotment God has for his people (Dan 12:13).

Chapter 12 also focuses on an aspect of the purpose of God's revelation through Scripture. Its words are closed to the wicked, who spurn it. But to the righteous, those who are wise in the way they live, the words of Scripture can be understood. They teach true wisdom that yields the fruit of life everlasting (cf. Rev 22). In this way, Daniel 12 parallels Ps 1. It can be tempting to follow the "counsel of the wicked" (Ps 1:1) when they seem to prosper and have the upper hand. True prosperity, though, is promised to those who faithfully follow God's instruction (Ps 1:2–3). One day the righteous will be gathered and the wicked will not stand among them (Ps 1:5). The wicked will perish, but God watches over the righteous (Ps 1:6), ensuring they receive their allotted portion.

## THE FOCUS OF DANIEL 12:3–13 FOR PREACHING AND TEACHING

As has been previously noted, a key difference between apocalyptic literature and prophetic literature is the finality of what is written. Apocalyptic literature emphasizes what has been determined—this is what will happen; prophetic literature, on the other hand, often emphasizes what will happen *if* things don't change. Daniel 12 concludes the apocalyptic section of the book. The events, and the timing of the events, have been determined. And though the timing of the events is not as clear as we might like them to be, the text is quite clear about their certainty. Therefore, as you prepare to preach/teach this pericope, pay attention to the clues in the text that emphasize certainty:

- "Close up these words by sealing the book until *the time of the end*." (v. 4)
- "For *a time, times, and half* (a time)." (v. 7)
- "And when the shattering of the power of the holy people *is complete*, all these (things) *will be finished*." (v. 7)
- "For these matters are closed up and sealed until *the time of the end*." (v. 9)
- "Now from *the time when the regular service is removed*. . .(there will be) *1290 days*. Any who wait and reach *1,335 days*. . ." (vss. 11–12)
- "And as for you, continue *to the end*." (v. 13)
- "You will rise to your allotted portion *at the end of days*." (v. 13)

In addition to the certainty communicated in this chapter, there is a thread of hope that ties a bow around the book of Daniel. These final chapters describe cataclysmic events that will unfold in the days ahead. Yet, rather than ending with words of doom and destruction, the book ends with these words of comfort to Daniel, "And as for you, continue to the end. You will rest, and you will rise to your allotted portion at the end of days." (v. 13) It's as if God is saying, "Daniel, don't worry. The end will come soon enough. You keep doing what you're doing. It's dark now, and you won't make it through the night. But trust me, when the new day dawns, I'll wake you up and we'll forever enjoy it together with all those who have put their trust in me." The sovereignty of God, as recorded in the book of Daniel, ensures much more than the defeat of evil; it assures the salvation of God's people.

## FROM TEXTUAL WORK TO TEACHING

## The Big Idea

- *Exegetical Idea:* Daniel is told that the shocking events of his final vision will play out for a predetermined period of time; while that happens, the wise will be purified, cleansed and refined, and the wicked will continue to act wickedly; in the meantime, Daniel is told to continue in faithfulness and look forward to being raised to everlasting life.
- *Theological Focus:* God has promised that while the shocking events of world history play out and the wicked continue to act wickedly, he will sanctify the wise, and eventually raise them to eternal life.
- *Preaching Idea:* Because of the hope we have, we can wisely persevere through the worst of times.

## Outline One: Following the Exegetical Flow

I. Only those who diligently seek God's wisdom will find it and those who do will have great reward in the kingdom of God.

    A. Only those who diligently seek God's wisdom will find it.

        1. We diligently seek God's wisdom by searching the Scriptures.

        2. We diligently seek God's wisdom by living faithfully.

    B. Those who seek God's wisdom will have great reward in the kingdom of God.

        1. The reward of honor

        2. The reward of turning others to righteousness

        3. The reward of everlasting life and an allotted portion

II. Those who trust in God need to remain faithful and wait for him to act, regardless of the circumstances, for the eschatological end.

    A. While the wicked prosper, trust in God leads to enduring faithfulness.

    B. While the wicked prosper, trust in God leads to hope-filled patience.

## Outline Two: Following a Theme

The sovereignty of God and the certainty of his decrees:

- "Close up these words by sealing the book until *the time of the end.*" (v. 4)
- "For *a time, times, and half* (a time)." (v. 7)
- "And when the shattering of the power of the holy people *is complete* all these (things) *will be finished.*" (v. 7)
- "For these matters are closed up and sealed until *the time of the end.*" (v. 9)
- "Now from *the time when the regular service is removed*...(there will be) *1290 days.* Any who wait and reach *1,335 days...*" (vss. 11–12)
- "And as for you, continue *to the end.*" (v. 13)
- "You will rise to your allotted portion *at the end of days.*" (v. 13)

In light of God's sovereignty and the certainty of his decrees, the way of the wise will always make a difference, now and forever. (12:3, 10, 12–13).

- Wisdom begins with knowledge of God.
- Wisdom is knowing that God has revealed mysteries.
- Wisdom is knowing that ultimate deliverance is in God's hands.
- Wisdom results in humility, not arrogance.
- Wisdom knows there is coming a day when this life will be totally exposed for what it was.

# Bibliography

Aharoni, Yohanan, and Michael Avi-Yonah, eds. *The Macmillan Bible Atlas*. New York: Macmillan, 1977.
Allen, Leslie C. *Psalms 101—150*. WBC. Vol. 21. Waco, TX: Word, 1983.
Allen, Lindsay. *The Persian Empire*. Chicago: University of Chicago Press, 2005.
Anderson, Sir Robert. *The Coming Prince: The Marvelous Prophecy of Daniel's Seventy Weeks Concerning the Antichrist*. 19th ed. Grand Rapids: Kregel, 1975.
Anderson, Steven D. *Darius the Mede: A Reappraisal*. Grand Rapids: self-published, 2014.
Archer, Gleason L., Jr. "Daniel." Pages 1–157 in vol. 7 of *EBC* (Daniel-Minor Prophets). Edited by Frank E. Gaebelein and Richard P. Polcyn. Grand Rapids: Zondervan, 1985.
———. "The Hebrew of Daniel Compared with the Qumran Sectarian Documents." Pages 470–81 in *The Law and the Prophets: Old Testament Studies Prepared in Honor of Oswald Thompson Allis*. Edited by John H. Skilton. N.p.: Presbyterian and Reformed, 1974.
———. Translator. *Jerome's Commentary on Daniel*. Grand Rapids: Baker, 1958.
———. "The Relationship between the Septuagint Translation and the Massoretic Text in Jeremiah." *Trinity Journal* 12 (1991): 139–50.
Ashley, Timothy R. *The Book of Numbers*. NICOT. Grand Rapids: Eerdmans, 1993.
*Assyrian and Babylonian Chronicles*. Edited by Albert Kirk Grayson. Locust Valley, NY: J. J. Augustin, 1975.
Austin, M. M. *The Hellenistic World from Alexander to the Roman Conquest: A selection of ancient sources in translation*. London: Cambridge University Press, 1981.
Baldwin, Joyce G. *Daniel: An Introduction and Commentary*. TOTC. Downers Grove, IL: InterVarsity, 1978.
Barnes, Cory. "Ancient Near Eastern Context and Theological Interpretation of Scripture: An Exploration in Daniel 7:1–14." *JETS* 65 (2022): 307–17.
Bartlett, J. R. "Edom." In *ABD*, edited by D. N. Freedman, 287–95. Vol. 2. New York: Doubleday, 1992.
Beale, G. K. *The Book of Revelation: A Commentary on the Greek Text*. NIGTC. Grand Rapids: Eerdmans, 1999.
Beaulieu, Paul-Alain. "The Babylonian Background of the Motif of the Fiery Furnace in Daniel 3." *JBL* 128 (2009): 273–90.
———. "King Nabonidus and the Neo-Babylonian Empire." Pages 969–79 in vol. 2 of *CANE*. Edited by Jack M. Sasson, et al. New York: Charles Scribner's Sons, 1995.

———. *The Reign of Nabonidus, King of Babylon, 556–539 B.C.* New Haven, CT: Yale University Press, 1989.
Beckwith, Carl L., ed. *Ezekiel, Daniel.* Vol 12. Reformation Commentary on Scripture, Old Testament. Downers Grove, IL: IVP Academic, 2012.
Beckwith, Roger T. *Calendar and Chronology, Jewish and Christian: Biblical, Intertestamental and Patristic Studies.* Boston, MA: Brill, 1996.
Bergsma, John Sietze. *The Jubilee from Leviticus to Qumran: A History of Interpretation.* VTSup, vol. 115. Boston: Brill, 2007.
———. "The Persian Period as Penitential Era: The 'Exegetical Logic' of Daniel 9:1–27." Pages 50–64 in *Exile and Restoration Revisited: Essays on the Babylonian and Persian Periods in Memory of Peter R. Ackroyd.* Edited by Gary N. Knoppers and Lester L. Grabbe, with Deirdre N. Fulton, 50–64. New York: T&T Clark, 2009.
Blasius, Andreas. "Antiochus IV Epiphanes and the Ptolemaic Triad: The Three Uprooted Horns in Dan 7:8, 20 and 24 Reconsidered." *JSJ* 37 (2006): 521–47.
Block, Daniel I. *The Book of Ezekiel: Chapters 1–24.* NICOT. Grand Rapids: Eerdmans, 1997.
———. *The Book of Ezekiel: Chapters 25–48.* NICOT. Grand Rapids: Eerdmans, 1998.
Blomberg, Craig L. "Interpreting Old Testament Prophetic Fulfillment in Matthew: Double Fulfillment." *TJ* 23 (2002): 17–33.
Bock, Darrell L. "The Use of Daniel 7 in Jesus' Trial, with Implications for His Self-understanding." Pages 70–100 in *'Who Is This Son of Man?' The Latest Scholarship on a Puzzling Expression of the Historical Jesus*, edited by Larry W. Hurtado and Paul L. Owen, Library of New Testament Studies 390. New York: T&T Clark, 2011.
Borland, James A. *Christ in the Old Testament.* Chicago: Moody, 1978.
Bracke, John M. "Nergal-Sharezer." Pages 1074–75 in vol. 4 of *ABD*. Edited by D. N. Freedman. New York: Doubleday, 1992.
Braverman, Jay. *Jerome's Commentary on Daniel: A Study of Comparative Jewish and Christian Interpretations of the Hebrew Bible.* CBQMS, no. 7. 1978.
Brendon, Piers. "Like Rome Before the Fall? Not Yet." *The New York Times.* February 24, 2010. https://www.nytimes.com/2010/02/25/opinion/25brendon.html?smid=url-share.
Brekelmans, C. H. W. "The Saints of the Most High." *Oudtestamentische Studiën* 14 (1965): 305–29.
Breneman, Marvin. *Ezra, Nehemiah, Esther.* NAC, vol. 10. Nashville: Broadman & Holman, 1993.
Briant, Pierre. *From Cyrus to Alexander: A History of the Persian Empire.* Translated by Peter T. Daniels. Winona Lake, IN: Eisenbrauns, 2002.
Bright, John. *A History of Israel.* 4th ed. Louisville, KY: Westminster John Knox, 2000.
Bulman, James M. "The Identification of Darius the Mede." *WTJ* 35 (1973): 247–67.
Burstein, Stanley M. *The Babyloniaca of Berossus.* Sources from the Ancient Near East, vol. 1, fascicle 5. Malibu, CA: Undena, 1978.
Buth, Randall. "A More Complete Semitic Background for בר־אנשא, 'Son of Man.'" Pages 176–89 in *The Function of Scripture in Early Jewish and Christian Tradition*, edited by Craig A. Evans and James A. Sanders. JSNTSup 154. Sheffield: Sheffield Academic Press, 1998.
Calvin, John. *Commentaries on the Book of the Prophet Daniel.* Translated by Thomas Myers. 2 vols. Grand Rapids: Eerdmans, 1948.
Carmignac, Jean. "Un aramaïsme biblique et Qumrânien: l'infinitif Placé après son complément d'objet." *RevQ* 5 (1996): 512–20.

Carpenter, Eugene, and Michael A. Grisanti. "בָּעַשׁ (7322)." Pages 706–10 in vol. 3 of *NIDOTTE*. Edited by W.A. VanGemeren. Grand Rapids: Zondervan, 1997.
Casey, Maurice. *The Solution to the 'Son of Man' Problem*. New York: T. & T. Clark, 2007.
———. *Son of Man: The interpretation and influence of Daniel 7*. London: SPCK, 1979.
Colless, Brian E. "Cyrus the Persian and Darius the Mede in the Book of Daniel." *JSOT* 56 (1992): 113–26.
Collins, Adela Yarbro. "The History of Interpretation: B. The Christian Interpretation." Pages 90–123 in *Daniel: A Commentary on the Book of Daniel*, by John J. Collins, edited by Frank Moore Cross. Hermeneia. Minneapolis: Fortress, 1993.
Collins, John J. *Daniel: A Commentary on the Book of Daniel*. Edited by Frank Moore Cross. Hermeneia. Minneapolis: Fortress, 1993.
———. "Introduction: Towards the Morphology of a Genre." Pages 1–20 in vol. 14 of *Semeia. Apocalypse: The Morphology of a Genre*, edited by John J. Collins. Semeia, vol. 14. Atlanta: Society of Biblical Literature, 1979.
———. "Stirring up the Great Sea: The Religio-Historical Background of Daniel 7." Pages 121–36 in vol. 106 of BETL. *The Book of Daniel in the Light of New Findings*. Edited by A. S. Van der Woude. Leuven: Leuven University Press, 1993.
Collins, John J., and Peter W. Flint, eds. *The Book of Daniel: Composition and Reception*. 2 vols. Boston: Brill, 2002.
Conrad, Edgar W. *Zechariah*. Sheffield, England: Sheffield Academic Press, 1999.
Cook, S. A., et al., eds. *The Hellenistic Monarchies and the Rise of Rome*. Vol. 7 of *The Cambridge Ancient History*. Cambridge, UK: Cambridge University Press, 1954.
Cook, Stephen L. *The Apocalyptic Literature*. Interpreting Biblical Texts. Nashville: Abingdon, 2003.
Cowley, A. *Aramaic Papyri of the Fifth Century B.C.* Eugene, OR: Wipf & Stock, 2005. [reprint of 1923 edition by the Clarendon Press]
Craige, P. C. *The Book of Deuteronomy*. NICOT. Grand Rapids: Eerdmans, 1976.
Culver, Robert D. *Daniel and the Latter Days*. Westwood, NJ: Fleming H. Revell, 1954.
Dalman, Gustaf. *Die Worte Jesu mit Berücksichtigung des nachkanonischen Jüdischen Schrifttums und der aramäischen Sprache*. Leipzig: J. C. Hinrichs'sche Buchhandlung, 1898.
Dandamaev, M. A. *A Political History of the Achaemenid Empire*. Translated by W. J. Vogelsang. New York: Brill, 1989.
Daniel, Andrew Glenn. "The Translator's Tell: Translation Technique, Verbal Syntax and the Myth of Old Greek Daniel's Alternate Semitic Vorlage." *JBL* 140 (2021): 733–49.
Davis, Dale Ralph. *The Message of Daniel: His kingdom cannot fail*. Edited by J. A. Motyer. The Bible Speaks Today. Downers Grove, IL: InterVarsity, 2013.
Diodorus Siculus. *Diodorus of Sicily*. Translated by Francis R. Walton. 12 vols. LCL. Cambridge, MA: Harvard University Press, 1968.
Dougherty, Raymond Philip. *Nabonidus and Belshazzar: a study of the closing events of the neo-Babylonian empire*. YOSR, vol. 15. New York: AMS, 1929.
Doukhan, Jacques B. *Daniel: The Vision of the End*. Rev. ed. Berrien Springs, MI: Andrews University Press, 1989.
Dressler, Harold H. P. "The Identification of the Ugaritic Dnil with the Daniel of Ezekiel." *VT* 29 (1979): 152–61.
Driver, S. R. *An Introduction to the Literature of the Old Testament*. 10th ed. International Theological Library. New York: Charles Scribner's Sons, 1900.

Easley, Kendell H. *Revelation*. Edited by Mark Anders. Holman New Testament Commentary. Nashville: Broadman & Holman, 1998.
Edwards, Ormond. "The Year of Jerusalem's Destruction. 2 Addaru 597 B.C. Reinterpreted." *ZAW* 104 (1992): 101–6.
Eichrodt, Walther. *Ezekiel: A Commentary*. Edited by G. Ernest Wright, et al. OTL. Philadelphia: Westminster, 1970.
Eusebius. *Preparation for the Gospel*. Translated by Edwin Hamilton Gifford. 2 vols. Grand Rapids: Baker, 1981.
Feinberg, Charles L. *Daniel: The Kingdom of the Lord*. Winona Lake, IN: BMH, 1981. Daniel
———. *God Remembers: A Study of the Book of Zechariah*. 4$^{th}$ ed. Portland, OR: Multnomah, 1979.
———. "Jeremiah." Vol. 6 in *Expositor's Bible Commentary*. Edited by Frank E. Gaebelein. Vol. 6. Grand Rapids, MI: Zondervan, 1986.
———. *The Prophecy of Ezekiel: The Glory of the Lord*. Chicago: Moody, 1969.
Feinberg, Paul D. "An Exegetical and Theological Study of Daniel 9:24–27." Pages 189–220 in *Tradition and Testament: Essays in Honor of Charles Lee Feinberg*. Edited by John S. and Paul D. Feinberg. Chicago: Moody, 1981.
Ferch, Arthur J. "Daniel 7 and Ugarit: A Reconsideration." *JBL* 99 (1980): 75–86.
———. "Porphyry: An heir to Christian Exegesis?" *ZNW* 73 (1982): 141–47.
Ferrari-D'Occhieppo, Konradin. "The Star of the Magi and Babylonian Astronomy." Pages 41–53 in *Chronos, Kairos, Christos: Nativity and Chronological Studies Presented to Jack Finegan*. Edited by Jerry Vardaman and Edwin M. Yamauchi. Winona Lake, IN: Eisenbrauns, 1989.
Fewell, Danna Nolan. *Circle of Sovereignty: Plotting Politics in the Book of Daniel*. Nashville: Abingdon, 1991.
Finegan, Jack. *Handbook of Biblical Chronology: Principles of Time Reckoning in the Ancient World and Problems of Chronology in the Bible*. Rev. ed. Peabody, MA: Hendrickson, 1999.
Finkelstein, J. J. "Mesopotamia." *JNES* 21 (1962): 73–92.
Finley, Thomas J. "The Book of Daniel in the Canon of Scripture." *Bibliotheca Sacra* 165 (2008): 195–208.
Fitzmyer, Joseph A. "Some Notes on Aramaic Epistolography." *JBL* 93 (1974): 201–25.
Flint, Peter W. "The Daniel Tradition at Qumran." Pages 329–67 in *The Book of Daniel: Composition and Reception*. Edited by John J. Collins and Peter W. Flint, 329–67. Vol 2. Boston: Brill, 2002.
Folmer, M. L. *The Aramaic Language in the Achaemenid Period: A Study in Linguistic Variation*. OLA, vol. 68. Leuven: Peeters Press & Department of Oriental Studies, 1995.
France, R. T. *Jesus and the Old Testament: His Application of Old Testament Passages to Himself and His Mission*. Downers Grove, IL: InterVarsity, 1971.
Frölich, Ida. *'Time and Times and Half a Time': Historical Consciousness in the Jewish Literature of the Persian and Hellenistic Eras*. JSPSup, no. 19. Sheffield, England: Sheffield Academic Press, 1996.
Frye, Northrop. *The Educated Imagination*. Bloomington, IN: Indiana University Press, 1964.
Gadd, C. J. "The Harran Inscriptions of Nabonidus." *Anatolian Studies* 8 (1958): 35–92.
Gaebelein, A. C. *The Prophet Daniel: A Key to the Visions and Prophecies of the Book of Daniel*. New York: Publication Office, "Our Hope," 1911.

Gardner, A. E. "Decoding Daniel: The Case of Dan 7.5." *Biblica* 88 (2007): 222–33.
Gera, Dov, and Wayne Horowitz. "Antiochus IV in Life and Death: Evidence from the Babylonian Astronomical Diaries." *JAOS* 117 (1997): 240–52.
*Gesenius' Hebrew Grammar*. Edited by E. Kautzsch. Edited and translated by A. E. Cowley. Oxford: Clarendon, 1910.
Goldingay, John E. *Daniel*. WBC, vol. 30. Dallas: Word, 1989.
Goldwurm, Hersh. *Daniel: A New Translation with a Commentary Anthologized from Talmudic, Midrashic and Rabbinic Sources*. 2$^{nd}$ ed. Brooklyn: Mesorah, 1980.
Goswell, Greg. "The Visions of Daniel and Their Historical Specificity." *Restoration Quarterly* 58, no. 3 (2016) 129–42.
Gowan, Donald E. *Daniel*. AOTC. Nashville: Abingdon, 2001.
Grabbe, Lester L. "Another Look at the *Gestalt* of 'Darius the Mede.'" *CBQ* 50 (1988b): 198–213.
———. "The Belshazzar of Daniel and the Belshazzar of History." *AUSS* 26 (1988a): 59–66.
Grainger, John D. *Seleukos Nikator: Constructing a Hellenistic Kingdom*. New York: Routledge, 1990.
Grayson, A. K. *Assyrian and Babylonian Chronicles*. TCS, vol. 5. Locust Valley, NY: J. J. Augustin, 1975.
Grayson, A. Kirk. "Tiglath-pileser." Page 533 in vol. 6 of *ABD*. Edited by D. N. Freedman. New York: Doubleday, 1992.
Groningen, Gerard van. *Messianic Revelation in the Old Testament*. Grand Rapids: Baker, 1990.
Gunkel, Hermann. *Creation and Chaos in the Primeval Era and the Eschaton: A Religio-Historical Study of Genesis 1 and Revelation 12*. Translated by K. William Whitney Jr. Grand Rapids: Eerdmans, 2006. [original German work published in 1895]
Gurney, Robert J. M. "The four kingdoms of Daniel 2 and 7." *Themelios* 2 (1977): 39–45.
Gzella, Holger, ed. "פרק *prq*." Pages 611–13 in vol. 16 (Aramaic Dictionary) of TDOT. Edited by G. Johannes Boterweck, Helmer Ringgren, and Heinz-Josef Fabry. Grand Rapids: Eerdmans, 2008.
Haag, Ernst. *Die Errettung Daniels aus der Löwengrube: Untersuchungen zum Ursprung der biblischen Danieltradition*. Stuttgarter Bibelstudien, vol. 110. Stuttgart, Germany: Verlag Katholisches Bibelwerk GmbH, 1983.
Hallo, William W., and William Kelly Simpson. *The Ancient Near East: A History*. 2$^{nd}$ ed. Belmont, CA: Thomson/Wadsworth, 1998.
Hamilton, James M., Jr. *With the Clouds of Heaven: The book of Daniel in biblical theology*. New Studies in Biblical Theology. Downers Grove, IL: InterVarsity, 2014.
Hanhart, K. "The Four Beasts of Daniel's Vision in the Night in the Light of Rev. 13.2." *NTS* 27 (1981): 576–83.
Harrison, R. K. *Introduction to the Old Testament: with a comprehensive review of Old Testament studies and a special supplement on the Apocrypha*. Grand Rapids: Eerdmans, 1964.
Hartman, Louis F., and Alexander A. Di Lella. *The Book of Daniel*. AB, vol. 23. Garden City, NY: Doubleday, 1978.
Hasel, Gerhard F. "The Book of Daniel and Matters of Language: Evidences Relating to Names, Words, and the Aramaic Language." *AUSS* 19 (1981): 211–25.
———. "The Identity of 'The Saints of the Most High' in Daniel 7." *Biblica* 56 (1975): 173–92.

# BIBLIOGRAPHY

———. "Resurrection in the Theology of Old Testament Apocalyptic." *ZAW* 92 (1980): 267–84.

Hassler, Mark A. "The Identity of the Little Horn in Daniel 8: Antiochus IV Epiphanes, Rome, or the Antichrist?" *Master's Seminary Journal* 27 (2016): 33–44.

Hays, Christopher B. "Chirps from the Dust: The Affliction of Nebuchadnezzar in Daniel 4:30 in Its Ancient Near Eastern Context." *JBL* 126 (2007): 305–25.

Hays, J. Daniel. "Jeremiah, the Septuagint, the Dead Sea Scrolls and Inerrancy." Pages 133–49 in *Evangelicals and Scripture: Tradition, Authority and Hermeneutics*. Edited by Vincent Bacote, et al. Downers Grove, IL: InterVarsity, 2004.

Heaton, Eric. *The Book of Daniel*. TBC. London: SCM, 1967.

Hebbard, Aaron B. *Reading Daniel as a Text in Theological Hermeneutics*. Princeton Theological Monograph Series. Eugene, OR: Pickwick, 2009.

Heiser, Michael S. "Deuteronomy 32:8 and the Sons of God." *Bibliotheca Sacra* 158 (2001): 52–74.

Hengel, Martin. *The Septuagint as Christian Scripture: Its Prehistory and the Problem of Its Canon*. Translated by Mark E. Biddle. Grand Rapids: Baker Academic, 2002.

Henze, Matthias. *The Madness of King Nebuchadnezzar: The Ancient Near Eastern Origins and Early History of Interpretation of Daniel 4*. JSOTSup, vol. 61. Boston: Brill, 1999.

Herodotus. *Herodotus*. Translated by A. D. Godley. Vol. 1. Books I–X. LCL. Cambridge, MA: Harvard University Press, 1946.

Hess, Richard S. "The Seventy Sevens of Daniel 9: A Timetable for the Future?" *BBR* 21, no. 3 (2011): 315–30.

Hill, Andrew E. "Daniel." Pages 19 to 212 in vol. 8 (Daniel-Malachi) of *Expositor's Bible Commentary*. Edited by Tremper Longman III and David E. Garland. Rev. ed. Grand Rapids: Zondervan, 2008.

Hippolytus (early 3rd century). In *Fathers of the Third Century: Hippolytus, Cyprian, Caius, Novatian, Appendix*. Edited by Alexander Roberts and James Donaldson. Vol. 5 of *Ante-Nicene Fathers*. Edited by Alexander Roberts and James Donaldson. Peabody, MA: Hendrickson.

Hoehner, Harold W. "Chronological Aspects of the Life of Christ, Part VI: Daniel's Seventy Weeks and New Testament Chronology." *Bibliotheca Sacra* 132, no. 525 (1975): 47–65.

Ironside, Harry A. *Lectures on Daniel the Prophet*. 2nd ed. Neptune, NJ: Loizeaus Brothers; New York: Bible Truth Depot, 1920.

Jerome, St. *Jerome's Commentary on Daniel*. Translated by Gleason L. Archer. Grand Rapids: Baker, 1958.

John of Antioch. *Ioannis Antiocheni Fragmenta quae Supersunt Omnia*. Edited and translated by Sergei Mariev. Berlin: Walter de Gruyter, 2008.

Johnson, Alan. "Revelation." Pages 399–603 in vol. 12 *Expositor's Bible Commentary*. Edited by Frank E. Gaebelein. Grand Rapids: Zondervan, 1981.

Johnston, Philip S. *Shades of Sheol: Death and Afterlife in the Old Testament*. Downers Grove, IL: InterVarsity (Apollos), 2002.

Jongeling, B., C. J. Labuschagne, and A. S. Van der Woude. *Aramaic Texts from Qumran: With Translations and Annotations*. Semitic Study Series, no. 4. Edited by J. H. Hospers, T. Jansma, and G. F. Pijper. Leiden: E. J. Brill, 1976.

Josephus. *Josephus*. Translated by Ralph Marcus. Vol. 7 of *Jewish Antiquities*. Books XII–XIV. LCL. Cambridge, MA: Harvard University Press, 1966.

# BIBLIOGRAPHY

Keck, Brian E. "Raphia." Page 622 in vol. 5 of *ABD*. Edited by D. N. Freedman. Vol. 5. New York: Doubleday, 1992.

Keil, C. F. *Ezekiel, Daniel*. Translated by James Martin and M. G. Easton. Vol. 9 of *Commentary on the Old Testament in Ten Volumes*. Grand Rapids: Eerdmans, 1983.

———. *Jeremiah, Lamentations*. Translated James Martin and M. G. Easton. Vol. 8 of *Commentary on the Old Testament in Ten Volumes*. Grand Rapids: Eerdmans, 1983b.

Kim, Young Hye. "The Jubilee: Its Reckoning and Inception Day." *VT* 60 (2010): 147–51.

Kitchen, K. A. "The Aramaic of Daniel." Pages 31–79 in *Notes on Some Problems in the Book of Daniel*. Edited by D. J. Wiseman, et al. London: Tyndale, 1965.

Klein, Neriah. "The Chronicler's Code: The Rise and Fall of Judah's Army in the Book of Chronicles." *JHebS* 3 (2017): 1–18.

Knowles, Louis E. "The Interpretation of the Seventy Weeks of Daniel in the Early Fathers." *WTJ* 7 (1945): 136–60.

Koch, Klaus. *Daniel 1–4*. BKAT, vol. 22, no. 1. Neukirchen-Vluyn, The Netherlands: Neukirchener Verlag, 2005.

Konkel, A. H. "983 בֹּהוּ." Pages 606–9 in vol. 1 of *NIDOTTE*. Edited by Willem A. VanGemeren. 5 vols. Grand Rapids: Zondervan, 1997.

Laato, Antii. "The Seventy Yearweeks in the Book of Daniel." *ZAW* 102 (1990): 212–25.

Lacocque, André. *The Book of Daniel*. Translated by David Pellauer. English rev. ed. Atlanta: John Knox, 1979.

Lebram, Jürgen-Christian. *Das Buch Daniel*. ZBKAT 23. Zürich: Theologischer Verlag, 1984.

Lenglet, A. "Le structure littéraire de Daniel 2–7." *Biblica* 53 (1972): 170–89.

Leupold, H. C. *Exposition of Daniel*. Columbus, OH: Wartburg, 1949.

Lindenberger, J. M. "Ahiqar (Seventh to Sixth Century b.c.)." In *OTP*. Edited by James H. Charlesworth. Vol 2. Garden City, NY: Doubleday, 1988.

———. *Ancient Aramaic and Hebrew Letters*. Edited by Kent Harold Richards. SBL Writings from the Ancient World, vol. 4. Atlanta: Scholars, 1994.

———. *The Aramaic Proverbs of Ahiqar*. JHNES. Baltimore: Johns Hopkins University Press, 1983.

Longacre, Robert E. *The Grammar of Discourse*. 2$^{nd}$ ed. Topics in Language and Linguistics. New York: Plenum, 1996.

Longman, Tremper III. *Daniel*. NIV Application Commentary. Grand Rapids: Zondervan, 1999.

Lucas, Ernest C. *Daniel*. ApOTC, vol. 20. Downers Grove, IL: InterVarsity, 2002.

———. "Daniel." In *Zondervan Illustrated Bible Backgrounds Commentary*. Edited by John H. Walton. Grand Rapids: Zondervan, 2009.

———. "The Origin of Daniel's Four Empires Scheme Re-examined." *TynBul* 40 (1989): 185–202.

Luck, G. Coleman. *Daniel*. Chicago: Moody, 1958.

Lundbom, Jack R. *Jeremiah 21–36: A New Translation with Introduction and Commentary*. AB, vol. 21B. New York: Doubleday, 2004.

Lust, Johan. "Cult and Sacrifice in Daniel. The Tamid and the Abomination of Desolation." Pages 671–88 in vol. 2 of *The Book of Daniel: Composition and Reception*. Edited by John J. Collins and Peter W. Flint. Boston: Brill, 2002.

Maalouf, Tony. *Arabs in the Shadow of Israel: The Unfolding of God's Prophetic Plan for Ishmael's Line.* Grand Rapids: Kregel, 2003.

MacArthur, John Jr. *Matthew 1–7.* The MacArthur New Testament Commentary. Chicago: Moody, 1985.

———. *Revelation 12—22.* The MacArthur New Testament Commentary. Chicago: Moody, 2000.

Martin, W. J. "The Hebrew of Daniel." Pages 28–30 in *Notes on Some Problems in the Book of Daniel.* Edited by D. J. Wiseman, et al. London: Tyndale, 1965.

Mathews, Kenneth A. *Genesis 1–11:26.* NAC, volume 1A. NP: Broadman & Holman, 1996.

McComiskey, Thomas Edward. "The Seventy 'Weeks' of Daniel against the Background of Ancient Near Eastern Literature." *WTJ* 47 (1985): 18–45.

McConville, J. G. *I & II Chronicles.* DSBOT. Philadelphia: Westminster, 1984.

Mendenhall, G. E. "Humility." Pages 659–60 in vol. 2 of *IDB.* Edited by George Arthur Buttrick. 4 vols. Nashville: Abingdon, 1976.

Meadowcroft, T. J. *Aramaic Daniel and Greek Daniel: A Literary Comparison.* Sheffield, England: Sheffield Academic Press, 1995.

Millard, Alan R. "Daniel in Babylon: An Accurate Record?" Pages 263–80 in *Do Historical Matters Matter to Faith? A Critical Appraisal of Modern and Postmodern Approaches to Scripture.* Edited by James K. Hoffmeier and Dennis R. Magary. Wheaton: Crossway, 2012.

Miller, Stephen R. *Daniel.* NAC, vol. 18. [Nashville]: Broadman & Holman, 1994.

Mitchell, T. C. and R. Joyce. "The Musical Instruments in Nebuchadrezzar's Orchestra." Pages 19–27 in *Notes on Some Problems in the Book of Daniel.* Edited by D. J. Wiseman, et al. London: Tyndale, 1965.

Mitchell, Terence C. "And the Band Played On . . . But What Did They Play On? Identifying the Instruments in Nebuchadnezzar's Orchestra." *BR* 15, no. 6 (1999): 32–49.

Montgomery, James A. *A Critical and Exegetical Commentary on the Book of Daniel.* ICC. Edinburgh, Scotland: T. & T. Clark, 1927.

Moore, Carey. *Daniel, Esther, and Jeremiah: The Additions.* AB 44. Garden City, NY: Doubleday, 1977.

Mørkholm, Otto. *Antiochus IV of Syria.* Classica et Mediaevalia, Dissertationes VIII. Kobenhavn, Denmark: Glydendalske Boghandel, 1966.

Most, Glenn W. Ed. and trans. *Hesiod: Theogony, Works and Days, Testimonia.* LCL 57. 2006.

Motyer, J. Alec *The Prophecy of Isaiah: An Introduction & Commentary.* Downers Grove, IL: InterVarsity, 1993.

Muscarella, Oscar White. "Miscellaneous Median Matters." In *Achaemenid History VIII: Continuity and Change: Proceedings of the Last Achaemenid History Workshop, April 6–8, 1990—Ann Arbor, Michigan.* Leiden, Netherlands: Nederlands Instituut voor het Nabije Oosten, 1994.

Myers, Jacob M. *II Chronicles: A New Translation with Introduction and Commentary.* AB 13. Garden City, NY: Doubleday, 1974.

Naudé, Jackie A. "2600 חָזָה." Pages 56–61 in vol. 2 of *NIDOTTE.* Edited by W. A. VanGemeren. 5 vols. Grand Rapids: Zondervan, 1997.

Nestle, Eberhard. "Zu Daniel." *ZAW* 4 (1884): 247–50.

Newman, J. H. *Praying by the Book: The Scripturalization of Prayer in Second Temple Judaism.* SBLEJL no. 14. Atlanta: Scholars, 1999.

Nicolò, San Mariano. *Beiträge zu einer Prosopographie neubabylonischer Beamten der Zivil- und Tempelverwaltung.* Sitzungsberichte der Bayerischen Akademie der Wissenschafter, Philosophisch-historische Abteilung. Vol. 2, no. 2. Munich: Verlag der Bayerischen Akademie der Wissenschaften, 1941.

Noth, Martin. "The Understanding of History in Old Testament Apocalyptic." Pages 194–214 in *The Laws in the Pentateuch and Other Studies.* Translated by D. R. Ap-Thomas, Ohiladelphia: Fortress, 1967.

Olmstead, A. T. *History of the Persian Empire [Achaemenid Period].* Chicago: University of Chicago Press, 1948.

Oppenheim, A. Leo. *Ancient Mesopotamia: Portrait of a Dead Civilization.* Rev. ed., completed by Erica Reiner. Chicago: University of Chicago Press, 1977.

———. *The Interpretation of Dreams in the Ancient Near East With a Translation of an Assyrian Dream-Book.* Transactions of the American Philosophical Society, NS, vol. 46, no. 3. Philadelphia: American Philosophical Society, 1956.

Pace, Sharon. *Daniel.* Smyth & Helwys Bible Commentary. Macon, GA: Smyth & Helwys, 2008.

———. *The Old Greek Translation of Daniel 7–12.* CBQMS 19. Washington, DC: The Catholic Biblical Association of America, 1988.

Parente, Fausto. "'Onias III' [sic!] death and the founding of the temple of Leontopolis." Pages 69–98 in *Josephus and the History of the Greco-Roman Period: Essays in Memory of Morton Smith.* Edited by Fausto Parente and Joseph Sievers. New York: E. J. Brill, 1994.

Parker, Richard A., and Waldo H. Dubberstein. *Babylonian Chronology: 626 B.C.–A.D. 75.* Providence, RI: Brown University Press, 1956.

Parker, Simon B., ed. *Ugaritic Narrative Poetry.* Translated by Mark S. Smith, et al. Writings from the Ancient World, vol. 9. [Atlanta]: Scholars, 1997.

Paul, Shalom M. "A Case Study of 'Neglected' Blasphemy." *JNES* 42 (1983): 291–94.

———. "Daniel 12:9: a technical Mesopotamian scribal term." Pages 115–18 in Sefer Moshe, the Moshe Weinfeld jubilee volume: studies in the Bible and the ancient Near East, Qumran, and post-biblical Judaism. Winona Lake, Ind: Eisenbrauns, 2004.

———. "The Mesopotamian Babylonian Background of Daniel 1—6." Pages 55–68 in vol. 1 of *The Book of Daniel: Composition and Reception.* Edited by John J. Collins and Peter W. Flint. Boston: Brill, 2002.

Payne, J. Barton. "The Goal of Daniel's Seventy Weeks." *JETS* 21 (1978): 97–115.

Pearce, Laurie E., and Cornelia Wunsch. *Document of Judean Exiles and West Semites in Babylonia in the collection of David Sofer.* Bethesda, MD: CDL, 2014.

Péter-Contesse, René, and John Ellington. *A Handbook on the Book of Daniel.* UBS Handbook Series. New York: United Bible Societies, 1993.

Phillips, John. *Exploring the Book of Daniel: An Expository Commentary.* Grand Rapids: Kregel, 2004.

Pierce, Ronald W. *Daniel.* Teach the Text. Edited by Mark L. Strauss and John H. Walton. Grand Rapids: Baker Books, 2015.

Polak, Frank H. "Style is More than the Person: Sociolinguistics, Literary Culture and the Distinction between Written and Oral Narrative." Pages 38–103 in *Biblical Hebrew: Studies in Chronology and Typology.* Edited by Ian Young. JSOTSup 369. New York: T&T Clark, 2003.

Polybius. *The Histories.* Translated by W. R. Paton. 6 vols. LCL. Cambridge, MA: Harvard University Press, 1954.

BIBLIOGRAPHY

Porada, Edith. "Why Cylinder Seals? Engraved Cylindrical Seal Stones of the Ancient Near East, Fourth to First Millennium B.C." *The Art Bulletin* 75 (1993): 563–82.
Porten, Bezalel, and Jerome A. Lund. *Aramaic Documents from Egypt: a key-word-in-context concordance.* Winona Lake, IN: Eisenbrauns, 2002.
Porteous, Norman W. *Daniel: A Commentary.* OTL. Philadelphia: Westminster, 1965.
Poythress, V. S. "The Holy Ones of the Most High in Daniel VII." *VT* 26 (1976): 203–13.
Pröbstle, Martin. "Truth and Terror: A text-oriented analysis of Daniel 8:9–14." Ph.D. diss., Andrews University, 2006.
Rad, Gerhard von. *Wisdom in Israel.* Nashville: Abingdon, 1972.
Reade, Julian. "Alexander the Great and the Hanging Gardens of Babylon." *Iraq* 62 (2000): 195–217.
Rosenthal, Franz. *A Grammar of Biblical Aramaic.* PLO, vol. 5. Wiesbaden, Germany: Otto Harrassowitz, 1968.
Rosscup, James E. "Prayer Relating to Prophecy in Daniel 9." *The Master's Seminary Journal* 3 (1992): 47–71.
Rowley, H. H. *Darius, the Mede and the Four World Empires in the Book of Daniel: A Historical Study of Contemporary Theories.* Rev. ed. Cardiff: University of Wales Press Board, 1959.
———. "The Unity of the Book of Daniel." Pages 235–68 in *The Servant of the Lord and Other Essays on the Old Testament.* London: Lutterworth, 1952.
Royer, Wilfred Sophrony. "The Ancient of Days: Patristic and Modern Views of Daniel 7:9–14." *St Vladimir's Theological Quarterly* 45 (2001): 137–62.
Russell, D. S. *Divine Disclosure: An Introduction to Jewish Apocalyptic.* Minneapolis: Fortress, 1992.
Sachs, A. J., and D. J. Wiseman. "A Babylonian King List of the Hellenistic Period." *Iraq* 16 (1954): 202–12.
San Nicolò, Mariano. *Beiträge zu einer Prosopographie neubabylonischer Beamten der Zivil- und Tempelverwaltung.* Sitzungsberichte der Bayerischen Akademie der Wissenschaften, Philosophisch-historische Abteilung. Vol. 2, no. 2. Munich: Verlag der Bayerischen Akademie der Wissenschaften, 1941.
Sancisi-Weerdenburg, Heleen. "The Orality of Herodotus' *Medikos Logos* or: the Median empire revisited." In *Achaemenid History VIII: Continuity and Change: Proceedings of the Last Achaemenid History Workshop, April 6–8, 1990—Ann Arbor, Michigan.* Leiden, Netherlands: Nederlands Instituut voor het Nabije Oosten, 1994.
Saucy, Robert L. *The Case for Progressive Dispensationalism.* Grand Rapids: Zondervan, 1993.
Saunders, E. W. "Heliodorus." Page 579 in vol. 2 of *IDB.* Edited by G.A. Buttrick. Nashville: Abingdon, 1962.
Sawyer, John F. A. "Hebrew Words for the Resurrection of the Dead." *VT* 23 (1973): 218–34.
Schiffman, Lawrence H. *From Text to Tradition: A History of Second Temple and Rabbinic Judaism.* Hoboken, NJ: Ktav, 1991.
Schwantes, S. J. "'Ereb Bōqer of Dan 8:14 Re-Examined." *AUSS* 16 (1978): 375–85.
Seow, C. L. *Daniel.* Westminster Bible Companion. Louisville: Westminster John Knox, 2003.
Shea, William H. "Bel(te)shazzar Meets Belshazzar." *AUSS* 26 (1988): 67–81.
———. "Daniel 3: Extra-Biblical Texts and the Convocation on the Plain of Dura." *AUSS* 20 (1982a): 29–52.

———. "Nabonidus, Belshazzar, and the Book of Daniel: An Update." *AUSS* 20 (1982b): 133–49.

———. "The Search for Darius the Mede (Concluded), or, the Time of the Answer to Daniel's Prayer and the Date of the Death of Darius the Mede." *Journal of the Adventist Theological Society* 12 (2001): 97–105.

———. "Wrestling with the Prince of Persia: A Study on Daniel 10." *AUSS* 21 (1983): 225–50.

Shedd, William G. T. *Dogmatic Theology*. Edited by Alan W. Gomes. 3$^{rd}$ ed. Phillipsburg, NJ: Presbyterian and Reformed, 2003.

Shepherd, Michael B. *Daniel in the Context of the Hebrew Bible*. Edited by Hemchand Gossai. StBibLit, vol. 123. New York: Peter Lang, 2009.

Slotki, Judah J. *Daniel-Ezra-Nehemiah: Hebrew Text & English Translation with Introductions and Commentary*. Soncino Books of the Bible. London: Soncino, 1951.

Sokoloff, Michael. *A Syriac Lexicon: A Translation from the Latin, Correction, Expansion, and Update of C. Brockelmann's* Lexicon Syriacum. Winona Lake, IN: Eisenbrauns, 2009.

Sprinkle, Joe M. *Daniel*. Edited by T. Desmond Alexander, Thomas Schreiner, and Andreas J. Köstenberger. Evangelical Biblical Theology Commentary. Bellingham, WA: Lexham, 2020.

Spronk, Klaas. *Beatific Afterlife in Ancient Israel and in the Ancient Near East*. Kevelaer, Germany: Butzon & Bercker, 1986.

Steinmann, Andrew E. *Daniel*. Concordia Commentary. Saint Louis: Concordia, 2008.

Stevenson, Kenneth, and Michael Glerup, eds. *Ezekiel, Daniel*. ACCSOT, vol. 13. Downers Grove, IL: InterVarsity, 2008.

Stolper, Matthew W. "The Governor of Babylon and Across-the-River in 486 B.C." *JNES* 48 (1989): 283–305.

Strack, Hermann L. and Paul Billerbeck. *Kommentar zum Neuen Testament aus Talmud und Midrasch*. Vol. 1 of *Das Evangelium nach Matthäus erläutert aus Talmud und Midrasch*. 2$^{nd}$ ed., unchanged. München: C. H. Beck'sche, 1926.

Strommenger, Eva. *5000 Years of the Art of Mesopotamia*. Photographs by Max Hirmer. Translated by Christina Haglund. New York: Harry M. Abrams, 1964.

Swain, Joseph Ward. "The Theory of the Four Monarchies: Opposition History under the Roman Empire." *Classical Philology* 25 (1940): 1–21.

Tate, Marvin E. *Psalms 51—100*. WBC 20. Dallas: Word, 1990.

Taylor, Joan E. "A Second Temple in Egypt: The Evidence for the Zadokite Temple of Onias." *JSJ* 29 (1998): 297–321.

Taylor, Richard A. *The Peshitta of Daniel*. Monographs of the Peshitta Institute, vol. 7. New York: E. J. Brill, 1994.

Theodoret of Cyrus. *Commentary on Daniel*. Translated with introduction and notes by Robert C. Hill. WGRW, no. 7. Atlanta: Society of Biblical Literature, 2006.

Thomas, Robert L. *Revelation 8–22: An Exegetical Commentary*. Chicago: Moody, 1995.

Thompson, Henry O. "Dura (Place) [Aram *dûraʾ*]." Page 241 in vol. 2 of *ABD*. Edited by D. N. Freedman. New York: Doubleday, 1992.

Toorn, Karel van der. "In the Lions' Den: The Babylonian Background of a Biblical Motif." *CBQ* 60 (1998): 626–40.

Toorn, Karel van der, and P. W. van der Horst. "Nimrod before and after the Bible." *HTR* 83 (1990): 1–29.

## BIBLIOGRAPHY

Towner, W. Sibley. *Daniel*. Interpretation. Atlanta: John Knox, 1984.

Tuplin, Christopher. "Persians as Medes." In *Achaemenid History VIII: Continuity and Change: Proceedings of the Last Achaemenid History Workshop, April 6–8, 1990—Ann Arbor, Michigan*. Leiden, Netherlands: Nederlands Instituut voor het Nabije Oosten, 1994.

Ulrich, Eugene. "The Text of Daniel in the Qumran Scrolls." Pages 572–85 in vol. 2 of *The Book of Daniel: Composition and Reception*. Edited by John J. Collins and Peter W. Flint. Boston: Brill, 2002.

VanderKam, James C. *The Dead Sea Scrolls Today*. 2$^{nd}$ ed. Grand Rapids: Eerdmans, 2010.

Venter, Pieter M. "Daniel 9: A Penitential Prayer in Apocalyptic Garb." Pages 33–49 in *Seeking the Favor of God. Volume 2, The Development of Penitential Prayer in Second Temple Judaism*, edited by Mark J. Boda, Daniel K. Falk, and Rodney A. Werline. Early Judaism and Its Literature, no. 22. Atlanta: Society of Biblical Literature, 2007.

Vermes, Geza. *The Complete Dead Sea Scrolls in English*. New York: Allen Lane, Penguin, 1997.

Wacholder, Ben Zion. "Chronomessianism: The Timing of Messianic Movements and the Calendar of Sabbatical Cycles." *HUCA* 46 (1975): 201–18.

Walbank, F. W. *The Hellenistic World*. Rev. ed. Cambridge, MA: Harvard University Press, 1993.

Wallace, Ronald S. *The Message of Daniel: The Lord is King*. The Bible Speaks Today. Downers Grove, IL: InterVarsity, 1979.

Waltke, Bruce K. *The Book of Proverbs, Chapters 15–31*. NICOT. Grand Rapids: Eerdmans, 2005.

Waltke, Bruce K., and M. O'Connor. *An Introduction to Biblical Hebrew Syntax*. Winona Lake, IN: Eisenbrauns, 2004.

Walton, John H. "The Decree of Darius the Mede in Daniel 6." *JETS* 31 (1988): 279–86.

———. "The Four Kingdoms of Daniel." *JETS* 29 (1986): 25–36. "Four Kingdoms of Daniel"

Walvoord, John F. "Biblical Kingdoms Compared and Contrasted." Pages 75–91 in *Issues in Dispensationalism*, edited by Wesley R. Willis and John R. Master. Chicago: Moody, 1994.

———. *Daniel: The Key to Prophetic Revelation*. Chicago: Moody, 1971.

Waters, Matt. "Cyrus and the Achaemenids." *Iran* 42 (2004): 91–102.

Watson, Duane F. "Michael (Angel)." Page 811 in vol. 4 of *ABD*, edited by D. N. Freedman. New York: Doubleday, 1992.

Wenham, David. "The Kingdom of God and Daniel." *Expository Times* 98 (1987): 132–34.

Whitcomb, John C. *Daniel*. Everyman's Bible Commentary. Chicago: Moody, 1985.

———. *Darius the Mede*. International Library of Philosophy and Theology: Biblical and Theological Studies. Phillipsburg, NJ: Presbyterian and Reformed, 1959.

Whitehorne, John. "Ptolemy (Person)." Pages 541–44 in vol. 6 of *ABD*. Edited by D. N. Freedman. New York: Doubleday, 1992.

———. "Seleucus (Person)." Pages 1076–77 in vol. 5 of *ABD*. Edited by D. N. Freedman. New York: Doubleday, 1992.

Widder, Wendy. *Daniel*. Vol. 20 of *The Story of God Commentary*. Grand Rapids: Zondervan, 2016.

Widengren, Geo. "The Persians." In *Peoples of Old Testament Times*, edited by D. J. Wiseman. Oxford, England: Clarendon, 1973.
Willard, Dallas. *The Spirit of the Disciplines: Understanding How God Changes Lives.* San Francisco: Harper & Row, 1988.
Williamson, H. G. M. *Ezra, Nehemiah.* Word Biblical Commentary, vol. 16. Dallas: Word, 1985.
Wilson, Gerald H. "The Prayer of Daniel 9: Reflection on Jeremiah 29." *JSOT* 48 (1990): 91–99.
Wilson, Robert Dick "On the Hebrew of Daniel." *Princeton Theological Review* 25 (1927): 177–99.
———. *Studies in the Book of Daniel*. Grand Rapids: Baker, 1972. [reprint of 1917 edition]
Wiseman, Donald J. *1 and 2 Kings*. TOTC. Downers Grove, IL: InterVarsity, 1993.
———. *Chronicles of Chaldaean Kings (626–556 b.c.) in the British Museum*. London: Trustees of the British Museum, 1956.
———. *Nebuchadrezzar and Babylon*. Schweich Lectures, 1983. Oxford, England: Oxford University Press, 1983.
———. "Some Historical Problems in the Book of Daniel." Pages 9–18 in *Notes on Some Problems in the Book of Daniel*. Edited by D. J. Wiseman, et al. London: Tyndale, 1965.
Wolters, Al. "The Riddle of the Scales in Daniel 5." *HUCA* 62 (1991): 155–77.
———. "Untying the King's Knots: Physiology and Wordplay in Daniel 5." *JBL* 110 (1991): 17–22.
Wood, Leon. *A Commentary on Daniel*. Grand Rapids: Zondervan, 1973.
Worschech, U. "Der assyrisch-babylonische Löwenmensch und der 'menschliche' Löwe aus Daniel 7,4." In *Ad bene et fideliter seminandum: Festgabe für Karlheinz Deller zum 21. Februar 1987*. AOAT, volume 220. Edited by Gerlinde Mauer and Ursula Magen. Neukirchen-Vluyn, Germany: Butzon & Bercker Kevelaer, 1988.
Wright, Christopher J. H. *The Mission of God: Unlocking the Bible's Grand Narrative*. Downers Grove, IL: InterVarsity, 2006.
Xenophon. *Cyropaedia*. Translated by Walter Miller. 2 vols. LCL. Cambridge, MA: Harvard University Press, 1953.
Yamauchi, Edwin M. *Persia and the Bible*. Grand Rapids: Baker, 1990.
Young, Cuyler T., Jr. "Cyrus." Pages 1231–32 in vol. 1 of *ABD*. Edited by D. N. Freedman. New York: Doubleday, 1992.
Young, Edward J. *The Prophecy of Daniel: A Commentary*. Grand Rapids: Eerdmans, 1949.
Young, Rodger C. "*Seder Olam* and the Sabbaticals associated with the two destructions of Jerusalem: Part II." *JBQ* 34 (2006): 252–59.
———. "When Did Jerusalem Fall?" *JETS* 47 (2004): 21–38.
Zahn, Molly M. *Genres of Rewriting in Second Temple Judaism: Scribal Composition and Transmission*. New York and Port Melbourne, Australia: Cambridge University Press, 2020.
Ziegler, Joseph, and Olivier Munnich, eds. *Susanna-Daniel-Bel et Draco*. Septuaginta, vol. 16, no. 2. Göttingen, Germany: Vandenhoeck & Ruprecht, 1999.
Zöckler, Otto. "The Book of the Prophet Daniel Theologically and Homiletically Expounded." Edited by John Peter Lange. Vol. 13 of *Ezekiel and Daniel*. Grand Rapids: Zondervan, 1960.

www.ingramcontent.com/pod-product-compliance
Lightning Source LLC
Chambersburg PA
CBHW071222290426
44108CB00013B/1266